W9-CCT-507

TŌKYŌ 東京
1ST EDITION

Where to Stay and Eat
for All Budgets

Must-See Sights
and Local Secrets

Ratings You Can Trust

Fodor's Travel Publications   New York, Toronto, London, Sydney, Auckland
www.fodors.com

FODOR'S TŌKYŌ
EDITORS: Emmanuelle Alspaugh, Deborah Kaufman

Editorial Contributors: Jared Lubarsky, Steve Trautlein, Dominic Al-Badri, Collin Campbell, Kazumi Pestka
Editorial Production: Linda K. Schmidt
Maps: David Lindroth, *cartographer*; Rebecca Baer and Robert Blake, *map editors*
Design: Fabrizio La Rocca, *creative director;* Guido Caroti, *art director;* Moon Sun Kim, *cover designer;* Melanie Marin, *senior picture editor*
Production/Manufacturing: Robert B. Shields
Cover Photograph: Stefano Cellai/agefotostock

SPECIAL SALES
This book is available for special discounts for bulk purchases for sales promotions or premiums. Special editions, including personalized covers, excerpts of existing books, and corporate imprints, can be created in large quantities for special needs. For more information, write to Special Markets/Premium Sales, 1745 Broadway, MD 6-2, New York, New York 10019, or e-mail specialmarkets@randomhouse.com.

AN IMPORTANT TIP & AN INVITATION
Although all prices, opening times, and other details in this book are based on information supplied to us at press time, changes occur all the time in the travel world, and Fodor's cannot accept responsibility for facts that become outdated or for inadvertent errors or omissions. So **always confirm information when it matters,** especially if you're making a detour to visit a specific place. Your experiences—positive and negative—matter to us. If we have missed or misstated something, **please write to us.** We follow up on all suggestions. Contact the Tokyo editor at editors@fodors.com or c/o Fodor's at 1745 Broadway, New York, New York 10019.

PRINTED IN THE UNITED STATES OF AMERICA

10 9 8 7 6 5 4 3 2 1

DESTINATION TŌKYŌ

ights, sushi, cell phones! Immense, frenetic, and endlessly fascinating, Japan's capital is a city of contrasts and contradictions. Here, kimono-clad shoppers walk the same streets as suited businesspeople. Shrines and gardens are pockets of calm between traffic-clogged streets. Gorgeous temples and avant-garde structures are juxtaposed with soaring office buildings and blocky housing projects. On one hand, Tōkyō is the seat of the influential Nikkei stock exchange and the base of operations for some of the most powerful electronics and automobile companies in the world; and on the other hand the city is home to Japan's wildly popular baseball teams and important sumō training stables. From mom-and-pop noodle houses to Western-style chain restaurants, from teahouses to techno clubs, Tōkyō is the place to witness age-old Japanese traditions blending with intense modernization.

Tim Jarrell, Publisher

CONTENTS

On the Road with Fodors *F7*
About this Book *F8*
What's Where *F14*
Great Itineraries *F16*
When to Go *F18*

On the Calendar *F19*
Pleasures and Pastimes *F21*
Fodor's Choice *F22*
Smart Travel Tips *F25*

1 Exploring Tōkyō   1

Imperial Palace District *4*
Akihabara & Jimbō-chō *18*
Ueno *23*
Asakusa *33*
Tsukiji & Shiodome *43*
Nihombashi, Ginza &
　Yūraku-chō *50*

Aoyama, Harajuku &
　Shibuya *59*
Shinjuku *69*
Elsewhere in Tōkyō *75*

2 Where to Eat   84

Akasaka *86*
Akasaka-mitsuke *89*
Aoyama *89*
Asakusa *92*
Azabu-jūban *92*
Daikanyama *94*
Ginza *94*
Ichiyaga *95*
Ikebukuro *95*
Kyō-bashi *97*
Meguro *97*
Niban-chō *98*

Nihombashi *98*
Omotesandō *98*
Roppongi *99*
Shibuya *101*
Shinagawa *102*
Shirokanedai *102*
Shōtō *103*
Tora-no-mon *103*
Tsukiji *103*
Uchisaiwai-chō *104*
Ueno *104*
Yūraku-chō *104*

3 Where to Stay   106

Akasaka-mitsuke *108*
Asakusa *108*
Ebisu *111*
Ginza *111*
Hakozaki *116*
Hibiya *116*
Higashi-Gotanda *117*
Higashi-Shinjuku *117*
Kyō-bashi *117*
Marunouchi *118*
Nagata-chō *119*
Ningyō-chō *119*

Nishi-Shinjuku *119*
Roppongi *121*
Sekiguchi *123*
Shiba Kōen *123*
Shinagawa *123*
Tora-no-mon *124*
Ueno *125*
Yaesu *125*
Yanaka *126*
Hostels *126*
Near Narita Airport *126*

(4) Nightlife & the Arts   129

Dance 131   Dance Clubs 143
Film 132   Izakaya 144
Modern Theater 133   Jazz Clubs 145
Music 134   Karaoke 146
Traditional Theater 136   Live Houses 146
Bars 141   Rooftop Bars 147
Beer Halls & Pubs 142

(5) Sports & the Outdoors   148

Baseball 149   Sumō 151
Golf 150   Swimming & Fitness 151
Running 150   Tennis 152
Soccer 150

(6) Shopping   154

Shopping Districts 155   Malls & Shopping Centers 160
Shopping Streets &   Department Stores 160
   Arcades 159   Specialty Stores 164

(7) Side Trips from Tōkyō   176

Nikkō 181   Fuji-Hakone-Izu
Kamakura 194   National Park 219
Yokohama 207

The Discreet Charm of Japanese Cuisine   239

The Essentials of a Japanese   Sushi, Sukiyaki, Tempura &
   Meal 241   Nabemono: A Comfortable
Culture: The Main Course 242   Middle Ground 243
Kaiseki Ryōri: Japanese Haute   Bentō, Soba, Udon &
   Cuisine 242   Robatayaki: Feasting on a
Shōjin Ryōri: Zen-Style   Budget 244
   Vegetarian Cuisine 243   Regional Differences 246
                                       The Bottom Line 246

Arts & Culture   248

Papermaking &   Ritual & Religion 255
   Calligraphy 249   The Tea Ceremony 257
Ceramics & Lacquerware 250   Geisha 258
Japanese Gardens 251   Japanese Society:
Japanese Textiles 253   A Factory of Fads 259
Bathing: An Immersion   Books & Movies 261
   Course 254

Facts & Figures   265

Japan at a Glance 266   Chronology 271
Tōkyō at a Glance 269

Vocabulary & Menu Guide   275

About Japanese 276   Menu Guide 283
Essential Phrases 278

Index   293

Maps

Japan F10–F11   Where to Eat in
Tōkyō Overview F12–F13   Tōkyō 90–91
Imperial Palace 6–7   Where to Stay in
Akihabara & Jimbo-chō 19   Tōkyō 112–113
Ueno 25   Tōkyō Shopping Districts 158
Asakusa 37   Nikkō Area 184
Tsukiji & Shiodome 47   Kamakura 198
Nihombashi, Ginza &   Yokohama 210
  Yūraku-chō 53   Fuji-Hakone-Izu
Aoyama, Harajuku &   National Park 221
  Shibuya 62–63   Tōkyō Subway
Shinjuku 71   inside back cover

CloseUps

Tōkyō Glossary 3   Lodging Alternatives 122
Etiquette and Behavior 14   Butō: Dance of Darkness 132
The Evolution of Tōkyō 34   Traditional Japanese Drama
Tsukiji Achievements 44   138
Teenybopper Shoppers of   Becoming a Sumō Wrestler 152
  Harajuku 60   Smart Souvenirs 161
On the Menu 88   Tōkyō Side Trips Glossary 178
Tips on Dining in Japan 93   The Downfall of
Beer, Wine, Sake & Spirits 96   Yoshitsune 201
Where to Refuel 100   Onsen 223
Choosing Your Hotel 114   Ryokan Etiquette 227

ON THE ROAD WITH FODOR'S

Our success in showing you every corner of Tōkyō is a credit to our extraordinary writers. Although there's no substitute for travel advice from a good friend who knows your style, our contributors are the next best thing—the kind of people you would poll for travel advice if you knew them.

Dominic Al-Badri studied biochemistry at the University of London's Imperial College, but after graduating he found himself a long way from both home and profession teaching English in rural Japan. Since 1997 he has been the editor of *Kansai Time Out,* Japan's oldest English-language monthly magazine. Dominic updated the Smart Travel Tips chapter, and he also covers Kōbe and Ōsaka for *Fodor's Japan.*

Paul Davidson studied Japanese drama at the University of Washington before coming to Japan in 1995 to work as an extra in a karate film by the B-movie director Pepe Baba. The picture went straight to video, and Paul went to Changsha, China. He lived in China and São Tomé, a small island nation off the coast of West Africa, until his return to Japan in 2000. Currently based in Yokohama, outside of Tōkyō, Paul works as a writer and translator when he isn't playing the *biwa* (Japanese lute) with the Tengu-kai sextet. He revised the essays at the end of this book, and he also contributed to several chapters of *Fodor's Japan.*

Jared Lubarsky, who worked on the Exploring, Where to Eat, Where to Stay, and Sports & the Outdoors chapters, has lived in Japan since 1973. He has worked for cultural exchange organizations, taught at public and private universities, and written extensively for travel publications. He still ponders the oddities of Japanese culture, wondering why, for instance, the signs that advise you not to ride in elevators during an earthquake are posted *inside* the elevators.

Steve Trautlein is a writer and editor at *Metropolis* magazine, a weekly publication focusing on entertainment and lifestyles in Japan. He has reviewed dozens of bars, restaurants, and shops in Tōkyō and the surrounding area. Steve revised the Nightlife, Shopping, and Side Trips chapters with Matt Wilce.

Matt Wilce first came to Japan in 1993 and has lived in Tōkyō since 1998. He has done everything from teaching government employees to being knifed by a yakuza on a TV police show, but prefers to stick to more sedate activities, such as writing. Matt has written and edited articles on the Japanese entertainment industry for *Eye-Ai* and *Metropolis* magazines, and he has also written features for *The Rochester Review, The Lantern, Ikebana International, POL Oxygen,* and *JapanInc.* He contributed to the Nightlife, Shopping, and Side Trips chapters.

ABOUT THIS BOOK

Once you've learned to find your way around our pages, you'll be in great shape to find your way around your destination.

RATINGS

Orange stars ★ denote sights and properties that our editors and writers consider the very best in the area covered by the entire book. These, the best of the best, are listed in the Fodor's Choice section in the front of the book. Black stars ★ highlight the sights and properties we deem Highly Recommended, the don't-miss sights within any region. It goes without saying that no property pays to be included.

SPECIAL SPOTS

Pleasures & Pastimes and text on chapter-title pages focus on experiences that reveal the spirit of the destination. Also watch for Off the Beaten Path sights. Some are out of the way, some are quirky, and all are worthwhile. When the munchies hit, look for Need a Break? suggestions.

TIME IT RIGHT

Check On the Calendar up front and chapters' Timing sections for weather and crowd overviews and best days and times to visit.

SEE IT ALL

Use Fodor's Great Itineraries as a model for your trip. Either follow those that begin the book, or mix regional itineraries from several chapters. In cities, Good Walks guide you to important sights in each neighborhood; ► indicates the starting points of walks and itineraries in the text and on the map.

BUDGET WELL

Hotel and restaurant price categories from ¢ to $$$$ are defined in the opening pages of each chapter—expect to find a balanced selection for every budget. For attractions, we always give standard adult admission fees; reductions are usually available for children, students, and senior citizens. Look in Discounts & Deals in Smart Travel Tips for information on destination-wide ticket schemes. Want to pay with plastic? AE, D, DC, MC, V following restaurant and hotel listings indicate whether American Express, Discover, Diner's Club, MasterCard, or Visa are accepted.

BASIC INFO

Smart Travel Tips lists travel essentials for the entire area covered by the book; city- and region-specific basics end each chapter. To find the best way to get around, see the transportation section; see individual modes of travel ("Car Travel," "Train Travel") for details.

ON THE MAPS

Maps throughout the book show you what's where and help you find your way around. Black and orange numbered bullets ❶ ❶ in the text correlate to bullets on maps.

BACKGROUND

We give background information within the chapters in the course of explaining sights as well as in CloseUp boxes and in the chapters at the end of the book. To get in the mood, review the Books & Movies section in the Arts & Culture chapter. The Vocabulary & Menu Guide at the end of the book can be invaluable.

FIND IT FAST

Within the Exploring Tōkyō chapter, sights are grouped by neighborhood, starting in central Tōkyō with the Imperial Palace District. The area divisions in this book are not always contiguous—Tōkyō is too spread out for that—but they generally border each other to a useful degree. Where to Eat and Where to Stay are also organized by neighborhood—Where to Eat is further divided by cuisine type. Sections in Nightlife & the Arts and Sports & the Outdoors are arranged alphabetically, and within Shopping, a description of the city's main shopping districts is followed by a list of specialty shops grouped according to their focus. The Side Trips from Tōkyō chapter explores Yokohama, Nikkō, Hakone, and other communities and natural areas outside the city.

DON'T FORGET

Restaurants are open for lunch and dinner daily unless we state otherwise; we mention dress only when there's a specific requirement and reservations only when they're essential or not accepted—it's always best to book ahead. Hotels have private baths, phone, TVs, and air-conditioning and operate on the European Plan (a.k.a. EP, meaning without meals). We always list facilities but not whether you'll be charged extra to use them, so when pricing accommodations, find out what's included.

SYMBOLS

Many Listings

★ Fodor's Choice
★ Highly recommended
⊠ Physical address
✦ Directions
⌖ Mailing address
☎ Telephone
🖷 Fax
⊕ On the Web
✉ E-mail
🎫 Admission fee
☉ Open/closed times
► Start of walk/itinerary
Ⓜ Metro stations
▭ Credit cards

Outdoors

🏌 Golf
⛺ Camping

Hotels & Restaurants

🏨 Hotel
🛏 Number of rooms
♨ Facilities
🍽 Meal plans
✕ Restaurant
🍴 Reservations
👗 Dress code
🚭 Smoking
🍷 BYOB
✕🏨 Hotel with restaurant that warrants a visit

Other

♟ Family-friendly
🖪 Contact information
⇨ See also
⊠ Branch address
☞ Take note

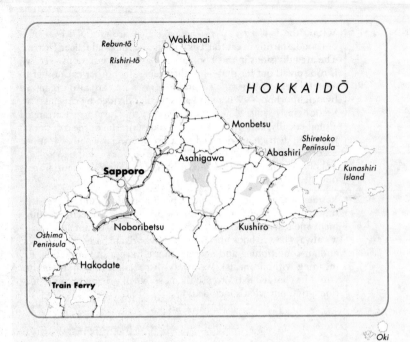

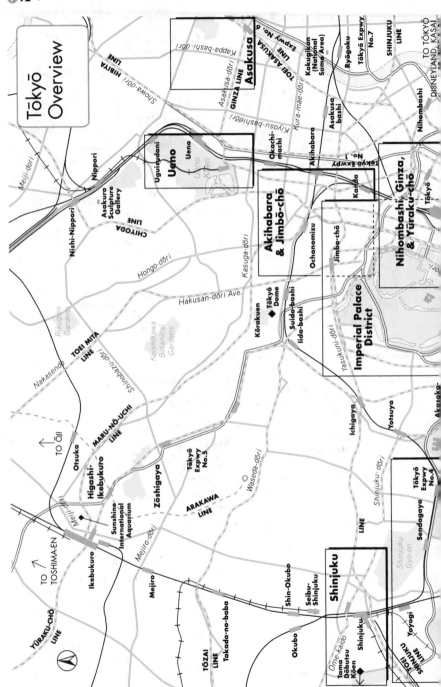

Tōkyō Overview

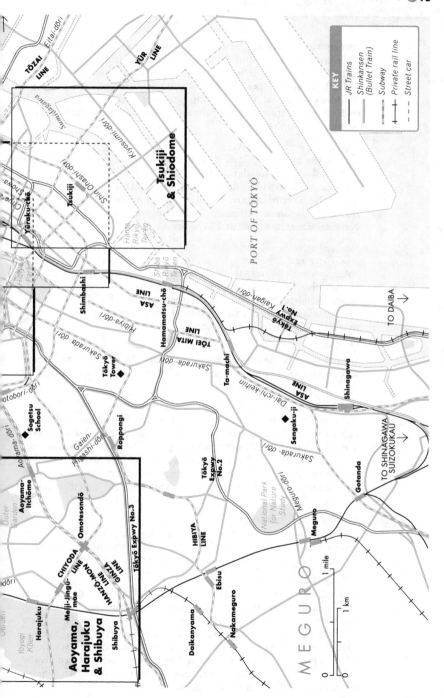

KEY

— JR Trains
| Shinkansen (Bullet Train)
Subway
+—+ Private rail line
– – – Street car

PORT OF TŌKYŌ

TOZAI LINE
Eitai-dōri

YŪR LINE

Sumidagawa

Kiyosumi-dōri

Tsukiji & Shiodome

Shin Ōhashi-dōri

Tsukiji

Chūō-dōri

Yūraku-chō

Shōwa-

Hama Rikyū Tei-en

Hibiya Park

Shiba Rikyū Tei-en

Shimbashi

Hibiya-dōri

ASA LINE

Hamamatsu-chō

TŌEI MITA LINE

Sakurada-dōri

Tōkyō Expwy No. 1

Kaigan-dōri

TO DAIBA →

Tōkyō Tower ◆

Dai-ichi-keihin

Ta-machi

ASA LINE

Shinagawa

Sengaku-ji ◆

TO SHINAGAWA SUIZOKUKAU →

Sotobori-dōri

Sogetsu School ◆

Gaien-Higashi-dōri

Roppongi

Sakurada-dōri

Gotanda

Tōkyō Expwy No. 2

Aoyama-dōri

Aoyama-Itchōme

Outer Garden

Meguro-dōri

National Park for Nature Study

Meguro

Aoyama, Harajuku & Shibuya

CHIYODA LINE

Omotesandō

HANZŌ-MON LINE

GINZA LINE

Tōkyō Expwy No. 3

HIBIYA LINE

Ebisu

Meguro

-dōri

Meiji-Jingū-mae

Harajuku

Shibuya

Daikanyama

Nakameguro

M E G U R O

Yoyogi Kōen

1 mile

1 km

0

Immense and sprawling, Tōkyō commands a prominent position in the Kantō region on the southern coast of Honshū, Japan's largest island. Some 12 million people live in or within commuting distance of the capital. Like most big cities, Tōkyō stitches together several colorful neighborhoods—Asakusa, Ginza, Tsukiji, Shinjuku, and dozens more—each with its own texture. A few of the most important neighborhoods for visitors are profiled below.

Imperial Palace District

Kōkyo, the Imperial Palace, is at the center of Tōkyō where Edo Castle once stood. Although the imperial residence is only open two days per year, you can explore the palace grounds and serene gardens at your leisure. Near the palace are several important museums, Yasukuni Jinja shrine, the Japanese parliament and supreme court buildings, and the National Theater, as well as Tōkyō Station.

Akihabara & Jimbō-chō

Akihabara and Jimbō-chō are the areas just northeast of the Imperial Palace grounds. Between them, these two neighborhoods have stores selling just about any electronic good or gadget you could possibly want. While Akihabara has most of the electronics vendors, Jimbō-chō has rows of booksellers selling anything printed, from antique wood-block books to cheap dictionaries in every language.

Ueno

Ueno Park, once the site of a defensive stronghold, is now home to three superb national museums, a university of fine arts, and a zoo. Ueno is directly north of Akihabara.

Asakusa

A trip to Asakusa in the northeastern part of the city is an essential Tōkyō experience, and not only because it's the home of the sublime temple, Sensō-ji. Once the city's suburban playground—for centuries urbanites stopped there for drinking, dancing, and Kabuki on their way to and from Sensō-ji—Asakusa is now where artists and hipsters come to live, among generations of locals fiercely proud of and loyal to their neighborhood.

Tsukiji & Shiodome

Tsukiji, in southeastern Tōkyō on the Sumida-gawa River, is the site of Tōkyō's largest fish market. Shiodome, a bit farther inland, is a massive development zone, with plenty of fashionable shops and restaurants.

Nihombashi, Ginza & Yūraku-chō

Nihombashi, east of the Imperial Palace, lays claim to the geographical and financial center of Tōkyō. Ginza, slightly to the south, is where to find some of Tōkyō's best shopping, in department stores and boutiques selling high-end traditional wares, plus hundreds of art galleries. Yūraku-chō, between Ginza and the Outer Garden of the Imperial Palace, flourished as black-market central when American GIs were posted nearby during World War II. Today it's an upscale commercial area with shops, restaurants, and a Western-style park.

Aoyama, Harajuku & Shibuya

Aoyama and Harajuku, west of the Imperial Palace, were developed for the 1964 Olympics and today they are chic neighborhoods saturated with designer and chain stores, independent boutiques, and malls. To the south, Shibuya is a major transportation hub with even more shops and restaurants.

Shinjuku

The edgy neighborhood of Shinjuku, north of Shibuya, is the nightlife capital of Tōkyō, with enough bars, clubs, and strip joints to entertain the whole city. It's also home to the towering Tōkyō Tochō complex, whose observation platforms provide sweeping views, and the Tōkyō Dome, whose bleachers envelope thousands of passionate baseball fans during home games.

Side Trips from Tōkyō

If Tōkyō were rows of Quonset huts, it would still be worth staying in for the side trips nearby. Start with lunch in **Yokohama's** Chinatown, where more than 150 restaurants serve every major regional Chinese cuisine. Here, silks, spices, herbal medicines, and all things Chinese beckon from a warren of shops in narrow lanes. Far removed from such urban bustle lie **Nikkō** and the **Tōshō-gū** shrine complex, stirring in its sheer scale alone. Some call it sublime, some excessive, but no one finds it dull. At a nearby national park, **Chūzenji-ko (Lake Chūzenji)** and waterfalls like Kegon-no-taki nourish the spirit. The national park and resort area of **Hakone** puts you close to majestic **Fuji-san,** which you can climb in summer without special gear. In **Hase,** the 37-foot Daibutsu—the Great Buddha—has sat for seven centuries, serenely gazing inward. The temples and shrines of nearby **Kamakura,** 13th-century capital of Japan, remind you that this was an important religious as well as political center. Break away from the tourists and enjoy a moment of peace: the clamor of Tōkyō falls silent here in the ancient heart of Japan.

Tōkyō in 3 Days

You need three days just to take in the highlights of Tōkyō and still have time for some shopping and nightlife. With four or five days you can explore the city in greater depth, wander off the beaten path, and appreciate Tōkyō's museums at leisure. More time would allow for day trips to the scenic and historical sights in communities outside the city.

DAY 1

Start *very* early (why waste your jet lag?) with a visit to the Tōkyō Central Wholesale Market (Tōkyō Chūō Oroshiuri Ichiba) while it's still in high gear; then use the rest of the day for a tour of the Imperial Palace and environs.

DAY 2

Spend the morning of Day 2 at Buddhist Sensō-ji in Asakusa, and from there head to Ueno for an afternoon with its many museums, vistas, and historic sites.

DAY 3

Start Day 3 with a morning stroll through Ginza to explore its fabled shops and depāto. In the afternoon, see the Shintō Meiji Jingū and take a leisurely walk through the nearby Harajuku and Omotesandō fashion districts to the Nezu Institute of Fine Arts—a perfect oasis for your last impressions of the city.

Tōkyō in 5 Days

DAY 4

Follow the itinerary above and add to it (or punctuate it with) a morning of browsing in Akihabara, Tōkyō's electronics discount quarter, visiting the nearby Shintō Kanda Myōjin as well. Spend the afternoon on the west side of Shinjuku, Tōkyō's 21st-century model city; savor the view from the observation deck of architect Kenzō Tange's monumental Tōkyō Metropolitan Government Office; and cap off the day with a walk through the greenery of Shinjuku Gyo-en National Garden.

DAY 5

The luxury of a fifth day would allow you to fill in the missing pieces that belong to no particular major tour: the Buddhist Sengaku-ji in Shinagawa, the remarkable Edo-Tōkyō Hakubutsukan in Ryōgoku, a tea ceremony, or any of the shops that haven't yet managed to stake a claim on your dwindling resources. See a sumō tournament, if there's one in town; failing that, you could still visit the Kokugikan, National Sumō Arena, in the Ryōgoku district, and some of the sumō stables in the neighborhood.

If You Have More Time

With a week or more, you can make Tōkyō your home base for a series of side trips (⇨ Chapter 7). After getting your fill of Tōkyō, take a train out to Yokohama, with its scenic port and Chinatown. A bit farther afield but still easily accessible by train is Kamakura, the 13th-century military capital of Japan. The Great Buddha (Daibutsu) of the Kōtoku-in is but one of the National Treasures of art and architecture here that draw millions of visitors a year. For both Yokohama and Kamakura, an early morning start will allow you to see most of the important sights in a full day and make it back to Tōkyō by late evening. As Kamakura is the most popular of excursions from Tōkyō, avoid the worst of the crowds by making the trip on a weekday.

Still farther off, but again an easy train trip, is Nikkō, where the founder of the Tokugawa shogunal dynasty is enshrined. Tōshō-gū is a monument unlike any other in Japan, and the picturesque Lake Chūzen-ji is in a forest above the shrine. Two full days, with an overnight stay, would allow you an ideal, leisurely exploration of both. Yet another option would be a trip to Hakone and a climb to the summit of Fuji-san (Mt. Fuji).

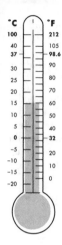

°C / °F

100 / 212
40 / 105
37 / 98.6
30 / 90
25 / 80
20 / 70
15 / 60
10 / 50
5 / 40
0 / 32
-5 / 20
-10 /
-15 / 10
-20 / 0

The best seasons to travel to Tōkyō are spring and fall, when the weather is at its best. Spring brings warm weather with only occasional showers, and flowers grace landscapes in both rural and urban areas. The first harbingers of spring are plum blossoms in early March; *sakura* (cherry blossoms) follow, beginning in Kyūshū and usually arriving in Tōkyō by mid-April. Summer brings on the rainy season, with particularly heavy rains and stifling humidity in July. Avoid July and August if at all possible. Fall is a welcome relief, with clear blue skies and glorious foliage. Occasionally a few surprise typhoons occur in early fall, but the storms are usually as quick to leave as they are to arrive. Winter is gray and chilly, with little snow in most areas along the Pacific Ocean.

To avoid crowds, do not plan a trip for times when most Japanese are vacationing. For the most part, Japanese cannot choose when they want to take their vacations; they tend to do so on the same holiday dates. As a result, airports, planes, trains, and hotels are booked far in advance. Many businesses, shops, and restaurants are closed during these holidays. Holiday periods include the few days before and after New Year's; Golden Week, which follows Greenery Day (April 29); and mid-August at the time of the Obon festivals, when many Japanese return to their hometowns.

Climate

The climate in Japan resembles that of the east coast of the United States. Spring is a beautiful and much celebrated time throughout the country. In Tōkyō the cherry blossoms open in early April, and festivals celebrating springtime last until June. Summer in Tōkyō can be unbearably hot in part due to the "heat island" effect, which occurs when exhausts from buildings in the crowded center affect the weather generally, raising the temperature and humidity to subtropical levels. Fall is very pleasant, and trees in and around the city turn bright red, orange, and yellow. Winter is chilly and dry. Western Japan receives plenty of snow, but Tōkyō doesn't get much at all. The following is a list of average daily maximum and minimum temperatures.

⚡ Forecasts **Weather Channel** ⊕ www.weather.com.

TŌKYŌ

Jan.	46F	8C	May	72F	22C	Sept.	78F	26C
	29	2		53	12		66	19
Feb.	48F	9C	June	75F	24C	Oct.	70F	21C
	30	1		62	17		56	13
Mar.	53F	12C	July	82F	28C	Nov.	60F	16C
	35	2		70	21		42	6
Apr.	62F	17C	Aug.	86F	30C	Dec.	51F	11C
	46	8		72	22		33	1

Matsuri (festivals) are very important to the Japanese, and hundreds of them are held throughout the year. Many originated in folk and religious rituals and date back hundreds of years. Gala matsuri take place annually at Buddhist temples and Shintō shrines, and many are associated with the changing of the seasons.

To find out specific matsuri dates, contact the Japan National Tourism Organization (☎ 212/757–5640 in U.S., 03/3201–3331 in Tōkyō). Note that when national holidays fall on Sunday, they are celebrated on the following Monday. Museums and sights are often closed the days after these holidays.

WINTER	
January 1	**New Year's Day,** along with the days preceding and following, is the festival of festivals for the Japanese. Some women dress in traditional kimonos, and many people visit shrines and hold family reunions. Although the day is solemn, streets are often decorated with pine twigs, plum branches, and bamboo stalks.
February 11	**National Foundation Day** celebrates accession to the throne by the first emperor.
SPRING	
On or near March 21	**Vernal Equinox Day** celebrates the start of spring. On or around this date, Buddhists visit family graves and tombs to remember and pay their respects to their ancestors.
April 29	Greenery Day marks the first day of **Golden Week**—when many Japanese take vacations, and hotels, trains, and attractions are booked solid. This is *not* a good time to visit Japan.
May 3	**Constitution Memorial Day** commemorates the adoption of the Japanese constitution.
May 5	On **Children's Day** families with little boys display paper or cloth carp on bamboo poles outside the house or a set of warrior dolls inside the home.
Weekend before May 15	The **Kanda Festival,** a loud Tōkyō blowout that takes place in odd-numbered years, is all about taking the Kanda shrine's gods out for some fresh air in their *mikoshi* (portable shrines)—not to mention drinking plenty of beer and having a great time.
3rd weekend of May	The **Sanja Festival,** held at Tōkyō's Asakusa Jinja, is the city's biggest party. Men, often naked to the waist, carry palanquins through the streets amid revelers. Many of these bare bearers bear the tattoos of the Yakuza, Japan's Mafia.

SUMMER	
3rd Monday of July	A recent addition to the calendar, Umi no hi (Marine Day) marks the start of school summer holidays.
August 13–16	During the Obon Festival, a time of Buddhist ceremonies in honor of ancestors, many Japanese take off the entire week to travel to their hometowns—try to avoid travel on these days.
FALL	
September 15	Keiro-no-hi is Respect for the Aged Day.
September 23 or 24	Shūbun-no-hi is Autumnal Equinox Day.
2nd Monday of October	Health-Sports Day commemorates the Tōkyō Olympics of 1964.
November 3	Culture Day, established after World War II, encourages the Japanese to cherish peace, freedom, and culture, both old and new.
December 23	On Tennō Tanjobi (the Emperor's Birthday) Emperor Akihito makes an appearance on the balcony of the Imperial Palace.
December 27	Travel is *not* recommended on the first day of the weeklong New Year celebrations.

PLEASURES & PASTIMES

Dining Japanese food is not only delicious and healthy but also arranged to please the eye. In fact the aesthetic experience of food is of utmost importance to the Japanese. Even the most humble box lunch (*bentō*) from a railway station or on a train will have been created with careful attention to color combinations and overall presentation. For an introduction to the delights of Japanese cooking, turn to Chapter 8, The Discreet Charm of Japanese Cuisine, and the English–Japanese Traveler's Vocabulary at the end of this guide, which includes names of food items in Japanese characters.

Language As difficult as it can be, learning Japanese is also a delight. For basic points on the language, *see* Language *in* Smart Travel Tips A to Z *and* the English–Japanese Traveler's Vocabulary at the end of this book.

Onsen No doubt the Japanese love of bathing has something to do with the hundreds of *onsen* (natural hot springs) that bubble out of their volcanic islands. Many onsen are surrounded by resorts, ranging from overlarge Western-style hotels to small, humble inns; all are extremely popular among Japanese tourists. Traditionally the curative value of hot-spring water was strongly emphasized. Add to that today's need to get away from the frantic pace of life and relax. At resorts, onsen water is usually piped in to hotel rooms or large, communal indoor baths. And some onsen have *rotemburo* (open-air baths) where you can soak outdoors in the midst of a snowy winter landscape. Some of the best-known spas near Tōkyō are at Atami, Hakone, Itō, and Nikkō.

Shopping Tōkyō's *depāto* (pronounced "deh-*pah*-to, meaning department stores) have to be seen to be believed—from their automatonlike white-gloved elevator operators to their elaborate wrapping of even the most humble purchase. Items made by every international designer you can name sit alongside the best of traditional Japanese arts-and-crafts items, and most stores have at least two basement levels devoted entirely to the selling of food, from international grocery fare to ready-to-eat Japanese delicacies.

For a view of how the middle class manages its daily shopping, head to one of the shopping arcades that are often an extension of urban and suburban train or subway stations. Everything—clothes, stationery, books, CDs, electronic goods, food, housewares—is sold in these arcades, which can be madhouses during the evening rush hour. Markets are another way to get closer to everyday Japanese life. The warrens of shops outside Tōkyō's fish market in Tsukiji are full of interesting wares.

Performing Arts Japan is justly proud of its music, dance, and theater traditions, which are unique. Unless you happen to catch one of the infrequent (and expensive) performances of a company on tour abroad, you'll never see the like of Kabuki, Nō, or Bunraku anywhere else. *See* Chapter 4, Nightlife & the Arts, for descriptions of Japanese performing arts and for information on where to view performances.

FODOR'S CHOICE

	The sights, restaurants, hotels, and other travel experiences on these pages are our writers' and editors' top picks—our Fodor's Choices.
Fodor's Choice ★	

LODGING

$$$$	**Grand Hyatt Tōkyō**, Roppongi. Luxurious materials, from sheets to showerheads, are the main claim to fame of this hotel.
$$$$	**Hotel Ōkura**, Tora-no-mon. The Ōkura is an old favorite among diplomats and business travelers for its good service, spacious rooms, and understated sophistication. There's a small museum on-site.
$$$–$$$$	**Four Seasons Hotel Chinzan-sō**, Sekiguchi. Every polished inch is evidence of the million dollars or so that it cost to complete each guest room here.
$$$–$$$$	**Yoshimizu Ginza**, Ginza. Artistic minimalism is the style of this simple, traditional inn, which aims to provide a total escape from the crowded streets of the city.

BUDGE LODGING

$	**Sawanoya Ryokan**, Yanaka. Rooms are basic and the bathroom is shared, but you can't beat the warm welcome at this family-run inn. Rooms book up quickly.

RESTAURANTS

$$–$$$$	**Inakaya**, Roppongi. Cooks in traditional dress grill skewers of meat, seafood, and vegetables as you look on.
$$–$$$$	**Tableaux**, Shibuya. Red leather meets antique gold at Tableaux. Although the design is over-the-top, it doesn't outshine the contemporary Asian-Italian dishes.
$$–$$$	**Robata**, Yūraku-chō. Home-style Japanese food, including steamed fish and beef stew, is served on beautiful pottery in this small eatery.
$$–$$$	**Sasashū**, Ikebukuro. This traditional-style pub pairs the finest sakes in Japan with the best izakaya food in town.
$$	**Ganchan**, Roppongi. Squeeze into this tiny, cluttered restaurant for some of the best charcoal-grilled yakitori in town.

BUDGET RESTAURANTS

$–$$	**Aoi-Marushin**, Asakusa. Loads of tempura are served fresh from the fryer at this Asakusa staple, a short walk from Sensō-ji temple. English menus make ordering a snap.
¢–$$	**Ume no Hana**, Aoyama. A traditional stone walkway lined with lanterns leads up to this restaurant, which takes the simple ingredient tofu and transforms it into delicious, creative dishes.

MUSEUMS

Nezu Institute of Fine Arts, Aoyama. A fantastic collection of Japanese and Chinese art, a lovely 5-acre garden, and several tea pavilions make the Nezu Institute the perfect destination for a leisurely afternoon.

Tōkyō National Museum, Ueno. This is where to get your fill of East Asian art and archaeology, including pottery, scrolls, swords, armor, and masks.

NATURAL WONDERS & PARKS

Fuji-san, in Fuji-Hakone-Izu National Park. Whether you climb to the summit or view it from afar, beautiful, symmetrical, snow-capped Mt. Fuji is bound to make an impression.

Imperial Palace East Garden. This wonderfully sculpted garden has tree-shaded walkways, rows of rhododendrons, a pond, a waterfall, several fine old structures, and unbeatable views of the Imperial Palace.

Kegon Falls, in Chūzenji. You can view Japan's most famous waterfall from either the top or the bottom of the 318-foot drop.

NIGHTLIFE

Kabuki-za, Ginza. A night of Kabuki is a quintessential Japanese experience and there's no better place to catch a performance than at this theater.

Montoak, Shibuya. This supercool lounge in the Omotesandō high-fashion district offers cocktails and canapés to those in the know.

Sekirei, Akasaka. On sunny days nothing beats having a drink at this inexpensive outdoor bar on the grounds of the Meiji-Kinenkan complex.

Sweet Basil 139, Roppongi. Come for dinner or just a drink and good music at this upscale jazz club, considered by many to be Tōkyō's best.

SHOPPING

Nippon Token, Toranomon. Come to this Meiji-era shop to check out its antique and reproduction swords, armor, and masks.

Takashimaya, Nihombashi. Japan's Bergdorf, this high-end department store sells designer clothing, traditional crafts, and luxury gifts.

Yamada Heiando, Shibuya. The authentic lacquerware bowls, boxes, and trays here are fairly priced and make perfect souvenirs.

SIGHTS & SCENES

Backstreet shops of Tsukiji. Besides its lively fish market, Tsukiji has countless small stores selling snacks, kitchenware, baskets, and knickknacks, plus dozens of tiny sushi bars.

Ryōgoku. A sumō tournament or the elaborate Edo-Tōkyō Museum may draw you out to this working-class neighborhood west of the Sumida-gawa River.

TEMPLES & SHRINES

Great Buddha statue, in Kamakura. This 37-foot, 700-year old bronze statue about 40 mi southwest of Tōkyō is one of Japan's most enduring symbols.

Hase-dera Temple, in Kamakura. The halls of this beautiful temple facing the sea enshrine three enormous statues: Jizō, the savior of children; Jūichimen Kannon, the 11-headed goddess of mercy; and Amida Buddha.

Sensō-ji, Asakusa. A walk through the serene gardens and Shintō shrine of this Edo-period temple complex is a must for any visitor to Tōkyō.

Tōshō-gū, in Nikkō. Anyone with more than four or five days to spend in Tōkyō should make a trip out to Nikkō to see the resplendent world-renowned shrine to Ieyasu Tokugawa.

SMART TRAVEL TIPS

ADDRESSES

The simplest way to decipher a Japanese address is to break it into parts. For example: 6-chōme 8–19, Chūō-ku, Fukuoka-shi, Fukuoka-ken. In this address the "chōme" indicates a precise area (a block, for example), and the numbers following "chōme" indicate the building within the area. Note that buildings aren't always numbered sequentially; numbers are often assigned as buildings are erected. Only local police officers and mail carriers in Japan seem to be familiar with the area defined by the chōme. Sometimes, instead of "chōme," "machi" (town) is used.

Written addresses in Japan have the opposite order of those in the West, with the city coming before the street. "Ku" refers to a ward (a district) of a city, "shi" refers to a city name, and "ken" indicates a prefecture, which is roughly equivalent to a state in the United States. It's not unusual for the prefecture and the city to have the same name, as in the above address. There are a few geographic areas in Japan that are not called ken. One is greater Tōkyō, which is called Tōkyō-to. Other exceptions are Kyōto and Ōsaka, which are followed by the suffix "-fu"—Kyōto-fu, Ōsaka-fu. Hokkaidō, Japan's northernmost island, is also not considered a ken. Not all addresses conform exactly to the above format. Rural addresses, for example, might use "gun" (county) where city addresses have "ku" (ward).

Even Japanese people cannot find a building based on the address alone. If you get in a taxi with a written address, do not assume the driver will be able to find your destination. Usually, people provide very detailed instructions or maps to explain their exact locations. It's always good to know the location of your destination in relation to a major building or department store.

AIR TRAVEL

You can fly nonstop to Tōkyō from Chicago, Detroit, New York, Los Angeles, San Francisco, Portland (OR), Seattle,

Addresses
Air Travel
Airports
Boat & Ferry Travel
Bus Travel
Business Hours
Cameras & Photography
Car Rental
Car Travel
Children in Japan
Computers on the Road
Consumer Protection
Customs & Duties
Disabilities & Accessibility
Discounts & Deals
Ecotourism
Electricity
Embassies
Emergencies
English-Language Media
Gay & Lesbian Travel
Health
Holidays
Insurance
Language
Lodging
Mail & Shipping
Money Matters
Packing
Passports & Visas
Restrooms
Safety
Senior-Citizen Travel
Shopping
Sightseeing Guides
Students in Japan
Subway Travel
Taxes
Taxis
Telephones
Time
Tipping
Tours & Packages
Train Travel to & from Tōkyō
Train Travel Within Tōkyō
Transportation Around Tōkyō
Travel Agencies
Visitor Information
Web Sites

Minneapolis, and Washington D.C. in the United States; from London; from Brisbane, Sydney, and Melbourne in Australia; and from Auckland in New Zealand. Because of the distance, fares to Japan from the United States tend to be expensive, usually between $900 and $1,200 for a seat in coach. But it's possible to get a ticket for as low as $700 from a discount travel Web site, depending on the time of year.

BOOKING
When you book, look for nonstop flights and remember that "direct" flights stop at least once. Try to avoid connecting flights, which require a change of plane. Two airlines may operate a connecting flight jointly, so ask whether your airline operates every segment of the trip; you may find that the carrier you prefer flies you only part of the way. To find more booking tips and to check prices and make online flight reservations, log on to www.fodors.com.

CARRIERS
Japan Airlines (JAL) and United Airlines are the major carriers between North America and Narita Airport in Tōkyō; Northwest, American Airlines, Delta Airlines, and All Nippon Airways (ANA) also link North American cities with Tōkyō. JAL, Cathay Pacific, Virgin Atlantic Airways, and British Airways fly between Narita and Great Britain; JAL, United, and Qantas fly between Narita and Australia; and JAL and Air New Zealand fly between Narita and New Zealand. Most of these airlines also fly into and out of Japan's number two international airport, Kansai International Airport, located south of Ōsaka.

🛫 Airlines & Contacts **Air Canada** ☎ 888/247-2262, 0120/048-048 in Japan ⊕ www.aircanada.ca. **All Nippon Airways** ☎ 800/235-9262 in U.S. and Canada, 0120/02-9222 in Japan for domestic flights, 0120/02-9333 in Japan for international flights ⊕ www.anaskyweb.com or www.ana.co.jp. **American** ☎ 800/433-7300, 0120/000-860 in Japan ⊕ www.aa.com. **British Airways** ☎ 0345/222-111 in U.K., 03/3593-8811 in Japan ⊕ www.british-airways.com. **Continental** ☎ 800/525-0280 ⊕ www.continental.com. **Delta** ☎ 800/221-1212 ⊕ www.delta.com. **Japan Airlines** ☎ 800/525-3663, 0845/7747-700 in U.K., 0120/255-931 international in Japan, 0120/255-971 domestic in Japan ⊕ www.jal.

co.jp. **Korean Air** ☎ 800/438-5000, 0800/413-000 in U.K., 03/5443-3311 in Japan ⊕ www.koreanair.com. **Lufthansa** ☎ 0870/837-7737 in U.K. ⊕ www.lufthansa.com. **Northwest** ☎ 800/447-4747, 03/3533-6000 or 0120/120-747 in Japan ⊕ www.nwa.com. **Swiss** ☎ 800/221-4750, 020/7434-7300 in U.K., 03/5156-9090 in Japan ⊕ www.swissair.com. **Thai Airways International** ☎ 800/426-5204, 020/7499-9113 in U.K., 03/3503-3311 in Japan ⊕ www.thaiair.com. **United** ☎ 800/241-6522, 0120/114-466 in Japan ⊕ www.united.com.

CHECK-IN & BOARDING
Always **find out your carrier's check-in policy.** Plan to arrive at the airport about 1½ hours before your scheduled departure time for domestic flights and 2½ hours before international flights. You may need to arrive earlier if you're flying from one of the busier airports or during peak air-traffic times. To avoid delays at airport-security checkpoints, try not to wear any metal. Shoes without laces that you can slip off and on are convenient when you have to pass them through the baggage scanners. Belt and other buckles, shoes with nails or steel toes, and keys are among the items that can set off detectors.

Assuming that not everyone with a ticket will show up, airlines routinely overbook planes. When everyone does, airlines ask for volunteers to give up their seats. In return, these volunteers usually get a several-hundred-dollar flight voucher, which can be used toward the purchase of another ticket, and are rebooked on the next flight out. If there are not enough volunteers, the airline must choose who will be denied boarding. The first to get bumped are passengers who checked in late and those flying on discounted tickets, so get to the gate and check in as early as possible, especially during peak periods.

Always **bring a government-issued photo ID** to the airport; even when it's not required, a passport is best.

CUTTING COSTS
The least expensive airfares to Tōkyō are priced for round-trip travel and must usually be purchased in advance. Airlines generally allow you to change your return date for a fee; most low-fare tickets, however,

are nonrefundable. It's smart to call a number of airlines and check the Internet; when you are quoted a good price, book it on the spot—the same fare may not be available the next day, or even the next hour. Always check different routings and look into using alternate airports. Also, price off-peak flights, which may be significantly less expensive than others. Travel agents, especially low-fare specialists (⇨ Discounts & Deals), are helpful.

Consolidators are another good source. They buy tickets for scheduled flights at reduced rates from the airlines, then sell them at prices that beat the best fare available directly from the airlines. (Many also offer reduced car-rental and hotel rates.) Sometimes you can even get your money back if you need to return the ticket. Carefully read the fine print detailing penalties for changes and cancellations, purchase the ticket with a credit card, and confirm your consolidator reservation with the airline.

When you fly as a courier, you trade your checked-luggage space for a ticket deeply subsidized by a courier service. There are restrictions on when you can book and how long you can stay. Some courier companies list with membership organizations, such as the Air Courier Association and the International Association of Air Travel Couriers; these require you to become a member before you can book a flight.

Many airlines, singly or in collaboration, offer discount air passes that allow foreigners to travel economically in a particular country or region. These visitor passes usually must be reserved and purchased before you leave home. Information about passes often can be found on most airlines' international Web pages, which tend to be aimed at travelers from outside the carrier's home country. Also, try typing the name of the pass into a search engine, or search for "pass" within the carrier's Web site.

Both of Japan's major carriers offer reduced prices for flights within the country, though tickets must be booked outside Japan. JAL offers the Yōkoso Japan Airpass while ANA has the Visit Japan Fare.

Consolidators **AirlineConsolidator.com** ☎ 888/468-5385 ⊕ www.airlineconsolidator.com, for international tickets. **Best Fares** ☎ 800/880-1234 or 800/576-8255 ⊕ www.bestfares.com; $59.90 annual membership. **Cheap Tickets** ☎ 800/377-1000 or 800/652-4327 ⊕ www.cheaptickets.com. **Expedia** ☎ 800/397-3342 or 404/728-8787 ⊕ www.expedia.com ⊕ www.hotwire.com. **Now Voyager Travel** ✉ 45 W. 21st St., Suite 5A, New York, NY 10010 ☎ 212/459-1616 🖷 212/243-2711 ⊕ www.nowvoyagertravel.com. **Onetravel.com** ⊕ www.onetravel.com. **Orbitz** ☎ 888/656-4546 ⊕ www.orbitz.com. **Priceline.com** ⊕ www.priceline.com. **Travelocity** ☎ 888/709-5983, 877/282-2925 in Canada, 0870/876-3876 in U.K. ⊕ www.travelocity.com.

Courier Resources **Air Courier Association/Cheaptrips.com** ☎ 800/280-5973 or 800/282-1202 ⊕ www.aircourier.org or www.cheaptrips.com; $34 annual membership. **International Association of Air Travel Couriers** ☎ 308/632-3273 in U.S. or 0800/0746-481 in U.K. ⊕ www.courier.org ⊕ www.aircourier.co.uk; $45 annual membership. **Now Voyager Travel** ✉ 45 W. 21st St., Suite 5A, New York, NY 10010 ☎ 212/459-1616 🖷 212/243-2711 ⊕ www.nowvoyagertravel.com.

Discount Passes **All Asia Pass** Cathay Pacific ☎ 800/233-2742, 800/268-6868 in Canada ⊕ www.cathay-usa.com or www.cathay.ca. **Visit Japan Fare** All Nippon Airways ☎ 800/235-9262 in U.S. and Canada, 870/837-8866 in U.K. ⊕ www.anaskyweb.com or www.ana.co.jp. **Yōkoso Japan Airpass** Japan Airlines ☎ 800/525-3663, 0845/7747-700 in U.K. ⊕ www.jal.co.jp.

ENJOYING THE FLIGHT
State your seat preference when purchasing your ticket, and then repeat it when you confirm and when you check in. For more legroom, you can request one of the few emergency-aisle seats at check-in, if you're capable of moving obstacles comparable in weight to an airplane exit door (usually between 35 pounds and 60 pounds)—a Federal Aviation Administration requirement of passengers in these seats. Seats behind a bulkhead also offer more legroom, but they don't have under-seat storage. Don't sit in the row in front of the emergency aisle or in front of a bulkhead, where seats may not recline.

Ask the airline whether a snack or meal is served on the flight. If you have dietary concerns, request special meals when booking. These can be vegetarian, low-cholesterol, or kosher, for example. It's a good idea to pack some healthful snacks and a small (plastic) bottle of water in your carry-on bag. On long flights, try to maintain a normal routine, to help fight jet lag. At night, get some sleep. By day, eat light meals, drink water (not alcohol), and **move around the cabin** to stretch your legs. For additional jet-lag tips consult *Fodor's FYI: Travel Fit & Healthy* (available at bookstores everywhere).

FLYING TIMES

Flying time to Tōkyō is 13¾ hours from New York, 12¾ hours from Chicago, 9½ hours from Los Angeles, 9½ hours from Sydney, 11–12 hours from the United Kingdom. Japan Airlines' GPS systems allow a more direct routing, which reduces its flight times by about 30 minutes. Your trip east, because of tailwinds, will be about 45 minutes shorter.

HOW TO COMPLAIN

If your baggage goes astray or your flight goes awry, complain right away. Most carriers require that you **file a claim immediately.** The Aviation Consumer Protection Division of the Department of Transportation publishes *Fly-Rights,* which discusses airlines and consumer issues and is available online. You can also find articles and information on mytravelrights.com, the Web site of the nonprofit Consumer Travel Rights Center.

🔀 Airline Complaints **Air Transport Users Council** ✉ For inquiries: FAA, Room K201, CAA House, 45–59 Kingsway, London, WC2B 6TE ☎ 020/7240-6061 ⊕ www.caa.co.uk/auc/. **Aviation Consumer Protection Division** ✉ U.S. Department of Transportation, Office of Aviation Enforcement and Proceedings, C-75, Room 4107, 400 7th St. SW, Washington, DC 20590 ☎ 202/366-2220 ⊕ aircon-sumer.ost.dot.gov. **Federal Aviation Administration Consumer Hotline** ✉ For inquiries: FAA, 800 Independence Ave. SW, Washington, DC 20591 ☎ 800/322-7873 ⊕ www.faa.gov.

RECONFIRMING

Check the status of your flight before you leave for the airport. You can do this on your carrier's Web site, by linking to a flight-status checker (many Web booking services offer these), or by calling your carrier or travel agent. Always confirm international flights at least 72 hours ahead of the scheduled departure time.

AIRPORTS

Tōkyō has two airports, Narita and Haneda. Narita, officially the New Tōkyō International Airport in Narita, is the major gateway to Japan, serving all international flights, except those operated by (Taiwan's) China Airways, which berths at Haneda. Narita is 80 km (50 mi) northeast of Tōkyō and has two fairly well-developed terminals, plus a central building of shops and restaurants. Traffic in and out of the airport is high, especially in December and August, when millions of Japanese take holidays abroad. Customs clearance delays of an hour or more are not uncommon.

Both terminals at Narita have ATMs and money exchange counters in the lobbies near Customs. Both terminals also have a Japan National Tourist Organization's Tourist Information Center, where you can get free maps, brochures, and other visitor information. Directly across from the customs-area exits at both terminals are the ticket counters for airport buses to Tōkyō.

✈ Airport Information **Haneda Airport (HND)** ☎ 03/5757-8111 ⊕ www.tokyo-airport-bldg.co.jp. **Narita Airport (NRT)** ☎ 0476/34-5000 ⊕ www.narita-airport.or.jp.

TRANSFERRING FROM NARITA AIRPORT TO TŌKYŌ

Directly across from the customs-area exits at both terminals are the ticket counters for buses to Tōkyō. Buses leave from platforms just outside terminal exits, exactly on schedule; the departure time is on the ticket. The Friendly Airport Limousine offers the only shuttle bus service from Narita to Tōkyō. Different buses stop at various major hotels in the $$$$ category and at the JR Tōkyō and Shinjuku train stations; the fare is ¥2,400–¥3,800 ($21–$35), depending on your destination. Even if you're not staying at one of the route's drop-off points, you can take the bus as far as the one closest to your hotel and then use a taxi for the remaining distance. The buses only run every hour or so and the last departure is at 11:30 PM. The trip is scheduled for 70–90 minutes but can take two hours in heavy traffic. A Friendly Airport Limousine bus to the Tōkyō City Air Terminal (TCAT) leaves approximately every 10–20 minutes from 6:55 AM to 11 PM; the fare is ¥2,900 ($26). TCAT is in Nihombashi in north-central Tōkyō, a bit far from most destinations, but from here you can connect directly with Suitengū station on the Hanzō-mon subway line, then to anywhere in the subway network. A taxi from TCAT to most major hotels will cost about ¥3,000 ($27).

Japan Railways trains stop at both Narita Airport terminals. The fastest and most comfortable is the Narita Limited Express (NEX), which makes 23 runs a day in each direction. Trains from the airport go directly to the central Tōkyō station in just under an hour, then continue to Yokohama and Ōfuna. Daily departures begin at 7:43 AM; the last train is at 9:43 PM. The one-way fare is ¥2,940 (¥4,980 for the first-class "Green Car" and ¥5,380 per person for a private compartment that seats four). All seats are reserved, and you'll need to reserve one for yourself in advance, as this train fills quickly. The less elegant *kaisoku* (rapid train) on JR's Narita Line also runs from the airport to Tōkyō station, by way of Chiba; there are 16 departures daily, starting at 7 AM. The fare to Tōkyō is ¥1,280 (¥2,210 for the Green Car); the ride takes 1 hour and 27 minutes.

The Keisei Skyliner train runs every 20–30 minutes between the airport terminals and Keisei-Ueno station. The trip takes 57 minutes and costs ¥1,920 ($17). The first Skyliner leaves Narita for Ueno at 9:21 AM, the last at 9:59 PM. There's also an early train from the airport, called the Morning Liner, which leaves at 7:49 AM and costs ¥1,400. From Ueno to Narita, the first Skyliner is at 6:32 AM, the last at 5:21 PM. All Skyliner seats are reserved. It only makes sense to take the Keisei, however, if your final destination is in the Ueno area; otherwise, you must change to the Tōkyō subway system or the Japan Railways loop line at Ueno (the station is adjacent to Keisei-Ueno station) or take a cab to your hotel.

You can take a taxi from Narita Airport to central Tōkyō, but it'll cost you ¥20,000 (about $180) or more, depending on traffic and where you're going. Private car service is also very expensive; from Narita Airport to the Imperial Hotel downtown, for example, will set you back about ¥35,000. **Airport Transport Service Co.** ☎ 03/3665-7232 in Tōkyō, 0476/32-8080 for Terminal 1, 0476/34-6311 for Terminal 2. **IAE Co.** ☎ 0476/32-7954 for Terminal 1, 0476/34-6886 for Terminal 2. **Japan Railways** ☎ 03/3423-0111 for JR East InfoLine ☉ weekdays 10-6. **Keisei Railway** ☎ 03/3831-0131 for Ueno information counter, 0476/32-8505 at Narita Airport.

TRANSFERRING FROM HANEDA AIRPORT TO TŌKYŌ

The monorail from Haneda Airport to Hamamatsu-chō station in Tōkyō is the fastest and cheapest way into town; the journey takes about 20 minutes, and trains run approximately every 4 to 5 minutes; the fare is ¥470 ($4). From Hamamatsu-chō station, change to a JR train or take a taxi to your destination.

A taxi to the center of Tōkyō takes about 40 minutes; the fare is approximately ¥8,000 ($73). **Tōkyō Monorail Co., Ltd.** ☎ 03/3434-3171.

BOAT & FERRY TRAVEL

The best ride in Tōkyō, hands down, is the *suijō basu* (river bus), operated by the Tōkyō Cruise Ship Company from Hinode Pier, from the mouth of the Sumida-gawa upstream to Asakusa. The glassed-in double-decker boats depart roughly every 20–40 minutes, weekdays 9:45–7:10, weekends and holidays 9:35–7:10 (with extended service to 7:50 July 9–September 23). The trip takes 40 minutes and costs ¥660. The pier is a seven-minute walk from Hamamatsu-chō station on the JR Yamanote Line.

The Sumida-gawa was once Tōkyō's lifeline, a busy highway for travelers and freight alike. The ferry service dates to 1885. Some people still take it to work, but today most passengers are Japanese tourists. On its way to Asakusa, the boat passes Tsukiji's Central Wholesale Market, the largest wholesale fish and produce market in the world; the old lumberyards and warehouses upstream; and the Kokugikan, with its distinctive green roof, which houses the sumō wrestling arena, the Sumō Museum, and headquarters of the Japan Sumō Association.

Another place to catch the ferry is at the Hama Rikyū Tei-en (Detached Palace Garden: open daily 9–4:30), a 15-minute walk from Ginza. Once part of the imperial estates, the gardens are open to the public for a separate ¥300 entrance fee—which you have to pay even if you are only using the ferry landing. The landing is a short walk to the left as you enter the main gate. Boats depart every 35–45 minutes every weekday 10:25–4:10; the fare between Asakusa and Hama Rikyū is ¥620.

In addition to the ferry to Asakusa, the Tōkyō Cruise Ship Company also operates four other lines from Hinode Pier. The Harbor Cruise Line stern-wheeler makes a 50-minute circuit under the Rainbow Bridge and around the inner harbor. Departures are at 10:30, 12:30, 1:30, and 3:30 (and 4:45 in August). The fare is ¥800. If you visit in August you should definitely opt for the evening cruise; the lights on the Rainbow Bridge and neighboring Odaiba are spectacular. Two lines connect Hinode to Odaiba itself, one at 20-minute intervals from 10:10 to 6:10 to Odaiba Seaside Park and the Museum of Maritime Science at Aomi Terminal (¥400–¥520), the other every 25 minutes from 9 to 5:40 to the shopping/amusement center at Palette Town and on to the Tōkyō Big Sight exhibition grounds at Ariake (¥350). The Kasai Sealife Park Line cruise leaves Hinode hourly from 10 to 4 and travels through the network of artificial islands in the harbor to the beach and aquarium at Kasai Rinkai Kōen in Chiba; the one-way fare is ¥800. The Canal Cruise Line connects Hinode with Shinagawa Suizokukan aquarium, south along the harborside. There are six departures daily except Tuesday between 10:15 and 4:50; the one-way fare is ¥800.

🚢 **Tōkyō Cruise Ship Company** ✉ 2-7-104 Kaigan, Minato-ku, Hinode Pier ☎ 03/3457-7830 at Hinode, 03/3841-9178 at Asakusa ⊕ www.suijobus.co.jp/english/cruise_e/index.html.

BUS TRAVEL

Bus routes within Tōkyō are impossibly complicated. The Tōkyō Municipal Government operates some of the lines; private companies run the rest. There's no telephone number even a native Japanese can call for help. And buses all have tiny seats and low ceilings. Unless you are a true Tōkyō veteran, forget about taking buses.

FARES & SCHEDULES

Some buses have a set cost, anywhere from ¥100 to ¥200, depending on the route and municipality, in which case you board at the front of the bus and pay as you get on. On other buses cost is determined by the distance you travel. You take a ticket when you board at the rear door of the bus; it bears the number of the stop at which you boarded. Your fare depends on your destination and is indicated by a board at the front of the bus.

🚌 **Bus Information** JR Kantō Bus ☎ 03/3516-1950. Nishinihon JR Bus ☎ 06/6466-9990.

BUSINESS HOURS

General business hours are weekdays 9–5. Many offices also open at least half of the day on Saturday but are generally closed on Sunday.

BANKS & OFFICES

Banks are open weekdays from 9 to at least 3, with some now staying open until 4 or 5. As with shops, there's a trend toward longer and later opening hours.

MUSEUMS & SIGHTS

Museums generally close on Monday and the day following national holidays. They are also closed the day following special exhibits and during the weeklong New Year celebrations.

SHOPS

Department stores are usually open 10–7 but close one day a week, which varies from store to store. Other stores are open from 10 or 11 to 7 or 8. Tōkyō has 24-hour convenience stores, many of which now have ATM facilities.

CAMERAS & PHOTOGRAPHY

If your camera or laptop was made in Japan, you should consider registering it with U.S. Customs (⇨ Customs & Duties) to avoid having to pay duties on it when returning home.

Fluorescent lighting, which is common in Japan, gives photographs a greenish tint. You can counteract this discoloration with an FL filter.

The Japanese love photography and taking photographs at temples or shrines is perfectly acceptable. Digital photography is all the rage now, and Japan is the world-leader in camera-equipped mobile phones. The *Kodak Guide to Shooting Great Travel Pictures* (available at bookstores everywhere) is loaded with tips.

Photo Help **Kodak Information Center** ☎ 800/242-2424 ⊕ www.kodak.com.

EQUIPMENT PRECAUTIONS
Don't pack film or equipment in checked luggage, where it is much more susceptible to damage. X-ray machines used to view checked luggage are extremely powerful and therefore are likely to ruin your film. Try to ask for hand inspection of film, which becomes clouded after repeated exposure to airport X-ray machines, and keep videotapes and computer disks away from metal detectors. Always keep film, tape, and computer disks out of the sun. Carry an extra supply of batteries, and be prepared to turn on your camera, camcorder, or laptop to prove to airport security personnel that the device is real.

FILM & DEVELOPING
Film is very easy to find, and is reasonably priced (a 36-exposure color print film costs ¥400, but cheap multipacks are very easy to find). Developing, however, can be a hit-and-miss affair, and is expensive compared to developing in the United States.

VIDEO
Japan uses the same standard for videotape as the U.S., so non-U.S. visitors should ensure an adequate supply of videotape. A 60-minute camcorder tape costs ¥1,300.

CAR RENTAL
Congestion, the infrequency of road signs in English, and the difficulty—not to say the expense—of parking make driving in Tōkyō impractical. That said, if you decide to rent a car, the following companies have locations all around Tōkyō and Japan: Budget Rent-A-Car, Dollar Rent-A-Car,

Hertz Asia Pacific (Japan), or Nippon Rent-A-Car Service. Be aware that their central business offices close at 6 PM or 7 PM, and that you're not guaranteed to reach anybody who can deal with you in English. Make your reservation via phone or on the Web before you come. With taxes, the cost of a mid-size sedan (1500 cc.) is about ¥12,000 ($110) per day. An international driver's license is required.

You can hire large and comfortable chauffeured cars (the Japanese call them *haiya*) for about ¥5,000 ($46) per hour for a mid-size car, up to ¥18,000 ($164) per hour for a Cadillac limousine. Call Hinomaru Limousine. The Imperial, Ōkura, and Palace hotels also have limousine services.

Local Agencies **Budget Rent-A-Car** ☎ 0120-150-801 toll-free ⊕ www.budget.com. **Dollar Rent-A-Car** ☎ 0120-117-801 toll-free ⊕ www.dollarcar.com. **Hertz Asia Pacific (Japan) Ltd.** ☎ 03/5401-7651 ⊕ www.hertz.com. **Hinomaru Limousine** ☎ 03/3212-0505 ⊕ www.hinomaru.co.jp. **Nippon Rent-A-Car** ☎ 03/3485-7196 ✉ intl-res@nipponrentacar.co.jp.

Major Agencies **Alamo** ☎ 800/522-9696 ⊕ www.alamo.com. **Avis** ☎ 800/331-1084, 800/879-2847 in Canada, 0870/606-0100 in U.K., 02/9353-9000 in Australia, 09/526-2847 in New Zealand ⊕ www.avis.com. **Budget** ☎ 800/527-0700, 0870/156-5656 in U.K. ⊕ www.budget.com. **Dollar** ☎ 800/800-6000, 0800/085-4578 in U.K. ⊕ www.dollar.com. **Hertz** ☎ 800/654-3001, 800/263-0600 in Canada, 0870/844-8844 in U.K., 02/9669-2444 in Australia, 09/256-8690 in New Zealand ⊕ www.hertz.com. **National Car Rental** ☎ 800/227-7368, 0870/600-6666 in U.K. ⊕ www.nationalcar.com.

Local Agencies **Ekiren–JR Tōkyō Station Branch** ☎ 03/3215-1717 ⊕ www.ekiren.co.jp. **Nippon Rentacar–JR Tōkyō Station Branch** ☎ 03/3271-6643 ⊕ www.nipponrentacar.co.jp.

INSURANCE
When driving a rented car you are generally responsible for any damage to or loss of the vehicle. You also may be liable for any property damage or personal injury that you may cause while driving. Before you rent, see what coverage you already have under the terms of your personal auto-insurance policy and credit cards.

REQUIREMENTS & RESTRICTIONS

In Japan your own driver's license is not acceptable. You need an international driver's permit; it's available from the American or Canadian Automobile Association, or, in the United Kingdom, from the Automobile Association or Royal Automobile Club (⇨ Auto Clubs *under* Car Travel, *below*). By law, car seats must be installed if the driver is travelling with a child under six.

SURCHARGES

To avoid a hefty refueling fee, fill the tank just before you turn in the car, but be aware that gas stations near the rental outlet may overcharge. It's almost never a deal to buy the tank of gas that's in the car when you rent it; the understanding is that you'll return it empty, but some fuel usually remains. Child seats generally cost about ¥500 a day, and must be ordered at the time of reservation.

CAR TRAVEL

You need an international driving permit (IDP) to drive in Japan. IDPs are available from the American and Canadian automobile associations and, in the United Kingdom, from the Automobile Association and Royal Automobile Club. These international permits, valid only in conjunction with your regular driver's license, are universally recognized; having one may save you a problem with local authorities.

Major roads in Japan are sufficiently marked in the roman alphabet, and on country roads there's usually someone to ask for help. However, it's a good idea to have a detailed map with town names written in *kanji* (Japanese characters) and *romaji* (romanized Japanese).

Car travel along the Tōkyō–Kyōto–Hiroshima corridor and in other built-up areas of Japan is not as convenient as the trains. Within the major cities, the trains and subways will get you to your destinations faster and more comfortably. Roads are congested, gas is expensive (about ¥110 per liter, or $4.80 per gallon), and highway tolls are exorbitant (tolls between Tōkyō and Kyōto amount to ¥10,550). In major cities, with the exception of main arteries, English signs are few and far between, one-way streets often lead you off the track,

and parking is often hard to find and usually expensive.

AUTO CLUBS

🔃 In Australia **Australian Automobile Association (AAA)** ☎ 02/6247-7311 ⊕ www.aaa.asn.au.
🔃 In Canada **Canadian Automobile Association (CAA)** ☎ 613/247-0117 ⊕ www.caa.ca.
🔃 In New Zealand **New Zealand Automobile Association** ☎ 09/377-4660 ⊕ www.aa.co.nz.
🔃 In the U.K. **Automobile Association (AA)** ☎ 0870/550-0600 ⊕ www.theaa.com. **Royal Automobile Club (RAC)** ☎ 0870/572-2722 ⊕ www.rac.co.uk.
🔃 In the U.S. **American Automobile Association (AAA)** ☎ 800/564-6222 ⊕ www.aaa.com.

EMERGENCY SERVICES

Emergency telephones along the highways can be used to contact the authorities. A nonprofit service, JHelp.com, offers a free, 24-hour emergency assistance hotline. Car rental agencies generally offer roadside assistance services.
🔃 **Police** ☎ 110. **Fire** ☎ 119. JHelp.com ☎ 0570/000-911.

GASOLINE

Gas stations are plentiful along Japan's toll roads, and prices are fairly uniform across the country. Credit cards are accepted everywhere and are even encouraged—there are discounts for them at some places. Self-service stations have recently become legal, so if you pump your own gas you may get a small discount. Often you pay after putting in the gas, but there are also machines where you put money in first and then use the receipt to get change back. Tipping is not customary.

ROAD CONDITIONS

Driving in Tōyō and other cities can be troublesome, as there are many narrow, one-way streets and little in the way of English road signs except on major arteries.

ROAD MAPS

Mapple is the most famous map company in Japan. Their maps can be found at any convenience store or bookshop, but they are only available in Japanese.

RULES OF THE ROAD

In Japan people **drive on the left.** Speed limits vary, but generally the limit is 80 kph

(50 mph) on highways, 40 kph (25 mph) in cities. Penalties for speeding are severe. By law, car seats must be installed if the driver is traveling with a child under six, while the driver and all passengers in cars must wear seat-belts at all times. Legislation banning the use of hand-held mobile phones is expected to be passed in 2005.

Many smaller streets lack sidewalks, so cars, bicycles, and pedestrians share the same space. Motorbikes with engines under 50 cc are allowed to travel against automobile traffic on one-way roads. Fortunately, considering the narrowness of the streets and the volume of traffic, most Japanese drivers are technically skilled. They may not allow quite as much distance between cars as you're used to. Be prepared for sudden lane changes by other drivers. When waiting at intersections after dark, many drivers, as a courtesy to other drivers, turn off their main headlights to prevent glare.

Japan has very strict laws concerning the consumption of alcohol prior to getting behind the wheel. Given the almost zero-tolerance for driving under the influence and the occasional evening police checkpoint set up along the roads, it's wisest to avoid alcohol entirely if you plan to drive.

CHILDREN IN JAPAN

Western children are adored in Japan and visitors with young children, especially blond ones, should expect lots of attention, especially in rural areas. If you are renting a car, don't forget to arrange for a car seat when you reserve. For general advice about traveling with children, consult *Fodor's FYI: Travel with Your Baby* (available in bookstores everywhere).

BABYSITTING

Some very expensive Western-style hotels and resorts have supervised playrooms where you can drop off your children. The babysitters, however, are unlikely to speak English. Child-care arrangements can also be made through your hotel's concierge, but some properties require up to a week's notice.

FLYING

If your children are two or older, ask about children's airfares. As a general rule, infants under two not occupying a seat fly at greatly reduced fares or even for free. But if you want to guarantee a seat for an infant, you have to pay full fare. Consider flying during off-peak days and times; most airlines will grant an infant a seat without a ticket if there are available seats. When booking, confirm carry-on allowances if you're traveling with infants. In general, for babies charged 10% to 50% of the adult fare you are allowed one carry-on bag and a collapsible stroller; if the flight is full, the stroller may have to be checked or you may be limited to less.

Experts agree that it's a good idea to use safety seats aloft for children weighing less than 40 pounds. Airlines set their own policies: if you use a safety seat, U.S. carriers usually require that the child be ticketed, even if he or she is young enough to ride free, because the seats must be strapped into regular seats. And even if you pay the full adult fare for the seat, it may be worth it, especially on longer trips. Do **check your airline's policy about using safety seats during takeoff and landing.** Safety seats are not allowed everywhere in the plane, so get your seat assignments as early as possible.

When reserving, request children's meals or a freestanding bassinet (not available at all airlines) if you need them. But note that bulkhead seats, where you must sit to use the bassinet, may lack an overhead bin or storage space on the floor.

FOOD

Western-style fast-food restaurants, coffee shops, and ice-cream chains are common in Japan. Many of the most popular U.S. chains are represented. Two very good local chains to watch out for are MOS Burger and Freshness Burger. First Kitchen is similar, but has more than just burgers, offering hot dogs and healthy sandwiches, too. Pizzas are readily available across the country. *Okonomiyaki*, a kind of pancake stuffed with beef, pork or shrimp and common in West Japan, is very popular with Japanese children.

LODGING

Most hotels in Japan allow children under a certain age (usually 12) to stay in their parents' room at no extra charge, but others charge for them as extra adults; be sure to find out the cutoff age for children's discounts.

SIGHTS & ATTRACTIONS

Places that are especially appealing to children are indicated by a rubber-duckie icon (🐤) in the margin.

SUPPLIES & EQUIPMENT

Disposable diapers are widely available in large supermarkets, pharmacies, and Toys R Us stores. Formula is available in powdered form, in tins or packs of sachets, which are more convenient for travelers.

COMPUTERS ON THE ROAD

Phone jacks are the same in Japan as in the U.S. Many hotels have ADSL or Ethernet connections for high-speed Internet access. Ethernet cables are usually available to buy at hotels if you don't bring your own. Wireless Internet access (Wi-Fi) is increasingly popular and available for free at certain coffee shops and in many hotel lobbies across the country.

CONSUMER PROTECTION

Honesty and integrity are important values in Japan, and tourist scams are uncommon. Note, however, that luxury-brand goods bought from street vendors are not likely to be the real thing.

Whether you're shopping for gifts or purchasing travel services, **pay with a major credit card** whenever possible, so you can cancel payment or get reimbursed if there's a problem (and you can provide documentation). If you're doing business with a particular company for the first time, contact your local Better Business Bureau and the attorney general's offices in your state and (for U.S. businesses) the company's home state as well. Have any complaints been filed? Finally, if you're buying a package or tour, always consider travel insurance that includes default coverage (⇨ Insurance).

🚩 BBB **Council of Better Business Bureaus** ✉ 4200 Wilson Blvd., Suite 800, Arlington, VA 22203 ☎ 703/276-0100 🖷 703/525-8277 ⊕ www. bbb.org.

CUSTOMS & DUTIES

When shopping abroad, keep receipts for all purchases. Upon reentering the country, **be ready to show customs officials what you've bought.** Pack purchases together in an easily accessible place. If you think a duty is incorrect, appeal the assessment. If you object to the way your clearance was handled, note the inspector's badge number. In either case, first ask to see a supervisor. If the problem isn't resolved, write to the appropriate authorities, beginning with the port director at your point of entry.

IN AUSTRALIA

Australian residents who are 18 or older may bring home A$400 worth of souvenirs and gifts (including jewelry), 250 cigarettes or 250 grams of cigars or other tobacco products, and 1,125 ml of alcohol (including wine, beer, and spirits). Residents under 18 may bring back A$200 worth of goods. Members of the same family traveling together may pool their allowances. Prohibited items include meat products. Seeds, plants, and fruits need to be declared upon arrival.

🚩 **Australian Customs Service** 🖉 Regional Director, Box 8, Sydney, NSW 2001 ☎ 02/9213-2000 or 1300/363263, 02/9364-7222 or 1800/020-504 quarantine-inquiry line 🖷 02/9213-4043 ⊕ www. customs.gov.au.

IN CANADA

Canadian residents who have been out of Canada for at least seven days may bring in C$750 worth of goods duty-free. If you've been away fewer than seven days but more than 48 hours, the duty-free allowance drops to C$200. If your trip lasts 24 to 48 hours, the allowance is C$50. You may not pool allowances with family members. Goods claimed under the C$750 exemption may follow you by mail; those claimed under the lesser exemptions must accompany you. Alcohol and tobacco products may be included in the seven-day and 48-hour exemptions but not in the 24-hour exemption. If you meet the age requirements of the province or territory through which you reenter Canada, you may bring in, duty-free, 1.5 liters of wine *or* 1.14 liters (40 imperial ounces) of liquor *or* 24 12-ounce cans or bottles of beer or ale. Also, if you meet the local age require-ment for tobacco products, you may bring in, duty-free, 200 cigarettes and 50 cigars. Check ahead of time with the Canada Cus-toms and Revenue Agency or the Depart-ment of Agriculture for policies regarding meat products, seeds, plants, and fruits.

You may send an unlimited number of gifts (only one gift per recipient, however) worth up to C$60 each duty-free to Canada. Label the package UNSOLICITED GIFT—VALUE UNDER $60. Alcohol and to-bacco are excluded.

Canada Customs and Revenue Agency ⊠ 2265 St. Laurent Blvd., Ottawa, Ontario K1G 4K3 ☎ 800/461-9999 in Canada, 204/983-3500 or 506/636-5064 ⊕ www.ccra.gc.ca.

IN JAPAN
Japan has strict regulations about bringing firearms, pornography, and narcotics into the country. Anyone caught with drugs is liable to be detained, deported, and refused reentry into Japan. Certain fresh fruits, vegetables, plants, and animals are also il-legal. Nonresidents are allowed to bring in duty-free: (1) 400 cigarettes or 100 cigars or 500 grams of tobacco; (2) three 760-ml bottles of alcohol; (3) 2 ounces of perfume; (4) other goods up to ¥200,000 value.

Ministry of Finance, Customs and Tariff Bu-reau ⊠ 3-1-1 Kasumigaseki, Chiyoda-ku TOKYO, Tōkyō, 100-8940 ☎ 03/3581-4111 ⊕ www.customs.go.jp/index_e.htm.

IN NEW ZEALAND
All homeward-bound residents may bring back NZ$700 worth of souvenirs and gifts; passengers may not pool their allowances, and children can claim only the concession on goods intended for their own use. For those 17 or older, the duty-free allowance also includes 4.5 liters of wine or beer; one 1,125-ml bottle of spirits; and either 200 cigarettes, 250 grams of tobacco, 50 cigars, *or* a combination of the three up to 250 grams. Meat products, seeds, plants, and fruits must be declared upon arrival to the Agricultural Services Department.

New Zealand Customs ⊠ Head office: The Cus-tomhouse, 17–21 Whitmore St., Box 2218, Wellington ☎ 09/300-5399 or 0800/428-786 ⊕ www.customs.govt.nz.

IN THE U.K.
From countries outside the European Union, including Japan, you may bring home, duty-free, 200 cigarettes, 50 cigars, 100 cigarillos, or 250 grams of tobacco; 1 liter of spirits or 2 liters of fortified or sparkling wine or liqueurs; 2 liters of still table wine; 60 ml of perfume; 250 ml of toilet water; plus £145 worth of other goods, including gifts and souvenirs. Pro-hibited items include meat and dairy prod-ucts, seeds, plants, and fruits.

HM Customs and Excise ⊠ Portcullis House, 21 Cowbridge Rd. E, Cardiff CF11 9SS ☎ 0845/010-9000 or 0208/929-0152 advice service, 0208/929-6731 or 0208/910-3602 complaints ⊕ www.hmce.gov.uk.

IN THE U.S.
U.S. residents who have been out of the country for at least 48 hours may bring home, for personal use, $800 worth of for-eign goods duty-free, as long as they haven't used the $800 allowance or any part of it in the past 30 days. This exemp-tion may include 1 liter of alcohol (for travelers 21 and older), 200 cigarettes, and 100 non-Cuban cigars. Family members from the same household who are traveling together may pool their $800 personal ex-emptions. For fewer than 48 hours, the duty-free allowance drops to $200, which may include 50 cigarettes, 10 non-Cuban cigars, and 150 ml of alcohol (or 150 ml of perfume containing alcohol). The $200 al-lowance cannot be combined with other in-dividuals' exemptions, and if you exceed it, the full value of all the goods will be taxed. Antiques, which U.S. Customs and Border Protection defines as objects more than 100 years old, enter duty-free, as do origi-nal works of art done entirely by hand, in-cluding paintings, drawings, and sculptures. This doesn't apply to folk art or handicrafts, which are in general dutiable.

You may also send packages home duty-free, with a limit of one parcel per ad-dressee per day (except alcohol or tobacco products or perfume worth more than $5). You can mail up to $200 worth of goods for personal use; label the package PER-SONAL USE and attach a list of its contents and their retail value. If the package con-tains your used personal belongings, mark it AMERICAN GOODS RETURNED to avoid paying duties. You may send up to $100 worth of goods as a gift; mark the package UNSOLICITED GIFT. Mailed items do not affect your duty-free allowance on your return.

To avoid paying duty on foreign-made high-ticket items you already own and will take on your trip, register them with Customs before you leave the country. Consider filing a Certificate of Registration for laptops, cameras, watches, and other digital devices identified with serial numbers or other permanent markings; you can keep the certificate for other trips. Otherwise, bring a sales receipt or insurance form to show that you owned the item before you left the United States.

For more about duties, restricted items, and other information about international travel, check out U.S. Customs and Border Protection's online brochure, *Know Before You Go*.

🗗 U.S. Customs and Border Protection ⊠ For inquiries and equipment registration, 1300 Pennsylvania Ave. NW, Washington, DC 20229 ⊕ www.cbp. gov ☎ 877/287-8667 or 202/354-1000 ⊠ For complaints, Customer Satisfaction Unit, 1300 Pennsylvania Ave. NW, Room 5.2C, Washington, DC 20229.

DISABILITIES & ACCESSIBILITY
Though wheelchair navigation is possible and elevators are common, the sheer number of people in Tōkyō may cause some frustration. However, strangers and service people are exceptionally kind and willing to help. Many shrines and temples are set on high ground, but most have ramps. Visit http://accessible.jp.org/tokyo/en for lists of accessible sights, hotels, shops, and more.

LODGING
Staying in a traditional Japanese inn, where guests sleep on futons laid out on *tatami*-mat floors and usually use a communal bath, is difficult, if not impossible, for those with mobility problems. In other hotels, ask for the lowest floor on which accessible services are offered. If you have a hearing impairment, check whether the hotel has devices to alert you visually to the ring of the telephone, a knock at the door, and a fire-emergency alarm. Some hotels provide these devices without charge. Discuss your needs with hotel personnel if this equipment isn't available, so that a staff member can personally alert you in the event of an emergency. In Tōkyō, the Imperial Hotel is the top choice for travelers with wheelchairs.

🗗 Best Choices Imperial Hotel ⊠ 1-1-1 Uchisaiwai-chō, Chiyoda-ku, Tōkyō 100-8558 ☎ 03/3504-1251 ⊕ www.imperialhotel.co.jp. **Hilton Ōsaka** ⊠ 8-8 Umeda 1-chōme, Kita-ku, Ōsaka 530-0001 ☎ 06/6347-7111 ⊕ www.hilton.co.jp/osaka. **Hotel New Hankyū** ⊠ 1-1-35 Shibata, Kita-ku, Ōsaka 530-8310 ☎ 06/6372-5101 ⊕ www.hotel.newhankyu.co.jp. **Westin Miyako Hotel** ⊠ Kachō-chō, Awadaguchi, Higashiyama-ku, Kyōto 605-0052 ☎ 075/771-7111 ⊕ www.westinmiyako-kyoto.com.

RESERVATIONS
When discussing accessibility with an operator or reservations agent, ask hard questions. Are there any stairs, inside *or* out? Are there grab bars next to the toilet *and* in the shower/tub? How wide is the doorway to the room? To the bathroom? For the most extensive facilities meeting the latest legal specifications, opt for newer accommodations. If you reserve through a toll-free number, consider also calling the hotel's local number to confirm the information from the central reservations office. Get confirmation in writing when you can.

TRANSPORTATION
Train stations often have elevators, and station staff will be happy to assist travelers using wheelchairs. Many private train and bus companies, including the Shinkansen (bullet train), are equipped to serve passengers with disabilities. Reservations are essential. Taxi trunks are large enough to hold folded wheelchairs.

🗗 Complaints Aviation Consumer Protection Division (⇨ Air Travel) for airline-related problems. **Departmental Office of Civil Rights** ⊠ For general inquiries, U.S. Department of Transportation, S-30, 400 7th St. SW, Room 10215, Washington, DC 20590 ☎ 202/366-4648 🖶 202/366-9371 ⊕ www.dot.gov/ost/docr/index.htm. **Disability Rights Section** ⊠ NYAV, U.S. Department of Justice, Civil Rights Division, 950 Pennsylvania Ave. NW, Washington, DC 20530 ☎ ADA information line 202/514-0301, 800/514-0301, 202/514-0383 TTY, 800/514-0383 TTY

⊕ www.ada.gov. **U.S. Department of Transporta-tion Hotline** ☎ For disability-related air-travel problems, 800/778-4838 or 800/455-9880 TTY.

TRAVEL AGENCIES

In the United States, the Americans with Disabilities Act requires that travel firms serve the needs of all travelers. Some agencies specialize in working with people with disabilities.

🔏 Travelers with Mobility Problems **Access Adventures/B. Roberts Travel** ✉ 206 Chestnut Ridge Rd., Scottsville, NY 14624 ☎ 585/889-9096 ⊕ www.brobertstravel.com ✍ dltravel@prodigy. net, run by a former physical-rehabilitation counselor. **Flying Wheels Travel** ✉ 143 W. Bridge St., Box 382, Owatonna, MN 55060 ☎ 507/451-5005 🖶 507/451-1685 ⊕ www.flyingwheelstravel.com.

DISCOUNTS & DEALS

Be a smart shopper and compare all your options before making decisions. A plane ticket bought with a promotional coupon from travel clubs, coupon books, and direct-mail offers or purchased on the Internet may not be cheaper than the least expensive fare from a discount ticket agency. And always keep in mind that what you get is just as important as what you save.

DISCOUNT RESERVATIONS

To save money, look into discount reservations services with Web sites and toll-free numbers, which use their buying power to get a better price on hotels, airline tickets (⇨ Air Travel), even car rentals. When booking a room, always **call the hotel's local toll-free number** (if one is available) rather than the central reservations number—you'll often get a better price. Always ask about special packages or corporate rates.

When shopping for the best deal on hotels and car rentals, look for guaranteed exchange rates, which protect you against a falling dollar. With your rate locked in, you won't pay more, even if the price goes up in the local currency.

🔏 Airline Tickets **Air 4 Less** ☎ 800/AIR4LESS, low-fare specialist.

🔏 Hotel Rooms **Accommodations Express** ☎ 800/444-7666 or 800/277-1064 ⊕ www.acex.net. **Hotels.com** ☎ 800/246-8357 ⊕ www.hotels.com. **Steigen-berger Reservation Service** ☎ 800/223-5652 ⊕ www.srs-worldhotels.com. **Turbotrip.com** ☎ 800/473-7829 ⊕ www.turbotrip.com. **Vacation-Land** ☎ 800/245-0050 ⊕ www.vacation-land.com.

PACKAGE DEALS

Don't confuse packages and guided tours. When you buy a package, you travel on your own, just as though you had planned the trip yourself. Fly-drive packages, which combine airfare and car rental, are often a good deal. In cities, ask the local visitor's bureau about hotel and local transportation packages that include tickets to major museum exhibits or other special events.

ECOTOURISM

Vending machines dispensing cans and bottles of juice, tea and beer can be found all over the country. They nearly always have a plastic recycling bin next to them for you to pop your empty container into afterward. These recycling bins can also be found in front of convenience stores.

ELECTRICITY

To use electric-powered equipment purchased in the U.S. or Canada, **bring a converter and adapter.** The electrical current in Japan is 100 volts, 50 cycles alternating current (AC) in eastern Japan, and 100 volts, 60 cycles in western Japan; the United States runs on 110-volt, 60-cycle AC current. Wall outlets in Japan accept plugs with two flat prongs, like in the United States, but do not accept U.S. three-prong plugs.

If your appliances are dual-voltage, you'll need only an adapter. Don't use 110-volt outlets marked FOR SHAVERS ONLY for high-wattage appliances such as blow-dryers. Most laptops operate equally well on 110 and 220 volts and so require only an adapter.

EMBASSIES

The following embassies and consulates are open weekdays, with one- to two-hour closings for lunch. Call for exact hours.

🔏 Australia **Australian Embassy and Consulate** ✉ 2-1-14 Mita, Minato-ku, Tōkyō ☎ 03/5232-4111 Ⓜ Toei Mita Line, Shiba-Kōen station [Exit A2]; Toei Ōedo and Nambuku lines, Azabu-jūban station [Exits 2 and 4].

Canada **Canadian Embassy and Consulate** ✉ 7-3-38 Akasaka, Minato-ku, Tōkyō ☎ 03/5412-6200 Ⓜ Hanzō-mon and Ginza lines, Aoyama-itchōme station [Exit 4].
New Zealand **New Zealand Embassy** ✉ 20-40 Kamiyama-chō, Shibuya-ku, Tōkyō ☎ 03/3467-2270 ⊕ www.nzembassy.com Ⓜ Chiyoda Line, Yoyogi-kōen station [Minami-guchi/South Exit].
United Kingdom **British Embassy and Consulate** ✉ 1 Ichiban-chō, Chiyoda-ku, Imperial Palace District ☎ 03/5211-1100 ⊕ www.uknow.or.jp Ⓜ Hanzō-mon Line, Hanzō-mon station [Exit 4].
United States **U.S. Embassy and Consulate** ✉ 1-10-5 Akasaka, Minato-ku, Toranomon ☎ 03/3224-500 ⊕ tokyo.usembassy.gov/ Ⓜ Namboku Line, Tameike-Sannō station [Exit 13].

EMERGENCIES

Assistance in English is available 24 hours a day on the Japan Helpline. The Tōkyō English Life Line (TELL) is a telephone service available daily 9 AM–4 PM and 7 PM–11 PM for anyone in distress who cannot communicate in Japanese. The service will relay your emergency to the appropriate Japanese authorities and/or will serve as a counselor. Operators who answer the 119 and 110 hotlines rarely speak English.
Ambulance and Fire ☎ 119. **Japan Helpline** ☎ 0120/461-997 or 0570/000-911. **Police** ☎ 110. **Tōkyō English Life Line (TELL)** ☎ 03/5774-0992.

DOCTORS & DENTISTS

The International Catholic Hospital (Seibō Byōin) accepts emergencies and takes regular appointments Monday–Saturday 8 AM–11 AM; outpatient services are closed the third Saturday of the month. The International Clinic also accepts emergencies. Appointments there are taken weekdays 9–noon and 2:30–5 and on Saturday 9–noon. St. Luke's International Hospital is a member of the American Hospital Association and accepts emergencies. Appointments are taken weekdays 8:30 AM–11 AM. The Tōkyō Medical and Surgical Clinic takes appointments weekdays 9–5 and Saturday 9–noon.

The Yamauchi Dental Clinic, a member of the American Dental Association, is open weekdays 9–12:30 and 3–5:30, Saturday 9–noon.
International Catholic Hospital (Seibō Byōin) ✉ 2-5-1 Naka Ochiai, Shinjuku District ☎ 03/

3951-1111 Ⓜ Seibu Shinjuku Line, Shimo-Ochiai station [Nishi-guchi/West Exit]. **International Clinic** ✉ 1-5-9 Azabu-dai, Minato-ku, Roppongi District ☎ 03/3582-2646 or 03/3583-7831 Ⓜ Hibiya Line, Roppongi station [Exit 3]. **St. Luke's International Hospital** ✉ 9-1 Akashi-chō, Chūō-ku, Tsukiji District ☎ 03/3541-5151 Ⓜ Hibiya Line, Tsukiji station [Exit 3]; Yūraku-chō Line, Shintomichō station [Exit 6]. **Tōkyō Medical and Surgical Clinic** ✉ 32 Mori Bldg., 3-4-30 Shiba Kōen, Minato-ku ☎ 03/3436-3028 Ⓜ Toei Mita Line, Onarimon station [Exit A1]; Hibiya Line, Kamiyachō station [Exit 1]; Toei Ōedo Line, Akabane-bashi station. **Yamauchi Dental Clinic** ✉ Shirokanedai Gloria Heights, 1st fl., 3-16-10 Shirokanedai, Minato-ku ☎ 03/3441-6377 Ⓜ JR Yamanote Line, Meguro station [Higashi-guchi/East Exit]; Namboku and Toei Mita lines, Shirokanedai station [Exit 1].

LATE-NIGHT PHARMACIES

No drugstores in Tōkyō are open 24 hours a day. The American Pharmacy, in two locations, stocks nonprescription Western products. Both locations are open weekdays 9 AM–9 PM and weekends 9 AM–8 PM. The Koyasu Drug Store in the Hotel Ōkura also offers some Western products and is open Monday–Saturday 8:30–9, Sunday and holidays 10–9. Many grocery and convenience stores carry basics such as aspirin and ibuprofen.

Nagai Yakkyoku is open daily (except Tuesday) 10–7 and will mix a Chinese and/or Japanese herbal medicine for you after a consultation. You can't have a doctor's prescription filled here, but you can find something for a headache or stomach pain. A little English is spoken.
American Pharmacy ✉ Marunouchi Bldg. B1F, 2-4-1 Marunouchi, Chiyoda-ku ☎ 03/5220-7716 ✉ Atore Ueno 1F, 7-1-1 Ueno, Taito-ku ☎ 03/5826-5874. **Koyasu Pharmacy** ✉ Hotel Ōkura, 2-10-4 Toranomon, Chiyoda-ku ☎ 03/3583-7958 Ⓜ Namboku Line, Tameike-Sannō station [Exit 13]. **Nagai Yakkyoku** ✉ 1-8-10 Azabu-jūban, Minato-ku. ☎ 03/3583-3889 Ⓜ Namboku and Toei Ōedo subway lines, Azabu-jūban station [Exit 7].

LOST & FOUND

The Central Lost and Found Office of the metropolitan police is open weekdays only, 8:30–5:15; someone should be able to speak English here. If you leave something on a JR train, report it to the lost-and-found office at any station. You can also call either of the two central JR Lost Property Offices, one at Tōkyō station (open daily 8:30–8), the other at Ueno station (open weekdays 10–6, Saturday 10–4). If you leave something on a subway car, contact the Eidan Subways Lost and Found Corner (open weekdays 9:30–7, Saturday 9:30–4). If you leave something in a taxi, contact the Tōkyō Taxi Kindaika Center. The center is open 24 hours, but only Japanese is spoken here.

⏷ Central Lost and Found Office ✉ 1-9-11, Kōraku, Bunkyō-ku ☏ 03/3814-4151. **JR Lost Property Office** ✉ Tōkyō Station, Marunouchi ☏ 03/3231-1880 ✉ Ueno Station, Ueno ☏ 03/3841-8069. **Eidan Subways Lost and Found Corner** ☏ 03/3834-5577. **Tōkyō Taxi Kindaika Center** ✉ 7-3-3 Minami-Suna, Koto-ku ☏ 03/3648-0300.

ENGLISH-LANGUAGE MEDIA

BOOKS
English-language books are easy to find at bookshops in Japan's major cities, but if you're planning an extended stay in the countryside, stock up before you go. Because almost all English-language books are imported, they are generally 20%-50% more expensive than at home.

NEWSPAPERS & MAGAZINES
The *Daily Yomiuri,* an English-language sibling of the *Yomiuri Shimbun*; the *Japan Times*, a daily English-language newspaper; and the *International Herald Tribune/Asahi Shimbun* are reliable for national and international news coverage, as well as for entertainment reviews and listings. They're available at newsstands and in bookstores that carry English-language books, and they have Web sites (⇨ *below*)—handy if you want to brush up on current events before your trip.

RADIO & TELEVISION
The national broadcaster, NHK, has a number of bilingual programs on TV, including the news. Popular international cable and satellite TV channels, like BBC World and CNN, are widely available in hotels. There's very little in English on the radio in Japan, though you will hear plenty of Western pop and classical music.

GAY & LESBIAN TRAVEL
A few words about the Japanese attitude toward homosexuality will help you in Japan. Because Japan does not have the religious opposition to homosexuality that the West does, the major barrier that continues to suppress gay lifestyle in Japan is the Confucian duty to continue the family line, to bring no shame to the family, and to fit into Japanese society. So gay and lesbian travelers aren't likely to stumble upon many establishments that cater to a gay clientele.

There *are* gay bars, karaoke lounges, discos, "snacks" (a type of bar), hostess bars, host bars, and drag king/queen bars—the trick is finding them. Even the gay district of Tōkyō, Shinjuku 2-chōme (a 15-minute walk west of Shinjuku Station) leaves you wondering if you've found the place. When you get there, look for people who live in the area, particularly Westerners, and approach them. The Japanese would never broach the subject except, perhaps, at the end of a night of drinking. In fact, it's a bad idea to broach the subject with a Japanese: it will cause much awkwardness, and the response will be nowhere near as sophisticated as it has become in the West. All of this said, homosexuality (as an interest but not a life choice) is more accepted in the realm of human expression than it is in the West. This may sound quite discouraging, but in actuality, Japan can prove to be an outlet of immense freedom for gays if you are successful in making friends in Tōkyō.

International Gay Friends is a gay meeting group in Tōkyō. Occur Help Line sets aside different days of the month for women and men. *Out in Japan* magazine is available at Tower Records in Tōkyō.

⏷ Contacts & Information International Gay Friends ☏ 03/5693-4569. **Occur Help Line** ☏ 03/3380-2269.

⏷ Gay- & Lesbian-Friendly Travel Agencies Different Roads Travel ✉ 8383 Wilshire Blvd., Suite 520, Beverly Hills, CA 90211 ☏ 323/651-5557 or 800/429-8747 (Ext. 14 for both) ☐ 323/651-5454 ✉ lgernert@tzell.com. **Kennedy Travel** ✉ 130 W. 42nd St., Suite 401, New York, NY 10036 ☏ 212/840-8659 or 800/237-7433 ☐ 212/730-2269 ⊕ www.kennedytravel.com. **Now, Voyager** ✉ 4406 18th St., San Francisco, CA 94114 ☏ 415/626-1169 or 800/

255-6951 🖷 415/626-8626 ⊕ www.nowvoyager.
com. **Skylink Travel and Tour/Flying Dutchmen
Travel** ✉ 1455 N. Dutton Ave., Suite A, Santa Rosa,
CA 95401 ☎ 707/546-9888 or 800/225-5759
🖷 707/636-0951, serving lesbian travelers.

HEALTH

Tap water everywhere is safe in Japan.
Medical treatment varies from highly
skilled and professional treatment at major
hospitals to somewhat less advanced procedures in small neighborhood clinics. At
larger hospitals you have a good chance of
encountering English-speaking doctors
who have been partly educated in the West.

OVER-THE-COUNTER REMEDIES

It may be difficult to buy the standard
over-the-counter remedies you're used to,
so it's best to bring with you any medications (in their proper packaging) you may
need. Medication can only be bought at
pharmacies in Japan, but every neighborhood seems to have at least one. *Kusuri-ya*
is the word for "pharmacy" in Japanese.
Pharmacists in Japan are usually able to
manage at least a few words of English,
and certainly are able to read some, so
have a pen and some paper ready, just in
case. In Japanese, aspirin is *asupirin* and
Tylenol is *Tairenōru*.

PESTS & OTHER HAZARDS

Mosquitoes can be a minor irritation during the rainy season, though you are never
at risk of contracting anything serious, like
malaria. If you're staying in a *ryokan* or
somewhere without air-conditioning, anti-
mosquito coils, or an electric-powered
spray will be provided. Dehydration and
heatstroke could be concerns if you spend
a long time outside during the summer
months, so isotonic sports drinks are readily available from the nation's ubiquitous
vending machines.

HOLIDAYS

As elsewhere, peak times for travel in
Japan tend to fall around holiday periods.
You'll want to avoid traveling during the
few days before and after New Year's; dur-
ing Golden Week, which follows Greenery
Day (April 29); and in mid-July and mid-
August, at the time of Obon festivals, when
many Japanese return to their hometowns

(Obon festivals are celebrated July or August 13–16, depending on the location).
Note that when a holiday falls on a Sunday, the following Monday is a holiday.

January 1 (*Ganjitsu*, New Year's Day); the
second Monday in January (*Senjin-no-hi*,
Coming of Age Day); February 11
(*Kenkoku Kinen-no-bi*, National Founda-
tion Day); March 20 or 21 (*Shumbun-no-
hi*, Vernal Equinox); April 29
(*Midori-no-hi*, Greenery Day); May 3
(*Kempo Kinen-bi*, Constitution Day); May
5 (*Kodomo-no-hi*, Children's Day); the
third Monday in July (*Umi-no-hi*, Marine
Day); the third Monday in September
(*Keirō-no-hi*, Respect for the Aged Day);
September 23 or 24 (*Shūbun-no-hi*, Au-
tumnal Equinox); the second Monday in
October (*Taiiku-no-hi*, Sports Day);
November 3 (*Bunka-no-hi*, Culture Day);
November 23 (*Kinro Kansha-no-hi*, Labor
Thanksgiving Day); December 23 (*Tennō
Tanjobi*, Emperor's Birthday).

INSURANCE

The most useful travel-insurance plan is a
comprehensive policy that includes coverage for trip cancellation and interruption,
default, trip delay, and medical expenses
(with a waiver for preexisting conditions).

Without insurance you'll lose all or most of
your money if you cancel your trip, regardless of the reason. Default insurance covers
you if your tour operator, airline, or cruise
line goes out of business—the chances of
which have been increasing. Trip-delay
covers expenses that arise because of bad
weather or mechanical delays. Study the
fine print when comparing policies.

If you're traveling internationally, a key
component of travel insurance is coverage
for medical bills incurred if you get sick on
the road. Such expenses aren't generally
covered by Medicare or private policies.
U.K. residents can buy a travel-insurance
policy valid for most vacations taken during the year in which it's purchased (but
check preexisting-condition coverage).
British and Australian citizens need extra
medical coverage when traveling overseas.

Always **buy travel policies directly from
the insurance company**; if you buy them
from a cruise line, airline, or tour operator

that goes out of business you probably won't be covered for the agency or operator's default, a major risk. Before making any purchase, review your existing health and home-owner's policies to find what they cover away from home.

🎫 Travel Insurers In the U.S.: **Access America** ✉ 2805 N. Parham Rd., Richmond, VA 23294 ☎ 800/284-8300 🖷 804/673-1491 or 800/346-9265 ⊕ www.accessamerica.com. **Travel Guard International** ✉ 1145 Clark St., Stevens Point, WI 54481 ☎ 715/345-0505 or 800/826-1300 🖷 800/955-8785 ⊕ www.travelguard.com.

🎫 Insurance Information In the U.K.: **Association of British Insurers** ✉ 51 Gresham St., London EC2V 7HQ ☎ 020/7600-3333 🖷 020/7696-8999 ⊕ www. abi.org.uk. In Canada: **RBC Insurance** ✉ 6880 Financial Dr., Mississauga, Ontario L5N 7Y5 ☎ 800/668-4342 or 905/816-2400 🖷 905/813-4704 ⊕ www.rbcinsurance.com. In Australia: **Insurance Council of Australia** ✉ Insurance Enquiries and Complaints, Level 12, Box 561, Collins St. W, Melbourne, VIC 8007 ☎ 1300/780808 or 03/9629-4109 🖷 03/9621-2060 ⊕ www.iecltd.com.au. In New Zealand: **Insurance Council of New Zealand** ✉ Level 7, 111-115 Customhouse Quay, Box 474, Wellington ☎ 04/472-5230 🖷 04/473-3011 ⊕ www.icnz.org.nz.

LANGUAGE

Communicating in Japan can be a challenge. This is not because the Japanese don't speak English but because most English speakers know little, if any, Japanese. Take some time before you leave home to **learn a few basic words,** such as where (*doko*), what time (*nan-ji*), bathroom (*o-te-arai*), thank you (*arigatō gozaimasu*), excuse me (*sumimasen*), and please (*one-gai shimasu*).

English is a required subject in Japanese schools, so most Japanese study English for at least six years. This does not mean everyone *speaks* English. Schools emphasize reading, writing, and grammar. As a result, many Japanese can read English but can speak only a few basic phrases. Furthermore, when asked, "Do you speak English?" many Japanese, out of modesty, say no, even if they do understand and speak a fair amount of it. It's usually best to simply ask what you really want to know slowly, clearly, and as simply as possible. If the person you ask understands, he or she will answer or perhaps take you where you need to go.

Although a local may understand your simple question, he or she cannot always give you an answer that requires complicated instructions. For example, you may ask someone on the subway how to get to a particular stop, and he may direct you to the train across the platform and then say something in Japanese that you do not understand. You may discover too late that the train runs express to the suburbs after the third stop; the person who gave you directions was trying to tell you to switch trains at the third stop. To avoid this kind of trouble, **ask more than one person for directions every step of the way.** You can avoid that trip to the suburbs if you ask someone *on* the train how to get to where you want to go. Also, remember that politeness is a matter of course in Japan and that the Japanese won't want to lose face by saying that they don't know how to get somewhere. If the situation gets confusing, **bow, say *arigatō gozaimashita* ("thank you" in the past tense), and ask someone else.** Even though you are communicating on a very basic level, misunderstandings can happen easily. When asking for directions, it's best to ask a "where is" type question—at least the person you've asked can point in the general direction, even if they can't explain themselves to you clearly.

Traveling in Japan can be problematic if you don't read Japanese. Before you leave home, **buy a phrase book** that shows English, English transliterations of Japanese (*romaji*), and Japanese characters (*kanji* and *kana*). You can read the romaji to pick up a few Japanese words and match the kanji and kana in the phrase book with characters on signs and menus. When all else fails, ask for help by pointing to the Japanese words in your book.

The Japan National Tourist Organization (JNTO) manages a free English-language tourist information line (0088/22–4800) in daily operation 9–5, and if there's an emergency you can always call the free, 24-hour Japan Helpline (0120/461–997 or 0570/000–911).

Learning Japanese is a major commitment. For information on pronouncing Japanese words, notes on how Japanese words are rendered in this guide, and a list of useful words and phrases, *see* An English-Japanese Traveler's Vocabulary *in* Chapter 11.

Note: There's some disagreement over the use of gaijin (literally, "outside person") as opposed to *gai-koku-jin* (literally, "outside country person") because the former has negative echoes of the days of Japanese isolationism. In the 17th and 18th centuries, when the Japanese had contact only with Dutch traders, Westerners were called *bata-kusai* (literally, "stinking of butter")—obviously a derogatory term. Gai-koku-jin, on the other hand, has a softer, more polite meaning, and many Westerners in Japan prefer it because it has no xenophobic taint.

Gaijin is used to translate the word *foreigner* throughout this guide for two reasons. First, it's commonly used in books written by Westerners who have lived in Japan, and as such it has wider recognition value. Second, as Japan becomes more global—especially its younger generation—gaijin is losing its negative sense. Many Japanese use gaijin as the one word they know to describe non-Japanese and most often mean no offense by it.

So if children giggle and point at the *gaijin-san,* know that it's meant with only the kindest fascination. And if you feel that extra politeness is appropriate, use gai-koku-jin with colleagues whom you respect—or with whomever might be using gaijin a bit too derogatorily.

LODGING

Tōkyō accommodations can be roughly divided into five categories: international (full-service) hotels, business hotels, *ryokan,* "capsule" hotels, and hostels. For a full description of each type of hotel, *see* Chapter 3, Where to Stay.

🚹 **Toll-Free Numbers** Best Western ☎ 800/528-1234 ⊕ www.bestwestern.com. Choice ☎ 800/424-6423 ⊕ www.choicehotels.com. Clarion ☎ 800/424-6423 ⊕ www.choicehotels.com. Comfort Inn ☎ 800/424-6423 ⊕ www.choicehotels.com. Four Seasons ☎ 800/332-3442 ⊕ www.fourseasons.com. Hilton ☎ 800/445-8667 ⊕ www.hilton.com.

Holiday Inn ☎ 800/465-4329 ⊕ www.ichotelsgroup.com. Hyatt Hotels & Resorts ☎ 800/233-1234 ⊕ www.hyatt.com. Inter-Continental ☎ 800/327-0200 ⊕ www.ichotelsgroup.com. Marriott ☎ 800/228-9290 ⊕ www.marriott.com. Le Meridien ☎ 800/543-4300 ⊕ www.lemeridien.com. Nikko Hotels International ☎ 800/645-5687 ⊕ www.nikkohotels.com. Radisson ☎ 800/333-3333 ⊕ www.radisson.com. Renaissance Hotels & Resorts ☎ 800/468-3571 ⊕ www.renaissancehotels.com/. Ritz-Carlton ☎ 800/241-3333 ⊕ www.ritzcarlton.com. Sheraton ☎ 800/325-3535 ⊕ www.starwood.com/sheraton. Sleep Inn ☎ 800/424-6423 ⊕ www.choicehotels.com. Tōkyū Hotels ☎ 03/3462-0109 ⊕ www.tokyuhotels.co.jp/en. Washington Hotels ☎ 03/3433-4253 ⊕ www.wh-rsv.com/english/index.html. Westin Hotels & Resorts ☎ 800/228-3000 ⊕ www.starwood.com/westin.

MAIL & SHIPPING

The Japanese postal service is very efficient. Airmail between Japan and the United States takes between five and eight days. Surface mail can take anywhere from four to eight weeks. Express service is also available through post offices.

Most hotels have stamps and will mail your letters and postcards; they will also give you directions to the nearest post office. Post offices are open weekdays 9–5 and Saturday 9–noon. Some of the central post offices have longer hours, such as the one in Tōkyō, located near Tōkyō Eki (train station), which is open 24 hours year-round. The main International Post Office is on the Imperial Palace side of JR Tōkyō station. Some of the smaller post offices are not equipped to send packages.

The Japanese postal service has implemented use of three-numeral-plus-four postal codes, but its policy is similar to that in the United States regarding ZIP-plus-fours; that is, mail addressed with the three-numeral code will still arrive at its destination, albeit perhaps one or two days later.

🚹 **International Post Office** ✉ 2-3-3 Ōte-machi, Chiyoda-ku ☎ 03/3241-4891 Ⓜ Tōkyō station.

OVERNIGHT SERVICES

FedEx has drop-off locations at branches of Kinko's all over Tōkyō. A 1 kg/2.2 lb package from central Tōkyō to Washington D.C. would cost about ¥7,200 ($64) and take two days to be delivered.

F Major Services **FedEx** ☎ 0120/00-320 toll-free, 043/298-1919 ⊕ www.fedex.com/jp_english.

POSTAL RATES

It costs ¥110 (98¢) to send a letter by air to North America and Europe. An airmail postcard costs ¥70 (63¢). Aerograms cost ¥90 (81¢).

RECEIVING MAIL

To get mail, have parcels and letters sent "poste restante" to the central post office in major cities; unclaimed mail is returned after 30 days.

SHIPPING PARCELS

The Japanese Post Office is very efficient and domestic mail rarely goes astray. To ship a 5 kg/11 lb parcel to the U.S., Canada, the U.K., Australia, or New Zealand costs ¥10,150 ($91) if sent by airmail, ¥7,300 ($65) by SAL (economy airmail) and ¥4,000 ($36) by sea. Allow a week for airmail, 2 to 3 weeks for SAL, and up to 6 weeks for packages sent by sea. Large shops usually ship domestically, but not overseas.

MONEY MATTERS

In terms of lodging, food, and transportation (except taxis), Tōkyō is about as expensive as New York or Paris. One good way to hold down expenses is to avoid taxis (they tend to get stuck in traffic anyway) and try the efficient, easy-to-use subway system. Restaurants for locals tend to be less expensive than those for tourists, so instead of going to a restaurant with Western-style food and menus in English, go to places where you can rely on your good old index finger to point to the dish you want, and try food that the Japanese eat (⇨ The Discreet Charm of Japanese Cuisine *in* Chapter 8).

Here are some sample prices: a regular cup of coffee costs ¥250–¥600 ($2–$5.50); a bottle of beer, ¥350–¥800 ($3–$7); a 2-km (1-mi) taxi ride, ¥660 ($6); a McDonald's hamburger, ¥84 (75¢); a bowl of noodles, ¥600 ($5.50); an average dinner, ¥2,500 ($22); a double room in Tōkyō, ¥11,000–¥45,000 ($98–$403).

Prices throughout this guide are given for adults. Substantially reduced fees are almost always available for children, students, and senior citizens. For information on taxes, *see* Taxes.

ATMS

ATMs at many Japanese banks do not accept foreign-issued cash or credit cards. Citibank has centrally located branches in most major Japanese cities and ATMs that are open 24 hours. Japan's most progressive bank, UFJ, is a member of the Plus network. Some convenience stores also have cash machines in the Plus network. Post offices have ATMs that accept Visa, MasterCard, American Express, Diners Club, and Cirrus cards. Elsewhere, especially in more rural areas, it's difficult to find suitable ATMs. PIN numbers in Japan are comprised of four digits. In Japanese, an ATM is commonly referred to by its English acronym, while PIN is *anshō bangō*.

CREDIT CARDS

MasterCard and Visa are the most widely accepted credit cards in Japan. Many vendors don't accept American Express. Throughout this guide, the following abbreviations are used: **AE**, American Express; **DC**, Diners Club; **MC**, MasterCard; and **V**, Visa.

F Reporting Lost Cards **American Express** ☎ 0120/020-120. **Diners Club** ☎ 0120/074-024. **MasterCard** ☎ 00531/113-886. **Visa** ☎ 0120/133-173.

CURRENCY

The unit of currency in Japan is the yen (¥). There are bills of ¥10,000, ¥5,000, ¥2,000, and ¥1,000. Coins are ¥500, ¥100, ¥50, ¥10, ¥5, and ¥1. Japanese currency floats on the international monetary exchange, so changes can be dramatic. Some vending machines will not accept the newly introduced ¥2,000 bill or the new version of the ¥500 coin, but these older machines are gradually being replaced.

CURRENCY EXCHANGE

At this writing, the exchange rate was ¥111 for U.S. $1, ¥84 for Canadian $1, ¥203 for British £1, ¥78 for Australian $1, and ¥71 for New Zealand $1.

Most hotels will change both traveler's checks and notes into yen. However, their rates are always less favorable than at banks. Because Tōkyō is largely free from street crime, you can safely consider changing even hefty sums into yen at any time; two places that may be familiar to you are American Express International and Citibank. The larger branches of most Japanese banks have foreign exchange counters where you can do this as well; the paperwork will be essentially the same. All major branch offices of the post office have ATM machines that accept Visa, Master-Card, American Express, Diners Club, and Cirrus cards. You can also use cards on the Cirrus network at Citibank ATMs. Banking hours are weekdays 9–3.

◪ Exchange Services **American Express International** ✉ 4-30-16 Ogikubo, Suginami-ku. ☎ 03/3220-6100 Ⓜ JR Chuo Line, Ogikubo station [Higashi-guchi/East Exit]. **Citibank** ✉ Ōte Center Bldg. 1F, 1-1-3 Ōte-machi, Chiyoda-ku. ☎ 0120/110-330 toll-free for account holders, 03/3215-0051 for other inquiries Ⓜ Chiyoda, Marunouchi, Hanzō-mon, Tōzai, and Mita subway lines; Ōte-machi station [Exit C-13B]. **International Currency Express** ✉ 427 N. Camden Dr., Suite F, Beverly Hills, CA 90210 ☎ 888/278-6628 orders 🖷 310/278-6410 ⊕ www.foreignmoney.com. **Travel Ex Currency Services** ☎ 800/287-7362 orders and retail locations ⊕ www.travelex.com.

TRAVELER'S CHECKS

Traveler's checks are widely accepted at major businesses in cities, though not in small businesses or rural areas. Lost or stolen checks can usually be replaced within 24 hours. To ensure a speedy refund, buy your own traveler's checks—don't let someone else pay for them: irregularities like this can cause delays. The person who bought the checks should make the call to request a refund.

PACKING

Because porters can be hard to find and baggage restrictions on international flights are tight, pack light. What you pack depends more on the time of year than on any dress code. For Tōkyō, pack as you would for any American or European city. At more expensive restaurants and nightclubs, men usually need to wear a jacket and tie. Wear conservative-color clothing at business meetings. Casual clothes are fine for sightseeing. Jeans are as popular in Japan as they are in the United States and are perfectly acceptable for informal dining and sightseeing.

Although there are no strict dress codes for visiting temples and shrines, you will be out of place in shorts or immodest outfits. For sightseeing leave sandals and open-toe shoes behind; you'll need sturdy walking shoes for the gravel pathways that surround temples and fill parks. Make sure to bring comfortable clothing that isn't too tight to wear in traditional Japanese restaurants, where you may need to sit on tatami-matted floors. For beach and mountain resorts pack informal clothes for both day and evening wear.

Japanese do not wear shoes in private homes or in any temples or traditional inns. Having shoes you can quickly slip in and out of is a decided advantage. Take some wool socks along to help you through those shoeless occasions in winter.

If you love coffee, **take along packets of instant coffee.** All lodgings provide a thermos of hot water and bags of green tea in every room, but for coffee you'll have to call room service (which can be expensive), buy sweet coffee in a can from a vending machine, or purchase instant coffee at a 24-hour convenience store. If you're staying in a Japanese inn, they probably won't have coffee.

Sunglasses, sunscreen lotions, and hats are readily available, and these days they're not much more expensive in Japan. It's a good idea to carry a couple of plastic bags to protect your camera and clothes during sudden cloudbursts.

Take along small gift items, such as scarves or perfume sachets, to thank hosts (on both business and pleasure trips), whether you've been invited to their home or out to a restaurant.

In your carry-on luggage, pack an extra pair of eyeglasses or contact lenses and enough of any medication you take to last a few days longer than the entire trip. You may also ask your doctor to write a spare prescription using the drug's generic name, as brand names may vary from country to country. In luggage to be checked, **never**

pack prescription drugs, valuables, or un-developed film. And don't forget to carry with you the addresses of offices that handle refunds of lost traveler's checks. Check *Fodor's How to Pack* (available at online retailers and bookstores everywhere) for more tips.

To avoid customs and security delays, carry medications in their original packaging. Don't pack any sharp objects in your carry-on luggage, including knives of any size or material, scissors, nail clippers, and corkscrews, or anything else that might arouse suspicion.

To avoid having your checked luggage chosen for hand inspection, don't cram bags full. The U.S. Transportation Security Administration suggests packing shoes on top and placing personal items you don't want touched in clear plastic bags.

CHECKING LUGGAGE

You're allowed to carry aboard one bag and one personal article, such as a purse or a laptop computer. Make sure what you carry on fits under your seat or in the overhead bin. Get to the gate early, so you can board as soon as possible, before the overhead bins fill up.

Baggage allowances vary by carrier, destination, and ticket class. On international flights, you're usually allowed to check two bags weighing up to 70 pounds (32 kilograms) each, although a few airlines allow checked bags of up to 88 pounds (40 kilograms) in first class. Some international carriers don't allow more than 66 pounds (30 kilograms) per bag in business class and 44 pounds (20 kilograms) in economy. On domestic flights, the limit is usually 50 to 70 pounds (23 to 32 kilograms) per bag. In general, carry-on bags shouldn't exceed 40 pounds (18 kilograms). Most airlines won't accept bags that weigh more than 100 pounds (45 kilograms) on domestic or international flights. Expect to pay a fee for baggage that exceeds weight limits. Check baggage restrictions with your carrier before you pack.

Airline liability for baggage is limited to $2,500 per person on flights within the United States. On international flights it amounts to $9.07 per pound or $20 per kilogram for checked baggage (roughly $640 per 70-pound bag), with a maximum of $634.90 per piece, and $400 per passenger for unchecked baggage. You can buy additional coverage at check-in for about $10 per $1,000 of coverage, but it often excludes a rather extensive list of items, shown on your airline ticket.

Before departure, itemize your bags' contents and their worth, and label the bags with your name, address, and phone number. (If you use your home address, cover it so potential thieves can't see it readily.) Include a label inside each bag and **pack a copy of your itinerary.** At check-in, make sure each bag is correctly tagged with the destination airport's three-letter code. Because some checked bags will be opened for hand inspection, the U.S. Transportation Security Administration recommends that you leave luggage unlocked or use the plastic locks offered at check-in. TSA screeners place an inspection notice inside searched bags, which are re-sealed with a special lock.

If your bag has been searched and contents are missing or damaged, file a claim with the TSA Consumer Response Center as soon as possible. If your bags arrive damaged or fail to arrive at all, file a written report with the airline before leaving the airport.

⑦ Complaints U.S. Transportation Security Administration Contact Center ☎ 866/289–9673 ⊕ www.tsa.gov.

PASSPORTS & VISAS

When traveling internationally, carry your passport even if you don't need one (it's always the best form of ID) and **make two photocopies of the data page** (one for someone at home and another for you, carried separately from your passport). If you lose your passport, promptly call the nearest embassy or consulate and the local police.

U.S. passport applications for children under age 14 require consent from both parents or legal guardians; both parents must appear together to sign the application. If only one parent appears, he or she must submit a written statement from the other parent authorizing passport issuance for the child. A parent with sole authority must present evidence of it when applying; acceptable documentation includes the child's certified birth certificate listing only the applying parent, a court order specifically permitting this parent's travel with the child, or a death certificate for the non-applying parent. Application forms and instructions are available on the Web site of the U.S. State Department's Bureau of Consular Affairs (⊕ travel.state.gov).

ENTERING JAPAN

Visitors from the United Kingdom can enter Japan and stay for up to six months with a valid passport; Canadian citizens are allowed three months; and visitors from the United States, Australia, and New Zealand can stay for 90 days; no visa is required.

PASSPORT OFFICES

The best time to apply for a passport or to renew is in fall and winter. Before any trip, check your passport's expiration date, and, if necessary, renew it as soon as possible.

🔝 Australian Citizens **Passports Australia** Australian Department of Foreign Affairs and Trade ☎ 131-232 ⊕ www.passports.gov.au.

🔝 Canadian Citizens **Passport Office** ✉ To mail in applications: 200 Promenade du Portage, Hull, Québec J8X 4B7 ☎ 819/994-3500 or 800/567-6868 ⊕ www.ppt.gc.ca.

🔝 New Zealand Citizens **New Zealand Passports Office** ☎ 0800/22-5050 or 04/474-8100 ⊕ www.passports.govt.nz.

🔝 U.K. Citizens **U.K. Passport Service** ☎ 0870/521-0410 ⊕ www.passport.gov.uk.

🔝 U.S. Citizens **National Passport Information Center** ☎ 877/487-2778, 888/874-7793 TDD/TTY ⊕ travel.state.gov.

RESTROOMS

The most hygienic restrooms are found in hotels and department stores and are usually clearly marked with international symbols. You may encounter Japanese-style toilets, with bowls recessed into the floor, over which you squat facing the hood. This may take some getting used to, but it's completely sanitary as you don't come into direct contact with the facility.

In many homes and Japanese-style public places, there will be a pair of slippers at the entrance to the restrooms. Change into these before entering the room, and change back when you exit.

Some public toilets don't have toilet paper, though there are dispensers where packets can be purchased for ¥50 (45¢) or so. Similarly, paper towel dispensers or hand dryers are not always installed, so a small handkerchief is useful to dry your hands.

SAFETY

Even in its major cities, Japan is a very safe country with one of the lowest crime rates in the world. You should, however, **avoid the back street of Kabuki-chō in Tōkyō's Shinjuku district and some of the large public parks at nighttime.**

Be aware that a money belt or a waist pack pegs you as a tourist, so be careful of placing money and valuables in these. A better idea is to distribute your cash and valuables (including your credit cards and passport) between a deep front pocket, an inside jacket or vest pocket, and a hidden money pouch.

Japan is generally a very safe country. Most criminals here would back down in the face of a forthright Western response. Shouting for help in English, for example, is likely to scare off any would-be attacker. Some basic precautions against crime include carrying a purse with a zipper and a strap that you can drape across your body; adjust the length so that the purse sits in front of you at or above hip level. Store only enough money in the purse to cover casual spending, and distribute the rest of your cash and any valuables between deep front pockets, inside jacket or vest pockets, and a concealed money pouch.

SENIOR-CITIZEN TRAVEL

Senior citizens often qualify for discounts at museums. To qualify for age-related discounts, mention your senior-citizen status up front when booking hotel reservations (not when checking out) and before you're seated in restaurants (not when paying the bill). Be sure to have identification on hand. When renting a car, ask about promotional car-rental discounts, which can be cheaper than senior-citizen rates.

🔝 Educational Programs **Elderhostel** ✉ 11 Ave. de Lafayette, Boston, MA 02111-1746 ☎ 877/426-8056,

978/323-4141 international callers, 877/426-2167 TTY 📠 877/426-2166 🌐 www.elderhostel.org. **Interhostel** ✉ University of New Hampshire, 6 Garrison Ave., Durham, NH 03824 ☎ 603/862-1147 or 800/733-9753 📠 603/862-1113 🌐 www.learn.unh.edu.

SHOPPING

Despite the high price of many goods, shopping is one of the great pleasures of a trip to Tōkyō. You may not find terrific bargains, but if you know where to go and what to look for, you can purchase unusual gifts and souvenirs at reasonable prices. In particular, **don't shop for items that are cheaper at home**; Japan is not the place to buy a Gucci bag. Electronics, too, are generally cheaper in the United States. Look for things that are Japanese made for Japanese people and sold in stores that do not cater primarily to tourists.

Don't pass up the chance to purchase Japanese crafts. Color, balance of form, and absolutely superb craftsmanship make these items exquisite and well worth the price you'll pay. Some items can be quite expensive; for example, Japanese lacquerware carries a hefty price. But if you like the shiny boxes, bowls, cups, and trays and consider that quality lacquerware is made to last a lifetime, the cost is justified. Be careful, though: some lacquer items are made from a pressed-wood product rather than solid wood, and only experts can tell the difference. If the price seems low, it probably means the quality is low, too. Note that, except at street markets, bargaining is not usually possible.

KEY DESTINATIONS

Akihabara is a must-visit destination for fans of computers and electrical gadgets; major department stores, like Daimaru or Hankyū are a safe bet for high-quality clothes, crafts, and pottery. The Shibuya district is an essential stopping-off point for the latest in teen fashion. For full shopping details, *see* Chapter 6, Shopping.

WATCH OUT

The export of antiques is controlled, and items such as firearms and Japanese swords cannot be exported without special documentation. A reputable dealer can advise about particular items and paperwork. Some street vendors purport to sell brand-name products at very cheap prices, but often the goods are fakes from China or Thailand.

SIGHTSEEING GUIDES

EXCURSIONS

Sunrise Tours, a division of the Japan Travel Bureau, runs a one-day bus tour to Nikkō on Monday, Tuesday, and Friday between April and October, at ¥13,500 (lunch included). Japan Amenity Travel and the Japan Gray Line conduct Mt. Fuji and Hakone tours, with return either by bus or train; one-day trips cost from ¥12,000 to ¥15,000 (lunch included), and two-day tours cost ¥26,500 (meals and accommodation included). Some of these tours include a quick visit to Kamakura. There are also excursions to Kyōto via Shinkansen that cost from ¥49,500 to ¥82,100; you can arrange these Shinkansen tours through Japan Amenity Travel or Japan Gray Line.

ORIENTATION TOUR

April–June and mid-September–November, Sunrise Tours conducts a Thursday-morning (8–12:30) "Experience Japanese Culture" bus-and-walking tour (¥7,000), which includes a calligraphy demonstration, a tea ceremony, and a visit to the Edo-Tōkyō Hakubutsukan. Both Sunrise Tours and the Japan Gray Line operate a number of other bus excursions around Tōkyō with English-speaking guides. The tours vary with the current demands of the market. Most include the Tōkyō Tower Observatory, the Imperial East Garden, a demonstration of flower arrangement at the Tasaki Pearl Gallery, and/or a Sumidagawa cruise to Sensō-ji in Asakusa. These are for the most part four-hour morning or afternoon tours; a full-day tour (seven hours) combines most of what is covered in half-day excursions with a tea ceremony at Happō Garden and lunch at the traditional Chinzan-sō restaurant. Costs range from ¥4,000 to ¥12,900. Tours are conducted in large, air-conditioned buses that set out from Hamamatsu-chō Bus Terminal, and there's also free pickup and return from major hotels. (If you travel independently and use the subway, you could probably manage the same full-day itinerary for under ¥3,000, including lunch.)

PERSONAL GUIDES

The Japan Guide Association will introduce you to English-speaking guides. You'll need to negotiate your own itinerary and price with the guide. Assume that the fee will be ¥25,000–¥30,000 for a full eight-hour day. The Japan National Tourist Organization can also put you in touch with various local volunteer groups that conduct tours in English; you need only to pay for the guide's travel expenses, admission fees to cultural sites, and meals if you eat together.

The Japan National Tourist Organization (JNTO) sponsors a Good-Will Guide program in which local citizens volunteer to show visitors around; this is a great way to meet Japanese people. These are not professional guides; they usually volunteer both because they enjoy welcoming foreigners to their town and because they want to practice their English. The services of Good-Will Guides are free, but you should pay for their travel costs, their admission fees, and any meals you eat with them while you are together. To participate in this program, make arrangements for a Good-Will Guide in advance through JNTO in the United States or through the tourist office in the area where you want the guide to meet you. The program operates in 75 towns and cities, including Tōkyō, Kyōto, Nara, Nagoya, Ōsaka, and Hiroshima.

SPECIAL-INTEREST TOURS

Sunrise Tours also offers a "Geisha Night" tour (4:30–7) of Tōkyō on Tuesday and Friday mid-March–November. Dinner is included. Other evening tours include Kabuki drama at the Kabuki-za, and sukiyaki dinner. Prices are ¥5,000–¥9,500, depending on which portions of the tour you select. Sunrise Tours has a free-schedule trip to Tōkyō Disneyland, but this operates only on Tuesday and Friday and works in only one direction: buses pick you up at major hotels but leave you to manage your own way back to Tōkyō at the end of the day. The cost for the trip is ¥9,500.

It's only possible to visit parts of the Imperial Palace Grounds by making online reservations in advance with the Imperial

Household Agency. The guided tour (in Japanese, but with a useful pamphlet and audio guide in English) takes about an hour and 15 minutes, and covers 11 of the buildings and sites on the west side of the Palace grounds, including the Fushimi Yagura watchtower and the Fujimi Tamon armory. Log on to the Imperial Household Agency Web site to make a reservation; do this well in advance, as the available slots fill up quickly. Visitors under 18 must be accompanied by an adult. The tours are given weekdays at 10:30 AM and 1:30 PM; admission is free. Tours start at the Nijūbashi Bridge, a minute's walk north of the subway; follow the moat to the courtyard in front of the gate.

🛐 Tour Contacts **Imperial Household Agency** ⊕ sankan.kunaicho.go.jp/order/index_EN.html. **Japan Amenity Travel** ✉ 5-13-12 Ginza, Chūō-ku ☏ 03/3542-7200 Ⓜ Hibiya subway line, Higashi-Ginza station [Exit 4]. **Japan Gray Line** ✉ 3-3-3 Nishi Shimbashi, Minato-ku ☏ 03/3433-5745 Ⓜ JR Yamanote Line, Shimbashi station [Nishi-guchi/West Exit]. **Japan Guide Association** ☏ 03/3213-2706. **Japan National Tourist Organization** ✉ Tōkyō International Forum B1, 3-5-1 Marunouchi, Chiyoda-ku ☏ 03/3201-3331 Ⓜ Yūraku-chō Line, Yūraku-chō station [Exit A-4B]. **Sunrise Tours Reservation Center, Japan Travel Bureau** ☏ 03/5620-9500.

STUDENTS IN JAPAN

Discounts for students are sometimes available at museums and other tourist attractions. You must show an International Student Identity Card.

🛐 IDs & Services **STA Travel** ✉ 10 Downing St., New York, NY 10014 ☏ 212/627-3111, 800/777-0112 24-hr service center ☏ 212/627-3387 ⊕ www.sta.com. **Travel Cuts** ✉ 187 College St., Toronto, Ontario M5T 1P7, Canada ☏ 800/592-2887 in U.S., 416/979-2406 or 866/246-9762 in Canada ☏ 416/979-8167 ⊕ www.travelcuts.com.

SUBWAY TRAVEL

Thirteen subway lines serve Tōkyō; nine of them are operated by the Rapid Transportation Authority (Eidan) and four by the Tōkyō Municipal Authority (Toei). Maps of the system, bilingual signs at entrances, and even the trains are color-coded for easy identification. Japan Travel Phone can provide information in English on subway travel. Subway trains run roughly every five minutes from about 5 AM to midnight; except during rush hours, the intervals are slightly longer on the newer Toei lines.

The network of interconnections (subway to subway and train to subway) is particularly good. One transfer—two at most—will take you in less than an hour to any part of the city you're likely to visit. At some stations—such as Ōte-machi, Ginza, and Iidabashi—long underground passageways connect the various lines, and it does take time to get from one to another. Directions, however, are clearly marked. Less helpful is the system of signs that tell you which of the 15 or 20 exits (exits are often numbered and alphabetized) from a large station will take you aboveground closest to your destination; only a few stations have such signs in English. Exit names or numbers have been included in the text where they'll be most useful. You can also try asking the agent when you turn in your ticket; she or he may understand enough of your question to come back with the exit number and letter (such as A3 or B12), which is all you need.

Subway fares begin at ¥160. Toei trains are generally a bit more expensive than Eidan trains, but both are competitive with JR lines. From Ueno across town to Shibuya on the old Ginza Line (orange), for example, is ¥190; the ride on the JR Yamanote Line will cost you the same. The Eidan (but *not* the Toei) has inaugurated an electronic card of its own, called Metrocard. The denominations are ¥1,000, ¥3,000, and ¥5,000. Automatic card dispensers are installed at some subway stations.

Remember to hold onto your ticket during your trip; you'll need it again to exit the station turnstile.

🇯 **Japan Travel Phone** ☎ 03/3201-3331.

TAXES

HOTELS

A 5% national consumption tax is added to all hotel bills. Another 3% local tax is added to the bill if it exceeds ¥15,000 (about $134). You may **save money by paying for your hotel meals separately** rather than charging them to your bill.

At first-class, full-service, and luxury hotels, a 10% service charge is added to the bill in place of individual tipping. At the more expensive ryokan, where individualized maid service is offered, the service charge is usually 15%. At business hotels, minshuku, youth hostels, and economy inns, no service charge is added to the bill.

SALES & VALUE-ADDED TAX

There's an across-the-board, nonrefundable 5% consumption tax levied on all sales, which is included in the ticket price. Authorized tax-free shops will knock the tax off purchases over ¥10,000 if you show your passport and a valid tourist visa. A large sign is displayed at such shops. A 5% tax is also added to all restaurant bills. Another 3% local tax is added to the bill if it exceeds ¥7,500 (about $67). At the more expensive restaurants, a 10%–15% service charge is added to the bill. Tipping is not customary.

TAXIS

In spite of the introduction of ¥340 initial-fare cabs, Tōkyō taxi fares remain among the highest in the world. Most meters start running at ¥660 and after the first 2 km (1 mi) tick away at the rate of ¥80 every 274 meters (about ⅙ mi). Keep in mind that the ¥340 taxis (which are a very small percentage of those on the street) are only cheaper for trips of 2 km (1 mi) or less; after that the fare catches up with the ¥660 cabs. The ¥340 taxis have a sticker on the left-rear window.

There are also smaller cabs, called *kogata,* that charge ¥640 and then ¥80 per 290 meters (⅙ mi). If your cab is caught in traffic—hardly an uncommon event—the meter registers another ¥80 for every 1½ minutes of immobility. Between 11 PM and 5 AM, a 30% surcharge is added to the fare.

You do get very good value for the money, though. Taxis are invariably clean and comfortable. The doors open automatically for you when you get in and out. Drivers take you where you want to go by the shortest route they know and do not expect a tip. Tōkyō cabbies are not, in general, a sociable species (you wouldn't be either if you had to drive for 10–12 hours a day in Tōkyō traffic), but you can always count on a minimum standard of courtesy. And if you forget something in the cab—a camera, a purse—your chances of getting it back are almost 100% (⇨ Lost and Found, *above*).

Hailing a taxi during the day is seldom a problem. You would have to be in a very remote part of town to wait more than five minutes for one to pass by. In Ginza, drivers are allowed to pick up passengers only in designated areas; look for short lines of cabs. Elsewhere, you need only step off the curb and raise your arm. If the cab already has a fare, there will be a green light on the dashboard, visible through the windshield; if not, the light will be red.

At night, when everyone's been out drinking and wants a ride home, the rules change a bit. Don't be astonished if a cab with a red light doesn't stop for you: the driver may have had a radio call, or he may be heading for an area where a long, profitable fare to the suburbs is more likely. (Or the cab driver may simply not feel like coping with a passenger in a foreign language. Refusing a fare is against the law—but it's done all the time.) Between 11 PM and 2 AM on Friday and Saturday nights, you have to be very lucky to get a cab in any of the major entertainment districts; in Ginza it's almost impossible.

Japanese taxis have automatic door-opening systems, so **do not try to open the taxi door.** Stand back when the cab comes to a stop—if you are too close, the door may slam into you. When you leave the cab, do not try to close the door; the driver will do it automatically. Only the curbside rear door opens. A red light on the dashboard indicates an available taxi, and a green light indicates an occupied taxi.

Unless you are going to a well-known destination such as a major hotel, it's advisable to **have a Japanese person write out your destination in Japanese.** Remember, there's no need to tip.

TELEPHONES

AREA & COUNTRY CODES
The country code for Japan is 81. When dialing a Japanese number from outside of Japan, drop the initial "0" from the local area code. The country code is 1 for the United States and Canada, 61 for Australia, 64 for New Zealand, and 44 for the United Kingdom.

DIRECTORY & OPERATOR ASSISTANCE
For directory information on Tōkyō telephone numbers, dial 104; for elsewhere in Japan, dial 105. These services are only in Japanese, but the NTT Information Customer Service Centre, open weekdays 9–5, has service representatives who speak English, French, Spanish, Portuguese, Korean, and Chinese.

🔲 **NTT Information Customer Service Centre** ☎ 0120/364–463 toll-free.

INTERNATIONAL CALLS
Many gray, multicolor, and green phones have gold plates indicating, in English, that they can be used for international calls. Three Japanese companies provide international service: KDDI (001), Japan Telecom (0041), and IDC (0061). Dial the company code + country code + city/area code and number of your party. Telephone credit cards are especially convenient for international calls. For operator assistance in English on long-distance calls, dial 0051.

LONG-DISTANCE SERVICES
AT&T, MCI, and Sprint access codes make calling long-distance relatively convenient, but you may find the local access number blocked in many hotel rooms. First ask the hotel operator to connect you. If the hotel operator balks, ask for an international operator, or dial the international operator yourself. One way to improve your odds of getting connected to your long-distance carrier is to travel with more than one company's calling card (a hotel may block Sprint, for example, but not MCI). If all else fails, call from a pay phone.

🔲 **Access Codes** For local access numbers abroad, contact one of the following: **AT&T Direct** ☎ 800/222-0300. **MCI WorldPhone** ☎ 800/444-4444. **Sprint International Access** ☎ 800/877-4646.

MOBILE PHONES
Japan is the world leader in mobile phone technology, but overseas visitors cannot easily use their handsets in Japan. Phones

can be rented on arrival at Vodafone out-lets at both Narita and Kansai airports. Rental rates start at ¥525 a day, excluding insurance.

PHONE CARDS

¥1,000 ($9) telephone cards can be bought at station kiosks or convenience stores and can be used in virtually all pub-lic telephones.

PUBLIC PHONES

Telephones come in various colors, includ-ing pink and green. Most pink-and-red phones, for local calls, accept only ¥10 coins. Green-and-gray phones accept ¥10 and ¥100 coins as well as prepaid tele-phone cards. Domestic long-distance rates are reduced as much as 50% after 9 PM (40% after 7 PM). Telephone cards, sold in vending machines, hotels, and a variety of stores, are tremendously convenient be-cause you will not have to search for the correct change.

TIME

All of Japan is in the same time zone, 1 hour behind Sydney, 9 hours ahead of Lon-don, 14 hours ahead of New York, and 17 hours ahead of San Francisco. Daylight saving time is not observed.

TIPPING

Tipping is not common in Japan. It's not necessary to tip taxi drivers, or at hair sa-lons, barbershops, bars, or nightclubs. A chauffeur for a hired car usually receives a tip of ¥500 ($4.50) for a half-day excur-sion and ¥1,000 ($9) for a full-day trip. Porters charge fees of ¥250–¥300 (about $2.50) per bag at railroad stations and ¥200 ($1.80) per piece at airports. It's not customary to tip employees of hotels, even porters, unless a special service has been rendered. In such cases, a gratuity of ¥2,000–¥3,000 ($18–$26) should be placed in an envelope and handed to the staff member discreetly.

TOURS & PACKAGES

Because everything is prearranged on a prepackaged tour or independent vacation, you spend less time planning—and often get it all at a good price.

BOOKING WITH AN AGENT

Travel agents are excellent resources. But it's a good idea to collect brochures from several agencies, as some agents' sugges-tions may be influenced by relationships with tour and package firms that reward them for volume sales. If you have a special interest, find an agent with expertise in that area; the American Society of Travel Agents (ASTA; ⇨ Travel Agencies) has a database of specialists worldwide. You can log on to the group's Web site to find an ASTA travel agent in your neighborhood.

Make sure your travel agent knows the ac-commodations and other services of the place being recommended. Ask about the hotel's location, room size, beds, and whether it has a pool, room service, or pro-grams for children, if you care about these. Has your agent been there in person or sent others whom you can contact?

Do some homework on your own, too: local tourism boards can provide infor-mation about lesser-known and small-niche operators, some of which may sell only direct.

BUYER BEWARE

Each year consumers are stranded or lose their money when tour operators—even large ones with excellent reputations—go out of business. So check out the operator. Ask several travel agents about its reputa-tion, and try to **book with a company that has a consumer-protection program.** (Look for information in the company's brochure.) In the United States, members of the United States Tour Operators Asso-ciation are required to set aside funds ($1 million) to help eligible customers cover payments and travel arrangements in the event that the company defaults. It's also a good idea to choose a company that partic-ipates in the American Society of Travel Agents' Tour Operator Program; ASTA will act as mediator in any disputes be-tween you and your tour operator.

Remember that the more your package or tour includes, the better you can predict the ultimate cost of your vacation. Make sure you know exactly what is covered, and beware of hidden costs. Are taxes, tips, and transfers included? Entertainment and excursions? These can add up.

🚩 Tour-Operator Recommendations **American Society of Travel Agents** (⇨ Travel Agencies). **National Tour Association (NTA)** ✉ 546 E. Main St., Lexington, KY 40508 ☎ 859/226–4444 or 800/682–8886 🖷 859/226–4404 ⊕ www.ntaonline.com. **United States Tour Operators Association (USTOA)** ✉ 275 Madison Ave., Suite 2014, New York, NY 10016 ☎ 212/599–6599 🖷 212/599–6744 ⊕ www.ustoa.com.

TRAIN TRAVEL TO & FROM TŌKYŌ

Riding Japanese trains is one of the pleasures of travel in the country. Efficient and convenient, trains run frequently and on schedule. The Shinkansen (bullet train), one of the fastest trains in the world, connects major cities north and south of Tōkyō. It's only slightly less expensive than flying but is in many ways more convenient because train stations are more centrally located than airports (and, if you have a Japan Rail Pass [⇨ Cutting Costs, *below*], it's extremely affordable). On the main line that runs west from Tōkyō, there are three types of Shinkansen. The *Nozomi* makes the fewest stops, which can cut as much as an hour from long, cross-country trips; it's the only Shinkansen on which you cannot use a JR Pass. The *Hikari* makes just a few more stops than the Nozomi. The *Kodama* is the equivalent of a Shinkansen local, making all stops along the Shinkansen lines. The same principal of faster and slower Shinkansen also applies on the line that runs north from Tōkyō to Morioka, in the Tōkyō region.

Other trains, though not as fast as the Shinkansen, are just as convenient and substantially cheaper. There are three types of train services: *futsū* (local service), *tokkyū* (limited express service), and *kyūkō* (express service). Both the tokkyū and the kyūkō offer a first-class compartment known as the Green Car. Smoking is allowed only in designated carriages on long-distance and Shinkansen trains. Local and commuter trains are entirely no-smoking.

Because there are no porters or carts at train stations, and the flights of stairs connecting train platforms can turn even the

lightest bag into a heavy burden, it's a good idea to **travel light when getting around by train.** Savvy travelers often have their main luggage sent ahead to a hotel that they plan to reach later in their wanderings. It's also good to know that every train station, however small, has luggage lockers, which cost about ¥300 for 24 hours.

CUTTING COSTS

If you plan to travel by rail, **get a Japan Rail Pass,** which offers unlimited travel on Japan Railways (JR) trains. You can purchase one-, two-, or three-week passes. A one-week pass is less expensive than a regular round-trip ticket from Tōkyō to Kyōto on the Shinkansen. You must **obtain a rail pass voucher prior to departure for Japan** (you cannot buy them in Japan), and the pass must be used within three months of purchase. The pass is available only to people with tourist visas, as opposed to business, student, and diplomatic visas.

When you arrive in Japan, you must exchange your voucher for the Japan Rail Pass. You can do this at the Japan Railways desk in the arrivals hall at Narita Airport or at the JR stations of major cities. When you make this exchange, you determine the day that you want the rail pass to begin, and, accordingly, when it ends. You do not have to begin travel on the day you make the exchange; instead, **pick the starting date to maximize use.** The Japan Rail Pass allows you to travel on all JR-operated trains (which cover most destinations in Japan) but not lines owned by other companies.

The JR Pass is also valid on buses operated by Japan Railways (⇨ Bus Travel, *above*). You can make seat reservations without paying a fee on all trains that have reserved-seat coaches, usually the long-distance trains. The Japan Rail Pass does not cover the cost of sleeping compartments on overnight trains (called blue trains), nor does it cover the newest and fastest of the Shinkansen trains, the *Nozomi,* which make only one or two stops on longer runs. The pass covers only the *Hikari* Shinkansen, which make a couple more stops than the *Nozomi,* and the *Kodama* Shinkansen, which stop at every station along the Shinkansen routes.

Japan Rail Passes are available in coach class and first class (Green Car), and as the difference in price between the two is relatively small, it's worth the splurge for first class, for real luxury, especially on the Shinkansen. A one-week pass costs ¥28,300 coach class, ¥37,800 first class; a two-week pass costs ¥45,100 coach class, ¥61,200 first class; and a three-week pass costs ¥57,700 coach class, ¥79,600 first class. Travelers under 18 pay lower rates. The pass pays for itself after one Tōkyō–Kyōto round-trip Shinkansen ride. Contact a travel agent or Japan Airlines to purchase the pass.

🚅 **Japan Railways Group** ✉ 1 Rockefeller Plaza, Suite 1622, New York, NY 10020 ☎ 212/332-8686 📠 212/332-8690.

🚅 Buying a Pass **Japan Airlines** (JAL) ✉ 655 5th Ave., New York, NY 10022 USA ☎ 212/838-4400. **Japan Travel Bureau** (JTB) ✉ 810 7th Ave., 34th fl., New York, NY 10019 ☎ 212/698-4900 or 800/223-6104. **Nippon Travel Agency** (NTA) ✉ 111 Pavonia Ave., Suite 317, Jersey City, NJ 07310 ☎ 201/420-6000 or 800/682-7872.

FARES & SCHEDULES

🚅 Train Information **JR Hotline** ☎ 03/3423-0111, is an English-language information service, open weekdays 10-6.

RESERVATIONS

Many travelers assume that rail passes guarantee them seats on the trains they wish to ride. Not so. If you're using a rail pass, there's no need to buy individual tickets, but you should **book seats ahead.** This guarantees you a seat and is also a useful reference for the times of train departures and arrivals. You can reserve up to two weeks in advance or just minutes before the train departs. If you fail to make a train, there's no penalty, and you can reserve again.

Seat reservations for any JR route may be made at any JR station except those in the tiniest villages. The reservation windows or offices, *midori-no-madoguchi,* have green signs in English and green-stripe windows. If you're traveling without a Japan Rail Pass, there's a surcharge of approximately ¥500 (depending upon distance traveled) for seat reservations, and if you miss the

train, you'll have to pay for another reservation. When making your seat reservation, you may request a no-smoking or smoking car. Your reservation ticket shows the date and departure time of your train as well as your car and seat number. On the platform you can figure out where to wait for a particular train car. Notice the markings painted on the platform or on little signs above the platform; ask someone which markings correspond to car numbers. If you don't have a reservation, ask which cars are unreserved. Sleeping berths, even with a rail pass, are additional. Unreserved tickets can be purchased at regular ticket windows. There are no reservations made on local service trains. For traveling short distances, tickets are usually sold at vending machines. A platform ticket is required if you go through the wicket gate onto the platform to meet someone coming off a train. The charge is ¥140 (in Tōkyō and Ōsaka, the tickets are ¥130).

Most clerks at train stations know a few basic words of English and can read Roman script. Moreover, they are invariably helpful in plotting your route. The complete railway timetable is a mammoth book written only in Japanese; however, you can **get an English-language train schedule from the Japan National Tourist Organization** (JNTO; ⇨ Visitor Information, *below*) that covers the Shinkansen and a few of the major JR Limited Express trains. JNTO's booklet *The Tourist's Handbook* provides helpful information about purchasing tickets in Japan.

TRAIN TRAVEL WITHIN TŌKYŌ

Japan Railways (JR) trains in Tōkyō are color-coded, making it easy to identify the different lines. The Yamanote Line (green or silver with green stripes) makes a 35-km (22-mi) loop around the central wards of the city in about an hour. The 29 stops include the major hub stations of Tōkyō, Yūraku-chō, Shimbashi, Shinagawa, Shibuya, Shinjuku, and Ueno.

The Chūō Line (orange) runs east to west through the loop from Tōkyō to the distant suburb of Takao. During the day, however, these are limited express trains that don't stop at most of the stations inside the loop.

For local cross-town service, which also extends east to neighboring Chiba Prefecture, you have to take the Sōbu Line (yellow).

The Keihin Tōhoku Line (blue) goes north to Ōmiya in Saitama Prefecture and south to Ōfuna in Kanagawa, running parallel to the Yamanote Line between Tabata and Shinagawa. Where they share the loop, the two lines usually use the same platform—Yamanote trains on one side and Keihin Tōhoku trains, headed in the same direction, on the other. This requires a little care. Suppose, for example, you want to take the loop line from Yūraku-chō around to Shibuya, and you board a blue train instead of a green one; four stops later, where the lines branch, you'll find yourself on an unexpected trip to Yokohama.

JR Yamanote Line fares start at ¥130; you can get anywhere on the loop for ¥260 or less. Most stations have a chart in English somewhere above the row of ticket vending machines, so you can check the fare to your destination. If not, you can simply buy the cheapest ticket and pay the difference at the other end. In any case, hold on to your ticket: you'll have to turn it in at the exit. Tickets are valid only on the day you buy them, but if you plan to use the JR a lot, you can save time and trouble with an Orange Card, available at any station office. The card is electronically coded; at vending machines with orange panels, you insert the card, punch the cost of the ticket, and that amount is automatically deducted. Orange Cards come in ¥1,000 and ¥3,000 denominations.

Shinjuku, Harajuku, and Shibuya are notorious for the long lines that form at ticket dispensers. If you're using a card, make sure you've lined up at a machine with an orange panel; if you're paying cash and have no change, make sure you've lined up at a machine that will change a ¥1,000 note—not all of them do.

Yamanote and Sōbu Line trains begin running about 4:30 AM and stop around 1 AM. The last departures are indicated at each station—but only in Japanese. Bear in mind that 7 AM–9:30 AM and 5 PM–7 PM trains are packed to bursting with commuters; avoid the trains at these times, if

possible. During these hours smoking is not allowed in JR stations or on platforms. ⓕ **Japan Railways** ☎ 03/3423-0111.

TRANSPORTATION AROUND TŌKYŌ

Daunting in its sheer size, Tōkyō is, in fact, an extremely easy city to negotiate. If you have any anxieties about getting from place to place, remind yourself first that a transportation system obliged to cope with 4 or 5 million commuters a day simply *has* to be efficient, extensive, and reasonably easy to understand. Remind yourself also that virtually any place you're likely to go as a visitor is within a 15-minute walk of a train or subway station—and that station stops are always marked in English. Of course, exceptions to the rule exist—the system has its flaws. In the outline here you'll find a few things to avoid and also a few pointers that will save you time—and money—as you go.

Excellent maps of the subway system, with major JR lines included as well, are available at any station office free of charge. Hotel kiosks and English-language bookstores stock a wide variety of pocket maps, some of which have suggested walking tours that also mark the locations of JR and subway stations along the way. A bit bulkier to carry around, but by far the best and most detailed resource, is the *Tōkyō City Atlas: A Bilingual Guide* (Kodansha International, fourth edition; ¥2,100), which contains subway and rail-system guides and area maps. Because all notations are in both English and Japanese, you can always get help on the street, even from people who do not speak your language, just by pointing at your destination. ⓕ **Japan Travel Phone** ☎ 03/3201-3331, 075/371-5649 for the Kyōto area. **JR East InfoLine** ☎ 03/3423-0111.

TRAVEL AGENCIES

A good travel agent puts your needs first. Look for an agency that has been in business at least five years, emphasizes customer service, and has someone on staff who specializes in your destination. In addition, **make sure the agency belongs to a professional trade organization.** The American

Society of Travel Agents (ASTA)—the largest and most influential in the field with more than 20,000 members in some 140 countries—maintains and enforces a strict code of ethics and will step in to help mediate any agent-client disputes involving ASTA members if necessary. ASTA also maintains a Web site that includes a directory of agents. (If a travel agency is also acting as your tour operator, *see* Buyer Beware *in* Tours & Packages.)

f Local Agent Referrals **American Society of Travel Agents (ASTA)** ✉ 1101 King St., Suite 200, Alexandria, VA 22314 ☎ 703/739–2782 or 800/965–2782 24-hr hotline 🖨 703/684–8319 ⊕ www. astanet.com. **Association of British Travel Agents** ✉ 68–71 Newman St., London W1T 3AH ☎ 020/7637–2444 🖨 020/7637–0713 ⊕ www.abta.com. **Association of Canadian Travel Agencies** ✉ 130 Albert St., Suite 1705, Ottawa, Ontario K1P 5G4 ☎ 613/237–3657 🖨 613/237–7052 ⊕ www.acta.ca. **Australian Federation of Travel Agents** ✉ Level 3, 309 Pitt St., Sydney, NSW 2000 ☎ 02/9264–3299 or 1300/363–416 🖨 02/9264–1085 ⊕ www.afta.com. au. **Travel Agents' Association of New Zealand** ✉ Level 5, Tourism and Travel House, 79 Boulcott St., Box 1888, Wellington 6001 ☎ 04/499–0104 🖨 04/499–0786 ⊕ www.taanz.org.nz.

VISITOR INFORMATION

For information before you go, contact the Japan National Tourist Organization (JNTO). You may also want to check out their Web site at www.jnto.go.jp. When you get there, call or stop by one of the Tourist Information Centers (TIC) for information on western or eastern Japan and use the Japan Travel Phone (daily 9–5); for recorded information 24 hours a day, call the Teletourist service.

The Tourist Information Center (TIC) in the Tōkyō Metropolitan Government Office is an extremely useful source of free maps and brochures. The center also advises on trip planning in Japan. Make a point of dropping by early in your stay in Tōkyō; it's open weekdays 9–5, Saturday 9–noon.

The Asakusa Tourist Information Center, opposite Kaminari-mon, has some English-speaking staff and plenty of maps and brochures; it's open daily 9:30–8.

A taped recording in English on festivals, performances, and other events in the Tōkyō area operates 24 hours a day and is updated weekly. Two free weekly magazines, the *Tour Companion* and *Metropolis*, available at hotels, book and music stores, some restaurants and cafés, and other locations, carry up-to-date announcements of what's going on in the city. The better of the two is *Metropolis*, which breaks its listings down in separate sections for Art & Exhibitions, Movies, TV, Music, and After Dark. *Tōkyō Journal* (¥600), available at newsstands in Narita Airport and at many bookstores that carry English-language books, is a monthly magazine with similar listings. The *Japan Times*, a daily English-language newspaper, is yet another resource for entertainment reviews and schedules.

NTT (Japanese Telephone Corporation) can help you find information (in English), such as telephone numbers, museum openings, and various other information available from its databases. It's open weekdays 9–5.

f Japan National Tourist Organization (JNTO) **Canada:** ✉ 165 University Ave., Toronto, Ontario M5H 3B8 ☎ 416/366–7140. **Japan:** ✉ 2-10-1 Yūrakuchō 1-chōme, Chiyoda-ku, Tōkyō ☎ 03/3502–1461 ✉ 9F, JR Kyōto Station Bldg., Hachijō-guchi, Minami-ku Kyōto ☎ 075/344–3300. **United Kingdom:** ✉ Heathcoat House, 20 Savile Row, London W1X 1AE ☎ 020/7734–9638. **United States:** ✉ 1 Rockefeller Plaza, Suite 1250, New York, NY 10020 ☎ 212/757–5640 ✉ 401 N. Michigan Ave., Suite 770, Chicago, IL 60611 ☎ 312/222–0874 ✉ 1 Daniel Burnham Court, San Francisco, CA 94109 ☎ 415/292–5686 ✉ 515 S. Figueroa St., Suite 1470, Los Angeles, CA 90071 ☎ 213/623–1952.

f Japan Travel Phone **Throughout Japan** ☎ 0088/22–4800 throughout Japan outside of Tōkyō and Kyōto, 03/3201–3331 in Tōkyō, 075/344–3300 in Kyōto.

f Teletourist Service **Tōkyō** ☎ 03/3201–2911.

f Tourist Information Centers (TIC) **Asakusa Tourist Information Center** ✉ 2-18-9 Kaminari-mon, Taitō-ku ☎ 03/3842–5566 Ⓜ Ginza Line, Asakusa station [Exit 2]. **Metropolis** ☎ 03/3423–6931 ⊕ www.metropolis.co.jp. **NTT** ☎ 0120/36–4463 toll-free. **Tourist Information Center** (TIC) ✉ Tōkyō International Forum, 3-5-1 Marunouchi, Chiyoda-ku ☎ 03/3201–3331 Ⓜ Yūraku-chō Line, Yūraku-chō station [Exit A-4B].

⁊ Government Advisories U.S. Department of State ✉ Overseas Citizens Services Office, 2100 Pennsylvania Ave. NW, 4th fl., Washington, DC 20520 ☎ 202/647−5225 interactive hotline, 888/407−4747 ⊕ www.travel.state.gov. **Consular Affairs Bureau of Canada** ☎ 800/267−6788 or 613/944−6788 ⊕ www. voyage.gc.ca. **U.K. Foreign and Commonwealth Office** ✉ Travel Advice Unit, Consular Division, Old Admiralty Bldg., London SW1A 2PA ☎ 0870/606−0290 or 020/7008−1500 ⊕ www.fco.gov.uk/travel. **Australian Department of Foreign Affairs and Trade** ☎ 300/139−281 travel advice, 02/6261−1299 Consular Travel Advice Faxback Service ⊕ www.dfat.gov.au. **New Zealand Ministry of Foreign Affairs and Trade** ☎ 04/439−8000 ⊕ www.mft.govt.nz.

WEB SITES

You can research prices and book plane tickets, hotel rooms, rental cars, vacation packages, and more at www.fodors.com. In addition, you can post your pressing questions in the Travel Talk section. Other planning tools include a currency converter and weather reports, and there are loads of links to travel resources.

Cultural resources and travel-planning tools abound for the cybertraveler to Japan. Good first stops include the Web sites of Japan's three major English-language daily newspapers, the *Asahi Shimbun* (⊕ www.asahi.com), *Daily Yomiuri* (⊕ www.yomiuri.co.jp/index-e.htm) the *Japan Times* (⊕ www.japantimes.co.jp).

For travel updates, visit the Web site of the Japan National Tourist Office (JNTO; ⊕ www.jnto.go.jp). You'll also find a links page, which connects you to an amusing if random assortment of sites that somehow relate to Japan.

Metropolis (⊕ metropolis.japantoday.com) and *Tokyo Journal* (⊕ www.tokyo.to/index.html) slick on-line magazines for the English expat community in Tōkyō, will catch you up on the latest goings-on in the capital city. Both have up-to-date arts, events, and dining listings. In the Kansai region, *Kansai Time Out* (⊕ www.kto.co.jp) is definitely worth a look.

On-line resources abound for information on traveling by public transportation.

Visit Jorudan's invaluable "Japanese Transport Guide" (⊕ www.jorudan.co.jp/english/norikae/e-norikeyin.html), which has a simple, uncluttered interface. You enter the station from which you're departing and your destination, and the planner presents you with the travel time, fare, and distance for all possible routes. Japan Rail's sites are handy planning tools as well, and provide fare and ticket information. Both the JR East (⊕ www.jreast.co.jp/e) and the JR West (⊕ www.westjr.co.jp/english/english/index.html) sites will direct you to detailed information about the Japan Rail Pass (⇨ Train Travel, *above*). For local info, RATP (⊕ www.subwaynavigator.com), the French rail-transit authority, maintains a useful subway navigator, which includes the subway systems in Ōsaka, Tōkyō and Sapporo. The Metropolitan Government Web site (⊕ www.metro.tokyo.jp), incidentally, is an excellent source of information on sightseeing and current events in Tōkyō.

On the Web site of the Japan City Hotel Association (⊕ www.jcha.or.jp/english), you can search member hotels by location and price and make reservations on-line. Japan Economy Hotels Reservation Service, Inc. (⊕ www.inn-info.co.jp/english/home.html) is another on-line lodging resource.

Japanese-Online (⊕ www.japanese-online.com) is a series of on-line language lessons that will help you pick up a bit of Japanese before your trip. (The site also, inexplicably, includes a sampling of typical Japanese junior high school math problems.) Kabuki for Everyone (⊕ www.fix.co.jp/kabuki/kabuki.html) provides a comprehensive and accessible introduction to the dramatic form; on the site you'll find video clips of Kabuki performances, summaries of major plays, an audio archive of Kabuki sounds, and a bibliography for further reading. Finally, for fun, stop by the Web site of Tōkyō's Tsukiji Central Wholesale Market (⊕ www.tsukiji-market.or.jp/tukiji_e.htm)—where else can you see tuna as big as cars on-line?

EXPLORING
TŌKYŌ 東京

1

MOST IMPORTANT TEMPLE COMPLEX
Sensō-ji in Asakusa ⇨*p.40*

PRETTIEST CITY GARDEN
Shinjuku Gyo-en National Garden ⇨*p.74*

SHARPEST WEAPON COLLECTION
Japanese Sword Museum in Shibuya ⇨*p.65*

POSHEST NEIGHBORHOOD
The mercantile streets of Ginza ⇨*p.56*

CRAZIEST TEEN FASHIONS
on the sidewalks of Harajuku ⇨*p.60*

LIVELIEST FISH MARKET
Tōkyō Central Wholesale Market ⇨*p.48*

By Jared
Lubarsky

TŌKYŌ: Of all major cities in the world, it is perhaps the hardest to understand or to see in any single perspective. To begin with, consider the sheer, outrageous size of it. Tōkyō incorporates 23 wards, 26 smaller cities, 7 towns, and 8 villages—altogether sprawling 88 km (55 mi) from east to west and 24 km (15 mi) from north to south. The wards alone enclose an area of 590 square km (228 square mi), which in turn house some 12 million people. More than 3 million of these residents pass through Shinjuku Station, one of the major hubs in the transportation network, every day.

Space, that most precious of commodities, is so scarce that pedestrians have to weave in and around utility poles as they walk along the narrow sidewalks—yet mile after mile, houses rise only one or two stories, their low uniformity broken here and there by the sore thumb of an apartment building. Begin with that observation, and you discover that the very fabric of life in this city is woven of countless, unfathomable contradictions.

Tōkyō is a state-of-the-art financial marketplace, where billions of dollars are whisked electronically around the globe every day in the blink of an eye—and where all but a handful of ATMs shut down at 9 PM. A city of astonishing beauty in its small details, Tōkyō also has some of the ugliest buildings on the planet and generates more than 20,000 tons of garbage a day. It installed its first electric light in 1877 yet still has hundreds of thousands of households without a bathtub.

Outsiders rarely venture very far into the labyrinths of residential Tōkyō. Especially for travelers, the city defines itself by its commercial, cultural, and entertainment centers: Ueno, Asakusa, Ginza, Roppongi, Shibuya, Harajuku, Shinjuku, and an ever-growing list of new developments. The attention of Tōkyō shifts constantly, seeking new patches of astronomically expensive land on which to realize its enormous commercial energy. Nowadays, you can't buy a square yard anywhere in the city's central wards for less than $1,000.

Tōkyō has no remarkable skyline, no prevailing style of architecture, no real context into which a new building can fit. Every new project is an environment unto itself. Architects revel in this anarchy, and so do the designers of neon signs, show windows, and interior spaces. The kind of creative energy you find in Tōkyō could flower only in an atmosphere where there are virtually no rules to break.

Not all of this is for the best. Many of the buildings in Tōkyō are merely grotesque, and most of them are supremely ugly. In the large scale, Tōkyō is not an attractive city—nor is it gracious, and it is certainly not serene. The pace of life is wedded to the one stupefying fact of population: within a 36-km (22-mi) radius of the Imperial Palace live almost 30 million souls, all of them in a hurry and all of them ferocious consumers—not merely of things but of culture and leisure. Still uncertain about who they are and where they are going, they consume to identify themselves—by what they wear, where they eat, and how they use their spare time.

Sooner or later everything shows up here: Van Gogh's *Sunflowers,* the Berlin Philharmonic, Chinese pandas, Mexican food. Even the Coney

TŌKYŌ GLOSSARY

Key Japanese words and suffixes in this chapter include

–bashi or –hashi	橋	bridge
bijutsukan	美術館	art museum
-chō	町 or 丁	street or block
-chōme	丁目	street
chūō	中央	central
depāto (deh-pah-to)	デパート	department store
-dōri	通	avenue
eki	駅	train station
gaijin	外人	foreigner
–gawa or -kawa	川 or 河	river
-gū	宮	Shintō shrine
deguchi	出口	exit
hakubutsukan	博物館	museum
higashi	東	east
-in	院	Buddhist temple
izakaya	居酒屋	pub
-ji	寺	Buddhist temple
-jima	島	island
jingū or jinja	神社	Shintō shrine
-jō	城	castle
kita	北	north
kōen	公園	park
ku	区	section or ward
kūkō	空港	airport
machi	町	town
matsuri	祭	festival
minami	南	south
-mon	門	gate
nishi	西	west
Shinkansen	新幹線	bullet train, literally "new trunk line"
shita	下	lower, downward
torii	鳥居	"to-ree-ee," gate
-ya	屋	shop, as in hon-ya, bookshop
yama	山	mountain
yamanote	山の手	the hilly part of town

Island carousel is here—lovingly restored down to the last gilded curlicue on the last prancing unicorn, back in action at an amusement park called Toshima-en. Tōkyō is a magnet, and now the magnet is drawing you. What follows here is an attempt to chart a few paths for you through this exciting and exasperating city.

Orientation

The distinctions of Shitamachi (literally "downtown," to the north and east) and Yamanote (literally "uptown," to the south and west) have shaped the character of Tōkyō since the 17th century and will guide you as you explore the city. At the risk of an easy generalization, it might be said that downtown has more to *see,* uptown more to *do.* Another way of putting it is that Tōkyō north and east of the Imperial Palace embodies more of the city's history and traditional way of life; the glitzy, ritzy side of contemporary, international Tōkyō generally lies south and west.

The city has been divided into eight exploring sections in this chapter, six in Shitamachi—starting in central Tōkyō with the Imperial Palace District—and two uptown in Yamanote. It can be exhausting to walk from one part of Tōkyō to another—you can look in vain for places outdoors just to sit and rest en route—and bus travel can be particularly tricky. Fortunately, no point on any of these itineraries is very far from a subway station, and you can use the city's efficient subway system to hop from one area to another, to cut a tour short, or to return to a tour the next day. The area divisions in this book are not always contiguous—Tōkyō is too spread out for that—but they generally border each other to a useful degree. As you plan your approach to the city, by all means skip parts of an area that don't appeal or combine parts of one tour with those of another to get the best of all worlds.

The listings in this chapter include subway and Japan Rail (JR) train lines and stops as well as station exit names and numbers in cases where they're most helpful—which is quite often, as several stations have multiple (sometimes more than 15) exits.

IMPERIAL PALACE DISTRICT 皇居近辺

Kōkyo, the Imperial Palace, occupies what were once the grounds of Edo Castle. When Ieyasu Tokugawa chose the site for his castle in 1590, he had two goals in mind. First, it would have to be impregnable. Second, it would have to reflect the power and glory of his position. He was lord of the Kantō, the richest fief in Japan, and would soon be shōgun, the military head of state. The fortifications he devised called for a triple system of moats and canals, incorporating the bay and the Sumida-gawa into a huge network of waterways that enclosed both the castle keep (the stronghold, or tower) and the palaces and villas of his court—in all, an area of 450 acres. The castle had 99 gates (36 in the outer wall), 21 watchtowers (of which 3 are still standing), and 28 armories. The outer defenses stretched from present-day Shimbashi Station to Kanda. Completed in 1640 (and later expanded), it was at the time the largest castle in the world.

The walls of Edo Castle and its moats were made of stone from the Izu Peninsula, about 96 km (60 mi) to the southwest. The great slabs were brought by barge—each of the largest was a cargo in itself—to the port of Edo (then much closer to the castle than the present port of Tōkyō is now) and hauled through the streets on sledges by teams of 100 or more men. Thousands of stonemasons were brought from all over the country to finish the work. Under the gates and castle buildings, the blocks of stone are said to have been shaped and fitted so precisely that a knife blade could not be slipped between them.

The inner walls divided the castle into four main areas, called *maru.* The *hon-maru,* the principle area, contained the shōgun's audience halls, his private residence, and, for want of a better word, his seraglio—the *ō-oku,* where he kept his wife and concubines, with their ladies-in-waiting, attendants, cooks, and servants. At any given time, as many as 1,000 women might be living in the ō-oku. Intrigue, more than sex, was its principal concern, and tales of the seraglio provided a rich source of material for the Japanese literary imagination. Below the hon-maru was the *ni-no-maru,* where the shōgun lived when he transferred his power to an heir and retired. Behind it was the *kita-no-maru,* the northern area, now a public park; south and west was the *nishi-no-maru,* a subsidiary fortress.

Not much of the Tokugawa glory remains. The shogunate was abolished in 1868, and when Emperor Meiji's moved from Kyōto to Edo, which he renamed Tōkyō, Edo Castle was chosen as the site of the Imperial Palace. Many of its buildings had been destroyed in the turmoil of the restoration of the emperor, others fell in the fires of 1872, and still others were simply torn down. Of the 28 original *tamon* (armories), only 2 have survived. The present-day Imperial Palace, which dates to 1968, is open to the general public only twice a year: on January 2 and December 23 (the Emperor's Birthday), when thousands of people assemble under the balcony to offer their good wishes to the imperial family. On other days during the year, the Imperial Household Agency conducts guided group tours of the palace grounds by reservation. In 1968, to mark the completion of the current palace, the area that once encompassed the hon-maru and ni-no-maru was opened to the public as the Imperial Palace East Garden. There are three entrance gates—Ōte-mon, Hirakawa-mon, and Kita-hane-bashi-mon. You can easily get to any of the three from the Ōte-machi or Takebashi subway station.

Numbers in the text correspond to numbers in the margin and on the Imperial Palace map.

A Good Walk

A good place to start is **Tōkyō Station** ❶ ☞. The Ōte-machi subway stop (on the Chiyoda, Marunouchi, Tōzai, Hanzō-mon, and Toei Mita lines) is a closer and handier connection, but the old redbrick Tōkyō Station building is a more compelling choice. Leave the station by the Marunouchi Central Exit, cross the street in front at the taxi stand, and walk up the broad divided avenue that leads to the Imperial Palace grounds. To your left is Marunouchi, to your right Ōte-machi: you're in the heart of Japan, Incorporated—the home of its major banks and investment

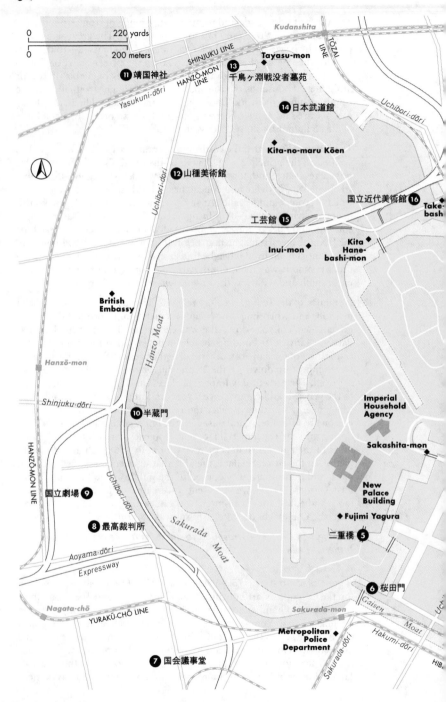

0

220 yards

0

200 meters

Kudanshita

SHINJUKU LINE

HANZŌ-MON LINE

TŌZAI LINE

Uchibori-dōri

Tayasu-mon

⑪ 靖国神社

⑬

千鳥ヶ淵戦没者墓苑

⑭ 日本武道館

Yasukuni-dōri

Kita-no-maru Kōen

Uchibori-dōri

⑫ 山種美術館

国立近代美術館 **⑯**

Take-bash

工芸館 ⑮

Inui-mon

Kita Hane-bashi-mon

British Embassy

Hanzo Moat

Hanzō-mon

Imperial Household Agency

Shinjuku-dōri

Sakashita-mon

⑩ 半蔵門

HANZŌ-MON LINE

Uchibori-dōri

New Palace Building

国立劇場 ⑨

◆ Fujimi Yagura

⑧ 最高裁判所

Sakurada Moat

二重橋 **⑤**

Aoyama-dōri

Expressway

⑥ 桜田門

Gaisen

Nagata-chō

YURAKŪ-CHŌ LINE

Sakurada-mon

Hakumi-dōri

Uch

Moat

Metropolitan Police Department

Sakurada-dōri

⑦ 国会議事堂

HIB

Chidori-ga-fuchi
National Memorial Garden **13**

Hanzō-mon (Hanzō Gate) **10**

Hirakawa-mon
(Hirakawa Gate) **17**

Imperial Palace East Garden
(Kōkyo Higashi Gyo-en) **3**

Imperial Palace Outer Garden
(Kōkyo-Gaien) **4**

Japan Martial Arts Hall
(Nippon Budōkan) **14**

Kōgeikan (Crafts Gallery
of the National Museum
of Modern Art) **15**

National Diet Building
(Kokkai-Gijidō) **7**

National Museum of
Modern Art, Tōkyō
(Tōkyō Kokuritsu
Kindai Bijutsukan) **16**

National Theater
(Kokuritsu Gekijō) **9**

Ōte-mon (Ōte Gate) **2**

Sakurada-mon (Gate of the
Field of Cherry Trees) **6**

Supreme Court
(Saikō Saibansho) **8**

Tōkyō Station **1**

Two-Tiered Bridge
(Ni-jū-bashi) **5**

Yamatane Museum of Art
(Yamatane Bijutsukan) **12**

Yasukuni Jinja (Shrine of Peace
for the Nation) **11**

houses, its insurance and trading companies. Take the second right, at the corner of the New Marunouchi Building; walk two blocks, past the gleaming brown-marble fortress of the Industrial Bank of Japan, and turn left. Ahead of you, across Uchibori-dōri (Inner Moat Avenue) from the Palace Hotel, is **Ōte-mon ❷**, one of three entrances to the **Imperial Palace East Garden ❸**.

Turn right as you leave the East Garden through Ōte-mon. Where the wall makes a right angle, you will see the Tatsumi, or Ni-jū Yagura (Double-Tiered Watchtower), one of three surviving watchtowers on the original fortifications. Here the sidewalk opens out to a parking lot for tour buses and the beginning of a broad promenade. In the far corner to your right, where the angle of the wall turns again, is the Kikyō-mon, a gate used primarily for deliveries to the palace. At the far end of the parking lot is Sakashita-mon, the gate used by the officials of the Imperial Household Agency.

From here to Hibiya Kōen (Hibiya Park), along both sides of Uchibori-dōri, stretches the concourse of the **Imperial Palace Outer Garden ❹**. This whole area once lay along the edge of Tōkyō Bay. Later, the shōgun had his most trusted retainers build their estates here. These in turn gave way to the office buildings of the Meiji government. In 1899 the buildings were relocated, and the promenade was planted with the wonderful stands of pine trees you see today.

Walk along the broad gravel path to the **Two-Tiered Bridge ❺** and the Sei-mon (Main Gate). The bridge makes its graceful arch over the moat here from the area inside the gate. The building in the background, completing the picture, is the Fushimi Yagura, built in the 17th century. It is the last of the three surviving original watchtowers.

Continue on the gravel walk past the Sei-mon, turn right, and pass through the gate known as **Sakurada-mon ❻**. Before you do, turn and look back down the concourse: you will not see another expanse of open space like this anywhere else in Tōkyō.

Look south across the street as you pass through the gate; the broad avenue that begins on the opposite side is Sakurada-dōri. World-renowned architect Kenzō Tange's Metropolitan Police Department building is on the west corner. The stately brick building on the east corner is the old Ministry of Justice. Sakurada-dōri runs through the heart of official Japan; between here and Kasumigaseki are the ministries—from Foreign Affairs and Education to International Trade and Industry—that compose the central government. Turn right at Sakurada-mon and follow the Sakurada Moat uphill along Uchibori-dōri.

A five-minute walk will bring you to where Roppongi-dōri branches in from the left; look in that direction and you will see the approach to the squat pyramid of the **National Diet Building ❼**, which houses the Japanese parliament. You might want to walk in for a closer look. If not, bear right as you continue to follow the moat along Uchibori-dōri to the next intersection, at Miya-zaka. Across the street are the gray-stone slabs of the **Supreme Court ❽**. This and the **National Theater ❾**, next door, are worth a short detour.

Over 700 monthly
furnished apartments
and guest houses
in Tokyo

Why SAKURA HOUSE ?

Economical - Monthly rents start from 80,000 yen for private apartments and 48,000 yen for guest houses, including utility expense and internet. Rents payable with VISA or MasterCard.

Easy - No key money, agent fee or guarantor required. All rooms furnished, just pop in with a suitcase.

Enjoyable - For guest houses, you will share a house with other sojourners from all over the world. Make friends, and share your Tokyo experience with them.

E-friendly - Check **http://www.sakura-house.com** for the latest availabilities. You can book a room online before coming to Japan.

✿ SAKURA HOUSE

Nishi-Shinjuku K-1 building 2F, 7-2-6 Nishi-Shinjuku, Shinjuku-ku, Tokyo
TEL: +81-3-5330-5250 (from abroad) / **03-5330-5250** (inside Japan)
For daily stays, check our sister hotel : **http://www.sakura-hotel.co.jp**

Cross back to the palace side of the street and continue north on Uchi-bori-dōri. At the top of the hill, on your right, a police contingent guards the road to the **Hanzō-mon** ⓿—the western gate to the new Imperial Palace. Here, where the road turns north again, begins the Hanzō Moat.

North along the Hanzō Moat is a narrow strip of park; facing it, across the street, is the British Embassy. Along this western edge of his fortress, the shōgun kept his personal retainers, called *hatamoto*, divided by *ban-chō* (district) into six regiments. Today these six ban-chō are among the most sought-after residential areas in Tōkyō, where high-rise apartments commonly fetch ¥100 million or more.

At the next intersection, review your priorities again. You can turn right and complete your circuit of the palace grounds by way of the Inui-mon, or you can continue straight north to the end of Uchibori-dōri to **Yasukuni Jinja** ⓫, the Shrine of Peace for the Nation.

If you do go to Yasukuni Jinja, make time for a short visit on the way to the **Yamatane Museum of Art** ⓬, a few minutes' walk past the inter-section on the east side of Samban-chō.

Leave Yasukuni Jinja the way you came in, cross the street, turn left, and walk down the hill. The entrance to **Chidori-ga-fuchi National Memorial Garden** ⓭ is about 50 yards from the intersection, on the right. The green strip of promenade is high on the edge of the moat, lined with cherry trees. Halfway along, it widens, and opposite the Fairmount Hotel a path leads down to the Chidori-ga-fuchi Boathouse. Beyond the boathouse, the promenade leads back in the direction of the Imperial Palace.

If you have the time and stamina for a longer tour, retrace your steps from the boathouse, leave Chidori-ga-fuchi the way you came in, turn right, and continue down the hill to the entrance to Kita-no-maru Kōen (Kita-no-maru Park), on the west side of the Imperial Palace. To get to this park you'll have to pass through Tayasu-mon, one of the largest and finest of the surviving *masu* (box) gates to the castle. The first building you come to in the park is the octagonal **Japan Martial Arts Hall** ⓮, site of major rock concerts and martial arts contests.

Opposite the main entrance to the Japan Martial Arts Hall, past the park-ing lot, a pathway leads off through the park back in the direction of the palace. Cross the bridge at the other end of the path, turn right, and then right again before you leave the park on the driveway that leads to the **Kōgeikan** ⓯. This museum is devoted to works of traditional craftsmanship by the great modern masters.

Return to the park exit and cross the street to the palace side. Ahead of you is the Inui-mon. This gate is used primarily by members of the im-perial family and by the fortunate few with special invitations to visit the palace itself. A driveway here leads to the Imperial Household Agency and the palace. A bit farther down the hill is the Kita-Hane-bashi-mon, one of the entrances to the Imperial Palace East Garden.

At the foot of the hill is Takebashi—although the name means Bamboo Bridge, the original construction has long since given way to reinforced concrete. Cross the street here to see the collection of modern Japanese and Western artwork in the **National Museum of Modern Art, Tōkyō** ⑯. On the palace side of Takebashi sits the finely reconstructed **Hirakawa-mon** ⑰, the East Garden's third entrance, which will complete the loop on this walk. From here follow the moat as it turns south again around the garden. In a few minutes you'll find yourself back at Ōte-mon, tired, perhaps, but triumphant.

TIMING   The Imperial Palace area covers a lot of ground—uphill and down—and even in its shorter versions the walk includes plenty to see. Allow at least an hour for the East Garden and Outer Garden of the palace itself. Plan to visit Yasukuni Jinja after lunch and spend at least an hour there. The Yūshūkan (at Yasukuni Jinja) and Kōgeikan museums are both small and should engage you for no more than a half hour each, but the modern art museum requires a more leisurely visit—particularly if there's a special exhibit. Set your own pace, but assume that this walk will take you the better part of a full day.

Avoid Monday, when the East Garden and museums are closed; the East Garden is also closed Friday. In July and August, heat will make the palace walk grueling—bring hats and bottled water.

What to See

⑬ **Chidori-ga-fuchi National Memorial Garden** (千鳥ヶ淵戦没者墓苑). High on the edge (*fuchi* means "edge") of the Imperial Palace moat, this park is pleasantly arrayed with cherry trees. Long before Edo Castle was built, there was a lovely little lake here, which Ieyasu Tokugawa incorporated into his system of defenses. Now you can rent a rowboat at **Chidori-ga-fuchi Boathouse,** roughly in the middle of the park, and explore it at your leisure. The park entrance is near Yasukuni Jinja, west and downhill from the corner of Yasukuni-dōri and Uchibori-dōri. ⊠ *Chiyoda-ku* ☎ *03/3234–1948* 🎫 *Park free, boat rental ¥500 for 30 min* ⊗ *Park daily sunrise–sunset, boathouse daily 10–5; opens at 9 in cherry-blossom season, usually late Mar.–early Apr.* Ⓜ *Hanzō-mon and Shinjuku subway lines, Kudanshita Station (Exit 2).*

⑩ **Hanzō-mon** (Hanzō Gate, 半蔵門). The house of the legendary Hattori Hanzō once sat at the foot of this small wooden gate. Hanzō was the leader of the shōgun's private corps of spies and infiltrators—and assassins, if need be. They were the menacing, black-clad ninja, perennial material for historical adventure films and television dramas. The gate is a minute's walk east from the subway. ⊠ *Chiyoda-ku* Ⓜ *Hanzō-mon subway line, Hanzō-mon Station (Exit 3).*

⑰ **Hirakawa-mon** (Hirakawa Gate, 平川門). The approach to this gate crosses the only wooden bridge that spans the Imperial Palace moat. The gate and bridge are reconstructions, but Hirakawa-mon is especially beautiful, looking much as it must have when the shōgun's wives and concubines used it on their rare excursions from the seraglio. Hirakawa-mon is the north gate to the East Garden, southeast of Bamboo Bridge. ⊠ *Chiyoda-ku* Ⓜ *Tōzai subway line, Takebashi Station (Exit 1A).*

③ **Imperial Palace East Garden** (Kōkyo Higashi Gyo-en, 皇居東御苑). The entrance to the East Garden is the ⇨ **Ōte-mon,** once the main gate of Ieyasu Tokugawa's castle. In lieu of an admission ticket, collect a plastic token

Fodor's Choice
★

at the office on the other side of the gate. As you walk up the driveway, you pass on the left the National Police Agency dōjō (martial arts hall). The hall was built in the Taishō period (1912–25) and is still used for kendō (Japanese fencing) practice. On the right is the Ōte Rest House, where for ¥100 you can buy a simple map of the garden.

There was once another gate at the top of the driveway, where feudal lords summoned to the palace would descend from their palanquins and proceed on foot. The gate itself is gone, but two 19th-century guardhouses survive, one outside the massive stone supports on the right and a longer one inside on the left. The latter, known as the **Hundred-Man Guardhouse,** was defended by four shifts of 100 soldiers each. Past it, to the right, is the entrance to what was once the ni-no-maru, the "second circle" of the fortress. It's now a grove and garden, its pathways defined by rows of perfect rhododendrons; a pond and a waterfall are in the northwest corner. At the far end is the **Suwa Tea Pavilion,** an early-19th-century building relocated here from another part of the castle grounds.

The steep stone walls of the **hon-maru** (the "inner circle"), with the Moat of Swans below (the swans actually swim in the outer waterways), dominate the west side of the garden. Halfway along, a steep path leads to an entrance in the wall to the upper fortress. This is **Shio-mi-zaka,** which translates roughly as "Briny View Hill," so named because in the Edo period the ocean could be seen from here.

Nothing remains on the broad expanse of the hon-maru's lawn to recall the scores of buildings that once stood here, connected by a network of corridors. What you see are the stone foundations of the castle keep at the far end of the grounds. Turn left and explore the wooded paths around the edges of the garden. Here are shade and quiet, and benches where you can sit and rest your weary feet. In the southwest corner, through the trees, you can see the back of the Fujimi Yagura, the only surviving watchtower of the hon-maru; farther along the path, on the west side, is the **Fujimi Tamon,** one of the two remaining armories.

The foundations of the keep make a platform with a fine view of Kitano-maru Kōen and the city to the north. The view must have been even finer from the keep itself. Built and rebuilt three times, it soared more than 250 feet over Edo. The other castle buildings were all plastered white; the keep was black, unadorned but for a golden roof. In 1657 a fire destroyed most of the city. Strong winds carried the flames across the moat, where it consumed the keep in a heat so fierce that it melted the gold in the vaults underneath. The keep was never rebuilt.

To the left of the keep foundations there's an exit from the hon-maru that leads northwest to the Kita-Hane-bashi-mon. To the right, another road leads past the **Tōka Music Hall**—an octagonal tower faced in mosaic tile, built in honor of the empress in 1966—down to the ni-no-maru and out of the gardens by way of the northern ⇨ **Hirakawa-mon.** If you decide to leave the hon-maru the way you came in, through the Ōtemon, stop for a moment at the rest house on the west side of the park before you surrender your token, and look at the photo collection. The pairs of before-and-after photographs of the castle, taken about 100 years apart, are fascinating. ⊠ *Chiyoda-ku* 🚇 *Free* 🕙 *Mar.–Oct., weekends and Tues.–Thurs. 9–4; Nov.–late Dec. and early Jan. and Feb., weekends and Tues.–Thurs. 9–3:30* Ⓜ *Tōzai, Marunouchi, and Chiyoda subway lines, Ōte-machi Station (Exit C13b).*

❹ **Imperial Palace Outer Garden** (Kōkyo-Gaien, 皇居外苑). When the office buildings of the Meiji government were moved from this area in 1899, the whole expanse along the east side of the palace was turned into a public promenade and planted with stands of pine. The Outer Garden affords the best view of the castle walls and their Tokugawa-period fortifications: Ni-jū-bashi and the Sei-mon, the 17th-century Fujimi Yagura watchtower, and the Sakurada-mon. ⊠ *Chiyoda-ku* 🚇 *Free* Ⓜ *Chiyoda subway line, Ni-jū-bashi-mae Station (Exit 2).*

⑭ **Japan Martial Arts Hall** (Nippon Budōkan, 日本武道館). With its eight-sided plan based on the Hall of Dreams of Hōryū-ji in Nara, the Budōkan was built as a martial arts arena for the Tōkyō Olympics of 1964. It still hosts tournaments and exhibitions of jūdō, karate, and kendō, as well as concerts. Tōkyō promoters are fortunate in their audiences, who don't seem to mind the exorbitant ticket prices and poor acoustics. To get here from the Kudanshita subway stop, walk west uphill toward Yasukuni Jinja; the entrance to Kita-no-Maru Kōen and the Budōkan is a few minutes' walk from the station, on the left. ⊠ *2–3 Kitano Maru Kōen, Chiyoda-ku* 📞 *03/3216–5100* Ⓜ *Tōzai, Hanzō-mon, and Shinjuku subway lines, Kudanshita Station (Exit 2).*

⑮ **Kōgeikan** (Crafts Gallery of the National Museum of Modern Art, 工芸館). Built in 1910, the Kōgeikan, once the headquarters of the Imperial Guard, is a rambling redbrick building, Gothic Revival in style, with exhibition halls on the second floor. The exhibits are all too few, but many of the craftspeople represented here—masters in the traditions of lacquerware, textiles, pottery, and metalwork—have been designated by the government as Living National Treasures. The most direct access to the gallery is from the Takebashi subway station on the Tōzai Line. Walk west and uphill about 10 minutes, on the avenue between Kita-no-maru Kōen and the Imperial Palace grounds; the entrance is on the right. ⊠ *1–1 Kita-no-maru Kōen, Chiyoda-ku* 📞 *03/3211–7781* 🚇 *¥420, includes admission to National Museum of Modern Art; additional fee for special exhibits; free 1st Sun. of month* 🕙 *Tues.–Sun. 10–5* Ⓜ *Hanzō-mon and Shinjuku subway lines, Kudanshita Station (Exit 2); Tōzai subway line, Takebashi Station (Exit 1b).*

❼ **National Diet Building** (Kokkai-Gijidō, 国会議事堂). This chunky pyramid, completed in 1936 after 17 years of work, houses the Japanese parliament. It's a building best contemplated from a distance. On a gloomy day it seems as if it might well have sprung from the screen of a German Expressionist movie. ⊠ *1–7–1 Nagata-chō, Chiyoda-ku* Ⓜ *Marunouchi subway line, Kokkai-Gijidō-mae Station (Exit 2).*

⑯ **National Museum of Modern Art, Tōkyō** (Tōkyō Kokuritsu Kindai Bijutsukan, 国立近代美術館). Founded in 1952 and moved to its present site in 1969, this was Japan's first national art museum. It mounts major exhibitions of 20th- and 21st-century Japanese and Western art throughout the year but tends to be rather stodgy about how it organizes and presents these exhibitions and is seldom on the cutting edge. The second through fourth floors house the permanent collection, which includes the painting, prints, and sculpture of Rousseau, Picasso, Tsuguji Fujita, Ryūzaburo Umehara, and Taikan Yokoyama. ✉ *3–1 Kita-no-maru Kōen, Chiyoda-ku* ☎ *03/ 3214–2561* ⊕ *www.momat.go.jp* 💷 *¥420, includes admission to the Kōgeikan); free 1st Sun. of month* ◷ *Tues.–Thurs. and weekends 10–5, Fri. 10–8* Ⓜ *Tōzai subway line, Takebashi Station (Exit 1b); Hanzō-mon and Shinjuku subway lines, Kudanshita Station (Exit 2).*

❾ **National Theater** (Kokuritsu Gekijō, 国立劇場). Architect Hiroyuki Iwamoto's winning entry in the design competition for the National Theater building (1966) is a rendition in concrete of the ancient *azekura* (storehouse) style, invoking the 8th-century Shōsōin Imperial Repository in Nara. The large hall seats 1,746 and presents primarily Kabuki theater, ancient court music, and dance. The small hall seats 630 and is used mainly for Bunraku puppet theater and traditional music. ✉ *4–1 Hayabusa-chō, Chiyoda-ku* ☎ *03/3265–7411* 💷 *Varies depending on performance* Ⓜ *Hanzō-mon subway line, Hanzō-mon Station (Exit 1).*

❷ **Ōte-mon** (Ōte Gate, 大手門). The main entrance to the Imperial Palace East Garden, Ōte-mon was in former days the principal gate of Ieyasu Tokugawa's castle. The masu style was typical of virtually all the approaches to the shōgun's impregnable fortress: the first portal leads to a narrow enclosure, with a second and larger gate beyond, offering the defenders inside a devastating field of fire upon any would-be intruders. Most of the gate was destroyed in 1945 but was rebuilt in 1967 on the original plans. The outer part of the gate, however, survived. ✉ *Chiyoda-ku* Ⓜ *Tōzai, Marunouchi, and Chiyoda subway lines, Ōte-machi Station (Exit C10).*

❻ **Sakurada-mon** (Gate of the Field of Cherry Trees, 桜田門). By hallowed use and custom, the small courtyard between the portals of this masu gate is where joggers warm up for their 5-km (3-mi) run around the palace. ✉ *Chiyoda-ku* Ⓜ *Yūraku-chō subway line, Sakurada-mon Station (Exit 3).*

❽ **Supreme Court** (Saikō Saibansho, 最高裁判所). The Supreme Court's fortresslike planes and angles, in granite and concrete, speak volumes of the role of the law in Japanese society—here is the very bastion of the established order. Designed by Shinichi Okada, the building was the last in a series of open architectural competitions sponsored by the various government agencies charged with the reconstruction of Tōkyō after World War II. Okada's winning design was one of 217 submitted. Before the building was finished, in 1974, the open competition had generated so much controversy that the government did not hold another one for almost 20 years. Guided tours are available, but under restrictive conditions: you must be at least 16 years old to take part, tours musts be reserved two weeks in advance, and there is no interpretation in English. Tours are conducted weekdays (except July 20–August 31 and national holidays); they begin at 3 and take about an hour. ✉ *4–2 Hayabusa-chō, Chiyoda-ku* ☎ *03/3264–8111 for public relations office (Kōhōka) for tours* Ⓜ *Hanzō-mon subway line, Hanzō-mon Station (Exit 1).*

ETIQUETTE & BEHAVIOR

PROPRIETY IS AN IMPORTANT PART OF JAPANESE SOCIETY. *Many Japanese expect foreigners to behave differently and are tolerant of faux pas, but they are pleasantly surprised when people acknowledge and observe their customs. The easiest way to ingratiate yourself with the Japanese is to take time to learn and respect Japanese ways.*

It's customary to **bow upon meeting someone.** The art of bowing is not simple; the depth of your bow depends on your social position with respect to that of the person you are meeting. Younger people and those of lesser status must bow more deeply to indicate their respect and acknowledge their position. You're not expected to understand the complexity of these rules, and a basic nod of the head will suffice. Many Japanese are familiar with Western customs and will offer a hand for a handshake.

Don't be offended if you're not invited to someone's home. Most entertaining among Japanese is done in restaurants and bars. It's an honor when you are invited to a home; this means your host feels comfortable and close to you. If you do receive an invitation, bring along a small gift—a souvenir from your country makes the best present, but food and liquor or anything that can be consumed (and not take up space in the home) is also appreciated. Upon entering a home, **remove your shoes in the foyer and put on the slippers that are provided**; in Japan, shoes are for outdoors only. Be sure your socks or stockings are in good condition.

Japanese restaurants often provide a small hot towel called an oshibori. This is to wipe your hands but not your face. You may see some Japanese wiping their faces with their oshibori, but sometimes this is considered bad form. If you must use your oshibori on your face, wipe your face first,

then your hands. When you are finished with your oshibori, do not just toss it back onto the table: fold or roll it up.

If you're not accustomed to eating with chopsticks, ask for a fork instead. When taking food from a shared dish, do not use the part of the chopstick that has entered your mouth to pick up a morsel. Instead, use the end that you have been holding in your hand. Never leave your chopsticks sticking upright in your food; this is how rice offerings at funerals are arranged. Instead, rest chopsticks on the edge of the tray, bowl, or plate between bites and at the end of the meal. For more information on dining etiquette, refer to The Discreet Charm of Japanese Cuisine at the back of this book.

Business Etiquette

Although many business practices are universal, certain customs are unique to Japan. It's not necessary to observe these precepts, but the Japanese always appreciate it if you do.

In Japan, meishi (business cards) are mandatory. Upon meeting someone for the first time, it's common to bow and to proffer your business card simultaneously. Although English will suffice on your business card, it's best to have one side printed in Japanese (there are businesses in Japan that provide this service in 24 hours). In a sense, the cards are simply a convenience. Japanese sometimes have difficulty with Western names, and referring to the cards is helpful. Also, in a society where hierarchy matters, Japanese like to know job titles and rank, so it's useful if your card indicates your position in your company. Japanese often place the business cards they have received in front of them on a table or desk as they conduct their meetings. Follow suit and do not simply shove the card in your pocket.

The concept of being fashionably late does not exist in Japan; it is extremely important to **be prompt for social and business occasions.** Japanese addresses tend to be complicated (⇨ Addresses, above), and traffic is often heavy, so allow adequate travel time. Most Japanese are not accustomed to using first names in business circumstances. Even coworkers of 20 years' standing use surnames. Unless you are sure that the Japanese person is extremely comfortable with Western customs, it's best to **stick to last names and use the honorific -san after the name,** as in Tanaka-san (Mr. or Mrs. Tanaka). Also, respect the hierarchy, and as much as possible address yourself to the most senior person in the room.

Don't be frustrated if decisions are not made instantly. Rarely empowered to make decisions, individual businesspeople must confer with their colleagues and superiors. Even if you are annoyed, **don't express anger or aggression.** Losing one's temper is equated with losing face in Japan.

A separation of business and private life is sacrosanct in Japan, and it's best not to ask about personal matters. Rather than asking about a person's family, it's better to **stick to neutral subjects in conversation.** This does not mean that you can only comment on the weather but rather that you should take care not to be nosy.

Because of cramped housing, again, many Japanese entertain in restaurants or bars. It's not customary for Japanese businessmen to bring wives along. If you are traveling with your spouse, do not assume that an invitation includes both of you. You may ask if it's acceptable to bring your spouse along, but remember that it's awkward for a Japanese person to say no. You should pose the question carefully, such as "Will your [wife or husband] come along, too?" This eliminates the need for a direct, personal refusal.

Usually, entertaining is done over dinner, followed by an evening on the town. Drinking is something of a national pastime in Japan. If you would rather not suffer from a hangover the next day, do not refuse your drink—sip, but keep your glass at least half full. Because the custom is for companions to pour drinks for each other, an empty glass is nearly the equivalent of requesting another drink. Whatever you do, **don't pour your own drink, and if a glass at your table happens to be empty, show your attentiveness by filling it for your companion.**

A special note to women traveling on business in Japan: remember that although the situation is gradually changing, many Japanese women do not have careers. Many Japanese businessmen do not yet know how to interact with Western businesswomen. They may be uncomfortable, aloof, or patronizing. Be patient and, if the need arises, gently remind them that, professionally, you expect to be treated as any man would be.

🏳 **❶ Tōkyō Station** (東京駅). The work of Kingo Tatsuno, one of Japan's first modern architects, Tōkyō Station was completed in 1914. Tatsuno modeled his creation on the railway station of Amsterdam. The building lost its original top story in the air raids of 1945, but it was promptly repaired. In the late 1990s, plans to tear it down entirely were scotched by a protest movement. Inside, it has been deepened and tunneled and redesigned any number of times to accommodate new commuter lines, but the lovely old redbrick facade remains untouched. The best thing about the place is the **Tōkyō Station Hotel,** on the west side on the second and third floors. ☒ *1–9–1 Marunouchi, Chiyoda-ku* ☎ *03/3231–2511.*

need a break?

If you're visiting Tōkyō Station in the morning, consider getting a bite to eat at the **Tōkyō Station Hotel,** which serves a fairly decent breakfast for ¥1,700. It's on the west side of the station. ☒ *1–9–1 Marunouchi, Chiyoda-ku* ☎ *03/3231–2511.*

❺ Two-Tiered Bridge (Ni-jū-bashi, 二重橋). Making a graceful arch across the moat, this bridge is surely the most photogenic spot on the grounds of the former Edo Castle. Normally you can approach no closer than the head of Sei-mon Sekkyō, a short stone bridge that arcs over the moat to the Sei-mon—the Main Gate. Ordinary mortals may pass through this gate only on December 23 and January 2 to pay their respects to the Imperial family. The guards in front of their small, octagonal, copper-roof sentry boxes change every hour on the hour—alas, with nothing like the pomp and ceremony of Buckingham Palace. ☒ *Chiyoda-ku* Ⓜ *Chiyoda subway line, Ni-jū-bashi-mae Station (Exit 2).*

⑫ Yamatane Museum of Art (Yamatane Bijutsukan, 山種美術館). The museum, which specializes in *Nihon-ga*—traditional Japanese painting—from the Meiji period and later, has a private collection of masterpieces by such painters as Taikan Yokoyama, Gyoshū Hayami, Kokei Kobayashi, and Gyokudō Kawai. The exhibits, which sometimes include works borrowed from other collections, change every two months. The decor and display at the Yamatane make it an oasis of quiet and elegance, and the chance to buy the lavish catalog of the collection is alone well worth the visit. The interior garden was designed by architect Yoshio Taniguchi, who also did the Museum of Modern Art. ☒ *2 Samban-chō, Chiyoda-ku* ☎ *03/3239–5911* 📠 *03/3239–5913* ☒ *¥500* ☉ *Tues.–Sun. 10–4:30* Ⓜ *Tōzai and Shinjuku subway lines, Kudanshita Station (Exit 2).*

★ **⑪ Yasukuni Jinja** (Shrine of Peace for the Nation, 靖国神社). Founded in 1869, this shrine is dedicated to the approximately 2.5 million Japanese who have died since then in war or military service. Since 1945 Yasukuni has been the periodic focus of passionate political debate, given that the Japanese constitution expressly renounces both militarism and state sponsorship of religion. Even so, hundreds of thousands of Japanese come here every year, simply to pray for the repose of friends and relatives they have lost.

The shrine is not one structure but a complex of buildings that include the **Main Hall** and the **Hall of Worship**—both built in the simple, unadorned style of the ancient Shintō shrines at Ise—and the **Yūshūkan,** a museum of documents and war memorabilia. Also here are a Nō theater and, in the far western corner, a sumō-wrestling ring. Both Nō and sumō have their origins in religious ritual, as performances offered to please and divert the gods. Sumō matches are held at Yasukuni in April, during the first of its three annual festivals.

You can pick up a pamphlet and simplified map of the shrine in English just inside the grounds. Just ahead of you, in a circle on the main avenue, is a statue of Masujiro Omura, commander of the imperial forces that subdued the Tokugawa loyalist resistance to the new Meiji government. From here, as you look down the avenue to your right, you can see the enormous steel outer torii of the main entrance to the shrine at Kudanshita; to the left is a bronze inner torii, erected in 1887. (These Shintō shrine arches are normally made of wood and painted red.) Beyond the inner torii is the gate to the shrine itself, with its 12 pillars and chrysanthemums—the imperial crest—embossed on the doors.

Refurbished in 2002, the Yūshūkan presents Japan at its most ambivalent—if not unrepentant—about its more recent militaristic past. Critics charge that the newer exhibits glorify the nation's role in the Pacific War as a noble struggle for independence; certainly there's an agenda here that's hard to reconcile with Japan's firm postwar rejection of war as an instrument of national policy. Many Japanese visitors are moved by such displays as the last letters and photographs of young kamikaze pilots; visitors from other countries tend to find the Yūshūkan a cautionary, rather than uplifting, experience.

Although some of the exhibits have English labels and notes, the English is not very helpful; most objects, however, speak clearly enough for themselves. Rooms on the second floor house an especially fine collection of medieval swords and armor. Perhaps the most bizarre exhibit is the *kaiten* (human torpedo) on the first floor. The kaiten was a black cylinder about 50 feet long and 3 feet in diameter, with 3,400 pounds of high explosives in the nose. The operator, squeezed into a seat with a periscope in the center of the tube, worked the directional vanes with his feet. The kaiten was carried into battle on the deck of a ship and launched, like a kamikaze plane, on its one-way journey.

If time permits, turn right as you leave the Yūshūkan and walk to the pond at the rear of the shrine. There's no general admittance to the teahouses on the far side, but the pond is among the most serene and beautiful in Tōkyō, especially in spring, when the irises are in bloom. ⊠ *3–1–1 Kudankita, Chiyoda-ku* ☎ *03/3261–8326* ☜ *¥800* ☉ *Grounds daily, usually 9–9. Museum Mar.–Oct., daily 9–5; Nov.–Feb., daily 9–4:30* Ⓜ *Hanzō-mon and Shinjuku subway lines, Kudanshita Station (Exit 1).*

need a
break?

The specialty at the moderately priced **Tony Roma's** (トニーローマ), as it is in this chain's umpteen locations, is charcoal-broiled spareribs. It's on the west side of Uchibori-dōri north of the British Embassy, at the intersection straight west of Inui-mon. ⊠ *1 Samban-chō, Chiyoda-ku* ☎ *03/3222–3440.*

AKIHABARA & JIMBŌ-CHŌ 秋葉原・神保町

This is it: the greatest sound-and-light show on earth. Akihabara is a merchandise mart for anything—and everything—that runs on electricity, from microprocessors and washing machines to television sets and gadgets that beep when your bathwater is hot. Wherever you go in the world, if people know nothing else about Japan, they recognize the country as a cornucopia of electronics equipment and household appliances. About 10% of what Japan's electronics industry makes for the domestic market passes through Akihabara.

Some 400 years ago this was a residential district for the lower-ranked samurai retainers of the Tokugawa military government. Later, it evolved into a commercial center—known especially for leather goods—and in 1929 the nation's largest wholesale produce market was located here. Surrounding the market were small shops making and selling vacuum tubes and radio parts for customers who wanted to build their own sets and catch the programs aired by the newly created Japan Broadcasting Corporation. Just after World War II a black market sprang up around the railroad station, where the Yamanote Line and the crosstown Sōbu Line intersect. In time, most of the stalls were doing a legitimate business in radio parts, and in 1951 they were all relocated in one dense clump under the tracks. Retail and wholesale suppliers then spread out into the adjacent blocks and made the area famous for cut-rate prices. In 1989 the produce market was torn down and relocated; still under construction on that site is the Akihabara Information Technology Center, slated for completion in 2006.

Few visitors to Tōkyō neglect this district; the mistake is to come here merely for shopping. Akihabara may be consumer heaven, but it's also the first stop on a walking tour through the general area known as Kanda—where the true Edokko, the born-and-bred Tōkyōites of the old town, claim their roots—to the bookstalls of Jimbō-chō. In a sense this tour is a journey through time: it's a morning's walk from satellite broadcast antennas to the hallowed precincts of the printed word.

Numbers in the text correspond to numbers in the margin and on the Akihabara & Jimbō-chō map.

A Good Walk

Start at the west exit of JR Akihabara Station. (There's also a stop, Nakaokachi-machi, nearby on the Hibiya subway line, but the JR provides much easier access.) Come out to the left after you pass through the wicket, head into the station square, turn right, and walk to the main thoroughfare. Ahead of you on the other side of the street you can see the **LAOX** ❶ ► building, one of the district's major discount stores.

Before you get to the corner, on the right is a little warren of stalls and tiny shops that cannot have changed an iota since the days of the black market—except for their merchandise. A stroll through the narrow passageways will reveal an astonishing array of switches, transformers, resistors, semiconductors, printed circuit cards, plugs, wires, connectors, and tools. The labyrinth is especially popular with domestic and for-

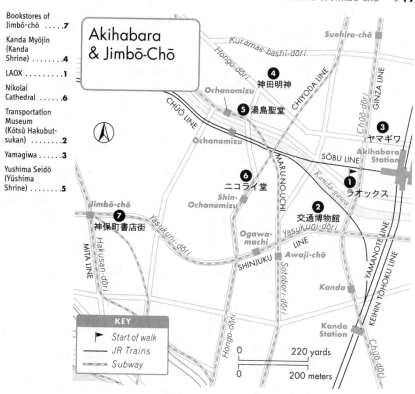

Bookstores of
Jimbō-chō **7**

Kanda Myōjin
(Kanda
Shrine) **4**

LAOX **1**

Nikolai
Cathedral **6**

Transportation
Museum
(Kōtsū Hakubut-
sukan) **2**

Yamagiwa **3**

Yushima Seidō
(Yūshima
Shrine) **5**

**Akihabara
& Jimbō-Chō**

eign techno mavens, the people who know—or want to know—what the latest in Japanese electronic technology looks like from the inside.

If you turn left at the corner and cross the small bridge over the Kanda-gawa (Kanda River), you'll soon come to the **Transportation Museum** ②— a detour you might want to make if you have children in tow. If not, turn right at the corner and walk north on Chūō-dōri. Music blares at you from hundreds of storefronts as you walk along; this is the heart of the district. Most larger stores on the main drag have one floor—or even an entire annex—of products for the foreign market, staffed by clerks who speak everything from English to Mandarin to Portuguese. Prices are duty-free (don't forget to bring your passport). One of the biggest selections can be found at **Yamagiwa** ③, just past the second intersection, on the right.

At Yamagiwa, cross the street, continue north to the Soto Kanda 5-chōme intersection (there's an entrance to the Suehiro-chō subway station on the corner), and turn left onto Kuramae-bashi-dōri. Walk about five minutes—you'll cross one more intersection with a traffic light—and in the middle of the next block you can see a flight of steps on the left, between two brick buildings. Red, green, and blue pennants flutter from the handrails. This is the back entrance to **Kanda Myōjin** ④.

Leave the shrine by the main gate. The seated figures in the alcoves on either side are its guardian gods; carved in camphor wood, they are depicted in Heian costume, holding long bows. From the gate down to the copper-clad torii on Hongo-dōri is a walk of a few yards. On either side are shops that sell the specialties famous in this neighborhood: pickles, miso, and sweet sake laced with ground ginger. On the other side of the avenue are the wall and wooded grounds of the **Yushima Seidō** ❺ Confucian shrine.

Cross Hongo-dōri and turn left, following the wall downhill. Turn right at the first narrow side street, and right again at the bottom; the entrance to Yushima Seidō is a few steps from the corner. As you walk up the path, you can see a statue of Confucius on your right; where the path ends, a flight of stone steps leads up to the main hall of the shrine.

Retrace your steps, turn right as you leave the shrine, and walk along the continuation of the wall on the side street leading up to Hijiri-bashi (Bridge of Sages), which spans the Kanda-gawa at Ochanomizu Station on the JR Sōbu Line. Cross the bridge—you're now back on Hongo-dōri— and ahead of you, just beyond the station on the right, you can see the dome of the Russian Orthodox **Nikolai Cathedral** ❻.

Continue south to the intersection of Hongo-dōri and Yasukuni-dōri. Surugadai, the area to your right as you walk down the hill, is a kind of fountainhead of Japanese higher education: two of the city's major private universities—Meiji and Nihon—occupy a good part of the hill. Not far from these are a score of elite high schools, public and private. In the 1880s several other universities were founded in this area. They have since moved away, but the student population here is still enormous.

Turn right on Yasukuni-dōri. Between you and your objective—the **bookstores of Jimbō-chō** ❼—are three blocks of stores devoted almost exclusively to electric guitars, records, travel bags, skis, and skiwear. The bookstores begin at the intersection called Surugadai-shita and continue along Yasukuni-dōri for about ½ km (¼ mi), most of them on the south (left) side of the street. This area is to print what Akihabara is to electronics.

What about that computer or CD player you didn't buy at the beginning of your walk because you didn't want to carry it all this way? No problem. There's a subway station (Mita Line) at the Jimbō-chō main intersection; go one stop north to Suidō-bashi, transfer to the JR Sōbu Line, and five minutes later you're back in Akihabara.

TIMING   Unless you do a lot of shopping, this walk should take you no more than a morning. Cultural landmarks are few, and you can explore them thoroughly in a half hour each. Getting from place to place will take up much of your time. Keep in mind that most stores in Akihabara do not open until 10 AM. Weekends draw hordes of shoppers, especially on Sunday, when the four central blocks of Chūō-dōri are closed to traffic and become a pedestrian mall.

What to See

❼ **Bookstores of Jimbō-chō** (神保町書店街). For the ultimate browse through art books, catalogs, scholarly monographs, secondhand paperbacks, and dictionaries in most known languages, the bookstores of Jimbō-chō are the place to go. A number of the antiquarian booksellers here carry not only rare typeset editions but also wood-block-printed books of the Edo period and individual prints. At shops like **Isseidō** (一誠堂) and **Ohya Shōbo** (大屋書房), both open Monday–Saturday 10–6, it's still possible to find genuine 19th- and 20th-century prints—if not in the best condition—at affordable prices. Many of Japan's most prestigious publishing houses make their home in this area as well. The bookstores run for ½ km (¼ mi) on Yasukuni-dōri beginning at the Surugadai-shita intersection. ⊠ *Isseidō: 1–7–4 Kanda Jimbō-chō, Chiyoda-ku* ☎ *03/3292–0071* ⊠ *Ohya Shōbō: 1–1 Kanda Jimbō-chō, Chiyoda-ku, Jimbō-chō* ☎ *03/3291–0062* Ⓜ *Shin-juku and Mita subway lines, Jimbō-chō Station (Exit A7).*

❹ **Kanda Myōjin** (Kanda Shrine, 神田明神). This shrine is said to have been founded in 730 in a village called Shibasaki, where the Ōte-machi financial district stands today. In 1616 it was relocated, a victim of Ieyasu Toku-gawa's ever-expanding system of fortifications. The present site was cho-sen, in accordance with Chinese geomancy, to afford the best view from Edo Castle and to protect the shrine from evil influences. The shrine it-self was destroyed in the Great Kantō Earthquake of 1923, and the present buildings reproduce in concrete the style of 1616. Ieyasu preferred the jazzier decorative effects of Chinese Buddhism to the simple lines of traditional Shintō architecture. This is especially evident in the curved, copper-tile roof of the main shrine and in the two-story front gate.

Three principle deities are enshrined here: Ōkuninushi-no-Mikoto and Sukunahikona-no-Mikoto, both of whom appear in the early Japanese creation myths, and Taira-no-Masakado. The last was a 10th-century warrior whose contentious spirit earned him a place in the Shintō pan-theon: he led a revolt against the Imperial Court in Kyōto, seized con-trol of the eastern provinces, declared himself emperor—and in 940 was beheaded for his rebellious ways. The townspeople of Kanda, con-tentious souls in their own right, made Taira-no-Masakado a kind of patron saint, and even today—overlooking somehow the fact that he lost—they appeal to him for victory when they face a tough encounter.

Some of the smaller buildings you see as you come up the steps and walk around the main hall contain the *mikoshi*—the portable shrines that are featured in one of Tōkyō's three great blowouts, the **Kanda Festival.** (The other two are the Sannō Festival of Hie Jinja in Nagata-chō and the Sanja Festival of Asakusa Shrine.) The essential shrine festival is a procession in which the gods, housed for the occasion in their mikoshi, pass through the streets and get a breath of fresh air. The Kanda Festival began in the early Edo period. Heading the procession then were 36 magnificent floats, most of which were destroyed in the fires that raged through the city after the earthquake of 1923. The floats that lead the procession today move in stately measure on wheeled carts, attended by the priests and officials of the shrine dressed in Heian-period (794–1185) costume. The mikoshi, some 70 of them, follow behind, bobbing and weaving, carried on the shoulders of the townspeople. Shrine festivals like Kanda's are a peculiarly competitive form of worship: piety is a matter of who can shout the loudest, drink the most beer, and have the best time. The festival takes place in August in odd-numbered years. Kanda Myōjin is on Kuramae-bashi-dōri, about a five-minute walk west of the Suehiro-chō subway stop. ⊠ *2–16–2 Soto Kanda, Chiyoda-ku* ☎ *03/3254–0753* Ⓜ *Ginza subway line, Suehiro-chō Station (Exit 3).*

▶ ❶ **LAOX** (ラオックス). Of all the discount stores in Akihabara, LAOX has the largest and most comprehensive selection, with four buildings in this area—one exclusively for musical instruments, another for duty-free appliances—and outlets in Yokohama and Narita. This is a good place to find the latest in digital cameras, watches, and games. ⊠ *1–2–9 Soto Kanda, Chiyoda-ku* ☎ *03/3253–7111* ⊙ *Mon.–Sat. 10–8, Sun. 10–7:30* Ⓜ *JR Akihabara Station (Nishi-guchi/West Exit).*

❻ **Nikolai Cathedral** (ニコライ堂). Formally, this is the Holy Resurrection Cathedral. The more familiar name derives from its founder, St. Nikolai Kassatkin (1836–1912), a Russian missionary who came to Japan in 1861 and spent the rest of his life here propagating the Russian Orthodox faith. The building, planned by a Russian engineer and executed by a British architect, was completed in 1891. Heavily damaged in the earthquake of 1923, the cathedral was restored with a dome much more modest than the original. Even so, it endows this otherwise featureless part of the city with the charm of the unexpected. ⊠ *4–1 Surugadai, Chiyoda-ku* ☎ *03/3291–1885* Ⓜ *Chiyoda subway line, Shin-Ochanomizu Station (Exit B1).*

☾ ❷ **Transportation Museum** (Kōtsū Hakubutsukan, 交通博物館). Displays at this fun museum explain the early development of the railway system and include a miniature layout of the rail services, as well as Japan's first airplane, which took off in 1903. To get here from JR Akihabara Station, cross the bridge on Chūō-dōri over the Kanda River, and turn right at the next corner. ⊠ *1–25 Kanda Sudachō, Chiyoda-ku* ☎ *03/3251–8481* 🎟 *¥310* ⊙ *Tues.–Sun. 9:30–5* Ⓜ *JR Akihabara Station (Denki-gai Exit).*

❸ **Yamagiwa** (ヤマギワ). Entire floors of this discount electronics giant are devoted to computer hardware and software, fax machines, and copiers. Yamagiwa has a particularly good selection of lighting fixtures, most of them 220 volts, but the annex has export models of the most popular appliances and devices, plus an English-speaking staff to assist you with selections. You should be able to bargain prices down a bit—especially if you're buying more than one big-ticket item. ⊠ *1–5–10 Soto Kanda, Chiyoda-ku* ☎ *03/3253–5111* ⊙ *Weekdays 11–7:30, weekends 10:30–7:30* Ⓜ *JR Akihabara Station (Nishi-guchi/West Exit).*

❺ **Yushima Seidō** (Yushima Shrine, 湯島聖堂). The origins of this shrine date to a hall, founded in 1632, for the study of the Chinese Confucian classics. The original building was in Ueno, and its headmaster was Hayashi Razan, the official Confucian scholar to the Tokugawa government. The shogunal dynasty found these Chinese teachings—with their emphasis on obedience and hierarchy—attractive enough to make Confucianism a kind of state ideology. Moved to its present site in 1691 (and destroyed by fire and rebuilt six times), the hall became an academy for the ruling elite. In a sense, nothing has changed: in 1872 the new Meiji government established the country's first teacher-training institute here, and that, in turn, evolved into Tōkyō University—the graduates of which still make up much of the ruling elite. The hall could almost be in China: painted black, weathered and somber, it looks like nothing else you're likely to see in Japan. ✉ *1–4–25 Yushima, Bunkyō-ku* ☎ *03/3251–4606* 💴 *Free* 🕓 *Apr.–Sept., Fri.–Wed. 10–5; Oct.–mid-Dec. and Jan.–Mar., Fri.–Wed. 10–4* Ⓜ *Marunouchi subway line, Ochanomizu Station (Exit B2).*

UENO 上野

JR Ueno Station is Tōkyō's version of the Gare du Nord: the gateway to and from Japan's northeast provinces. Since its completion in 1883, the station has served as a terminus in the great migration to the city by villagers in pursuit of a better life.

Ueno was a place of prominence long before the coming of the railroad. When Ieyasu Tokugawa established his capital here in 1603, it was merely a wooded promontory, called Shinobu-ga-oka (Hill of Endurance), overlooking the bay. Ieyasu gave a large tract of land on the hill to one of his most important vassals, Takatora Toda, who designed and built Edo Castle. Ieyasu's heir, Hidetada, later commanded the founding of a temple on the hill. Shinobu-ga-oka was in the northeast corner of the capital. In Chinese geomancy, the northeast approach required a particularly strong defense against evil influences.

That defense was entrusted to Tenkai (1536–1643), a priest of the Tendai sect of Buddhism and an adviser of great influence to the first three Tokugawa shōguns. The temple he built on Shinobu-ga-oka was called Kan-ei-ji, and he became the first abbot. The patronage of the Tokugawas and their vassal barons made Kan-ei-ji a seat of power and glory. By the end of the 17th century it occupied most of the hill. To the magnificent Main Hall were added scores of other buildings—including a pagoda and a shrine to Ieyasu—and 36 subsidiary temples. The city of Edo itself expanded to the foot of the hill, where Kan-ei-ji's main gate once stood. And most of what is now Ueno was called *Mon-zen-machi*: "the town in front of the gate."

The power and glory of Kan-ei-ji came to an end in just one day: April 11, 1868. An army of clan forces from the western part of Japan, bearing a mandate from Emperor Meiji, arrived in Edo and demanded the surrender of the castle. The shogunate was by then a tottering regime; it capitulated, and with it went everything that had depended on the favor of the Tokugawas. The Meiji Restoration began with a bloodless coup.

A band of some 2,000 Tokugawa loyalists assembled on Ueno Hill, however, and defied the new government. On May 15 the imperial army attacked. The Shōgitai (loyalists), outnumbered and surrounded, soon discovered that right was on the side of modern artillery. A few survivors fled; the rest committed ritual suicide, and took Kan-ei-ji with them— torching the temple and most of its outbuildings.

The new Meiji government turned Ueno Hill into one of the nation's first public parks. The intention was not merely to provide a bit of greenery but to make the park an instrument of civic improvement and to show off the achievements of an emerging modern state. It would serve as the site of trade and industrial expositions; it would have a national museum, a library, a university of fine arts, and a zoo. The modernization of Ueno still continues, but the park is more than the sum of its museums. The Shōgitai failed to take everything with them: some of the most important buildings in the temple complex survived or were restored and should not be missed.

Numbers in the text correspond to numbers in the margin and on the Ueno map.

A Good Walk

The best way to begin is to head to JR Ueno Station on the JR Yamanote Line and leave the station by the Kōen-guchi (Park Exit), upstairs. Directly across from the exit is the Tōkyō Metropolitan Festival Hall, one of the city's major venues for classical music. Follow the path to the right of the hall to the information booth, where you can pick up a useful detailed map of the park in English; northwest of the booth (turn left, away from Ueno Station) is the **National Museum of Western Art** ❶ ▶. The Rodins in the courtyard—*The Gate of Hell, The Thinker,* and the magnificent *Burghers of Calais*—are authentic castings from Rodin's original molds.

Turn right at the far corner of the museum and walk along a stretch of wooded park; you come next to the **National Science Museum** ❷. At the next corner is the main street that cuts through the park. Turn left on this street, and cross at the traffic signal some 50 yards west to the main entrance of the **Tōkyō National Museum** ❸, which has one of the world's greatest collections of East Asian art and archaeology.

Turn right as you leave the museum complex, walk west, and turn right at the first corner; this road dead-ends in about five minutes in the far northwest corner of the park, opposite the gate to **Kan-ei-ji** ❹. (The gate is usually locked; use the side entrance to the left.) Stretching away to the right is the cemetery of Kan-ei-ji, where several Tokugawa shōguns had their mausoleums. These were destroyed in the air raids of 1945, but the gate that led to the tomb of the fourth shōgun, Ietsuna, remains.

Retrace your steps to the main gate of the Tōkyō National Museum, and cross the street to the long esplanade, with its fountain and reflecting pool. Keep to the right as you walk south. The first path to the right brings you to the **Tōkyō Metropolitan Art Museum** ❺ and its small but impressive permanent collection of modern Japanese painting.

At the south end of the esplanade is the central plaza of the park. (Look to your left for the police substation, a small steel-gray building of futuristic design.) To the right is the entrance to **Ueno Zoo** ❻. Opened in 1882, the zoo gradually expanded to its present 35 acres, and the original section here on the hill was connected to the one below, along the edge of **Shinobazu Pond** ❼, by a bridge and a monorail.

A few steps farther south, on the continuation of the esplanade, is the path that leads to **Tōshō-gū** ❽—the shrine to the first Tokugawa shōgun, Ieyasu. The entrance to the shrine is marked by a stone torii built in 1633.

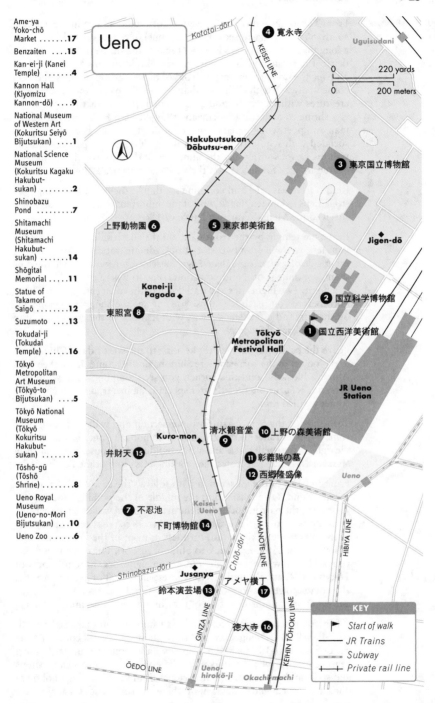

Ame-ya Yoko-chō Market **17**

Benzaiten **15**

Kan-ei-ji (Kanei Temple) **4**

Kannon Hall (Kiyomizu Kannon-dō) **9**

National Museum of Western Art (Kokuritsu Seiyō Bijutsukan) **1**

National Science Museum (Kokuritsu Kagaku Hakubut-sukan) **2**

Shinobazu Pond **7**

Shitamachi Museum (Shitamachi Hakubut-sukan) **14**

Shōgitai Memorial **11**

Statue of Takamori Saigō **12**

Suzumoto **13**

Tokudai-ji (Tokudai Temple) **16**

Tōkyō Metropolitan Art Museum (Tōkyō-to Bijutsukan) **5**

Tōkyō National Museum (Tōkyō Kokuritsu Hakubut-sukan) **3**

Tōshō-gū (Tōshō Shrine) **8**

Ueno Royal Museum (Ueno-no-Mori Bijutsukan) . . . **10**

Ueno Zoo **6**

Ueno

Kototoi-dōri

KEISEI LINE

④ 寛永寺

Uguisudani

0   220 yards

0   200 meters

Hakubutsukan-Dōbutsu-en

③ 東京国立博物館

上野動物園 **⑥**

⑤ 東京都美術館

Jigen-dō

Kanei-ji Pagoda ◆

② 国立科学博物館

東照宮 **⑧**

① 国立西洋美術館

Tōkyō Metropolitan Festival Hall

JR Ueno Station

清水観音堂 **⑩** 上野の森美術館

Kuro-mon ◆ **⑨**

弁財天 **⑮**

⑪ 彰義隊の墓

⑫ 西郷隆盛像

Ueno

⑦ 不忍池

Keisei-Ueno

YAMANOTE LINE

HIBIYA LINE

下町博物館 **⑭**

Shinobazu-dōri

Chūō-dōri

◆ **Jusanya**

鈴本演芸場 **⑬**

アメヤ横丁 **⑰**

KEIHIN TŌHOKU LINE

徳大寺 **⑯**

	KEY
▶	*Start of walk*
—	*JR Trains*
⚏	*Subway*
+++	*Private rail line*

GINZA LINE

ŌEDO LINE

Ueno-hirokō-ji

Okachi-machi

From Tōshō-gū, return to the avenue, turn right, and continue walking south. Shortly you can see a kind of tunnel of red-lacquered torii, with a long flight of stone steps leading down to the shrine to Inari, a Shintō deity of harvests and family prosperity. Shrines of this kind are found all over the downtown part of Tōkyō, tucked away in alleys and odd corners, always with their guardian statues of foxes—the mischievous creatures with which the god is associated. Just below the Inari shrine is a shrine to Sugawara Michizane (854–903), a Heian-period nobleman and poet worshipped as the Shintō deity Tenjin. Because he is associated with scholarship and literary achievement, Japanese students visit his various shrines by the hundreds of thousands in February and March to pray for success on their college entrance exams.

Return to the avenue and continue south. On the left side is a flight of stone steps to **Kannon Hall** 9, one of the important temple structures that survived the Meiji-Tokugawa battle of 1868.

Leave the temple by the front gate, on the south side. As you look to your left, you will see a two-story brick administration building, on the other side of which is the **Ueno Royal Museum** 10. After a stop in the museum, continue south, and you soon come to where the park narrows to a point. Two flights of steps lead down to the main entrance on Chūō-dōri. Before you reach the steps, you can see the **Shōgitai Memorial** 11, on the left, and a few steps away, with its back to the gravestone, the **statue of Takamori Saigō** 12.

Leave the park and walk south, keeping to the west side of Chūō-dōri, until you get to the corner where Shinobazu-dōri comes in on the right. About a block beyond this corner, you see a building hung with banners; this is **Suzumoto** 13, a theater specializing in a traditional narrative comedy called *rakugo*.

Turn right at the Shinobazu-dōri intersection and walk west until you come to an entrance to the grounds of Shinobazu Pond; just inside, on the right, is the small black-and-white building that houses the **Shitamachi Museum** 14, which celebrates the working-class folk of the Edo period.

From in front of the museum, a path follows the eastern shore of Shinobazu Pond. On the island in the middle of the pond is **Benzaiten** 15, a shrine to the patron goddess of the arts. You can walk up the east side of the embankment to the causeway and cross to the shrine. Then cross to the other side of the pond, turn left in front of the boathouse, and follow the embankment back to Shinobazu-dōri. Off to your right as you walk, a few blocks away and out of sight, begin the precincts of Tōkyō University, the nation's most prestigious seat of higher learning, alma mater to generations of bureaucrats. Turn left as you leave the park and walk back in the direction of the Shitamachi Museum.

When you reach the intersection, cross Chūō-dōri and turn right; walk past the ABAB clothing store and turn left at the second corner. At the end of this street is **Tokudai-ji** 16, a temple over a supermarket, and the bustling heart of **Ame-ya Yoko-chō Market** 17. There are more than 500 little shops and stalls in this market, which stretches from the beginning of Shōwa-dōri at the north end to Okachi-machi at the south end. Okachi-machi means "Okachi Town"; the *okachi*—the "honorable infantry," the samurai of lowest rank in the shōgun's service—lived in the area.

From here follow the JR tracks as you wander north. In a few minutes you'll find yourself back in front of Ueno Station.

TIMING   Exploring Ueno can be one excursion or two: an afternoon of cultural browsing or a full day of discoveries in one of the great centers of the city. Avoid Monday, when most of the museums are closed. Ueno out of doors is no fun at all in February or the rainy season (late June–mid-July); mid-August can be brutally hot and muggy. In April, the cherry blossoms of Ueno Kōen are glorious.

What to See

⑰ **Ame-ya Yoko-chō Market** (アメヤ横丁). The history of Ame-ya Yoko-chō (often shortened to Ameyoko) begins in the desperate days immediately after World War II. Ueno Station had survived the bombings—virtually everything around it was rubble—and anyone who could make it here from the countryside with rice and other small supplies of food could sell them at exorbitant black-market prices. Sugar was a commodity that couldn't be found at any price in postwar Tōkyō. Before long, there were hundreds of stalls in the black market selling various kinds of *ame* (confections), most of them made from sweet potatoes. These stalls gave the market its name: Ame-ya Yoko-chō means "Confectioners' Alley."

Shortly before the Korean War, the market was legalized, and soon the stalls were carrying watches, chocolate, ballpoint pens, blue jeans, and T-shirts that had somehow been "liberated" from American PXs. In years to come the merchants of Ameyoko diversified still further—to fine Swiss timepieces and French designer luggage of dubious authenticity, cosmetics, jewelry, fresh fruit, and fish. The market became especially famous for the traditional prepared foods of the New Year, and during the last few days of December, as many as half a million people crowd into the narrow alleys under the railroad tracks to stock up for the holiday. ⊠ *Ueno 4-chōme, Taitō-ku* ⊘ *Most shops and stalls daily 10–7* Ⓜ *JR Ueno Station (Hirokō-ji Exit).*

⑮ **Benzaiten** (弁財天). Perched in the middle of Shinobazu Pond, this shrine is dedicated to the goddess Benten, one of the Seven Gods of Good Luck, a pantheon that emerged some time in the medieval period from a jumble of Indian, Chinese, and Japanese mythology. As matron goddess of the arts, she is depicted holding a lutelike musical instrument called a *biwa*. The shrine, which was built by Abbot Tenkai, who also built Kan-ei-ji, was destroyed in the bombings of 1945; the present version, with its distinctive octagonal roof, is a faithful copy. You can rent rowboats and pedal boats at a nearby boathouse. ⊠ *Taitō-ku* ☎ *03/3828–9502 for boathouse* 🎫 *Rowboats ¥600 for 1 hr, pedal boats ¥600 for 30 min, swan boats ¥700 for 30 min* ⊘ *Boathouse daily 10–5:30* Ⓜ *JR Ueno Station (Kōen-guchi/Park Exit); Keisei private rail line, Keisei-Ueno Station (Ikenohata Exit).*

❹ **Kan-ei-ji** (Kanei Temple, 寛永寺). In 1638 the second Tokugawa shōgun, Hidetada, commissioned the priest Tenkai to build a temple on the hill known as Shinobu-ga-oka in Ueno to defend his city from evil spirits.

Tenkai turned for his model to the great temple complex of Enryaku-ji in Kyōto, established centuries earlier on Mt. Hiei to protect the imperial capital. The main hall of Tenkai's temple, called Kan-ei-ji, was moved to Ueno from the town of Kawagoe, about 40 km (25 mi) away, where he had once been a priest; it was moved again, to its present site, in 1879, and looks a bit weary of its travels. The only remarkable remaining structure here is the ornately carved vermilion gate to what was the mausoleum of Tsunayoshi, the fifth shōgun. Tsunayoshi is famous in the annals of Tokugawa history for his disastrous fiscal mismanagement and his *Shōrui Awaremi no Rei* (Edicts on Compassion for Living Things), which, among other things, made it a capital offense for a human being to kill a dog. ⊠ *1–14–11 Ueno Sakuragi, Taitō-ku* ☎ *03/ 3821–1259* ✉ *Free, contributions welcome* ⊙ *Daily 9–5* Ⓜ *JR Ueno Station (Kōen-guchi/Park Exit), JR Uguisudani Station.*

❾ Kannon Hall (Kiyomizu Kannon-dō, 清水観音堂). This National Treasure was a part of Abbot Tenkai's grand attempt to echo in Ueno the grandeur of Kyōto, but the echo is a little weak. The model for it was Kyōto's magnificent Kiyomizu-dera, but where the original rests on enormous wood pillars over a gorge, the Ueno version merely perches on the lip of a little hill. And the hall would have a grand view of Shinobazu Pond— which itself was landscaped to recall Biwa-ko (Lake Biwa), near Kyōto— if the trees in front of the terrace were not too high and too full most of the year to afford any view at all. The principal Buddhist image of worship here is the Senjū Kannon (Thousand-Armed Goddess of Mercy). Another figure, however, receives greater homage. This is the Kosodate Kannon, who is believed to answer the prayers of women having difficulty conceiving children. If their prayers are answered, they return to Kiyomizu and leave a doll, as both an offering of thanks and a prayer for the child's health. In a ceremony held every September 25, the dolls that have accumulated during the year are burned in a bonfire. ⊠ *1–29 Ueno Kōen, Taitō-ku* ☎ *03/3821–4749* ✉ *Free* ⊙ *Daily 7–5* Ⓜ *JR Ueno Station (Kōen-guchi/Park Exit).*

★ ⌐ ❶ National Museum of Western Art (Kokuritsu Seiyō Bijutsukan, 国立西洋美術館). Along with castings from the original molds of Rodin's *Gate of Hell, The Burghers of Calais,* and *The Thinker,* the wealthy businessman Matsukata Kojiro (1865–1950) acquired some 850 paintings, sketches, and prints by such masters as Renoir, Monet, Gauguin, Van Gogh, Delacroix, and Cézanne. Matsukata kept the collection in Europe, but he left it to Japan in his will. The French government sent the artwork to Japan after World War II, and the collection opened to the public in 1959 in a building designed by Swiss-born architect Le Corbusier. Since then, the museum has diversified a bit; more recent acquisitions include works by Reubens, Tintoretto, El Greco, Max Ernst, and Jackson Pollock. The Seiyō is one of the best-organized, most pleasant museums to visit in Tōkyō. ⊠ *7-7 Ueno Kōen, Taitō-ku* ☎ *03/3828–5131* ⊕ *www.nmwa.go.jp* ✉ *¥420; additional fee for special exhibits* ⊙ *Tues.–Thurs. and weekends 9:30–4:30, Fri. 9:30–7:30* Ⓜ *JR Ueno Station (Kōen-guchi/Park Exit).*

🐦 **②** **National Science Museum** (Kokuritsu Kagaku Hakubutsukan, 国立科学博物館). The six buildings of this museum complex house everything from fossils to moon rocks. And what self-respecting institution of its kind would be without a dinosaur collection? Look for them in the B2F Exhibition Hall, in the newest annex. Although the museum occasionally outdoes itself with special exhibits, it's pretty conventional, and provides relatively little in the way of hands-on learning experiences. Kids seem to like it anyway—but this is not a place to linger if your time is short. ⊠ 7–20 Ueno Kōen, Taitō-ku ☎ 03/3822–0111 ⊕ www.kahaku.go.jp/english ☜ ¥420; additional fees for special exhibits ⊙ Tues.–Thurs. 9–5, Fri. 9–8, weekends 9–6 Ⓜ JR Ueno Station (Kōen-guchi/Park Exit).

⑦ **Shinobazu Pond** (不忍池). Shinobazu was once an inlet of Tōkyō Bay. When the area was reclaimed, it became a freshwater pond. Abbot Tenkai, founder of Kan-ei-ji on the hill above the pond, had an island made in the middle of it, on which he built ⇨ **Benzaiten** for the goddess of the arts. Later improvements included a causeway to the island, embankments, and even a racecourse (1884–93). Today the pond is in three sections. The first, with its famous lotus plants, is a sanctuary for about 15 species of birds, including pintail ducks, cormorants, great egrets, and grebes. Some 5,000 wild ducks migrate here from as far away as Siberia, sticking around from September to April. The second section, to the north, belongs to Ueno Zoo; the third, to the west, is a small lake for boating.

During the first week of June, a path here is lined on both sides with the stalls of the annual All-Japan Azalea Fair, a spectacular display of flowering bonsai shrubs and trees. Gardeners in *happi* (work coats) sell plants, seedlings, bonsai vessels, and ornamental stones. ⊠ *Shinobazu-dōri, Taitō-ku* ☜ *Free* ⊙ *Daily sunrise–sunset* Ⓜ *JR Ueno Station (Kōen-guchi/Park Exit); Keisei private rail line, Keisei-Ueno Station (Higashi-guchi/East Exit).*

★ **⑭** **Shitamachi Museum** (Shitamachi Hakubutsukan, 下町博物館). Japanese society in the days of the Tokugawa shōguns was rigidly stratified. Some 80% of the city was allotted to the warrior class and to temples and shrines. The remaining 20% of the space—between Ieyasu's fortifications on the west, and the Sumida-gawa on the east—was known as Shitamachi, literally, "downtown" or the "lower town" (as it expanded, Shitamachi came to include what today constitutes the Chūō, Taitō, Sumida, and Kōtō wards). It was here that the common folk, who made up more than half the population, lived. Most of them inhabited long, single-story tenements called *nagaya,* one jammed up against the next along the narrow alleys and unplanned streets of Ueno and the areas nearby. They developed a unique culture and way of life. The people here were hardworking, short-tempered, free-spending, quick to help a neighbor in trouble, and remarkably stubborn about their way of life. The Shitamachi Museum preserves and exhibits what remained of that way of life as late as 1940.

The two main displays on the first floor are a merchant house and a tenement, intact with all their furnishings. This is a hands-on museum:

you can take your shoes off and step up into the rooms. On the second floor are displays of toys, tools, and utensils donated, in most cases, by people who had grown up with them and used them all their lives. There are also photographs of Shitamachi and video documentaries of crafts-people at work. Occasionally various traditional skills are demon-strated, and you're welcome to take part. This don't-miss museum makes great use of its space, and there are even volunteer guides (avail-able starting at 10) who speak passable English. ⊠ *2–1 Ueno Kōen, Taitō-ku* ☎ *03/3823–7451* ✉ *¥300* ⊗ *Tues.–Sun. 9:30–4:30* Ⓜ *JR Ueno Station (Kōen-guchi/Park Exit); Keisei private rail line, Keisei-Ueno Station (Higashi-guchi/East Exit).*

⓫ **Shōgitai Memorial** (彰義隊の墓). Time seems to heal wounds very quickly in Japan. Only six years after the Shōgitai had destroyed most of Ueno Hill in 1868, the Meiji government permitted these Tokugawa loyalists to be honored with a gravestone, erected on the spot where their bod-ies had been cremated. ⊠ *Taitō-ku* Ⓜ *JR Ueno Station (Kōen-guchi/Park Exit); Keisei private rail line, Keisei-Ueno Station (Higashi-guchi/East Exit).*

⓬ **Statue of Takamori Saigō** (西郷隆盛像). As chief of staff of the Meiji im-perial army, Takamori Saigō (1827–77) played a key role in forcing the surrender of Edo and the overthrow of the shogunate. Ironically, Saigō himself fell out with the other leaders of the new Meiji government and was killed in an unsuccessful rebellion of his own. The sculptor Taka-mura Kōun's bronze, made in 1893, sensibly avoids presenting Saigō in uniform. ⊠ *Taitō-ku* Ⓜ *JR Ueno Station (Kōen-guchi/Park Exit); Kei-sei private rail line, Keisei-Ueno Station (Higashi-guchi/East Exit).*

⓭ **Suzumoto** (鈴本演芸場). Originally built around 1857 for Japanese comic monologue performances called rakugo and since rebuilt, Suzumoto is the oldest theater operation of its kind in Tōkyō. A rakugo comedian sits on a purple cushion, dressed in a kimono, and tells stories that have been handed down for centuries. Using only a few simple props—a fan, a pipe, a handkerchief—the storyteller becomes a whole cast of char-acters, with all their different voices and facial expressions. There's no English interpretation, and even for the Japanese themselves, the mono-logues are difficult to follow, filled with puns and expressions in dialect—but don't let that deter you. For a slice of traditional pop culture, rakugo at Suzumoto is worth seeing, even if you don't understand a word. The theater is on Chūō-dōri, a few blocks north of the Ginza Line's Ueno Hirokō-ji stop. ⊠ *2–7–12 Ueno, Taitō-ku* ☎ *03/3834–5906* ✉ *¥2,000* ⊗ *Continual performances daily 12:20–4:30 and 5:20–9:10* Ⓜ *Ginza subway line, Ueno Hirokō-ji Station (Exit 3).*

⓰ **Tokudai-ji** (Tokudai Temple, 徳大寺). This is a curiosity in a neighbor-hood of curiosities: a temple on the second floor of a supermarket. Two deities are worshipped here. One is the bodhisattva Jizō, and the act of washing this statue is believed to help safeguard your health. The other, principal image is of the Indian goddess Marici, a daughter of Brahma, usually depicted with three faces and four arms. She is believed to help worshippers overcome various sorts of difficulties and to help them pros-per in business. ⊠ *4–6–2 Ueno, Taitō-ku* Ⓜ *JR Yamanote and Keihin-*

tōhoku lines, Okachi-machi Station (Higashi-guchi/East Exit) or Ueno Station (Hirokō-ji Exit).

⑤ Tōkyō Metropolitan Art Museum (Tōkyō-to Bijutsukan, 東京都美術館). The museum displays its own collection of modern Japanese art on the lower level and rents out the remaining two floors to various art institutes and organizations. At any given time, there can be at least five exhibits in the building: work by promising young painters, for example, or new forms and materials in sculpture or modern calligraphy. Completed in 1975, the museum was designed by Maekawa Kunio, who also did the nearby Metropolitan Festival Hall. ⊠ *8–36 Ueno Kōen, Taitō-ku* ☎ *03/3823–6921* ⊕ *www.tobikan.jp* ☜ *Permanent collection free; fees vary for other exhibits (usually ¥300–¥800)* ⊙ *Daily 9–5; closed 3rd Mon. of month* Ⓜ *JR Ueno Station (Kōen-guchi/Park Exit).*

③ Tōkyō National Museum (Tōkyō Kokuritsu Hakubutsukan, 東京国立博物館).

Fodor'sChoice
★

This complex of four buildings grouped around a courtyard is one of the world's great repositories of East Asian art and archaeology. Altogether, the museum has some 87,000 objects in its permanent collection, with several thousand more on loan from shrines, temples, and private owners.

The Western-style building on the left (if you're standing at the main gate), with its bronze cupolas, is the **Hyōkeikan.** Built in 1909, it was devoted to archaeological exhibits; aside from the occasional special exhibition, the building is closed today. The larger **Heiseikan,** behind the Hyōkeikan, now houses the archaeological exhibits. Look for the flame-like sculpted rims and elaborate markings of Middle Jōmon–period pottery (circa 3500 BC–2000 BC)—so different from anything produced in Japan before or since. Also look for the terra-cotta figures called *haniwa,* unearthed at burial sites dating from the 4th to the 7th century. The figures are deceptively simple in shape, and mysterious and comical at the same time in effect.

In the far left corner of the museum complex is the **Hōryū-ji Hōmotsukan** (Gallery of Hōryū-ji Treasures). In 1878 the 7th-century Hōryū-ji in Nara presented 319 works of art in its possession—sculpture, scrolls, masks, and other objects—to the Imperial Household. These were transferred to the National Museum in 2000 and now reside in this gallery designed by Yoshio Taniguchi. There's a useful guide to the collection in English, and the exhibits are well explained. Don't miss the hall of carved wooden *gigaku* (Buddhist processional) masks.

The central building in the complex, the 1937 **Honkan,** houses Japanese art exclusively: paintings, calligraphy, sculpture, textiles, ceramics, swords, and armor. Also here are 84 objects designated by the government as National Treasures. The Honkan rotates the works on display several times during the year. It also hosts two special exhibitions a year (April and May or June, and October and November), which feature important collections from both Japanese and foreign museums. These, unfortunately, can be an ordeal: the lighting in the Honkan is not particularly good, the explanations in English are sketchy at best, and the hordes of visitors make it impossible to linger over a work you especially want to study. The more attractive **Tōyōkan,** to the right of the Honkan, completed in 1968, is devoted to the art of other Asian cultures. ✉ *13–9 Ueno Kōen, Taitō-ku* ☎ *03/3822–1111* ⊕ *www.tnm.go.jp/en* 🎟 *¥420* ☽ *Tues.–Sat. 9:30–5, Sun. 9:30–6* Ⓜ *JR Ueno Station (Kōen-guchi/Park Exit).*

★ ❽ **Tōshō-gū** (Tōshō Shrine, 東照宮). Ieyasu, the first Tokugawa shōgun, died in 1616 and the following year was given the posthumous name Tōshō-Daigongen (The Great Incarnation Who Illuminates the East). The Imperial Court declared him a divinity of the first rank, thenceforth to be worshipped at Nikkō, in the mountains north of his city, at a shrine he had commissioned before his death. That shrine is the first and foremost Tōshō-gū. The one here, built in the ornate style called *gongenzukuri,* dates to 1627. Miraculously, it survived the disasters that destroyed most of the other original buildings on the hill—the fires, the 1868 revolt, the 1923 earthquake, the 1945 bombings—making it one of the few early-Edo-period buildings in Tōkyō. The shrine and most of its art are designated National Treasures.

Two hundred *ishidōrō* (stone lanterns) line the path from the stone entry arch to the shrine itself. One of them, just outside the arch to the left, is more than 18 feet high—one of the three largest in Japan. This particular lantern is called *obaketōrō* (ghost lantern) because of a story connected to it: it seems that one night a samurai on guard duty slashed at the ghost (*obake*) that was believed to haunt the lantern. His sword was so good it left a nick in the stone, which can still be seen. Beyond these lanterns is a double row of 50 copper lanterns, presented by the feudal lords of the 17th century as expressions of their piety and loyalty to the regime.

The first room inside the shrine is the **Hall of Worship;** the four paintings in gold on wooden panels are by Tan'yū, one of the famous Kano family of artists who enjoyed the patronage of emperors and shōguns from the late 15th century to the end of the Edo period. Tan'yū was appointed *goyō eshi* (official court painter) in 1617. His commissions included the Tokugawa castles at Edo and Nagoya as well as the Nikkō Tōshō-gū. The framed tablet between the walls, with the name of the shrine in gold, is in the calligraphy of Emperor Go-Mizuno-o (1596–1680). Other works of calligraphy are by the abbots of Kan-ei-ji. Behind the Hall of Worship, connected by a passage called the *haiden,* is the sanctuary, where the spirit of Ieyasu is said to be enshrined.

The real glories of Tōshō-gū are its so-called **Chinese Gate,** which you reach at the end of your tour of the building, and the fence on either side. Like its counterpart at Nikkō, the fence is a kind of natural history lesson, with carvings of birds, animals, fish, and shells of every description; unlike the one at Nikkō, this fence was left unpainted. The two long panels of the gate, with their dragons carved in relief, are attributed to Hidari Jingoro—a brilliant sculptor of the early Edo period whose real name is unknown (*hidari* means "left"; Jingoro was reportedly left-handed). The lifelike appearance of his dragons has inspired a legend. Every morning they were found mysteriously dripping with water. Finally it was discovered that they were sneaking out at night to drink from the nearby Shinobazu Pond, and wire cages were put up around them to curtail this disquieting habit. ✉ *9–88 Ueno Kōen, Taitō-ku* ☎ *03/3822–3455* 🎟 *¥200* ☽ *Daily 9–5* Ⓜ *JR Ueno Station (Kōen-guchi/Park Exit).*

❿ **Ueno Royal Museum** (Ueno-no-Mori Bijutsukan, 上野の森美術館). Although the museum has no permanent collection of its own, it makes its galleries available to various groups, primarily for exhibitions of modern painting and calligraphy. ✉ *1–2 Ueno Kōen, Taitō-ku* ☎ *03/3833–4191* 💰 *Prices vary depending on exhibition, but usually ¥400–¥800* 🕐 *Sun.–Wed. 10–5, Thurs.–Sat. 10–7:30* Ⓜ *JR Ueno Station (Kōen-guchi/Park Exit).*

🖐 ❻ **Ueno Zoo** (上野動物園). The zoo houses some 900 different species, most of which look less than enthusiastic about being here. First built in 1882 and several times expanded without really being modernized, Ueno is not among the most attractive zoos in the world. But it does have a giant panda (quartered near the main entrance), and you might decide the zoo is worth a visit on that score alone. On a pleasant Sunday afternoon, however, upward of 20,000 Japanese are likely to share your opinion; don't expect to have a leisurely view. The process of the zoo's expansion somehow left within its confines the 120-foot, five-story Kan-ei-ji Pagoda, built in 1631 and rebuilt after a fire in 1639. ✉ *9–83 Ueno Kōen, Taitō-ku* ☎ *03/3828–5171* 💰 *¥600; free on Mar. 20, Apr. 29, and Oct. 1* 🕐 *Tues.–Sun. 9:30–4* Ⓜ *JR Ueno Station (Kōen-guchi/Park Exit); Keisei private rail line, Ueno Station (Dōbutsu-en Exit).*

ASAKUSA 浅草

In the year 628, so the legend goes, two brothers named Hamanari and Takenari Hikonuma were fishing on the lower reaches of the Sumida-gawa when they dragged up a small, gilded statue of Kannon—an aspect of the Buddha worshipped as the goddess of mercy. They took the statue to their master, Naji-no-Nakamoto, who enshrined it in his house. Later, a temple was built for it in nearby Asakusa. Called Sensō-ji, the temple was rebuilt and enlarged several times over the next 10 centuries—but Asakusa itself remained just a village on a river crossing a few hours' walk from Edo.

Then Ieyasu Tokugawa made Edo his capital and Asakusa blossomed. Suddenly, it was the party that never ended, the place where the free-spending townspeople of the new capital came to empty their pockets. For the next 300 years it was the wellspring of almost everything we associate with Japanese popular culture.

The first step in that transformation came in 1657, when Yoshiwara—the licensed brothel quarter not far from Nihombashi—was moved to the countryside farther north: Asakusa found itself square in the road, more or less halfway between the city and its only nightlife. The village became a suburb and a pleasure quarter in its own right. In the narrow streets and alleys around Sensō-ji, there were stalls selling toys, souvenirs, and sweets; acrobats, jugglers, and strolling musicians; and sake shops and teahouses—where the waitresses often provided more than tea. (The Japanese have never worried much about the impropriety of such things; the approach to a temple is still a venue for very secular enterprises of all sorts.) Then, in 1841, the Kabuki theaters—which the government looked upon as a source of dissipation second only to Yoshiwara—moved to Asakusa.

THE EVOLUTION OF TŌKYŌ

IFE WAS SIMPLER here in the 12th century, when Tōkyō was a little fishing village called Edo (pronounced eh-doh), near the mouth of the Sumida-gawa (Sumida River) on the Kantō Plain. The Kantō was a strategic granary, large and fertile; over the next 400 years it was governed by a succession of warlords and other rulers. One of them, Dōkan Ōta, built the first castle in Edo in 1457. That act is still officially regarded as the founding of the city, but the honor really belongs to Ieyasu (ee-eh-ya-su), the first Tokugawa shōgun, who arrived in 1590. A key figure in the civil wars of the 16th century, he had been awarded the eight provinces of Kantō in eastern Japan in exchange for three provinces closer to Kyōto, the imperial capital. Ieyasu was a farsighted soldier; the swap was fine with him. On the site of Ōta's stronghold, he built a mighty fortress of his own—from which, 10 years later, he was effectively ruling the whole country.

By 1680 there were more than a million people here, and a great city had grown up out of the reeds in the marshy lowlands of Edo Bay. Tōkyō can only really be understood as a jō-ka-machi—a castle town. Ieyasu had fought his way to the shogunate, and he had a warrior's concern for the geography of his capital. Edo Castle had the high ground, but that wasn't enough; all around it, at strategic points, he gave large estates to allies and trusted retainers. These lesser lords' villas also served as garrisons, outposts on a perimeter of defense.

Farther out, Ieyasu kept the barons he trusted least of all—whom he controlled by bleeding their treasuries. He required them to keep large, expensive establishments in Edo; to contribute generously to the temples he endowed; to come and go in alternate years in great pomp and ceremony; and, when they returned to their estates, to leave their families—in effect, hostages—behind.

All this, the Edo of feudal estates, of villas and gardens and temples, lay south and west of Edo Castle. It was called Yamanote—the Bluff, the uptown. Here, all was order, discipline, and ceremony; every man had his rank and duties (very few women were within the garrisons). Those duties were less military than bureaucratic. Ieyasu's precautions worked like a charm, and the Tokugawa dynasty enjoyed some 250 years of unbroken peace, during which nothing very interesting ever happened uptown.

But Yamanote was only the demand side of the economy: somebody had to bring in the fish, weed the gardens, weave the mats, and entertain the bureaucrats. To serve the noble houses, common people flowed into Edo from all over Japan. Their allotted quarters of the city were jumbles of narrow streets, alleys, and cul-de-sacs in the low-lying estuarine lands to the north and east. Often enough, the land assigned to them wasn't even there; they had to make it by draining and filling the marshes (the first reclamation project in Edo dates to 1457). The result was Shitamachi—literally "downtown"—the part below the castle, which sat on a hill. Bustling, brawling Shitamachi was the supply side: it had the lumberyards, markets, and workshops; the wood-block printers, kimono makers, and moneylenders. The people here gossiped over the back fence in the earthy, colorful Edo dialect. They went to Yoshiwara—a walled and moated area on the outskirts of Edo where prostitution was under official control (Yoshiwara was for a time the biggest licensed brothel area in the world). They supported the bathhouses and Kabuki theaters and reveled in their spectacular summer fireworks festivals. The city and spirit of the Edokko—the people of Shitamachi—have survived, while the great estates uptown are now mostly parks and hotels.

The shogunate was overthrown in 1867 by supporters of Emperor Meiji. The following year, the emperor moved his court from Kyōto to Edo and renamed it Tōkyō: the Eastern Capital. By now the city was home to nearly 2 million people, and the geography was vastly more complex. As it grew, it became not one but many smaller cities, with different centers of commerce, government, entertainment, and transportation. In Yamanote rose the commercial emporia, office buildings, and public halls that made up the architecture of an emerging modern state. The workshops of Shitamachi multiplied, some of them becoming small jobbers and family-run factories. Still, there was no planning, no grid. The neighborhoods and subcenters were worlds unto themselves, and a traveler from one was soon hopelessly lost in another.

The firebombings of 1945 left Tōkyō, for the most part, in rubble and ashes. That utter destruction could have been an opportunity to rebuild on the rational order of cities like Kyōto, Barcelona, or Washington. No such plan was ever made. Tōkyō reverted to type: it became once again an aggregation of small towns and villages. One village was much like any other; the nucleus was always the shōten-gai, the shopping arcade. Each arcade had at least one fishmonger, grocer, rice dealer, mat maker, barber, florist, and bookseller. You could live your whole life in the neighborhood of the shōten-gai. It was sufficient to your needs.

People seldom moved out of these villages. The vast waves of new residents who arrived after World War II—about three-quarters of the people in the Tōkyō metropolitan area today were born elsewhere—just created more villages. People who lived in the villages knew their way around, so there was no particular need to name the streets. Houses were numbered not in sequence but in the order in which they were built. No. 3 might well share a mailbox with No. 12. People still take their local geography for granted—the closer you get to the place you're looking for, the harder it is to get coherent directions. Away from main streets and landmarks, even a taxi driver can get hopelessly lost.

Fortunately, there are the kōban: small police boxes, or substations, usually with two or three officers assigned to each of them full time, to look after the affairs of the neighborhood. You can't go far in any direction without finding a kōban. The officer on duty knows where everything is and is glad to point the way. (The substation system, incidentally, is one important reason for the legendary safety of Tōkyō: on foot or on white bicycles, the police are a visible presence, covering the beat. Burglaries are not unknown, of course, but street crime is very rare.)

Tōkyō is still really two areas, Shitamachi and Yamanote. The heart of Shitamachi, proud and stubborn in its Edo ways, is Asakusa; the dividing line is Ginza, west of which lie the boutiques and department stores, the banks and engines of government, the pleasure domes and cafés. Today there are 13 subway lines in full operation that weave the two areas together.

Highborn and lowborn, the people of Edo flocked to Kabuki. They loved its extravagant spectacle, its bravado, and its brilliant language. They cheered its heroes and hissed its villains. They bought wood-block prints, called *ukiyo-e,* of their favorite actors. Asakusa was home to the Kabuki theaters for only a short time, but that was enough to establish it as *the* entertainment quarter of the city—a reputation it held unchallenged until World War II.

When Japan ended its long, self-imposed isolation in 1868, where else would the novelties and amusements of the outside world first take root but in Asakusa? The country's first photography studios appeared here in 1875. Japan's first skyscraper, a 12-story mart called the Jū-ni-kai, was built in Asakusa in 1890 and filled with shops selling imported goods. The area around Sensō-ji had by this time been designated a public park and was divided into seven sections; the sixth section, called Rok-ku, was Tōkyō's equivalent of 42nd Street and Times Square. The nation's first movie theater opened here in 1903—to be joined by dozens more, and these in turn were followed by music halls, cabarets, and revues. The first drinking establishment in Japan to call itself a "bar" was started in Asakusa in 1880; it still exists.

Most of this area was destroyed in 1945. As an entertainment district, it never really recovered, but Sensō-ji was rebuilt almost immediately. The people here would never dream of living without it—just as they would never dream of living anywhere else. This is the heart and soul of Shitamachi, where you can still hear the rich, breezy downtown Tōkyō accent of the 17th and 18th centuries. Where, if you sneeze in the middle of the night, your neighbor will demand to know the next morning why you aren't taking better care of yourself. Where a carpenter will refuse a well-paid job if he doesn't think the clients have the mother wit to appreciate good work when they see it. Where you can still go out for a good meal and not have to pay through the nose for a lot of uptown pretensions. Even today the temple precinct embraces an area of narrow streets, arcades, restaurants, shops, stalls, playgrounds, and gardens. It's home to a population of artisans and small entrepreneurs, neighborhood children and their grandmothers, and hipsters and hucksters and mendicant priests. In short, if you have any time at all to spend in Tōkyō, you really should devote at least a day of it to Asakusa.

Numbers in the text correspond to numbers in the margin and on the Asakusa map.

A Good Walk

For more information on individual shops mentioned in this walk, *see* Chapter 6.

Start at Asakusa Station, at the end of the Ginza Line. Opened in 1927, this was Tōkyō's first subway, running from Asakusa to Ueno; it later became known as the Ginza Line when it was extended through Ginza to Shimbashi and Shibuya. Follow the signs, clearly marked in English, to Exit 1. When you come up to the street level, turn right and walk west along Kaminari-mon-dōri. In a few steps you come to a gate on

The Sensō-ji Complex ▼

Asakusa Jinja (Asakusa Shrine) **3**

Belfry (Toki-no-kane Shōrō) **4**

Dembō-in (Dembo Temple) **5**

Kaminari-mon (Thunder God Gate) **1**

Sensō-ji Main Hall **2**

Elsewhere in Asakusa ▼

Kappa-bashi **6**

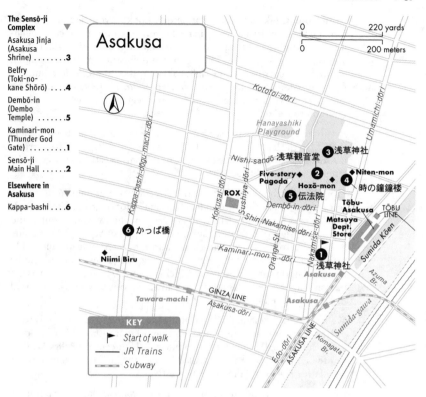

your right with two huge red lanterns hanging from it: this is **Kaminari-mon ❶** ▶, the main entrance to the grounds of Sensō-ji.

Another way to get to Kaminari-mon is via the "river bus" ferry from Hinode Pier, which stops in Asakusa at the southwest corner of the park called Sumida Kōen. Walk out to the three-way intersection, cross two sides of the triangle, and turn right. Kaminari-mon is in the middle of the second block.

Take note of the Asakusa Tourist Information Center (Asakusa Bunka Kankō Center), across the street from Kaminari-mon. A volunteer staff with some English is on duty here daily 10–5 and will happily load you down with maps and brochures.

From Kaminari-mon, Nakamise-dōri—a long, narrow avenue lined on both sides with small shops—leads to the courtyard of Sensō-ji. One shop worth stopping at is Ichiban-ya, about 100 yards down on the right, for its handmade, toasted *sembei* (rice crackers) and its seven-pepper spices in gourd-shape bottles of zelkova wood. At the end of Nakamise-dōri, on the right, is Sukeroku, which specializes in traditional hand-made dolls and models clothed in the costumes of the Edo period. Just beyond Sukeroku is a two-story gate called Hōzō-mon.

At this point, take an important detour. Look to your left as you pass through the gate. Tucked away in the far corner is a vermilion-color building in the traditional temple style (just to the left of the pagoda, behind an iron railing) that houses the Sensō-ji administrative offices: walk in, go down the corridor on the right to the third door on the left, and ask for permission to see the Garden of Dembō-in. There's no charge. You simply enter your name and address in a register and receive a ticket. Hold on to the ticket: you'll need it later.

Return to Hōzō-mon and walk across the courtyard to the **Sensō-ji Main Hall ❷**. To the left of the Main Hall is the Five-Story Pagoda. To the right is **Asakusa Jinja ❸**; near the entrance to this shrine is the east gate to the temple grounds, Niten-mon.

From Niten-mon, walk back in the direction of Kaminari-mon to the southeast corner of the grounds. On a small plot of ground here stands the shrine to Kume-no-Heinai, a 17th-century outlaw who repented and became a priest of one of the subsidiary temples of Sensō-ji. Late in life he carved a stone statue of himself and buried it where many people would walk over it. In his will, he expressed the hope that his image would be trampled upon forever. Somehow, Heinai came to be worshipped as the patron god of lovers—as mystifying an apotheosis as you will ever find in Japanese religion.

Walk south from Heinai's shrine along the narrow street that runs back to Kaminari-mon-dōri, parallel to Nakamise-dōri. On the left you pass a tiny hillock called Benten-yama and the 17th-century **Belfry ❹**. Opposite Benten-yama is a shop called Naka-ya, which sells all manner of regalia for Sensō-ji's annual Sanja Festival.

Next door is Kuremutsu, a tiny century-old *nomiya* (Japanese pub); it's open only in the evening, but is worth admiring any time of day as a remnant of the Meiji era. Just up the street from Kuremutsu is Hyaku-suke (百助), an unusual shop selling traditional Japanese cosmetics. Three doors up, on the same side of the street, is Fuji-ya (ふじや), a shop that deals exclusively in *tenugui*: cotton hand towels, hand-printed from original stencil designs.

Turn right at the corner past Fuji-ya and walk west on Dembō-in-dōri until you cross Nakamise-dōri. On the other side of the intersection, on the left, is Yono-ya, purveyor of pricey handmade boxwood combs for traditional Japanese coiffures and wigs. Some combs are carved with auspicious motifs, like peonies, hollyhocks, or cranes, and all are engraved with the family benchmark.

Now it's time to cash in the ticket you've been carrying around. Walk west another 70 yards or so, and on the right you can see an old dark wooden gate; this is the side entrance to **Dembō-in ❺**, the living quarters of the abbot of Sensō-ji. The only part of the grounds you can visit is the garden: go through the small door in the gate, across the courtyard and through the door on the opposite side, and present your ticket to the caretaker in the house at the end of the alley. The entrance to the garden is down a short flight of stone steps to the left.

Turn right as you leave Dembō-in and continue walking west on Dembō-in-dōri. You pass a small Shintō shrine with numerous little statues of the bodhisattva Jizō; this is a shrine for prayers for the repose of the souls of *mizuko*—literally "water children"—those who were aborted or miscarried.

Farther on, at the corner of Orange-dōri, is the redbrick Asakusa Public Hall; performances of Kabuki and traditional dance are sometimes held here, as well as exhibitions on life in Asakusa before World War II. Across the street is Nakase, one of the best of Asakusa's many fine tempura restaurants.

If you have the time and energy, you might want to explore the warren of streets and covered arcades on the south and west sides of Dembō-in, where you can find kimonos and *yukata* (cotton kimono) fabrics, traditional accessories and festival costumes, and purveyors of crackers, seaweed, and tea. Otherwise, walk south, away from Dembō-in, on any of these arcades to return to Kaminari-mon-dōri; turn right, and walk to the end of the avenue. Cross Kokusai-dōri, turn left, and then right at the next major intersection onto Asakusa-dōri; on the corner is the entrance to Tawara-machi Station on the Ginza subway line. Head west on Asakusa-dōri; at the second traffic light, you can see the Niimi Building across the street, crowned with the guardian god of the Kappa-bashi neighborhood: an enormous plastic chef's head, 30 feet high, beaming, mustached, and crowned, as every chef in Japan is crowned, with a tall white hat. Turn right onto Kappa-bashi-dōgu-machi-dōri to explore the shops of **Kappa-bashi** ⑥, Tōkyō's wholesale-restaurant-supply district.

At the second intersection, on the right, is the main showroom of **Maizuru** (まいづる), virtuosos in the art of counterfeit cuisine—the plastic food models displayed at many Japanese restaurants. A few doors down is **Biken Kōgei** (美研工芸), a good place to look for the folding red-paper lanterns that grace the front of inexpensive bars and restaurants. Across the street from Maizuru is **Nishimura** (西村), a shop specializing in the traditional restaurant entrance curtains called *noren*.

On the next block, on the right (east) side of the street, is **Kondo Shōten** (近藤商店), which sells all sorts of bamboo trays, baskets, scoops, and containers. A block farther, look for **Iida Shōten** (飯田商店), with a good selection of embossed cast-iron kettles and casseroles, called *nambu* ware. On the far corner is Union Company, which sells everything you need to run a coffee shop (or the make-believe one in your own kitchen): roasters, grinders, beans, flasks, and filters of every kind.

There's more of Kappa-bashi to the north, but you can safely ignore it. Continue east, straight past Union Company down the narrow side street. On the next block, on the left, look for **Tsubaya Hōchōten** (つば屋包丁店), which sells cutlery for professionals. Continue on this street east to Kokusai-dōri and then turn right (south). As you walk, you can see several shops selling *butsudan,* Buddhist household altars. The most elaborate of these, hand-carved in ebony and covered with gold leaf, are made in Toyama Prefecture and can cost as much as ¥1 million. No proper Japanese household is without at least a modest butsudan; it's the spiritual center of the family, where reverence for ancestors and continuity of the family traditions are expressed. In a few moments, you'll be back at Tawara-machi Station—the end of the Asakusa walk.

TIMING   Unlike most of the other areas to explore on foot in Tōkyō, Sensō-ji is admirably compact. You can easily see the temple and environs in a morning. The garden at Dembō-in is worth a half hour. If you decide to include Kappa-bashi, allow yourself an hour more for the tour. Some of the shopping arcades in this area are covered, but Asakusa is essentially an outdoor experience. Be prepared for rain in June, heat and humidity in July and August.

What to See

The Sensō-ji Complex   浅草寺

Fodor'sChoice   Dedicated to the goddess Kannon, the Sensō-ji Complex is the heart and
★   soul of Asakusa. Come for its local and historical importance, its garden, its 17th-century Shintō shrine, and the wild Sanja Festival in May. ⊠ *2-3-1 Asakusa, Taitō-ku* ☏ *03/3842–0181* ☎ *Free* ☾ *Temple grounds daily 6–sunset* Ⓜ *Ginza subway line, Asakusa Station (Exit 1/ Kaminari-mon Exit).*

❸ **Asakusa Jinja** (Asakusa Shrine, 浅草神社). Several structures in the temple complex survived the bombings of 1945. The largest, to the right of the Main Hall, is this Shintō shrine to the Hikonuma brothers and their master, Naji-no-Nakamoto—the putative founders of Sensō-ji. In Japan, Buddhism and Shintoism have enjoyed a comfortable coexistence since the former arrived from China in the 6th century. It's the rule, rather than the exception, to find a Shintō shrine on the same grounds as a Buddhist temple. The shrine, built in 1649, is also known as Sanja Sanma (Shrine of the Three Guardians). The **Sanja Festival,** held every year on the third weekend in May, is the biggest, loudest, wildest party in Tōkyō. Each of the neighborhoods under Sanja Sama's protection has its own mikoshi, and on the second day of the festival, these palanquins are paraded through the streets of Asakusa to the shrine, bouncing and swaying on the shoulders of the participants all the way. Many of the "parishioners" take part naked to the waist, or with the sleeves of their tunics rolled up, to expose fantastic red-and-black tattoo patterns that sometimes cover their entire backs and shoulders. These are the tribal markings of the Japanese underworld.

Near the entrance to Asakusa Shrine is another survivor of World War II: the east gate to the temple grounds, **Niten-mon,** built in 1618 for a shrine to Ieyasu Tokugawa (the shrine itself no longer exists) and designated by the government as an Important Cultural Property. ⊠ *Taitō-ku.*

❹ **Belfry** (Toki-no-kane Shōrō, 時の鐘鐘楼). The tiny hillock Benten-yama, with its shrine to the goddess of good fortune, is the site of this 17th-century belfry. The bell here used to toll the hours for the people of the district, and it was said that you could hear it anywhere within a radius of some 6 km (4 mi). The bell still sounds at 6 AM every day, when the temple grounds open. It also rings on New Year's Eve—108 strokes in all, beginning just before midnight, to "ring out" the 108 sins and frailties of humankind and make a clean start for the coming year. Benten-yama and the belfry are at the beginning of the narrow street that parallels Nakamise-dōri. ✉ *Taitō-ku.*

need a break?

Originally a teahouse, **Kuremuttsu** (暮六つ), a tiny pub, has been sitting—precariously—on its site, a stone's throw from the Asakusa Kannon Temple, for more than 100 years. Narrow your field of vision, to shut out the buildings on either side, and you could be back in the waning days of Meiji-period Japan. Open only in the evenings, 4–10 (closed Mon.), Kuremuttsu specializes in premium sake, with set courses of food and drink that range from ¥5,000 to ¥10,000. ✉ *2–2–13 Asakusa, Taitō-ku* ☎ *03/3842–0906.*

★ ❺ **Dembō-in** (Dembo Temple, 伝法院). Believed to have been made in the 17th century by Kōbori Enshū, the genius of Zen landscape design, the garden of Dembō-in, part of the living quarters of the abbot of Sensō-ji, is the best-kept secret in Asakusa. Anyone can see the front entrance to Dembō-in from Nakamise-dōri—behind an iron fence in the last block of shops—but the thousands of Japanese visitors passing by seem to have no idea what it is. (And if they do, it somehow never occurs to them to visit it themselves.) The garden of Dembō-in is usually empty and always utterly serene, an island of privacy in a sea of pilgrims. Spring, when the wisteria blooms, is the ideal time to be here. As you walk along the path that circles the pond, a different vista presents itself at every turn. The only sounds are the cries of birds and the splashing of carp.

A sign in English on Dembō-in-dōri, about 150 yards west of the intersection with Naka-mise-dōri, indicates the entrance, through the side door of a large wooden gate. For permission to see the abbot's garden, you must first apply at the temple administration building, between Hōzō-mon and the Five-Story Pagoda, in the far corner. ✉ *Taitō-ku* ☎ *03/ 3842–0181 for reservations* 🎫 *Free* ��� *Daily 9–4; may be closed if abbot has guests.*

need a break?

The tatami-mat rooms in **Nakase** (中瀬), a fine tempura restaurant, look out on a perfect little interior garden that's hung in May with great fragrant bunches of white wisteria. Carp and goldfish swim in the pond, and you can almost lean out from your room and trail your fingers in the water as you listen to the fountain. Nakase is expensive: lunch (11:30–3) at the tables inside starts at ¥3,000; more elaborate meals by the garden start at ¥7,000. It's across Orange-dōri from the redbrick Asakusa Public Hall. ✉ *1–39–13 Asakusa, Taitō-ku* ☎ *03/ 3841–4015* 🍽 *No credit cards* ☽ *Closed Tues. and 2nd and 4th Mon. of month.*

▶ ❶ **Kaminari-mon** (Thunder God Gate, 雷門). This is the proper Sensō-ji entrance, with its huge red-paper lantern hanging in the center. The original gate was destroyed by fire in 1865; the replica you see today was built after World War II. Traditionally, two fearsome guardian gods are installed in the alcoves of Buddhist temple gates to ward off evil spirits. The Thunder God (Kaminari-no-Kami) of the Sensō-ji main gate is on the left. He shares his duties with the Wind God (Kaze-no-Kami) on the right. Few Japanese visitors neglect to stop at **Tokiwa-dō** (常盤堂), the shop on the west side of the gate, to buy some of Tōkyō's most famous souvenirs: *kaminari okoshi* (thunder crackers), made of rice, millet, sugar, and beans.

Kaminari-mon also marks the southern extent of **Nakamise-dōri** (仲見世通り), the Street of Inside Shops. The area from Kaminari-mon to the inner gate of the temple was once composed of stalls leased to the townspeople who cleaned and swept the temple grounds. The rows of redbrick buildings now technically belong to the municipal government, but the leases are, in effect, hereditary: some of the shops have been in the same families since the Edo period. ⊠ *Taitō-ku.*

❷ **Sensō-ji Main Hall** (浅草観音堂). The Main Hall and Five-Story Pagoda of Sensō-ji are both faithful copies in concrete of originals that burned down in 1945. During a time when most of the people of Asakusa were still rebuilding their own bombed-out lives, it took 13 years to raise money for the restoration of their beloved Sensō-ji. To them—and especially to those involved in the world of entertainment—it's far more than a tourist attraction: Kabuki actors still come here before a new season of performances, and sumō wrestlers visit before a tournament to pay their respects. The large lanterns in the Main Hall were donated by the geisha associations of Asakusa and nearby Yanagi-bashi. Most Japanese stop at the huge bronze incense burner, in front of the Main Hall, to bathe their hands and faces in the smoke—it's a charm to ward off illnesses—before climbing the stairs to offer their prayers.

The Main Hall, about 115 feet long and 108 feet wide, is not an especially impressive piece of architecture. Unlike in many other temples, however, part of the inside has a concrete floor, so you can come and go without removing your shoes. In this area hang Sensō-ji's chief claims to artistic importance: a collection of 18th- and 19th-century votive paintings on wood. Plaques of this kind, called *ema,* are still offered to the gods at shrines and temples, but they are commonly simpler and smaller. The worshipper buys a little tablet of wood with the picture already painted on one side and inscribes a prayer on the other. The temple owns more than 50 of these works, which were removed to safety in 1945 and so escaped the air raids. Only eight of them, depicting scenes from Japanese history and mythology, are on display. A catalog of the collection is on sale in the hall, but the text is in Japanese only.

Lighting is poor in the Main Hall, and the actual works are difficult to see. This is also true of the ceiling, done by two contemporary masters of Nihon-ga (traditional Japanese-style painting); the dragon is by Ryūshi Kawabata, and the motif of angels and lotus blossoms is by Inshō Dōmoto. One thing that visitors cannot see at all is the holy image of Kannon itself, which supposedly lies buried somewhere deep under the temple. Not even the priests of Sensō-ji have ever seen it, and there is in fact no conclusive evidence that it actually exists.

Hōzō-mon (宝蔵門), the gate to the temple courtyard, is also a repository for sutras (Buddhist texts) and other treasures of Sensō-ji. This gate, too, has its guardian gods; should either god decide to leave his post for a stroll, he can use the enormous pair of sandals hanging on the back wall—the gift of a Yamagata Prefecture village famous for its straw weaving. ✉ *Taitō-ku.*

Elsewhere in Asakusa

★ ❻ **Kappa-bashi** (かっぱ橋). In the 19th century, so the story goes, a river (crossed by a bridge) ran through the present-day Kappa-bashi district. The surrounding area was poorly drained and was often flooded. A local shopkeeper began a project to improve the drainage, investing all his own money, but met with little success until a troupe of *kappa*—mischievous green water sprites—emerged from the river to help him. A more prosaic explanation for the name of the district points out that the lower-ranking retainers of the local lord used to earn extra money by making straw raincoats, also called kappa, that they spread to dry on the bridge.

Today, Kappa-bashi's more than 200 wholesale dealers sell everything the city's restaurant and bar trade could possibly need to do business, from paper supplies and steam tables to signs and soup tureens. In their wildest dreams the Japanese themselves would never have cast Kappa-bashi as a tourist attraction, but indeed it is.

For one thing, it is *the* place to buy plastic food. The custom of putting in restaurant windows models of the food served inside is said to date to the early days of the Meiji Restoration, when anatomical models made of wax first came to Japan as teaching aids in the new schools of Western medicine. A businessman from Nara decided that wax models would also make good point-of-purchase advertising for restaurants. He was right: the industry grew in a modest way at first, making models mostly of Japanese food. In the boom years after 1960, restaurants began to serve all sorts of dishes most people had never seen before, and the models provided much-needed reassurance: "So *that's* a cheeseburger. It doesn't look as bad as it sounds. Let's go in and try one." By the mid-1970s, the makers of plastic food were turning out creations of astonishing virtuosity and realism, and foreigners had discovered in them a form of pop art. ✉ *Nishi-Asakusa 1-chōme and 2-chōme, Taitō-ku* ☉ *Most shops daily 9–6* Ⓜ *Ginza subway line, Tawara-machi Station (Exit 1).*

TSUKIJI & SHIODOME 築地・汐留

Although it's best known today as the site of the largest fish market in Asia, Tsukiji is also a reminder of the awesome disaster of the great fire of 1657. In the space of two days, it killed more than 100,000 people and leveled almost 70% of Ieyasu Tokugawa's new capital. Ieyasu was not a man to be discouraged by mere catastrophe, however; he took it as an opportunity to plan an even bigger and better city, one that would incorporate the marshes east of his castle. Tsukiji, in fact, means "reclaimed land," and a substantial block of land it was, laboriously drained and filled, from present-day Ginza to the bay.

The common people of the tenements and alleys, who had suffered most in the great fire, benefited not at all from this project; land was first allotted to feudal lords and to temples. After 1853, when Japan opened

TSUKIJI ACHIEVEMENTS

T WAS IN TSUKIJI, on the estate of their patron, Lord Okudaira, that the scholars Ryōtaku Maeno (1723–1803) and Gempaku Sugita (1733–1817) translated the first work of European science into Japanese: a Dutch book on human anatomy Maeno had acquired in Nagasaki in 1770. At this time Japan was still officially closed to the outside world, and the trickle of scientific knowledge accessible through the Dutch trading post at Nagasaki—the only authorized foreign settlement—was enormously frustrating to the eager scholars who wanted to modernize Japan. Maeno, Sugita, and their colleagues began with barely a few hundred words of Dutch among them and had no reference works or resources on which to base their translation, except the diagrams in the book. It must have been an agonizing task, but the publication in 1774 of Kaitai Shinsho (New Book of Anatomy) had a tremendous influence.

From this time on, Japan would turn away from classical Chinese scholarship and begin to take its lessons in science from the West.

Another achievement associated with Tsukiji was the founding of Keiō University by Yukichi Fukuzawa (1835–1901), the most influential educator and social thinker of the Meiji period. The son of a low-ranking samurai, Fukuzawa was ordered by his lord to start a school of Western learning, which he opened in Tsukiji in 1858. Later the school was moved west to Mita, where the university is today. Fukuzawa's famous statement: HEAVEN CREATED NO MAN ABOVE ANOTHER, NOR BELOW, uttered when the feudal Tokugawa regime was still in power, was an enormously daring thought. It took Japan almost a century to catch up with his liberal and egalitarian vision.

its doors to the outside world, Tsukiji became Tōkyō's first foreign settlement—the site of the American legation and an elegant two-story brick hotel, and home to missionaries, teachers, and doctors.

To the west of Tsukiji lie Shiodome and Shimbashi. In the period after the Meiji Restoration, Shimbashi was one of the most famous geisha districts of the new capital. Its reputation as a pleasure quarter is even older. In the Edo period, when there was a network of canals and waterways here, it was the height of luxury to charter a covered boat (called a *yakata-bune*) from one of the Shimbashi boathouses for a cruise on the river; a local restaurant would cater the excursion, and a local geisha house would provide the companionship. Almost nothing remains in Shimbashi to recall that golden age, but as its luster has faded, adjacent Shiodome has risen—literally—in its place as one of the most ambitious redevelopment projects of 21st-century Tōkyō.

Shiodome (literally "where the tide stops") was an area of saltwater flats on which in 1872 the Meiji government built the Tōkyō terminal—the original Shimbashi Station—on Japan's first railway line, which ran for 29 km (18 mi) to nearby Yokohama. Later a freight yard, the area eventually became Japan Rail's (JR) most notorious white elephant: a staggeringly valuable hunk of real estate, smack in the middle of the world's most expensive city, that JR no longer needed and couldn't seem to sell. By 1997 a bewildering succession of receivers, public development corporations, and zoning commissions had evolved an urban renewal plan for the area, and the land was auctioned off. Among the buyers were Nippon Television and Dentsū, the largest advertising agency in Asia and the fourth largest in the world.

In 2002 Dentsū consolidated its scattered offices into the centerpiece of the Shiodome project: a 47-story tower and annex designed by Jean Nouvel. With the annex, known as the Caretta Shiodome, Dentsu aspired not just to a new corporate address, but an "investment in community," a complex of cultural facilities, shops, and restaurants that has turned Shiodome into one of the most fashionable places in the city to see and be seen. The 1,200-seat Dentsū Shiki Theater SEA here has become one of Tōkyō's major venues for live performances; its resident repertory company regularly brings long-running Broadway hits like *Mamma Mia* to eager Japanese audiences.

Numbers in the text correspond to numbers in the margin and on the Tsukiji & Shiodome map.

A Good Walk

TSUKIJI
築地

Take the Ōedo Line to Tsukiji-shijō Station. Leave the station by Exit A1 onto Shin-Ōhashi-dōri and turn right. After walking about 30 paces, you come to the back gate of the fish market, which extends from here southeast toward the bay. Alternatively, take the Hibiya Line to Tsukiji Station (FISH MARKET signs in English are posted in the station), come up on Shin-Ōhashi-dōri (Exit 1), and turn southeast. Cross Harumi-dōri, walk along the covered sidewalk for about 110 yards to the traffic light, and turn left. Walk to the end of the street (you can see the stone torii of a small shrine) and turn right. If you reach this point at precisely 5 AM, you can hear the signal for the start of Tōkyō's greatest ongoing open-air spectacle: the fish auction at the **Tōkyō Central Wholesale Market** ❶ ☞.

By 9 AM the business of the fish market is largely finished for the day, but there's still plenty to see and do in the area. After the auctions, you can explore the **backstreet shops of Tsukiji** ❷, in the maze of alleys between the market and Harumi-dōri. Here you can find a fascinating collection of small restaurants, stalls, fish markets, and other stores. For a close-up view of Japanese daily life, this is one of the best places in Tōkyō to visit.

Return to Shin-Ōhashi-dōri and walk northeast, past Harumi-dōri. On the right, as you approach the Hibiya subway line's Tsukiji Station, are the grounds of **Tsukiji Hongan-ji** ❸. Looking much like a transplant from India, this temple is the main branch in Tōkyō of Kyōto's Nishi Hongan-ji. A short walk north of Tsukiji Hongan-ji are the grounds of St. Luke's International Hospital (founded in 1900 by Dr. Rudolf Teusler, an American medical missionary), which are not in themselves worth a detour but are of historical note. It was here in the 18th century that Ryōtaku Maeno and Gempaku Sugita translated the Dutch book on anatomy, thereby ushering in Japan's interest in Western science. Covering the several square blocks north of the hospital was the foreign settlement created after the signing of the U.S.-Japan Treaty of Commerce in 1858. Among the residents here in the late 19th century was a Scottish surgeon and missionary named Henry Faulds. Intrigued by the Japanese custom of putting their thumbprints on documents for authentication, he began the research that established for the first time that no two people's fingerprints are alike. In 1880 he wrote a paper for *Nature* magazine suggesting that this fact might be of some use in criminal investigation.

After visiting Tsukiji Hongan-ji, walk southwest on Shin-Ōhashi-dōri, past the Asahi Newspapers Building and the National Institute for Cancer Research on your right. The street will curve to the right; dead ahead, across the intersection of Kaigan-dōri at Shiosaki-bashi, are Shiodome and the skyscraper headquarters of the advertising giant Dentsu. Just before the intersection, on the left, the old Nanmon-bashi stone bridge crosses a canal to the entrance of the **Hama Rikyū Tei-en** ④. (The path to the left as you enter the garden leads to the "river bus" ferry landing, from which you can leave this excursion and begin another: up the Sumida to Asakusa.)

SHIODOME
汐留

From the Hama Rikyū Tei-en, cross Shōwa-dōri by the pedestrian bridge and spend some time exploring the shops and arcades of Caretta Shiodome, adjacent to the Dentsu headquarters building. The **Advertising Museum Tokyo** ⑤, on the B1 level of Caretta, is especially worth visiting. It presents Japan's unique sense of graphic design in the context of some 300 years of advertising history.

Return to Shōwa-dōri and turn left. (If you were to turn right instead, you'd come to an O marker commemorating the starting point of the 1872 railway service to Yokohama.) At the next major intersection turn right and then left at the third corner. Walk northeast in the direction of Higashi-Ginza Station. On the second block, on your right, is the Shimbashi Enbujō, which hosts Kabuki performances and other traditional theater. On the left is the Nissan Motor Company headquarters.

A brisk minute's walk will bring you to the intersection of Harumi-dōri. Turn left, and on the next block, on the right, you can see the **Kabuki-za** ⑥, built especially for Kabuki performances.

Just in front of the Kabuki-za is the Hibiya subway's Higashi-Ginza stop, where you can make your way back from whence you came.

TIMING

The Tsukiji walk has few places to spend time *in*; getting from point to point, however, can consume most of a morning. The backstreet shops will probably require no more than an hour. Allow yourself about an hour to explore the fish market; if fish in all its diversity holds a special fascination for you, take two hours. Remember that in order to see the fish auction in action, you need to get to the market before 6:30 AM; by 9 AM the business of the market is largely finished for the day.

This part of the city can be brutally hot and muggy in August; during the O-bon holiday, in the middle of the month, Tsukiji is comparatively lifeless. Mid-April and early October are best for strolls in the Hama Rikyū Tei-en.

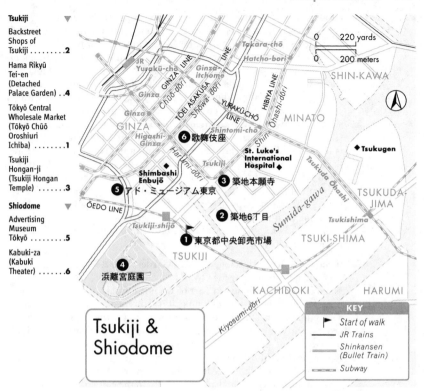

Tsukiji ▼

Backstreet
Shops of
Tsukiji 2

Hama Rikyū
Tei-en
(Detached
Palace Garden) . .4

Tōkyō Central
Wholesale Market
(Tōkyō Chūō
Oroshiuri
Ichiba) 1

Tsukiji
Hongan-ji
(Tsukiji Hongan
Temple) 3

Shiodome ▼

Advertising
Museum
Tōkyō 5

Kabuki-za
(Kabuki
Theater) 6

Tsukiji &
Shiodome

KEY

► *Start of walk*

━━ *JR Trains*

═══ *Shinkansen
(Bullet Train)*

▭▭▭ *Subway*

What to See

❺ Advertising Museum Tōkyō (アド・ミュージアム東京). ADMT puts the unique Japanese gift for graphic and commercial design into historical perspective, from the sponsored "placements" in 18th-century wood-block prints to the postmodern visions of fashion photographers and video directors. The museum is maintained by a foundation established in honor of Hideo Yoshida, fourth president of the mammoth Dentsu Advertising Company, and includes a digital library of some 130,000 entries on everything you ever wanted to know about hype. There are no explanatory panels in English—but this in itself is a test of how well the visual vocabulary of consumer media can communicate across cultures. ⊠ *1–8–2 Higashi-Shimbashi, Caretta Shiodome B1F–B2F, Chūō-ku* ☎ *03/6218–2500* ⊕ *www.admt.jp* ☞ *Free* ⊘ *Tues.–Fri. 11–6:30, Sat. 11–4:30* Ⓜ *Ōedo subway line, Shiodome Station (Exit 7); JR (Shiodome Exit) and Asakusa and Ginza lines (Exit 4), Shimbashi Station.*

❷ Backstreet shops of Tsukiji (築地6丁目). Tōkyō's markets provide a vital counterpoint to the museums and monuments of conventional sightseeing: they let you see how people really live in the city. If you have time for only one market, this is the one to see. The three square blocks between the Tōkyō Central Wholesale Market and Harumi-dōri have, naturally

Fodor's Choice

★

enough, scores of fishmongers, but also shops and restaurants. Stores sell pickles, tea, crackers and snacks, cutlery (what better place to pick up a professional sushi knife?), baskets, and kitchenware. Hole-in-the-wall sushi bars here have set menus ranging from ¥1,000 to ¥2,100; look for the plastic models of food in glass cases out front. The area includes the row of little counter restaurants, barely more than street stalls, under the arcade along the east side of Shin-Ōhashi-dōri, each with its one specialty. If you haven't had breakfast by this point in your walk, stop at **Segawa** (瀬川) for *maguro donburi*—a bowl of fresh raw tuna slices served over rice and garnished with bits of dried seaweed (Segawa is in the middle of the arcade, but without any distinguishing features or English signage; your best bet is to ask someone). Some 100 of the small retailers and restaurants in this area are members of the Tsukiji Meiten-kai (Association of Notable Shops), and promote themselves by selling illustrated maps of the area for ¥50; the maps are all in Japanese, but with proper frames they make great souvenirs. ⊠ *Tsukiji 4-chōme, Chūō-ku* Ⓜ *Ōedo subway line, Tsukiji-shijō Station (Exit A1); Hibiya subway line, Tsukiji Station (Exit 1).*

❹ **Hama Rikyū Tei-en** (Detached Palace Garden, 浜離宮庭園). The land here was originally owned by the Owari branch of the Tokugawa family from Nagoya, and it extended to part of what is now the fish market. When one of the family became shōgun in 1709, his residence was turned into a shogunal palace—with pavilions, ornamental gardens, pine and cherry groves, and duck ponds. The garden became a public park in 1945, although a good portion of it is fenced off as a nature preserve. None of the original buildings has survived, but on the island in the large pond is a reproduction of the pavilion where former U.S. president Ulysses S. Grant and Mrs. Grant had an audience with the emperor Meiji in 1879. The building can now be rented for parties. The path to the left as you enter the garden leads to the "river bus" ferry landing, from which you can leave this excursion and begin another: up the Sumida-gawa to Asakusa. Note that you must pay the admission to the garden even if you're just using the ferry. ⊠ *1–1 Hamarikyū–Teien, Chūō-ku* ☎ *03/ 3541–0200* 🖾 *¥300* ⊙ *Daily 9–4:30* Ⓜ *Ōedo subway line, Shiodome Station (Exit 8).*

★ ❻ **Kabuki-za** (Kabuki Theater, 歌舞伎座). Soon after the Meiji Restoration and its enforced exile in Asakusa, Kabuki began to reestablish itself in this part of the city. The first Kabuki-za was built in 1889, with a European facade. Here, two of the hereditary theater families, Ichikawa and Onoe, developed a brilliant new repertoire that brought Kabuki into the modern era. In 1912 the Kabuki-za was taken over by the Shochiku theatrical management company, which replaced the old theater building in 1925. Designed by architect Shin'ichirō Okada, it was damaged during World War II but was restored soon after. ⊠ *4–12–15 Ginza, Chūō-ku* ☎ *03/3541–3131* ⊕ *www.shochiku.co.jp/play/kabukiza/ theater* Ⓜ *Hibiya subway line, Higashi-Ginza Station (Exit 3).*

★ ▶ ❶ **Tōkyō Central Wholesale Market** (Tōkyō Chūō Oroshiuri Ichiba, 東京都中央卸売市場). The city's fish market used to be farther uptown, in Nihombashi. It was moved to Tsukiji after the Great Kantō Earthquake of 1923, and it occupies the site of what was once Japan's first naval training academy. Today the market sprawls over some 54 acres of reclaimed land and employs approximately 15,000 people, making it the largest fish market in the world. Its warren of buildings houses about 1,200 wholesale shops, supplying 90% of the seafood consumed in Tōkyō every day—some 2,400 tons of it. Most of the seafood sold in Tsukiji comes in by truck, arriving through the night from fishing ports all over the country.

What makes Tsukiji a great show is the auction system. The catch—more than 100 varieties of fish in all, including whole frozen tuna, Styrofoam cases of shrimp and squid, and crates of crabs—is laid out in the long covered area between the river and the main building. Then the bidding begins. Only members of the wholesalers' association can take part. Wearing license numbers fastened to the front of their caps, they register their bids in a kind of sign language, shouting to draw the attention of the auctioneer and making furious combinations in the air with their fingers. The auctioneer keeps the action moving in a hoarse croak that sounds like no known language, and spot quotations change too fast for ordinary mortals to follow.

Different fish are auctioned off at different times and locations, and by 6:30 AM or so, this part of the day's business is over, and the wholesalers fetch their purchases back into the market in barrows. Restaurant owners and retailers arrive about 7, making the rounds of favorite suppliers for their requirements. Chaos seems to reign, but everybody here knows everybody else, and they all have it down to a system.

A word to the wise: the 52,000 or so buyers, wholesalers, and shippers who work at the market may be a lot more receptive to casual visitors than they were in the past, but they are not running a tourist attraction. They're in the fish business, moving more than 600,000 tons of it a year to retailers and restaurants all over the city, and this is their busiest time of day. The cheerful banter they use with each other can turn snappish if you get in their way. Also bear in mind that you are not allowed to take photographs while the auctions are under way (flashes are a distraction). The market is kept spotlessly clean, which means the water hoses are running all the time. Boots are helpful, but if you don't want to carry them, bring a pair of heavy-duty trash bags to slip over your shoes and secure them above your ankles with rubber bands. ⊠ *5–2–1 Tsukiji, Chūō-ku* ☎ *03/3542–1111* ⊕ *www.shijou.metro.tokyo.jp* ⊠ *Free* ☉ *Business hrs Mon.–Sat. (except 2nd and 4th Wed. of month) 5 AM–3 PM* Ⓜ *Ōedo subway line, Tsukiji-shijō Station (Exit A1); Hibiya subway line, Tsukiji Station (Exit 1).*

❸ **Tsukiji Hongan-ji** (Tsukiji Hongan Temple, 築地本願寺). Disaster seemed to follow this temple, the main branch in Tōkyō of Kyōto's Nishi Hongan-ji, since it was first located here in 1657: it was destroyed at least five times thereafter, and reconstruction in wood was finally abandoned after the Great Kantō Earthquake of 1923. The present stone building dates from 1935. It was designed by Chūta Ito, a pupil of Tatsuno Kingo, who built Tōkyō Station. Ito's other credits include the Meiji Shrine in Harajuku; he also lobbied for Japan's first law for the preservation of historic buildings. Ito traveled extensively in Asia; the evocations of classical Hindu architecture in the temple's domes and ornaments were his homage to India as the cradle of Buddhism. But with stained-glass windows and a pipe organ as well, the building is nothing if not eclectic. ✉ *3–15–1 Tsukiji, Chūo-ku* ☎ *03/3541–1131* ✆ *Free* ⊙ *Daily 6–4* Ⓜ *Hibiya subway line, Tsukiji Station (Exit 1).*

need a break?   **Edo-Gin** (江戸銀), one of the area's older sushi bars, founded in 1924, is legendary for its portions—slices of raw fish that almost hide the balls of rice on which they sit. Dinner is pricey, but the set menu at lunch is a certifiable *bāgen* (bargain) at ¥1,000. Walk southwest on Shin-Ōhashi-dōri from its intersection with Harumi-dōri. Take the first right and look for Edo-Gin just past the next corner, on the left. ✉ *4–5–1 Tsukiji, Chūo-ku* ☎ *03/3543–4401* ☰ *AE, MC, V* ⊙ *Closed early Jan.* Ⓜ *Hibiya subway line, Tsukiji Station (Exit 1); Ōedo subway line, Tsukiji-shijō Station (Exit A1).*

NIHOMBASHI, GINZA & YŪRAKU-CHŌ
日本橋・銀座・有楽町

Tōkyō is a city of many centers. The municipal administrative center is in Shinjuku. The national government center is in Kasumigaseki. For almost 350 years Japan was ruled from Edo Castle, and the great stone ramparts still define—for travelers, at least—the heart of the city. History, entertainment, fashion, traditional culture: every tail you could want to pin on the donkey goes in a different spot. Geographically speaking, however, there's one and only one center of Tōkyō: a tall, black, iron pole on the north side of Nihombashi—and if the tail you were holding represented high finance, you would have to pin that one right here as well.

When Ieyasu Tokugawa had the first bridge constructed at Nihombashi, he designated it the starting point for the five great roads leading out of his city, the point from which all distances were to be measured. His decree is still in force: the black pole on the present bridge, erected in 1911, is the Zero Kilometer marker for all the national highways.

In the early days of the Tokugawa Shogunate, Edo had no port; almost everything the city needed was shipped here. The bay shore was marshy and full of tidal flats, so heavily laden ships would come only as far as Shinagawa, a few miles down the coast, and unload to smaller vessels. These in turn would take the cargo into the city through a network of canals to wharves and warehouses at Nihombashi. The bridge and the area south and east became a wholesale distribution center, not only for manufactured goods but also for foodstuffs. The city's first fish market, in fact, was established at Nihombashi in 1628 and remained here until the Great Earthquake of 1923.

All through the Edo period, this area was part of Shitamachi. Except for a few blocks between Nihombashi and Kyō-bashi, where the city's deputy magistrates had their villas, it belonged to the common people—not all of whom lived elbow to elbow in poverty. There were fortunes to be made in the markets, and the early millionaires of Edo built their homes in the Nihombashi area. Some, like the legendary timber magnate Bunzaemon Kinokuniya, spent everything they made in the pleasure quarters of Yoshiwara and died penniless. Others founded the great trading houses of today—Mitsui, Mitsubishi, Sumitomo—which still have warehouses nearby.

It was appropriate, then, that when Japan's first corporations were created and the Meiji government developed a modern system of capital formation, the Tōkyō Stock Exchange (Shōken Torihikijo) would go up on the west bank of the Nihombashi-gawa (Nihombashi River). A stone's throw from the exchange now are the home offices of most of the country's major securities companies, which in the hyperinflated bubble economy of the 1980s and early '90s were moving billions of yen around the world electronically—a far cry from the early years of high finance, when the length of a trading day was determined by a section of rope burning on the floor of the exchange. Trading finished when the rope had smoldered down to the end.

A little farther west, money—the problems of making it and of moving it around—shaped the area in a somewhat different way. In the Edo period there were three types of currency in circulation: gold, silver, and copper, each with its various denominations. Determined to unify the system, Ieyasu Tokugawa started minting his own silver coins in 1598 in his home province of Suruga, even before he became shōgun. In 1601 he established a gold mint; the building was only a few hundred yards from Nihombashi, on the site of what is now the Bank of Japan. In 1612 he relocated the Suruga plant to a patch of reclaimed land west of his castle. The area soon came to be known informally as Ginza (Silver Mint).

The value of these various currencies fluctuated. There were profits to be made in the changing of money, and this business eventually came under the control of a few large merchant houses. One of the most successful of these merchants was a man named Takatoshi Mitsui, who had a dry-goods shop in Kyōto and opened a branch in Edo in 1673. The shop, called Echigo-ya, was just north of Nihombashi. By the end of the 17th century it was the base of a commercial empire—in retailing, banking, and trading—known today as the Mitsui Group. Not far from the site of Echigo-ya stands its direct descendant: Mitsukoshi department store.

"*Rui wa tomo wo yobu*" goes the Japanese expression: "like calls to like." From Nihombashi through Ginza to Shimbashi is the domain of all the noble houses that trace their ancestry back to the dry-goods and kimono shops of the Edo period: Mitsukoshi, Takashimaya, Matsuzakaya, Matsuya. All are intensely proud of being at the top of the retail business, as purveyors of an astonishing range of goods and services.

The district called Yūraku-chō lies west of Ginza's Sukiya-bashi, stretching from Sotobori-dōri to Hibiya Kōen and the Outer Garden of the Imperial Palace. The name derives from one Urakusai Oda, younger brother of the warlord who had once been Ieyasu Tokugawa's commander. Urakusai, a Tea Master of some note (he was a student of Sen no Rikyū, who developed the tea ceremony) had a town house here, beneath the castle ramparts, on land reclaimed from the tidal flats of the bay. He soon left Edo for the more refined comforts of Kyōto, but his name stayed behind, becoming Yūraku-chō—the Pleasure (*yūraku*) Quarter (*chō*)—in the process. Sukiya-bashi was the name of the long-gone bridge near Urakusai's villa that led over the moat to the Silver Mint.

The "pleasures" associated with this district in the early postwar period stemmed from the fact that a number of the buildings here survived the air raids of 1945 and were requisitioned by the Allied forces. Yūraku-chō quickly became the haunt of the so-called *pan-pan* women, who provided the GIs with female company. Because it was so close to the military post exchange in Ginza, the area under the railroad tracks became one of the city's largest black markets. Later, the black market gave way to clusters of cheap restaurants, most of them little more than counters and a few stools, serving yakitori and beer. Office workers on meager budgets and journalists from the nearby *Mainichi, Asahi,* and *Yomiuri* newspaper headquarters would gather here at night. Yūraku-chō-under-the-tracks was smoky, loud, and friendly—a kind of open-air substitute for the local taproom. The area has long since become upscale, and no more than a handful of the yakitori stalls remains.

Numbers in the text correspond to numbers in the margin and on the Nihombashi, Ginza, and Yūraku-chō map.

A Good Walk

For more information on department stores and individual shops mentioned in this walk, *see* Chapter 6.

NIHOMBASHI
日本橋

Begin at Tōkyō Station. Take the Yaesu Central Exit on the east side of the building, cross the broad avenue in front of you (Sotobori-dōri), and turn left. Walk north until you cross a bridge under the Shuto Expressway and turn right at the second corner, at the **Bank of Japan** ❶ ▶. From here walk east two blocks to the main intersection at Chūō-dōri. On your left is the Mitsui Bank, and on your right is **Mitsukoshi** ❷ department store. The small area around the store, formerly called Suruga-chō, is the birthplace of the Mitsui conglomerate.

Turn right on Chūō-dōri. As you walk south, you can see on the left a shop founded in 1849, called Yamamoto Noriten, which specializes in *nori,* the ubiquitous dried seaweed used to wrap *maki* (sushi rolls) and *onigiri* (rice balls); nori was once the most famous product of Tōkyō Bay.

At the end of the next block is **Nihombashi** ❸ (this is the name of the bridge itself, as well as the neighborhood), shaken but not stirred by the incessant rumbling of the expressway overhead. Before you cross the bridge, notice on your left the small statue of a sea princess seated by a pine tree: a monument to the fish market that stood here before the 1923 quake. To the right is the Zero Kilometer marker, from which all highway distances are measured. On the other side, also to the right, is a plaque depicting the old wooden bridge. In the Edo period the south end of the bridge was set aside for posting public announcements—and for displaying the heads of criminals.

Turn left as soon as you cross the bridge and walk past the Nomura Securities Building to where the expressway loops overhead and turns south.

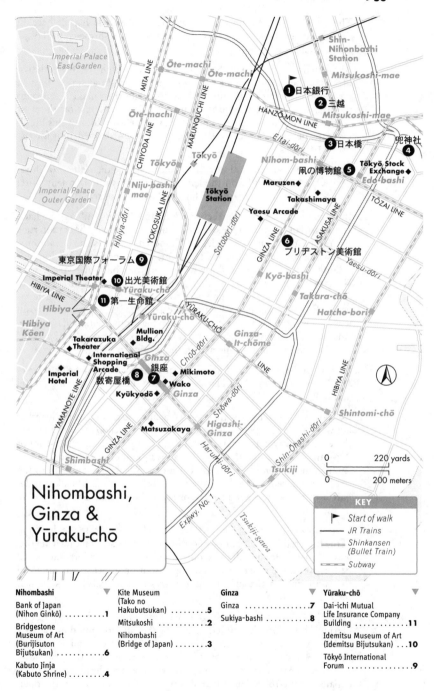

Imperial Palace East Garden

Imperial Palace Outer Garden

MITA LINE

MARUNOUCHI LINE

CHIYODA LINE

Ōte-machi

Ōte-machi

Ōte-machi

HANZŌ-MON LINE

Eitai-dōri

Shin-Nihonbashi Station

Mitsukoshi-mae

❶ 日本銀行

❷ 三越

Mitsukoshi-mae

❸ 日本橋

❹ 兜神社

Nihom-bashi

凧の博物館 ❺

Maruzen ◆

❻ Tōkyō Stock Exchange ◆

Edo-bashi

Tōkyō

Niju-bashi mae

Tōkyō

Tōkyō Station

YOKOSUKA LINE

Hibiya-dōri

Sotobori-dōri

GINZA LINE

ASAKUSA LINE

Takashimaya ◆

Yaesu Arcade

❻ ブリヂストン美術館

Yaesu-dōri

TŌZAI LINE

東京国際フォーラム ❾

Imperial Theater ◆

❿ 出光美術館

Yūraku-chō

Kyō-bashi

HIBIYA LINE

Hibiya

⓫ 第一生命館

Hibiya Kōen

Yūraku-chō

YŪRAKU-CHŌ

Takara-chō

Hatcho-bori

Takarazuka Theater ◆

Mullion Bldg.

Ginza-It-chōme

LINE

International Shopping Arcade

Ginza

銀座

Imperial Hotel

❽ 数寄屋橋

❼ 銀座

◆ **Mikimoto**

Chō-dōri

YAMANOTE LINE

Wako

Kyūkyodō ◆

Ginza

Shōwa-dōri

HIBIYA LINE

Shintomi-chō

GINZA LINE

Matsuzakaya

Higashi-Ginza

Shin-Ōhashi-dōri

Shimbashi

Harumi-dōri

Tsukiji

Expwy. No. 1

Tsukiji-gawa

| 0 | 220 yards |
| 0 | 200 meters |

Nihombashi, Ginza & Yūraku-chō

Nihombashi ▼

Bank of Japan (Nihon Ginkō) 1

Bridgestone Museum of Art (Burijisuton Bijutsukan) 6

Kabuto Jinja (Kabuto Shrine) 4

Kite Museum (Tako no Hakubutsukan) 5

Mitsukoshi 2

Nihombashi (Bridge of Japan) 3

Ginza ▼

Ginza 7

Sukiya-bashi 8

Yūraku-chō ▼

Dai-ichi Mutual Life Insurance Company Building 11

Idemitsu Museum of Art (Idemitsu Bijutsukan) ...10

Tōkyō International Forum 9

This area is called Kabuto-chō, after the small **Kabuto Jinja** ④ here on the left, under the loop. Across the street from the shrine is the Tōkyō Stock Exchange.

At the main entrance to the Stock Exchange, turn right. Walk south two blocks to the intersection at Eitai-dōri and turn right again. Walk west on Eitai-dōri, turn right onto Shōwa-dōri, and then make a left onto the first small street behind the Bank of Hiroshima. Just off the next corner is a restaurant called Taimeiken. On the fifth floor of this building is the delightful little **Kite Museum** ⑤—well worth the detour for visitors of all ages.

Retrace your steps to Eitai-dōri, continue west, and turn left onto Chūō-dōri. One block south, on the left, is Takashimaya department store; on the right is Maruzen, one of Japan's largest booksellers.

Look right at the next intersection; you can see that you've come back almost to Tōkyō Station. Below the avenue from here to the station runs the Yaesu Underground Arcade, with hundreds of shops and restaurants. The whole area here, west of Chūō-dōri, was named after Jan Joosten, a Dutch sailor who was shipwrecked on the coast of Kyūshū with William Adams—hero of James Clavell's novel *Shōgun*—in 1600. Like Adams, Joosten became an adviser to Ieyasu Tokugawa, took a Japanese wife, and was given a villa near the castle. "Yaesu" (originally Yayosu) was as close as the Japanese could come to the pronunciation of his name. Adams, an Englishman, lived out his life in Japan; Joosten drowned off the coast of Indonesia while attempting to return home.

On the southeast corner of the intersection is the **Bridgestone Museum of Art** ⑥, one of Japan's best private collections of early modern painting and sculpture, both Western and Japanese.

GINZA
銀座

Consider your feet. By now they may be telling you that you'd really rather not walk to the next point on this excursion. If so, get on the Ginza Line—there's a subway entrance right in front of the Bridgestone Museum of Art—and ride one stop to **Ginza** ⑦. Take any exit directing you to the 4-chōme intersection (yon-*chō*-me *kō*-sa-ten). When you come up to the street level, orient yourself by the Ginza branch of the Mitsukoshi department store, on the northeast corner, and the round San-aī Building on the southwest.

From Ginza 4-chōme, walk northwest on Harumi-dōri in the direction of the Imperial Palace. From Chūō-dōri to the intersection called **Sukiya-bashi** ⑧, named for a bridge that once stood here, your exploration should be free-form: the side streets and north–south parallel streets are ideal for wandering, particularly if you're interested in art galleries—of which there are 300 or more in this part of Ginza.

YŪRAKU-CHŌ
有楽町

From the Sukiya-bashi intersection, walk northwest on the right side of Harumi-dōri. Pass the curved facade of the Mullion Building department store complex and cross the intersection. After passing through the tunnel under the JR Yamanote Line tracks, turn right. Walk two long blocks east, parallel to the tracks, until you come to the gleaming white expanse of the **Tōkyō International Forum** ⑨. You can relax in the open space of the Forum's plaza and perhaps grab a pastry and coffee at Café Wien, next to the Plaza Information Center.

From the southwest corner of the Forum, turn left and walk halfway down the block to the main entrance of the International Building, which houses the **Idemitsu Museum of Art** ⑩ on the ninth floor. After a stop inside, continue west along the side of the International Building toward the Imperial Palace to Hibiya-dōri. Turn left; less than a minute's walk along Hibiya-dōri will bring you to the **Dai-ichi Mutual Life Insurance Company Building** ⑪, where you can visit the preserved former office of General Douglas MacArthur. Across the avenue is Hibiya Kōen, Japan's first Western-style public park, which dates to 1903. Its lawns and fountains make a pretty place for office workers from nearby buildings to have lunch on a warm spring afternoon, but it doesn't provide compelling reasons for you to make a detour. Press on, past the Hibiya police station, across the Harumi-dōri intersection; at the second corner, just before you come to the Imperial Hotel, turn left.

At the end of the block, on the corner, is the Takarazuka Theater, where all-female casts take the art of musical review to the highest levels of camp. Continue southeast, and on the next block, on both sides of the street (just under the railroad bridge), are entrances to the International Shopping Arcade. Stores here sell kimonos and happi coats, pearls and cloisonné, prints, cameras, and consumer electronics: one-stop shopping for presents and souvenirs.

Turn left down the narrow side street that runs along the side of the arcade to the Hankyū department store—the horned monstrosity in the pocket park on the corner is by sculptor Taro Okamoto—and you can find yourself back on Harumi-dōri, just a few steps from the Sukiyabashi crossing. From here you can return to your hotel by subway, or a minute's walk will bring you to JR Yūraku-chō station.

TIMING   There's something about this part of Tōkyō—the traffic, the number of people, the way it exhorts you to keep moving—that can make you feel you've covered a lot more ground than you really have. Take this walk in the morning; when you're done, you can better assess the energy you have left for the rest of the day. None of the stops along the way, with the possible exception of the Bridgestone and Idemitsu museums, should take you more than 45 minutes. The time you spend shopping, of course, is up to you. In summer make a point of starting early, even though many stores and attractions don't open until 10 or 11: by midday the heat and humidity can be brutal. On weekend afternoons (October–March, Saturday 3–5 and Sunday noon–5; April–September, Saturday 2–6 and Sunday noon–6), Chūō-dōri is closed to traffic from Shimbashi all the way to Kyō-bashi and becomes a pedestrian mall with tables and chairs set out along the street. Keep in mind that some of the museums and other sights in the area close on Sunday.

What to See

▶ ❶ **Bank of Japan** (Nihon Ginkō, 日本銀行). The older part of the Bank of Japan is the work of Tatsuno Kingo, who also designed Tōkyō Station. Completed in 1896, on the site of what had been the Edo-period gold mint, the bank is one of the few surviving Meiji-era Western buildings in the city. The annex building houses the **Currency Museum,** a historical collection of rare gold and silver coins from Japan and other East Asian countries. There's little English information here, but the setting of muted lighting and plush red carpets evokes the days when the only kind of money around was the kind you could heft in your hand. ✉ *2–1–1 Nihombashi Hongoku-chō, Chūō-ku* ☎ *03/3279–1111 bank, 03/3277–3037 museum* ⊕ *www.boj.or.jp/en* 🎫 *Free* ☉ *Museum Tues.–Sun. 9:30–4:30* Ⓜ *Ginza (Exit A5) and Hanzō-mon (Exit B1) subway lines, Mitsukoshi-mae Station.*

❻ Bridgestone Museum of Art (Burijisuton Bijutsukan, ブリヂストン美術館). This is one of Japan's best private collections of French impressionist art and sculpture and of post-Meiji Japanese painting in Western styles by such artists as Shigeru Aoki and Tsuguji Fujita. The collection, assembled by Bridgestone Tire Company founder Shōjiro Ishibashi, also includes work by Rembrandt, Picasso, Utrillo, and Modigliani. The small gallery devoted to ancient art has a breathtaking Egyptian cat sculpture dating to between 950 and 660 BC. The Bridgestone also puts on major exhibits from private collections and museums abroad. ✉ *1–10–1 Kyō-bashi, Chūō-ku* ☎ *03/3563–0241* ⊕ *www.bridgestone-museum.gr.jp/e/* 🎫 *¥700* ☉ *Tues.–Sat. 10–8, Sun. 10–6* Ⓜ *Ginza subway line, Kyō-bashi Station (Meijiya Exit) or Nihombashi Station (Takashimaya Exit).*

⓫ Dai-ichi Mutual Life Insurance Company Building (第一生命館). Built like a fortress, this edifice survived World War II virtually intact and was taken over by the Supreme Command of the Allied powers. From his office here, General Douglas MacArthur directed the affairs of Japan from 1945 to 1951. The room is kept exactly as it was then. It can be visited by individuals and small groups without appointment; you need only to sign in at the reception desk in the lobby. ✉ *1–13–1 Yūraku-chō, Chiyoda-ku* ☎ *03/3216–1211* 🎫 *Free* ☉ *Weekdays 10–4:30* Ⓜ *Hibiya subway line, Hibiya Station (Exit B1).*

❼ Ginza (銀座). Ieyasu's Silver Mint moved out of this area in 1800. The name Ginza remained, but only much later did it begin to acquire any cachet for wealth and style. The turning point was 1872, when a fire destroyed most of the old houses here. The main street of Ginza, together with a grid of parallel and cross streets, was rebuilt as a Western quarter. It had two-story brick houses with balconies, the nation's first sidewalks and horse-drawn streetcars, gaslights, and, later, telephone poles. Before the turn of the 20th century, Ginza was already home to the great mercantile establishments that still define its character. The **Wako** (和光) department store, for example, on the northwest corner of the 4-chōme intersection, established itself here as Hattori, purveyors of clocks and watches. The clock on the present building was first installed in the Hattori clock tower, a Ginza landmark, in 1894.

Many of the nearby shops have lineages almost as old, or older, than Wako's. A few steps north of the intersection, on Chūō-dōri, **Mikimoto** (ミキモト) sells the famous cultured pearls first developed by Kōkichi Mikimoto in 1883. His first shop in Tōkyō dates to 1899. South of the intersection, next door to the Sanai Building, **Kyūkyodō** (鳩居堂) carries a variety of handmade Japanese papers and related goods. Kyūkyodō has been in business since 1663 and on Ginza since 1880. Across the street and one block south is the **Matsuzakaya** (松坂屋) department store, which began as a kimono shop in Nagoya in 1611.

There's even a name for browsing this area: Gin-bura, or "Ginza wandering." The best times to wander here are Saturday afternoons and Sunday from noon to 5 or 6 (depending on the season), when Chūō-dōri is closed to traffic between Shimbashi and Kyō-bashi. ⊠ *Chūō-ku* Ⓜ *Ginza and Hibiya subway lines, Ginza Station.*

★ ⑩ **Idemitsu Museum of Art** (Idemitsu Bijutsukan, 出光美術館). The strength of the collection in these four spacious, well-designed rooms lies in the Tang- and Song-dynasty Chinese porcelain and in the Japanese ceramics—including works by Nonomura Ninsei and Ogata Kenzan. On display are masterpieces of Old Seto, Oribe, Old Kutani, Karatsu, and Kakiemon ware. The museum also houses outstanding examples of Zen painting and calligraphy, wood-block prints, and genre paintings of the Edo period. Of special interest to scholars is the resource collection of shards from virtually every pottery-making culture of the ancient world. The museum is on the ninth floor of the Teikoku Gekijō building. ⊠ *3–1–1 Marunouchi, Chiyoda-ku* ☎*03/3213–9402* *¥800* ◷ *Tues.–Sun. 10–4:30* Ⓜ *Yūraku-chō subway line, Yūraku-chō Station (Exit A1).*

④ **Kabuto Jinja** (Kabuto Shrine, 兜神社). This shrine, like the Nihombashi itself, is another bit of history lurking in the shadows of the expressway. Legend has it that a noble warrior of the 11th century, sent by the Imperial Court in Kyōto to subdue the barbarians of the north, stopped here and prayed for assistance. His expedition was successful, and on the way back he buried a *kabuto,* a golden helmet, on this spot as an offering of thanks. Few Japanese are aware of this legend, and the monument of choice in Kabuto-chō today is the nearby Tōkyō Stock Exchange. ⊠ *1–8 Kabuto-chō, Nihombashi, Chūō-ku* Ⓜ *Tōzai subway line, Kayaba-chō Station (Exit 10).*

⊕ ⑤ **Kite Museum** (Tako no Hakubutsukan, 凧の博物館). Kite flying is an old tradition in Japan. The collection here includes examples of every shape and variety of kite from all over the country, hand-painted in brilliant colors with figures of birds, geometric patterns, and motifs from Chinese and Japanese mythology. You can call ahead to arrange a kite-making workshop (in Japanese) for groups of children. ⊠ *1–12–10 Nihombashi, Chūō-ku* ☎ *03/3271–2465* ⊕ *www.tako.gr.jp* *¥210* ◷ *Mon.–Sat. 11–5* Ⓜ *Tōzai subway line, Nihombashi Station (Exit C5).*

② **Mitsukoshi** (三越). Takatoshi Mitsui made his fortune by revolutionizing the retail system for kimono fabrics. The drapers of his day usually did business on account, taking payments semiannually. In his store (then called Echigo-ya), Mitsui started the practice of unit pricing, and his customers paid cash on the spot. As time went on, the store was always ready to adapt to changing needs and merchandising styles: garments made to order, home delivery, imported goods, and even—as the 20th century opened and Echigo-ya changed its name to Mitsukoshi—the hiring of women to the sales force. The emergence of Mitsukoshi as Tōkyō's first *depāto* (department store), also called *hyakkaten* (hundred-kinds-of-goods emporium), actually dates to 1908, with the construction of a three-story Western building modeled on Harrods of London. This was replaced in 1914 by a five-story structure with Japan's first escalator. The present flagship store is vintage 1935. Even if you don't plan to shop, this branch merits a visit. Two bronze lions, modeled on those at London's Trafalgar Square, flank the main entrance and serve as one of Tōkyō's best-known meeting places. Inside, a sublime statue of Magokoro, a Japanese goddess of sincerity, rises four stories through the store's central atrium. ⊠ *1–4–1 Nihombashi Muro-machi, Chūō-ku* ☎ *03/ 3241–3311* ⊙ *Daily 10–7:30* Ⓜ *Ginza and Hanzō-mon subway lines, Mitsukoshi-mae Station (Exits A3 and A5).*

❸ **Nihombashi** (Bridge of Japan, 日本橋). Why the expressway *had* to be routed directly over this lovely old landmark back in 1962 is one of the mysteries of Tōkyō and its city planning—or lack thereof. There were protests and petitions, but they had no effect. At that time Tōkyō had only two years left to prepare for the Olympics, and the traffic congestion was already out of control. So the bridge, with its graceful double arch, ornate lamps, and bronze Chinese lions and unicorns, was doomed to bear the perpetual rumble of trucks overhead—its claims overruled by concrete ramps and pillars. ⊠ *Chūō-ku* Ⓜ *Tōzai and Ginza subway lines, Nihombashi Station (Exits B5 and B6); Ginza and Hanzō-mon subway lines, Mitsukoshi-mae Station (Exits B5 and B6).*

❽ **Sukiya-bashi** (数寄屋橋). The side streets of the Sukiya-bashi area are full of art galleries, which operate a bit differently here than they do in most of the world's art markets. A few, like the venerable **Nichidō** (日動画廊, 5–3–16 Ginza), **Gekkōso** (月光荘, 7–2–8 Ginza), **Yoseidō** (養清堂画廊, 5–5–15 Ginza, and **Kabuto-ya** (兜屋画廊, 8–8–7 Ginza), actually function as dealers, representing particular artists, as well as acquiring and selling art. The majority, however, are rental spaces. Artists or groups pay for the gallery by the week, publicize their shows themselves, and in some cases even hang their own work. It's not unreasonable to suspect that a lot of these shows, even in so prestigious a venue as Ginza, are vanity exhibitions by amateurs with money to spare—but that's not always the case. The rental spaces are also the only way for serious professionals, independent of the various art organizations that might otherwise sponsor their work, to get any critical attention; if they're lucky, they can at least recoup their expenses with an occasional sale. ⊠ *Chiyoda-ku* Ⓜ *Ginza, Hibiya, and Marunouchi subway lines, Ginza Station (Exit C4).*

❾ **Tōkyō International Forum** (東京国際フォーラム). This postmodern masterpiece, the work of Uruguay-born American architect Raphael Viñoly, is the first major convention and art center of its kind in Tōkyō. Viñoly's design was selected in a 1989 competition that drew nearly 400 entries from 50 countries. The plaza of the Forum is that rarest of Tōkyō rarities, civilized open space: a long, tree-shaded central courtyard with comfortable benches. Freestanding sculpture, triumphant architecture, and people strolling—actually *strolling*—past in both directions are all here. The Forum itself is really two buildings. On the east side of the plaza is

Glass Hall, the main exhibition space—an atrium with an 180-foot ceiling, a magnificent curved wooden wall, and 34 upper-floor conference rooms. The west building has six halls for international conferences, exhibitions, receptions, and concert performances—the largest with seating for 5,012. ✉ *3–5–1 Marunouchi, Chiyoda-ku* ☎ *03/5221–9000* ⊕ *www.t-i-forum.co.jp/english* Ⓜ *Yūraku-chō subway line, Yūraku-chō Station (Exit A-4B).*

need a break?

Amid all of Tōkyō's bustle and crush, you actually can catch your breath in the open space of the plaza of the Tōkyō International Forum. If you also feel like having coffee and a bite of pastry, stop in at **Café Wien** (カフェ・ウィーン), next to the Plaza Information Center. ✉ *3–5–1 Marunouchi, Chiyoda-ku* ☎ *03/3211–3111* ◷ *Daily 10 AM–10 PM* Ⓜ *Yūraku-chō subway line, Yūraku-chō Station (Exit A-4B).*

AOYAMA, HARAJUKU & SHIBUYA 青山・原宿・渋谷

Who would have known? As late as 1960, this was as unlikely a candidate as any area in Tōkyō to develop into anything remotely chic. True, there was the Meiji Shrine, which gave the neighborhood a certain solemnity and drew the occasional festival crowd. Between the shrine and the Aoyama Cemetery to the east, however, the area was so unpromising that the municipal government designated a substantial chunk of it for low-cost public housing. Another chunk, called Washington Heights, was being used by U.S. occupation forces—who spent their money elsewhere. The few young Japanese people in Harajuku and Aoyama were either hanging around Washington Heights to practice their English or attending the Methodist-founded Aoyama Gakuin (Aoyama University)—and seeking their leisure farther south in Shibuya.

Then Tōkyō won its bid to host the 1964 Olympics, and Washington Heights was turned over to the city for the construction of Olympic Village. Aoyama-dōri, the avenue through the center of the area, was improved. Under it ran the extension of the Ginza Line subway and later the Hanzō-mon Line. Public transportation is the chief ingredient in Tōkyō's commercial alchemy: suddenly, people could get to Aoyama and Harajuku easily, and they did—in larger and larger numbers, drawn by the Western-style fashion houses, boutiques, and design studios that decided this was the place to be. By the 1980s the area was positively *smart*. Today, most of the older buildings along Omotesandō, many of them put up originally as low-cost public housing, are long gone, and in their place are the glass-and-marble emporia of *the* preeminent fashion houses of Europe: Louis Vuitton, Chanel, Armani, and the like. Their showrooms here are the Japanese cash cows of their worldwide empires.

Shibuya is south and west of Harajuku and Aoyama. Two subway lines, three private railways, the JR Yamanote Line, and two bus terminals move about a million people a day through Shibuya. Shops, restaurants, and amusements in this area target a population of university students, young office workers, and consumers younger still.

CloseUp
TEENYBOPPER SHOPPERS OF HARAJUKU

On weekends the heart of Harajuku, particularly the street called Takeshita-dōri, belongs to high school and junior high school shoppers, who flock here with hoarded sums of pocket money and for whom last week was ancient history. Harajuku is where market researchers come, pick 20 teenagers off the street at random, give them ¥2,000, and ask them to buy a tote bag. Whole industries convulse themselves to keep pace with those adolescent decisions. Stroll through Harajuku—with its outdoor cafés, its designer-ice-cream and Belgian-waffle stands, its profusion of stores with names like Rap City and Octopus Army, its ever-changing profusion of mascots and logos—and you may find it impossible to believe that Japan is in fact the most rapidly aging society in the industrial world.

Numbers in the text correspond to numbers in the margin and on the Aoyama, Harajuku & Shibuya map.

A Good Walk

For more information on department stores and individual shops mentioned in this walk, *see* Chapter 6.

AOYAMA
青山

Begin outside of the Gaien-mae subway station on Aoyama-dōri. This is also the stop for the Jingū Baseball Stadium, home field of the Yakult Swallows. You can see it across the street from the Chichibu-no-miya Rugby and Football Ground. The stadium is actually within the **Meiji Shrine Outer Gardens ❶ ▶**. The National Stadium—Japan's largest stadium, with room for 75,000 people, and the seat from which the city hosted the 1964 Summer Olympics—sits on the other side of this park.

From Gaien-mae, walk west some five blocks toward Shibuya, and turn left at the intersection where you see the Omotesandō subway station on the right-hand side of the avenue. Hold tight to your credit cards here: this is the east end of Omotesandō, Tōkyō's premier fashion boulevard, lined on both sides with the boutiques of couturiers like Issey Miyake, Missoni, Calvin Klein, and Comme des Garçons. Midway along the avenue is the quirky, high-tech (to some critics, even fetishistic) Tōkyō showroom of the Prada fashion house, built by Swiss-based architects Jacques Herzog and Pierre de Meuron. At the far end of the street (a 15-minute walk at a brisk pace), across the intersection to the right, you can see the walls of the **Nezu Institute of Fine Arts ❷**.

From the Nezu Institute of Fine Arts, retrace your steps to Aoyama-dōri. If you turned left here, you would come in due course (it's a longish walk) to Shibuya, by way of the Aoyama Gakuin University campus on the left. To make your way to Harajuku, continue straight across Aoyama-dōri northwest on Omotesandō.

HARAJUKU   North of Aoyama-dōri, Omotesandō becomes a broad divided boulevard lined with ginkgo trees, sloping gently downhill to the intersection with Meiji-dōri and to the neighborhood of Harajuku. Upscale brands have laid claim to the higher ground of the boulevard, but the commercial pulse of this area beats faster in the maze of side streets and alleys off to the left (south side) of Omotesandō; here, the hole-in-the-wall boutiques of hundreds of domestic designers cater to a young market. Japan's adolescents may have less to spend than a couturier's clientele, but they still take their apprenticeship as consumers very seriously.

On the left side of the boulevard as you approach the Meiji-dōri intersection is the Oriental Bazaar, a store especially popular with foreign visitors for its extensive stock of Japanese, Korean, and Chinese souvenirs at reasonable prices; browse here for scroll paintings and screens, kimono fabrics, antiques, ceramics, and lacquerware. A few doors down is Kiddy Land, one of the city's largest toy stores. On the northwest corner of the intersection itself is La Foret. With some 110 boutiques on five floors, this was one of the earliest of Tōkyō's characteristic vertical malls.

Here you might want to make a brief detour to the right on Meiji-dōri and left at the corner of the third narrow side street, called Takeshita-dōri, which rises to JR Harajuku station at the other end. This is where the youngest of Harajuku's consumers gather from all over Tōkyō and the nearby prefectures, packing the street from side to side and end to end, filling the coffers of countless faddish shops. If Japanese parents ever pause to wonder where their offspring might be on a Saturday afternoon, Takeshita-dōri is the likely answer.

Retrace your steps to La Foret, turn right, and walk uphill on the right side of Omotesandō to the first corner. Turn right again, and a few steps from the corner on this small street you can find the **Ōta Memorial Museum of Art** ❸—an unlikely setting for an important collection of traditional wood-block prints. Return to Omotesandō and walk up (northwest) to the intersection at the top. Across the street to your right look for JR Harajuku Station; straight ahead is the entrance to the Meiji Shrine Inner Garden and the **Meiji Shrine** ❹ itself.

When you finish exploring the grounds of the shrine, you have two options. You can leave the Inner Garden on the northwest side and walk west about five minutes from Sangū-bashi Station along the private Odakyū railway line to the **Japanese Sword Museum** ❺ to see its collection of swords. From there you can return to Sangū-bashi Station and take the train two stops north to Shinjuku, the next major exploring section. The other possibility is to return to Harajuku Station and take the JR Yamanote Line one stop south to Shibuya.

SHIBUYA   Begin your exploration of this area at JR Shibuya Station; use the **statue**
渋谷   **of Hachiko** ❻, on the plaza on the north side of the station, as a starting point. Cross the intersection and walk southwest on Dōgen-zaka. In a minute the street will fork at a vertical mall called the 109 Fashion Community; bear right on Bunka-mura-dōri and walk about four blocks to where the street suddenly narrows. Ahead of you will be the main

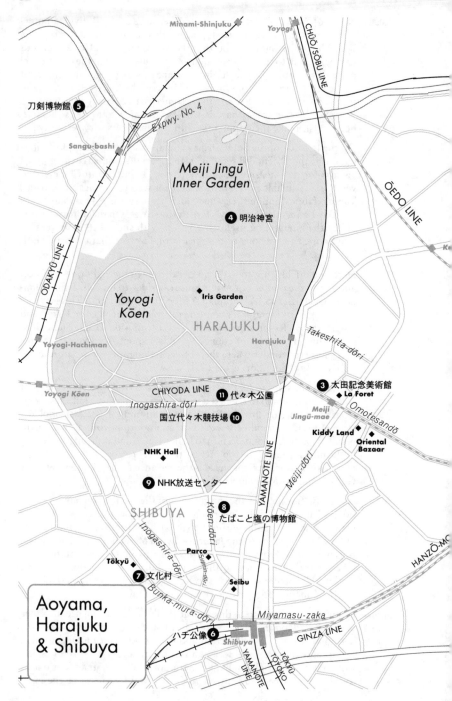

Minami-Shinjuku

Yoyogi

CHŪŌ/SŌBU LINE

刀剣博物館 **5**

Sangu-bashi

Expwy. No. 4

Meiji Jingū Inner Garden

ŌEDO LINE

4 明治神宮

ODAKYŪ LINE

Ke

Yoyogi Kōen

◆ Iris Garden

HARAJUKU

Yoyogi-Hachiman

Harajuku

Takeshita-dōri

Yoyogi Kōen

CHIYODA LINE

11 代々木公園

Inogashira-dōri

国立代々木競技場 **10**

3 太田記念美術館
◆ La Foret

Omotesandō

Meiji Jingū-mae

Kiddy Land ◆

◆ Oriental Bazaar

NHK Hall ◆

YAMANOTE LINE

Meiji-dōri

9 NHK放送センター

SHIBUYA

8

たばこと塩の博物館

Inogashira-dōri

Kōen-dōri

Parco ◆

HANZŌ-MO

Tōkyū ◆

7 文化村

Seibu ◆

Bunka-mura-dōri

Miyamasu-zaka

Aoyama, Harajuku & Shibuya

ハチ公像 **6**

Shibuya

GINZA LINE

YAMANOTE LINE

TŌKYŪ TŌYOKO

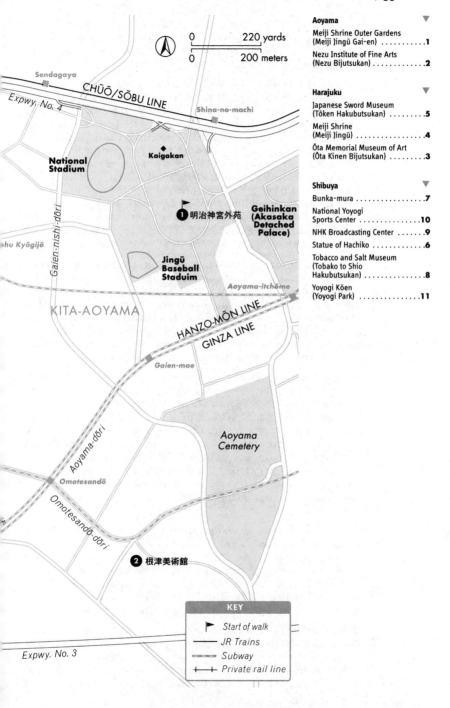

Aoyama ▼

Meiji Shrine Outer Gardens
(Meiji Jingū Gai-en) **1**

Nezu Institute of Fine Arts
(Nezu Bijutsukan) **2**

Harajuku ▼

Japanese Sword Museum
(Tōken Hakubutsukan) **5**

Meiji Shrine
(Meiji Jingū) **4**

Ōta Memorial Museum of Art
(Ōta Kinen Bijutsukan) **3**

Shibuya ▼

Bunka-mura **7**

National Yoyogi
Sports Center **10**

NHK Broadcasting Center **9**

Statue of Hachiko **6**

Tobacco and Salt Museum
(Tobako to Shio
Hakubutsukan) **8**

Yoyogi Kōen
(Yoyogi Park) **11**

Sendagaya

CHŪŌ/SŌBU LINE

Expwy. No. 4

Shina-no-machi

National Stadium

◆ **Kaigakan**

❶ 明治神宮外苑

Geihinkan (Akasaka Detached Palace)

Gaien-nishi-dōri

shu Kyōgijō

Jingū Baseball Staduim

Aoyama-itchōme

KITA-AOYAMA

HANZO-MŌN LINE

GINZA LINE

Gaien-mae

Aoyama-dōri

Aoyama Cemetery

Omotesandō

Omotesandō-dōri

❷ 根津美術館

Expwy. No. 3

KEY

▶ *Start of walk*

— *JR Trains*

═ *Subway*

┼┼ *Private rail line*

branch of the Tōkyū department store chain. Cross to the entrance and turn left to reach the **Bunka-mura** ❼ complex of theaters, exhibition halls, shops, and restaurants on the next corner. Les Deux Magots, in the sunken courtyard of the complex, is a good place for a light meal.

Return to Bunka-mura-dōri and walk back toward Shibuya Station on the left side of the street to the second corner. Turn left at the first traffic light and walk north, crossing Sentā-gai, a street lined with fast-food shops, downscale clothing stores, and game centers, to Inogashira-dōri. Ahead of you, across the street, will be the entrance to Supein-dōri, the heart of Shibuya's appeal to young consumers: a narrow brick-paved passageway climbing to a flight of steps at the other end, supposedly inspired by the Spanish Steps in Rome. Supein-dōri leads to Kōen-dōri, the smartest street in the neighborhood, by way of Parco (on the left), a vertical mall developed by the Seibu department store conglomerate. The Parco Theater, on the top floor, has an interesting calendar of plays and art films. Farther up Kōen-dōri, on the right, is the **Tobacco and Salt Museum** ❽, an interesting paean of sorts to the uses of tobacco and salt.

Turn left at the top of Kōen-dōri and you can see the **NHK Broadcasting Center** ❾ across the street on your right. The building next to it, at the far north corner, is the 4,000-seat NHK Hall, the pride of which is a 7,640-pipe organ, the foremost of its kind in the world. West of NHK Hall, across the street, is the **National Yoyogi Sports Center** ❿. From here you can finish off Shibuya in either of two ways: retrace your steps to JR Shibuya Station, or walk through **Yoyogi Kōen** ⓫ along the extension of Omotesandō to Harajuku and the JR station there.

TIMING   Aoyama and Harajuku together make a long walk, with considerable distances between the sights. Ideally, you should devote an entire day to these two areas, giving yourself plenty of time to browse in shops. You can see Meiji Shrine in less than an hour; the Nezu Institute warrants a leisurely two-hour visit. Don't be afraid to visit on weekends; there are more people on the streets, of course, but people-watching is a large part of the experience of Harajuku. Spring is the best time of year for the Meiji Jingu Inner Garden. As with any other walk in Tōkyō, the June rainy season is horrendous, and the humid heat of midsummer can quickly drain your energy and add hours to the time you need for a comfortable walk.

Shibuya is fairly compact, so you can easily cover it in about two hours. Unless you switch into shopping mode, no particular stop along the way should occupy you for more than a half hour; allow a full hour for the NHK Broadcasting Center, however, if you decide to take the guided tour. Spring is the best time of year for Yoyogi Kōen, and Sunday the best day. The area will be crowded, but Sunday affords the best opportunity to observe Japan's younger generation on display.

What to See

❼ **Bunka-mura** (文化村). One of the liveliest venues in Tōkyō for music and art, this six-story theater-and-gallery complex, a venture of the next-door Tōkyū department store, hosts everything from science-fiction film festivals and opera to ballet and big bands. The design of the building would be impressive if there were any vantage point from which to see it whole. The museum on the lower-level Garden Floor often has well-planned, interesting exhibits on loan from major European museums. ✉ *2–24–1 Dōgen-zaka, Shibuya-ku* ☎ *03/3477–9111, 03/3477–9999 ticket center* 🎟 *Theater admission and exhibit prices vary with events* ☉ *Lobby ticket counter daily 10–7* Ⓜ *JR Yamanote Line, Ginza and Hanzō-mon subway lines, and private rail lines; Shibuya Station (Exits 5 and 8 for Hanzō-mon subway line, Kita-guchi/North Exit for all others).*

need a break?

Les Deux Magots (ドゥ・マゴ・パリ), sister of the famed Paris café, in the Bunka-mura complex, serves a good selection of beers and wines, sandwiches, salads, quiches, tarts, and coffee. There's a fine art bookstore next door, and the tables in the courtyard are perfect for people-watching. ✉ *Bunka-mura, lower courtyard, 2–24–1 Dōgen-zaka, Shibuya-ku* ☎ *03/3477–9124* Ⓜ *JR Yamanote Line, Ginza and Hanzō-mon subway lines, and private rail lines; Shibuya Station (Exits 5 and 8 for Hanzō-mon subway line, Kita-guchi/ North Exit for all others).*

★ ❺ **Japanese Sword Museum** (Tōken Hakubutsukan, 刀剣博物館). It's said that in the late 16th century, before Japan closed its doors to the West, the Spanish tried to establish a trade here in weapons of their famous Toledo steel. The Japanese were politely uninterested; they had been making blades of incomparably better quality for more than 600 years. Early Japanese swordsmiths learned the art of refining steel from a pure iron sand called *tamahagane,* carefully controlling the carbon content by adding straw to the fire in the forge. The block of steel was repeatedly folded, hammered, and cross-welded to an extraordinary strength, then "wrapped" around a core of softer steel for flexibility. At one time there were some 200 schools of sword making in Japan; swords were prized not only for their effectiveness in battle but for the beauty of the blades and fittings and as symbols of the higher spirituality of the warrior caste. There are few inheritors of this art today. The Japanese Sword Museum offers a unique opportunity to see the works of noted sword smiths, ancient and modern. ✉ *4–25–10 Yoyogi, Shibuya-ku* ☎ *03/3379–1386* 🎟 *¥525* ☉ *Tues.–Sun. 10–4:30* Ⓜ *Odakyū private rail line, Sangū-bashi Station.*

★ ❹ **Meiji Shrine** (Meiji Jingū, 明治神宮). The Meiji Shrine honors the spirits of Emperor Meiji, who died in 1912, and Empress Shōken. It was established by a resolution of the Imperial Diet the year after the emperor's death to commemorate his role in ending the long isolation of Japan under the Tokugawa Shogunate and setting the country on the road to modernization. Completed in 1920 and virtually destroyed in an air raid in 1945, it was rebuilt in 1958 with funds raised in a nationwide public subscription.

Made from 1,700-year-old cypress trees from Mt. Ari in Taiwan, the two torii at the entrance to the grounds of the shrine rise 40 feet high; the crosspieces are 56 feet long. Torii are meant to symbolize the separation of the everyday secular world from the spiritual world of the Shintō shrine. The buildings in the shrine complex, with their curving green copper roofs, are also made of cypress wood. The surrounding gardens have some 100,000 flowering shrubs and trees, many of which were donated by private citizens.

An annual festival at the shrine takes place on November 3, Emperor Meiji's birthday, which is a national holiday. On the festival day and at New Year's, as many as a million people come to offer prayers and pay their respects. Several other festivals and ceremonial events are held here throughout the year; check by phone or on the shrine Web site to see what's scheduled during your visit. Even on a normal weekend the shrine draws thousands of visitors, but this seldom disturbs its mood of quiet gravitas: the faster and more unpredictable the pace of modern life, the more respectable the Japanese seem to find the certainties of the Meiji era.

The peaceful **Inner Garden** (Jingū Nai-en, 神宮内苑), where the irises are in full bloom in the latter half of June, is on the left as you walk in from the main gates, before you reach the shrine. Beyond the shrine is the **Treasure House** (宝物殿), a repository for the personal effects and clothes of Emperor and Empress Meiji—perhaps of less interest to foreign visitors than to the Japanese. ☒ *1–1 Kamizono-chō, Yoyogi, Shibuya-ku* ☎ *03/ 3379–9222* ⊕ *www.meijijingu.or.jp* ☒ *Shrine free, Inner Garden ¥500, Treasure House ¥500* ☉ *Shrine daily sunrise–sunset; Inner Garden Mar.–Nov., daily 9–4; Treasure House daily 10–4* ☉ *Closed 3rd Fri. of month* Ⓜ *Chiyoda subway line, Meiji-jingū-mae Station; JR Yamanote Line, Harajuku Station (Exit 2).*

▶ ➊ **Meiji Shrine Outer Gardens** (Meiji Jingū Gai-en, 明治神宮外苑). This rare expanse of open space is devoted to outdoor sports of all sorts. The Yakult Swallows play at **Jingū Baseball Stadium** (神宮球場, ☒ 13 Kasumigaoka, Shinjuku-ku ☎ 03/3404–8999); the Japanese baseball season runs from April to October. The main venue of the 1964 Summer Olympics, **National Stadium** (国立競技場, ☒ 10 Kasumigaoka, Shinjuku-ku ☎ 03/ 3403–1151) now hosts soccer matches. Some of the major World Cup matches were played here when Japan cohosted the event with Korea in autumn 2002. The **Meiji Memorial Picture Gallery** (Kaigakan, 絵画館; ☒ 9 Kasumigaoka, Shinjuku-ku, Aoyama ☎ 03/3401–5179), across the street from the National Stadium, doesn't hold much interest unless you're a fan of Emperor Meiji and don't want to miss some 80 otherwise undistinguished paintings depicting events in his life. It's open daily 9–4:30 and costs ¥500. ☒ *Shinjuku-ku* Ⓜ *Ginza and Hanzō-mon subway lines, Gai-en-mae Station (Exit 2); JR Chūō Line, Shina-no-machi Station.*

➓ **National Yoyogi Sports Center** (国立代々木競技場). The center consists of two paired structures created by Kenzō Tange for the 1964 Olympics. Tange's design of flowing ferroconcrete shell structures and cable-and-steel suspension roofing successfully fuses traditional and modern Japanese aesthetics. The stadium, which can accommodate 15,000 spectators for swimming and diving events, and the annex, which houses a basketball court with a seating capacity of 4,000, are open to visitors when there are no competitions. ☒ *2–1–1 Jinnan, Shibuya-ku* ☎ *03/3468–1171* ☒ *Pool ¥550* ☉ *Weekdays noon–9, Sat. 10–4, Sun. 10–7* Ⓜ *JR Yamanote Line, Harajuku Station (Exit 2).*

② **Nezu Institute of Fine Arts** (Nezu Bijutsukan, 根津美術館). This museum

Fodor'sChoice houses the private art collection of Meiji-period railroad magnate and

★ politician Kaichirō Nezu. The permanent display in the main building and the annex includes superb examples of Japanese painting, calligraphy, and ceramics—some of which are registered as National Treasures—plus Chinese bronzes, sculpture, and lacquerware. The institute also has one of Tōkyō's finest gardens, with more than 5 acres of shade trees and flowering shrubs, ponds, and waterfalls, as well as seven tea pavilions. To get here walk southeast on Omotesandō-dōri from the intersection of Aoyama-dōri for about 10 minutes to where the street curves away to the left. The Nezu Institute is opposite the intersection, on the right, behind a low sandstone-gray wall. ✉ *6–5–1 Minami-Aoyama, Minato-ku* ☎ *03/3400–2536* ⊕ *www.nezu-muse. or.jp/index_e.html* 💴 *¥1,000* 🕐 *Tues.–Sun. 9–4* Ⓜ *Ginza and Hanzō-mon subway lines, Omotesandō Station (Exit A5).*

need a break? How can you resist a café with a name like **Yokku Mokku** (ヨックモック)? Tables in the tree-shaded courtyard continue to make this place, which established itself as Japan's primo confectionery just after World War II, an Aoyama favorite. Its blue-tile front is on Omotesandō-dōri near the Nezu Institute. As you approach, you'll probably notice a steady stream of very smartly dressed young people on their way in and out. The café is open daily 10–7. ✉ *5–3–3 Minami-Aoyama, Shibuya-ku* ☎ *03/ 5485–3340* Ⓜ *Ginza, Chiyoda, and Hanzō-mon subway lines, Omotesandō Station (Exit A4).*

❾ **NHK Broadcasting Center** (NHK放送センター). The 23-story Japanese National Public Television facility was built as the Olympic Information Center in 1964. NHK (Nippon Hōsō Kyōkai) runs a "Studio Park" tour, in Japanese only, in the main building, where you can see the latest developments in broadcast technology. The center is a 15-minute walk north on Kōen-dōri from Shibuya Station. ✉ *2–2–1 Jinnan, Shibuya-ku* ☎ *03/ 3485–8034* 💴 *¥200* 🕐 *Daily 10–5:30* 🕐 *Closed 3rd Mon. of month, except Aug.* Ⓜ *Subway, JR, and private rail lines, Shibuya Station (Kita-guchi/North Exit).*

★ **❸** **Ōta Memorial Museum of Art** (Ōta Kinen Bijutsukan, 太田記念美術館). The gift of former Tōhō Mutual Life Insurance chairman Seizō Ōta, this is probably the city's finest private collection of ukiyo-e, traditional Edo-period wood-block prints. *Ukiyo* means "the floating world" of everyday life; *e* means "picture." The genre flourished in the 18th and 19th centuries. The works on display are selected and changed periodically from the 12,000 prints in the collection, which includes some extremely rare work by artists such as Hiroshige, Sharaku, and Utamaro. From JR Harajuku station, walk southwest downhill on Omotesandō-dōri and turn left on the narrow street before the intersection of Meiji-dōri. The museum is less than a minute's walk from the corner, on the left. ✉ *1–10–10 Jingū-mae, Shibuya-ku* ☎ *03/3403–0880* 💴 *¥500–¥800, depending on exhibition* 🕐 *Tues.–Sun. 10:30–5; may be closed 1st–4th of the month for new installations, so call ahead.*

⑥ Statue of Hachiko (ハチ公像). The subject of at least one three-hanky motion picture, Hachiko is Japan's version of the archetypal faithful dog. Hachiko's master, a professor at Tōkyō University, would take the dog with him every morning as far as Shibuya Station on his way to work, and Hachiko would go back to the station every evening to greet him on his return. One day in 1925 the professor failed to appear: he had died that day of a stroke. Every evening for the next seven years, Hachiko would go to Shibuya and wait there hopefully until the last train had pulled out of the station. Then the dog died, too, and his story made the newspapers. A handsome bronze statute of Hachiko was installed in front of the station, funded by thousands of small donations from readers all over the country. The present version is a replica—the original was melted down for its metal in World War II—but it remains a familiar landmark where young people in particular arrange to meet. ⊠ *JR Shibuya Station, West Plaza, Shibuya-ku.*

⑧ Tobacco and Salt Museum (Tobako to Shio Hakubutsukan, たばこと塩の博物館). A museum that displays examples of every conceivable artifact associated with tobacco and salt since the days of the Maya might not seem, at first, to serve a compelling social need, but the existence of the T&S reflects one of the more interesting facts of Japanese political life. Tobacco and salt were both made government monopolies at the beginning of the 20th century. Sales and distribution were eventually liberalized, but production remained under exclusive state control until 1985 through the Japan Tobacco and Salt Public Corporation. The corporation was then privatized. Renamed Nihon Tabako Sangyō (Japan Tobacco, Inc.), it continues to provide comfortable, well-paying second careers—called *amakudari* (literally "descent from Heaven")—for retired public officials. It remains Japan's exclusive producer of cigarettes, still holds a monopoly on the sale of salt, and dabbles in real estate, gardening supplies, and pharmaceuticals—ringing up sales of some $17 billion a year. Japan Tobacco, Inc., in short, has more money than it knows what to do with: so why not put up a museum? What makes this museum noteworthy is the special exhibit on the fourth floor of ukiyo-e on the themes of smoking and traditional salt production. T&S is a 10-minute walk on Kōen-dōri from Shibuya Station. ⊠ *1–16–8 Jinnan, Shibuya-ku* ☎ *03/3476–2041* ⊕ *www.jtnet.ad.jp/Culture/museum/Welcome.html* ☞ *¥100* ⊙ *Tues.–Sun. 10–5:30* Ⓜ *Subway, JR, and private rail lines, Shibuya Station (Kita-guchi/North Exit).*

⑪ Yoyogi Kōen (Yoyogi Park, 代々木公園). This area was once a parade ground for the Imperial Japanese Army, but in the postwar period it was appropriated by the occupying forces for military housing and was known as Washington Heights. During the 1964 Olympics, it served as the site of Olympic Village, and in 1967 it became a public park. On Sunday and holidays, there's a flea market in the park, along the main thoroughfare that runs through it, opposite the National Yoyogi Sports Center. ⊠ *Jinnan 2-chōme, Shibuya-ku* Ⓜ *Chiyoda subway line, Meiji Jingū-mae Station (Exit 2); JR Yamanote Line, Harajuku Station (Omotesandō Exit).*

SHINJUKU 新宿

If you have a certain sort of love for big cities, you're bound to love Shinjuku. Come here, and for the first time Tōkyō begins to seem *real*. Shinjuku is where all the celebrated virtues of Japanese society—its safety and order, its grace and beauty, its cleanliness and civility—fray at the edges.

To be fair, the area has been on the fringes of respectability for centuries. When Ieyasu, the first Tokugawa shōgun, made Edo his capital, Shinjuku was at the junction of two important arteries leading into the city from the west. It became a thriving post station, where travelers would rest and refresh themselves for the last leg of their journey; the appeal of this suburban pit stop was its "teahouses," where the waitresses dispensed a good bit more than sympathy with the tea.

When the Tokugawa dynasty collapsed in 1868, 16-year-old Emperor Meiji moved his capital to Edo, renaming it Tōkyō, and modern Shinjuku became the railhead connecting it to Japan's western provinces. As the haunt of artists, writers, and students, it remained on the fringes of respectability; in the 1930s Shinjuku was Tōkyō's bohemian quarter. The area was virtually leveled during the firebombings of 1945—a blank slate on which developers could write, as Tōkyō surged west after the war. By the 1970s property values in Shinjuku were the nation's highest, outstripping even those of Ginza.

Today three subways and seven railway lines converge here. Every day more than 3 million commuters pass through Shinjuku Station, making this the city's busiest and most heavily populated commercial center. The hub at Shinjuku—a vast, interconnected complex of tracks and terminals, department store and shops—divides the area into two distinctly different subcities, Nishi-Shinjuku (West Shinjuku) and Higashi-Shinjuku (East Shinjuku).

After the Great Kantō Earthquake of 1923, Nishi-Shinjuku was virtually the only part of Tōkyō left standing; the whims of nature had given this one small area a gift of better bedrock. That priceless geological stability remained largely unexploited until the late 1960s, when technological advances in engineering gave architects the freedom to soar. Some 20 skyscrapers have been built here since then, including the Tōkyō Metropolitan Government Office complex, and Nishi-Shinjuku has become Tōkyō's 21st-century administrative center.

By day the quarter east of Shinjuku Station is an astonishing concentration of retail stores, vertical malls, and discounters of every stripe and description. By night it's an equally astonishing collection of bars and clubs, strip joints, hole-in-the-wall restaurants, pinball parlors, and peep shows—just about anything that amuses, arouses, alters, or intoxicates is for sale in Higashi-Shinjuku, if you know where to look. Drunken fistfights are hardly unusual here, and petty theft is not unknown. Not surprisingly, Higashi-Shinjuku has the city's largest—and busiest—police substation.

Numbers in the text correspond to numbers in the margin and on the Shinjuku map.

A Good Walk

For more information on department stores and individual shops mentioned in this walk, *see* Chapter 6.

NISHI-SHINJUKU
JR trains and subways will drop you off belowground at Shinjuku Station; head for the west exit. You need to get up to the street level in front of the Odakyū department store, with the Keiō department store on your left, to avoid the passageway under the plaza. Walk across the plaza, through the bus terminal, or take the pedestrian bridge on the north side. Traffic in front of the station is rather confusing—what you're looking for is the wide, divided, east–west avenue on the other side, called Chūō-dōri (YON-GŌ GAIRO on some street markers), between the Fuji Bank on the left and the Dai-ichi Kangyō Bank on the right. Walk west on Chūō-dōri one block to the Shinjuku Center Building, cross at the traffic light, and turn right. On the next block is the tapering shape of the Yasuda Fire and Marine Insurance Building; the **Seiji Tōgō Memorial Sompo Japan Museum of Art ①** ☞ is on the 42nd floor.

Retrace your steps to Chūō-dōri, turn right, and walk west to where the avenue dead-ends at Kyū-gō Gairo, also called Higashi-dōri. You can see the 52-story Shinjuku Sumitomo Building, ahead of you to the right, and to the left the unmistakable shape of the Tōkyō Metropolitan Government Office complex—but you need to make a slight detour to reach it. Cross Kyū-gō Gairo, turn left, and walk south past the front of the Keiō Plaza Inter-Continental, the first of the high-rise hotels to be built in the area, to the next corner.

Across the street you can see the blue phallic shape of the sculpture in front of the Shinjuku Monolith Building. Turn right and walk downhill on Fureai-dōri. In the middle of this next block, on the left, is the Shinjuku NS Building. Opposite the NS Building, to the right, are the steps to the Citizens' Plaza of the adored and reviled **Tōkyō Metropolitan Government Office ②**.

From here you have two options. You can turn east and walk along any of the streets parallel to Chūō-dōri that lead back to Shinjuku Station. You may want to stop (especially if you haven't included Akihabara on your Tōkyō itinerary) at one of the giant discount electronics stores in the area—Yodobashi and Doi are a block from the station—to get an eye- or bagful of the latest gadgets that Japan is churning out.

Or if you have energy to spare, leave the Tōkyō Metropolitan Government Office complex the way you came in, turn right, and walk west to Kōen-dōri, which runs along the east side of Shinjuku Chūō Kōen. Cross Kōen-dōri, turn left, and walk south about five minutes, past the end of the park (avoiding the expressway on-ramp), to the **Shinjuku Park Tower Building ③**, at the corner of Kōshū Kaidō (Kōshū Highway). The Park Hyatt, on the topmost floors of this building, is a good place to stop for lunch or high tea.

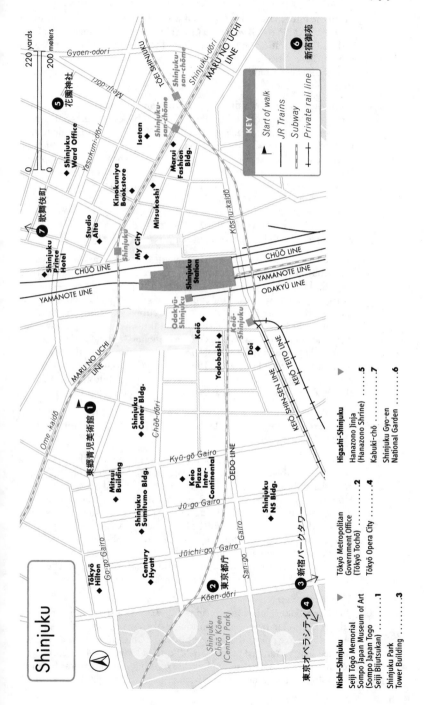

Shinjuku

220 yards
200 meters

Gyoen-odori

新宿御苑 **6**

KEY
- ▶ Start of walk
- JR Trains
- Subway
- Private rail line

花園神社 **5**

Shinjuku Ward Office ◆

Yasukuni-dōri

Isetan ◆

Shinjuku-san-chōme

TŌEI SHINJUKU

MARU NO UCHI LINE

Shinjuku-dōri

Shinjuku-san-chōme

Meiji-dōri

Marui Fashion Bldg. ◆

Kinokuniya Bookstore ◆

Mitsukoshi ◆

歌舞伎町 **7**

Studio Alta ◆

My City ◆

Shinjuku Prince Hotel ◆

CHŪŌ LINE

Shinjuku

Shinjuku Station

Kōshū-kaidō

CHŪŌ LINE

YAMANOTE LINE

ODAKYŪ LINE

YAMANOTE LINE

Odakyū-Shinjuku

Keiō ◆

Keiō-Shinjuku

Doi ◆

Yodobashi ◆

KEIŌ SHIN-SEN LINE

KEIŌ TEITO LINE

MARU NO UCHI LINE

東郷青児美術館 **1**

Ome-kaidō

Shinjuku Center Bldg. ◆

Mitsui Building ◆

Chūō-dōri

Kyū-gō Gairo

Keio Plaza Inter-Continental ◆

Shinjuku Sumitomo Bldg. ◆

Jū-go Gairo

ŌEDO LINE

Shinjuku N5 Bldg. ◆

Tōkyō Hilton ◆

Go-go Gairo

Century Hyatt ◆

Jūichi-go Gairo

San-gō Gairo

東京都庁 **2**

Kōen-dōri

新宿オペラシティ **4**

東京パークタワー **3**

Shinjuku Chūō Kōen (Central Park)

Nishi-Shinjuku
Seiji Tōgō Memorial
Sompo Japan Museum of Art
(Sompo Japan Togo
Seiji Bijutsukan) **1**

Shinjuku Park
Tower Building **3**

▶ Tōkyō Metropolitan
Government Office
(Tōkyō Tochō) **2**

Tōkyō Opera City **4**

Higashi-Shinjuku
Hanazono Jinja
(Hanazono Shrine) **5**

Kabuki-chō **7**

Shinjuku Gyo-en
National Garden **6**

From the intersection turn right and walk about five minutes southwest on Kōshū Kaidō to **Tōkyō Opera City** ❹. There's an entrance to the Hatsudai subway station on the west side of the courtyard. Stop in at Tōkyō Opera City to see the architecture of the performance spaces of the New National Theater, and then ride the Keiō Shin-sen Line one stop back to Shinjuku Station.

HIGASHI-
SHINJUKU From the east exit of Shinjuku Station, you can't miss the huge video screen on the facade of Studio Alta. Under this building begins Subnade—the most extensive underground arcade in Tōkyō, full of shops and restaurants. Studio Alta is at the northwest end of Shinjuku-dōri, which on Sunday, when the area is closed to traffic, becomes a sea of shoppers. Turn right, and as you walk southeast, Kinokuniya Bookstore looms up on your left; the sixth floor is devoted to foreign-language books, including some 40,000 titles in English. On the next block, on the same side of the street, is Isetan department store, with a foreign customer-service counter on the fifth floor. Mitsukoshi department store and the Marui Fashion Building are on the opposite side of Shinjuk-dōri.

At the Isetan corner, turn left onto Meiji-dōri and walk north. Cross Yasukuni-dōri and walk for another minute until you reach **Hanazono Jinja** ❺. From here you can head in two different directions—indeed, to two different worlds. You can retrace your steps to Isetan department store and the Shinjuku-san-chōme subway station, and take the Marunouchi Line one stop east to Shinjuku-Gyo-en-mae, a few steps from the north end of **Shinjuku Gyo-en National Garden** ❻. Visit the gardens and take the subway back to Shinjuku Station. Another option is to walk back from Hanazono Jinja as far as Yasukuni-dōri and take a right. Two blocks farther is the south end of rough-and-tumble **Kabuki-chō** ❼. From here you can easily return to Shinjuku Station on foot.

If you'd like to finish the day with a kaiseki or *bentō* (box) meal, head for **Yaozen** (八百膳), on the 14th floor of Takashimaya Times Square (5–24–2 Sendagaya).

TIMING Plan at least a full day for Shinjuku if you want to see both the east and west sides. Subway rides can save you time and energy on the longer versions of these walks, but walking distances are still considerable. The Shinjuku Gyo-en National Garden is worth at least an hour, especially if you come in early April, during *sakura* (cherry blossom) season. The Tōkyō Metropolitan Government Office complex can take longer than you might expect; lines for the elevators to the observation decks are often excruciatingly long. Sunday, when shopping streets are closed to traffic, is the best time to tramp around Higashi-Shinjuku. The rainy season in late June and the sweltering heat of August are best avoided.

What to See

❺ **Hanazono Jinja** (Hanazono Shrine, 花園神社). Constructed in the early Edo period, Hanazono is not among Tōkyō's most imposing shrines, but it does have one of the longest histories. Chief among the deities enshrined here is Yamato-takeru-no-Mikoto, a legendary 4th-century imperial prince, whose heroic exploits are recounted in the earliest Japanese mythologies. His fame rests on the conquest of aboriginal tribes, which he did at the bidding of the Yamato Court. When he died, legends say, his soul took the form of a swan and flew away. Prayers offered here are believed to bring prosperity in business. The shrine is a five-minute walk north on Meiji-dōri from the Shinjuku-san-chōme subway station. The block just to the west (5-chōme 1) has the last embattled remaining bars of the "Golden-Gai": a district of tiny, unpretentious, even seedy, nomiya that in the '60s and '70s commanded the fierce loyalty of fiction writers, artists, freelance journalists, and expat Japanophiles—the city's hard-core outsiders. ⊠ *5–17–3 Shinjuku, Shinjuku-ku* ☎ *03/3209–5265* 🎫 *Free* ☉ *Daily sunrise–sunset* Ⓜ *Marunouchi subway line, Shinjuku-san-chōme Station (Exits B2 and B3).*

❼ **Kabuki-chō** (歌舞伎町). In 1872 the Tokugawa-period formalities governing geisha entertainment were dissolved, and Kabuki-chō became Japan's largest center of prostitution. Later, when vice laws got stricter, prostitution just went a bit deeper underground, where it remains—deeply deplored and widely tolerated.

In an attempt to change the area's image after World War II, plans were made to replace Ginza's fire-gutted Kabuki-za with a new one in Shinjuku. The plans were never realized, however, as the old theater was rebuilt. But the project gave the area its present name. Kabuki-chō's own multipurpose theater is the 2,000-seat **Koma Gekijō** (コマ劇場), ⊠ 1–19–1 Kabuki-chō, Shinjuku-ku ☎ 03/3200–2213). The building, which also houses several discos and bars, is a central landmark for the quarter.

Kabuki-chō means unrefined nightlife at its best and raunchy seediness at its worst. Neon signs flash; shills proclaim the pleasures of the places you particularly want to shun. Even when a place looks respectable, ask about prices first: *bottakuri*—overcharging for food and drink—is the regional sport here, and watered-down drinks can set you back ¥5,000 or more in a hostess club. Avoid the cheap nomiya under the railway tracks; chances are there's a client in at least one of them looking for a fight. All that said, you needn't be intimidated by the area: use your streetsmarts, and it *can* be fun. ⊠ *Shinjuku-ku* Ⓜ *JR (Higashi-guchi/East Exit) and Marunouchi subway line (Exits B10, B11, B12, and B13), Shinjuku Station.*

▶ ❶ **Seiji Tōgō Memorial Sompo Japan Museum of Art** (Sompo Japan Togo Seiji Bijutsukan, 東郷青児美術館). The painter Seiji Tōgō (1897–1978) was a master of putting on canvas the grace and charm of young maidens. More than 100 of his works from the museum collection are on display here at any given time, along with other Japanese and Western artists. The museum also houses Van Gogh's *Sunflowers*. Yasuda Fire & Marine Insurance Company CEO Yasuo Gotō acquired the painting in 1987 for ¥5.3 billion—at the time the highest price ever paid at auction for a work of art. He later created considerable stir in the media with the ill-considered remark that he'd like the painting cremated with him when he died. The gallery has an especially good view of the old part of Shinjuku. ⊠ *Yasuda Fire and Marine Insurance Bldg., 42nd fl., 1–26–1 Nishi-Shinjuku, Shinjuku-ku* ☎ *03/5777–8600* ⊕ *www.sompo-japan. co.jp/museum/english/index.html* 🎫 *¥500; additional fees for special exhibits* ☉ *Tues.–Sun. 10–6* Ⓜ *Marunouchi and Shinjuku subway lines,*

JR, and Keiō Shin-sen and Teitō private rail lines; Shinjuku Station (Exit A18 for subway lines, Nishi-guchi/West Exit or Exit N4 from the underground passageway for all others).

★ ❻ **Shinjuku Gyo-en National Garden** (新宿御苑). This lovely 150-acre park was once the estate of the powerful Naitō family of feudal lords, who were among the most trusted retainers of the Tokugawa shōguns. In 1871, after the Meiji Restoration, the family gave the grounds to the government, which—not quite ready yet to put such gems at the disposal of ordinary people—made it an imperial property. After World War II, the grounds were finally opened to the public. It's a perfect place for leisurely walks: paths wind past ponds and bridges, artificial hills, thoughtfully placed stone lanterns, and more than 3,000 kinds of plants, shrubs, and trees. There are different gardens in Japanese, French, and English styles, as well as a greenhouse (the nation's first, built in 1885) filled with tropical plants. The best times to visit are April, when 75 different species of cherry trees—some 1,500 trees in all—are in bloom, and the first two weeks of November, during the chrysanthemum exhibition. ✉ *11 Naitō-chō, Shinjuku-ku* ☎ *03/3350–0151* 💴 *¥200* 🕙 *Tues.–Sun. 9–4; also open Mon. 9–4 in cherry-blossom season (Mar. 25–Apr. 24) and for chrysanthemum show (Nov. 1–15)* Ⓜ *Marunouchi subway line, Shinjuku Gyo-en-mae Station (Exit 1).*

❸ **Shinjuku Park Tower Building** (新宿パークタワー). The Shinjuku Park Tower has in some ways the most arrogant, hard-edged design of any of the skyscrapers in Nishi-Shinjuku, but it does provide any number of opportunities to rest and take on fuel. Some days there are free chamber-music concerts in the atrium. **Kushinobo** (串の坊, ☎ 03/5322–6400), on the lower level, serves delicately deep-fried bamboo skewers of fish and vegetables for lunch. In the afternoon, you can ride up to the skylighted bamboo garden of the Peak Lounge on the 41st floor of the **Park Hyatt Hotel** (パークハイアット東京, ☎ 03/5322–1234) for high tea and a spectacular view of the city. The **Cafe Excelsior** (エクセルシオール カフェ, ☎ 03/5323–3936) is a nice place to stop in for a drink in the evening. ✉ *3–7–1 Nishi-Shinjuku, Shinjuku-ku* Ⓜ *JR Shinjuku Station (Nishi-guchi/West Exit).*

★ ❷ **Tōkyō Metropolitan Government Office** (Tōkyō Tochō, 東京都庁). Dominating the western Shinjuku skyline and built at a cost of ¥157 billion, Kenzō Tange's grandiose city hall complex is clearly meant to remind observers that Tōkyō's annual budget is bigger than that of the average developing country. The late-20th-century complex consists of a main office building, an annex, the Metropolitan Assembly building, and a huge central courtyard, often the venue of open-air concerts and exhibitions. The design has inspired a passionate controversy: Tōkyōites either love it or hate it. The main building soars 48 stories, splitting on the 33rd floor into two towers. On a clear day, from the observation decks on the 45th floors of both towers, you can see all the way to Mt. Fuji and to the Bōsō Peninsula in Chiba Prefecture. Several other skyscrapers in the area have free observation floors—among them the Shinjuku Center Building, the Shinjuku Nomura Building, and the Shinjuku Sumitomo Building—but city hall is the best of the lot. The Metropolitan Government Web site, incidentally, is an excellent source of information on sightseeing and current events in Tōkyō. ✉ *2–8–1 Nishi-Shinjuku, Shinjuku-ku* ☎ *03/5321–1111* ⊕ *www.metro.tokyo.jp* 🎫 *Free* 🕐 *North observation deck daily 9:30–10:30; south observation deck daily 9:30–5:30* Ⓜ *Marunouchi and Shinjuku subway lines, JR, Keiō Shin-sen and Teitō private rail lines; Shinjuku Station (Nishi-guchi/West Exit).*

❹ **Tōkyō Opera City** (東京オペラシティ). Completed in 1997, this is certain to be the last major cultural project in Tōkyō for the foreseeable future. The west side of the complex is the New National Theater (Shin Koku-ritsu Gekijō), consisting of the 1,810-seat Opera House, the 1,038-seat Playhouse, and an intimate performance space called the Pit, with seating for 468. Architect Helmut Jacoby's design for this building, with its reflecting pools and galleries and granite planes of wall, deserves real plaudits: the New National Theater is monumental and approachable at the same time.

The east side of the complex consists of a 54-story office tower—an uninspired atrium-style slab, forgettable in almost every respect—flanked by a sunken garden and art museum on one side and a concert hall on the other. The museum focuses rather narrowly on post–World War II Japanese abstract painting. The 1632-seat concert hall is arguably the most impressive classical-music venue in Tōkyō, with tiers of polished-oak panels, and excellent acoustics despite the venue's daring vertical design. ✉ *3–20–2 Nishi-Shinjuku, Shinjuku-ku* ☎ *03/5353–0700 concert hall, 03/5351–3011 New National Theater* ⊕ *www.operacity.jp* Ⓜ *Keiō Shin-sen private rail line, Hatsudai Station (Higashi-guchi/East Exit).*

ELSEWHERE IN TŌKYŌ

The sheer size of the city and the diversity of its institutions make it impossible to fit all of Tōkyō's interesting sights into neighborhoods and walking tours. Plenty of worthy places—from Tōkyō Disneyland to sumō stables to the old Ōji district—fall outside the city's neighborhood repertoire. Yet no guide to Tōkyō would be complete without them. The sights below are marked on the Tōkyō Overview map at the beginning of this chapter.

Amusement Centers

🕐 **Kasai Seaside Park** (葛西臨海公園). With two artificial beaches, a bird sanctuary, and the ⇨ **Tōkyō Sea Life Park** aquarium spread over a stretch of landfill between the Arakawa and the Kyū-Edogawa rivers, Kasai Seaside Park is one of the major landmarks in the vast effort to transform Tōkyō Bay into Fun City. The **Great Ferris Wheel of Diamonds and Flowers** (Daia to Hana no Dai-kanransha), the tallest Ferris wheel in Japan, takes passengers on a 17-minute ride to the apex, 384 feet above the ground, for a spectacular view of the city. On a clear day you can see all the way to Mt. Fuji; at night, if you're lucky, you reach the top just in time for a bird's-eye view of the fireworks over the Magic Kingdom, across the river. To get here, take the JR Keiyō Line local train from Tōkyō Station to Kasai Rinkai Kōen Station; the park is a five-minute walk from the south exit. ⊠ *Rinkai-chō, Edogawa-ku* ☎ *03/3686–6911* 🎫 *Free, Ferris wheel ¥700* 🕙 *Ferris wheel Sept.–July, Tues.–Fri. 10–8, weekends 10–9; Aug., weekdays 10–8, weekends 10–9.*

🌀 **Kōrakuen** (後楽園遊園地). The Kōrakuen stop on the Marunouchi subway line, about 10 minutes from Tōkyō Station, lets you out in front of the **Tōkyō Dome,** Japan's first air-supported indoor stadium, built in 1988 and home to the Tōkyō Giants baseball team. Across the Tōkyō Expressway from the stadium is **LaQua,** formerly the Kōrakuen Amusement Park. It's chiefly noted for its stomach-churning Thunder Dolphin giant roller coaster, which runs at one point straight through what the management touts as the world's first centerless Ferris wheel. ⊠ *1–3–61 Kōraku, Bunkyō-ku* ☎ *03/5800–9999* 🎫 *LaQua: ¥4,000 for full day, ¥3,000 after 5 PM* 🕙 *LaQua daily 10–10.*

🌀 **Tōkyō Disneyland** (東京デイズニーランド). At Tōkyō Disneyland, Mickey-san and his coterie of Disney characters entertain just the way they do in the California and Florida Disney parks. When the park was built in 1983 it was much smaller than its counterparts in the United States, but the construction in 2001 of the adjacent DisneySea, with its seven "Ports of Call" with different nautical themes and rides, added more than 100 acres to this multifaceted Magic Kingdom.

There are several types of admission tickets. Most people buy the One-Day Passport, at ¥5,500 for adults, which gives you unlimited access to the attractions and shows at one or the other of the two parks; also available are a weekday after–6 PM pass, at ¥2,900, and a weekend (and national holiday) after–3 PM pass, at ¥4,500. There's also a two-day pass, good for both parks, for ¥9,800. You can buy tickets in advance in Tōkyō Station, near the Yaesu North Exit—look for red-jacketed attendants standing outside the booth—or from any travel agent, such as the Japan Travel Bureau.

The simplest way to get to Disneyland is by JR Keiyō Line from Tōkyō Station to Maihama; the park is just a few steps from the station exit. From Nihombashi you can also take the Tōzai subway line to Urayasu and walk over to the Tōkyō Disneyland Bus Terminal for the 25-minute ride, which costs ¥230. ⊠ *1–1 Maihama, Urayasu-shi* ☎ *045/683–3333* ⊕ *www.tokyodisneyresort.co.jp* 🕙 *Daily 9–10; seasonal closings in Dec. and Jan. may vary, so check before you go.*

🌀 **Tōkyō Tower** (東京タワー). In 1958 Tōkyō's fledgling TV networks needed a tall antenna array to transmit signals. Trying to emerge from the devastation of World War II, the nation's capital was also hungry for a landmark—a symbol for the aspirations of a city still without a skyline. The result was the 1,093-foot-high Tōkyō Tower: an unabashed (though taller) knockoff of Paris's Eiffel Tower. The Grand Observation Platform, at an elevation of 492 feet, and the Special Observation Platform, at an elevation of 820 feet, quickly became major tourist attractions; they still draw some 3 million visitors a year, the vast majority of them Japanese youngsters on their first trip to the big city. A modest aquarium and a wax museum round out the tower's appeal as an amusement complex. The tower does provide a spectacular view of the city, and it gives

Godzilla something to demolish periodically. This is a good diversion for kids, but get here soon: the antennas were originally built for analog broadcasting, and with Japan set to convert entirely to digital communications by 2010, a real demolition is already on the planning board. ⊠ *4–2–8 Shiba-Kōen, Minato-ku* ☎ *03/3433–5111* ✆ *¥820 for Grand Observation Platform, ¥600 extra for Special Observation Platform; aquarium ¥1,000; wax museum ¥870* ◷ *Tower, daily 9–10. Wax museum, daily 10–9. Aquarium, Sept.–July, daily 10–7; Aug., daily 10–8* Ⓜ *Hibiya subway line, Kamiyachō Station (Exit 2).*

◷ **Toshima-en** (としまえん). This large, well-equipped amusement park in the northwestern part of Tōkyō has four roller coasters, a haunted house, and seven swimming pools. What makes it special is the authentic Coney Island carousel—left to rot in a New York warehouse, discovered and rescued by a Japanese entrepreneur, and lovingly restored down to the last gilded curlicue on the last prancing unicorn. From Shinjuku, the Ōedo subway line goes directly to the park. ⊠ *3–25–1 Koyama, Nerima-ku* ☎ *03/3990–3131* ✆ *Day pass ¥3,800* ◷ *Thurs.–Mon. 10–6.*

Zoo & Aquariums

◷ **Shinagawa Aquarium** (Shinagawa Suizokukan, しながわ水族館). The fun part of this aquarium in southwestern Tōkyō is walking through an underwater glass tunnel while some 450 species of fish swim around and above you. There are no pamphlets or explanation panels in English, however. Avoid Sunday, when the dolphin and sea lion shows draw crowds in impossible numbers. Take the local Keihin-Kyūkō private rail line from Shinagawa to Ōmori-kaigan Station. Turn left as you exit the station and follow the ceramic fish on the sidewalk to the first traffic light; then turn right. You can also take the JR Tōkaidō Line to Oimachi Station; board a free shuttle to the aquarium from the No. 6 platform at the bus terminal just outside Oimachi Station. ⊠ *3–2–1 Katsushima, Shinagawa-ku* ☎ *03/3762–3433* ✆ *¥1,100* ◷ *Wed.–Mon. 10–4:30; dolphin and sea lion shows 3 times daily, on varying schedule.*

◷ **Sunshine International Aquarium** (サンシャイン国際水族館). The Sunshine International Aquarium has some 750 kinds of sea creatures on display, plus sea lion performances four times a day (except when it rains). An English-language pamphlet is available, and most of the exhibits have some English explanation. Take the JR Yamanote Line to Ikebukuro Station (Exit 35) and walk about eight minutes west to the Sunshine City complex. You can also take the Yūraku-chō subway to Higashi-Ikebukuro Station (Exit 2); Sunshine City and the aquarium are about a three-minute walk north. ⊠ *3–1–3 Higashi-Ikebukuro, Toshima-ku* ☎ *03/3989–3331* ✆ *¥1,600* ◷ *Weekdays 10–6, weekends 10–6:30.*

◷ **Tama Zoo** (Tama Dōbutsu Kōen, 多摩動物公園). More a wildlife park than a zoo, this facility in western Tōkyō gives animals room to roam; moats typically separate them from you. You can ride through the Lion Park in a minibus. To get here, take a Keiō Line train toward Takao from Shinjuku Station and transfer at Takahata-Fudō Station for the one-stop branch line that serves the park. ⊠ *7–1–1 Hodokubo, Hino-shi* ☎ *0425/91–1611* ✆ *¥600* ◷ *Thurs.–Tues. 9:30–4.*

Ⓒ **Tōkyō Sea Life Park** (葛西臨海水族園). The three-story cylindrical complex of this aquarium houses more than 540 species of fish and other sea creatures within three different areas: "Voyagers of the Sea" ("Maguro no Kaiyū"), with migratory species; "Seas of the World" ("Sekai no Umi"), with species from foreign waters; and the "Sea of Tōkyō" ("Tōkyō no Umi"), devoted to the creatures of the bay and nearby waters. To get here, take the JR Keiyō Line local train from Tōkyō Station to Kasai Rinkai Kōen Station; the aquarium is a 10-minute walk or so from the south exit. ✉ *6–2–3 Rinkai-chō, Edogawa-ku* ☎ *03/3869–5152* 🎫*¥700* ⊙ *Thurs.–Tues. 9:30–5.*

Off the Beaten Path

Asakura Sculpture Gallery (朝倉彫刻館). Outsiders have long since discovered the Nezu and Yanaka areas of Shitamachi—much to the dismay of the handful of foreigners who have lived for years in this charming, inexpensive section of the city. Part of the areas' appeals lie in the fact that some of the giants of modern Japanese culture lived and died here, including novelists Ōgai Mori, Sōseki Natsume, and Ryūnosuke Akutagawa; scholar Tenshin Okakura, who founded the Japan Art Institute; painter Taikan Yokoyama; and sculptors Kōun Takamura and Fumio Asakura. If there's one single attraction here, it's probably Asakura's home and studio, which was converted into a gallery after his death in 1964 and now houses many of his most famous pieces. The tearoom on the opposite side of the courtyard is a quiet place from which to contemplate his garden.

From the north wicket (Nishi-guchi/West Exit) of JR Nippori Station, walk west—Tennō-ji temple will be on the left side of the street—until you reach a police box. Turn right, then right again at the end of the street. The museum is a three-story black building on the right, a few hundred yards from the corner. ✉ *7–18–10 Yanaka, Taitō-ku* ☎ *03/ 3821–4549* 🎫 *¥400* ⊙ *Tues.–Thurs. and weekends 9:30–4:30.*

Odaiba (お台場). Tōkyō's "offshore" leisure and commercial-development complex rises on more than 1,000 acres of landfill, connected to the city by the Yurikamome monorail from Shimbashi. People come here for the arcades, shopping malls, and museums, as well as the city's longest (albeit artificial) stretch of sand beach, along the boat harbor. There's also a Ferris wheel—a neon phantasmagoric beacon for anyone driving into the city across the Rainbow Bridge. With hotels and apartment buildings as well, this is arguably the most successful of the megaprojects on Tōkyō Bay.

From Shimbashi Station (JR, Karasumori Exit; Asakusa subway line, Exit A2; Ginza subway line, Exit 4) follow the blue seagull signs to the monorail. You can pick up a map of Odaiba in English at the entrance. The Yurikamome Line makes 10 stops between Shimbashi and the terminus at Ariake; fares range from ¥310 to ¥370, but the best strategy is to buy a ¥1,000 prepaid card that allows you to make multiple stops at different points in Odaiba. The monorail runs every three to five minutes from 5:46 AM to 11:56 AM.

The first monorail stop on the island is **Odaiba Kaihin Kōen** (お台場海浜公園), the closest point to the beach and the site of two massive shopping complexes. Aqua City has four floors of boutiques, movie theaters, cafés, and eateries—including a Starbucks and Hanashibe, an excellent sake-brewery restaurant on the third level. Overlooking the harbor is Decks Tōkyō Beach, a five-story complex of shops, restaurants, and boardwalks in two connected malls. Daiba Little Hong Kong, on the sixth and seventh floors of the Island Mall, has a collection of Cantonese restaurants and dim sum joints on neon-lit "streets" designed to evoke the real Hong Kong. At the Seaside Mall, a table by the window in any of the restaurants affords a delightful view of the harbor, especially at sunset, when the yakata-bune drift down the Sumida-gawa from Yanagibashi and Ryōgoku.

Architecture buffs should make time for Daiba, the second stop on the monorail, if only to contemplate the futuristic **Fuji Television Nippon Broadcasting Building** (フジテレビ, ✉ 2–4–8 Daiba, Minato-ku ☎ 03/5500–8888 💳 ¥500 🕐 Tues.–Sun. 10–8). From its fifth-floor Studio Promenade, you can watch programs being produced. The observation deck on the 25th floor affords a spectacular view of the bay and the graceful curve of the Rainbow Bridge.

The third stop on the monorail from Shimbashi is the **Museum of Maritime Science** (Fune-no-Kagakukan, 船の科学館; ✉ 3–1 Higashi-Yashio, Shinagawa-ku ☎ 03/5500–1111 💳 ¥1,000 🕐 Weekdays 10–5, weekends 10–6), which houses an impressive collection of models and displays on the history of Japanese shipbuilding and navigation. Built in the shape of an ocean liner, the museum is huge; if you're interested in ships, plan at least an hour here to do it justice. There are no English-language explanations at the museum. Anchored alongside the museum are the ferry *Yōtei-maru*, which for some 30 years plied the narrow straits between Aomori and Hokkaidō, and the icebreaker *Sōya-maru,* the first Japanese ship to cross the Arctic Circle.

The fun part of the **National Museum of Emerging Science and Innovation** (Nihon Gagaku Miraikan, 日本科学未来館; ✉ 2–41 Aomi, Kōtō-ku ☎ 03/3570–9151 💳 ¥500 🕐 Mon. and Wed.–Sat. 10–7, Sun. 10–5), the third stop on the monorail from Shimbashi, is on the third floor, where you can watch robots in action, write with light pens, and play with various things that move. The rest of the museum is what the Japanese call *ō-majime* (deeply sincere)—five floors of thematic displays on environment-friendly technologies, life sciences, and the like with high seriousness and not much fun. The director of this facility, Dr. Mamoru Mohri, was Japan's first astronaut, who in 1992 logged some 460 hours in space aboard the NASA Spacelab-J Endeavor. Some of the exhibits have English-language explanations. It's a short walk here from the Museum of Maritime Science.

A two-minute walk south from the fourth stop on the monorail, at Telecom Center, brings you to **Odaiba's Hot Spring Theme Park** (Ōedo Onsen Monogatari, 大江戸温泉物語); ✉ 2–57 Ōmi, Kōtō-ku ☎ 03/5500–1126 💳 ¥2,700; ¥1,500 surcharge for entrance after midnight). Once upon a time, when bathtubs in private homes were a rarity, the great defining social institution of Japanese urban life was the *sento*: the local public bath. At the end of a hard day of work, there was no pleasure like sinking to your neck in hot water with your friends and neighbors, soaking your cares away, and sitting around afterward for beer and gossip. And if the sento was also an *onsen*—a thermal spring—with waters drawn from some mineral-rich underground supply, the delight was even greater. No more than a handful of such places survives in Tōkyō, but the Ōedo Onsen managed to tap a source some 4,600 feet below the bay, and parlayed this into a tourist attraction that should not be missed.

At the entrance, designed to evoke an Edo-era gate, remove your shoes and store them in a locker. Attendants in period wigs and *hakama* (culottes) guide you to a dressing room, where you exchange your street clothes for a yukata, which you can wear for the rest of your stay in the park. Choose from several indoor and outdoor pools, with different temperatures and motifs—but remember that you must soap up and rinse off before you enter any of them. Follow up with a massage and a stroll through the food court—modeled on a street in Yoshiwara, the licensed red-light district of the Edo period—for sushi or noodles. On any given day, Ōedo Onsen draws 2,000 to 4,000 visitors; getting naked with strangers may be daunting at first, but the baths are gender-segregated, and hygiene is absolutely no problem. The park is open daily from 11 AM to 9 AM; the front desk closes at 2 AM. Charges include the rental of a yukata and a towel.

The fifth stop on the monorail circuit of Odaiba is Aomi, gateway to the **Palette Town** complex of malls and amusements at the east end of the island. The uncontested landmark here is the the 377-foot-high Ferris wheel, modeled after the London Eye, the biggest in the world; it's open daily 10–10 and costs ¥900. Adjacent to the Ferris wheel is Mega Web, ostensibly a complex of rides and multimedia amusements but in fact a showcase for the Toyota Motor Corporation. You can ride a car (hands off—the ride is electronically controlled) over a 1-km (½-mi) course configured like a roller coaster but moving at a stately pace. You can have any car you want, of course, as long as it's a Toyota. The shopping mall **Venus Fort** (ビーナスフォート, ⊠ Palette Town 1-chōme, Aomi, Kōtō-ku ☎ 03/3599–0700) at Aomi consists of galleries designed to suggest an Italian Renaissance palazzo, with arches and cupolas, marble fountains and statuary, and painted vault ceilings. The mall is chockfull of boutiques by the likes of Jean Paul Gaultier, Calvin Klein, Ralph Lauren, and all the other usual suspects.

Roppongi Hills (六本木ヒルズ). During the last quarter of the 20th century, Roppongi was a better-heeled, better-behaved version of Shinjuku or Shibuya, without the shopping: not much happening by day, but by night an irresistible draw for young clubbers with foreign sports cars and wads of disposable income. In 2003, Mori Building Company—Japan's biggest commercial landlord—transformed this area and created Roppongi Hills, a complex of shops, restaurants, residential and commercial towers, a nine-screen cineplex, a luxury hotel, and a major art museum, wrapped around the TV Asahi studios and sprawled out in five zones from the Roppongi intersection to Azabu-jūban. To navigate this minicity, you need a 12-page floor guide with color-coded maps; luckily, the guide is available in English, and most of the staff members at the omnipresent information counters speak a modicum of English as well. At the center of Roppongi Hills is the 54-story (**Mori Tower** 森タワー, ☎ 03/5777–8600 ✉ Museum and observation promenade ¥1,800 weekdays, ¥2,000 weekends ☉ Mon., Wed., and Thurs. 10–10; Fri.–Sun. 10–5). On a clear day, from the Tokyo City View observation promenade on the 52nd floor, you can see Mt. Fuji in the distance, and by night the panoramic view of the city is spectacular. The promenade encircles three of the nine galleries of the Mori Art Museum, which showcases contemporary art in several different media. You enter the six main galleries, where the major exhibitions are mounted, from the floor above. The Mori is well-designed, intelligently curated, and hospitable to big crowds. ✉ *6–10–1 Roppongi, Minato-ku* ⊕ *www.roppongihills.com* Ⓜ *Hibiya subway line, Roppongi Station (Exit C-1).*

Fodor's Choice ★ **Ryōgoku** (両国). Two things make this working-class Shitamachi neighborhood worth a special trip: this is the center of the world of sumō wrestling as well as the site of the extraordinary Edo-Tōkyō Museum. Five minutes from Akihabara on the JR Sōbu Line, Ryōgoku is easy to get to, and if you've budgeted a leisurely stay in the city, it's well worth a morning's expedition.

The **Edo-Tōkyō Museum** (江戸東京博物館, ✉ 1–4–1 Yokoami, Sumida-ku ☎ 03/3626–9974 ⊕ www.edo-tokyo-museum.or.jp ✉ ¥600; additional fees for special exhibits ☉ Tues., Wed., and weekends 9:30–5; Thurs. and Fri. 9:30–8; closed Tues. when Mon. is a national holiday) opened in 1993, more or less coinciding with the collapse of the economic bubble that had made the project possible. Money was no object in those days; much of the large museum site is open plaza—an unthinkably lavish use of space. From the plaza the museum rises on massive pillars to the permanent exhibit areas on the fifth and sixth floors. The escalator takes you directly to the sixth floor—and back in time 300 years. You cross a replica of the Edo-period Nihombashi Bridge into a truly remarkable collection of dioramas, scale models, cutaway rooms, and even whole buildings: an intimate and convincing experience of everyday life in the capital of the Tokugawa shōguns. Equally elaborate are the fifth-floor re-creations of early modern Tōkyō, the "enlightenment" of Japan's headlong embrace of the West, and the twin devastations of the Great Kantō Earthquake and World War II. If you only visit one nonart museum in Tōkyō, make this it.

To get to the museum, leave Ryōgoku Station by the west exit, immediately turn right, and follow the signs. The moving sidewalk and the stairs bring you to the plaza on the third level; to request an English-speaking volunteer guide, use the entrance to the left of the stairs instead, and ask at the General Information counter in front of the first-floor Special Exhibition Gallery.

Walk straight out to the main street in front of the west exit of Ryōgoku station, turn right, and you come almost at once to the Kokugikan (National Sumō Arena), with its distinctive copper-green roof. If you can't attend one of the Tōkyō sumō tournaments, you may want to at least pay a short visit to the **Sumō Museum** (相撲博物館, ✉ 1-3-28 Yokoami,

Sumida-ku ☎ 03/3622–0366 📧 Free 🕐 Weekdays 10–4:30), in the south wing of the arena. There are no explanations in English, but the museum's collection of sumō-related wood-block prints, paintings, and illustrated scrolls includes some outstanding examples of traditional Japanese fine art.

Sumō wrestlers are not free agents; they must belong to one or another of the **sumo stables** officially recognized by the Sumō Association. Although the tournaments and exhibition matches take place in different parts of the country at different times, all the stables—now some 30 in number—are in Tōkyō, most of them concentrated on both sides of the Sumida-gawa near the Kokugikan. Wander this area when the wrestlers are in town (January, May, and September are your best bets) and you're more than likely to see some of them on the streets, in their wood clogs and kimonos. Come 7 AM–11 AM, and you can peer through the doors and windows of the stables to watch them in practice sessions. One of the easiest to find is the **Tatsunami Stable** (立浪部屋, 3–26–2 Ryōgoku), only a few steps from the west end of Ryōgoku Station (turn left when you go through the turnstile and left again as you come out on the street; then walk along the station building to the second street on the right). Another, a few blocks farther south, where the Shuto Expressway passes overhead, is the **Izutsu Stable** (井筒部屋, 2–2–7 Ryōgoku).

★ **Sengaku-ji** (Sengaku Temple, 泉岳寺). One day in the year 1701, a young provincial baron named Asano Takumi-no-Kami, serving an official term of duty at the shōgun's court, attacked and seriously wounded a courtier named Yoshinaka Kira. Kira had demanded the usual tokens of esteem that someone in his high position would expect for his goodwill; Asano refused, and Kira humiliated him in public to the point that he could no longer contain his rage.

Kira survived the attack. Asano, for daring to draw his sword in the confines of Edo Castle, was ordered to commit suicide. His family line was abolished and his fief confiscated. Headed by Kuranosuke Ōishi, the clan steward, 47 of Asano's loyal retainers vowed revenge. Kira was rich and well protected; Asano's retainers were *rōnin*—masterless samurai. It took them almost two years of planning, subterfuge, and hardship, but on the night of December 14, 1702, they stormed Kira's villa in Edo, cut off his head, and brought it in triumph to Asano's tomb at Sengaku-ji, the family temple. Ōishi and his followers were sentenced to commit suicide—which they accepted as the reward, not the price, of their honorable vendetta—and were buried in the temple graveyard with their lord.

The event captured the imagination of the Japanese like nothing else in their history. Through the centuries it has become the national epic, the last word on the subject of loyalty and sacrifice, celebrated in every medium from Kabuki to film. The temple still stands, and the graveyard is wreathed in smoke from the bundles of incense that visitors still lay reverently on the tombstones.

The story gets even better. There's a small museum on the temple grounds with a collection of weapons and other memorabilia of the event. One of these items dispels forever the myth of Japanese vagueness and indirection in the matter of contracts and formal documents. Kira's family, naturally, wanted to give him a proper burial, but the law insisted this could not be done without his head. They asked for it back, and Ōishi—mirror of chivalry that he was—agreed. He entrusted it to the temple, and the priests wrote him a receipt, which survives even now in the corner of a dusty glass case. "Item," it begins, "One head."

Take the Asakusa subway line to Sengaku-ji Station (Exit A2), turn right when you come to street level, and walk up the hill. The temple is past the first traffic light, on the left. ✉ *2–11–1 Takanawa, Minato-ku* ☎ *03/3441–5560* ✆ *Temple and grounds free, museum ¥200* ⊘ *Temple Apr.–Sept., daily 7–6; Oct.–Mar., daily 7–5. Museum daily 9–4.*

Sōgetsu School (Sōgetsu Kaikan, 草月会館). The schools of ikebana, like those of other traditional arts, from music and dance to calligraphy and tea ceremony, are highly stratified organizations. Students rise through levels of proficiency, paying handsomely for lessons and certifications as they go, until they can become teachers themselves. At the top of the hierarchy is the *iemoto,* the head of the school, a title usually held within a family for generations. The Sōgetsu School of flower arrangement is a relative newcomer to all this. It was founded by Sōfū Teshigahara in 1927, and, compared to the older schools, it espouses a style flamboyant, free-form, and even radical. Detractors call it overblown, but it draws students and admirers from the world over, and it has made itself wealthy in the process. Lessons in flower arrangement are given in English on Monday from 10 to noon. Reservations must be made a day in advance. The main hall of the Sōgetsu Kaikan, created by the late Isamu Noguchi, one of the masters of modern sculpture, is well worth a visit. Noguchi's moving composition of carved stone slabs, cantilevered walkways, and flowing water is typical of his later career and reflects the influence of Zen aesthetics. Sōgetsu Kaikan is a 10-minute walk west on Aoyama-dōri from the Akasaka-mitsuke intersection or east from the Aoyama-itchōme subway stop. ✉ *7–2–21 Akasaka, Minato-ku* ☎ *03/3408–1209* ✆ *¥4,850 for 1st lesson, ¥3,800 per lesson thereafter* Ⓜ *Ginza and Marunouchi subway lines, Akasaka-mitsuke Station; Ginza and Hanzō-mon subway lines, Aoyama-itchōme Station (Exit 4).*

Toden Arakawa Line (都電荒川線). Want to take a trip back in time? Take the JR Yamanote Line to Ōtsuka, cross the street in front of the station, and change to the Toden Arakawa Line—Tōkyō's last surviving trolley. Heading east, the trolley takes you through the back gardens of old neighborhoods on its way to Ōji—once the site of Japan's first Western-style paper mill, built in 1875 by Ōji Paper Company, the nation's oldest joint-stock company. The mill is long gone, but the memory lingers on at the **Asuka-yama Ōji Paper Museum** (紙の博物館). Some exhibits here show the process of milling paper from pulp. Others illustrate the astonishing variety of products that can be made from paper. The museum is a minute's walk from the trolley stop at Asuka-yama Kōen: you can also get here from the JR Ōji Station (Minami-guchi/South Exit) on the Keihin–Tōhoku Line, or the Nishigahara Station (Asuka-yama Exit) on the Namboku subway line. ✉ *1–1–3 Ōji, Kita-ku* ☎ *03/ 3916–2320* ✆ *¥300* ⊘ *Tues.–Sun. 10–4:30.*

WHERE TO EAT

2

BEST SUSHI BAR
Edo-Gin in Tsukuji ⇨ *p.101*

MOST CREATIVE WAYS TO PREPARE TOFU
Ume no Hama in Aoyama ⇨ *p.92*

FLASHIEST TRENDSETTER
Tableaux in Daikanyama ⇨ *p.94*

MOST MODEST NOODLE SHOP
Naokyu in Ginza ⇨ *p.95*

FRESH FROM THE FRYER
Tempura at Aoi-Marushin in Asakusa ⇨ *p.92*

THEATER IN THE ROUND
Inakaya in Roppongi ⇨ *p.100*

NOISIEST YAKITORI JOINT
Ganchan in Roppongi ⇨ *p.101*

BEST PLACE FOR SAKE TASTING
Sasashū in Ikebukuro ⇨ *p.95*

By Jared
Lubarsky

AT LAST COUNT there were more than 200,000 bars and restaurants in Tōkyō. Since the collapse of the bubble economy in the 1990s, you might expect people to be a bit more cautious with their disposable income, but Tōkyōites seem—on the surface, at least—undismayed. Megalithic development projects, like those in Shiodome, Roppongi, Odaiba, and Ebisu, continue to rise and vie amongst themselves for tenant lists of first-rate places to wine and dine. The high end of the market (especially in the "anchor" luxury hotels of these major developments) can be grotesquely expensive, but Tōkyō's myriad choices also include a fair number of bargains—good cooking of all sorts that you can enjoy even on a modest budget. Food and drink, even at street stalls, are safe wherever you go.

For an international city, Tōkyō is still stubbornly provincial in many ways. Whatever the rest of the world has pronounced good, however, eventually makes its way here: French, Italian, Chinese, Indian, Middle Eastern, Latin American. It's hard to think of a cuisine of any prominence that goes unrepresented, as Japanese chefs by the thousand go abroad, hone their craft, and bring it home.

Restaurants in Japan naturally expect most of their clients to be Japanese, and the Japanese are the world's champion modifiers. Only the most serious restaurateurs refrain from editing some of the authenticity out of foreign cuisines; in areas like Shibuya, Harajuku, and Shinjuku, all too many of the foreign restaurants cater to students and young office workers who come mainly for the *fun'iki* (atmosphere). Choose a French bistro or Italian trattoria in these areas carefully, and expect to pay dearly for the real thing. That said, you can count on the fact that the city's best foreign cuisine is world-class. Several of France's two- and three-star restaurants, for example, have established branches and joint ventures in Tōkyō, and they regularly send their chefs over to supervise. The style almost everywhere is still nouvelle cuisine: small portions, with picture-perfect garnishes and light sauces. More and more, you find interesting fusions of French and Japanese culinary traditions. Meals are served in poetically beautiful presentations, in bowls and dishes of different shapes and patterns. Recipes make imaginative use of fresh Japanese ingredients, like *shimeji* mushrooms and local wild vegetables.

Tōkyōites have also had more and more opportunities to experience the range and virtuosity of Italian cuisine; chances are good that the finer trattorias here will measure up to even Tuscan standards. Indian food is also consistently good—and relatively inexpensive. Chinese food is the most consistently modified; it can be very good, but for repertoire and richness of taste, it pales in comparison to Hong Kong or Beijing fare. Significantly, Tōkyō has no Chinatown. Many of the city's newest restaurants can only be classified as "fusion" or "eclectic," quoting liberally—like California cuisine—from several Eastern and Western culinary traditions.

The quintessential Japanese restaurant is the *ryōtei,* something like a villa, most often walled off from the bustle of the outside world and divided into several small, private dining rooms. These rooms are traditional in style, with tatami-mat floors, low tables, and a hanging scroll or a flower arrangement in the alcove. One or more of the staff is assigned to each room to serve the many dishes that compose the meal, pour your sake, and provide light conversation. Think of a ryōtei as an adventure, an encounter with foods you've likely never seen before and with a centuries-old graceful, almost ritualized style of service unique to Japan. Many parts of the city are proverbial for their ryōtei; the top houses tend to be in Akasaka, Tsukiji, Asakusa and nearby Yanagi-bashi, and Shimbashi.

A few pointers are in order on the geography of food and drink. The farther "downtown" you go—into Shitamachi—the less likely you are to find the real thing in foreign cuisine. There's superb Japanese food all over the city, but aficionados of sushi swear (with excellent reason) by Tsukiji, where the fish market supplies the neighborhood's restaurants with the freshest ingredients; the restaurants in turn serve the biggest portions and charge the most reasonable prices. Asakusa takes pride in its tempura restaurants, but tempura is reliable almost everywhere, especially at branches of the well-established, citywide chains. Every department store and skyscraper office building in Tōkyō devotes at least one floor to restaurants; none of them stand out, but all are inexpensive and quite passable places to lunch. When in doubt for dinner, note that Tōkyō's top-rated international hotels also have some of the city's best places to eat and drink.

Akasaka 赤坂

Indian

★ $$ ✕ **Moti** (モティ). Vegetarian dishes at Moti, especially the lentil and eggplant curries, are very good; so is the chicken masala, cooked in butter and spices. The chefs here are recruited from India by a family member who runs a restaurant in Delhi. As its reputation for reasonably priced North Indian cuisine grew, Moti established branches in nearby Akasaka-mitsuke, Roppongi, and farther afield in Yokohama. They all have the inevitable Indian friezes, copper bowls, and white elephants, but this one—popular at lunch with the office crowd from the nearby Tōkyō Broadcasting System headquarters—puts the least into decor. ⊠ *Kimpa Bldg., 3rd fl., 2–14–31 Akasaka, Minato-ku* ☎ *03/3584–6640* ⊟ *AE, DC, MC, V* Ⓜ *Chiyoda subway line, Akasaka Station (Exit 2).*

Italian

$$$–$$$$ ✕ **La Granata** (ラ・グラナータ). In the Tōkyō Broadcasting System Garden building, La Granata is very popular with the media crowd in this neighborhood, and deservedly so: the chefs prepare some of the most accomplished, professional Italian food in town. La Granata is decked out trattoria style, with brickwork arches, red-checkered tablecloths, and a display of antipasti to whet the appetite. Whether you order the *tagliolini* (thin ribbon noodles) with porcini mushrooms, the spaghetti with garlic and red pepper, or another dish as your main meal, start with an appetizer of the wonderful batter-fried zucchini flowers filled with mozzarella and asparagus. ⊠ *5–1–3 Akasaka, Minato-ku* ☎ *03/ 3582–5891* ⊟ *AE, MC, V* Ⓜ *Chiyoda subway line, Akasaka Station (Exit 1A).*

For more general information on dining in Japan, *see* The Discreet Charm of Japanese Cuisine *in* Chapter 8.

Dress

Dining out in Tōkyō does not ordinarily demand a great deal in the way of formal attire. If it's a business meal, of course, and your hosts or guests are Japanese, dress conservatively: for men, a suit and tie; for women, a dress or suit in a basic color and a minimum of jewelry. On your own, follow the unspoken dress codes you'd observe at home and you're unlikely to go wrong. We mention dress only when men are required to wear a jacket or a jacket and tie.

For Japanese-style dining on tatami floors, keep two things in mind: wear shoes that slip on and off easily and presentable socks, and choose clothing you'll be comfortable in for a few hours with your legs gathered under you.

Reservations

Unless otherwise noted, the restaurants listed in this guide are open daily for lunch and dinner. Reservations are always a good idea: we mention them only when they're essential or not accepted. Book as far ahead as you can, and reconfirm as soon as you arrive.

Prices

Eating at hotels and famous restaurants is costly; however, you can eat well and reasonably at standard restaurants that may not have signs in English. Many less expensive restaurants display in their front windows plastic replicas of the dishes they serve, so you can always point to what you want to eat if the language barrier is insurmountable. Good places to look for moderately priced dining spots are in the restaurant concourses of department stores, usually on the first and/or second basement levels and the top floors.

The restaurants we list are the cream of the crop in each price category. Price-category estimates are based on the cost of a main course at dinner, excluding drinks, taxes, and service charges. Note that Japanese-style restaurants often serve set meals, which may include rice, soup, and pickled vegetables in addition to the main course—this can also drive up the cost. You can sometimes request the main dish without the sides, but then you'd be missing out on the beauty and harmony of a Japanese meal. Credit cards are becoming more widely accepted at cheaper establishments, but definitely check before sitting down.

WHAT IT COSTS In yen				
$$$$	$$$	$$	$	¢
AT DINNER over 3,000	2,000–3,000	1,000–2,000	800–1,000	under 800

Prices are per person for a main course.

Water & Restrooms

Japanese restaurants are very clean (standards of hygiene are very high), and tap water is safe to drink. Restaurants may have Japanese-style toilets, with bowls recessed into the floor, over which you must squat.

ON THE MENU

FIRST, THINK SUSHI. *The style popular now everywhere—slices of raw fish or shellfish on a hand-formed portion of vinegared rice, with a dab of wasabi for zest—developed in Edo (present-day Tōkyō) in the early 19th century. The local name for this style, in fact, is Edo-mae. (Go west, to Ōsaka or Kyōto, and you find a very different kettle of fish, called oshi-zushi: the fish and rice are pressed together in a box mold, then sliced into individual servings.) Originally, Edo-mae was pure street food, sold at stalls as a quick snack; today the best sushi restaurants send buyers early every morning to the Central Wholesale Market in Tsukiji for the freshest ingredients: maguro (tuna) and hamachi (yellowtail), tako (octopus) and eka (squid), ikura (salmon roe) and uni (sea urchin), ebi (shrimp) and anago (conger eel).*

Next, think tempura: fresh fish, shellfish, and vegetables delicately batter-fried in

oil. This kind of cooking dates to the mid-16th century, with the earliest influences of Spanish and Portuguese culture on Japan, and you find it today all over the country. But nowhere is it better than in Tōkyō, and nowhere in Tōkyō is it better than in the tempura stalls and restaurants of Shitamachi—the older commercial and working-class districts of the eastern wards—or in the restaurants that began there in the 19th century and moved upscale. Typical ingredients are shrimp, kisu (smelt), shirauo (whitebait), shiitake mushrooms, lotus root, and green peppers. To really enjoy tempura, you want to be at the counter, in front of the chef: these individual portions should be served and eaten the moment they emerge from the oil.

Japanese

$$$–$$$$ ✕ **Kisoji** (木曽路). The specialty here is shabu-shabu: thin slices of beef cooked in boiling water at your table and dipped in sauce. Normally this is an informal, if pricey, sort of meal; after all, you do get to play with your food a bit. Kisoji, however, adds a dimension of posh to the experience, with all the tasteful appointments of a traditional ryōtei— private dining rooms with tatami seating (at a 10% surcharge), elegant little rock gardens, and alcoves with flower arrangements. ✉ *3–10 Akasaka, Minato-ku* ☎ *03/3588–0071* ⊟ *AE, MC, V* Ⓜ *Ginza and Marunouchi subway lines, Akasaka-mitsuke Station (Belle Vie Akasaka Exit).*

$$–$$$ ✕ **Jidaiya** (時代屋). Like the Jidaiya in Roppongi, these two Akasaka branches serve various prix-fixe courses, including shabu-shabu, tempura, sushi, and steamed rice with seafood. The food is nothing fancy, but it's delicious and filling. ✉ *Naritaya Bldg. 1F, Akasaka 3–14–3, Minato-ku* ☎ *03/3588–0489* ⊟ *AE, DC, MC, V* ⊘ *No lunch weekends* Ⓜ *Ginza and Marunouchi subway lines, Akasaka-mitsuke Station (Belle Vie Akasaka Exit)* ✉ *Isomura Bldg. B1, Akasaka 5–1–4, Minato-ku* ☎ *03/3224–1505* ⊟ *AE, DC, MC, V* ⊘ *No lunch weekends* Ⓜ *Chiyoda subway line, Akasaka Station (Exit 1A).*

Akasaka-mitsuke 赤坂見附

Indian

$$ ✕ **Moti** (モテイ). Like the branch in Akasaka, this Moti serves delicious vegetarian dishes, especially the lentil and eggplant curries. The chicken masala, cooked in butter and spices, is also good. Indian friezes, copper bowls, and white elephants decorate the dining room. ✉ *Akasaka Floral Plaza 2F, 3–8–8 Akasaka, Minato-ku* ☎ *03/3584–3760* ▭ *AE, DC, MC, V* Ⓜ *Ginza and Marunouchi subway lines, Akasaka-mitsuke Station (Belle Vie Akasaka Exit).*

Japanese

¢–$$ ✕ **Sawanoi** (澤乃井). The homemade udon noodles here, served in a broth with seafood, vegetables, or chicken, make a perfect light meal or midnight snack. Try the *inaka* (country-style) udon, which has bonito, seaweed flakes, radish shavings, and a raw egg dropped in to cook in the hot broth. For a heartier meal, chose the *tenkama* set: hot udon and shrimp tempura with a delicate soy-based sauce. A bit rundown, Sawanoi is one of the last remaining neighborhood shops in what is now an upscale business and entertainment district. It stays open until 3 AM, and a menu is available in English. ✉ *Shimno Bldg., 1st fl., 3–7–13 Akasaka, Minato-ku* ☎ *03/3582–2080* ▭ *No credit cards* ✆ *Closed Sun.* Ⓜ *Ginza and Marunouchi subway lines, Akasaka-mitsuke Station (Belle Vie Akasaka Exit).*

Aoyama 青山

Japanese

$$$ ✕ **Higo-no-ya** (肥後の屋). The specialty of the house is *kushi-yaki*: small servings of meat, fish, and vegetables cut into bits and grilled on bamboo skewers. There's nothing ceremonious or elegant about kushi-yaki; it resembles the more familiar yakitori, with somewhat more variety to the ingredients. Higo-no-ya's helpful English menu guides you to other delicacies like shiitake mushrooms stuffed with minced chicken; bacon-wrapped scallops; and bonito, shrimp, and eggplant with ginger. The restaurant is a postmodern-traditional cross, with wood beams painted black, paper lanterns, and sliding paper screens. There's tatami, table, and counter seating. ✉ *AG Bldg. B1, 3–18–17 Minami-Aoyama, Minato-ku* ☎ *03/3423–4461* ▭ *AE, DC, MC, V* ✆ *No lunch* Ⓜ *Ginza, Chiyoda, and Hanzō-mon subway lines, Omotesandō Station (Exit A4).*

$–$$ ✕ **Maisen** (まい泉). Converted from a *sentō* (public bathhouse), Maisen still has the old high ceiling (built for ventilation) and the original signs instructing bathers where to change out of their street clothes. Bouquets of seasonal flowers help transform the large, airy space into a pleasant dining room. Maisen's specialty is *tonkatsu*: tender, juicy, deep-fried pork cutlets served with a spicy sauce, shredded cabbage, miso soup, and rice. A popular alternative is the *Suruga-zen* set, a main course of fried fish served with sashimi, soup, and rice. There are no-smoking rooms upstairs. ✉ *4–8–5 Jingū-mae, Shibuya-ku* ☎ *03/3470–0071* ▭ *AE, DC,*

Where to Eat in Tōkyō

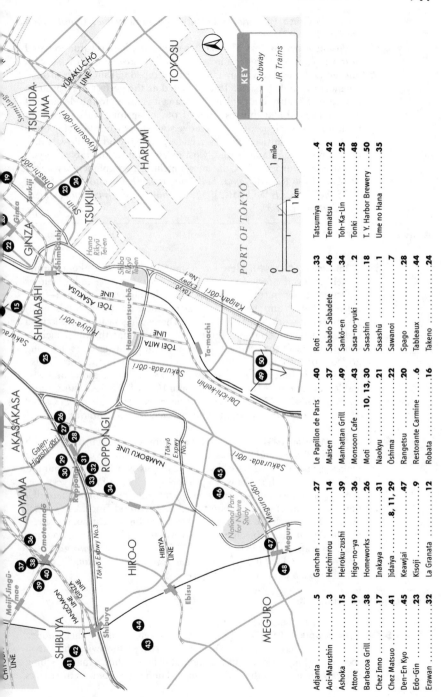

KEY

- - - - Subway
——— JR Trains

Hama Rikyū Tei-en
Shiba Rikyū Teien

PORT OF TŌKYŌ

0   1 km
0   1 mile

Adjanta	5	Ganchan	27	Le Papillon de Paris	40	Roti	33	Tatsumiya	4

Adjanta 5
Aoi-Marushin 3
Ashoka 15
Attore 19
Barbacoa Grill 38
Chez Inno 17
Chez Matsuo 41
Den-En Kyo 45
Edo-Gin 23
Erawan 32

Ganchan 27
Heichinrou 14
Heiroku-zushi 39
Higo-no-ya 36
Homeworks 26
Inakaya 31
Jidaiya 8, 11, 29
Keawjai 47
Kisoji 9
La Granata 12

Le Papillon de Paris 40
Maisen 37
Manhattan Grill 49
Monsoon Cafe 43
Moti 10, 13, 30
Naokyu 21
Ōshima 22
Rangetsu 20
Restorante Carmine 6
Robata 16

Roti 33
Sabado Sabadete 46
Sankō-en 34
Sasa-no-yuki 2
Sasashin 18
Sasashū 1
Sawanoi 7
Spago 28
Tableaux 44
Takeno 24

Tatsumiya 4
Tenmatsu 42
Toh-Ka-Lin 25
Tonki 48
T. Y. Harbor Brewery 50
Ume no Hana 35

MC, V Ⓜ *Ginza, Chiyoda, and Hanzō-mon subway lines, Omotesandō Station (Exit A2).*

¢–$$ ✕**Ume no Hana** (梅の花). The exclusive specialty here is tofu, prepared
Fodor'sChoice   in more ways than you can imagine—boiled, steamed, stir-fried with
★   minced crabmeat, served in a custard, wrapped in thin layers around
a delicate whitefish paste. Tofu is touted as the perfect high-protein,
low-calorie health food; at Ume no Hana it is raised to the elegance of
haute cuisine. Enter this restaurant from a flagstone walk lined with
traditional stone lanterns, and remove your shoes when you step up to
the main room; latticed wood screens separate the tables. Private din-
ing rooms have tatami seating with recesses under the tables so you
can stretch your legs. Prix-fixe meals include a complimentary aperi-
tif. ⊠ *2–14–6 Kita-Aoyama, Bell Commons 6F, Minato Ward* ☎ *03/
3475–8077* ⊟ *AE, DC, MC, V* ⤸ *No smoking* Ⓜ *Ginza Line, Gaien-
mae Station (Exit 3).*

Asakusa 浅草

Japanese

$$ ✕**Tatsumiya** (たつみや). Here's a restaurant that's run like a formal
ryōtei but has the feel of a rough-cut *izakaya* (Japanese pub). Neither
inaccessible nor outrageously expensive, Tatsumiya is adorned—nay,
cluttered—with antique chests, braziers, clocks, lanterns, bowls, utensils, and craft work, some of it for sale. The evening meal is in the kaiseki
style, with seven courses: tradition demands that the meal include
something raw, something boiled, something vinegared, something
grilled. You must arrive before 8:30 for the kaiseki, but Tatsumiya also
serves a light lunch, plus a variety of *nabe* (one-pot seafood and vegetable stews, prepared at your table) until 10. ⊠ *1–33–5 Asakusa, Taitō-
ku* ☎ *03/3842–7373* 👔 *Jacket and tie* ⊟ *No credit cards* ◷ *Closed
Mon.* Ⓜ *Ginza and Asakusa subway lines, Asakusa Station (Exits 1
and 3).*

$–$$ ✕**Aoi-Marushin** (葵丸進). The largest tempura restaurant in Tōkyō, with
Fodor'sChoice   six floors of table and tatami seating, welcomes foreign customers and
★   makes a visit easy with English menus. This is a family restaurant.
Don't expect much in the way of decor—just lots of food at very reasonable prices. Asakusa is a must on any itinerary, and tempura *teishoku*
(an assortment of delicate batter-fried fish, seafood, and fresh vegetables) is the specialty of the district. Aoi-Marushin's location, just a few
minutes' walk from the entrance to Sensō-ji temple, makes it an obvi-
ous choice after a visit to the temple. ⊠ *1–4–4 Asakusa, Taitō-ku* ☎ *03/
3841–0110* ⊟ *AE, MC, V* Ⓜ *Ginza and Asakusa subway lines, Asakusa
Station (Exit 1).*

Azabu-jūban 麻布十番

American/Casual

$–$$ ✕**Homeworks** (ホームワークス). Every so often, even on alien shores,
you've got to have a burger. When the urge strikes, the Swiss-and-bacon
special at Homeworks is an incomparably better choice than anything
you can get at one of the global chains. Hamburgers come in three sizes

TIPS ON DINING IN JAPAN

- There's no taboo against slurping your noodle soup, though women are generally less boisterous about it than men.

- Pick up the soup bowl and drink directly from it, rather than leaning over the table to sip it. Take the fish or vegetables from it with your chopsticks. Return the lid to the soup bowl when you are finished. The rice bowl, too, is to be picked up and held in one hand while you eat from it.

- Don't point or gesture with chopsticks. Licking the ends of your chopsticks is rude, as is taking food from a common serving plate with the end of the chopstick you've had in your mouth. Don't stick your chopsticks upright in your food when you're done using them; instead, allow them to rest on the side of your dish or bowl.

- When drinking with a friend, don't pour your own. Take the bottle and pour for the other person. She will in turn reach for the

bottle and pour for you. The Japanese will attempt to top your drink off after every few sips.

- The Japanese don't pour sauces on their rice in a traditional meal. Sauces are intended for dipping foods lightly, not for dunking or soaking.

- Among faux pas that are considered nearly unpardonable, the worst perhaps is blowing your nose. Excuse yourself and leave the room if this becomes necessary.

- Although McDonald's and Häagen-Dazs have made great inroads on the custom of never eating in public, it's still considered gauche to munch on a hamburger (or an ice-cream cone) as you walk along a public street.

on white or wheat buns, with a variety of toppings. There are also hot teriyaki chicken and pastrami sandwiches and vegetarian options like hummus and eggplant. Desserts, alas, are so-so. With its hardwood banquettes and French doors open to the street in good weather, Homeworks is a pleasant place to linger over lunch. ⊠ *Vesta Bldg. 1F, 1–5–8 Azabu-jūban, Minato-ku* ☎ *03/3405–9884* 🚫 *No credit cards* Ⓜ *Namboku and Ōedo subway lines, Azabu-jūban Station (Exit 4).*

Korean

$$–$$$$ ✕**Sankō-en** (三幸園). With the embassy of South Korea a few blocks away, Sankō-en stands out in a neighborhood thick with Korean-barbecue joints. Customers—not just from the neighborhood but from nearby trendy Roppongi as well—line up at all hours (from 11:30 AM to midnight) to get in. Korean barbecue is a smoky affair; you cook your own food, usually thin slices of beef and vegetables, on a gas grill at your table. The *karubi* (brisket), which is accompanied by a great salad, is the best thing to order. ⊠ *1–8–7 Azabu-jūban, Minato-ku* ☎ *03/3585–6306* 🗪 *Reservations not accepted* 🚫 *MC, V* ⊘ *Closed Wed.* Ⓜ *Namboku and Ōedo subway lines, Azabu-jūban Station (Exit 4).*

Daikanyama 代官山

Contemporary

$$–$$$$
Fodor$Choice
★
✕**Tableaux** (タブローズ). The mural in the bar depicts the fall of Pompeii, the banquettes are upholstered in red leather, and the walls are papered in antique gold. So with ponytailed waiters gliding about, you suspect that somebody here really *believes* in Los Angeles. Tableaux may lay on more glitz than is necessary, but the service is cordial and professional, and the food is superb. Try batter-fried zucchini flowers with mozzarella and anchovy; spaghettini with baby clams, lobster meat, and green olives; or the miso-glazed black cod with sour-plum sauce, garnished with mushrooms and shrimp wontons. The bar is open until 1:30 AM. ⊠ *Sunroser Daikanyama Bldg. B1, 11–6 Sarugaku-chō, Shibuya-ku* ☎ *03/5489–2201* ⊟ *AE, DC, MC, V* ⊘ *No lunch* Ⓜ *Tōkyū Tōyoko private rail line, Daikanyama Station (Kita-guchi/North Exit).*

Pan-Asian

¢–$$
✕**Monsoon Cafe** (モンスーンカフェ). The demand for "ethnic" food—which by local definition means spicy and primarily Southeast Asian—continues apace in Tōkyō. With several locations, the Monsoon Cafe meets that demand. Complementing the eclectic Pan-Asian food are rattan furniture, brass tableware from Thailand, colorful papier-mâché parrots on gilded stands, Balinese carvings, and ceiling fans. The best seats in the house here at the original Monsoon are on the balcony that runs around the four sides of the atrium-style central space. Try the Vietnamese steamed spring rolls, Indonesian grilled chicken with peanut sauce, or Chinese-style beef with oyster sauce. ⊠ *15–4 Hachiyama-chō, Shibuya-ku* ☎ *03/5489–3789* ⊟ *AE, DC, MC, V* Ⓜ *Tōkyū Tōyoko private rail line, Daikanyama Station (Kita-guchi/North Exit).*

Ginza 銀座

Indian

$$–$$$$
✕**Ashoka** (アショカ). Since 1968, Ashoka has staked out the high ground for Indian cuisine in Tōkyō—with a dining room suited to its fashionable Ginza location. The room is hushed and spacious, incense perfumes the air, the lighting is recessed, the carpets are thick, and the servers wear spiffy uniforms. The best thing to order here is the *thali,* a selection of curries, tandoori chicken, and nan served on a figured brass tray. The Goan fish curry is also excellent, as is the chicken tikka: boneless chunks marinated and cooked in the tandoor. ⊠ *Ginza Inns Bldg., 1st and 2nd fl., 3–1 Nishi Ginza, Chūō-ku* ☎ *03/ 3572–2377* ⊟ *AE, DC, MC, V* Ⓜ *Marunouchi and Ginza subway lines, Ginza Station (Exit A4).*

Japanese

$$$$
✕**Ōshima** (大志満). The draw at Ōshima is the *Kaga ryōri* cooking of Kanazawa, a small city on the Sea of Japan known as "Little Kyōto" for its rich craft traditions. Waitresses dress in kimonos of Kanazawa's famous Yuzen dyed silk; Kutani porcelain and Wajima lacquerware grace the exquisite table settings. Seafood at Ōshima is superb, but don't ignore the specialty of the house: a stew of duck and potatoes called

jibuni. Kaiseki full-course meals are pricey, but there's a reasonable lunchtime set menu for ¥1,800. ⊠ *Ginza Core Bldg. 9F, 5–8–20 Ginza, Chūō-ku* ☎ *03/3574–8080* ⊟ *AE, MC, V* Ⓜ *Ginza, Hibiya, and Marunouchi subway lines, Ginza Station (Exit A5).*

$$$–$$$$ ✕**Rangetsu** (らん月). Japan enjoys a special reputation for its lovingly raised, tender, marbled domestic beef. Try it, if your budget will bear the weight, at Rangetsu, in the form of this elegant Ginza restaurant's signature shabu-shabu or sukiyaki course. Call ahead to reserve a private alcove, where you can cook for yourself, or have a kaiseki meal brought to your table by kimono-clad attendants. Rangetsu is a block from the Ginza 4-chōme crossing, opposite the Matsuya Department Store. ⊠ *3–5–8 Ginza, Chūō-ku* ☎ *03/3567–1021* ⊟ *AE, DC, MC, V* Ⓜ *Marunouchi and Ginza subway lines, Ginza Station (Exits A9 and A10).*

¢ ✕**Naokyū** (直久). Ramen is the quintessential Japanese fast food in a bowl: thick Chinese noodles in a savory broth, with soybean paste, diced leeks, slices of pork loin, and spinach. No neighborhood in Tōkyō is without at least one ramen joint—often serving only at a counter, where you eat standing up. In Ginza, the hands-down favorite—for prices that have hardly changed since the 1970s, as well as for taste—is Naokyū, in the basement of Hankyū Department Store. There's limited seating here at the Formica-top tables; at lunch, the line of waiting customers extends halfway down the corridor. ⊠ *Hankyū Department Store H2, 5–2–1 Ginza, Chūō-ku* ☎ *03/3571–0957* ⊟ *MC, V* Ⓜ *Marunouchi and Ginza subway lines, Ginza Station (Sukiyabashi Exit C3 for Ginza Palmy).*

Ichiyaga   市ヶ谷

Italian

$$ ✕**Restorante Carmine** (カルミネ). Everybody pitched in, so the story goes, when chef Carmine Cozzolino left his job at an upscale restaurant in Aoyama and opened this unpretentious neighborhood bistro in 1987: friends designed the logo and the interior, painted the walls (black and white), and hung the graphics, swapping their labor for meals. The five-course dinner (¥3,800–¥5,000) here could be the best deal in town. The menu changes daily; specialties of the house include pasta twists with tomato-and-caper sauce, and veal scallopini à la Marsala. The wine list is well chosen, and the tiramisu is a serious dessert. ⊠ *1–19 Saiku-chō, Shinjuku-ku* ☎ *03/3260–5066* ⊟ *AE, MC, V* Ⓜ *Ōedo subway line, Ushigome-Kagurazaka Station (Exit 1).*

Ikebukuro   池袋

Japanese

$$–$$$
FodorʼsChoice
★
✕**Sasashū** (笹周). This traditional-style pub is noteworthy for stocking only the finest and rarest, the Latours and Mouton-Rothschilds, of sake: these are the rice wines that take gold medals in the annual sake competition year after year. It also serves some of the best izakaya food in town—and the Japanese wouldn't dream of drinking well without eating well. Sasashū purports to be the only restaurant in Tōkyō that

CloseUp

BEER, WINE, SAKE & SPIRITS

JAPAN HAS FOUR large breweries, Asahi, Kirin, Sapporo, and Suntory. Asahi and Kirin are the two heavyweights, constantly battling for the much coveted title of "Japan's No. 1 Brewery," but many beer fans rate Suntory's Malts brand and Sapporo's Yebisu brand as the tastiest brews in the land. Since a change in the law in the early 1990s, an increasing number of microbreweries have sprung up across Japan, but locally produced brews can still be hard to find, even when you know they exist.

Japan produces a small amount of domestic wine, but imports far more from both the Old and New Worlds. Wine is easy to find in neighborhood liquor shops and 24-hour convenience stores, but department stores boast the best selections.

Shōchū, a liquor made from grain and particularly associated with the southern island of Kyūshū, is drunk either on the rocks or mixed with water, hot or cold. Sometimes a wedge of lemon or a small pickled apricot, known as umeboshi, is added as well. It can also be mixed with club soda and served cold.

Japan's number one alcoholic beverage is sake (pronounced sa-kay), the "beverage of the samurai," as one brewery puts it. There are more than 2,000 different brands of sake produced throughout Japan. Like other kinds of wine, sake comes in sweet (amakuchi) and dry (karakuchi) varieties; these are graded tokkyū (superior class), ikkyū (first class), and nikkyū (second class) and are priced accordingly. (Connoisseurs say this ranking is for tax purposes and is not necessarily a true indication of quality.)

Best drunk at room temperature (nurukan) so as not to alter the flavor, sake is also served heated (atsukan) or with ice (rokku de). It's poured from tokkuri (small ceramic vessels) into tiny cups called choko. The diminutive size of these cups shouldn't mislead you into thinking you can't drink too much. The custom of making sure that your companion's cup never runs dry often leads the novice astray.

Junmaishu is the term for pure rice wine, a blend of rice, yeast, and water to which no extra alcohol has been added. Junmaishu has the strongest and most distinctive flavor, compared with various other methods of brewing and is preferred by the sake tsū, as connoisseurs are known.

Apart from the nomiya (bars) and restaurants, the place to sample sake is the izakaya, a drinking establishment that serves only sake, usually dozens of different kinds, including a selection of jizake, the kind produced in limited quantities by small regional breweries throughout the country. For more about sake, see The Discreet Charm of Japanese Cuisine in Chapter 8.

serves wild duck, brushed with sake and soy sauce and broiled over a hibachi. This is a rambling, two-story, traditional-style building, with thick beams and tatami floors. ✉ *2–2–6 Ikebukuro, Toshima-ku* ☎ *03/3971–6796* ▤ *AE, DC, V* ⊗ *Closed Sun. No lunch* Ⓜ *JR Yamanote Line; Yūraku-chō, Marunouchi, and Ōedo subway lines: Ikebukuro Station (Exit 19).*

Kyō-bashi 京橋

French

$$$$ ✕ **Chez Inno** (シェ・イノ). Chef Noboru Inoue studied his craft at Maxim's in Paris and Les Frères Troisgros in Roanne; the result is brilliant, innovative French food. Try fresh lamb in wine sauce with truffles and finely chopped herbs, or lobster with caviar. The main dining room, with seating for 28, has velvet banquettes, white-stucco walls, and stained-glass windows. A smaller room can accommodate private parties. Across the street is the elegant Hotel Seiyō Ginza—making this block the locus of the very utmost in Tōkyō upscale. ✉ *Daihyaku Seimei Bldg. 1F, 3–2–11 Kyō-bashi, Chūō-ku* ☎ *03/3274–2020* ⌕ *Reservations essential* 🎩 *Jacket and tie* ▤ *AE, DC, MC, V* ⊗ *Closed Sun.* Ⓜ *Ginza subway line, Kyō-bashi Station (Exit 2); Yūraku-chō subway line, Ginza-Itchōme Station (Exit 7).*

Italian

$$–$$$ ✕ **Attore** (アトーレ). This Italian restaurant in the elegant Hotel Seiyō Ginza is divided into two sections. The "casual" side has a bar counter, banquettes, and a see-through glass wall to the kitchen; the "formal" side has mauve wall panels and carpets, armchairs, and soft recessed lighting. On either side of the room, you get some of the best Italian cuisine in Tōkyō. Try pâté of pheasant and porcini mushrooms with white-truffle cheese sauce or the walnut-smoked lamb chops with sun-dried tomatoes. The menu is simpler and cheaper on the casual side of the restaurant. ✉ *1–11–2 Ginza, Chūō-ku* ☎ *03/3535–1111* ⌕ *Reservations essential* 🎩 *Jacket and tie* ▤ *AE, DC, MC, V* Ⓜ *Ginza subway line, Kyō-bashi Station (Exit 2); Yūraku-chō subway line, Ginza-Itchōme Station (Exit 7).*

Meguro 目黒

Japanese

★ ¢–$$ ✕ **Tonki** (とんき). Meguro, a neighborhood distinguished for almost nothing else culinary, has arguably the best tonkatsu restaurant in Tōkyō. It's a family joint, with Formica-top tables and a server who comes around to take your order while you wait the requisite 10 minutes in line. And people do wait in line, every night until the place closes at 10:45. Tonki is a success that never went conglomerate or added frills to what it does best: deep-fried pork cutlets, soup, raw cabbage salad, rice, pickles, and tea. That's the standard course, and almost everybody orders it, with good reason. ✉ *1–1–2 Shimo-Meguro, Meguro-ku* ☎ *03/3491–9928* ▤ *DC, V* ⊗ *Closed Tues. and 3rd Mon. of month* Ⓜ *JR Yamanote and Namboku subway lines, Meguro Station (Nishi-guchi/West Exit).*

Thai

★ $$ ✕ **Keawjai** (ゲウチャイ). Blink and you miss the faded sign of this little basement restaurant a minute's walk from Meguro Station. Keawjai is one of the few places in Tōkyō to specialize in the subtle complexities of Royal Thai cuisine, and despite its size—only eight tables and four banquettes—it serves a remarkable range of dishes in different regional styles. The spicy beef salad is excellent (and *really* spicy), as are the baked rice and crabmeat served in a whole pineapple, and the red-curry chicken in coconut milk with cashews. The staff is Thai, and the service is friendly and unhurried. ✉ *Meguro Kōwa Bldg. B1, 2–14–9 Kami Ōsaki, Meguro-ku* ☎ *03/5420–7727* ▭ *AE, DC, MC, V* ⊘ *Closed 2nd and 3rd Mon. of month* Ⓜ *JR Yamanote and Namboku subway lines, Meguro Station (Higashi-guchi/East Exit).*

Niban-chō　二番町

Indian

$$ ✕ **Adjanta** (アジャンタ). In the mid-20th century, the owner of Adjanta came to Tōkyō to study electrical engineering. He ended up changing careers and establishing what is today one of the oldest and best Indian restaurants in town. There's no decor to speak of at this 24-hour restaurant. The emphasis instead is on the variety and intricacy of Indian cooking—and none of its dressier rivals can match Adjanta's menu for sheer depth. The curries are hot to begin with, but you can order them even hotter. There's a small boutique in one corner, where saris and imported Indian foodstuffs are sold. ✉ *3–11 Niban-chō, Chiyoda-ku* ☎ *03/3264–6955* ▭ *AE, DC, MC, V* Ⓜ *Yūraku-chō subway line, Kōji-machi Station (Exit 5).*

Nihombashi　日本橋

Japanese

$$ ✕ **Sasashin** (笹新). Like most izakaya, Sasashin spurns the notion of decor: there's a counter laden with platters of the evening's fare, a clutter of rough wooden tables, and not much else. It's noisy, smoky, crowded—and great fun. Like izakaya fare in general, the food is best described as professional home cooking, and is meant mainly as ballast for the earnest consumption of beer and sake. Try the sashimi, the grilled fish, or the fried tofu; you really can't go wrong by just pointing your finger to anything on the counter that takes your fancy. ✉ *2–20–3 Nihombashi-Ningyōchō, Chūō-ku* ☎ *03/3668–2456* ⌂ *Reservations not accepted* ▭ *No credit cards* ⊘ *Closed Sun. and 3rd Sat. of month. No lunch* Ⓜ *Hanzō-mon subway line, Suitengū-mae Station (Exit 7); Hibiya and Asakusa subway lines, Ningyōchō Station (Exits A1 and A3).*

Omotesandō　表参道

Brazilian

$$–$$$ ✕ **Barbacoa Grill** (バルバッコアグリル). Carnivores flock here for the great-value all-you-can-eat Brazilian grilled chicken and barbecued beef, which the efficient waiters will keep bringing to your table on skewers

until you tell them to stop. Those with lighter appetites can choose the less-expensive salad buffet and feijoada pork stew with black beans; both are bargains. Barbacoa has hardwood floors, lithographs of bull motifs, warm lighting, salmon-color tablecloths, and roomy seating. This popular spot is just off Omotesandō-dōri on the Harajuku 2-chōme shopping street (on the north side of Omotesandō-dōri), about 50 yards down on the left. ⊠ *4–3–24 Jingū-mae, Shibuya-ku* ☏ *03/3796–0571* ☰ *AE, DC, MC, V* Ⓜ *Ginza, Chiyoda, and Hanzō-mon subway lines, Omotesandō Station (Exit A2).*

French

$$$$ ✕ **Le Papillon de Paris** (ル・パピヨン・ド・パリ). This very fashion-minded restaurant is a joint venture of L'Orangerie in Paris and couturier Mori Hanae. Muted elegance marks the dining room, with cream walls and deep brown carpets; mirrors add depth to a room that actually seats only 40. The ambitious prix-fixe menus change every two weeks; the recurring salad of sautéed sweetbreads is excellent. This is a particularly good place to be on Sunday between 11 and 2:30, for the buffet brunch (¥3,500), during which you can graze through to what is arguably the best dessert tray in town. ⊠ *Hanae Mori Bldg., 5th fl., 3–6–1 Kita–Aoyama, Minato-ku* ☏ *03/3407–7461* ⌲ *Reservations essential* ☰ *AE, DC, MC, V* ☺ *No dinner Sun.* Ⓜ *Ginza, Chiyoda and Hanzō-mon subway lines, Omotesandō Station (Exit A1).*

Sushi

$$ ✕ **Heiroku-zushi** (平禄寿司). Ordinarily, a meal of sushi is a costly indulgence. The rock-bottom alternative is a *kaiten-zushi*, where sushi is literally served assembly-line style. The chefs inside the circular counter maintain a constant supply on the revolving belt on plates color-coded for price; just choose whatever takes your fancy as dishes pass by. Heiroku-zushi is a bustling, cheerful example of the genre, with fresh fish and no pretensions at all to decor. When you're done, the server counts up your plates and calculates your bill (¥126 for staples like tuna and squid to ¥367 for delicacies like eel and salmon roe). ⊠ *5–8–5 Jingū-mae, Shibuya-ku* ☏ *03/3498–3968* ☰ *MC, V* Ⓜ *Ginza, Chiyoda, and Hanzō-mon subway lines, Omotesandō Station (Exit A1).*

Roppongi 六本木

American

$$$$ ✕ **Spago** (スパゴ). Celebrity-chef Wolfgang Puck, who created the original Spago in Los Angeles, still checks in periodically to oversee the authenticity of his California cuisine at this Tōkyō branch. Most diners here content themselves with a starter like mango-and-Brie quesadilla with tomato salsa, and an equally eclectic pasta or pizza—but such entrées as grilled snapper with lemongrass and chardonnay or roast duck breast with Cointreau sauce and beet risotto are not to be ignored. This is a clean, well-lighted place, painted pink and white and adorned with potted palms. The best seats in the house are on the glassed-in veranda. ⊠ *5–7–8 Roppongi, Minato-ku* ☏ *03/3423–4025* ☰ *AE, DC, MC, V* Ⓜ *Hibiya subway line, Roppongi Station (Exit 3).*

WHERE TO REFUEL

WHEN YOU don't have time for a leisurely meal, you might want to try a local chain restaurant. **Yoshinoya,** popular with Tokyoites, serves grilled salmon, rice, and miso soup for breakfast (until 10), and then hearty portions of rice and beef for the rest of the day. **Sen Zushi, Chiyoda Sushi,** and **Kyoutaru** dish out sushi and sashimi, and at **Ichiran** you can customize a bowl of ramen. Nearly all of these counter-service restaurants also sell rice balls, the easiest snack to pick up when you're on the go. Often shaped like a thick triangle small enough to fit in your palm, the sticky rice balls come stuffed with a bit of meat or vegetable and wrapped in nori, so you can handle them. Rice balls cost about ¥100. If you want to eat something familiar, check out **MOS Burger, Freshness Burger,** or **First Kitchen,** which serve classic hamburgers as well as some Japanese snacks.

Contemporary

$$–$$$ ✕ **Roti** (ロティ). Billing itself a "modern American brasserie," Roti takes pride in the creative use of simple, fresh ingredients, and a fusing of Eastern and Western elements. For an appetizer, try the Vietnamese sea-bass carpaccio with crisp noodles and roasted garlic, or the calamari batter-fried in ale with red-chili tartar sauce. Don't neglect dessert: the espresso-chocolate tart is to die for. Roti stocks some 60 Californian wines, microbrewed ales from the famed Rogue brewery in Oregon, and Cuban cigars. The best seats in the house are in fact outside at one of the dozen tables around the big glass pyramid on the terrace. ⊠ *Piramide Bldg. 1F, 6–6–9 Roppongi, Minato-ku* ☎ *03/5785–3671* ▤ *AE, MC, V* Ⓜ *Hibiya subway line, Roppongi Station (Exit 1).*

Indian

$$ ✕ **Moti** (モテイ). Like the branch in Akasaka, this Moti serves delicious vegetarian dishes, especially the lentil and eggplant curries. The chicken masala, cooked in butter and spices, is also good. Indian friezes, copper bowls, and white elephants decorate the dining room. ⊠ *Roppongi Hama Bldg. 3F, 6–2–35 Roppongi, Minato-ku* ☎ *03/3479–1939* ▤ *AE, DC, MC, V* Ⓜ *Hibiya subway line, Roppongi Station (Exit 1).*

Japanese

$$–$$$$ ✕ **Inakaya** (田舎屋). The style here is *robatayaki*, a dining experience that
FodorsChoice segues into pure theater. Inside a large U-shape counter, two cooks in
★ traditional garb sit on cushions behind a grill, with a cornucopia of food spread out in front of them: fresh vegetables, seafood, skewers of beef and chicken. You point to what you want, and your server shouts out the order. The cook bellows back your order, plucks your selection up out of the pit, prepares it, and hands it across on an 8-foot wooden paddle. Inakaya is open from 5 PM to 5 AM, and fills up fast after 7. ⊠ *Reine Bldg., 1st fl., 5–3–4 Roppongi, Minato-ku* ☎ *03/3408–5040* ⟳ *Reser-*

vations not accepted ⊟ AE, DC, MC, V ⊘ *No lunch* Ⓜ *Hibiya subway line, Roppongi Station (Exit 3).*

$$-$$$ ✕ **Jidaiya** (時代屋). The Roppongi branch of this restaurant evokes the feeling of an Edo-period tavern with a good collection of antiques: *akadansu* (red-lacquered chests), Nambu ironware kettles, and low *horigotatsu* tables, with recesses beneath which you can stretch out your legs. All the tables are for six people or more; you're bound to be sharing yours. The later you dine (the place stays open until 4 AM), the more boisterous and friendly your tablemates will be. Jidaiya serves a bit of everything in its prix-fixe courses: shabu-shabu, tempura, sushi, steamed rice with seafood. The food is nothing fancy, but it's delicious and filling. ⊠ *Uni Roppongi Bldg., B1, 7–15–17 Roppongi, Minato-ku* ☎ 03/3403–3563 ⊟ AE, DC, MC, V Ⓜ *Hibiya subway line, Roppongi Station (Exit 2).*

$$ ✕ **Ganchan** (がんちゃん). The Japanese expect their yakitori joints—restaurants that specialize in bits of charcoal-broiled chicken and
Fodor'sChoice vegetables—to be just like Ganchan: smoky, noisy, and cluttered. The
★ counter here seats barely 15, and you have to squeeze to get to the chairs in back. Festival masks, paper kites and lanterns, and greeting cards from celebrity patrons adorn the walls. The cooks yell at each other, fan the grill, and serve up enormous schooners of beer. Try the *tsukune* (balls of minced chicken) and the fresh asparagus wrapped in bacon. The place stays open until 1 AM (11 PM on Sunday). ⊠ *6–8–23 Roppongi, Minato-ku* ☎ 03/3478–0092 ⊟ MC, V Ⓜ *Hibiya subway line, Roppongi Station (Exit 1A).*

Thai

$$-$$$ ✕ **Erawan** (エラワン). Window tables at this sprawling Thai "brasserie" on the top floor of a popular Roppongi vertical mall afford a wonderful view of the Tōkyō skyline at night. Black-painted wood floors, ceiling fans, Thai antiques, and rattan chairs establish the mood, and the space is nicely broken up into large and small dining areas and private rooms. The service is cheerful and professional. Specialties of the house include deep-fried prawn and crabmeat cakes, spicy roast-beef salad, sirloin tips with mango sauce, and a terrific dish of stir-fried lobster meat with cashews. For window seating, it's best to reserve ahead. ⊠ *Roi Bldg. 13F, 5–5–1 Roppongi, Minato-ku* ☎ 03/3404–5741 ⊟ AE, DC, M, V Ⓜ *Hibiya subway line, Roppongi Station (Exit 3).*

Shibuya 渋谷

Japanese

★ **$$-$$$** ✕ **Tenmatsu** (天松). The best seats in the house at Tenmatsu, as in any tempura-*ya*, are at the immaculate wooden counter, where your tidbits of choice are taken straight from the oil and served up immediately. You also get to watch the chef in action. Tenmatsu's brand of good-natured professional hospitality adds to the enjoyment of the meal. Here you can rely on a set menu or order à la carte tempura delicacies like lotus root, shrimp, *unagi* (eel), and *kisu* (a small white freshwater fish). Call ahead to reserve counter seating or a full-course kaiseki dinner in a private tatami room. ⊠ *1–6–1 Dōgen-zaka, Shibuya-ku* ☎ 03/3462–2815 ⊟ DC, MC,

V Ⓜ *JR Yamanote Line, Shibuya Station (Minami-guchi/South Exit); Ginza and Hanzō-mon subway lines, Shibuya Station (Exit 3A).*

Shinagawa 品川

Contemporary

$$–$$$$ ✕ **Manhattan Grill** (マンハッタングリル). Only in hypereclectic Japan can you have a French-Indonesian meal at a restaurant called the Manhattan Grill in a food court dubbed the "Foodium." Chef Wayan Surbrata, who trained at the Four Seasons Resort in Bali, has a delicate, deft touch with such dishes as spicy roast-chicken salad, and steak marinated in cinnamon and soy sauce, served with shiitake mushrooms and *gado-gado* (shrimp-flavor rice crackers). One side of the minimalist restaurant is open to the food court; the floor-to-ceiling windows on the other side don't afford much of a view. The square black-and-white ceramics set off the food especially well. ⊠ *Atré 4F, 2–18–1 Konan, Minato-ku* ☎ *03/ 6717–0922* ⊟ *AE, MC, V* Ⓜ *JR Shinagawa Station (Higashi-guchi/ East Exit).*

★ **$$–$$$** ✕ **T. Y. Harbor Brewery** (T.Y.ハーバーブルワリーレストラン). A converted warehouse on the waterfront houses this restaurant, a Tōkyō hot spot for private parties. Chef David Chiddo refined his signature California-Thai cuisine at some of the best restaurants in Los Angeles. Don't miss his grilled mahimahi with green rice and mango salsa, or the grilled jumbo-shrimp brochettes with tabbouleh. True to its name, T. Y. Harbor brews its own beer, in a tank that reaches all the way to the 46-foot-high ceiling. The best seats in the house are on the bay-side deck, open from May to October. Reservations are a good idea on weekends. ⊠ *2–1–3 Higashi-Shinagawa, Shinagawa-ku* ☎ *03/5479–4555* ⊟ *AE, DC, MC, V* Ⓜ *Tōkyō Monorail or Rinkai Line, Ten-nōz Isle Station (Exit B).*

Shirokanedai 白金台

Chinese

$$–$$$ ✕ **Den-En Kyo** (田燕居). Pale-green walls with black trim, antique chests, and chic geometric screens announce that this is not your typical Chinese-food joint. Chef Son You-Ting puts forth the high cuisine of his native Beijing, varied with the spicy style of Szechuan Province. There's no English menu, but you can always order the seven-course set meal (for two people or more), which includes Den-En Kyo's wonderful fried spring rolls with minced shrimp, and braised pork with lotus root. The 11-course menu features quail-egg soup, Peking duck, and jumbo scallops braised in brandy. ⊠ *Creer Bldg. 2F, above the Garden supermarket, 3–16–8 Shirokanedai, Minato-ku* ☎ *03/3440–6635* ⊟ *DC, MC, V* Ⓜ *Mita and Namboku subway lines, Shirokanedai Station (Exit 2).*

Spanish

$$ ✕ **Sabado Sabadete** (サバドサバデテ). Catalan jewelry designer Mañuel Benito used to rent a bar in Aoyama on Saturday nights and cook for his friends, just for the fun of it. Word got around: eventually there wasn't room in the bar to lift a fork. Inspired by this success, Benito opened this Spanish restaurant. The highlight of every evening is still the moment when the chef, in his bright red cap, shouts out "Gohan desu yo!"—

the Japanese equivalent of "Soup's on!"—and dishes out his bubbling-hot paella. Don't miss the empanadas or the *escalivada* (Spanish ratatouille with red peppers, onions, and eggplant). ✉ *Genteel Shirokanedai Bldg., 2nd fl., 5–3–2 Shirokanedai, Minato-ku* ☎ *03/3445–9353* ▭ *No credit cards* ⊘ *Closed Sun.* Ⓜ *Mita and Namboku subway lines, Shirokanedai Station (Exit 1).*

Shōtō 松濤

French

$$$$ ✕ **Chez Matsuo** (シェ・松尾). With its stately homes, Shōtō, a sedate sort of Beverly Hills, is the kind of area you don't expect Tōkyō to have—at least not so close to Shibuya Station. In the middle of it all is Chez Matsuo, in a lovely two-story Western-style house. The dining rooms overlook the garden, where you can dine by candlelight on spring and autumn evenings. Owner-chef Matsuo studied as a sommelier in London and perfected his culinary finesse in Paris. His pricey food is nouvelle; the specialty of the house is *suprême* (breast and wing) of duck. ✉ *1–23–15 Shōtō, Shibuya-ku* ☎ *03/3465–0610* ✎ *Reservations essential* ▭ *AE, DC, MC, V* Ⓜ *JR Yamanote Line, Ginza and Hanzō-mon subway lines, and private rail lines: Shibuya Station (Exits 5 and 8 for Hanzō-mon, Kita-guchi/North Exit for all others).*

Tora-no-mon 虎ノ門

Chinese

$$–$$$$ ✕ **Toh-Ka-Lin** (桃花林). Business travelers consistently rate the Ōkura as one of the best hotels in Asia. That judgment has to do with its polish, its human scale, its impeccable standards of service, and, to judge by Toh-Ka-Lin, the quality of its restaurants. The style of the cuisine here is eclectic; two stellar examples are the Peking duck and the sautéed quail wrapped in lettuce leaf. The restaurant also has a not-too-expensive midafternoon meal ($$) of assorted dim sum and other delicacies—and one of the most extensive wine lists in town. ✉ *Hotel Ōkura, 2–10–4 Tora-no-mon, Minato-ku* ☎ *03/3505–6068* ▭ *AE, DC, MC, V* Ⓜ *Hibiya subway line, Kamiya-chō Station (Exit 4B); Ginza subway line, Tora-no-mon Station (Exit 3).*

Tsukiji 築地

Japanese

★ $–$$$ ✕ **Edo-Gin** (江戸銀). In an area that teems with sushi bars, this one maintains its reputation as one of the best. Edo-Gin serves generous slabs of fish that drape over the vinegared rice rather than perch demurely on top. The centerpiece of the main room is a huge tank in which the day's ingredients swim about until they are required; it doesn't get any fresher than this. Set menus here are reasonable, especially for lunch, but a big appetite for specialties like sea urchin and *ōtoro* tuna can put a dent in your budget. ✉ *4–5–1 Tsukiji, Chūō-ku* ☎ *03/3543–4401* ✎ *Reservations not accepted* ▭ *AE, DC, MC, V* ⊘ *Closed early Jan.* Ⓜ *Hibiya subway line, Tsukiji Station (Exit 1); Ōedo subway line, Tsukiji-shijō Station (Exit A1).*

¢–$ ✕ Takeno (たけの). Just a stone's throw from the Tōkyō fish market, Takeno is a rough-cut neighborhood restaurant that tends to fill up at noon with the market's wholesalers and auctioneers and personnel from the nearby Asahi Newspaper offices. There's nothing here but the freshest and the best—big portions of it, at very reasonable prices. Sushi and sashimi are the staples, but there's also a wonderful *tendon* bowl, with shrimp and eel tempura on rice. Prices are not posted because they vary with the costs that morning in the market. ✉ *6–21–2 Tsukiji, Chūo-ku* ☎ *03/3541–8698* ⌣ *Reservations not accepted* ▤ *No credit cards* ☺ *Closed Sun.* Ⓜ *Hibiya subway line, Tsukiji Station (Exit 1); Ōedo subway line, Tsukiji-shijō Station (Exit A1).*

Uchisaiwai-chō 内幸町

Chinese

★ $$–$$$$ ✕ Heichinrou (聘珍楼). A short walk from the Imperial Hotel, this branch of one of Yokohama's oldest and best Chinese restaurants commands a spectacular view of the Imperial Palace grounds. Call ahead to reserve a table by the window. The cuisine is Cantonese; pride of place goes to the *kaisen ryōri*, a banquet of steamed sea bass, lobster, shrimp, scallops, abalone, and other seafood dishes. Much of the clientele comes from the law offices, securities firms, and foreign banks in the building. The VIP room at Heichinrou, with its soft lighting and impeccable linens, is a popular venue for power lunches. ✉ *Fukoku Seimei Bldg., 28th fl., 2–2–2 Uchisaiwai-chō, Chiyoda-ku* ☎ *03/3508–0555* ▤ *AE, DC, MC, V* ☺ *Closed Sun.* Ⓜ *Mita Line, Uchisaiwai-chō Station (Exit A6).*

Ueno 上野

Japanese

$$–$$$ ✕ Sasa-no-yuki (笹の雪). In the heart of Shitamachi, Tōkyō's old downtown working-class neighborhood, Sasa-no-yuki has been serving meals based on homemade tofu for the past 300 years. The food is inspired in part by *shōjin ryōri* (Buddhist vegetarian cuisine). The basic three-course set menu includes *ankake* (bean curd in sweet soy sauce), *uzumi* tofu (scrambled with rice and green tea), and *unsui* (a creamy tofu crepe filled with sea scallops, shrimp, and minced red pepper). For bigger appetites, there's also an eight-course banquet. The seating is on tatami, and the garden has a waterfall. ✉ *2–15–10 Negishi, Taitō-ku* ☎ *03/3873–1145* ▤ *AE, DC, V* ☺ *Closed Mon.* Ⓜ *JR Uguisudani Station (Kita-guchi/North Exit).*

Yūraku-chō 有楽町

Japanese

$$–$$$ ✕ Robata (炉端). Old, funky, and more than a little cramped, Robata is
Fodor's Choice a bit daunting at first. But fourth-generation chef-owner Takao Inoue
★ holds forth here with an inspired version of Japanese home cooking. He's also a connoisseur of pottery; he serves his food on pieces acquired at famous kilns all over the country. There's no menu; just tell Inoue-san (who speaks some English) how much you want to spend, and leave the

rest to him. A meal at Robata—like the pottery—is simple to the eye but subtle and fulfilling. Typical dishes include steamed fish with vegetables, stews of beef or pork, and seafood salads. ⊠ *1–3–8 Yūraku-chō, Chiyoda-ku* ☎ *03/3591–1905* ▭ *No credit cards* ⊙ *Closed 3rd Mon. of month. No lunch* Ⓜ *JR Yūraku-chō Station (Hibiya Exit); Hibiya, Chiyoda, and Mita subway lines, Hibiya Station (Exit A4).*

WHERE TO STAY

3

MOST REGAL SETTING
Imperial Hotel in the heart of Tōkyō ⇨*p.116*

BEST MINIMALIST ESCAPE
the elegant Yoshimizu Ginza ⇨*p.111*

ONLY IF YOU DARE
Green Plaza Shinjuku ⇨*p.117*

LOST IN TRANSLATION BEHEMOTH
Park Hyatt Tōkyō in Shinjuku ⇨*p.120*

BEST PLACE TO CATCH A TEA CEREMONY
Hotel Ōkura in Tora-no-mon ⇨*p.125*

SIMPLE AND FRIENDLY
Sawanoya Ryokan in Yanaka ⇨*p.126*

MOST BEAUTIFUL GARDEN
Four Seasons Hotel Chinzan-sō ⇨*p.120*

By Jared
Lubarsky

THERE ARE THREE THINGS you can take for granted almost anywhere you set down your bags in Tōkyō: cleanliness, safety, and good service. The factors that will probably determine your choice of lodging, then, are cost and location.

It's not at all easy to find a *moderately* priced lodging in this city. The cost of commercial real estate in Tōkyō has come down from the insane levels of the 1980s and early 1990s, but lodging prices never really took a nosedive. It doesn't pay to build small or to convert an existing structure to a boutique hotel; when developers build, they build on a grand scale, and when the project includes a hotel—more often than not, nowadays, on the upper floors of an office tower—it's invariably at the high end of the market. Most of the hotels that have opened in Tōkyō since 2002, or are slated to open by 2006, are managed by international luxury chains like the Hyatt, Four Seasons, and Mandarin Oriental groups.

These ventures add pricy lodgings to the overall supply at an astonishing rate: analysts predict that by 2007 travelers will have some 84,000 rooms at their disposal. Does that presage a glut? Bargains to be had? Probably not. Hoteliers are predicting that visitors to Tōkyō are willing to pay well to be pampered, and the spare-no-expense approach to hotel design remains the norm: soaring atriums, concierges, oceans of marble, interior decorators fetched in from London, New York, and Milan. The results—some of which are listed here—rival the quality of luxury accommodations anywhere in the world.

Hotels in the middle market provide less in the way of services and decor, but this affects the cost of accommodations less than you might imagine. Deluxe hotels make a substantial part of their profits from their banquet and dining facilities; they charge you more, but they can also give you more space. Farther down the scale, you pay less—but not remarkably less—and the rooms are disproportionately smaller. By and large, these are the hotels that remain under local management and ownership; some of them, aware at last of the threat posed by their international rivals, are undertaking major expansion and renovation projects to stay competitive.

With Tōkyō's down-market business hotels, inns, and guesthouses, what you sacrifice is essentially location. You pay significantly less for the minimal benefits of a roof overhead, but you might have to travel farther to and from sights you want to see. That said, the sacrifice is not really very great. Many of these accommodations are still within the central wards; some of them have an old-fashioned charm and personal touch the upscale hotels can't offer. Nor should transportation be a concern: wherever you're staying, Tōkyō's subway and train system—comfortable (except in rush hours), efficient, inexpensive, and safe—will get you back and forth.

Akasaka-mitsuke   赤坂見附

$$$$ 🏨 **Akasaka Prince Hotel** (赤坂プリンスホテル). Rooms from the 20th to the 30th floor of this hotel, designed by world-renowned architect Kenzō Tange, afford the best views of the city, especially at night. A white-and-pale-gray color scheme accentuates the light from the wide windows that run the length of the rooms. This affords a feeling of spaciousness, though the rooms—oddly shaped because of Tange's attempt to give every accommodation a "corner" location—are a bit small compared to those in other deluxe hotels. The marble and off-white reception areas on the ground floor are pristine—maybe even a bit sterile. ✉ *1–2 Kioi-chō, Chiyoda-ku, Tōkyō-to 102-0094* ☎ *03/3234–1111* 🖷 *03/3205–5163* ⊕ *www.princehotelsjapan.com* 🛏 *693 rooms, 68 suites* ⚫ *8 restaurants, coffee shop, room service, some in-room data ports, minibars, refrigerators, cable TV with movies, pool, hair salon, massage, 2 bars, lounges, shops, laundry service, concierge, business services, convention center, travel services, no-smoking floors* ▤ *AE, DC, MC, V* Ⓜ *Ginza and Marunouchi subway lines, Akasaka-mitsuke Station (Exit 7).*

$$$$ 🏨 **Hotel New Ōtani Tōkyō and Towers** (ホテルニューオータニ). The New Ōtani is virtually a city unto itself. When the house is full and all the banquet facilities are in use, the traffic in the restaurants and shopping arcades seems like rush hour at a busy railway station. The hotel's redeeming feature is its spectacular 10-acre Japanese garden, complete with a pond and a red-lacquer bridge; the rooms overlooking the garden are the best in the house. Among the many restaurants and bars are La Tour d'Argent, Japan's first Trader Vic's, and the revolving Sky Lounge. ✉ *4–1 Kioi-chō, Chiyoda-ku, Tōkyō-to 102-0094* ☎ *03/3265–1111, 0120/112–211 toll-free* 🖷 *03/3221–2619* ⊕ *www.newotani.co.jp* 🛏 *1,549 rooms, 51 suites* ⚫ *33 restaurants, coffee shop, room service, in-room data ports, in-room safes, minibars, refrigerators, cable TV with movies, driving range, 2 tennis courts, indoor pool, health club, hair salon, 4 bars, beer garden, shops, babysitting, laundry service, business services, convention center, travel services, no-smoking rooms* ▤ *AE, DC, MC, V* Ⓜ *Ginza and Marunouchi subway lines, Akasaka-mitsuke Station (Exit 7).*

Asakusa   浅草

$$$–$$$$ 🏨 **Asakusa View Hotel** (浅草ビューホテル). Upscale Western-style accommodations are rare in Asakusa, so the Asakusa View pretty much has this end of the market to itself. Off the smart marble lobby a harpist plays in the tea lounge, and expensive boutiques line the second floor. The communal *hinoki* (Japanese-cypress) baths on the sixth floor, which also houses the Japanese-style tatami suites, overlook a Japanese garden. The best of the Western-style rooms are on the 22nd and 23rd floors, with a view of the Sensō-ji pagoda and temple grounds. There's a top-floor lounge with live entertainment. ✉ *3–17–1 Nishi-Asakusa, Taitō-ku, Tōkyō-to 111-8765* ☎ *03/3847–1111* 🖷 *03/3842–2117* ⊕ *www.viewhotels.co.jp/asakusa/english* 🛏 *330 Western-style rooms, 7 Japanese-style suites* ⚫ *3 restaurants, coffee shop, pool, health club, Japanese baths, 2 bars, lounge, shops, concierge floor, no-smoking rooms* ▤ *AE, DC, MC, V* Ⓜ *Ginza subway line, Tawara-machi Station (Exit 3).*

Facilities Unless otherwise specified, all rooms at the hotels listed in this book have private baths and are Western-style. In listings, we always name the facilities that are available, but we don't specify whether they cost extra. When pricing accommodations, try to find out what's included and what entails an additional charge.

Assume that hotels operate on the European Plan (EP, with no meals) unless we specify that they use the Continental Plan (CP, with a Continental breakfast), Breakfast Plan (BP, with a full breakfast), Modified American Plan (MAP, with breakfast and dinner), or the Full American Plan (FAP, with all meals).

Reservations The **Japanese Inn Group** (Ryokan Asakusa Shigetsu ✉ 1-31-11 Nishi-Asakusa, Taito-ku, Tōkyō 111-0032 ☏ 03/3252-1717 ⊕ www. jpinn.com) is a nationwide association of small ryokan and family-owned tourist hotels. Because they tend to be slightly out of the way and provide few amenities, these accommodations are priced to attract budget-minded travelers. The association has the active support of the Japan National Tourist Organization. The best way to get information about the member inns in Tōkyō and throughout Japan—and arrange bookings on the spot—is to visit the **JNTO Tourist Information Center** (✉ Tōkyō Kōtsū Kaikan, 10F, 2–10–1 Yūraku-chō, Chiyoda-ku ☏ 03/3201-3331 ⊕ www.jnto.go.jp Ⓜ JR Yamanote Line [Higashi-guchi/East Exit] and Yūraku-chō subway line [Exit A-8], Yūraku-chō Station), open weekdays 9–5 and Saturday 9–noon. The JNTO publishes a listing of some 700 reasonably priced accommodations. To be listed, properties must meet Japanese fire codes and charge less than ¥8,000 (about $70) per person without meals. For the most part, the properties charge ¥5,000–¥6,000 ($44–$54). These properties welcome foreigners (many Japanese hotels and ryokan do not like to have foreign guests because they might not be familiar with traditional-inn etiquette). Properties include business hotels, *ryokan* of a very rudimentary nature, *minshuku* (Japanese bed-and-breakfasts), and pensions. It's the luck of the draw whether you choose a good or less-than-good property. In most cases rooms are clean but very small. Except in business hotels, shared baths are the norm, and you are expected to have your room lights out by 10 PM.

Many establishments on the list of reasonably priced accommodations—and many that are not on the list—can be reserved through the nonprofit **Welcome Inn Reservation Center** (✉ Tōkyō International Forum B1, 3–5–1 Marunouchi, Chiyoda-ku, Tōkyō 100–0005 ☏ 03/3211-4201 📠 03/3211-9009 ⊕ www. itcj.or.jp). Reservation forms are available from JNTO office. The center must receive reservation requests at least one week before your departure to allow processing time. If you are already in Tōkyō, JNTO's Tourist Information Centers (TICs) at Narita Airport, Kansai International Airport, and downtown can make immediate reservations for you.

The **Japan Ryokan Association** (✉ 1–8–3 Maru-no-uchi, Chiyoda-ku, Tōkyō ☏ 03/3231-5310 ⊕ www.ryokan.or.jp) has a listing of traditional ryokans all over the country plus literature on ryokan etiquette. You can inquire about reservations at member inns via an online form.

The **Japan Minshuku Center** (✉ Tōkyō Kōtsū Kaikan Bldg., B1, 2–10–1 Yūrakuchō, Chiyoda-ku, Tōkyō ☎ 03/3216–6556 🖶 03/3216–6557 ⊕ www. minshuku.jp) will reserve your stay in a minshuku. Call for information first, then fill out a reservation request form, available from the Web site or office.

In some 4,500 locations in more than 70 countries around the world, **Hostelling International (HI),** the umbrella group for a number of national youth-hostel associations, offers single-sex, dorm-style beds and, at many hostels, rooms for couples and families. Membership in any HI national hostel association, open to travelers of all ages, allows you to stay in HI-affiliated hostels at member rates. A one-year membership to HI–USA (☎ 301/495–1240 ⊕ www.hiusa. org) is about $28 for adults. A two-year minimum membership to HI–Canada (☎ 613/237–7884 or 800/663–5777 ⊕ www.hihostels.ca) costs C$35. Membership to YHA England and Wales (☎ 0870/870–8808, 0870/770–8868, or 0162/959–2600 ⊕ www.yha.org.uk) costs £14. Membership to YHA Australia (☎ 02/9261–1111 ⊕ www.yha.com.au) costs A$52. Membership to YHA New Zealand (☎ 03/379–9970 or 0800/278–299 ⊕ www.yha.org. nz) costs NZ$40. Whether you're a member or not, you'll most likely be directed to the organization Japan Youth Hostels, Inc. (✉ Suidō-bashi Nishiguchi Kaikan, 2–20–7 Misaki-chō, Chiyoda-ku, Tōkyō 101–0061 ☎ 03/3288–1417) for listings and reservations.

Some useful words when checking into a hotel: air-conditioning *eakon,* private baths *o-furo,* showers *shawā,* double beds *daburubeddo,* twin beds *tsuinbeddo,* separate *betsu,* pushed together *kuttsukerareta,* queen bed *kuīn saizun-no-beddo,* king bed *kingu saizu-no-beddo.*

Prices

	WHAT IT COSTS In yen				
	$$$$	$$$	$$	$	¢
FOR 2 PEOPLE	over 22,000	18,000–22,000	12,000–18,000	8,000–12,000	under 8,000

Price categories are assigned based on the range between the least and most expensive standard double rooms in nonholiday high season. Taxes (5%, plus 3% for bills over ¥15,000) are extra.

★ **$$** 🏠**Ryokan Shigetsu** (旅館指月). Just off Nakamise-dōri and inside the Sensō-ji grounds, this small inn could not be better located for a visit to the temple. The best options are the rooms with futon bedding and tatami floors; the Western rooms, plainly but comfortably furnished, are less expensive. All rooms have private baths; there's also a Japanese-style wooden communal bath on the sixth floor with a view of the Sensō-ji pagoda. ✉ *1–31–11 Asakusa, Taitō-ku, Tōkyō-to 111-0032* ☎ *03/3843–2345* 🖷 *03/3483–2348* 🌐 *www.roy.hi-ho.ne.jp/shigetsu* 🛏 *14 Western-style rooms, 10 Japanese-style rooms* 👃 *Restaurant, Japanese baths* 🝙 *AE, MC, V* Ⓜ *Ginza subway line, Asakusa Station (Exit 1/ Kaminari-mon Exit).*

Ebisu 恵比寿

$$$$ 🏨 **Westin Tōkyō** (ウエスティンホテル東京). In the pharaonic Yebisu Garden Place development, the Westin provides easy access to Mitsukoshi department store, the Tōkyō Metropolitan Museum of Photography, an elegant concert hall, and the Taillevent-Robuchon restaurant (in a full-scale reproduction of a Louis XV château). The style of the hotel is updated art nouveau, with an excess of marble and bronze. The rooms are spacious, and the suites are huge by Japanese standards. You can arrange for privileges at the nearby Club at Yebisu Garden, a fitness center with a spa, squash courts, and a pool. ✉ *1–4 Mita 1-chōme, Meguro-ku, Tōkyō-to 153-0062* ☎ *03/5423–7000* 🖷 *03/5423–7600* 🌐 *www.westin.co.jp/english/* 🛏 *445 rooms, 20 suites* 👃 *5 restaurants, coffee shop, room service, in-room data ports, some in-room faxes, in-room safes, minibars, refrigerators, cable TV with movies, massage, bar, lounge, shops, dry cleaning, laundry service, concierge floor, business services, convention center, travel services, no-smoking rooms* 🝙 *AE, DC, MC, V* Ⓜ *JR, Hibiya subway line; Ebisu Station (Higashi-guchi/ East Exit).*

Ginza 銀座

$$$$ 🏨 **Renaissance Tōkyō Hotel Ginza Tōbu** (ルネッサンス東京ホテル銀座東武). Relatively reasonable prices, friendly service, and comfortable rooms make the Renaissance something of a bargain for the Ginza area. Blond-wood furniture and pastel quilted bedspreads decorate the standard rooms. The pricier concierge floors have much larger rooms, with such extras as terry robes and hair dryers; breakfast, afternoon tea, and complimentary cocktails in the lounge are part of the package. ✉ *6–13–10 Ginza, Chūō-ku, Tōkyō-to 104-0061* ☎ *03/3546–0111* 🖷 *03/3546–8990* 🌐 *http://marriott.com* 🛏 *197 rooms, 9 suites* 👃 *2 restaurants, coffee shop, room service, minibars, refrigerators, cable TV with movies, hair salon, massage, 2 bars, lounge, dry cleaning, laundry service, concierge floor, business services, travel services, no-smoking rooms* 🝙 *AE, DC, MC, V* Ⓜ *Hibiya and Asakusa subway lines, Higashi-Ginza Station (Exit A1).*

$$$–$$$$ 🏨 **Yoshimizu Ginza** (銀座吉水). You're expected to fold up your own
Fodor'sChoice futon at this modest traditional inn inspired by owner Yoshimi Naka-
★ gawa's experience living the simple life at a commune in Woodstock, New York, in the 1970s. The money that isn't spent on service has been spent—with exquisite taste—on simple, natural appointments: wooden floors dyed pale indigo, hand-painted shōji screens, basins of Shigaraki

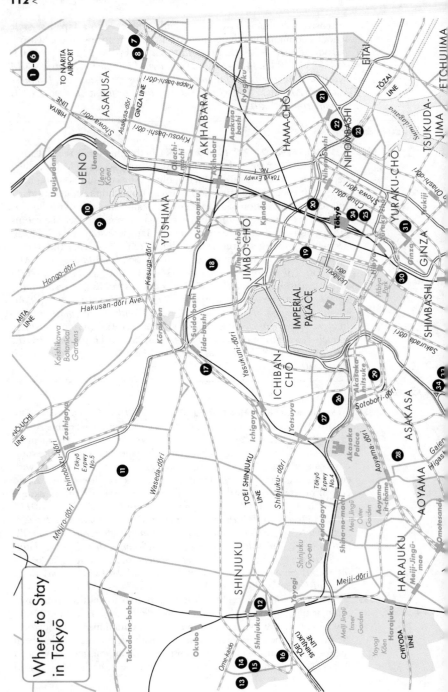

Where to Stay in Tōkyō

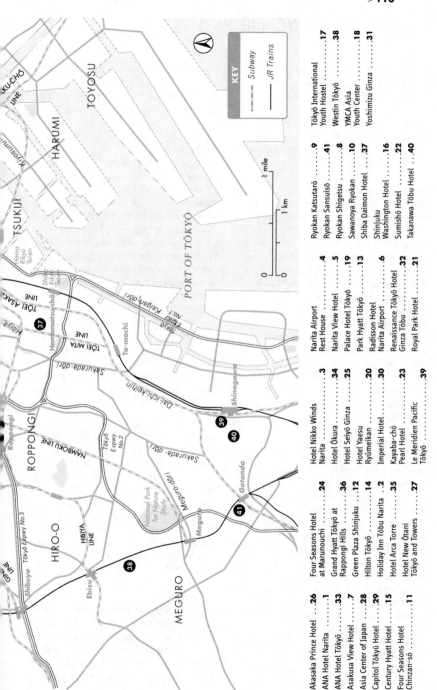

CHOOSING YOUR HOTEL

ACCOMMODATIONS IN TŌKYŌ can be roughly divided into five categories: international (full-service) hotels, business hotels, ryokan, "capsule" hotels, and hostels. Which you choose to stay in depends on your budget and the type of experience you're looking for.

International Hotels

Full-service, first-class international hotels in Japan resemble their counterparts all over the world, and because many of the staff members speak English, these are the easiest places for foreigners to stay. They are also among the most expensive, tending to fall into the $$$ and $$$$ categories. Virtually all have Western and Japanese restaurants, room service, in-room data ports, minibars, yukata (cotton bedroom kimonos), concierge services, and porters. Most have business and fitness centers. A few also have swimming pools. At least 90% of the guest rooms are Western style; the few Japanese rooms available (with tatami mats and futons) are more expensive.

Business Hotels

Business hotels are meant primarily for travelers who need no more than a place to leave luggage, sleep, and change. Rooms are small; a single traveler will often take a double rather than suffer the claustrophobia of a single. Each room has a telephone, a small writing desk, a television (sometimes the pay-as-you-watch variety; though rarely with English-language channels), slippers, a yukata, and a prefabricated plastic bathroom unit with tub, shower, and washbasin; the bathrooms are scrupulously clean, but if you're basketball-player size, you might have trouble standing up inside. The hotel facilities are limited usually to one restaurant and a 24-hour receptionist who probably doesn't speak English, with no room service or porters. Business hotels are often conveniently located near the railway station. Most of fall into the $$ (and sometimes $$$) price category.

Ryokan

There are two kinds of ryokan. One is an expensive traditional inn, with impeccable personal service, where you are served dinner and breakfast in your room. The other is an inexpensive hostelry that offers rooms with tatami mats on the floors and futon beds; meals might be served in rooms, but more often they aren't. Tōkyō ryokan fall in the latter category. They are often family-run lodgings, where service is less a matter of professionalism than of good will. Many offer the choice of rooms with or without baths. Because they have few rooms and the owners are usually on hand to answer questions, these small, relatively inexpensive ryokan are hospitable places to stay and are especially popular with younger travelers. The expensive, full-service type of ryokan is best found outside Tōkyō.

A genuine traditional ryokan with exemplary service is exorbitant—more than ¥30,000 ($270) per person per night with two meals. In lesser-priced inns, which run from ¥5,000 ($44) for a single room to ¥7,000 ($54) for a double, tubs are likely to be plastic rather than cedarwood, and small rooms might overlook a street rather than a garden. Rooms have tatami straw-mat floors, futon bedding, and a scroll or flower arrangement in its rightful place.

Minshuku

Minshuku are private homes that accept guests. Usually they cost about ¥6,000 (about $54) per person, including two meals. Although in a traditional ryokan you need not lift a finger, don't be surprised if you are expected to lay out and put away your own bedding in a minshuku. Meals are often served in communal dining rooms. Minshuku vary in size and atmosphere; some are private homes that take in only a few guests, while others are more like no-frill inns. Some of your most memorable stays could be at a minshuku, as they offer a chance to become acquainted with a Japanese family and their hospitality.

Hostels

Hostels in Japan run about ¥2,000–¥3,000 per night for members, usually ¥1,000 more for nonmembers. The quality of hostels varies a lot in Japan, though the bad ones are never truly terrible, and the good ones offer memorable experiences. Most offer private rooms for couples or families, though you should call ahead to be sure. Tourist information offices can direct you to a local hostel. Note that hostels tend to be crowded during school holidays, when university students are traveling around the country.

Capsule Hotels

Capsule hotels consist of plastic cubicles stacked one on top of another. The rooms are a mere 3½ feet wide, 3½ feet high, and 7¼ feet long, and they are used by very junior business travelers, backpackers on shoestring budgets, and late-night revelers or commuters who have missed the last train home. The capsule has a bed, an intercom, an alarm clock, and (in the luxury models) a TV. Washing and toilet facilities are shared. Capsule hotels offer single accommodations only and generally have no facilities for women. Although you may want to try sleeping in a capsule, you probably won't want to spend a week in one.

ware in the washrooms. The two stone communal Japanese baths on the ninth floor can be reserved for a private relaxing soak for two. The inn is few minutes' walk from the Kabuki-za and the fashionable heart of Ginza. Book early. ⊠ *3–11–3 Ginza, Chūō-ku, Tōkyō-to 104-0061* ☏ *03/3248–4432* 🖷 *03/3248–4431* ⊕ *www.yoshimizu.com* ⇦ *12 Japanese-style rooms without bath* ⚒ *2 restaurants, Japanese baths; no room phones, no room TVs, no smoking* ⊟ *AE, MC, V* ⦿️ *BP* Ⓜ *Hibiya subway line, Higashi-Ginza Station (Exit 3 or A2).*

Hakozaki 箱崎

★ **$$$$** 🏨 **Royal Park Hotel** (ロイヤルパークホテル). The bonus feature of this hotel is its connecting passageway to the Tōkyō City Air Terminal, where you can check in for your flight before boarding the bus to Narita. Pack, ring for the porter, and you won't have to touch your baggage again until it comes off the conveyor belt back home. The comfortable, spacious marble-clad lobby has wood-panel columns and brass trim. Neutral grays and browns decorate the well-proportioned rooms. The best rooms are those on the executive floors (16–18) with a view of the Sumida-gawa, and those on floors 6–8 overlooking the hotel's delightful Japanese garden. ⊠ *2–1–1 Nihombashi, Kakigara-chō, Chūō-ku, Tōkyō-to 103-0014* ☏ *03/3667–1111* 🖷 *03/3667–1115* ⊕ *www.rph. co.jp* ⇦ *450 rooms, 9 suites* ⚒ *7 restaurants, coffee shop, room service, some in-room data ports, minibars, refrigerators, cable TV with movies, 1 bar, lounge, shops, dry cleaning, laundry services, concierge floor, business services, convention center, travel services, no-smoking rooms* ⊟ *AE, DC, MC, V* Ⓜ *Hanzō-mon subway line, Suitengū-mae Station (Exit 4).*

$$–$$$ 🏨 **Kayaba-chō Pearl Hotel** (茅場町パールホテル). Some 90% of the small rooms in the Pearl are singles, designed with the lone (and budget-conscious) Japanese business traveler in mind. Given its location—five minutes' walk across the bridge to Tōkyō City Air Terminal and seven minutes on the subway to Ginza—the hotel is a bargain. Don't be tempted to sleep late, however: there's a hefty surcharge on your room rate for checkout after 10 AM. Avoid the so-called "semi-double": it's a claustrophobic single in disguise. ⊠ *1–2–5 Shinkawa, Tōkyō-to, Chūō-ku 104-0033* ☏ *03/3553–2211* 🖷 *03/3555–1849* ⊕ *www.pearlhotel.co.jp* ⇦ *262 rooms* ⚒ *Restaurant, refrigerators, room TVs with movies, massage, Internet, business services, meeting room* ⊟ *AE, DC, MC, V* Ⓜ *Hibiya and Tōzai subways lines, Kayaba-chō Station (Exit 4b).*

Hibiya 日比谷

$$$$ 🏨 **Imperial Hotel** (帝国ホテル). You can't beat the location of these prestigious quarters: in the heart of central Tōkyō, between the Imperial Palace and Ginza. The finest rooms, on the 30th floor in the New Tower, afford views of the palace grounds. The Old Imperial Bar incorporates elements from the 1922 version of the hotel, which Frank Lloyd Wright designed. The Imperial opened its doors in 1891, and from the outset the hotel has been justly proud of its Western-style facilities and personalized Japanese service. Rooms range from standard doubles to suites that are larger than many homes. ⊠ *1–1–1 Uchisaiwai-chō, Chiyoda-ku, Tōkyō-to 100-0011* ☎*03/3504–1111* 🖷*03/3581–9146* ⊕*www. imperialhotel.co.jp* ⤳ *1,005 rooms, 54 suites* ♧ *13 restaurants, cable TV with movies, indoor pool, health club, massage, 4 bars, shops, concierge floor, business services, travel services, no-smoking rooms* ▤ *AE, DC, MC, V* Ⓜ *Hibiya subway line, Hibiya Station (Exit 5).*

Higashi-Gotanda　東五反田

$ 🏨 **Ryokan Sansuisō** (旅館山水荘). Budgeteers appreciate this basic ryokan, a two-story building near Gotanda Station. The proprietor will greet you with a warm smile and a bow and escort you to a small tatami room with a pay TV and a rather noisy heater–air-conditioner mounted on the wall. Some rooms are stuffy, and only two have private baths, but the Sansuisō is clean, easy to find, and only 20 minutes by train from Tōkyō Station or Ginza. The midnight curfew poses a problem for night owls. The Japan National Tourist Organization can help you make reservations at this Japanese Inn Group property. ⊠ *2–9–5 Higashi-Gotanda, Shinagawa-ku, Tōkyō-to 141-0022* ☎*03/3441–7475, 03/3201–3331 for Japan National Tourist Organization* 🖷*03/3449–1944* ⊕ *www.itcj.or.jp/facility/3/facil/313007.html* ⤳ *10 rooms, 2 with bath* ♧ *Room TVs with movies, Japanese baths* ▤ *AE, V* Ⓜ *Asakusa subway line (Exit A3) and JR Yamanote Line (Higashi-guchi/East Exit), Gotanda Station.*

Higashi-Shinjuku　東新宿

¢ 🏨 **Green Plaza Shinjuku** (グリーンプラザ新宿). The Green Plaza is the only capsule we recommend. Staying in any capsule is a no-frills experience taken to the extreme, but if you want to try it out, the Green Plaza is the place to do it. It's the largest capsule hotel in Tōkyō, not far from the east exits of Shinjuku Station, and like in most others, women are not allowed. You leave your luggage and clothes in a locker, change into a yukata, and settle into your "room"—a plastic burrow 3 feet wide by 6½ feet deep, with a TV screen in the ceiling. There's no door—just a curtain—and you pay extra for the coin-operated communal showers. Many clients arrive after midnight, often having had too much to drink. The Green Plaza is not tranquil, but it's clean, safe, and cheap. ⊠ *1–29–3 Kabuki-chō, Shinjuku-ku, Tōkyō-to 160–0021* ☎*03/3207–5411* ⤳ *660 capsules, without bath* ♧ *Snack bar, sauna, lounge; no room phones* ▤ *AE, MC, V.*

Kyō-bashi　京橋

$$$$ 🏨 **Hotel Seiyō Ginza** (ホテル西洋銀座). The grand marble staircase, the thick pile of the carpets, the profusion of cut flowers, the reception staff in coats and tails: all combine to create an atmosphere more like an elegant private club than a hotel. Along with this elegance, location and personalized service are the best reasons to choose the exclusive Seiyō, tucked away on a side street a few minutes from Ginza. Individually decorated rooms have walk-in closets, huge shower stalls, and a direct line to a personal secretary who takes care of your every need. The accommodations, however, are smaller than what you might expect for the price. ☒ *1–11–2 Ginza, Chūō-ku, Tōkyō-to 104-0061* ☏ *03/3535–1111* 🖷 *03/3535–1110* ⊕ *www.seiyo-ginza.com/* ⤺ *51 rooms, 26 suites* ⚒ *3 restaurants, patisserie, room service, in-room data ports, in-room safes, minibars, refrigerators, cable TV with movies, health club, bar, lounge, babysitting, dry cleaning, laundry service, concierge, business services, convention center, travel services, no-smoking rooms* ▤ *AE, DC, MC, V* Ⓜ *Ginza subway line, Kyō-bashi Station (Exit 2); Yūraku-chō Line, Ginza-Itchōme Station (Exit 7).*

Marunouchi   丸の内

$$$$ 🖭 **Four Seasons Hotel Tōkyō at Marunouchi** (フォーシーズンズホテル丸の内東京). The unusual "top-down" design of this ultramodern glass tower means that the first floor is merely a transfer lobby, reception is on the seventh floor, and the guest rooms are on the five floors in between. The muted beige-and-bronze reception area feels like a comfortable private club, with deep-pile carpets, plush brocade sofas, and sumptuous armchairs. Chic black-lacquer doors lead to the spacious guest rooms; beds have brown-leather-covered headboards that continue partway across the ceiling for a canopy effect. Design really *matters* here—but so does high-tech luxury, in touches like plasma screen TVs and variable lighting. The staff speaks fluent English, and the service is spot-on. ☒ *1–11–1 Marunouchi, Chiyoda-ku, Tōkyō-to 100-6277* ☏ *03/5222–7222* 🖷 *03/ 5222–1255* ⊕ *www.fourseasons.com/marunouchi/* ⤺ *48 rooms, 9 suites* ⚒ *Restaurant, room service, in-room data ports, in-room fax, in-room safes, minibars, refrigerators, cable TV with movies, in-room DVD/VCR players, health club, Japanese baths, spa, steam room, bar, lounge, dry cleaning, laundry service, concierge, business services, meeting rooms, no-smoking rooms* ▤ *AE, DC, MC, V* Ⓜ *JR Tōkyō Station (Yaesu South Exit).*

★ **$$$$** 🖭 **Palace Hotel** (パレスホテル). The service here is extremely helpful and professional; much of the staff has been with the hotel for more than 10 years. The location is ideal: only a moat separates the hotel from the outer gardens of the Imperial Palace, and Ginza and the financial districts of Marunouchi are both a short taxi or subway ride away. An air of calm conservatism bespeaks the Palace's half century as an accommodation for the well-to-do and well connected. The tasteful, low-key guest rooms are spacious; ask for one on the upper floors, facing the Imperial Palace. ☒ *1–1–1 Marunouchi, Chiyoda-ku, Tōkyō-to 100-0005* ☏ *03/3211–5211* 🖷 *03/3211–6987* ⊕ *www.palacehotel.co.jp/ english/* ⤺ *384 rooms, 5 suites* ⚒ *7 restaurants, coffee shop, room service, in-room data ports, in-room fax, in-room safes, minibars, refrigerators, cable TV with movies, in-room VCRs, indoor pool, health club, massage, sauna, bar, lounge, shops, dry cleaning, laundry service, concierge, business services, travel services, no-smoking floors* ▤ *AE, DC, MC, V* Ⓜ *Chiyoda, Marunouchi, Hanzō-mon, Tōzai, and Mita subway lines; Ōte-machi Station (Exit C-13B).*

Nagata-chō 永田町

$$$$ ☒ **Capitol Tōkyū Hotel** (キャピトル東急ホテル). The Capitol was built in 1963, but it feels a bit like a grand hotel of a bygone era and maintains a loyal repeat clientele among foreign business travelers. Traditional touches include an ikebana arrangement dominating the lobby, and an exquisite small garden and fishpond. With two staff members to every guest, the service is excellent. Dark-wood furnishings fill the rooms, but shōji on the windows creates a feeling of soft warmth and light. Request a room overlooking the Hie Jinja shrine. The hotel commands its high prices in part because of its proximity to the National Diet and government offices. ⊠ *2–10–3 Nagata-chō, Chiyoda-ku, Tōkyō-to 100-0014* ☏ *03/3581–4511* 🖷 *03/3581–5822* ⊕ *www.capitoltokyu.com/ english* ⌕ *440 rooms, 19 suites* ♢ *4 restaurants, café, coffee shop, room service, in-room data ports, in-room safes, minibars, refrigerators, cable TV with movies, pool, gym, hair salon, spa, bar, shops, dry cleaning, laundry service, concierge floor, business services, convention center, travel services, no-smoking rooms* ⊟ *AE, DC, MC, V* Ⓜ *Chiyoda and Marunouchi subway lines, Kokkai Gijidō-mae Station (Exit 5); Ginza and Namboku subway lines, Tameike-Sannō Station (Exit 5).*

Ningyō-chō 人形町

$–$$ ☒ **Sumishō Hotel** (住庄ホテル). This hotel in a down-to-earth, friendly Shitamachi neighborhood is popular with budget-minded foreign visitors. Expect no graces here: even the biggest twin rooms are long and narrow, and the bathrooms are tiny units with low ceilings. The best accommodations are the three tatami rooms on the second floor overlooking a small Japanese garden. The hotel is a bit hard to find: from Exit A5 of Ningyō-chō Station, turn right and take the first small right-hand street past the second traffic light; the Sumishō is on the left. ⊠ *9–14 Nihombashi-Kobunachō, Chūō-ku, Tōkyō-to 103-0024* ☏ *03/ 3661–4603* 🖷 *03/3661–4639* ⊕ *www.sumisho-hotel.co.jp* ⌕ *72 Western-style rooms, 11 Japanese-style rooms* ♢ *Restaurant, in-room data ports, cable TV, Japanese baths, no-smoking rooms* ⊟ *AE, MC, V* Ⓜ *Hibiya and Asakusa subway lines, Ningyō-chō Station (Exit A5).*

Nishi-Shinjuku 西新宿

★ **$$$$** ☒ **Hilton Tōkyō** (ヒルトン東京). The Hilton, which is a short walk from the megalithic Tōkyō Metropolitan Government Office, is a particular favorite of Western business travelers. When it opened in 1984, it was the largest Hilton in Asia but opted away from the prevailing atrium style in favor of more guest rooms and banquet facilities; as a result, the lobby is on a comfortable, human scale. A copper-clad spiral staircase reaching to the mezzanine floor above highlights the bar-lounge. Shōji screens instead of curtains bathe the guest rooms in soft, relaxing light. ⊠ *6–6–2 Nishi-Shinjuku, Shinjuku-ku, Tōkyō-to 160-0023* ☏ *03/ 3344–5111, 0120/489–992 toll-free* 🖷 *03/3342–6094* ⊕ *www.hilton. com* ⌕ *677 rooms, 129 suites* ♢ *6 restaurants, room service, in-room* *data ports, in-room fax, some in-room safes, minibars, refrigerators, cable TV with movies, 2 tennis courts, pool, gym, hair salon, massage, sauna, bar, cabaret, dance club, shops, babysitting, dry cleaning, laundry service, concierge, business services, travel services, meeting rooms, no-smoking rooms ▤ AE, DC, MC, V Ⓜ Shinjuku Station (Nishi-guchi/West Exit); Marunouchi subway line, Nishi-Shinjuku Station (Exit C8); Ōedo subway line, Tochō-mae Station (all exits).*

$$$$　▣ **Park Hyatt Tōkyō** (パークハイアット東京). An elevator whisks you to the 41st floor, where the hotel—immortalized in the 2003 film *Lost in Translation*—begins with an atrium lounge enclosed on three sides by floor-to-ceiling plate-glass windows. The panorama of Shinjuku spreads out before you. Service is efficient and personal, and the mood of the hotel is contemporary and understated. Guest rooms are large by any standard. King-size beds have Egyptian-cotton sheets and down-feather duvets; other appointments include pale olive-green carpets, black-lacquer cabinets, and huge plasma-screen TVs. Among the hotel's several restaurants is the popular New York Grill, with its open kitchen and steak-and-seafood menu. ✉ *3–7–1–2 Nishi-Shinjuku, Shinjuku-ku, Tōkyō-to 163-1090* ☎ *03/5322–1234* ⊟ *03/5322–1288* ⊕ *http://tokyo. park.hyatt.com/* ⇨ *155 rooms, 23 suites ⌂ 3 restaurants, coffee shop, patisserie, room service, in-room data ports, in-room fax, in-room safes, minibars, refrigerators, cable TV with movies, in-room DVD/VCR players, indoor pool, health club, sauna, spa, 2 bars, library, dry cleaning, laundry service, concierge, Internet, business services, convention center, airport shuttle, travel services, no-smoking rooms ▤ AE, DC, MC, V* Ⓜ *Shinjuku Station (Nishi-guchi/West Exit).*

$$$–$$$$　▣ **Century Hyatt Hotel** (センチュリーハイアットホテル). The Century has the trademark Hyatt atrium-style lobby: seven stories high, with open-glass elevators soaring upward and three huge chandeliers suspended from above. The rooms are spacious for the price, though unremarkable in design; the best choices are the View Rooms (10th–26th floors), which overlook Shinjuku Kōen (Shinjuku Park). The Hyatt emphasizes its cuisine; at any given time, there's almost sure to be a "gourmet fair" in progress, celebrating the food of one country or another and supervised by visiting celebrity chefs. ✉ *2–7–2 Nishi-Shinjuku, Shinjuku-ku, Tōkyō-to 160-0023* ☎ *03/3349–0111* ⊟ *03/3344–5575* ⊕ *http://tokyo. century.hyatt.com/* ⇨ *750 rooms, 16 suites ⌂ 7 restaurants, coffee shop, room service, in-room data ports, in-room safes, minibars, refrigerators, cable TV with movies, indoor pool, gym, hair salon, massage, 2 bars, lounge, shops, dry cleaning, laundry service, concierge floor, business services, convention center, travel services, no-smoking rooms* ▤ *AE, DC, MC, V* Ⓜ *Shinjuku Station (Nishi-guchi/West Exit).*

$$–$$$　▣ **Shinjuku Washington Hotel** (新宿ワシントンホテル). This is the very model of a modern Japanese business hotel, where service is computerized as much as possible and the rooms—utterly devoid of superfluous features—are just about big enough for the furniture and your luggage. The third-floor lobby has an automated check-in and check-out system; you are assigned a room and provided with a plastic card that opens the door and the minibar. The clerk at the counter will ex-

plain the process, but after that you're on your own. ✉ *3–2–9 Nishi-Shinjuku, Shinjuku-ku, Tōkyō-to 160-0023* ☎ *03/3343–3111* 📠 *03/3340–1804* ⊕ *www.wh-rsv.com/english/shinjuku/* 🛏 *1,630 rooms, 3 suites* ♿ *4 restaurants, coffee shop, grocery, room service, some in-room data ports, minibars, refrigerators, room TVs with movies, in-room VCRs, massage, bar, no-smoking rooms* ☐ *AE, DC, MC, V* Ⓜ *Shinjuku Station (Minami-guchi/South Exit).*

Roppongi 六本木

$$$$ 🏨 **Grand Hyatt Tōkyō at Roppongi Hills** (グランドハイアット東京). The

Fodor'sChoice Grand Hyatt is a class act—a hotel designed with every imaginable

★ convenience and comfort. A drawer in the mahogany dresser in each room, for example, has laptop cables and adaptors. The showers have two delivery systems, one through a luxurious "rain-shower" head affixed to the ceiling. No expense has been spared on materials, from the Egyptian-cotton bed linens to the red-granite pool in the spa. Rooms are huge, with high ceilings, black-out blinds, and muted earth tones of brown, beige, and yellow. Weather permitting, the rooms on the west side on the 10th floor and higher afford a view of Mt. Fuji. ✉ *6–10–3 Roppongi, Minato-ku, Tōkyō-to 106–0032* ☎ *03/4333–1234* 📠 *03/4333–8123* ⊕ *www.grandhyatttokyo.com* 🛏 *361 rooms, 24 suites* ♿ *5 restaurants, 2 cafés, patisserie, room service, in-room data ports, in-room fax, in-room safes, minibars, refrigerators, cable TV with movies, in-room DVD players, indoor pool, gym, health club, hair salon, Japanese baths, spa, 3 bars, shops, babysitting, dry cleaning, laundry service, concierge, business services, convention center, airport shuttle, travel services, no-smoking rooms* ☐ *AE, DC, MC, V* Ⓜ *Hibiya subway line, Roppongi Station (Roppongi Hills Exit).*

$$–$$$ 🏨 **Hotel Arca Torre** (ホテルアルカトーレ). With a little more staff training, the Arca Torre, opened in 2002, could be a great deal. It sits on a coveted location in the heart of one of Tōkyō's premier nightlife quarters, just a few minutes' walk from the Roppongi Hills shopping-and-entertainment complex. The accommodations are ample for the price (twins are much roomier than doubles), with nice little touches like built-in hot plates for making tea and coffee, and retractable clotheslines in the bathrooms. There are, however, no closets—just some coat hooks on the wall. The reception desk is chronically shorthanded, and few staff members speak good English. ✉ *6–1–23 Roppongi, Minato-ku, Tōkyō-to 106-0032* ☎ *03/3404–5111* 📠 *03/3404–5115* ⊕ *www.arktower.co.jp* 🛏 *77 rooms* ♿ *Restaurant, coffee shop, in-room data ports, refrigerators, cable TV, no-smoking floor* ☐ *AE, MC, V* Ⓜ *Hibiya subway line, Roppongi Station (Exit 4a).*

★ **$$** 🏨 **Asia Center of Japan** (アジア会館). Established mainly for Asian students and travelers on limited budgets, these accommodations have become generally popular with many international travelers for their good value and easy access (a 15-minute walk) to the nightlife of Roppongi. The "semi-doubles" here are really small singles, but twins and doubles are quite spacious for the price. Appointments are a bit spar-

CloseUp

LODGING ALTERNATIVES

Apartment & House Rentals

If you want a home base that's roomy enough for a family and comes with cooking facilities, consider a furnished rental. These can save you money, especially if you're traveling with a group. Home-exchange directories sometimes list rentals as well as exchanges.

In addition to the agents listed below, English language-newspapers and magazines, such as the Hiragana Times, Kansai Time Out or Metropolis, or the City-Source English Telephone Directory may be helpful in locating a rental property. Note that renting apartments or houses in Japan is not that common a way to spend a vacation.

International Agents: Hideaways International (☎ 603/430–4433 or 800/843–4433 🖷 603/430–4444 ⊕ www.hideaways.com 🖃 $145 annual membership). *Moveandstay* (☎ 02/235–6624 🖷 02/235–6626 ⊕ www.moveandstay.com).

Local Agent: The Mansions (⊠ 3–8–5 Roppongi, Minato-ku, Tōkyō 106-0032 ☎ 03/5414–7070 🖷 03/5414–7088 ⊠ 2–1–3 Azabudai, Minato-ku, Tōkyō 106-0041 ☎ 03/5575–3232 🖷 03/5575–3233 ⊕ www.themansions.jp).

Rental Listings: Metropolis (☎ 03/3423–6932 ⊕ www.metropolis.japantoday.com). Hiragana Times (☎ 03/3341–8989 ⊕ www.hiraganatimes.com) Kansai Time Out (☎ 078/232–4517 ⊕ www.kto.co.jp).

Home Exchanges

If you would like to exchange your home for someone else's, join a home-exchange organization, which will send you its updated listings of available exchanges for a year and will include your own listing in at least one of them. It's up to you to make specific arrangements.

Exchange Club: Intervac U.S. (⊠ 30 Corte San Fernando, Tiburon, CA 94920 ☎ 800/756–4663 🖷 415/435–7440 ⊕ www.intervacus.com 🖃 $65 per year for a listing and online access, $60 catalog).

Home Visits

Through the home visit system, travelers can get a sense of domestic life in Japan by visiting a local family in their home. The program is voluntary on the home owner's part, and there's no charge for a visit. The system is active in many cities throughout the country, including Tōkyō, Yokohama, Nagoya, Kyōto, Ōsaka, Hiroshima, Nagasaki, and Sapporo. To make a reservation, apply in writing for a home visit at least a day in advance to the Japan National Tourist Organization (⊠ Tōkyō Kōtsū Kaikan, 10F, 2–10–1 Yūraku-chō, Chiyoda-ku ☎ 03/3201–3331 ⊕ www.jnto.go.jp). Contact the JNTO before leaving for Japan for more information on the program.

Temples

You can also arrange accommodations in Buddhist temples. JNTO has lists of temples that accept guests. A stay at a temple generally costs ¥3,000–¥9,000 ($27–$80) per night, including two meals. Some temples offer instruction in meditation or allow you to observe their religious practices, while others simply offer a room. The Japanese-style rooms are very simple and range from beautiful, quiet havens to not-so-comfortable, basic cubicles. Either way, temples provide a taste of traditional Japan.

tan—off-white walls, mass-market veneer furniture—but the rooms have plenty of basic amenities like hair dryers, electric kettles, and yukatas. ⊠ *8–10–32 Akasaka, Minato-ku, Tōkyō-to 107-0052* ☎ *03/ 3402–6111* 🖷 *03/3402–0738* 🌐 *www.asiacenter.or.jp* 🛏 *172 rooms, 1 suite* 🍴 *Restaurant, in-room data ports, refrigerators, cable TV with movies, massage, dry cleaning, laundry service, no-smoking rooms* 🚭 *AE, MC, V* Ⓜ *Ginza and Hanzō-mon subway lines, Aoyama-itchōme Station (Exit 4).*

Sekiguchi 関口

$$$$ 🏨 **Four Seasons Hotel Chinzan-sō** (フォーシーズンズホテル椿山荘). Where

Fodor'sChoice else can you sleep in a million-dollar room? That's about what it costs,

★ on average, to build and furnish each spacious room in this elegant hotel. The spectacular fifth-floor Conservatory Rooms have bay windows overlooking private Japanese-garden terraces. The solarium pool, with its columns, tropical plants, and retractable glass roof, is straight out of Xanadu. Built on the former estate of an imperial prince, Chinzan-sō rejoices in one of the most beautiful settings in Tōkyō; in summer the gardens are famous for their fireflies. Complimentary shuttle service connects you to the subway and Tōkyō Station. ⊠ *2–10–8 Sekiguchi, Bunkyō-ku, Tōkyō-to 112-0014* ☎ *03/3943–2222* 🖷 *03/ 3943–2300* 🌐 *www.fourseasons.com/tokyo* 🛏 *283 rooms, 51 suites* 🍴 *4 restaurants, room service, in-room data ports, some in-room faxes, in-room safes, minibars, refrigerators, cable TV with movies, indoor pool, health club, Japanese baths, spa, lounge, shops, babysitting, dry cleaning, laundry service, concierge, business services, convention center, travel services, no-smoking floors* 🚭 *AE, DC, MC, V* Ⓜ *Yūraku-chō subway line, Edogawa-bashi Station (Exit 1A).*

Shiba Kōen 芝公園

$$ 🏨 **Shiba Daimon Hotel** (芝大門ホテル). This moderately priced hotel a minute's walk from Zōjō-ji temple is popular with Japanese travelers. The staff is a bit ill at ease with guests who cannot speak Japanese but no less willing to help. The ubiquitous blond-veneer-on-pressboard furniture and floral-print bedspreads fill the unremarkable rooms, which are reasonably spacious for the price. A good restaurant on the ground floor serves Japanese and Chinese breakfasts and Chinese fare in the evening. ⊠ *2–3–6 Shiba-kōen, Minato-ku, Tōkyō-to 105-0011* ☎ *03/ 3431–3716* 🖷 *03/3434–5177* 🌐 *www4.famille.ne.jp/~tyo-stay/e-nikkanren/sdh1.htm* 🛏 *92 Western-style rooms, 4 Japanese-style rooms* 🍴 *Restaurant, some in-room data ports, refrigerators, room TVs with movies, massage, laundry service, no-smoking rooms* 🚭 *AE, DC, MC, V* Ⓜ *JR Hamamatsu-chō Station (Kita-guchi/North Exit); Asakusa subway line, Daimon Station (Exit A3).*

Shinagawa 品川

$$$$ 🏨 **Le Meridien Pacific Tōkyō** (ホテルパシフィック東京). Just across the street from JR Shinagawa Station, the Meridien sits on grounds that were once part of an imperial-family estate. The hotel gears much of its marketing effort toward booking banquets, wedding receptions, conventions, and tour groups; rooms are comfortable, but public spaces tend to carry a lot of traffic. The Sky Lounge on the 30th floor affords a fine view of Tōkyō Bay. The entire back wall of the ground-floor lounge is glass, the better to contemplate a Japanese garden, sculpted with rocks and waterfalls. ⊠ *3–13–3 Takanawa, Minato-ku, Tōkyō-to 108-0074* ☎ *03/ 3445–6711* 🖷 *03/3445–5137* ⊕ *www.lemeridien.com* ➪ *900 rooms, 40 suites* ♨ *5 restaurants, coffee shop, grocery, room service, in-room data ports, minibars, refrigerators, cable TV with movies, pool, hair salon, massage, bar, lounge, shops, dry cleaning, laundry service, concierge, business services, convention center, travel services, no-smoking rooms* 🖃 *AE, DC, MC, V* Ⓜ *JR Yamanote Line, Shinagawa Station (West Exit).*

$$$–$$$$ 🏨 **Takanawa Tōbu Hotel** (高輪東武ホテル). The Takanawa Tōbu, a five-minute walk from JR Shinagawa Station, provides good value for the price—particularly since the rate includes a buffet breakfast. Rooms are smallish and uninspired, the bathrooms are the claustrophobic prefabricated plastic units beloved of business hotels, and there's no proper sitting area in the lobby, but the hotel atones for these shortcomings with a friendly staff (which speaks a bit of English) and a cozy bar. There's also a small Western restaurant, the Boulogne. ⊠ *4–7–6 Takanawa, Minato-ku, Tōkyō-to 108-0074* ☎ *03/3447–0111* 🖷 *03/3447–0117* ⊕ *www.tobuhotel.co.jp* ➪ *190 rooms* ♨ *Restaurant, in-room data ports, refrigerators, room TVs with movies, bar, meeting room, no-smoking rooms* 🖃 *DC, V* ⦿| *BP* Ⓜ *JR Yamanote Line, Shinagawa Station (Nishi-guchi/West Exit).*

Tora-no-mon   虎ノ門

$$$$ 🏨 **ANA Hotel Tōkyō** (東京全日空ホテル). The ANA typifies the ziggurat-atrium style that seems to have been a requirement for hotel architecture from the mid-'80s. The reception floor, with its two-story fountain, is clad in enough marble to have depleted an Italian quarry. In general, though, the interior designers have made skillful use of artwork and furnishings to take some of the chill off the hotel's relentless modernism. Guest rooms are airy and spacious. There are Chinese, French, and Japanese restaurants. The Astral Lounge on the top (37th) floor affords a superb view of the city. The hotel is a short walk from the U.S. Embassy. ⊠ *1–12–33 Akasaka, Minato-ku, Tōkyō-to 107-0052* ☎ *03/ 3505–1111, 0120/029–501 toll-free* 🖷 *03/3505–1155* ⊕ *www. anahoteltokyo.jp* ➪ *867 rooms, 16 suites* ♨ *12 restaurants, cafeteria, coffee shop, food court, room service, in-room data ports, in-room fax, minibars, refrigerators, cable TV with movies, indoor pool, health club, hair salon, massage, sauna, 4 bars, shops, dry cleaning, laundry service, concierge floor, business services, meeting room, travel services, no-smoking floors* 🖃 *AE, DC, MC, V* Ⓜ *Ginza and Namboku subway lines, Tameike-Sannō Station (Exit 13); Namboku subway line, Roppongi-itchō Station (Exit 3).*

$$$$ 🏨 **Hotel Ōkura** (ホテルオークラ). Year after year, a poll of business trav-
Fodor'sChoice elers ranks the Ōkura among the best hotels in Asia for its exemplary
★ yet unobtrusive service. The hotel opened just before the 1964 Olympics,
and, understated in its sophistication, human in its scale, it remains a
favorite of diplomatic visitors. Amenities in the tasteful, spacious rooms
include remote-control draperies and terry robes. The odd-number
rooms, 871–889 inclusive, overlook a small Japanese landscaped garden. The on-site museum houses fine antique porcelain, mother-of-
pearl, and ceramics; tea ceremonies take place here Monday–Saturday
11–4 (¥1,000). The main building is preferable to the south wing, which
you reach by an underground shopping arcade. ⊠ *2–10–4 Tora-no-*
mon, Minato-ku, Tōkyō-to 105-0001 ☎ *03/3582–0111, 0120/003–*
751 toll-free 🖷 *03/3582–3707* ⊕ *www.okura.com/tokyo* ⇨ *855*
rooms, 47 suites ♿ *8 restaurants, cafeteria, coffee shop, room service,*
in-room data ports, in-room fax, in-room safes, minibars, refrigerators,
cable TV with movies, in-room VCRs, indoor pool, health club, spa, 3
bars, shops, dry cleaning, laundry service, concierge, business services,
convention center, travel services, no-smoking rooms ▤ *AE, DC, MC,*
V Ⓜ *Hibiya subway line, Kamiya-chō Station (Exit 3); Ginza subway*
line, Tora-no-mon Station (Exit 4B).

Ueno　上野

$ 🏨 **Ryokan Katsutarō** (旅館勝太郎). This small, simple, economical hotel
is a five-minute walk from the entrance to Ueno Kōen (Ueno Park) and
a 10-minute walk from the Tōkyō National Museum. The quietest
rooms are in the back, away from the main street. A simple breakfast
of toast, eggs, and coffee is served for only ¥500. To get here, leave the
Nezu subway station by Exit 2, cross the road, take the street running
northeast, and turn right at the "T" intersection; Ryokan Katsutarō is
25 yards along Dōbutsuen-uramon-dōri, on the left-hand side. ⊠ *4–16–8*
Ikenohata, Taitō-ku, Tōkyō-to 110-0008 ☎ *03/3821–9808* 🖷 *03/*
3891–4789 ⊕ *www.katsutaro.com/katsu-index.html* ⇨ *7 Japanese-*
style rooms, 4 with bath ♿ *In-room data ports, Japanese baths; no a/c*
in some rooms, no TV in some rooms ▤ *AE, MC, V* Ⓜ *Chiyoda sub-*
way line, Nezu Station (Exit 2).

Yaesu　八重洲

★ **$$–$$$** 🏨 **Hotel Yaesu Ryūmeikan** (ホテル八重洲龍名館). It's amazing that this
ryokan near Tōkyō Station has survived in the heart of the city's financial
district, where the price of real estate is astronomical. A friendly, professional staff goes the extra mile to make you feel comfortable; weekday evenings, someone who speaks English is usually on duty. Amenities
are few, but for price and location this inn is hard to beat. Room rates
include a Japanese-style breakfast; ¥800 per person is deducted from
your bill if you'd rather skip it. Checkout is at 10 AM sharp; there's a
¥1,500 surcharge for each hour you overstay. ⊠ *1–3–22 Yaesu, Chūo-*
ku, Tōkyō-to 103-0028 ☎ *03/3271–0971* 🖷 *03/3271–0977* ⊕ *www.*
ryumeikan.co.jp/yaesu_e.htm ⇨ *21 Japanese-style rooms, 9 Western-*

style rooms ♿ *2 restaurants, in-room data ports, refrigerators, Japanese baths* ⊟ *AE, MC, V* ⏐◐⏐ *BP* Ⓜ *JR Line and Marunouchi subway line, Tōkyō Station (Yaesu North Exit); Tōzai subway line, Nihombashi Station (Exit A3).*

Yanaka 谷中

$ ⌧ **Sawanoya Ryokan** (澤の屋旅館). The Shitamachi area is known for its
Fodor'sChoice down-to-earth friendliness, which you get in full measure at Sawanoya.
★ This little inn is a family business: everybody pitches in to help you plan excursions and book hotels for the next leg of your journey, and they even organize cultural events in the lobby. The inn is very popular with budget travelers, so reserve well in advance by fax or online. To get here from Nezu Station, walk 300 yards north along Shinobazu-dōri and take the street on the right; Sawanoya is 180 yards ahead on the right. ⊠ *2–3–11 Yanaka, Taitō-ku, Tōkyō-to 110-0001* ☏ *03/3822–2251* 🖷 *03/3822–2252* ⊕ *www.sawanoya.com* ↘ *12 Japanese-style rooms, 2 with bath* ♿ *Dining room, in-room data ports, Japanese baths* ⊟ *AE, MC, V* Ⓜ *Chiyoda subway line, Nezu Station (Exit 1).*

Hostels

$ ⌧ **YMCA Asia Youth Center** (YMCAアジア青少年センター). Both men and women can stay here, and all rooms are private and have private baths. The hostel is an eight-minute walk from Suidō-bashi Station. ⊠ *2–5–5 Saragaku, Chiyoda-ku, Tōkyō-to 101-0064* ☏ *03/3233–0611* 🖷 *03/3233–0633* ⊕ *http://ymcajapan.org/ayc* ↘ *55 rooms* ⊟ *MC, V* Ⓜ *JR Mita Line, Suidō-bashi Station.*

¢ ⌧ **Tōkyō International Youth Hostel** (東京国際ユースホステル). In typical hostel style, you're required to be off the premises between 10 AM and 3 PM. Less typical is the fact that for an additional ¥1,200 over the standard rate, you can eat breakfast and dinner in the hostel cafeteria. TIYH is a few minutes' walk from Iidabashi Station. ⊠ *Central Plaza Bldg., 18th fl., 1–1 Kagura-kashi, Shinjuku-ku, Tōkyō-to 162-0823* ☏ *03/3235–1107* 🖷 *03/3267–4000* ⊕ *www.tokyo-yh.jp/engl/e_top.html* ↘ *138 bunk beds without bath* ♿ *Dining room, Japanese baths* ⊟ *No credit cards* Ⓜ *JR; Tōzai, Namboku, and Yūraku-chō subway lines: Iidabashi Station (Exit B2b).*

Near Narita Airport

Transportation between Narita Airport and Tōkyō proper takes at least an hour and a half. In heavy traffic, a limousine bus or taxi ride can stretch to two hours or more. A sensible strategy for visitors with early-morning flights home would be to spend the night before at one of the hotels near the airport, all of which have courtesy shuttles to the departure terminals; these hotels are also a boon to visitors en route elsewhere with layovers in Narita.

$$$$ ⌧ **ANA Hotel Narita** (成田全日空ホテル). This hotel, like many others in the ANA chain, aspires to architecture in the grand style; expect the cost of brass and marble to show up on your bill. The amenities measure

up, and the proximity to the airport (about 15 minutes by shuttle bus) makes this a good choice if you're in transit. If you're flying ANA, you can check in for your flight in the lobby. ✉ *68 Hori-no-uchi, Narita-shi, Chiba-ken 286-0107* ☎ *0476/33–1311, 0120/029–501 toll-free* 📠 *0476/33–0244* ⊕ *www.anahotel-narita.com/english* 🛏 *422 rooms* ⚥ *3 restaurants, coffee shop, room service, in-room data ports, mini-bars, cable TV with movies, tennis court, indoor pool, gym, sauna, shops, airport shuttle, no-smoking rooms* 🖃 *AE, DC, MC, V.*

$$–$$$$ ▣ **Holiday Inn Tōbu Narita** (ホリデイ・イン東武成田). The Western-style accommodations at this hotel, a 10-minute ride by shuttle bus from the airport, provide the standard—if unremarkable—range of ameni-ties. You can also rent one of its soundproof twin rooms for daytime-only use (11 AM–6 PM, ¥13,000). ✉ *320–1 Tokkō, Narita-shi, Chiba-ken 286-0106* ☎ *0476/32–1234* 📠 *0476/32–0617* ⊕ *www.basshotels.com* 🛏 *500 rooms* ⚥ *2 restaurants, coffee shop, tennis court, pool, hair salon, massage, steam room, bar, no-smoking rooms* 🖃 *AE, DC, MC, V.*

$$–$$$$ ▣ **Hotel Nikkō Winds Narita** (ホテル日航ウインズ成田). A regular shuttle bus (at Terminal 1, Bus Stop 14; Terminal 2, Bus Stop 31) makes the 10-minute trip from the airport to the Nikkō Winds, and you can check in for Japan Airlines flights right at the hotel. Basic, cheap furnishings fill the rooms in the main building, and there's barely room to pass be-tween the bed and the dresser en route to the bathroom—but the rooms are thoroughly soundproof. Rooms in the "Executive" building are nicer but pricier. ✉ *560 Tokkō, Narita-shi, Chiba-ken 286-1016* ☎ *0476/33–1111, 0120/582–586 toll-free* 📠 *0476/33–1108* ⊕ *www.jalhnn.co.jp/hnn-e* 🛏 *308 rooms, 9 suites* ⚥ *3 restaurants, coffee shop, grocery, room service, in-room data ports, minibars, refrigerators, cable TV with movies, 2 tennis courts, pool, hair salon, massage, lounge, shops, meeting room, airport shuttle, no-smoking rooms* 🖃 *AE, DC, MC, V.*

$$–$$$$ ▣ **Radisson Hotel Narita Airport** (ラディソンホテル成田エアポート). Set on 72 spacious acres of land, this modern hotel feels somewhat like a re-sort, and it has Narita's largest outdoor pool. A shuttle bus runs between the Radisson and the airport every 20 minutes or so; the hotel also op-erates ten buses daily directly to and from Tōkyō Station. ✉ *650–35 Nanae, Tomisato-machi, Inaba-gun, Chiba-ken 286-0222* ☎ *0476/93–1234* 📠 *0476/93–4834* ⊕ *www.radisson.com/tokyojp_narita* 🛏 *493 rooms* ⚥ *Restaurant, coffee shop, room service, in-room data ports, mini-bars, refrigerators, cable TV with movies, 2 tennis courts, indoor-out-door pool, gym, sauna, bar, beer garden, lounge, shops, dry cleaning, laundry service, business services, convention center, airport shuttle, travel services, no-smoking rooms* 🖃 *AE, DC, MC, V.*

$$–$$$ ▣ **Narita View Hotel** (成田ビューホテル). Boxy and uninspired, the Narita View offers no view of anything in particular but can be reached by shut-tle bus from the airport in about 15 minutes. Short on charm, it tends to rely on promotional discount "campaigns" to draw a clientele. Rooms are soundproof. ✉ *700 Kosuge, Narita-shi, Chiba-ken 286-0127* ☎ *0476/32–1111* 📠 *0476/32–1078* ⊕ *www.viewhotels.co.jp/narita/english/* 🛏 *504 rooms* ⚥ *4 restaurants, coffee shop, refrigerators, room TVs with movies, hair salon, massage, no-smoking rooms* 🖃 *AE, DC, MC, V.*

$ ▦ **Narita Airport Rest House** (成田エアポートレストハウス). A basic business hotel without much in the way of frills, the Rest House offers the closest accommodations to the airport itself, less than five minutes away by shuttle bus. You can also rent one of its soundproof rooms for daytime-only use from 9 to 5 for about ¥5,000. ⊠ *New Tōkyō International Airport, Narita-shi, Chiba-ken 286-0000* ☎ *0476/32–1212* 🖷 *0476/32–1209* 🖘 *129 rooms* 🖒 *Restaurant, coffee shop, bar, nosmoking rooms* 🖃 *AE, DC, MC, V.*

NIGHTLIFE &
THE ARTS

4

MOST COLORFUL DRAMAS
Performances at Kabuki-za in Ginza ⇨*p.136*

RITZIEST LOUNGES AND CLUBS
the Ginza district ⇨*p.140*

DECADENT, SKETCHY, AND NEON-LIT
Kabuki-chō in Shinjuku ⇨*p.141*

BEST OUTDOOR CAFÉ
Sekirei in Akasaka ⇨*p.142*

HIPPER-THAN-THOU DJs
Womb in Shibuya ⇨*p.144*

WHEN IN JAPAN, SING KARAOKE
Smash Hits in Shibuya ⇨*p.146*

Updated by
Steve Trautlein
and Matt
Wilce

UNDER A RAINBOW OF NEON, Tōkyō comes alive at night. This city has more sheer diversity of nightlife than any other Japanese city. It seems as if every neighborhood is packed with secret drinking dens, swank bars, jazz spots, pubs, clubs, hostess bars, and other entertainments. Whether you're a punk rocker, disco diva, or bar-hopper, you'll be in good company if you venture out after dark.

Despite the popularity of *nomunication* (communication through drink), not all of the city's nightlife revolves around Suntory whiskey and Asahi beer. Tōkyō has an incredibly diverse performing-arts scene that spans everything from the traditional arts to Western musicals to avant-garde theater. Japan's own great stage traditions—Kabuki, Nō, Bunraku puppet drama, and various forms of music and dance—take you back in time as they bring to life the histories and folktales of old Japan.

THE ARTS

An astonishing variety of dance and music, both classical and popular, can be found in Tōkyō, alongside the must-see traditional Japanese arts of Kabuki, Nō, and Bunraku. The city is a proving ground for local talent and a magnet for orchestras and concert soloists from all over the world. Eric Clapton, Yo-Yo Ma, Wynton Marsalis: whenever you visit, the headliners will be here. Tōkyō also has modern theater—in somewhat limited choices, to be sure, unless you can follow dialogue in Japanese, but Western repertory companies can always find receptive audiences here for plays in English. And it doesn't take long for a hit show from New York or London to open in Tōkyō. In recent years musicals such as *The Lion King* have found enormous popularity here—although you'll find Simba speaks Japanese.

Japan has yet to develop any real strength of its own in ballet and has only just begun to devote serious resources to opera, but for that reason touring companies like the Metropolitan, the Bolshoi, Sadler's Wells, and the Bayerische Staatsoper find Tōkyō a very compelling venue—as well they might when even seats at ¥30,000 or more sell out far in advance. One domestic company that's making a name for itself is the Asami Maki Ballet, whose dancers are known for their technical proficiency and expressiveness; the company often performs at the Tōkyō Metropolitan Festival Hall. Latin dance also has a strong following in Tōkyō, and flamenco heart-throb Joaquin Cortés visits regularly to wide acclaim and packed houses.

Film presents a much broader range of possibilities than it did in the past. The major commercial distributors bring in the movies they expect will draw the biggest receipts—these days, that's as likely to be a big Asian hit as an American blockbuster or Oscar nominee. The increased diversity brought by smaller distributors, and the current vogue for Korean, Chinese, and Hong Kong cinema have helped to develop vibrant small theaters that cater to a sophisticated audience of art house fans. New multiplexes have also brought new screens to the capital, offering a more comfortable film-going experience than some of the older Japanese theaters.

Information & Tickets

One of Tōkyō's best English-language performance guides is *Metropolis*, a free weekly magazine that has up-to-date listings of what's going on in the city; it's available at hotels, book and music stores, some restaurants and cafés, and other locations. Another source, rather less complete, is the *Tour Companion,* a tabloid visitor guide published every two weeks, available free of charge at hotels and at Japan National Tourist Organization offices. For coverage of all aspects of Tōkyō's performance-art scene, visit ⊕ www.artindex.metro.tokyo.jp.

If your hotel cannot help you with concert and performance bookings, call **Ticket Pia** (☎ 03/5237–9999) for assistance in English. Note, however, that this is one of the city's major ticket agencies, and the lines are frequently busy. The **Playguide Agency** (✉ Playguide Bldg., 2–6–4 Ginza, Chūō-ku ☎ 03/3561–8821 📠 03/3567–0263 Ⓜ Yūraku-chō subway line, Ginza Itchōme Station, Exit 4) sells tickets to cultural events via outlets in most department stores and in other locations throughout the city; you can stop in at the main office and ask for the nearest counter. Note that agencies normally do not have tickets for same-day performances but only for advance booking.

Dance

Traditional Japanese dance, like flower arranging and the tea ceremony, is divided into dozens of styles, ancient of lineage and fiercely proud of their differences from each other. In fact, only the aficionado can really tell them apart. They survive not so much as performing arts but as schools, offering dance as a cultured accomplishment to interested amateurs. At least once a year, teachers and their students in each of these schools hold a recital, so that on any given evening there's very likely to be one somewhere in Tōkyō. Truly professional performances are given at the Kokuritsu Gekijō and the Shimbashi Enbujō; the most important of the classical schools, however, developed as an aspect of Kabuki, and if you attend a play at the Kabuki-za, you are almost guaranteed to see a representative example.

Ballet began to attract a Japanese following in 1920, when Anna Pavlova danced *The Dying Swan* at the old Imperial Theater. The well-known companies that come to Tōkyō from abroad perform to full houses, usually at the Tōkyō Metropolitan Festival Hall in Ueno. There are now about 15 professional Japanese ballet companies, including the Tōkyō Ballet—which performs at the Tōkyō Metropolitan Festival Hall and regularly tours abroad—but this has yet to become an art form on which Japan has had much of an impact.

Modern dance, on the other hand, is a different story. The modern Japanese dance form known as Butō, in particular, with its contorted and expressive body movements, is acclaimed internationally and domestically. Butō performances are held periodically at a variety of event spaces and small theaters. For details, check with ticket agencies and the local English-language press.

CloseUp

BUTŌ: DANCE OF DARKNESS

THE STORY OF MODERN DANCE in Japan began with a visit in 1955 by the Martha Graham Dance Company. The decade that followed was one of great turmoil in Japan, a period of dissatisfaction—political, intellectual, artistic—with old forms and conventions. The work of pioneers like Graham inspired talented dancers and choreographers to explore new avenues of self-expression. One of the fruits of that exploration was Butō, a movement that was at once uniquely Japanese and a major contribution to the world of modern dance.

The father of Butō was the dancer Tatsumi Hijikata (1928–86), who sought to create a form entirely different from traditional Japanese and classical and modern Western styles of dance. The watershed work was his Revolt of the Flesh, which premiered in 1968. Others soon followed:

Kazuo Ōno, Min Tanaka, Akaji Maro and the Dai Rakuda Kan troupe, and Ushio Amagatsu and the Sankai Juku. To most Japanese, their work was inexplicably grotesque. Dancers performed with shaved heads, dressed in rags or with naked bodies painted completely white, their movements agonized and contorted. The images were dark and demonic, violent and explicitly sexual (the form was originally called Ankoku Butō, literally "dance of darkness"). Butō was an exploration of the unconscious: its gods were the gods of the Japanese village and the gods of prehistory; its literary inspirations came from Mishima, Genet, Artaud. Like many other modern Japanese artists, Butō dancers and choreographers were largely ignored by the mainstream until they began to appear abroad—to thunderous critical acclaim. Now they are equally honored at home.

Film

One of the best things about foreign films in Japan is that the distributors invariably add Japanese subtitles rather than dub their offerings. Exceptions include kids' movies and big blockbusters that are released in both versions—if there are two screenings close to each other, that's a sign one may be dubbed. The original sound track, of course, may not be all that helpful to you if the film is Polish or Italian, but the majority of first-run foreign films here are made in the United States. Choices range from the usual Hollywood fare to independent movies, but many films take so long to open in Tōkyō that you've probably seen them all already at home. And tickets are expensive: around ¥1,800 for general admission and ¥2,500–¥3,000 for a reserved seat, called a *shitei-seki*. Slightly discounted tickets, usually ¥1,600, can be purchased from the ticket counters found in many department stores.

The Japanese film industry is currently experiencing a renaissance, with high-profile wins at Cannes, the 2001 *Spirited Away*'s Academy Award, and the 2002 American remake of the 1998 horror hit *Ringu* (*The Ring*) boosting recognition overseas. Director-actor Takeshi Kitano's works have garnered critical acclaim and a following in Europe, and he remains one of the country's foremost auteurs—although this doesn't stop him from dressing up in outlandish costumes on TV. Although many of the major Japanese studios continue to struggle to compete with big-budget U.S. fare, anime remains strong and each year sees several major domestic successes. Unless your Japanese is top-notch, most domestic films will be off-limits, but if you happen to be in town during one of the many film festivals you may be able to catch a screening with English subtitles. Festival season is in the fall, with the Tōkyō International Film Festival taking over the Shibuya district in October and a slew of other more specialized festivals screening more outré fare.

First-run theaters that have new releases, both Japanese and foreign, are clustered for the most part in three areas: Shinjuku, Shibuya, and Yūraku-chō-Hibiya-Ginza. At most of them, the last showing of the evening starts at around 7. This is not the case, however, with the best news on the Tōkyō film scene: the handful of small theaters that take a special interest in classics, revivals, and serious imports. Somewhere on the premises will also be a chrome-and-marble coffee shop, a fashionable little bar, or even a decent restaurant. Most of these small theaters have a midnight show—at least on the weekends.

Bunka-mura. The complex in Shibuya has two movie theaters, a concert auditorium (Orchard Hall), and a performance space (Theater Cocoon); it's the principal venue for many of Tōkyō's film festivals. ⊠ *2–24–1 Dōgenzaka, Shibuya-ku* ☎ *03/3477–9999* Ⓜ *JR Yamanote Line, Ginza and Hanzō-mon subway lines, and private rail lines; Shibuya Station (Exits 5 and 8 for Hanzō-mon Line, Kita-guchi/North Exit for all others).*

Chanter Cine. A three-screen cinema complex, Chanter Cine tends to show British and American films by independent producers but also showcases fine work by filmmakers from Asia and the Middle East. ⊠ *1–2–2 Yūraku-chō, Chiyoda-ku* ☎ *03/3591–1511* Ⓜ *Hibiya, Chiyoda, and Mita subway lines, Hibiya Station (Exit A5).*

Cine Saison Shibuya. In addition to popular films, this theater occasionally screens recent releases by award-winning directors from such countries as Iran, China, and South Korea. ⊠ *Prime Bldg., 2–29–5 Dōgenzaka, Shibuya-ku* ☎ *03/3770–1721* Ⓜ *JR Yamanote Line, Shibuya Station (Hachiko Exit).*

Haiyū-za. This is primarily a repertory theater, but on Haiyū-za Talkie Nights it screens notable foreign films. ⊠ *4–9–2 Roppongi, Minato-ku* ☎ *03/3401–4073* Ⓜ *Hibiya subway line, Roppongi Station (Exit 4A).*

Virgin Cinemas. In Roppongi Hills, this complex offers comfort, plus six screens, VIP seats, and late shows on weekends. There are plenty of bars in the area for post-movie discussions. ⊠ *Keyakizaka Complex, 6–10–2 Roppongi, Minato-ku* ☎ *03/5775–6090* Ⓜ *Hibiya and Ōedo subway lines, Roppongi Station (Roppongi Hills Exit).*

Modern Theater

The Shingeki (Modern Theater) movement began in Japan at about the turn of the 20th century, coping at first with the lack of native repertoire by performing translations of Western dramatists from Shakespeare to Shaw. It wasn't until around 1915 that Japanese playwrights began writing for the Shingeki stage, but modern drama did not really develop a voice of its own here until after World War II.

The watershed years came around 1965, when experimental theater companies, unable to find commercial space, began taking their work to young audiences in various unusual ways: street plays and "happenings," dramatic readings in underground malls and rented lofts, tents put up on vacant lots for unannounced performances (miraculously filled to capacity by word of mouth) and taken down the next day. It was during this period that surrealist playwright Kōbō Abe found his stride and director Tadashi Suzuki developed the unique system of training that now draws aspiring actors from all over the world to his "theater community" in the mountains of Toyama Prefecture. Japanese drama today is a lively art indeed; theaters small and large, in unexpected pockets all over Tōkyō, attest to its vitality.

Most of these performances, however, are in Japanese, for Japanese audiences. You're unlikely to find one with program notes in English to help you follow it. Unless it's a play you already know well, and you're curious to see how it translates, you might do well to think of some other way to spend your evenings out if you don't understand Japanese. Language is less of a barrier, however, to enjoyment of the Takarazuka comedic troupe.

Takarazuka. Japan's own wonderfully goofy all-female troupe was founded in the Ōsaka suburb of Takarazuka in 1913 and has been going strong ever since; today it has not one but five companies, one of them with a permanent home in Tōkyō at the 2,069-seat Tōkyō Takarazuka Theater. Everybody sings; everybody dances; the sets are breathtaking; the costumes are swell. Where else but at the Takarazuka could you see *Gone With the Wind*, sung in Japanese, with a young woman in a mustache and a frock coat playing Rhett Butler? Tickets cost ¥3,800–¥10,000 for regular performances, ¥2,000–¥5,000 for debut performances with the company's budding ingenues. ⊠ *1–1–3 Yūraku-chō, Chiyoda-ku* ☎ *03/5251–2001* Ⓜ *JR Yamanote Line, Yūraku-chō Station (Hibiya-guchi Exit); Hibiya subway line, Hibiya Station (Exit A5); Chiyoda and Mita subway line, Hibiya Station (Exit A13).*

Music

Information in English about venues for traditional Japanese music (koto, shamisen, and so forth) can be a bit hard to find; check newspaper listings, particularly the Friday and Saturday editions, for concerts and school recitals. Western music poses no such problem: during the 1980s and early 1990s a considerable number of new concert halls and performance spaces sprang up all over the city, adding to what was already an excellent roster of public auditoriums. The following are a few of the most important.

Casals Hall. The last of the fine small auditoriums built for chamber music, before the Japanese bubble economy burst in the early '90s, was designed by architect Arata Isozaki—justly famous for the Museum of Contemporary Art in Los Angeles. In addition to chamber music, Casals draws piano, guitar, cello, and voice soloists. ✉ *1–6 Kanda Surugadai, Chiyoda-ku* ☎ *03/3294–1229* Ⓜ *JR Chūō Line and Marunouchi subway line, Ochanomizu Station (Exit 2).*

Iino Hall. Built before Japan fell fatally in love with marble, Iino Hall maintains a reputation for comfort, intelligent programming, and excellent acoustics. The venue hosts chamber music and Japanese concert soloists. ✉ *2–1–1 Uchisaiwai-chō, Chiyoda-ku* ☎ *03/3506–3251* Ⓜ *Chiyoda and Hibiya subway lines, Kasumigaseki Station (Exit C4); Marunouchi subway line, Kasumigaseki Station (Exit B2); Ginza subway line, Toranomon Station (Exit 9); Mita subway line, Uchisaiwai-chō Station (Exit A7).*

Nakano Sun Plaza. Everything from rock to Argentine tango music is staged at this hall. ✉ *4–1–1 Nakano, Nakano-ku* ☎ *03/3388–1151* Ⓜ *JR and Tōzai subway lines, Nakano Station (Kita-guchi/North Exit).*

New National Theater and Tōkyō Opera City Concert Hall. With its 1,810-seat main auditorium, this venue nourishes Japan's fledgling efforts to make a name for itself in the world of opera. The Opera City Concert Hall has a massive pipe organ and hosts visiting orchestras and performers. Large-scale operatic productions such as *Carmen* draw crowds at the New National Theater's Opera House, while the Pit and Playhouse theaters showcase musicals and more intimate dramatic works. Ticket prices range from ¥1,500 to ¥21,000. The complex also includes an art gallery. ✉ *3–20–2 Nishi-Shinjuku, Shinjuku-ku* ☎ *03/5353–0788, 03/5353–9999 for tickets* ⊕ *www.operacity.jp* Ⓜ *Keiō Shin-sen private rail line, Hatsudai Station (Higashi-guchi/East Exit).*

NHK Hall. The home base for the Japan Broadcasting Corporation's NHK Symphony Orchestra is probably the auditorium most familiar to Japanese lovers of classical music, as performances here are routinely rebroadcast on NHK-TV. ✉ *2–2–1 Jinnan, Shibuya-ku* ☎ *03/3465–1751* Ⓜ *JR Yamanote Line, Shibuya Station (Hachiko Exit); Ginza and Hanzō-mon subway lines, Shibuya Station (Exits 6 and 7).*

Suntory Hall. This lavishly appointed concert auditorium in the Ark Hills complex has one of the best locations for theatergoers who want to extend their evening out: there's an abundance of good restaurants and bars nearby. ✉ *1–13–1 Akasaka, Minato-ku* ☎ *03/3505–1001* Ⓜ *Ginza and Namboku subway lines, Tameike-Sannō Station (Exit 13).*

Tōkyō Dome. A 55,000-seat sports arena, the dome hosts the biggest acts from abroad in rock and popular music. ✉ *1–3–61 Kōraku, Bunkyō-ku* ☎ *03/5800–9999* Ⓜ *Marunouchi and Namboku subway lines, Kōraku-en Station (Exit 2); Ōedo and Mita subway lines, Kasuga Station (Exit A2); JR Suidō-bashi Station (Nishi-guchi/West Exit).*

Tōkyō Metropolitan Festival Hall (Tōkyō Bunka Kaikan). In the 1960s and '70s this hall was one of the city's premier showcases for orchestral music and visiting soloists. It still gets major bookings. ✉ *5–45 Ueno Kōen,*

Taitō-ku ☎ *03/3828–2111* Ⓜ *JR Yamanote Line, Ueno Station (Kōen-guchi/Park Exit).*

Traditional Theater

Bunraku

Bunraku puppet theater is one of Japan's most accessible traditional arts. Incredibly intricate puppets give performances so realistic that you may soon forget they're being guided by black-clad puppet masters. The spiritual center of Bunraku today is Ōsaka, rather than Tōkyō, but there are a number of performances in the small hall of the Kokuritsu Gekijō. The art form has come into vogue with younger audiences, and Bunraku troupes will occasionally perform in trendier locations. Consult *Metropolis* magazine or check with one of the English-speaking ticket agencies for performance schedules.

Kabuki

Kabuki has been pleasing Japanese audiences from all walks of life for more than 300 years. It's the kind of theater—a combination of music, dance, and drama, with spectacular costumes and acrobatics, duels, and quick changes and special effects thrown in—that you can enjoy without understanding a word the actors say.

Fodor'sChoice ★ **Kabuki-za.** The best place to see Kabuki is at this theater, built especially for this purpose, with its *hanamichi* (runway) passing diagonally through the audience to the revolving stage. Built in 1925, the Kabuki-za was destroyed in an air raid in 1945 and rebuilt in the identical style in 1951. Matinees usually begin at 11 and end at 4; evening performances start at 4:30 and end around 9. Reserved seats are expensive and can be hard to come by on short notice (reserve tickets by at least 6 PM the day before you wish to attend). For a mere ¥800 to ¥1,000, however, you can buy an unreserved ticket that allows you to see one act of a play from the topmost gallery. Bring binoculars—the gallery is very far from the stage. You might also want to rent an earphone set (¥650; deposit ¥1,000) to follow the play in English, but for some this is more of an intrusion than a help—and you can't use the set in the topmost galleries. ✉ *4-12–15 Ginza, Chūō-ku* ☎ *03/5565–6000 or 03/3541–3131* ⊕ *www.shochiku.co.jp/play/kabukiza/theater* Ⓜ *Hibiya and Asakusa subway lines, Higashi-Ginza Station (Exit 3).*

Kokuritsu Gekijō. This theater hosts Kabuki companies based elsewhere; it also has a training program for young people who may not have one of the hereditary family connections but want to break into this closely guarded profession. Debut performances, called *kao-mise*, are worth watching to catch the stars of the next generation. Reserved seats are usually ¥1,500–¥9,000. Tickets can be reserved by phone up until the day of the performance by calling the theater box office between 10 and 5. ✉ *4-1 Hayabusa-chō, Chiyoda-ku* ☎ *03/3230–3000* Ⓜ *Hanzō-mon subway line, Hanzō-mon Station (Exit 1).*

Shimbashi Enbujō. Dating to 1925, this theater was built for the geisha of the Shimbashi quarter to present their spring and autumn performances of traditional music and dance. It's a bigger house than the Kabuki-za, and it presents a lot of traditional dance, *kyogen* (traditional Nō-style comic skits), and conventional Japanese drama as well as Kabuki. Reserved seats commonly run ¥2,100–¥16,800, and there's no gallery. ⊠ *6–18–2 Ginza, Chūo-ku* ☎ *03/5565–6000* Ⓜ *Hibiya and Asakusa subway lines, Higashi-Ginza Station (Exit A6).*

Nō

Performances of Nō, with its slow, ritualized movements and archaic language, are given at various times during the year, generally in the theaters of the individual schools. The schools also often teach their dance and recitation styles to amateurs. Consult the *Tour Companion* listings. Tickets to Takigi Nō (held outdoors in temple courtyards) sell out quickly and are normally available only through the temples.

Kanze Nō-gakudō. Founded in the 14th century, this is among the most important of the Nō family schools in Tōkyō. The current *iemoto* (head) of the school is the 26th in his line. ⊠ *1–16–4 Shōtō, Shibuya-ku* ☎ *03/3469–5241* Ⓜ *Ginza and Hanzō-mon subway lines, Shibuya Station (Exit 3A).*

National Nō Theater. This is one of the few public halls to host Nō performances. ⊠ *4–18–1 Sendagaya, Shibuya-ku* ☎ *03/3423–1331* Ⓜ *JR Chūō Line, Sendagaya Station (Minami-guchi/South Exit); Ōedo subway line, Kokuritsu-Kyōgijō Station (Exit A4).*

Umewaka Nō-gakuin. Johnny-come-lately in the world of Nō is the Umewaka School, founded in 1921. Classes and performances are held here. ⊠ *2–6–14 Higashi-Nakano, Nakano-ku* ☎ *03/3363–7748* Ⓜ *JR Chūō Line, Higashi-Nakano Station (Exit 2); Marunouchi and Ōedo subway lines, Nakano-saka-ue Station (Exit A1).*

Rakugo

A *rakugo* comedian sits on a cushion and, with the help of such simple props as fans and pipes, relates stories that have been handed down for centuries. Using different voices and facial expressions, the storyteller acts out the parts of different characters within the stories. There's generally no English interpretation, and the monologues, filled with puns and expressions in dialect, can even be difficult for the Japanese themselves. A performance of rakugo is still worth seeing, however, for a slice of traditional pop culture.

Suzumoto. Built around 1857 and later rebuilt, Suzumoto is the oldest rakugo theater in Tōkyō. It's on Chūō-dōri, a few blocks north of the Ginza Line's Ueno Hirokō-ji stop. Tickets cost ¥2,000, and performances run continually throughout the day 12:20–4:30 and 5:20–9:10. ⊠ *2–7–12 Ueno, Taitō-ku* ☎ *03/3834–5906* Ⓜ *Ginza subway line, Ueno Hirokō-ji Station (Exit 3).*

NIGHTLIFE

Most bars and clubs in the main entertainment districts have printed price lists, many in English. Drinks generally cost ¥600–¥1,200, although some small exclusive bars and clubs will set you back a lot more. Be wary of establishments without visible price lists. Hostess clubs and small

TRADITIONAL JAPANESE DRAMA

Kabuki

Kabuki emerged as a popular form of entertainment by women dancing lewdly in the early 17th century; before long, it had been banned by the authorities as a threat to public order. Eventually it cleaned up its act, and by the latter half of the 18th century it had become popular with common folks—especially the townspeople of bustling, hustling Edo, which would grow into Tōkyō. Kabuki had music, dance, and spectacle; it had acrobatics and sword fights; it had pathos and tragedy and historical romance and social satire. It no longer had bawdy beauties, however—women have been banned from the Kabuki stage since 1629—but in recompense it developed a professional role for female impersonators, who train for years to project a seductive, dazzling femininity. It had—and still has—superstars and quick-change artists and legions of fans, who bring their lunch to the theater, stay all day, and shout out the names of their favorite actors at the stirring moments in their favorite plays.

Edo is now Tōkyō, but Kabuki is still here, just as it has been for centuries. The traditions are passed down from generation to generation in a small group of families; the roles and great stage names are hereditary. The Kabuki repertoire does not really grow or change, but stars like Ennosuke Ichikawa and Tamasaburo Bando have put exciting, personal stamps on their performances that continue to draw audiences young and old. If you don't know Japanese, you can still enjoy a performance: Tōkyō's Kabuki-za (Kabuki Theater) has simultaneous English translation of its plays available on headphones. Reading: The Kabuki Guide, by Masakatsu Gunji.

Nō

Nō is a dramatic tradition far older than Kabuki: it reached a point of formal perfection in the 14th century and survives virtually unchanged from that period. Somewhat like Kabuki, Nō has a number of schools, the traditions of which developed as the exclusive property of hereditary families. Whereas Kabuki was theater for the masses, however, Nō developed for the most part under the patronage of the warrior class. It's dignified, ritualized, and symbolic. Many of the plays in the repertoire are drawn from classical literature or tales of the supernatural, and the texts are richly poetic. Some understanding of the plot of each play is necessary to enjoy a performance, which moves at a nearly glacial pace—the pace of ritual time—as it's solemnly chanted. The major Nō theaters often provide synopses of the plays in English.

Whereas the Kabuki actor is usually in brightly colored makeup derived from the Chinese opera, the principal character in a Nō play wears a carved wooden mask. Such is the skill of the actor—and the mysterious effect of the play—that the mask itself may appear expressionless until the actor "brings it to life," at which point the mask seems to express a considerable range of emotions. As in Kabuki, the various roles of the Nō repertoire all have specific costumes—robes of silk brocade with intricate patterns that are works of art in themselves. Nō is not a very accessible kind of theater: its language is archaic, its conventions are obscure, and its measured, stately pace can put even Japanese audiences to sleep.

The best way to see Nō is in the open air, at torchlight performances called Takigi Nō, held in the courtyards of temples. The setting and the aesthetics of the drama combine to produce an eerie theatrical experience. In Tōkyō, as a contrast to the rest of the city, Nō will provide an experience of Japan as an ancient, sophisticated culture.

Kyōgen are shorter, lighter plays that are often interspersed in between Nō performances and are much more accessible than Nō. If Nō doesn't appeal to you, consider taking advantage of opportunities to see kyōgen instead.

Bunraku

The third major form of traditional Japanese drama is Bunraku puppet theater. Itinerant puppeteers were plying their trade in Japan as early as the 10th century. Sometime in the late 16th century, a form of narrative ballad called jōruri, performed to the accompaniment of a three-string banjolike instrument called the shamisen, was grafted onto their art, and Bunraku was born. The golden age of Bunraku came some 200 years later, when most of the form's great plays were written and the puppets themselves evolved to their present form—so expressive and intricate in their movements that they require three people at one time to manipulate them. Puppeteers and narrators, who deliver their lines in a kind of high-pitched croak from deep in the throat, train for many years to master this difficult and unusual genre of popular entertainment. Puppets are about two-thirds human size and are large enough to cover the puppeteers underneath them. Elaborately dressed in period costume, each puppet is made up of interchangeable parts: a head, shoulder piece, trunk, legs, and arms. Various puppet heads are used for roles of different sex, age, and character, and a certain hairstyle will indicate a puppet's position in life.

To operate one puppet, three puppeteers must act in complete unison. The omozukai controls the expression on the puppet's face and its right arm and hand.

The hidarizukai controls the puppet's left arm and hand along with any props that it's carrying. The ashizukai moves the puppet's legs. This last task is the easiest. The most difficult task belongs to the omozukai. It takes about 30 years to become an expert. A puppeteer must spend 10 years as ashizukai, an additional 10 as hidarizukai, and then 10 more years as omozukai. These master puppeteers not only skillfully manipulate the puppets' arms and legs but also roll the eyes and move the lips so that the puppets express fear, joy, and sadness.

— Jared Lubarsky and David Miles

backstreet bars known as "snacks" or "pubs" can be particularly treacherous territory for the unprepared. That drink you've just ordered could set you back a reasonable ¥1,000; you might, on the other hand, have wandered unknowingly into a place that charges you ¥15,000 up front for a whole bottle—and slaps a ¥20,000 cover charge on top. If the bar has hostesses, it's often unclear what the companionship of one will cost you, or whether she is there just for conversation. Ignore the persuasive shills on the streets of Roppongi and Kabuki-chō, who will try to hook you into their establishment. There is, of course, a certain amount of safe ground: hotel lounges, jazz clubs, and cabarets where foreigners come out to play are pretty much the way they are anywhere else. But wandering off the beaten path in Tōkyō can be like shopping for a yacht: if you have to ask how much it costs, you probably can't afford it anyhow.

There are five major districts in Tōkyō that have extensive nightlife, including places that welcome foreigners. The *kinds* of entertainment will not vary much from one to another; the tone, style, and prices will.

Akasaka

Nightlife in Akasaka concentrates mainly on two streets—Ta-machi-dōri and Hitotsugi-dōri—and the small alleys connecting them. The area has several cabarets and nightclubs, plus wine bars, coffee shops, late-night restaurants, pubs, and "snacks"—counter bars that will serve (and charge you for) small portions of food with your drinks, whether you order them or not. It's also renowned for its many Korean barbecue restaurants, which tend to be on the pricy side. Akasaka is sophisticated and upscale—which is not surprising for an old geisha district—but not quite as expensive as Ginza and not as popular as Roppongi. Being fairly compact, it makes a convenient venue for testing the waters of Japanese nightlife.

Ginza

This is probably the city's most well-known entertainment district, and one of the most—if not *the* most—expensive in the world. It does have affordable restaurants and pubs, but its reputation rests on the exclusive hostess clubs where only the highest of high rollers on corporate expense accounts can take their clients. Many corporations have been taking a harder look at those accounts, however, and Ginza as a nightlife destination has shifted its focus more to affluent young women and trendy couples. Expect to find everything from old-style corporate hangouts and traditional Japanese fare to contemporary dining and tony bars.

Roppongi

At one time Roppongi was the haunt of the rich and the beautiful. Although no longer the unanimous first choice for those seeking a rollicking night on the town, the area remains an indispensable part of the city's nightlife. Sure, the sleaze factor is high—but so are the options. Bars, clubs, cafés, karaoke rooms, restaurants, hostess bars, dinner theater, and comedy acts are all here, and Roppongi is still the part of Tōkyō where Westerners are most likely to feel at home. The 2003 unveiling of the Roppongi Hills complex, with its shops and restaurants, even managed to restore a bit of the old luster to the area.

Shibuya

Less expensive than Roppongi and not as raunchy as Shinjuku, Shibuya attracts mainly students and young professionals. An up-and-coming neighborhood that is already a center of teen fashion, Shibuya is making a name for itself with a newly vibrant nightlife scene that includes some of Tōkyō's top nightclubs, plus inexpensive bars and restaurants. This is a great place to drink, eat, people-watch, and take in the city's vibrant youth culture.

Shinjuku

Long a favorite drinking spot for artists and businesspeople alike, Shinjuku offers everything from glamorous high-rise bars to sleazy dens. The Golden-Gai area is the haunt of writers, artists, and filmmakers. Nearby Kabuki-chō is the city's wildest nightlife venue—just steer clear of places with English-speaking touts out front and you'll be fine. The 2-chōme area (near Shinjuku Gyo-en National Garden and away from the rowdiness of Kabuki-chō) is a popular nightlife spot for the gay community. Although it's limited to a block or so of small bars and clubs, there is a diverse scene.

Bars

Bandol. This stylish wine bar on Aoyama-dōri has a helpful English-speaking staff and an urbane yet unstuffy clientele. Several dozen vintages from France, Italy, Spain, and New Zealand—most available by the glass—share menu space with reasonably priced Continental cuisine (eight-course dinners for ¥3,900). Weekend brunch is also available. Drinks start at ¥900. ⊠ *2–12–16 Minami-Aoyama, Minato-ku* ☎ *03/5785–3722* ☉ *Weekdays 6 PM–2 AM, weekends noon–2 AM* Ⓜ *Ginza subway line, Gaien-mae Station (Exit 4).*

D-Zone. Patrons of the D-Zone, part of the Vision Network complex of shops, restaurants, and a gallery space, sport tattoos and neckties in equal measure. The vibe here is inclusive, convivial, and arty, and the terrace restaurant Las Chicas is a popular date spot. The leafy backstreet location, across from the design shop Sputnik Pad, is one of Tōkyō's best. ⊠ *5–47–6 Jingū-mae, Shibuya-ku* ☎ *03/3407–6845* ☉ *Daily 6 PM–early morning* Ⓜ *Chiyoda, Ginza, and Hanzō-mon subway lines, Omotesandō Station (Exit B2).*

Heartland. Tōkyō's best-looking pickup bar sits in a somewhat disregarded corner of Roppongi Hills, but that doesn't stop the crowd—mostly white-collar *gaijin* (foreign) guys and Japanese women—from spilling out onto the patio. The funky white interior, with its long curving bar and wall-length couch, is done mostly in white, with emerald-green detailing. Drinks start at ¥500. ⊠ *Roppongi Hills West Walk, 1F, 6–10–1 Roppongi, Minato-ku* ☎ *03/5772–7600* ☉ *Daily 11 AM–5 AM* Ⓜ *Hibiya and Ōedo subway lines, Roppongi Station (Roppongi Hills Exit).*

Fodor'sChoice ★ **Montoak.** At the intersection of the Omotesandō high-fashion district and the scruffy strip known as Cat Street, Montoak distills the essence of both neighborhoods into an atmosphere of refined cool. Smoky floor-to-ceiling windows, sleek black couches and cushy armchairs, and a hipper-than-thou clientele that has included the likes of a kimono-clad Sofia Coppola make for a thoroughly appealing scene. The bar food consists of canapés, salads, cheese plates, and the like. ⊠ *6–1–9 Jingū-mae, Shibuya-ku* ☎ *03/5468–5928* ⊙ *Daily 11:30 AM–midnight* Ⓜ *Chiyoda subway line, Meiji Jingū-mae Station (Exit 4).*

Moph. Part of the Parco department store complex, this café-bar is an excellent post-shopping space in which to relax alongside a crowd of young Shibuya-ites lounging on Claudio Colucci–designed furniture. Three walls of windows are great for people-watching. Drinks start at ¥700, and the food is cheap. ⊠ *Shibuya Parco Part 1, 15–1 Udagawa-chō, Shibuya-ku* ☎ *03/5456–8244* ⊙ *Mon.–Sat. 10 AM–midnight* Ⓜ *Ginza and Hanzō-mon subway lines, Shibuya Station (Exits 6 and 7).*

Mu-Mu. A sophisticated clientele and a good selection of sake and other kinds of Japanese liquor are the hallmarks of this sleek bar-restaurant in the heart of Ginza. Drinks start at ¥660. ⊠ *Ginza 646 Bldg., 6–4–6 Ginza, Chūō-ku* ☎ *03/3569–0006* ⊙ *Mon.–Sat. 6 PM–4 AM, Sun. 5 PM–10:30 PM* Ⓜ *Ginza, Hibiya, and Marunouchi subway lines, Ginza Station (Exit C3).*

★ **Old Imperial Bar.** Comfortable and sedate, this is the pride of the Imperial Hotel, decorated with elements saved from Frank Lloyd Wright's earlier version of the building—alas, long since torn down. Drinks start at ¥1,000. ⊠ *Imperial Hotel, 1–1–1 Uchisaiwai-chō, Chiyoda-ku* ☎ *03/3504–1111* ⊙ *Daily 11:30 AM–midnight* Ⓜ *Hibiya Line, Hibiya Station (Exit 5).*

FodorsChoice **Sekirei.** Few Tōkyō experiences are more pleasurable than reclining in
★ this outdoor bar on the leafy grounds of the Meiji-Kinenkan complex and watching traditionally garbed *nihon-buyō* dancers perform to the strains of shamisen music. Sekirei serves inexpensive drinks and Japanese- and Western-style food to a mix of after-work types and tourists. Drinks cost less than ¥1,000. ⊠ *2–2–23 Moto-Akasaka, Minato-ku* ☎ *03/ 3746–7723* ⊙ *June–Sept., weekdays 4:30 PM–10:30 PM, weekends 5:30 PM–10:30 PM; dancers perform two or three times nightly at varying times* Ⓜ *JR Chūō Line, Shinanomachi Station.*

Beer Halls & Pubs

Clubhouse. Weekly darts matches and above-average pub food make this Shinjuku sports bar stand out from a crowded field. The clientele, an interesting mix of locals and foreigners, is a bit more restrained than what you'll find at similar venues. ⊠ *3–7–3 Shinjuku, 3F, Shinjuku-ku* ☎ *03/3359–7785* ⊙ *Daily 5 PM–midnight* Ⓜ *Marunouchi subway line, Shinjuku-Sanchōme Station (Exit 3).*

Ginza Lion. This bar, in business since 1899 and occupying the same stately Chūō-dōri location since 1934, is remarkably inexpensive for one of Tōkyō's toniest addresses. Ginza shoppers and office workers alike drop by for beer and ballast—anything from yakitori to spaghetti. Beers start at ¥590. ⊠ *7–9–20 Ginza, Chūō-ku* ☎ *03/3571–2590* ⊙ *Mon.–Sat. 11:30–11* Ⓜ *Ginza, Hibiya, and Marunouchi subway lines, Ginza Station (Exit A3).*

What the Dickens. This pub is nearly always packed with a fun-seeking mix of locals and foreigners. It's in a former Aum Shinri Kyō (the cult held responsible for the gas attack in the Tōkyō subway in 1995) headquarters in Ebisu. ✉ *Roob 6 Bldg., 4th fl., 1–13–3 Ebisu-Nishi, Shibuya-ku* ☎ *03/3780–2099* ⊘ *Tues.–Wed. 5 PM–1 AM, Thurs.–Sat. 5 PM–2 AM, Sun. 5 PM–midnight* Ⓜ *Hibiya subway line, Ebisu Station (Nishi-guchi/West Exit).*

Dance Clubs

Tōkyō's club scene draws internationally renowned DJs who spin all genres and who come for the enthusiastic crowds and the stylish venues. Just about every weekend, a big name will be manning the decks somewhere in town. Tōkyō clubbers tend to be more passionate about their music than they are about cruising. Most nightclubs are not pickup joints or places to preen: instead, it's the music that counts.

Dance clubs in Tōkyō are ephemeral ventures, disappearing fairly regularly only to open again with new identities, stranger names, and different selling points, although the money behind them is usually the same. Even those listed here come with no guarantee they'll be around when you arrive, but if the club you seek is gone, a new and better one may have opened up in its place.

★ **Ageha.** More than a nightclub, Ageha is a bay-side venue that has several distinct leisure zones. The cavernous Arena hosts well-known house and techno DJs, the Rose Room plays hip-hop, a summer-only swimming-pool area has reggae, and inside a chill-out tent there's ambient and trance music. After enjoying well-known DJs like Junior Velasquez, who spin until the early hours, the twentysomething crowd watches the sunrise before catching the first train back to town. Free buses to Ageha depart every half hour between 11 PM and 4:30 AM from the Shibuya police station on Roppongi-dōri, a three-minute walk from Shibuya Station (there are also return buses every half hour from 11:30 PM to 5 AM). ✉ *2–2–10 Shin-Kiba, Kotō-ku* ☎ *03/5534–1515* ⊕ *www.ageha.com* 💰 *Around ¥3,500* ⊘ *10 PM–early morning* Ⓜ *Yūraku-chō subway line, Shin-Kiba Station.*

Harlem. Hip-hop is the main flavor at this spacious Shibuya club, which hosts local emcees, DJs, and R&B artists. ✉ *2–4 Maruyama-chō, Shibuya-ku* ☎ *03/3461–8806* 💰 *Admission varies* ⊘ *Daily 9 PM–5 AM* Ⓜ *JR Yamanote Line, Ginza and Hanzō-mon subway lines, Shibuya Station (Hachiko Exit for JR and Ginza, Exit 3a for Hanzō-mon Line).*

La Fabrique. A continental crowd gathers at the late-night parties at this small, dressy, French restaurant–cum–club in Shibuya's Zero Gate complex. The music is mostly French house. ✉ *B1F, 16–9 Udagawachō, Shibuya-ku* ☎ *03/5428–5100* 💰 *¥3,000–¥3,500* ⊘ *Daily 11 AM–5 AM* Ⓜ *JR Yamanote Line, Ginza and Hanzō-mon subway lines, Shibuya Station (Hachiko Exit for JR and Ginza, Exit 6 for Hanzō-mon Line).*

Lexington Queen. To Tōkyō's hipster club kids, Lexington Queen is something of an embarrassment: the music hasn't really changed since the place opened in 1980. But to visiting movie stars, fashion models, and other members of the international jet set, the Lex is the place to party hard and go wild—and be seen doing it. ✉ *3–13–14 Roppongi, Minato-ku* ☎ *03/3401–1661* ⊕ *www.lexingtonqueen.com* 🗐 *Admission varies* ⊘ *Daily 8 PM–5 AM* Ⓜ *Hibiya and Ōedo subway lines, Roppongi Station (Exit 5); Namboku subway line, Roppongi-Itchōme Station (Exit 1).*

911. A great central-Roppongi location and no cover charge make 911 popular as both an early- and late-night singles' spot. Across from the Roi Building, this is a good starting point for a night of barhopping. ✉ *3–14–12 Roppongi, B1F, Minato-ku* ☎ *03/5772–8882* ⊘ *Daily 6 PM–6 AM* 🗐 *No cover charge* Ⓜ *Hibiya and Ōedo subway lines, Roppongi Station (Exit 3).*

Space Lab Yellow. Yellow, as this club is known, can be counted on for A-list DJs, well-regarded progressive house parties, and the occasional drum 'n' bass event. An international crowd flocks here to dance and lounge late-night in the multilevel, multiroom interior—one of Tōkyō's biggest. ✉ *1–10–11 Nishi-Azabu, Minato-ku* ☎ *03/3479–0690* ⊕ *www.club-yellow.com* ⊘ *10 PM–early morning* 🗐 *¥3,500–¥4,000* Ⓜ *Chiyoda subway line, Nogizaka Station (Exit 5); Hibiya and Ōedo subway lines, Roppongi Station (Exit 2).*

★ **Womb.** Well-known techno and break-beat DJs make a point of stopping by this Shibuya über club on their way through town. The turntable talent, including the likes of Danny Howells and Richie Hawtin, and four floors of dance and lounge space make Womb Tōkyō's most consistently rewarding club experience. ✉ *2–16 Maruyama-chō, Shibuya-ku* ☎ *03/5459–0039* ⊕ *www.womb.co.jp* 🗐 *Around ¥3,500* ⊘ *Daily 10 PM–early morning* Ⓜ *JR Yamanote Line, Ginza and Hanzō-mon subway lines, Shibuya Station (Hachiko Exit for JR and Ginza, Exit 3a for Hanzō-mon Line).*

Izakaya

Izakaya (literally "drinking place") are Japanese pubs that can be found on just about every block in Tōkyō. If you're in the mood for elegant decor and sedate surroundings, look elsewhere; these drinking dens are often noisy, bright, and smoky. But for a taste of authentic Japanese-style partying, a visit to an izakaya is a must—this is where young people start their nights out, office workers gather on their way home, and students take a break to grab a cheap meal and a drink.

Typically, izakaya have a full lineup of cocktails, a good selection of sake, draft beer, and lots of good Japanese and Western food; rarely does anything cost more than ¥1,000. Picture menus make ordering easy, and because most cocktails retain their Western names, communicating drink preferences shouldn't be too difficult. Chances are, though, that the boisterous and slightly tipsy group at the next table will help you out.

Amataro. The Center Gai location of this ubiquitous izakaya chain impresses with a huge, dimly lit interior. On weekends the crowd is young, boisterous, and fun. ✉ *2–3F Tōkyō Kaikan Bldg., 33–1 Udagawachō, Shibuya-ku* ☎ *03/5784–4660* ⊘ *Daily 5 PM–5 AM* Ⓜ *JR Yamanote*

Line, Ginza and Hanzō-mon subway lines, Shibuya Station (Hachiko Exit for JR and Ginza, Exit 3a for Hanzō-mon Line).

Takara. This high-class izakaya in the sumptuous Tōkyō International Forum is a favorite with foreigners because of its English-language menu and extensive sake list. ☒ *B1, 3–5–1 Marunouchi, Chiyoda-ku* ☎ *03/5223–9888* ☉ *Weekdays 11:30–2:30 and 5–11, weekends 11:30–3:30 and 5–10* Ⓜ *Yūraku-chō subway line, Yūraku-chō Station (Exit A-4B).*

Watami. One of Tōkyō's big izakaya chains—with a half-dozen branches in the youth entertainment district of Shibuya alone—Watami is popular for its seriously inexpensive menu. Seating at this location ranges from a communal island bar to Western-style tables to more private areas. ☒ *Satose Bldg., 4F, 13–8 Udagawachō, Shibuya-ku* ☎ *03/6415–6516* ☉ *Sun.–Thurs. 5 PM–3 AM, Fri.–Sat. 5 PM–5 AM* Ⓜ *JR Yamanote Line, Ginza and Hanzō-mon subway lines, Shibuya Station (Hachiko Exit for JR and Ginza, Exit 6 for Hanzō-mon Line).*

Jazz Clubs

Tōkyō has one of the best jazz scenes in Asia. The clubs here attract world-class performers and innovative local acts.

Blue Note Tōkyō. The Blue Note sees everyone from the Count Basie Orchestra to Herbie Hancock perform to packed houses. The "Sunday Special" series showcases fresh Japanese talent. Prices here are typically high; expect to pay upwards of ¥13,000 to see acts like Natalie Cole. ☒ *6–3–16 Minami-Aoyama, Minato-ku* ☎ *03/5485–0088* ☉ *Shows usually Mon.–Sat. at 7 and 9:30, Sun. at 6:30 and 9* ⊕ *www.bluenote.co.jp* Ⓜ *Chiyoda, Ginza, and Hanzō-mon subway lines, Omotesandō Station (Exit A3).*

Shinjuku Pit Inn. This veteran club stages mostly mainstream fare with the odd foray into the avant-garde. Afternoon admission is ¥1,300 weekdays, ¥2,500 weekends; evening entry is typically ¥3,000. Better-known local acts are often a little more. ☒ *B1 Accord Shinjuku Bldg., 2–12–4 Shinjuku, Shinjuku-ku* ☎ *03/3354–2024* ☉ *Daily, hrs vary* Ⓜ *Marunouchi subway line, Shinjuku-san-chōme Station.*

Fodor'sChoice **Sweet Basil 139.** Although it's not related to New York City's Sweet Basil, ★ Tōkyō's own jazz hot spot is fast gaining a reputation to rival the famous Greenwich Village venue. An upscale jazz club near Roppongi Crossing, Sweet Basil 139 is renowned for local and international acts that run the musical gamut from smooth jazz and fusion to classical. A large, formal dining area serves Italian dishes that are as good as the jazz, making this spot an excellent choice for a complete night out. With a spacious interior and standing room for 500 on the main floor, this is one of the largest and most accessible jazz bars in town. Prices range from ¥2,857 to ¥12,000 depending on who's headlining. ☒ *6–7–11 Roppongi, Minato-ku* ☎ *03/5474–0139* ⊕ *http://stb139.co.jp* ☉ *Mon.–Sat. 6 PM–11 PM; shows at 8* Ⓜ *Hibiya and Ōedo subway lines, Roppongi Station (Exit 3).*

Karaoke

Karaoke may be the only activity in which the normally reserved Japanese lose all abandon—and it's truly a sight to behold. Unlike most karaoke bars in the United States, in which singers perform in front of a crowd of strangers, karaoke in Japan is usually enjoyed by groups of friends or coworkers in the seclusion of private rooms. Basic hourly charges vary but are usually less than ¥1,000. Most establishments have a large selection of English songs, stay open late, and serve inexpensive food and drink.

Big Echo. One of Tōkyō's largest karaoke chains, Big Echo has dozens of locations throughout the city. Cheap hourly rates and late closing times make it popular with youngsters. The Roppongi branch is spread over three floors. ⊠ *7–14–12 Roppongi, Minato-ku* ☎ *03/5770–7700* ⧖ *¥500–¥600 per hr* ☉ *Daily 6 PM–5 AM* Ⓜ *Hibiya and Ōedo subway lines, Roppongi Station (Exit 4).*

Pasela. This 10-story entertainment complex on the main Roppongi drag of Gaien-Higashi-dōri has seven floors of karaoke rooms with more than 10,000 foreign-song titles. A Mexican-theme bar and a restaurant are also on the premises. ⊠ *5–16–3 Roppongi, Minato-ku* ☎ *0120/911–086* ⧖ *¥500 per hr* ☉ *Daily 5 PM–10 AM* Ⓜ *Hibiya and Ōedo subway lines, Roppongi Station (Exit 3).*

Shidax. The Shidax chain's corporate headquarters—in an excellent Shibuya location, across from Tower Records—has 130 private karaoke rooms, a café, and a restaurant. ⊠ *1–12–13 Jinnan, Shibuya-ku* ☎ *03/5784–8881* ⧖ *¥760 per hr* ☉ *Daily 11 AM–8 AM* Ⓜ *JR, Ginza and Hanzō-mon subway lines, Shibuya Station (Exit 6).*

Smash Hits. Smash Hits is an expat favorite, with thousands of English songs and a central performance stage. The cover charge gets you two drinks and no time limit. ⊠ *5–2–26 Hiro-o, Shibuya-ku* ☎ *03/3444–0432* ⧖ *¥3,000* ☉ *Mon.–Sat. 7 PM–3 AM* ⊕ *www.smashhits.jp* Ⓜ *Hibiya Line, Hiro-o Station.*

Live Houses

Tōkyō has numerous small music clubs known as "live houses." These basement spots range from the very basic to miniclub venues, and they showcase the best emerging talent on the local scene. Many of the best live houses can be found in the Kichijōji, Kōenji, and Nakano areas, although they are tucked away in basements citywide. One of the great things about the live house scene is the variety: a single "amateur night" set can include everything from experimental ethnic dance to thrash rock. Cover charges vary depending on who's performing but are typically ¥3,000–¥5,000.

Manda-la. Relaxed and intimate, this local favorite in Kichijōji attracts an eclectic group of performers. Cover charges range from ¥1,800 to ¥4,000. ⊠ *2–8–6 Kichijōji-Minami-cho, Musashino-shi* ☎ *0422/42–1579* ☉ *6:30 PM to closing time, which varies* Ⓜ *Keiō Inokashira private rail* *line, JR Chūō and JR Sōbu lines, Kichijōji Station (Kōen-guchi/Park Exit, on Suehiro-dōri).*

Milk. One of the city's larger live houses—it can handle 400 music fans—has three levels and more of a clublike vibe than other venues. Ticket prices are in the ¥2,500–¥3,000 range. ✉ *1–13–3 Nishi-Ebisu, Shibuya-ku* ☎ *03/5458–2826* ☉ *Weekends 9–early morning* Ⓜ *JR Yamanote Line and Hibiya subway line, Ebisu Station (Nishi-guchi/West Exit).*

Showboat. A small, basic venue that's been going strong for more than a decade, Showboat attracts both amateur and semiprofessional performers. Ticket prices vary by act but are typically around ¥2,000 and often include one drink. ✉ *B1 Oak Bldg. Kōenji, 3–17–2 Kita Kōenji Suginami-ku* ☎ *03/3337–5745* ☉ *Daily 6 PM—early morning* Ⓜ *JR Sōbu and JR Chūō lines, Kōenji Station (Kita-guchi/North Exit).*

Rooftop Bars

Bellovisto. This 40th-floor lounge bar atop the Cerulean Tower draws a mixed crowd of tourists and local couples, who come for the grand views out over Shibuya and beyond. Drinks start at ¥1,000. ✉ *26–1 Sakuragaoka-chō, Shibuya-ku* ☎ *03/3476–3398* ☉ *Daily 4 PM–midnight* Ⓜ *JR, Ginza and Hanzō-mon subway lines, Shibuya Station (Minami-guchi/South Exit for JR and Ginza, Exit 8 for Hanzō-mon Line).*

★ **New York Bar.** Even before *Lost in Translation* introduced the Park Hyatt's signature lounge to filmgoers worldwide, New York Bar was a local Tōkyō favorite. All the style you would expect of one of the city's top hotels combined with superior views of Shinjuku's skyscrapers and neon-lighted streets make this one of the city's premier nighttime venues. The quality of the jazz on offer equals that of the view. Drinks start at ¥800, and there's a cover charge of ¥2,000 after 8 PM (7 PM on Sunday). ✉ *Park Hyatt Hotel 52F, 3–7–1–2 Nishi-Shinjuku, Shinjuku-ku* ☎ *03/5322–1234* ☉ *Sun.–Wed. 5 PM–midnight, Thurs.–Sat. 5 PM–1 AM* Ⓜ *Ōedo subway line, Tochō-mae Station.*

Sorasiso. The Kenji Kumaki–designed interior of this 46th-floor bar-restaurant in Shiodome is almost as impressive as the view out over Tōkyō Bay. Sorasiso attracts a well-heeled crowd. Drinks start at ¥1,000. ✉ *1–8–2 Higashi-Shimbashi, Caretta Shiodome B1F–B2F, Chūō-ku* ☎ *03/6215–8055* ☉ *Daily 11–11* Ⓜ *Ōedo subway line, Shiodome Station (Exit 7); JR (Shiodome Exit) and Asakusa and Ginza lines (Exit 4), Shimbashi Station.*

Top of Akasaka. On the 40th floor of the Akasaka Prince Hotel, you can enjoy some of the finest views of Tōkyō. If you can time your visit for dusk, the price of one drink gets you two views—the daylight sprawl of buildings and the twinkling lights of evening. Drinks start at ¥1,000, and there's a table charge of ¥800 per person. ✉ *Akasaka Prince, 1–2 Kioi-chō, Chiyoda-ku* ☎ *03/3234–1111* ☉ *Weekdays noon–2 AM, weekends noon–midnight* Ⓜ *Ginza and Marunouchi subway lines, Akasakamitsuke Station (Exit D).*

SPORTS &
THE OUTDOORS

5

BEST PLACE TO SEE PRO BASEBALL
Tōkyō Dome at Kōraku-en ⇨*p.149*

REVERBERATING WRESTLING MATCH
Kokugikan National Sumō Arena ⇨*p.151*

RUNNING WITH A VIEW
Imperial Palace Outer Garden track ⇨*p.150*

Updated by
Jared Lubarsky

IT'S FAIR TO SAY THAT BASEBALL is as much a national pastime in Japan as it is stateside. If you're a fan—and perhaps even if you aren't—you may want to take in a game in Japan: the way the Japanese have adopted and adapted this Western sport makes it a fascinating and easy-to-grasp microcosm of both their culture and their overall relationship to things Western. The team names alone—the Orix BlueWave and the Hiroshima Carp, for example—have an amusing appeal to Westerners accustomed to such monikers as the Yankees and the Indians, and the fans' cheers are different and chanted more in unison than in U.S. ballparks. Amateur baseball, from high school leagues to corporate teams, has a huge following, and the competition to be a player is fierce, even at the primary-school level. Indeed, sports in general are considered very *kakko-ii* ("cool"), especially by young urbanites. Among people in their teens and twenties, there's an active cohort for pretty much any sport you can imagine, from rollerblading to windsurfing, from soccer to squash. And Tōkyō's young actives are willing to spend on the necessary clothes and equipment, too. The Mizuno Corporation, Japan's leading maker of sporting goods, footwear and uniforms, racked up sales of some $1.1 billion in 2003, and shows no signs of slowing down.

By the time they've joined the workforce, and started families, most Japanese have made the transition from participants to fans. Golf remains the game of choice for the aspiring salaryman, but noticeably less so than a generation ago; overpriced and overextended in the boom years of the 1990s, country clubs all over the country are in trouble. But despite the interest in sports and the general notion of fitness, Tōkyō actually has very few green spaces dedicated to active leisure. Every ward maintains at least one substantial sports facility for its own residents, but otherwise fitness is the province of private clubs where memberships are expensive and peak hours are crowded. Besides walking, visitors are mainly limited to their hotel gyms. The few outlets available for participant and spectator sports are listed below.

Baseball

Tōkyō Dome at Kōraku-en is the place to see pro ball in the big city. An afternoon in the bleachers, when a despised rival like the Hanshin Tigers are in town from Ōsaka to play the Yomiuri Giants, will give you insights into a Japanese passion like nothing else.

The Japanese baseball season runs between April and October. Same-day tickets are hard to come by; try the ticket agency **Playguide** (☎ 03/3561–8821). **Ticket Pia** (☎ 03/5237–9999) handles mainly music and theater but can also book and sell tickets to sporting events. Depending on the stadium, the date, and the seat location, expect to pay from ¥1,500 to ¥8,000 for an afternoon at the ballpark.

Baseball fans in Tōkyō are blessed with a choice of three home teams. The Yomiuri Giants and the Nippon Ham Fighters both play at the 55,000-seat **Tōkyō Dome.** ✉ *1–3–61 Kōraku, Bunkyō-ku* ☎ *03/5800–9999* Ⓜ *Marunouchi and Namboku lines, Kōraku-en Station (Exit 2); Ōedo and Toei Mita lines, Kasuga Station (Exit A2); JR Suidō-bashi Station (West Exit).*

The home ground of the Yakult Swallows is **Jingū Baseball Stadium,** in the Outer Gardens of Meiji Jingū. ⊠ *13 Kasumigaoka, Shinjuku-ku* ☎ *03/ 3404–8999* Ⓜ *Ginza Line, Gaien-mae Station (Exit 2).*

Golf

Golfing can be a daunting prospect for the casual visitor to Tōkyō: The few public courses are far from the city, and booking a tee time on even a week's notice is almost impossible. What you can do, however, if the golf bug is in your blood, is groove your swing at one of the many practice ranges in Tōkyō itself. Most driving ranges are open from 11 AM to 7 or 8 at night and will rent you a club for around ¥200. At **Golf Range Pinflag** (⊠ 1–7–13 Tsukiji, Chūō-ku, ☎ 03/3542–2936 Ⓜ Hibiya subway line, Tsukiji Station [Exit 4]), a bucket of 24 balls costs ¥350, and you can generally get a tee without waiting very long. At the **Meguro Gorufu-jō** (⊠ 5–6–22 Kami-Meguro, Meguro-ku ☎ 03/3713–2805 Ⓜ Tōkyū Tōyoko private railway line, Nakameguro Station), you buy a prepaid card for ¥2,000, which allows you to hit up to 142 balls.

Running

The venue of choice for runners who work in the central wards of Chūō-ku and Chiyoda-ku is the **Imperial Palace Outer garden.** Sakurada-mon, at the west end of the park, is the traditional starting point for the 5-km (3-mi) run around the palace—though you can join in anywhere along the route. Jogging around the palace is a ritual that begins as early as 6 AM and goes on throughout the day, no matter what the weather. Almost everybody runs the course counterclockwise. Now and then you may spot someone going the opposite way, but freethinking of this sort is frowned upon in Japan.

Soccer

Soccer is one of the marketing miracles of Japan. It was launched as a full-fledged professional sport only in 1993, and within three years—buoyed by a stunningly successful media hype—was drawing crowds of 6 million spectators a season. Much of that success was due to superstars like Gary Linaker and Dragan Stojkovic, who came to Japan to finish out their careers and train the inexperienced local teams. By 1990, the J. League had 26 teams in two divisions, and European and Latin American clubs were scouting for talented Japanese players. The popularity of soccer waned for a time but has revived again—thanks in part to Japan's successful bid to cohost the 2002 World Cup, and in part by the introduction in 2001 of legalized gambling on the results of the J. League's 13 weekly matches. (The biggest payoff in the "Toto" pools is ¥100 million.)

The original J. League marketing plan called for the fledgling soccer clubs to be sponsored by small cities in the provinces, many of them with moribund economies and declining populations; these cities would build modest stadiums for their clubs and ride the popularity of soccer back to prosperity. The plan worked, with one odd result: Tōkyō never acquired a home team. Now it has two, FC Tōkyō and Tōkyō Verde, both of which play at the 50,000-seat **Tōkyō Stadium** in Tama. The J. League season has two 15-week schedules, one beginning in mid-March and the other in mid-August; visitors to Tōkyō have a pretty fair window of opportunity to see a match. Tickets cost ¥1,000–¥6,000 and can be ordered through **Playguide** (☎ 03/3561–8821) or **Ticket Pia** (☎ 0570/02–9966), or purchased directly at most Seven-Eleven, Family Mart, or Lawson convenience stores. ⊠ *376–3 Nishi-machi, Chōfu City* ☎ *0424/40–0555* Ⓜ *JR Keiō Line, Tobitakyū Station.*

Sumō

Sumō wrestling dates back some 1,500 years. Originally it was not merely a sport but a religious rite, performed at shrines to entertain the gods that presided over the harvest. Ritual and ceremony are still important elements of sumō matches—contestants in unique regalia, referees in gorgeous costumes, elaborately choreographed openings and closings. To the casual spectator a match itself can look like a mostly naked free-for-all. Stripped down to silk loincloths, the two wrestlers square off in a dirt ring about 15 feet in diameter and charge straight at each other; the first one to step out of the ring or touch the ground with anything but the soles of his feet loses. Other than that, there are no rules—not even weight divisions: a runt of merely 250 pounds can find himself facing an opponent twice his size.

Of the six Grand Tournaments (called *basho*) that take place during the year, Tōkyō hosts three of them: in early January, mid-May, and mid-September. The tournaments take place in the **Kokugikan,** the National Sumō Arena, in the Ryōgoku district on the east side of the Sumida-gawa. Matches go from early afternoon, when the novices wrestle, to the titanic clashes of the upper ranks at around 6 PM. The price of admission buys you a whole day of sumō; the most expensive seats, closest to the ring, are tatami-floor loges for four people, called *sajiki*. The loges are terribly cramped, but the cost (¥9,200–¥11,300 per person) includes all sorts of food and drink and souvenirs, brought around to you by Kokugikan attendants in traditional costume. The cheapest seats cost ¥3,600 for advance sales, ¥2,100 for same-day box office sales. For same-day box office sales you should line up an hour in advance of the tournament. You can also reserve tickets through **Playguide** (☎03/5802–9999) or **Ticket Pia** (☎ 03/5237–9955 or 0570/02–9977), or at Seven-Eleven, Family Mart, or Lawson convenience stores. ⊠ *1–3–28 Yokoami, Sumida-ku* ☎ *03/3622–1100* ⊕ *www.sumo.or.jp/eng/ticket/index.html* Ⓜ *JR Sōbu Line, Ryōgoku Station (West Exit).*

Swimming & Fitness

The vast majority of pools and fitness centers in Tōkyō are for members only. Major international hotels have facilities of their own, but if your accommodations are further downscale, places to swim or work out are harder to find. The fitness center at **Big Box Seibu Sports Plaza Athletic Club** (⊠ 1–35–3 Takadano-baba, Shinjuku-ku ☎03/3208–7171) is open to nonmembers for ¥4,000; use of the pool, which is only available on Sunday 10–6, is an additional ¥1,500.

CloseUp

BECOMING A SUMŌ WRESTLER

THE CENTURIES-OLD NATIONAL SPORT of sumō is not to be taken lightly—as anyone who has ever seen a sumō wrestler will testify. Indeed, sheer weight is almost a prerequisite to success. Contenders in the upper ranks tip the scales at an average of 350 pounds, and there are no upper limits. There are various techniques of pushing, gripping, and throwing in sumō, but the basic rules are very simple: except for hitting below the belt (which is all a sumō wrestler wears), grabbing your opponent by the hair, or striking with a closed fist, almost anything goes. If you get thrown down or forced out of the ring, you lose.

There are no free agents in sumō. To compete, you must belong to a heya (stable) run by a retired wrestler who has purchased that right from the Japan Sumō Association. Sumō is very much a closed world, hierarchical and formal. Youngsters recruited into the sport live in the stable dormitory, doing all the community chores and waiting on their seniors while they learn. When they rise high enough in tournament rankings, they acquire servant-apprentices of their own.

Tournaments and exhibitions are held in different parts of the country at different times, but all stables in the Sumō Association—now some 30 in number—are in Tōkyō. Most are clustered on both sides of the Sumida River near the green-roofed Kokugikan (National Sumō Arena), in the areas called Asakusabashi and Ryōgoku. When wrestlers are in town in January, May, and September, you are likely to see some of them on the streets, cleaving the air like leviathans in their wood clogs and kimonos.

The **Clark Hatch Fitness Center** (⌧ 2–1–3 Azabu-dai, Minato-ku ☎ 03/3584–4092) has a full array of machines and charges ¥2,600 for non-members. It does not have a pool. You don't necessarily have to be a resident to use one of the facilities operated by the various wards of Tōkyō, though the registration formalities can be a hassle (bring your passport or a photo ID). One of the best of these is the **Minato Ward Shiba Pool** (⌧ 2–7–2 Shiba Kōen, Minato-ku ☎ 03/3435–0470), which is open Tuesday–Saturday 9:30–8 and Sunday–Monday 9:30–5. The pool charges only ¥300 for two hours of swimming.

Tennis

So near and yet so far: the central wards of Tōkyō have literally hundreds of public tennis courts—all of which require you to sign up for court time in advance (usually in mid-month for a one-hour slot in the following month); for some, you can only sign up by lottery. The courts will only hold a phone reservation for one day, for you to appear in person and pay to confirm it—typically from ¥3,000 to ¥5,000, depending on the time of day you request.

A few private clubs are available to nonmembers. The **Sun Plaza Nakano** (✉ 4–1–1 Nakano, Nakano-ku ☎ 03/3388-1151 Ext. 211 Ⓜ JR Chūō Line, Nakano Station), has one artificial grass court, available at limited times on weekdays for ¥5,000 per hour. The **Taishō Central Tennis Club** (✉ 1–55–14 Honmachi, Shibuya-ku ☎ 03/3320–8631 Ⓜ Keiō New Line, Hatsudai Station [North Exit] ☯ Tues.–Sun.), has eight hard courts, which can be booked for ¥8,000 for 90 minutes during the day and ¥15,000 for two hours evenings from 6.

That leaves the hotels. The **Tōkyō Hilton** (✉ 6–5–2 Nishi-Shinjuku, Shinjuku-ku ☎ 03/3344-5111), has two courts, in principle only for the use of guests, but if they're otherwise unreserved you can book them for ¥2,000 per hour per person (¥2,500 weekends), plus a general facilities fee of ¥2,500. The **Hotel New Ōtani Tōkyō** (✉ 4–1 Kioi-chō, Chiyoda-ku ☎ 03/3265–1111), also has two courts, at its Golden Spa fitness club; club privileges for registered guests are ¥5,000 plus an additional ¥1,000 per hour (¥4,000 weekends) for court time. The **Shinagawa Prince Hotel** (✉ 4–10–30 Takanawa, Minato-ku ☎ 03/3441–0020), has nine indoor courts, open 24 hours (Thurs.–Fri. 6 AM–2 AM) to guests and nonguests alike for ¥7,000–¥14,000 an hour per court, depending on when you book.

SHOPPING

6

BEST JAPANESE ANTIQUES
Fuji-Torii in Shibuya ⇨*p.164*

THE ULTIMATE BROWSE
in the bookstores of Jimbō-chō ⇨*p.165*

WIDEST SELECTION OF AUTHENTIC CRAFTS
Bingo-ya in Shinjuku ⇨*p.166*

NEWEST GADGETS AND GAMES
The Sony Building in Ginza ⇨*p.168*

LOVELIEST LACQUERWARE
Yamada Heiando on Daikanyama ⇨*p.172*

MOST AFFORDABLE SILK KIMONOS
Tansu-ya in Ginza ⇨*p.172*

Updated by
Steve Trautlein
and Matt
Wilce

HORROR STORIES ABOUND about prices in Japan—and some of them are true. Yes, a cup of coffee can cost $10, if you pick the wrong coffee shop. A gift-wrapped melon from a department-store gourmet counter can cost $70. And a taxi ride from the airport to central Tōkyō does cost about $200. But most people take the convenient airport train for $9, and if you shop around, you can find plenty of gifts and souvenirs at fair prices.

Some items are better bought at home: why go all the way to Tōkyō to buy European designer clothing? Instead, look for items that are Japanese made for Japanese people and sold in stores that do not cater primarily to tourists. Don't pass up the chance to purchase Japanese crafts. Color, balance of form, and superb workmanship make these items exquisite and well worth the price you'll pay. Some can be quite expensive; for example, Japanese lacquerware carries a hefty price tag. But if you like the shiny boxes, bowls, cups, and trays and consider that quality lacquerware is made to last a lifetime, the cost is justified.

Shopping in Japan is an exercise in elegance and refinement. Note the care taken with items after you purchase them, especially in department stores and boutiques. Goods will be wrapped, wrapped again, bagged, and sealed. Sure, the packaging can be excessive—does anybody really need three plastic bags for one croissant?—but such a focus on presentation has deep roots in Japanese culture.

Salespeople are invariably helpful and polite. In the larger stores they greet you with a bow when you arrive, and many of them speak at least enough English to help you find what you're looking for. There's a saying in Japan: *o-kyaku-sama wa kami-sama,* "the customer is a god"—and since the competition for your business is fierce, people do take it to heart.

Japan has been slow to embrace the use of credit cards, and even though plastic is now accepted at big retailers, many smaller shops only take cash. So when you go souvenir hunting, bring along cash; Tōkyō's low crime rates make this a low-risk proposition. The dishonor associated with theft is so strong, in fact, that it's considered bad form to conspicuously count change in front of cashiers.

Japan has an across-the-board 5% value-added tax (V.A.T.) imposed on luxury goods as well as on restaurant and hotel bills. This tax can be avoided at some duty-free shops in the city (don't forget to bring your passport). It's also waived in the duty-free shops at the international airports, but because these places tend to have higher profit margins, your tax savings there are likely to be offset by the higher markups.

Stores in Tōkyō generally open at 10 or 11 AM and close at 8 or 9 PM.

Shopping Districts

Akihabara & Jimbō-chō

Akihabara was at one time the only place Tōkyōites would go to buy cutting-edge electronic gadgets, but the area has lost its aura of exclusivity thanks to big discount chains that have sprung up around the city.

Still, for its sheer variety of products and foreigner-friendliness, Akihabara has the newcomers beat—and a visit remains essential to any Tōkyō shopping spree. Salesclerks speak English at most of the major shops (and many of the smaller ones), and the big chains offer duty-free and export items. Be sure to poke around the backstreets for smaller stores that sell used and unusual electronic goods. West of Akihabara, in the used-bookstore district of Jimbō-chō, you'll find pretty much whatever you're looking for in dictionaries and art books, rare and out-of-print editions (Western and Japanese), and prints. Ⓜ *For Akihabara: JR Yamanote, Keihin Tōhoku, and Sōbu lines, Akihabara Station (Denki-gai Exit); Hibiya subway line, Akihabara Station. For Jimbō-chō: Hanzō-mon, Shinjuku, and Mita subway lines, Jimbō-chō Station.*

Aoyama

Shopping in Aoyama can empty your wallet in no time: this is where many of the leading Japanese and Western designers have their cash-cow boutiques, and there are lots of elegant and pricey antiques shops on Aoyama's Kottō-dōri. European and American imports will be high, but Japanese designer clothes are usually 30%–40% lower than they are elsewhere. Aoyama tends to be a showcase not merely of high fashion but also of the latest concepts in commercial architecture and interior design. Ⓜ *Chiyoda, Ginza, and Hanzō-mon subway lines, Omotesandō Station (Exits A4, A5, B1, B2, and B3).*

Asakusa

While sightseeing in this area, take time to stroll through its arcades. Many of the goods sold here are the kinds of souvenirs you can find in any tourist trap, but look a little harder and you can find small backstreet shops that have been making beautiful wooden combs, delicate fans, and other items of fine traditional craftsmanship for generations. Also here are the cookware shops of Kappa-bashi, where you can load up on everything from sushi knives to plastic lobsters. Ⓜ *Asakusa subway line, Asakusa Station (Kaminari-mon Exit); Ginza subway line, Asakusa Station (Exit 1) and Tawara-machi Station (Exit 3).*

Ginza

This world-renowned entertainment and shopping district dates to the Edo period (1603–1868), when it consisted of long, willow-lined avenues. The willows have long since gone, and the streets are now lined with department stores and boutiques. The exclusive shops in this area—including flagship stores for major jewelers like Tiffany & Co., Harry Winston, and Mikimoto—sell quality merchandise at high prices. Ⓜ *Marunouchi, Ginza, and Hibiya subway lines, Ginza Station (Exits A1–A10); Yūraku-chō subway line, Ginza Itchōme Station; JR Yamanote Line, Yūraku-chō Station.*

Harajuku

The average shopper in Harajuku is under 20; a substantial percentage is under 16. Most stores focus on moderately priced clothing and accessories, with a lot of kitsch mixed in, but there are also several upscale fashion houses in the area—and more on the way. This shopping and residential area extends southeast from Harajuku Station along both sides of Omotesandō and Meiji-dōri; the shops that target the youngest

6

Start your day, as so many Japanese do, at the south exit of Shinjuku Station, said to be the busiest in the world. Cross the street (Kōshu-kaidō) at the light, take a left, and make your way to Takashimaya Times Square, which is the large shopping center off to your right. If you make it to **Takashimaya** when the doors open at 10 AM sharp, you'll receive a formal greeting as you enter this stylish department store with Western and Japanese clothes, jewelry, crafts, and accessories. The back end of the store connects to the housewares-and-hobby emporium **Tōkyū Hands,** a good place to buy talking cigarette lighters and other kitsch keepsakes. Take the escalator to the fifth floor and cross a walkway to **Kinokuniya** bookstore; you'll enter at the English-language section, which has everything from haiku translations to coffee-table tomes on Japanese gardens. Exit the doors near the first-floor elevators, cross the street, and bear right to the taxi stand outside Tōkyū Hands. Take a short cab ride to Harajuku Station; ask the driver to drop you off at **Takeshita-dōri** (at the west end, which is closest to the station), where you can go elbow-to-elbow with Tōkyō's youthful and trendy consumers.

At the east end of Takeshita-dōri, turn right onto Meiji-dōri (it's at the first light). The next big intersection is Omotesandō. Cross it, take a left on the opposite side, and in quick succession you'll come upon **Kiddy Land** (toys), **Fuji-Torii** (antiques), and **Oriental Bazaar** (traditional crafts). Walking farther (southeast) along tree-lined Omotesandō takes you past some of Tōkyō's most exclusive fashion and accessories boutiques. Stop in the basement of the **Hanae Mori Building,** on Omotesandō, for more antiques.

High-fashion heaven continues after you cross the next big intersection at Aoyama-dōri. Don't miss the bizarre **Comme Des Garçons** shop one block farther along on your right. Then take a right (two blocks past Aoyama-dōri) at the stunning, glass-encased Prada building. The side streets here lead to more boutiques (including the first right, where you'll find **Bape Exclusive Aoyama**). After passing the trendy shopping center **Glassarea** on your left, you'll come to "Antiques Road": Kottō-dōri. Home to some of Tōkyō's best antiques dealers, this area also has many cafés and restaurants.

At the intersection of Kottō-dōri and Aoyama-dōri, turn right and head to the Omotesandō subway station. A ¥160 ticket buys you passage on the Ginza subway line to Ginza Station. Take Exit A2 for the main Chūō-dōri thoroughfare and traditional stationer **Kyūkyodō** (on your right as you exit the station). Shop here for *washi* (paper), calligraphy goods, scrolls, and all manner of decorative paper items. One block behind Kyūkyodō, between Harumi-dōri and Miyuki-dōri, is the traditional sword shop **Tōken Shibata.** After certifying your samurai credentials, swing back to Chūō-dōri, walk southwest, and get cultured in a different way at **Mikimoto.** Walk farther up the street and duck into the alley behind the Apple Store, where you can shop for traditional clothes at the small kimono store **Tansuya.** If you have any leftover energy—or, more importantly, money—you may want to visit the **Matsuya, Wako,** and **Matsuzakaya** department stores, all set around Ginza Station. Or take a break at the second-floor café in **Mitsukoshi,** which affords an excellent view over one of Tōkyō's busiest intersections.

Akihabara &
Jimbō-chō 2
Aoyama 7
Asakusa 1
Ginza 8
Harajuku 4
Omotesandō 5
Shibuya 6
Shinjuku 3
Tsukiji 9

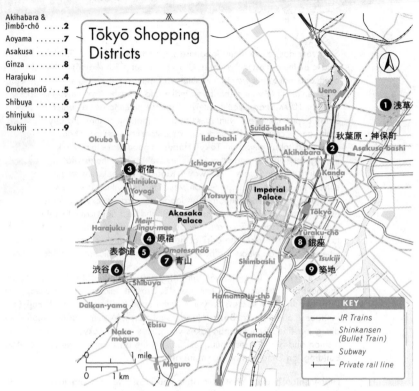

Tōkyō Shopping Districts

KEY

- JR Trains
- Shinkansen (Bullet Train)
- Subway
- Private rail line

consumers concentrate especially on the narrow street called Takeshita-dōri. Tōkyō's most exciting neighborhood for youth fashion and design lies along the promenade known as Kyū Shibuya-gawa Hodō, commonly referred to as Cat Street. Ⓜ *Chiyoda subway line, Meiji Jingū-mae Station (Exits 1–5); JR Yamanote Line, Harajuku Station.*

Omotesandō

Known as the Champs-Elysées of Tōkyō, this long, wide avenue running from Aoyama-dōri to Meiji Jingū is lined with cafés and designer boutiques. There are also several antiques and souvenir shops here. Omotesandō is perfect for browsing, window-shopping, and lingering over a café au lait before strolling to your next destination. Ⓜ *Chiyoda, Ginza, and Hanzō-mon lines, Omotesandō Station (Exits A4, A5, B1, B2, and B3).*

Shibuya

This is primarily an entertainment and retail district geared toward teenagers and young adults. The shopping scene in Shibuya caters to these groups with many reasonably priced smaller shops and a few department stores that are casual yet chic. Ⓜ *JR Yamanote Line; Tōkyū and Keiō private rail lines; Ginza and Hanzō-mon subway lines: Shibuya Station (Nishi-guchi/West Exit for JR, Exits 3–8 for subway lines).*

Shinjuku

Shinjuku is not without its honky-tonk and sleaze, but it also has some of the city's most popular department stores. Shinjuku's merchandise reflects the crowds—young, stylish, and hip. Surrounding the station are several discount electronics and home-appliance outlets. Ⓜ *JR Yamanote Line; Odakyū private rail line; Marunouchi, Shinjuku, and Ōedo subway lines: Shinjuku Station.*

Tsukiji

Best known for its daily fish-market auctions, Tsukiji also has a warren of streets that carry useful, everyday items that serve as a window onto the lives of the Japanese. This is a fascinating area to poke around after seeing the fish auction and before stopping in the neighborhood for a fresh-as-can-be sushi lunch. Ⓜ *Ōedo subway line, Tsukiji-shijō Station (Exit A1); Hibiya subway line, Tsukiji Station (Exit 1).*

Shopping Streets & Arcades

Most Japanese villages have pedestrian shopping streets known as *shotengai,* and Tōkyō, a big city made up of smaller neighborhoods, is no different. But you won't find everyday retailers like pharmacies and grocery stores in these areas—Tōkyō's shotengai are thick with boutiques, accessory shops, and cafés. Just like their surrounding neighborhoods, these streets can be classy, trendy, or a bit shabby.

Ame-ya Yoko-chō Market. Everything from fresh fish to cheap import clothing is for sale at this bustling warren of side streets between Okachi-machi and Ueno stations. The name of the market is often shortened to Ameyoko. Most shops and stalls are open daily 10–7. ✉ *Ueno 4-chōme, Taitō-ku* Ⓜ *JR Ueno Station (Hirokō-ji Exit), JR Okachi-machi Station (Exit A7).*

International Shopping Arcade. A somewhat ragtag collection of shops in Hibiya, this arcade holds a range of goods, including cameras, electronics, pearls, and kimonos. The shops are duty-free, and most of the sales staff speaks English. It's near the Imperial Hotel. ✉ *1–7–23 Uchisaiwai-chō, Chiyoda-ku* Ⓜ *Chiyoda and Hibiya subway lines, Hibiya Station (Exit A13).*

Kyū Shibuya-gawa Hodō. With its avant-garde crafts stores, funky T-shirt shops, and hipster boutiques, this pedestrian strip, also known as Cat Street, serves as a showcase for Japan's au courant designers and artisans. Cat Street is the place to experience bohemian Tōkyō in all its exuberance. ✉ *Between Jingū-mae 3-chōme and Jingū-mae 6-chōme, Shibuya-ku* Ⓜ *Chiyoda subway line, Meiji Jingū-mae Station (Exits 4 and 5).*

Nishi-Sandō. Kimono and *yukata* (cotton kimonos) fabrics, traditional accessories, swords, and festival costumes at very reasonable prices are all for sale at this Asakusa arcade. It runs east of the area's movie theaters, between Rok-ku and the Sensō-ji complex. ✉ *Asakusa 2-chōme, Taitō-ku* Ⓜ *Ginza subway line, Asakusa Station (Exit 1).*

Takeshita-dōri. Teenybopper fashion is all the rage along this Harajuku mainstay, where crowds of high school kids look for the newest addition to their wardrobes. ✉ *Jingū-mae 1-chōme Shibuya-ku* Ⓜ *JR Harajuku Station (Takeshita-dōri Exit).*

Malls & Shopping Centers

Most of these self-contained retail zones carry both foreign and Japanese brands and, like the city's department stores, house cafés, bars, and restaurants. If you don't have the time or energy to dash about Tōkyō in search of the perfect gifts, consider dropping by one of these shopping centers, where you can find a wide selection of merchandise. Most are used to dealing with foreigners.

★ **Axis.** Classy and cutting-edge housewares, fabrics, and ceramics are sold at this multistory design center on the main Roppongi drag of Gaien-Higashi-dōri. Living Motif is a home-furnishings shop with exquisite foreign and Japanese goods. Savoir Vivre has an excellent selection of ceramics. The small Yoshikin sells its own brand of professional-grade cutlery. ⊠ *5–17–1 Roppongi, Minato-ku* ☎ *03/3587–2781* ⊙ *Most shops Mon.–Sat. 11–7* Ⓜ *Hibiya and Ōedo subway lines, Roppongi Station (Exit 3); Namboku subway line, Roppongi Itchōme Station (Exit 1).*

Coredo. Unlike other big stores in the Ginza and Nihombashi areas, this sparkling mall has a contemporary feel thanks to an open layout and extensive use of glass and wood. Housewares, toys, and fashion can all be found here. ⊠ *1–4–1 Nihombashi, Chūo-ku* ☎ *03/3272–4939* ⊙ *Mon.–Sat. 11–9, Sun. 11–8* Ⓜ *Ginza, Tōzai, and Asakusa subway lines, Nihombashi Station (Exit B10).*

Glassarea. Virtually defining Aoyama elegance is this cobblestone shopping center, which draws well-heeled Aoyama housewives to its boutiques, restaurants, and housewares shops. ⊠ *5–4 Minami-Aoyama, Minato-ku* ⊙ *Most shops daily 11–8* Ⓜ *Ginza, Chiyoda, and Hanzō-mon subway lines, Omotesandō Station (Exit B1).*

Marunouchi Building. Opened in 2003, this 37-story shopping, office, and dining complex has brought some much-needed retail dazzle to the area between Tōkyō Station and the Imperial Palace. The ground-floor Beams shop is part of a well-respected Tōkyō fashion chain, and the second-floor Aquagirl boutique sells trendy clothes for women. ⊠ *2–4–1 Marunouchi, Chūo-ku, Tōkyō* ☎ *03/5218–5199* ⊙ *Mon.–Sat. 11–9, Sun. 11–8* Ⓜ *Marunouchi subway line, Marunouchi Station (Marunouchi Building Exit); JR Yamanote Line, Tōkyō Station (Marunouchi Minami-guchi/South Exit).*

Roppongi Hills. You could easily spend a whole day exploring the retail areas of Tōkyō's newest minicity, opened in 2003. The shops here emphasize eye-catching design and chi-chi brands. ⊙ *Most shops daily 11–8* Ⓜ *Hibiya and Ōedo subway lines, Roppongi Station (Roppongi Hills Exit).*

Department Stores

Most Japanese *depāto* (department stores) are parts of conglomerates that include railways, real estate, and leisure industries. The stores themselves commonly have travel agencies, theaters, and art galleries on the premises, as well as reasonably priced and strategically placed restaurants and cafés.

SMART SOUVENIRS

TEMS MADE OF *WASHI*—hand-molded paper—are one of the best buys in Japan. Delicate sheets of almost-transparent stationery, greeting cards, money holders, and wrapping paper are available at traditional crafts stores, stationery stores, and department stores. Small washi-covered boxes (suitable for jewelry and other keepsakes) and pencil cases are also strong candidates for gifts and personal souvenirs.

At first glance, Japanese ceramics may seem priced for a prince's table. Doubtless some are, but if you keep shopping, you can find reasonably priced functional and decorative items that are generally far superior in design to what is available at home. Sale items are often amazingly good bargains. Vases, sake sets consisting of one or two small bottles and a number of cups, and chopstick rests all make good gifts.

Printed fabric, whether by the yard or in the form of finished scarves, napkins, tablecloths, or pillow coverings, is another item worth purchasing in Japan. The complexity of the designs and the quality of the printing make the fabric, both silk and cotton, special. Furoshiki—square pieces of cloth used for wrapping, storing, and carrying things—make great wall hangings.

A visit to a Japanese department store is not merely a shopping excursion—it's a lesson in Japanese culture. Plan to arrive just before it opens: promptly on the hour, immaculately groomed young women face the customers from inside, bow ceremoniously, and unlock the doors. As you walk through the store, all the sales assistants will be standing at attention, in postures of nearly reverent welcome. Notice the uniform angle of incline: many stores have training sessions to teach their new employees the precise and proper degree at which to bend from the waist.

On the top floor of many department stores you'll find gift packages containing Japan's best-loved brands of sake, rice crackers, and other food items. Department stores also typically devote one floor to traditional Japanese crafts, including ceramics, paintings, and lacquerware. If you're pressed for time, these are great places to pick up a variety of souvenirs.

Don't miss the food departments on the lower levels, where you'll encounter an overwhelming selection of Japanese and Western delicacies. No locals in their right minds would shop here regularly for their groceries. A brief exploration, however, will give you a pretty good picture of what people might select for a special occasion—and the price they're prepared to pay for it. Many stalls have small samples out on the counter, and nobody will raise a fuss if you help yourself, even if you don't make a purchase.

Major department stores accept credit cards and provide shipping services. Some salesclerks speak English. If you're having communication difficulties, someone will eventually come to the rescue. On the first floor you'll invariably find a general information booth with useful maps of the store in English. Some department stores close one or two days a month. To be on the safe side, call ahead.

Ginza/Nihombashi

Matsuya. On the fourth floor, the gleaming Matsuya houses an excellent selection of Japanese fashion, including Issey Miyake, Yohji Yamamoto, and Comme Ça Du Mode. The second-floor Louis Vuitton shop is particularly popular with Tōkyō's brand-obsessed shoppers. ⊠ *3–6–1 Ginza, Chūō-ku* ☎ *03/3567–1211* ✆ *Sat.–Thurs. 10–8, Fri. 10–9* Ⓜ *Ginza, Marunouchi, and Hibiya subway lines, Ginza Station (Exits A12 and A13).*

Matsuzakaya. The Matsuzakaya conglomerate was founded in Nagoya and still commands the loyalties of shoppers with origins in western Japan. Style-conscious Tōkyōites tend to find the sense of fashion here a bit countrified. ⊠*6–10–1 Ginza, Chūō-ku* ☎*03/3572–1111* ✆*Mon.–Thurs. 10:30–7:30, Fri. and Sat. 10:30–8, Sun. 10:30–7* Ⓜ *Ginza, Marunouchi, and Hibiya subway lines, Ginza Station (Exits A3 and A4).*

★ **Mitsukoshi.** Founded in 1673 as a dry-goods store, Mitsukoshi later played one of the leading roles in introducing Western merchandise to Japan. It has retained its image of quality and excellence, with a particularly strong representation of Western fashion designers. The store also stocks fine traditional Japanese goods—don't miss the art gallery and the crafts area on the sixth floor. With its own subway stop, bronze lions at the entrance, and an atrium sculpture of the Japanese goddess Magokoro, the remarkable Nihombashi flagship store merits a visit even if you're not planning on buying anything. ⊠ *1–4–1 Nihombashi Muromachi, Chūō-ku* ☎ *03/3241–3311* ✆ *Daily 10–7:30* Ⓜ *Ginza and Hanzō-mon subway lines, Mitsukoshi-mae Station (Exits A3 and A5)* ⊠ *4–6–16 Ginza, Chūō-ku* ☎ *03/3562–1111* ✆ *Mon.–Sat. 10–8, Sun. 10–7:30* Ⓜ *Ginza, Marunouchi, and Hibiya subway lines, Ginza Station (Exits A6, A7, A8).*

Fodor'sChoice **Takashimaya.** In Japanese, *taka* means "high"—a fitting word for this
★ store, which is beloved for its superior quality and prestige. Gift-givers all over Japan seek out this department store; a present that comes in a Takashimaya bag makes a statement regardless of what's inside. The second floor, with shops by Christian Dior, Prada, Chanel, Cartier, and many others, is one of the toniest retail spaces in a shopping district celebrated for its exclusivity. The seventh floor has a complete selection of traditional crafts, antiques, and curios. The lower-level food court carries every gastronomic delight imaginable, from Japanese crackers and green tea to Miyazaki beef and plump melons. ⊠ *2–4–1 Nihombashi, Chūō-ku* ☎ *03/3211–4111* ✆ *Daily 10–8* Ⓜ *Ginza subway line, Nihombashi Station (Exits B1 and B2)* ⊠ *Takashimaya Times Sq., 5–24–2*

Sendagaya, Shibuya-ku ☎ *03/5361–1111* ⊘ *Daily 10–8* Ⓜ *JR Yamanote Line, Shinjuku Station (Minami-guchi/South Exit).*

Wako. Confining itself to a limited selections of goods at the top end of the market, Wako is particularly known for its glassware, jewelry, and accessories—and for some of the handsomest, most sophisticated window displays in town. ⊠ *4–5–11 Ginza, Chūō-ku* ☎ *03/3562–2111* ⊘ *Mon.–Sat. 10:30–6* Ⓜ *Ginza, Marunouchi, and Hibiya subway lines, Ginza Station (Exits A9 and A10).*

Ikebukuro & Shibuya

Parco. Parco, owned by the Seibu conglomerate, is actually not one store but four vertical malls filled with small retail shops and boutiques, all in hailing distance of one another in the commercial heart of Shibuya. Parco Part 1 and Part 4 (Quattro) cater to a younger crowd, stocking "generic" unbranded casual clothing, crafts fabrics, and accessories; Quattro even has a club that hosts live music. Part 2 is devoted mainly to interiors and fashion, and Part 3 sells a mixture of men's and women's fashions, tableware, and household furnishings. The nearby Zero Gate complex houses the basement restaurant-nightclub La Fabrique. ⊠ *15–1 Udagawa-chō, Shibuya-ku* ☎ *03/3464–5111* ⊘ *Parts 1, 2, and 3 daily 10–8:30; Quattro daily 11–9* Ⓜ *Ginza and Hanzō-mon subway lines, Shibuya Station (Exits 6 and 7).*

Seibu. The mammoth main branch of this department store—where even many Japanese customers get lost—is in Ikebukuro. The Shibuya branch, which still carries an impressive array of merchandise, is smaller and more manageable. Seibu has an excellent selection of household goods, from furniture to china and lacquerware, in its stand-alone Loft shops (often next door to Seibu branches, or occasionally within the department store itself). ⊠ *1–28–1 Minami Ikebukuro, Toshima-ku* ☎ *03/3981–0111* ⊘ *Mon.–Sat. 10–9, Sun. 10–8* Ⓜ *JR, Marunouchi and Yūrakuchō subway lines, Ikebukuro Station (Minami-guchi/South Exit); Seibu Ikebukuro private rail line, Seibu Ikebukuro Station (Seibu Department Store Exit); Tōbu Tōjō private rail line, Tōbu Ikebukuro Station (Minami-guchi/South Exit)* ⊠ *21–1 Udagawa-chō, Shibuya-ku* ☎ *03/3462–0111* ⊘ *Mon.–Sat. 10–9, Sun. 10–8* Ⓜ *JR (Hachiko Exit), Ginza and Hanzō-mon subway lines (Exits 6 and 7), Shibuya Station.*

Shinjuku

Isetan. One of Tōkyō's oldest and largest department stores, Isetan is known for its mix of high-end and affordable fashions. The department store even stocks clothing for women (Clovertown) and men (Supermale) in slightly larger sizes for those not quite petite enough for the standard Japanese range. ⊠ *3–14–1 Shinjuku, Shinjuku-ku* ☎ *03/3352–1111* ⊘ *Daily 10–8* Ⓜ *JR (Higashi-guchi/East Exit), Marunouchi subway line (Exits B2, B3, B4, and B5), Shinjuku Station.*

Marui. Marui, easily recognized by its red-and-white OI logo, burst onto the department store scene in the 1980s by introducing an in-store credit card—one of the first stores in Japan to do so. Branches typically occupy separate buildings near big stations; there are six big shops in Shinjuku with names like Marui Young, Marui City, and Marui One. Youngsters flock to the stores in search of petite clothing, accessories, and sportswear. The main Shinjuku location, Marui Zacca, carries furniture and products for the home. ✉ *3–1–3 Shinjuku, Shinjuku-ku* ☎ *03/3354–0101* ⊙ *Daily 11–8* Ⓜ *JR, Shinjuku Station (Higashi-guchi/East Exit); Marunouchi subway line, Shinjuku San-chōme Station (Exit A1).*

Specialty Stores

Antiques

From ornate *tansu* (traditional chests used to store clothing) to Meiji-era Nō masks, Tōkyō's antiques shops are stocked with fine examples of traditional Japanese craftsmanship. The two best areas for antiques are Nishi-Ogikubo (also known as Nishiogi), which is just outside of Shinjuku, and Aoyama. The elegant shops along Kottō-dōri—Aoyama's "Antiques Road"—are the places to hunt down exquisite ¥100,000 vases and other pricey items. The slapdash array of more than 60 antiques shops in Nishi-Ogikubo has an anything-goes feel. When visiting Nishi-Ogikubo, which you can reach by taking the Sōbu Line to Nishi-Ogikubo Station, your best bet is to pick up the free printed area guide available at the police box outside the train station's north exit. Even though it's mostly in Japanese, the map provides easy-to-follow directions to all stores. Dealers are evenly clustered in each of the four districts around the station, so plan on spending at least half a day in Nishi-Ogikubo if you want to see them all.

Antiquers can also find great buys at Tōkyō's flea markets, which are often held on the grounds of the city's shrines.

★ **Fuji-Torii.** An English-speaking staff, a central Omotesandō location, and antiques ranging from ceramics to swords are the big draws at this shop, in business since 1948. In particular, Fuji-Torii has an excellent selection of folding screens, lacquerware, and *ukiyo-e* (wood-block prints). ✉ *6–1–10 Jingū-mae, Shibuya-ku* ☎ *03/3400–2777* ⊙ *Wed.–Mon. 11–6; closed 3rd Mon. of month* Ⓜ *Chiyoda subway line, Meiji Jingū-mae Station (Exit 4).*

Hanae Mori Building. The basement floor of this Kenzō Tange–designed emporium houses more than a dozen small antiques shops. The emphasis is on European goods, but Japanese offerings include a tasteful sword shop and ceramics dealers. Upstairs, fashion hounds can shop for designs from Mori Hanae, the doyenne of Japanese designers. ✉ *3–6–1 Kita-Aoyama, Minato-ku* ☎ *03/3406–1021* ⊙ *Daily 10:30–7* Ⓜ *Ginza, Chiyoda, and Hanzō-mon subway lines, Omotesandō Station (Exit A1).*

Lee Bong Rae. Stately Korean furniture and ceramics are on offer at this small Aoyama shop just up the road from the designer-housewares store Idee. ✉ *6–2–5 Minami-Aoyama, Minato-ku* ☎ *03/3407–6420* ⊙ *Mon.–Sat. 10–6* Ⓜ *Ginza, Chiyoda, and Hanzō-mon subway lines, Omotesandō Station (Exit B1).*

Morita. This Aoyama shop carries antique and new *mingei* (Japanese folk crafts) in addition to a large stock of textiles from throughout Asia. ✉ *5–12–2 Minami-Aoyama, Minato-ku* ☎ *03/3407–6420* ⊙ *Daily*

10–7 [M] *Ginza, Chiyoda, and Hanzō-mon subway lines, Omotesandō Station (Exit B1).*

Tōgō Jinja. One of the city's biggest flea markets—where you can often find antiques—takes place at this shrine near Harajuku's Takeshita-dōri, on the first, fourth, and fifth Sunday of the month from sunrise to sunset. ✉ *1–5 Jingū-mae, Shibuya-ku* ☎ *03/3425–7965* [M] *Chiyoda subway line, Meiji-jingū-mae Station; JR Harajuku Station (Takeshita-dōri Exit).*

Yasukuni Jinja. You can search for antiques at the large flea market at Yasukuni, the Shrine of Peace for the Nation, every second and third Sunday of the month from sunrise to sunset. ✉ *3–1 Kudan-Kita, Chiyoda-ku* ☎ *090/2723–0687* [M] *Hanzō-mon and Shinjuku subway lines, Kudanshita Station (Exit 1).*

Books

If you want to read while you're in Tōkyō, it's best to bring your books and magazines with you; foreign titles are often marked up by as much as 300%. All the shops listed below are open daily.

Bookstores of Jimbō-chō. The site of one of the largest concentrations of used bookstores in the world, the Jimbō-chō area is a bibliophile's dream. In the ½-km (¼-mi) strip along Yasukuni-dōri and its side streets you can find centuries-old Japanese prints, vintage manga (sophisticated comic books), and even complete sets of the *Oxford English Dictionary*. Most shops have predominately Japanese-language selections, but almost all stock some foreign titles, with a few devoting major floor space to English books. Kitazawa Shoten, recognizable by its stately entranceway, carries lots of humanities titles. Tokyo Random Walk is the retail outlet of Tuttle Publishing, which puts out books on Japanese language and culture. The large Japanese publisher Sanseidō has its flagship store here; the fifth floor sells magazines and postcards in addition to books. The stores in the area are usually open 9 or 9:30 to 5:30 or 6, and many of the smaller shops close on Monday or Sunday. [M] *Mita, Shinjuku, and Hanzō-mon subway lines, Jimbō-chō Station (Exit A5).*

Kinokuniya. The mammoth Kinokuniya bookstore near the south exit of Shinjuku Station devotes most of its fifth floor to English titles, with an excellent selection of travel guides, magazines, and books on Japan. ✉ *Takashimaya Times Sq., 5–24–2 Sendagaya, Shibuya-ku* ☎ *03/ 5361–3301* ◷ *Daily 10–8* [M] *JR Yamanote Line, Shinjuku Station (Minami-guchi/South Exit).*

Maruzen. There are English titles on the fourth floor, and art books in English and Japanese on the second floor of this well-known bookstore. ✉ *2–3–10 Nihombashi, Chūō-ku* ☎ *03/3272–7211* ◷ *Mon.–Sat. 10–8, Sun. 10–6* [M] *JR Tōkyō Station (Yaesu North Exit 16); Ginza and Tōzai subway lines, Nihombashi Station (Exit B3).*

Tower Records. This branch of the U.S.-based chain carries an eclectic collection of English-language books at more reasonable prices than most bookstores in town. It also has the best selection of foreign magazines in Tōkyō. ✉ *1–22–14 Jinnan, Shibuya-ku* ☎ *03/3496–3661* ◷ *Daily*

10–11 Ⓜ *JR Yamanote, Hanzō-mon and Ginza subway lines, Shibuya Station (Exit 6).*

Yaesu Book Center. English-language paperbacks, art books, and calendars are available on the seventh floor of this celebrated bookstore. ✉ *2–5–1 Yaesu, Chūō-ku* ☎ *03/3281–1811* ⊗ *Mon.–Sat. 10–9, Sun. 10–8* Ⓜ *JR Tōkyō Station (Yaesu South Exit 5).*

Ceramics

The Japanese have been crafting extraordinary pottery for more than 2,000 years, but this art form really began to flourish in the 16th century with the popularity and demand for tea-ceremony utensils. Feudal lords competed for possession of the finest pieces, and distinctive styles of pottery developed in regions all over the country. Some of the more prominent styles are those of the village of Arita in Kyūshū, with painted patterns of flowers and birds; Mashiko, in Tochigi Prefecture, with its rough textures and simple, warm colors; rugged Hagi ware, from the eponymous Western Honshū city; and Kasama, in Ibaraki Prefecture, with glazes made from ash and ground rocks. Tōkyō's specialty shops and department stores carry fairly complete selections of these and other wares.

Noritake. The Akasaka showroom of this internationally renowned brand carries fine china and glassware in a spacious setting. ✉ *7–8–5 Akasaka, Minato-ku* ☎ *03/3586–0059* ⊗ *Weekdays 10–6* Ⓜ *Chiyoda subway line, Akasaka Station (Exit 7).*

Savoir Vivre. In Roppongi's ultratrendy Axis Building, this store sells contemporary and antique tea sets, cups, bowls, and glassware. ✉ *Axis Bldg., 3F, 5–17–1 Roppongi, Minato-ku* ☎ *03/3585–7365* ⊗ *Mon.–Sat. 11–7, Sun. 11–6:30* Ⓜ *Hibiya and Ōedo subway lines, Roppongi Station (Exit 3).*

Tsutaya. *Ikebana* (flower arrangement) and *sadō* (tea ceremony) goods are the only items sold at this Kottō-dōri shop, but they come in such stunning variety that a visit is definitely worthwhile. Vases in surprising shapes and traditional ceramic tea sets make for unique souvenirs. ✉ *5–10–5 Minami-Aoyama, Minato-ku* ☎ *03/3400–3815* ⊗ *Daily 10–6:30* Ⓜ *Ginza, Chiyoda, and Hanzō-mon subway lines, Omotesandō Station (Exit B1).*

Clothing Boutiques

Japanese boutiques pay as much attention to interior design as they do to the clothing they sell; like anywhere else, it's the image that moves the merchandise. Although many mainstream Japanese designers are represented in the major upscale department stores, you may enjoy your shopping more in the elegant boutiques of Aoyama and Omotesandō—most of which are within walking distance of one another.

Bape Exclusive Aoyama. Since the late 1990s, no brand has been more coveted by Harajuku scenesters than the A Bathing Ape label (shortened to Bape) from DJ–fashion designer Nigo. At the height of the craze, hopefuls would line up outside Nigo's well-hidden boutiques for the chance to plop down ¥7,000 for a T-shirt festooned with a simian visage or a *Planet of the Apes* quote. Bape has since gone above-ground, with Nigo expanding his business empire to Singapore, Hong Kong, and

London. Here in Tōkyō, you can see what all the fuss is about at a spacious boutique that houses the Bape Gallery on the second floor. ✉ *5–5–8 Minami-Aoyama, Minato-ku* ☎ *03/3407–2145* ☉ *Daily 11–7* Ⓜ *Ginza and Hanzō-mon subway lines, Omotesandō Station (Exit A5).*

Busy Workshop Harajuku. This Harajuku spot sells the trendy Bape clothing line and has an avant-garde interior by noted local designers Wonderwall. ✉ *B1F, 4–28–22 Jingū-mae, Minato-ku* ☎ *03/5474–0204* ☉ *Daily 11–7* Ⓜ *Chiyoda line, Meiji-jingū-mae Station (Exit 5); JR Harajuku Station (Takeshita-dori Exit).*

★ **Comme des Garçons.** Sinuous low walls snake through Rei Kawakubo's flagship store, a minimalist labyrinth that houses the designer's signature clothes, shoes, and accessories. Staff members will do their best to ignore you, but that's no reason to stay away from one of Tōkyō's funkiest retail spaces. ✉ *5–2–1 Minami-Aoyama, Minato-ku* ☎ *03/3406–3951* ☉ *Daily 11–8* Ⓜ *Ginza, Chiyoda, and Hanzō-mon subway lines, Omotesandō Station (Exit A5).*

Issey Miyake. The otherworldly creations of internationally renowned designer Miyake are on display at her flagship store in Aoyama, which carries the full Paris line. ✉ *3–18–11 Minami-Aoyama, Minato-ku* ☎ *03/3423–1407* ☉ *Daily 11–8* Ⓜ *Ginza, Chiyoda, and Hanzō-mon subway lines, Omotesandō Station (Exit A4).*

10 Corso Como Comme des Garçons. Milanese lifestyle guru Carla Sozzani helped create this spacious boutique for designer Rei Kawakubo's Comme des Garçons lines, which include Junya Watanabe menswear and womens wear. Also on offer are Vivienne Westwood and Balenciaga brands, and the staff isn't too busy being hip to help you out. ✉ *5–3 Minami-Aoyama, Minato-ku* ☎ *03/5774–7800* ☉ *Daily 11–8* Ⓜ *Ginza, Chiyoda, and Hanzō-mon subway lines, Omotesandō Station (Exit A5).*

Under Cover. This stark shop houses Paris darling Jun Takahashi's cult clothing, with enormously high racks of men's and women's clothing with a tatty punk look. ✉ *5–3–18 Minami-Aoyama, Minato-ku* ☎ *03/3407–1232* ☉ *Daily 11–8* Ⓜ *Ginza, Chiyoda, and Hanzō-mon subway lines, Omotesandō Station (Exit A5).*

Y's Roppongi Hills. With its glossy surfaces and spare lines, the interior of this Ron Arad–designed shop on Roppongi's Keyakizaka-dōri serves as a suitable showcase for Yohji Yamamoto's austere fashions. ✉ *6–12–4 Roppongi, Minato-ku* ☎ *03/5416–3434* ☉ *Daily 11–9* Ⓜ *Hibiya and Ōedo subway lines, Roppongi Station (Roppongi Hills Exit).*

Dolls

Many types of traditional dolls are available in Japan, each with its own charm. Kokeshi dolls, which date from the Edo period, are long, cylindrical, painted, and made of wood, with no arms or legs. Daruma, papier-mâché dolls with rounded bottoms and faces, are often painted with amusing expressions. Legend has it they are modeled after a Buddhist priest who remained seated in the lotus position for so long that his arms and legs atrophied. Hakata dolls, from Kyūshū, are ceramic figurines in traditional costume, such as geisha, samurai, or festival dancers.

Kyūgetsu. In business for more than a century, Kyūgetsu sells every kind of doll imaginable. ✉ *1–20–4 Yanagibashi, Taitō-ku* ☎ *03/3861–5511* ⊙ *Weekdays 9:15–6, weekends 9:15–5:15* Ⓜ *Asakusa subway line, Asakusa-bashi Station (Exit A3).*

Electronics

The area around Akihabara Station has more than 200 stores with discount prices on stereos, digital cameras, PCs, DVD players, and anything else that runs on electricity. The larger shops have sections or floors (or even whole annexes) of goods made for export. Products come with instructions in most major languages, and if you have a tourist visa in your passport, you can purchase them duty-free.

Bic Camera. A large discount-electronics chain in the Odakyū Halc building, Bic Camera has low prices. ✉ *1–5–1 Nishi-Shinjuku, Shinjuku-ku* ☎ *03/5326–1111* ⊙ *Daily 11–9* Ⓜ *Marunouchi and Shinjuku subway lines; JR; Keiō Shin-sen and Teitō private rail lines: Shinjuku Station (Nishi-guchi/West Exit).*

LAOX. One of the big Akihabara chains, LAOX has several locations in the area. The "Duty Free Akihabara" branch on the main Chūō-dōri strip carries a full six floors of export models. English-speaking staff members are always on call. ✉ *1–15–3 Soto-Kanda, Chiyoda-ku* ☎ *03/ 3255–5301* ⊙ *Daily 10–8* Ⓜ *JR Akihabara Station (Denki-gai Exit).*

Softmap. One Akihabara retailer that actually benefited from the bursting of Japan's economic bubble in the early '90s is Softmap, a used-PC and -software chain with a heavy presence in Tōkyō. Most branches are open daily until 7:30 or 8. ✉ *3–14–10 Soto-Kanda, Chiyoda-ku* ☎ *03/ 3253–3030* ⊙ *Daily 11–8* Ⓜ *JR Akihabara Station (Denki-gai Exit).*

Ⓒ **Sony Building.** You can take the latest Sony gadgets for a test drive at this retail and entertainment space in the heart of Ginza. Kids enjoy trying out the latest, not-yet-released PlayStation games, while their parents fiddle with digital cameras and stereos from Japan's electronics leader. ✉ *5–3–1 Ginza, Chūō-ku* ☎ *03/3573–2371* ⊙ *Daily 11–7* Ⓜ *Ginza, Hibiya, and Marunouchi subway lines, Ginza Station (Exit B9).*

Yamagiwa. Like LAOX, Yamagiwa has branches and annexes throughout Akihabara, and the upper floors of the main store sell items for foreign markets. ✉ *4–1–1 Soto-Kanda, Chiyoda-ku* ☎ *03/3253–2111* ⊙ *Daily 10–8* Ⓜ *JR Akihabara Station (Denki-gai Exit).*

Yodobashi Camera. This discount-electronics superstore near Shinjuku Station carries a selection comparable to Akihabara's big boys. ✉ *1–11–1 Nishi-Shinjuku, Shinjuku-ku* ☎ *03/3346–1010* ⊙ *Daily 11–9* Ⓜ *Marunouchi and Shinjuku subway lines; JR; Keiō Shin-sen and Teitō private rail lines: Shinjuku Station (Nishi-guchi/West Exit).*

Folk Crafts

Japanese folk crafts, called mingei—among them bamboo vases and baskets, fabrics, paper boxes, dolls, and toys—achieve a unique beauty in their simple and sturdy designs. Be aware, however, that simple does not mean cheap. Long hours of labor go into these objects, and every year there are fewer craftspeople left, producing their work in smaller and smaller quantities. Include these items in your budget ahead of time: the best—worth every cent—can be fairly expensive.

★ **Bingo-ya.** You may be able to complete all of your souvenir shopping in one trip to this tasteful four-floor shop, which carries traditional handicrafts from all over Japan, including ceramics, toys, lacquerware, Nō masks, fabrics, and lots more. ✉ *10–6 Wakamatsu-chō, Shinjuku-ku* ☎ *03/3202–8778* ⊘ *Tues.–Sun. 10–7* Ⓜ *Ōedo subway line, Wakamatsu Kawada Station (Wakamatsu-chō Exit).*

★ **Oriental Bazaar.** The four floors of this popular tourist destination are packed with just about anything you could want as a traditional Japanese (or Chinese or Korean) handicraft souvenir: painted screens, pottery, chopsticks, dolls, and more, all at very reasonable prices. ✉ *5–9–13 Jingū-mae, Shibuya-ku* ☎ *03/3400–3933* ⊘ *Fri.–Wed. 10–7* Ⓜ *Chiyoda subway line, Meiji Jingū-mae Station (Exit 4).*

Foodstuffs & Wares

This hybrid category includes everything from crackers and dried seaweed to cast-iron kettles, paper lanterns, and essential food kitsch like plastic sushi sets.

Backstreet Shops of Tsukiji. In Tsukiji, between the Central Wholesale Market and Harumi-dōri, among the many fishmongers, you can also find stores selling pickles, tea, crackers, kitchen knives, baskets, and crockery. The area is a real slice of Japanese life. ✉ *Tsukiji 4-chōme, Chūō-ku* Ⓜ *Ōedo subway line, Tsukiji-shijō Station (Exit A1); Hibiya subway line, Tsukiji Station (Exit 1).*

Tea-Tsu. Some people ascribe Japanese longevity to the beneficial effects of green tea. Tea-Tsu, which has five branches in Tōkyō, sells a variety of leaves in attractive canisters that make unique gifts. The main Aoyama branch also sells tea sets and other ceramics, and the staff will serve you a complimentary cup of *cha* (tea) as you make your selection. ✉ *3–18–3 Minami-Aoyama, Minato-ku* ☎ *03/5772–2662* ⊘ *Tues.–Sat. 11–8* Ⓜ *Ginza, Chiyoda, and Hanzō-mon subway lines, Omotesandō Station (Exit A4).*

Tokiwa-dō. Come here to buy some of Tōkyō's most famous souvenirs: *kaminari okoshi* (thunder crackers), made of rice, millet, sugar, and beans. The shop is on the west side of Asakusa's Thunder God Gate, the Kaminari-mon entrance to Sensō-ji. ✉ *1–3 Asakusa, Taitō-ku* ☎ *03/3841–5656* ⊘ *Daily 9–8:45* Ⓜ *Ginza subway line, Asakusa Station (Exit 1).*

Yamamoto Noriten. The Japanese are resourceful in their uses of products from the sea. Nori, the paper-thin dried seaweed used to wrap maki sushi and *onigiri* (rice balls), is the specialty here. If you plan to bring some home with you, buy unroasted nori and toast it yourself at home; the flavor will be far better than that of the preroasted sheets. ✉ *1–6–3 Nihombashi Muromachi, Chūō-ku* ☎ *03/3241–0261* ⊘ *Daily 9–6:30* Ⓜ *Hanzō-mon and Ginza subway lines, Mitsukoshi-mae Station (Exit A1).*

KAPPA-BASHI   A wholesale-restaurant-supply district might not sound like a promising shopping destination, but Kappa-bashi, about a 10-minute walk west of the temples and pagodas of Asakusa, is worth a look. Ceramics, cutlery, cookware, folding lanterns, and even kimonos can all be found here, along with the kitschy plastic food models that appear in restaurant windows throughout Japan. The best strategy is to stroll up and down the 1-km (½-mi) length of Kappa-bashi-dōgu-machi-dōri and visit any shop that looks interesting. Most stores here emphasize function over charm, but some manage to stand out for their stylish spaces as well. Most Kappabashi shops are open until 5:30; some close on Sunday. To get here, take the Ginza subway line to Tawara-machi Station.

Kappa-bashi Sōshoku. Come here for *aka-chōchin* (folding red-paper lanterns) like the ones that hang in front of inexpensive bars and restaurants. ✉ *3–1–1 Matsugaya, Taitō-ku* ☎ *03/3844–1973* 🕐 *Mon.–Sat. 9:30–5:30* Ⓜ *Ginza subway line, Tawara-machi Station (Exit 3).*

Kawahara Shōten. The brightly colored bulk packages of rice crackers, shrimp-flavored chips, and other Japanese snacks sold here make offbeat gifts. ✉ *3–9–2 Nishi-Asakusa, Taitō-ku* ☎ *03/3842–0841* 🕐 *Mon.–Sat. 9–5:30* Ⓜ *Ginza subway line, Tawara-machi Station (Exit 3).*

🔁 **Maizuru.** This perennial tourist favorite manufactures the plastic food that's displayed outside almost every Tōkyō restaurant. Ersatz sushi, noodles, and even beer cost just a few hundred yen. You can buy tiny plastic key holders and earrings, or splurge on a whole Pacific lobster, perfect in coloration and detail down to the tiniest spines on its legs. ✉ *1–5–17 Nishi-Asakusa, Taitō-ku* ☎ *03/3843–1686* 🕐 *Daily 9–6* Ⓜ *Ginza subway line, Tawara-machi Station (Exit 3).*

Soi. The selection of lacquerware, ceramics, and antiques sold at this Kappa-bashi shop is modest, but Soi displays the items in a primitivist setting of stone walls and and exposed wood beams, with up-tempo jazz in the background. ✉ *3–17–3 Matsugaya, Taitō-ku* ☎ *03/3843–9555* 🕐 *Daily 10–6* Ⓜ *Ginza subway line, Tawara-machi Station (Exit 3).*

Sōtei Yabukita. In addition to kitchenware, this tasteful shop sells lamps and decorative fountains. ✉ *2–1–12 Matsugaya, Taitō-ku* ☎ *03/ 5828–5082* Ⓜ *Ginza subway line, Tawara-machi Station (Exit 3).*

Housewares

Tōkyōites appreciate fine design, both the kind they can wear and the kind they can display in their homes. This passion is reflected in the exuberance of the city's *zakka* shops—retailers that sell small housewares. The Daikanyama and Aoyama areas positively brim with these stores, but trendy zakka can be found throughout the city.

Idee. Local design giant Teruo Kurosaki's shop, which is just off Kottō-dōri, carries housewares, fabrics, and ceramics by some of Japan's most celebrated young craftspeople. The third-floor café-restaurant is a favorite meeting place of Aoyama creative types. ✉ *6–1–6 Minami-Aoyama, Minato-ku* ☎ *03/3409–6581* 🕐 *Sat.–Thurs. 11–7, Fri. 11–9* Ⓜ *Ginza, Chiyoda, and Hanzō-mon subway lines, Omotesandō Station (Exit B1).*

Nishimura. This Kappa-bashi shop specializes in *noren*—the curtains that shops and restaurants hang to announce they're open. The curtains are typically cotton, linen, or silk, most often dyed to order for individual shops. Nishimura also sells premade noren of an entertaining variety—from white-on-blue landscapes to geisha and sumō wrestlers in polychromatic splendor—for home decorating. They make wonderful wall hangings and dividers. ✉ *1–10–10 Matsugaya, Taitō-ku* ☎ *03/3844–9954* ◷ *Mon.–Sat. 10–5* Ⓜ *Ginza subway line, Tawara-machi Station (Exit 3).*

Sempre. Playful, colorful, and bright describe both the products and the space of this Kottō-dōri housewares dealer. Among the great finds here are interesting tableware, glassware, lamps, office goods, and jewelry. ✉ *5–13–3 Minami-Aoyama, Minato-ku* ☎ *03/5464–5655* ◷ *Mon.–Sat. 11–8, Sun. 11–7* Ⓜ *Ginza, Chiyoda, and Hanzō-mon subway lines, Omotesandō Station (Exit B1).*

Serendipity. Alessi products and other Western brands are sold at this spacious housewares store in the Coredo shopping center. ✉ *1–4–1 Nihombashi, Chūō-ku* ☎ *03/3272–4939* ◷ *Mon.–Sat. 11–9, Sun. 11–8* Ⓜ *Ginza, Tōzai, and Asakusa subway lines, Nihombashi Station (Exit B10).*

Sputnik Pad. One of local designer Teruo Kurosaki's shops, Sputnik is Tōkyō's ultimate housewares destination. It carries funky and functional interiors products from big international designers like Marc Newson. Low, a trendy "rice café," is in the basement, and the Vision Network entertainment complex is across the street. ✉ *5–46–14 Jingū-mae, Minato-ku* ☎ *03/6418–1330* ◷ *Daily 11–7* Ⓜ *Ginza, Chiyoda, and Hanzō-mon subway lines, Omotesandō Station (Exit B1).*

Ⓒ **Tōkyū Hands.** Billing itself as a "Creative Lifestyle Store," this do-it-yourself hobby chain stocks an excellent selection of bric-a-brac for the Tōkyō apartment dweller. Tourists find it to be a great spot to pick up inexpensive knickknacks with a Japanese flavor, like toys, picture frames, and kitchen goods. Tōkyū Hands has branches near most big stations. ✉ *Takashimaya Times Sq., 5–24–2 Sendagaya, Shibuya-ku* ☎ *03/5361–3111* ◷ *Daily 10–8* Ⓜ *JR Yamanote Line, Shinjuku Station (Minami-guchi/South Exit).*

Kimonos

Traditional clothing has experienced something of a comeback among Tōkyō's youth, but most Japanese women, unless they work in traditional restaurants, now wear kimonos only on special occasions. Like tuxedos in the United States, they are often rented, not purchased outright, for social events such as weddings or graduations. Kimonos are extremely expensive and difficult to maintain. A wedding kimono, for example, can cost as much as ¥1 million.

Most visitors, naturally unwilling to pay this much for a garment that they probably want to use as a bathrobe or a conversation piece, settle for a secondhand or antique silk kimono. You can pay as little as ¥1,000 in a flea market, but to find one in decent condition, you should expect to pay about ¥10,000. However, cotton summer kimonos, called yukata, in a wide variety of colorful and attractive designs, can be bought new for ¥7,000–¥10,000.

Hayashi. This store in the Yūraku-chō International Arcade specializes in ready-made kimonos, sashes, and dyed yukata. ✉ *2–1–1 Yūraku-chō, Chiyoda-ku* ☎ *03/3501–4012* ◷ *Mon.–Sat. 10–7, Sun. 10–6* Ⓜ *Ginza, Hibiya, and Marunouchi subway lines, Ginza Station (Exit C1).*

Kawano Gallery. Kawano, in the high-fashion district of Omotesandō, sells kimonos and kimono fabric in a variety of patterns. ✉ *4–4–9 Jingū-mae, Shibuya-ku* ☎ *03/3470–3305* ◷ *Daily 11–6* Ⓜ *Ginza, Chiyoda, and Hanzō-mon subway lines, Omotesandō Station (Exit A2).*

Tansu-ya. This small but pleasant Ginza shop, part of a chain with locations throughout Japan and abroad, has attractive used kimonos, yukata, and other traditional clothing in many fabrics, colors, and patterns. The helpful staff can acquaint you with the somewhat complicated method of putting on the clothes. ✉ *3–4–5 Ginza, Chūō-ku* ☎ *03/3561–8529* ◷ *Daily 11–8* Ⓜ *Ginza, Hibiya, and Marunouchi subway lines, Ginza Station (Exit A13).*

Lacquerware

For its history, diversity, and fine workmanship, lacquerware rivals ceramics as the traditional Japanese craft nonpareil. One warning: lacquerware thrives on humidity. Cheaper pieces usually have plastic rather than wood underneath. Because these won't shrink and crack in dry climates, they make safer—and no less attractive—buys.

Fodor'sChoice **Yamada Heiando.** With a spacious, airy layout and lovely lacquerware
★ goods, this fashionable Daikanyama shop is a must for souvenir hunters— and anyone else who appreciates fine design. Rice bowls, sushi trays, *bento* lunch boxes, *hashioki* (chopstick rests), and jewelry cases come in traditional blacks and reds, as well as patterns both subtle and bold. Prices are fair—many items cost less than ¥10,000—but these are the kinds of goods for which devotees of Japanese craftsmanship would be willing to pay a lot. ✉ *Hillside Terrace G Block, 18–12 Sarugakuchō, Shibuya-ku* ☎ *03/3463–5541* ◷ *Mon.–Sat. 10:30–7, Sun. 10:30–6:30* Ⓜ *Tōkyū Tōyoko line, Daikanyama Station (Komazawa-dōri Exit).*

Miscellaneous

Handmade combs, towels, and cosmetics are other uniquely Japanese treasures to consider picking up while in Tōkyō.

★ **Fuji-ya.** Master textile creator Keiji Kawakami's cotton *tenugui* (teh-*noo*-goo-ee) hand towels are collector's items, often as not framed instead of used as towels. Kawakami is an expert on the hundreds of traditional towel motifs that have come down from the Edo period: geometric patterns, plants and animals, and scenes from Kabuki plays and festivals. When Kawakami feels he has made enough of one pattern of his own design, he destroys the stencil. The shop is near the corner of Dembō-in-dōri on Naka-mise-dōri. ✉ *2–2–15 Asakusa, Taitō-ku* ☎ *03/3841–2283* ◷ *Fri.–Wed. 10–6* Ⓜ *Ginza subway line, Asakusa Station (Exit 6).*

Hyaku-suke. This is the last place in Tōkyō to carry government-approved skin cleanser made from powdered nightingale droppings. Ladies of the Edo period—especially the geisha—swore by the cleanser. These days this 100-year-old-plus cosmetics shop sells little of the nightingale powder, but its theatrical makeup for Kabuki actors, geisha, and traditional weddings—as well as unique items like seaweed shampoo, camellia oil, and handcrafted combs and cosmetic brushes—makes it a worthy addition to your Asakusa shopping itinerary. ✉ *2–2–14 Asakusa, Taitō-*

ku ☎ *03/3841–7058* ⊙ *Thurs.–Tues. 10–6* Ⓜ *Ginza subway line, Asakusa Station (Exit 6).*

Jusan-ya. A shop selling handmade boxwood combs, this business was started in 1736 by a samurai who couldn't support himself as a feudal retainer. It has been in the same family ever since. Jusan-ya is on Shinobazu-dōri, a few doors west of its intersection with Chūō-dōri in Ueno. ⊠ *2–12–21 Ueno, Taitō-ku* ☎ *03/3831–3238* ⊙ *Mon.–Sat. 10–7* Ⓜ *Ginza subway line, Ueno Hirokō-ji Station (Exit 6); JR Ueno Station (Shinobazu Exit).*

Naka-ya. If you want to equip yourself for Sensō-ji's annual Sanja Festival in May, this is the place to come. Best buys here are *sashiko hanten,* which are thick woven firemen's jackets, and *happi* coats, cotton tunics printed in bright colors with Japanese characters. Some items are available in children's sizes. ⊠ *2–2–12 Asakusa, Taitō-ku* ☎ *03/3841–7877* ⊙ *Daily 10–7* Ⓜ *Ginza subway line, Asakusa Station (Exit 6).*

Yono-ya. Traditional Japanese coiffures and wigs are very complicated, and they require a variety of tools to shape them properly. Tatsumi Minekawa, the current master at Yono-ya—the family line goes back 300 years—deftly crafts and decorates very fine boxwood combs. Some combs are carved with auspicious motifs, such as peonies, hollyhocks, or cranes, and all are engraved with the family benchmark. ⊠ *1–37–10 Asakusa, Taitō-ku* ☎ *03/3844–1755* ⊙ *Daily 10–6; occasionally closed on Wed. or Thurs.* Ⓜ *Ginza subway line, Asakusa Station (Exit 1).*

Paper

What packs light and flat in your suitcase, won't break, doesn't cost much, and makes a great gift? The answer is traditional handmade *washi* (paper), which the Japanese make in thousands of colors, textures, and designs and fashion into an astonishing number of useful and decorative objects.

Kami Hyakka. Operated by the Ōkura Sankō wholesale paper company, which was founded in the late 19th century, this showroom displays some 512 different types and colors of paper—made primarily for stationery, notes, and cards rather than as crafts material. You can pick up three free samples when you visit. ⊠*2–4–9 Ginza, Chūō-ku* ☎*03/3538–5025* ⊙*Tues.–Sat. 10:30–7* Ⓜ *Yūraku-chō subway line, Ginza-Itchōme Station (Exit 5); Ginza, Hibiya, and Marunouchi subway lines, Ginza Station (Exit B4).*

Kami-no-Takamura. Specialists in washi and other papers printed in traditional Japanese designs, this shop also carries brushes, inkstones, and other tools for calligraphy. ⊠ *1–1–2 Higashi-Ikebukuro, Toshima-ku* ☎ *03/3971–7111* ⊙ *Daily 11–6:45* Ⓜ *Ikebukuro Station (Exit 35).*

★ **Kyūkyodō.** Kyūkyodō has been in business since 1663—in Ginza since 1880—selling its wonderful handmade Japanese papers, paper products, incense, brushes, and other materials for calligraphy. ⊠ *5–7–4 Ginza, Chūō-ku* ☎ *03/3571–4429* ⊙ *Mon.–Sat. 10–7:30, Sun. 11–7* Ⓜ *Ginza, Hibiya, and Marunouchi subway lines, Ginza Station (Exit A2).*

Ozu Washi. This shop, which was opened in the 17th century, has one of the largest washi showrooms in the city and its own gallery of antique papers. ✉ *2–6–3 Nihombashi-Honchō, Chūo-ku* ☎ *03/3663–8788* 🕐 *Mon.–Sat. 10–6* Ⓜ *Ginza subway line, Mitsukoshi-mae Station (Exit A4).*

Yushima no Kobayashi. Here, in addition to shopping for paper goods, you can also tour a papermaking workshop and learn the art of origami. ✉ *1–7–14 Yushima, Bunkyō-ku* ☎ *03/3811–4025* 🕐 *Mon.–Sat. 9–6* Ⓜ *Chiyoda subway line, Yushima Station (Exit 5).*

Pearls

Japan is one of the best places in the world to buy cultured pearls. They will not be inexpensive, but pearls of the same quality cost considerably more elsewhere.

★ **Mikimoto.** Kōkichi Mikimoto created his technique for cultured pearls in 1893. Since then his name has been associated with the best quality in the industry. Mikimoto's flagship store in Ginza is less a jewelry shop than a boutique devoted to nature's ready-made gems. ✉ *4–5–5 Ginza, Chūo-ku* ☎ *03/3535–4611* 🕐 *Mon.–Sat. 11–7:30, Sun. 11–7; occasionally closed on Wed.* Ⓜ *Ginza, Hibiya, and Marunouchi subway lines, Ginza Station (Exit A9).*

Tasaki Pearl Gallery. Tasaki sells pearls at slightly lower prices than Mikimoto. The store has several showrooms and hosts English-language tours that demonstrate the technique of culturing pearls and explain how to maintain and care for them. ✉ *1–3–3 Akasaka, Minato-ku* ☎ *03/5561–8881* 🕐 *Daily 9–6* Ⓜ *Ginza subway line, Tameike-Sannō Station (Exit 9).*

Swords & Knives

Supplying the tools of the trade to samurai and sushi chefs alike, Japanese metalworkers have played a significant role in the nation's military and culinary history. The remarkable knives on offer from the shops below are comparable in both quality and price to the best Western brands. For swords, you can pay thousands of dollars for a good-quality antique, but far more reasonably priced reproductions are available as well. Consult with your airline on how best to transport these items home.

Ichiryō-ya. A small, cluttered souvenir shop in the Nishi-Sandō arcade, Ichiryō-ya carries antique swords and reproductions and has some English-speaking salesclerks. ✉ *2–7–13 Asakusa, Taitō-ku* ☎ *03/3843–0051* 🕐 *Wed. and Fri.–Mon. 11–6* Ⓜ *Ginza subway line, Asakusa Station (Exit 1) or Tawara-machi Station (Exit 3).*

Kiya. Workers shape and hone blades in one corner of this Ginza shop, which carries cutlery, pocketknives, saws, and more. Scissors with handles in the shape of Japanese cranes are among the many unique gift items sold here, and custom-made knives are available on the second floor. ✉ *1–5–6 Nihombashi-Muromachi, Chūo-ku* ☎ *03/3241–0110* 🕐 *Mon.–Sat. 10–6, Sun. 11:15–5:45* Ⓜ *Ginza subway line, Mitsukoshi-mae Station (Exit A4).*

FodorśChoice **Nippon Tōken** (Japan Sword). Wannabe samurai can learn how to tell
★ their *tōshin* (blades) from their *tsuka* (sword handles) with help from
the English-speaking staff at this small shop, which has been open since
the Meiji era. Items range from a circa-1390 samurai sword to inexpensive
reproductions to armor and masks. ⊠ *3–8–1 Toranomon, Minato-ku*
☎ *03/3434–4321* ⊙ *Weekdays 9:30–6, Sat. 9:30–5* Ⓜ *Hibiya and
Ginza subway lines, Toranomon Station (Exit 2).*

Tōken Shibata. A tiny, threadbare shop incongruously situated near
Ginza's glittering department stores, Tōken Shibata sells well-worn antique swords. ⊠ *5–6–8 Ginza, Chūō-ku* ☎ *03/3573–2801* ⊙ *Mon.–Sat.
10–6:30* Ⓜ *Ginza, Hibiya, and Marunouchi subway lines, Ginza Station (Exit A1).*

★ **Tsubaya Hōchōten.** Tsubaya sells high-quality cutlery for professionals.
Its remarkable selection is designed for every imaginable use, as the art
of food presentation in Japan requires a great variety of cutting imple-
ments. The best of these carry the Traditional Craft Association seal:
hand-forged tools of tempered blue steel, set in handles banded with deer
horn to keep the wood from splitting. Be prepared to pay the premium
for these items: a cleaver just for slicing soba can cost as much as
¥50,000. ⊠ *3–7–2 Nishi-Asakusa, Taitō-ku* ☎ *03/3845–2005*
⊙ *Mon.–Sat. 9–5:45, Sun. 9–5* Ⓜ *Ginza subway line, Tawara-machi
Station (Exit 3).*

Yoshikin. This small shop sells Japan's Global-brand knives, which,
thanks to their handiness and maneuverability, have been winning over
chefs worldwide at the expense of traditional European cutlers. ⊠ *Axis
Bldg., 2F, 5–17–1 Roppongi, Minato-ku* ☎ *03/3568–2336* ⊙ *Mon.–Sat.
11–7* Ⓜ *Hibiya and Ōedo subway lines, Roppongi Station (Exit 3); Namboku subway line, Roppongi Itchōme Station (Exit 1).*

Toys

ⓒ **Garage.** A hands-on toy and hobby shop in the sleek Coredo shopping
center, Garage carries everything from telescopes to robots. ⊠ *1–4–1
Nihombashi, Chūō-ku* ☎ *03/3272–4939* ⊙ *Mon.–Sat. 11–9, Sun.
11–8* Ⓜ *Ginza, Tōzai, and Asakusa subway lines, Nihombashi Station
(Exit B10).*

ⓒ **Hakuhinkan.** This is reputedly the largest toy store in Japan, with lots
of homegrown-character goods like Hello Kitty in addition to Western
products. It's on Chūō-dōri, the main axis of the Ginza shopping area.
⊠ *8–8–11 Ginza, Chūō-ku* ☎ *03/3571–8008* ⊙ *Daily 11–8* Ⓜ *Ginza
and Asakusa subway lines, Shimbashi Station (Exit 1).*

ⓒ **Kiddy Land.** Commonly regarded as Tōkyō's best toy store, Kiddy Land
also carries kitsch items that draw in Harajuku's teen brigade. ⊠ *6–1
Jingū-mae, Shibuya-ku* ☎ *03/3409–3431* ⊙ *Daily 11–8* Ⓜ *Chiyoda subway line, Meiji Jingū-mae Station (Exit 4).*

SIDE TRIPS
FROM TŌKYŌ

7

THE ULTIMATE SHRINE
Elaborate, gold-covered Tōshō-gū ⇨*p.185*

BEST RE-CREATION OF AN 18TH-C. TOWN
Nikkō Edo Village ⇨*p.188*

MOST DRAMATIC WATERFALLS
Kegon Falls at Chuzenji near Nikkō ⇨*p.190*

WHAT BUDDHIST MONKS WOULD EAT
vegetarian fare at Gyōshintei ⇨*p.190*

LARGEST ZEN MONASTERY
Engaku-ji in Kamakura ⇨*p.196*

THE CAN'T-MISS JAPANESE ICON
12,388-foot, white-capped Fuji-san ⇨*p.219*

By Jared
Lubarsky

Updated by
Steve Trautlein
and Matt
Wilce

NIKKŌ—which means "sunlight"—is the site not simply of the Tokugawa shrine but also of a national park, Nikkō Kokuritsu Kōen, on the heights above it. The centerpiece of the park is Chūzenji-ko, a deep lake some 21 km (13 mi) around, and the 318-foot-high Kegon Falls, Japan's most famous waterfall. "Think nothing splendid," asserts an old Japanese proverb, "until you have seen Nikkō." Whoever said it first might well have been thinking more of the park than of the shrine below.

One caveat: the term "national park" does not quite mean what it does elsewhere in the world. In Japan pristine grandeur is hard to come by; there are few places in this country where intrepid hikers can go to contemplate the beauty of nature for very long in solitude. If a thing's worth seeing, it's worth developing. This world view tends to fill the national parks with bus caravans, ropeways and gondolas, scenic overlooks with coin-fed telescopes, signs that tell you where you may and may not walk, fried-noodle joints and vending machines, and shacks full of kitschy souvenirs. That's true of Nikkō, and it's true as well of Fuji-Hakone-Izu National Park, southwest of Tōkyō, another of Japan's most popular resort areas.

The park's chief attraction is, of course, Fuji-san—spellbinding in its perfect symmetry, immortalized by centuries of poets and artists. South of Mt. Fuji, the Izu Peninsula projects out into the Pacific, with Suruga Bay to the west and Sagami Bay to the east. The beaches and rugged shoreline of Izu, its forests and highland meadows, and its numerous hot-springs inns and resorts (*izu* means "spring") make the region a favorite destination for the Japanese.

Kamakura and Yokohama, both close enough to Tōkyō to provide ideal day trips, could not make for more contrasting experiences. Kamakura is an ancient city—the birthplace, one could argue, of the samurai way of life. Its place in Japanese history begins late in the 12th century, when Minamoto no Yoritomo became the country's first shōgun and chose this site, with its rugged hills and narrow passes, as the seat of his military government. The warrior elite of the Kamakura period took much of their ideology—and their aesthetics—from Zen Buddhism, endowing splendid temples that still exist today. A walking tour of Kamakura's Zen temples and Shintō shrines is a must for anyone with a day to spend out of Tōkyō. Yokohama, too, can lay claim to an important place in Japanese history: in 1869, after centuries of isolation, this city became the first important port for trade with the West and the site of the first major foreign settlement. Twice destroyed, the city retains very few remnants of that history, but it remains Japan's largest port and has an international character that rivals—if not surpasses—that of Tōkyō. Its waterfront park and its ambitious Minato Mirai bay-side development project draw visitors from all over the world.

About the Restaurants

The local specialty in Nikkō is a kind of bean curd called *yuba*; dozens of restaurants in Nikkō serve it in a variety of dishes you might not have believed possible for so prosaic an ingredient. Other local favorites are soba (buckwheat) and udon (wheat-flour) noodles—both inexpensive, filling, and tasty options for lunch.

TŌKYŌ SIDE TRIPS GLOSSARY

Key Japanese words and suffixes in this chapter include the following:

banchi	番地	street number
bijutsukan	美術館	art museum
-chō	町 or 丁	street or block
-chōme	丁目	street
chūō	中央	central
daimyō	大名	feudal lord
-den	殿	hall
-dō	堂	temple or hall
-dōri	通	avenue
eki	駅	train station
gaijin	外人	foreigner
-gawa or -kawa	川 or 河	river
-gū	神宮 or 神社	Shintō shrine
-gun	郡	district
-hama	浜	beach
-hantō	半島	peninsula
-hara	原	plain
higashi	東	east
-in	院	Buddhist temple
izakaya	居酒屋	pub
-ji (Tera)	寺	temple
-jima or -shima	島	island
jingū or jinja	神宮 or 神社	Shintō shrine
-kan	館	museum
-ken	県	prefecture
kita	北	north
-ko	湖	lake
kōen	公園	park
-ku	区	section or ward
-kūkō	空港	airport

machi	町 or 街	town
michi	道	street
minami	南	south
-misaki	岬	cape
-mon	門	gate
Nihon-kai	日本海	Sea of Japan
nishi	西	west
Ohotsuku-kai	オホーツク海	Sea of Ohotsuku
onsen	温泉	hot spring
rotemburo	露天風呂	outdoor hot spring
ryūhyō	流氷	ice floes
sakura	桜	cherry blossoms
-shi	市	city or municipality
-shima	島	island
Shinkansen	新幹線	bullet train, literally "new trunk line"
shōgun	将軍	commander in chief
-take or -dake (tah-keh or dah-keh)	岳	peak
-tō	島	island
tōge	峠	pass
torii	門	gate
-yama	山	mountain
-zan (san)	山	mountain

Three things about Kamakura make it a good place in which to eat. It's on the ocean (properly speaking, on Sagami Bay), which means that fresh seafood is everywhere; it's a major tourist stop; and it has long been a prestigious place to live among Japan's worldly and well-to-do (many successful writers, artists, and intellectuals call Kamakura home). On a day trip from Tōkyō, you can feel confident picking a place for lunch almost at random.

Yokohama, as befits a city of more than 3 million people, lacks little in the way of food, from quick-fix lunch counters to elegant dining rooms, and has almost every imaginable cuisine. Your best bet is Chinatown—Japan's largest Chinese community—with more than 100 restaurants representing every regional style. If you fancy Greek, Italian, or Indian instead, this international port is still guaranteed to provide an eminently satisfying meal.

About the Hotels

Yokohama and Kamakura are treated here as day trips, and as it's unlikely that you'll stay overnight in either city, no accommodations are listed for them. Nikkō is something of a toss-up: you can easily see Tōshō-gū and be back in Tōkyō by evening. But when the weather turns glorious in spring or autumn, why not spend some time in the national park, staying overnight at Chūzenji, and returning to the city the next day? Mt. Fuji and Hakone, on the other hand—and more especially the Izu Peninsula—are pure resort destinations. Staying overnight is an intrinsic part of the experience, and it makes little sense to go without hotel reservations confirmed in advance.

In both Nikkō and the Fuji-Hakone-Izu area, there are modern, Western-style hotels that operate in a fairly standard international style. More common, however, are the Japanese-style *kankō* (literally, "sightseeing") hotels and the traditional *ryokan* (inns). The undisputed pleasure of a ryokan is to return to it at the end of a hard day of sightseeing, luxuriate for an hour in a hot bath with your own garden view, put on the *nemaki* (sleeping gown) provided for you, and sit down to a catered private dinner party. There's little point to staying at a kankō, on the other hand, beyond being able to say you've had the experience and survived with your good humor intact. Like everywhere else in Japan, these places do most of their business with big, boisterous tour groups. The turnover of guests is ruthless at kankō hotels, and the cost is way out of proportion to the service they provide.

The price categories listed below are for double occupancy, but you'll find that most kankō and ryokan normally quote per-person rates, which include breakfast and dinner. Remember to stipulate whether you want a Japanese or Western breakfast. If you don't want dinner at your hotel, it's usually possible to renegotiate the price, but the management will not be happy about it; the two meals are a fixture of their business. The typical ryokan takes great pride in its cuisine, usually with good reason: the evening meal is an elaborate affair of 10 or more different dishes, based on the fresh produce and specialties of the region, served to you—nay, *orchestrated*—in your room on a wonderful variety of trays and tableware designed to celebrate the season.

WHAT IT COSTS In yen					
	$$$$	$$$	$$	$	¢
RESTAURANTS	over 3,000	2,000–3,000	1,000–2,000	800–1,000	under 800
HOTELS	over 22,000	18,000–22,000	12,000–18,000	8,000–12,000	under 8,000

Restaurant prices are per person for a main course at dinner. Hotel price categories reflect the range of least- to most-expensive standard double rooms in non-holiday high season, based on the European Plan (with no meals) unless otherwise noted. Taxes (5%) are included.

NIKKŌ 日光

Nikkō is a popular vacation spot for the Japanese, for good reason: its gorgeous sights include a breathtaking waterfall and one of the country's best-known shrines. In addition, Nikkō combines the rustic charm of a countryside village (complete with wild monkeys that have the run of the place) with a convenient location not far from Tōkyō.

At Nikkō there's a monument to a warlord who was so splendid and powerful that he became a god. In 1600, Ieyasu Tokugawa (1543–1616) won a battle at a place called Seki-ga-hara, in the mountains of south-central Japan, that left him the undisputed ruler of the archipelago. He died 16 years later, but the Tokugawa Shogunate would last another 252 years, holding in its sway a peaceful, prosperous, and united country.

The founder of such a dynasty required a fitting resting place. Ieyasu (ee-eh-*ya*-su) had provided for one in his will: a mausoleum at Nikkō, in a forest of tall cedars, where a religious center had been founded more than eight centuries earlier. The year after his death, in accordance with Buddhist custom, he was given a *kaimyō*—an honorific name to bear in the afterlife. Thenceforth, he was Tōshō-Daigongen: the Great Incarnation Who Illuminates the East. The imperial court at Kyōto declared him a god, and his remains were taken in a procession of great pomp and ceremony to be enshrined at Nikkō.

The dynasty he left behind was enormously rich. Ieyasu's personal fief, on the Kantō Plain, was worth 2.5 million *koku* of rice. One koku, in monetary terms, was equivalent to the cost of keeping one retainer in the necessities of life for a year. The shogunate itself, however, was still an uncertainty. It had only recently taken control after more than a century of civil war. The founder's tomb had a political purpose: to inspire awe and to make manifest the power of the Tokugawas. It was Ieyasu's legacy, a statement of his family's right to rule.

Tōshō-gū was built by his grandson, the third shōgun, Iemitsu (it was Iemitsu who established the policy of national isolation, which closed the doors of Japan to the outside world for more than 200 years). The mausoleum and shrine required the labor of 15,000 people for two years (1634–36). Craftsmen and artists of the first rank were assembled from all over the country. Every surface was carved and painted and lacquered in the most intricate detail imaginable. Tōshō-gū shimmers with the reflections of 2,489,000 sheets of gold leaf. Roof beams and rafter ends with dragon heads, lions, and elephants in bas-relief; friezes of phoenixes, wild ducks, and monkeys; inlaid pillars and red-lacquer corridors: Tōshō-gū is everything a 17th-century warlord would consider gorgeous, and the inspiration is very Chinese.

Foreign visitors have differed about the effect Iemitsu achieved. Victorian-era traveler Isabella Bird, who came to Nikkō in 1878, was unrestrained in her enthusiasm. "To pass from court to court," she writes in her *Unbeaten Tracks in Japan,* "is to pass from splendour to splendour; one is almost glad to feel that this is the last, and that the strain on one's capacity for admiration is nearly over." Fosco Mariani, a more recent visitor, felt somewhat different: "You are taken aback," he observes in his *Meeting with Japan* (1959). "You ask yourself whether it is a joke, or a nightmare, or a huge wedding cake, a masterpiece of sugar icing made for some extravagant prince with a perverse, rococo taste, who wished to alarm and entertain his guests." Clearly, it is impossible to feel indifferent about Tōshō-gū. Perhaps, in the end, that is all Ieyasu could ever really have expected.

Exploring Nikkō

The town of Nikkō is essentially one long avenue—Sugi Namiki (Cryptomeria Avenue)—extending for about 2 km (1 mi) from the railway stations to Tōshō-gū. You can easily walk to most places within town. Tourist inns and shops line the street, and if you have time, you might want to make this a leisurely stroll. The antiques shops along the way may turn up interesting—but expensive—pieces like armor fittings, hibachi, pottery, and dolls. The souvenir shops here sell ample selections of local wood carvings.

Buses and taxis can take you from Nikkō to the village of Chūzenji and nearby Lake Chūzenji.

Numbers in the text correspond to numbers in the margin and on the Nikkō Area map.

Tōshō-gū Area   東照宮

The best way to see the Tōshō-gū precincts is to buy a multiple-entry ticket: ¥1,000 for Rinnō-ji (Rinnō Temple), the Taiyū-in Mausoleum, and Futara-san Jinja (Futara-san Shrine); ¥1,300 for these sights as well as the Sleeping Cat and Ieyasu's tomb at Taiyū-in (separate fees are charged for admission to other sights). There are two places to purchase the multiple-entry ticket: one is at the entrance to Rinnō Temple, in the corner of the parking lot, at the top of the path called the Higashi-sandō (East Approach) that begins across the highway from the Sacred Bridge; the other is at the entrance to Tōshō-gū, at the top of the broad Omotesandō (Central Approach), which begins about 100 yards farther west.

❶ Built in 1636 for shōguns and imperial messengers visiting the shrine, the original **Sacred Bridge** (Shinkyō, 神橋) was destroyed in a flood; the present red-lacquer wooden structure dates to 1907. Buses leaving from either railway station at Nikkō go straight up the main street to the bridge, opposite the first of the main entrances to Tōshō-gū. The fare is ¥190. The Sacred Bridge is just to the left of a modern bridge, where the road curves and crosses the Daiya-gawa (Daiya River).

❷ A Nikkō landmark, the **Nikkō Kanaya Hotel** (金谷ホテル, ✉ 1300 Kami Hatsuishi-machi) has been in the same family for more than 100 years. The main building is a delightful, rambling Victorian structure that has hosted royalty and other important personages—as the guest book attests—from around the world. The long driveway that winds up to the hotel at the top of the hill is just below the Sacred Bridge, on the same side of the street.

The **Monument to Masatuna Matsudaira** (松平正綱の杉並木寄進碑)—opposite the Sacred Bridge, at the east entrance to the grounds of Tōshō-gū—pays tribute to one of the two feudal lords charged with the construction of Tōshō-gū. Matsudaira's great contribution was the planting of the wonderful cryptomeria trees (Japanese cedars) surrounding the shrine and along all the approaches to it. The project took 20 years, from 1628 to 1648, and the result was some 36 km (22 mi) of cedar-lined avenues—planted with more than 15,000 trees in all. Fire and time have taken their toll, but thousands of these trees still stand in the shrine precincts, creating a setting of solemn majesty the buildings alone could never have achieved. Thousands more line Route 119 east of Nikkō on the way to Shimo-Imaichi.

★ ❸ **Rinnō-ji** (Rinnō Temple, 輪王寺) belongs to the Tendai sect of Buddhism, the head temple of which is Enryaku-ji, on Mt. Hiei near Kyōto. The main hall of Rinnō Temple, called the **Sanbutsu-dō,** is the largest single building at Tōshō-gū; it enshrines an image of Amida Nyorai, the Buddha of the Western Paradise, flanked on the right by Senju (Thousand-Armed) Kannon, the goddess of mercy, and on the left by Bato-Kannon, regarded as the protector of animals. These three images are lacquered in gold and date from the early part of the 17th century. The original Sanbutsu-dō is said to have been built in 848 by the priest Ennin (794–864), also known as Jikaku-Daishi. The present building dates from 1648.

In the southwest corner of the Rinnō Temple compound, behind the abbot's residence, is an especially fine Japanese garden called **Shōyō-en,** created in 1815 and thoughtfully designed to present a different perspective of its rocks, ponds, and flowering plants from every turn on its path. To the right of the entrance to the garden is the **Treasure Hall** (Hōmotsu-den) of Rinnō Temple, a museum with a collection of some 6,000 works of lacquerware, painting, and Buddhist sculpture. The museum is rather small, and only a few of the pieces in the collection—many of them designated National Treasures and Important Cultural Properties—are on display at any given time.

Gohōten-dō, in the northeast corner of Rinnō Temple, behind the Sanbutsu-dō, enshrines three of the Seven Gods of Good Fortune. These three Buddhist deities are derived from Chinese folk mythology: Daikoku-ten and Bishamon-ten, who bring wealth and good harvests, and Benzai-ten, patroness of music and the arts. ✉ *Rinnō Temple ¥1,000, multiple-entry ticket includes admission to the Taiyū-in Mausoleum*

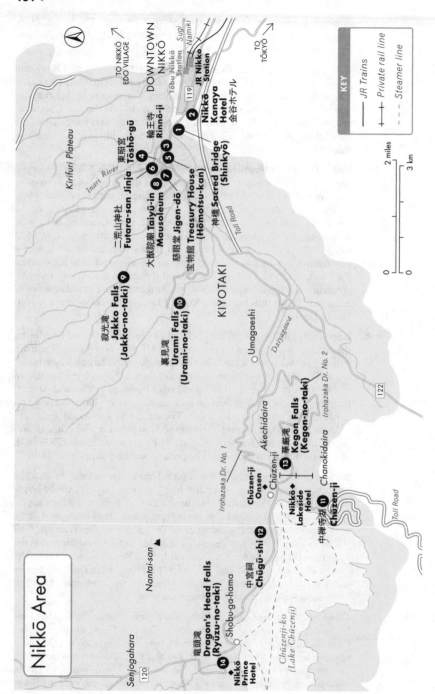

Nikkō Area

TO NIKKŌ
EDO VILLAGE

DOWNTOWN
NIKKŌ

Sugi

Namiki

Tōbu Nikkō Station

119

JR Nikko Station

TO TOKYO

Nikkō Kanaya Hotel
金谷ホテル

輪王寺 Rinnō-ji **1**

2

Kirifuri Plateau

東照宮 Tōshō-gū **4**

5 **3**

神橋 Sacred Bridge (Shinkyō)

Imari River

二荒山神社 Futara-san Jinja

6

8 **7**

Toll Road

大猷院廟 Taiyū-in Mausoleum

慈眼堂 Jigen-dō

宝物館 Treasury House (Hōmotsu-kan)

KIYOTAKI

寂光滝 Jakko Falls (Jakko-no-taki) **9**

裏見滝 Urami Falls (Urami-no-taki) **10**

Daiyagawa

Umagaeshi

Irohazaka Dr. No. 2

122

Irohazaka Dr. No. 1

Akechidaira

Chūzenji Onsen

Chūzen-ji

華厳滝 Kegon Falls (Kegon-no-taki) **13**

Chanokidaira

Nikkō Lakeside Hotel

Toll Road

中禅寺湖 Chūzen-ji **11**

Senjogahara

▲ *Nantai-san*

中宮祠 Chūgū-shi **12**

Shobu-ga-hama

竜頭滝 Dragon's Head Falls (Ryūzu-no-taki) **14**

Nikkō Prince Hotel

120

Chūzenji-ko (Lake Chūzenji)

KEY

—— JR Trains
—+—+— Private rail line
- - - - Steamer line

2 miles

3 km

0

and Futara-san Shrine; Shōyō-en and Treasure Hall ¥300 ⊘ Apr.–Oct., daily 8–5, last entry at 4; Nov.–Mar., daily 8–4, last entry at 3.

❹

FodorsChoice

★

With its riot of colors and carvings, inlaid pillars, red-lacquer corridors, and extensive use of gold leaf, **Tōshō-gū** (東照宮), the 17th-century shrine to Ieyasu Tokugawa, is magnificent, astonishing, and never for a moment dull.

The west gate of Rinnō Temple brings you out onto Omote-sandō, which leads uphill to the stone torii of the shrine. The **Five-Story Pagoda** of Tōshō-gū—a reconstruction dating from 1818—is on the left as you approach the shrine. The 12 signs of the zodiac decorate the first story. The black-lacquer doors above each sign bear the three hollyhock leaves of the Tokugawa family crest.

From the torii a flight of stone steps brings you to the front gate of the shrine—the Omote-mon, also called the Nio-mon (Gate of the Deva Kings), with its fearsome pair of red-painted guardian gods. From here the path turns to the left. In the first group of buildings you reach on the left is the **Sacred Stable** (Shinkyū). Housed here is the white horse—symbol of purity—that figures in many of the shrine's ceremonial events. Carvings of pine trees and monkeys adorn the panels over the stable. The second panel from the left is the famous group of three monkeys—"Hear no evil, see no evil, speak no evil"—that has become something of a trademark for Nikkō, reproduced endlessly on plaques, bags, and souvenirs of every sort. A few steps farther, where the path turns to the right, is a granite font where visitors purify themselves before entering the inner precincts of Tōshō-gū. The **Sutra Library** (Rinzō), just beyond the font, is a repository for some 7,000 Buddhist scriptures, kept in a huge revolving bookcase nearly 20 feet high; it's not open to the public.

As you pass under the second (bronze) torii and up the steps, you'll see on the right a belfry and a tall bronze candelabrum; on the left is a drum tower and a bronze revolving lantern. The two works in bronze were presented to the shrine by the Dutch government in the mid-17th century. (Under the policy of national seclusion, only the Dutch retained trading privileges with Japan, and even they were confined to the tiny artificial island of Dejima, in the port of Nagasaki. They regularly sent tokens of their esteem to the shogunate to keep their precarious monopoly.) Behind the drum tower is the **Yakushi-dō**, which enshrines a manifestation of the Buddha as Yakushi Nyorai, the healer of illnesses. The original 17th-century building was famous for a huge India-ink painting on the ceiling of the nave, *The Roaring Dragon,* so named for the rumbling echoes it seemed to emit when visitors clapped their hands beneath it. The painting was by Yasunobu Enshin Kanō (1613–85), from a family of artists that dominated the profession for 400 years. The Kanō school was founded in the late 15th century and patronized by successive military governments until the fall of the Tokugawa Shogunate in 1868. The leadership was hereditary; the artists who trained in the Kanō ateliers specialized in Chinese-style ink paintings, landscapes, and decorative figures of birds and animals—typically for screens and the paneled sliding doors that stand as the interior "walls" of Japanese villas and temples. The Yakushi-dō was destroyed by fire in 1961, then rebuilt; the dragon on the ceiling now is by Nampu Katayama (1887–1980).

The centerpiece of Tōshō-gū is the **Gate of Sunlight** (Yōmei-mon), at the top of the second flight of stone steps. A designated National Treasure, it's also called the Twilight Gate (Higurashi-mon)—implying that you could spend all day until sunset looking at its richness of detail. And rich it is indeed: dazzling white, 36 feet high, the gate has 12 columns, beams, and roof brackets carved with dragons, lions, clouds, peonies, Chinese sages, and demigods, painted in vivid hues of red, blue, green, and gold. On one of the central columns, there are two carved tigers; the natural grain of the wood is used to bring out the "fur." To the right and left of the Yomei-mon as you enter, there are galleries running east and west for some 700 feet, their paneled fences also carved and painted with a profusion of motifs from nature: pine and plum branches, pheasants, cranes, and wild ducks.

The portable shrines that appear in the annual Tōshō-gū Festival on May 17–18 are kept in the **Shin-yosha,** a storeroom to the left as you come through the Twilight Gate into the heart of the shrine. The paintings on the ceiling, of *tennin* (Buddhist angels) playing harps, are by Ryōtaku Kanō.

The "official" entrance to the Tōshō-gū inner shrine, through which mere mortals may not pass, is the **Chinese Gate** (Kara-mon). Like its counterpart, the Yomei-mon, on the opposite side of the courtyard, the Kara-mon is a National Treasure—and, like the Yomei-mon, carved and painted in elaborate detail with dragons and other auspicious figures. The Main Hall of Tōshō-gū is enclosed by a wall of painted and carved panel screens; opposite the right-hand corner of the wall, facing the shrine, is the **Kitō-den,** a hall where annual prayers were once offered for the peace of the nation. For a very modest fee, Japanese couples can be married here in a traditional Shintō ceremony, with an ensemble of drums and reed flutes and shrine maidens to attend them.

The **Main Hall** (Hon-den) of Tōshō-gū is the ultimate purpose of the shrine. You approach it from the rows of lockers at the far end of the enclosure; here you remove and store your shoes, step up into the shrine, and follow a winding corridor to the Oratory (Hai-den)—the anteroom, resplendent in its lacquered pillars, carved friezes, and coffered ceilings bedecked with dragons. Over the lintels are paintings by Mitsuoki Tosa (1617–91) of the 36 great poets of the Heian period, with their poems in the calligraphy of Emperor Go-Mizuno-o. Deeper yet, at the back of the Oratory, is the Inner Chamber (Nai-jin)—repository of the Sacred Mirror that represents the spirit of the deity enshrined here. To the right is a room that was reserved for members of the three principal branches of the Tokugawa family; the room on the left was for the chief abbot of Rinnō Temple, who was always a prince of the imperial line.

Behind the Inner Chamber is the Innermost Chamber (Nai-Nai-jin). No visitors come this far. Here, in the very heart of Tōshō-gū, is the gold-lacquer shrine where the spirit of Ieyasu resides—along with two other deities, whom the Tokugawas later decided were fit companions. One was Hideyoshi Toyotomi, Ieyasu's mentor and liege lord in the long wars of unification at the end of the 16th century. The other was Minamoto no Yoritomo, brilliant military tactician and founder of the earlier (12th-century) Kamakura Shogunate (Ieyasu, born Takechiyo Matsudaira, son of a lesser baron in what is today Aichi Prefecture, claimed Yoritomo for an ancestor).

Recover your shoes and return to the courtyard. Between the Goma-dō and the **Kagura-den** (a hall where ceremonial dances are performed to honor the gods) is a passage to the **Gate at the Foot of the Hill** (Sakashita-mon). Above the gateway is another famous symbol of Tōshō-gū, the Sleeping Cat—a small panel said to have been carved by Hidari Jingoro (Jingoro the Left-handed), a late-16th-century master carpenter and sculptor credited with important contributions to numerous Tokugawa-period temples, shrines, and palaces. A separate admission charge (¥520) is levied to go beyond the Sleeping Cat, up the flight of 200 stone steps through a forest of cryptomeria to **Ieyasu's tomb**. The climb is worth making for the view of the Yomei-mon and Kara-mon from above; the tomb itself is unimpressive. 🖼 *Free; Ieyasu's tomb ¥520 ⊙ Apr.–Oct., daily 8–5; Nov.–Mar., daily 8–4.*

An unhurried visit to the precincts of Tōshō-gū should definitely include the **Treasury House** (Hōmotsu-kan, 宝物館), which contains a collection of antiquities from its various shrines and temples. From the west gate of Rinnō Temple, turn left off Omote-sandō, just below the pagoda, onto the cedar-lined avenue to Futara-san Jinja. A minute's walk will bring you to the museum, on the left. 🖼 *¥500 ⊙ Apr.–Oct., daily 9–5; Nov.–Mar., daily 9–4.*

The holy ground at Nikkō is far older than the Tokugawa dynasty, in whose honor it was improved upon. To the gods enshrined at the 8th-century **Futara-san Jinja** (Futara-san Shrine, 二荒山神社), Ieyasu Tokugawa must seem but a callow newcomer. Futara-san is sacred to the Shintō deities Okuni-nushi-no-Mikoto (god of the rice fields, bestower of prosperity), his consort Tagorihime-no-Mikoto, and their son Ajisukitaka-hikone-no-Mikoto. Futara-san actually has three locations: the Hon-sha (Main Shrine), at Tōshō-gū; the Chū-gushi (Middle Shrine), at Chūzenji-ko; and the Okumiya (Inner Shrine), on top of Mt. Nantai.

The bronze torii at the entrance to the shrine leads to the **Chinese Gate** (Kara-mon) and the **Sanctum** (Hon-den)—the present version of which dates from 1619. To the left, in the corner of the enclosure, is an antique bronze lantern, some 7 feet high, under a canopy. Legend has it that the lantern would assume the shape of a goblin at night; the deep nicks in the bronze were inflicted by swordsmen of the Edo period—on guard duty, perhaps, startled into action by a flickering shape in the dark. This proves, if not the existence of goblins, the incredible cutting power of the Japanese blade, a peerlessly forged weapon. To get to Futara-san, take the avenue to the left as you're standing before the stone torii at Tōshō-gū and follow it to the end. 🖼 *¥200, ¥1,000 multiple-entry ticket includes admission to Rinnō Temple and Taiyū-in Mausoleum ⊙ Apr.–Oct., daily 8–5; Nov.–Mar., daily 9–4.*

Tenkai (1536–1643), the first abbot of Rinnō Temple, has his own place
❼ of honor at Tōshō-gū: the **Jigen-dō** (慈眼堂). The hall, which was founded
in 848, now holds many of Rinnō Temple's artistic treasures. To reach
it, take the path opposite the south entrance to Futara-san Shrine that
passes between the two subtemples called Jōgyō-dō and Hokke-dō. Connected by a corridor, these two buildings are otherwise known as the Fu-
tatsu-dō (Twin Halls) of Rinnō Temple and are designated a National
Cultural Property. The path between the Twin Halls leads roughly south
and west to the Jigen-dō compound; the hall itself is at the north end of
the compound, to the right. At the west end sits the Go-ōden, a shrine
to Prince Yoshihisa Kitashirakawa (1847–95), the last of the imperial
princes to serve as abbot. Behind it are his tomb and the tombs of his 13
predecessors. 🎫 *Free* ⏰ *Apr.–Nov., daily 8–5; Dec.–Mar., daily 9–4.*

★ ❽ The grandiose **Taiyū-in Mausoleum** (大猷院廟) is the resting place of the
third Tokugawa shōgun, Iemitsu (1604–51), who imposed a policy of
national isolation on Japan that was to last more than 200 years.
Iemitsu, one suspects, had it in mind to upstage his illustrious grand-
father; he marked the approach to his own tomb with no fewer than
six different decorative gates. The first is another Niō-mon—a Gate of
the Deva Kings—like the one at Tōshō-gū. The dragon painted on the
ceiling is by Yasunobu Kanō (1613–85). A flight of stone steps leads from
here to the second gate, the Niten-mon, a two-story structure protected
front and back by carved and painted images of guardian gods. Beyond
it, two more flights of steps lead to the middle courtyard. As you climb
the last steps to Iemitsu's shrine, you'll pass a bell tower on the right
and a drum tower on the left; directly ahead is the third gate, the remarkable **Yasha-mon,** so named for the figures of *yasha* (she-demons)
in the four niches. This structure is also known as the Peony Gate
(Botan-mon) for the carvings that decorate it.

On the other side of the courtyard is the **Chinese Gate** (Kara-mon),
gilded and elaborately carved; beyond it is the **Hai-den,** the shrine's oratory. The Hai-den, too, is richly carved and decorated, with a dragon-
covered ceiling. The Chinese lions on the panels at the rear are by two
distinguished painters of the Kanō school. From the oratory of the Taiyū-
in a connecting passage leads to the **Sanctum** (Hon-den). Designated a
National Treasure, it houses a gilded and lacquered Buddhist altar some
9 feet high, decorated with paintings of animals, birds, and flowers, in
which resides the object of all this veneration: a seated wooden figure of
Iemitsu himself.

As you exit the shrine, on the west side, you come to the fifth gate: the
Kōka-mon, built in the style of the late Ming dynasty of China. The gate
is normally closed, but from here another flight of stone steps leads to
the sixth and last gate—the cast copper **Inuki-mon,** inscribed with characters in Sanskrit—and Iemitsu's tomb. 🎫 *¥1,000 multiple-entry ticket
includes admission to Rinnō Temple and Futara-san Shrine* ⏰ *Apr.–Oct.,
daily 8–5; Nov.–Mar., daily 8–4.*

🜨 **Nikkō Edo Village** (Nikkō Edo Mura, 日光江戸村), a living-history theme
park a short taxi ride from downtown, re-creates an 18th-century Jap-

anese village. The complex includes sculpted gardens with waterfalls and ponds and 22 vintage buildings, where actors in traditional dress stage martial arts exhibitions, historical theatrical performances, and comedy acts. You can even observe Japanese tea ceremony rituals in gorgeous tatami-floored houses, as well as people dressed as geisha and samurai. Strolling stuffed animal characters and acrobatic ninjas keep kids happy. Nikkō Edo Mura has one large restaurant and 15 small food stalls serving period cuisine like *yakisoba* (fried soba) and *dango* (dumplings). ⊠ *470–2 Egura, Fujiwara-chō, Shiodani-gun* ☎ *0288/77–1777* 💰 *¥2,300 general admission, plus extra for rides and shows; ¥6,300 unlimited day pass includes rides and shows* ⊙ *Mid-Mar.–Nov., daily 9–5; Dec.–mid-Mar., daily 9:30–4.*

To Chūzenji-ko (Lake Chūzenji)

More than 3,900 feet above sea level, at the base of the volcano known as Nantai-san, is Lake Chūzenji, renowned for its clean waters and fresh air. People come to boat and fish on the lake and to enjoy the surrounding scenic woodlands, waterfalls, and hills.

Falling water is one of the special charms of the Nikkō National Park area; people going by bus or car from Tōshō-gū to Lake Chūzenji often **❾** stop off en route to see **Jakkō Falls** (Jakkō-no-taki, 寂光滝), which descend in a series of seven terraced stages, forming a sheet of water about 100 feet high. About 1 km (½ mi) from the shrine precincts, at the Tamozawa bus stop, a narrow road to the right leads to an uphill walk of some 3 km (2 mi) to the falls.

❿ "The water," wrote the great 17th-century poet Bashō about the **Urami Falls** (Urami-no-taki, 裏見滝), "seemed to take a flying leap and drop a hundred feet from the top of a cave into a green pool surrounded by a thousand rocks. One was supposed to inch one's way into the cave and enjoy the falls from behind." It's a steep climb to the cave, which begins at the Arasawa bus stop, with a turn to the right off the Chūzenji road. The falls and the gorge are striking—but you should make the climb only if you have good hiking shoes and are willing to get wet in the process.

The real climb to Lake Chūzenji begins at **Umagaeshi** (馬返し, literally, "horse return"). Here, in the old days, the road became too rough for horse riding, so riders had to alight and proceed on foot. The lake is 4,165 feet above sea level. From Umagaeshi the bus climbs a one-way toll road up the pass; the old road has been widened and is used for the traffic coming down. The two roads are full of steep hairpin turns, and on a clear day the view up and down the valley is magnificent—especially from the halfway point at **Akechi-daira** (Akechi Plain), from which you can see the summit of **Nantai-san** (Mt. Nantai), reaching 8,149 feet. Hiking season lasts from May through mid-October; if you push it, you can make the ascent in about four hours. Note that wild monkeys make their homes in these mountains, and they've learned the convenience of mooching from visitors along the route. Be careful—they have a way of not taking no for an answer. Umagaeshi is about 10 km (6 mi) from Tōbu Station in Nikkō, or 8 km (5 mi) from Tōshō-gū.

⑪ The bus trip from Nikkō to the national park area ends at Chūzenji village, which shares its name with the temple established here in 784. **Chūzenji** (Chūzen Temple, 中禅寺) is a subtemple of Rinnō Temple, at Tōshō-gū. The principal object of worship at Chūzen-ji is the **Tachi-ki Kannon,** a 17-foot-tall standing statue of the Buddhist goddess of mercy, said to have been carved more than 1,000 years ago by the priest Shōdō from the living trunk of a single Judas tree. You reach the temple grounds by turning left (south) as you leave the village of Chūzenji and walking about 1½ km (1 mi) along the eastern shore of the lake. *¥300 ⊙ Apr.–Oct., daily 8–5; Mar. and Nov., daily 8–4; Dec.–Feb., daily 8–3:30.*

⑫ **Chūgū-shi** (中宮祠), a subshrine of the Futara-san Shrine at Tōshō-gū, is the major religious center on the north side of Lake Chūzenji, about 1½ km (1 mi) west of the village. The **Treasure House** (Hōmotsu-den) contains an interesting historical collection, including swords, lacquerware, and medieval shrine palanquins. *Shrine free, Treasure House ¥300 ⊙ Apr.–Oct., daily 8–5; Nov.–Mar., daily 9–4.*

Near the bus stop at Chūzenji village is a **gondola** (ゴンドラ, ¥900 round-trip) to the Chanoki-daira (Chanoki plateau). About 1,000 feet above the lake, it commands a wonderful view of the surrounding area. A few minutes' walk from the gondola terminus is a small botanical garden. *⊙ Daily 8–5.*

⑬ More than anything else, **Kegon Falls** (Kegon-no-taki, 華厳滝), the country's most famous falls, are what draw the crowds of Japanese visitors to Chūzenji. Fed by the eastward flow of the lake, the falls drop 318 feet into a rugged gorge; an elevator (¥530) takes you to an observation platform at the bottom. The volume of water over the falls is carefully regulated, but it's especially impressive after a summer rain or a typhoon. In winter the falls do not freeze completely but form a beautiful cascade of icicles. The elevator is just a few minutes' walk east from the bus stop at Chūzenji village, downhill and off to the right at the far end of the parking lot. *⊙ Daily 8–5.*

Fodor'sChoice ★

If you've budgeted an extra day for Nikkō, you might want to consider a walk around the lake. A paved road along the north shore extends for about 8 km (5 mi), one-third of the whole distance, as far as the "beach" at Shōbu-ga-hama. Here, where the road branches off to the ⑭ north for Senjōgahara, are the lovely cascades of **Dragon's Head Falls** (Ryūzu-no-taki, 竜頭滝). The falls are less dramatic than Kegon, perhaps, but they're blessed with a charming woodland setting and a rustic coffee shop where you can sit and enjoy the play of the waters as they tumble into the lake. To the left is a steep footpath that continues around the lake to Senju-ga-hama and then to a campsite at Asegata. The path is well marked but can get rough in places. From Asegata it's less than an hour's walk back to Chūzenji village.

Where to Eat

Nikkō

$$$$ ✕ **Gyōshintei** (尭心亭). This is the only restaurant in Nikkō devoted to *shōjin ryōri,* the Buddhist-temple vegetarian fare that evolved centuries

ago into haute cuisine. Gyōshintei is decorated in the style of a *ryōtei* (traditional inn), with all-tatami seating. It differs from a ryōtei in that it has one large, open space where many guests are served at once, rather than a number of rooms for private dining. Dinner is served until 7. ⊠ *2339–1 Sannai, Nikkō* ☎ *0288/53–3751* ▭ *AE, DC, MC, V* ☺ *Closed Thurs.*

$$$–$$$$ ✕ **Fujimoto** (ふじもと). At what may be Nikkō's most formal Western-style restaurant, finer touches include plush carpets, art deco fixtures, stained and frosted glass, a thoughtful wine list, and a maître d' in black tie. The menu combines elements of French and Japanese cooking styles and ingredients; the fillet of beef in mustard sauce is particularly excellent. Fujimoto closes at 7:30, so plan on eating early. ⊠ *2339–1 Sannai, Nikkō* ☎ *0288/53–3754* ▭ *AE, DC, MC, V* ☺ *Closed Fri.*

$$$–$$$$ ✕ **Masudaya** (ゆば亭ますだや). Masudaya started out as a sake maker more than a century ago, but for four generations now, it has been the town's best-known restaurant. The specialty is *yuba* (bean curd), which the chefs transform, with the help of local vegetables and fresh fish, into sumptuous high cuisine. The building is traditional, with a lovely interior garden; the assembly-line-style service, however, detracts from the ambience. Masudaya serves one nine-course kaiseki-style meal; the kitchen simply stops serving when the food is gone. It's on the main street of Nikkō, halfway between the railway stations and Tōshō-gū. ⊠ *439–2 Ishiyamachi, Nikkō* ☎ *0288/54–2151* ☜ *Reservations essential* ▭ *No credit cards* ☺ *Closed Thurs. No dinner.*

$$$–$$$$ ✕ **Meiji-no-Yakata** (明治の館). Not far from the east entrance to Rinnō Temple, Meiji-no-Yakata is an elegant 19th-century Western-style stone house, originally built as a summer retreat for an American diplomat. The food, too, is Western style; specialties of the house include fresh rainbow trout from Lake Chūzenji, roast lamb with pepper sauce, and melt-in-your-mouth filet mignon made from local Tochigi beef. High ceilings, hardwood floors, and an air of informality make this a very pleasant place to dine. The restaurant closes at 7:30. ⊠ *2339–1 Sannai, Nikkō* ☎ *0288/53–3751* ▭ *AE, DC, MC, V* ☺ *Closed Wed.*

$$–$$$ ✕ **Sawamoto** (澤本). Charcoal-broiled *unagi* (eel) is an acquired taste, and there's no better place in Nikkō to acquire it than at this restaurant. The place is small and unpretentious, with only five plain-wood tables, and service can be lukewarm, but Sawamoto is reliable for a light lunch or dinner of unagi on a bed of rice, served in an elegant lacquered box. Eel is considered a stamina builder: just right for the weary visitor on a hot summer day. Sawamoto closes at 7. ⊠ *Kami Hatsuishi-machi, Nikkō* ☎ *0288/54–0163* ▭ *No credit cards.*

Where to Stay

Nikkō

★ **$$–$$$$** ▨ **Nikkō Kanaya Hotel** (日光金谷ホテル). A little worn around the edges after a century of operation, the Kanaya still has the best location in town: across the street from Tōshō-gū. The hotel is very touristy; daytime visitors browse through the old building and its gift shops. The helpful staff is better at giving area information than the tourist office. Rooms vary a great deal, as do their prices. The more expensive rooms are spacious and comfortable, with wonderful high ceilings; in the annex the sound of the Daiya-gawa murmuring below the Sacred Bridge lulls you to sleep. Horseback riding and golf are available nearby. ☒ *1300 Kami Hatsuishi-machi, Nikkō, Tochigi-ken 321-1401* ☏ *0288/54–0001* 🖷 *0288/53–2487* ⊕ *www.kanayahotel.co.jp/nkh/index-e.html* 🛏 *77 rooms, 62 with bath* ⚐ *2 restaurants, coffee shop, pool, bar* ▭ *AE, DC, MC, V.*

¢   ▥ **Turtle Inn Nikkō** (タートルイン日光). This member of the Japanese Inn Group provides friendly, modest, cost-conscious Western- and Japanese-style accommodations with or without a private bath. Simple, cheap breakfasts and dinners are served in the dining room, but you needn't opt for these if you'd rather eat out. Rates go up about 10% in high season (late July and August). To get here, take the bus bound for Chūzenji from either railway station and get off at the Sōgō Kaikan-mae bus stop. The inn is two minutes from the bus stop and within walking distance of Tōshō-gū. ☒ *2–16 Takumi-chō, Nikkō, Tochigi-ken 321-1433* ☏ *0288/53–3168* 🖷 *0288/53–3883* 🛏 *7 Western-style rooms, 3 with bath; 5 Japanese-style rooms without bath* ⊕ *www.turtle-nikko.com* ⚐ *Restaurant, Japanese baths, Internet* ▭ *AE, MC, V.*

Chūzenji

$$$$ ▥ **Chūzenji Kanaya** (中禅寺金谷). A boathouse and restaurant on the lake give this branch of the Nikkō Kanaya on the road from the village to Shōbu-ga-hama the air of a private yacht club. Pastel colors decorate the simple, tasteful rooms, which have floor-to-ceiling windows overlooking the lake or grounds. ☒ *2482 Chū-gūshi, Nikkō, Tochigi-ken 321-1661* ☏ *0288/51–0001* 🖷 *0288/51–0011* ⊕ *www.kanayahotel.co.jp/ckh/index-e.html* 🛏 *60 rooms, 54 with bath* ⚐ *Restaurant, boating, waterskiing, fishing* ▭ *AE, DC, MC, V* ⦿ *MAP.*

$$–$$$ ▥ **Nikkō Lakeside Hotel** (日光レイクサイドホテル). In the village of Chūzenji at the foot of the lake, the Nikkō Lakeside has no particular character, but the views are good and the transportation connections (to buses and excursion boats) are ideal. Prices vary considerably from weekday to weekend and season to season. ☒ *2482 Chū-gūshi, Nikkō, Tochigi-ken 321-1661* ☏ *0288/55–0321* 🖷 *0288/55–0771* 🛏 *100 rooms with bath* ⚐ *2 restaurants, tennis court, boating, fishing, bicycles, bar* ▭ *AE, DC, MC, V* ⦿ *MAP.*

Shōbu-ga-hama

$$ ▥ **Nikkō Prince Hotel** (日光プリンスホテル). On the shore of Lake Chūzenji, this hotel, part of a large Japanese chain, is within walking distance of the Dragon's Head Falls. With many of its accommodations in two-story maisonettes and rustic detached cottages, the Prince chain markets itself to families and small groups of younger excursionists. The architecture favors high ceilings and wooden beams, with lots of glass in the public areas to take advantage of the view of the lake and Mt. Nantai. ☒ *Shōbu-ga-hama, Chū-gūshi, Nikkō, Tochigi-ken 321-1692* ☏ *0288/55–1111* 🖷 *0288/55–0669* ⊕ *www.princehotels.co.jp* 🛏 *60 rooms with bath* ⚐ *Restaurant, 2 tennis courts, pool, skiing, bar, lounge* ▭ *AE, DC, MC, V* ⦿ *MAP.*

Nikkō A to Z

To research prices, get advice from other travelers, and book travel arrangements, visit www.fodors.com.

BUS TRAVEL

Local buses leave Tōbu Nikkō Station for Lake Chūzenji, stopping just above the entrance to Tōshō-gū, approximately every 30 minutes from 6:15 AM. The fare to Chūzenji is ¥1,100, and the ride takes about 40 minutes. The last return bus from the lake leaves at 7:39 PM, arriving back at Tōbu Nikkō Station at 9:17.

CAR TRAVEL

It's possible, but unwise, to travel by car from Tōkyō to Nikkō. The trip will take at least three hours, and merely getting from central Tōkyō to the toll-road system can be a nightmare. Coming back, especially on a Saturday or Sunday evening, is even worse. If you absolutely *must* drive, take the Tōkyō Expressway 5 (Ikebukuro Line) north to the Tōkyō Gaikandō, go east on this ring road to the Kawaguchi interchange, and pick up the Tōhoku Expressway northbound. Take the Tōhoku to Utsunomiya and change again at Exit 10 (marked in English) for the Nikkō–Utsunomiya Toll Road, which runs into Nikkō.

TOURS

From Tōkyō, Sunrise Tours operates one-day bus tours to Nikkō, which take you to Tōshō-gū and Lake Chūzenji for ¥13,500 (lunch included). The tour schedule varies widely from season to season, so check the Web site or call well in advance.

🔒 **Sunrise Tours** ☎ 03/5796–5454 🖷 03/5495–0680 ⊕ www.jtb.co.jp/sunrisetour.

TAXIS

Cabs are readily available in Nikkō; the one-way fare from Tōbu Nikkō Station to Chūzenji is about ¥6,000.

TRAIN TRAVEL

The limited express train of the Tōbu Railway has two direct connections from Tōkyō to Nikkō every morning, starting at 7:30 AM from Tōbu Asakusa Station, a minute's walk from the last stop on Tōkyō's Ginza subway line; there are additional trains on weekends, holidays, and in high season. The one-way fare is ¥2,740. All seats are reserved. Bookings are not accepted over the phone; consult your hotel or a travel agent. The trip from Asakusa to the Tōbu Nikkō Station takes about two hours, which is quicker than the JR trains. If you're visiting Nikkō on a day trip, note that the last return trains are at 4:29 PM (direct express) and 7:42 PM (with a transfer at 7:52 at Shimo-Imaichi).

If you have a JR Pass, use JR (Japan Railways) service, which connects Tōkyō and Nikkō, from Ueno Station. Take the Tōhoku–Honsen Line limited express to Utsunomiya (about 1½ hours) and transfer to the train for JR Nikkō Station (45 minutes). The earliest departure from Ueno is at 5:10 AM; the last connection back leaves Nikkō at 8:03 PM and brings you into Ueno at 10:48 PM. (If you're not using the JR Pass, the one-way fare will cost ¥2,520).

More expensive but faster is the Yamabiko train on the north extension of the Shinkansen; the one-way fare, including the surcharge for the express, is ¥5,430. The first one leaves Tōkyō Station at 6:04 AM (or Ueno at 6:10 AM) and takes about 50 minutes to Utsunomiya; change there to the train to Nikkō Station. To return, take the 9:43 PM train from Nikkō to Utsunomiya and catch the last Yamabiko back at 10:53 PM, arriving in Ueno at 11:38 PM.

🚆 Japan Railways ☎ 03/3423-0111 ⊕ www.japanrail.com.

VISITOR INFORMATION

You can do a lot of preplanning for your visit to Nikkō with a stop at the Japan National Tourist Organization office in Tōkyō, where the helpful English-speaking staff will ply you with pamphlets and field your questions about things to see and do. Closer to the source is the Tourist Information and Hospitality Center in Nikkō itself, about halfway up the main street of town between the railway stations and Tōshō-gū, on the left; don't expect too much in the way of help in English, but the center does have a good array of guides to local restaurants and shops, registers of inns and hotels, and mapped-out walking tours.

🚆 Tourist Information **Japan National Tourist Organization** ⊠ Tōkyō Kōtsū Kaikan, 10F, 2-10-1 Yūraku-chō, Chiyoda-ku, Tōkyō ☎ 03/3201-3331 ⊕ www.jnto.go.jp Ⓜ JR Yamanote Line [Higashi-guchi/East Exit] and Yūraku-chō subway line [Exit A-8], Yūraku-chō Station. **Nikkō Tourist Information and Hospitality Center** ☎ 0288/54-2496.

KAMAKURA 鎌倉

Kamakura, about 40 km (25 mi) southwest of Tōkyō, is an object lesson in what happens when you set the fox to guard the henhouse.

For the aristocrats of the Heian-era Japan (794–1185), life was defined by the imperial court in Kyōto. Who in their right mind would venture elsewhere? In Kyōto there was grace and beauty and poignant affairs of the heart; everything beyond was howling wilderness. Unfortunately, it was the howling wilderness that had all the estates: the large grants of land, called *shōen*, without which there would be no income to pay for all that grace and beauty. Somebody had to go *out there,* to govern the provinces and collect the rents, to keep the restive local families in line, and to subdue the barbarians at the fringes of the empire. Over time many of the lesser noble families consigned to the provinces began to produce not only good poets and courtiers but also good administrators. To the later dismay of their fellow aristocrats, some of them—with their various clan connections, vassals, and commanders in the field—also turned out to be extremely good fighters.

By the 12th century two clans—the Taira (*ta*-ee-ra) and the Minamoto, themselves both offshoots of the imperial line—had come to dominate the affairs of the Heian court and were at each other's throats in a struggle for supremacy. In 1160 the Taira won a major battle that should have secured their absolute control over Japan, but in the process they made one serious mistake: having killed the Minamoto leader Yoshitomo, they spared his 13-year-old son, Yoritomo, and sent him into exile. Yoritomo bided his time, gathered support against the Taira, and planned his revenge. In 1180 he launched a rebellion and chose Kamakura—a superb natural fortress, surrounded on three sides by hills and guarded on the fourth by the sea—as his base of operations.

The rivalry between the two clans became an all-out war. By 1185 Yoritomo and his half-brother, Yoshitsune, had destroyed the Taira utterly, and the Minamoto were masters of all Japan. In 1192 Yoritomo forced the imperial court to name him shōgun; he was now de facto and de jure the military head of state. The emperor was left as a figurehead in Kyōto, and the little fishing village of Kamakura became—and for 141 years remained—the seat of Japan's first shogunal government.

The Minamoto line came to an end when Yoritomo's two sons were assassinated. Power passed to the Hōjō family, who remained in control, often as regents for figurehead shōguns, for the next 100 years. In 1274 and again in 1281 Japan was invaded by the Mongol armies of China's Yuan dynasty. On both occasions typhoons—the original kamikaze (literally, "divine wind")—destroyed the Mongol fleets, but the Hōjō family was still obliged to reward the various clans that had rallied to the defense of the realm. A number of these clans were unhappy with their portions—and with Hōjō rule in general. The end came suddenly, in 1333, when two vassals assigned to put down a revolt switched sides. The Hōjō regent committed suicide, and the center of power returned to Kyōto.

Kamakura reverted to being a sleepy backwater on the edge of the sea. It remained relatively isolated until the Yokosuka Railway line was built in 1889. After World War II the town began to develop as a residential area for the well-to-do. Nothing secular survives from the days of the Minamoto and Hōjō; there wasn't much there to begin with. The warriors of Kamakura had little use for courtiers, or their palaces and gardened villas; the shogunate's name for itself, in fact, was the Bakufu—literally, the "tent government." As a religious center, however, the town presents an extraordinary legacy. The Bakufu endowed shrines and temples by the score in Kamakura, especially temples of the Rinzai sect of Zen Buddhism. The austerity of Zen, its directness and self-discipline, had a powerful appeal for a warrior class that in some ways imagined itself on perpetual bivouac. Most of those temples and shrines are in settings of remarkable beauty; many are designated National Treasures. If you can afford the time for only one day trip from Tōkyō, you should probably spend it here.

Exploring Kamakura

There are three principal areas in Kamakura, and you can easily get from one to another by train. From Tōkyō head first to Kita-Kamakura for most of the important Zen temples, including Engaku-ji (Engaku Temple) and Kenchō-ji (Kencho Temple). The second area is downtown Kamakura, with its shops and museums and the venerated shrine Tsuru-ga-oka Hachiman-gū. The third is Hase, to the southwest, a 10-minute train ride from Kamakura on the Enoden Line. Hase's main attractions are the great bronze figure of the Amida Buddha, at Kōtoku-in, and the Kannon Hall of Hase-dera. There's a lot to see in Kamakura, and even to hit just the highlights will take you most of a busy day. You may need to edit your choices—especially if you want to leave yourself enough time for the Enoshima resort area, in Sagumi Bay.

If your time is limited, you may want to visit only Engaku Temple and Tōkei Temple in Kita-Kamakura before riding the train one stop to Kamakura. If not, follow the main road all the way to Tsuru-ga-oka Hachiman-gū and visit four additional temples en route.

Numbers in the text correspond to numbers in the margin and on the Kamakura map.

Kita-Kamakura (North Kamakura) 北鎌倉

Hierarchies were important to the Kamakura Shogunate. In the 14th century it established a ranking system called Go-zan (literally, "Five Mountains") for the Zen Buddhist monasteries under its official sponsorship. The largest of the Zen monasteries in Kamakura, **Engaku-ji** (Engaku Temple, 円覚寺), founded in 1282, ranked second in the Five Mountains hierarchy. Here, prayers were to be offered regularly for the prosperity and well-being of the government; Engaku Temple's special role was to pray for the souls of those who died resisting the Mongol invasions in 1274 and 1281. The temple complex once contained as many as 50 buildings. Often damaged in fires and earthquakes, it has been completely restored.

Engaku Temple belongs to the Rinzai sect of Zen Buddhism. Introduced into Japan from China at the beginning of the Kamakura period (1192–1333), the ideas of Zen were quickly embraced by the emerging warrior class. The samurai especially admired the Rinzai sect, with its emphasis on the ascetic life as a path to self-transcendence. The monks of Engaku Temple played an important role as advisers to the shogunate in matters spiritual, artistic, and political. The majestic old cedars of the temple complex bespeak an age when this was both a haven of quietude and a pillar of the state.

Among the National Treasures at Engaku Temple is the **Hall of the Holy Relic of Buddha** (Shari-den), with its remarkable Chinese-inspired thatched roof. Built in 1282, it was destroyed by fire in 1558 but rebuilt in its original form soon after, in 1563. The hall is said to enshrine a tooth of the Gautama Buddha himself, but it's not on display. In fact, except for the first three days of the New Year, you won't be able to go any farther into the hall than the main gate. Such is the case, alas, with much of the Engaku Temple complex: this is still a functioning monastic center, and many of its most impressive buildings are not open to the public. The accessible National Treasure at Engaku Temple is the **Great Bell** (Kōshō), on the hilltop on the southeast side of the complex. The bell—Kamakura's most famous—was cast in 1301 and stands 8 feet tall. It's rung only on special occasions, such as New Year's Eve. Reaching the bell requires a trek up a long staircase, but once you've made it to the top you can enjoy tea and traditional Japanese sweets at a small outdoor café. The views from here are tremendous.

The two buildings open to the public at Engaku Temple are the **Butsunichi-an,** which has a long ceremonial hall where you can enjoy the

Japanese tea ceremony, and the Ōbai-in. The latter is the mausoleum of the last three regents of the Kamakura Shogunate: Hōjō Tokimune, who led the defense of Japan against the Mongol invasions; his son Sadatoki; and his grandson Takatoki. Off to the side of the mausoleum is a quiet garden with apricot trees, which bloom in February. As you exit Kita-Kamakura Station, you'll see the stairway to Engaku Temple just in front of you. ⊠ *409 Yama-no-uchi* ☎ *0467/22–0478* ✉ *Engaku Temple ¥200, Butsunichi-an additional ¥300* ⊙ *Nov.–Mar., daily 8–4; Apr.–Oct., daily 8–5.*

★ ❷ **Tōkei-ji** (Tōkei Temple, 東慶寺), a Zen temple of the Rinzai sect, holds special significance for the study of feminism in medieval Japan. More popularly known as the Enkiri-dera, or Divorce Temple, it was founded in 1285 by the widow of the Hōjō regent Tokimune as a refuge for the victims of unhappy marriages. Under the shogunate, a husband of the warrior class could obtain a divorce simply by sending his wife back to her family. Not so for the wife; no matter what cruel and unusual treatment her husband meted out, she was stuck with him. If she ran away, however, and managed to reach Tōkei Temple without being caught, she could receive sanctuary at the temple and remain there as a nun. After three years (later reduced to two), she was officially declared divorced. The temple survived as a convent through the Meiji Restoration of 1868. The last abbess died in 1902; her headstone is in the cemetery behind the temple, beneath the plum trees that blossom in February. Tōkei Temple was later reestablished as a monastery.

The **Matsugaoka Treasure House** (Matsugaoka Hōzō) of Tōkei Temple displays several Kamakura-period wooden Buddhas, ink paintings, scrolls, and works of calligraphy, some of which have been designated by the government as Important Cultural Objects. The library, called the Matsugaoka Bunko, was established in memory of the great Zen scholar D. T. Suzuki (1870–1966).

Tōkei Temple is on the southwest side of the JR tracks (the side opposite Engaku Temple), less than a five-minute walk south from the station on the main road to Kamakura (Route 21–the Kamakura Kaidō), on the right. ⊠ *1367 Yama-no-uchi* ☎ *0467/22–1663* ✉ *Tōkei Temple ¥300, Matsugaoka Treasure House additional ¥300* ⊙ *Tōkei Temple Apr.–Oct., daily 8:30–5; Nov.–Mar., daily 8:30–4. Matsugaoka Treasure House Tues.–Sun. 9:30–3:30.*

❸ In June, when the hydrangeas are in bloom, **Meigetsu-in** (Meigetsu Temple, 明月院) becomes one of the most popular places in Kamakura. The gardens transform into a sea of color—pink, white, and blue—and visitors can number in the thousands. A typical Kamakura light rain shouldn't deter you; it only showcases this incredible floral display to best advantage. From Tōkei Temple walk along Route 21 toward Kamakura for about 20 minutes until you cross the railway tracks; take the immediate left turn onto the narrow side street that doubles back along the tracks. This street bends to the right and follows the course of a little stream called the Meigetsu-gawa to the temple gate. ⊠ *189 Yama-no-uchi* ☎ *0467/24–3437* ✉ *¥300* ⊙ *Apr., May and July–Oct., daily 9–4:30; June, daily 8:30–5; Nov.–Mar., daily 9–4.*

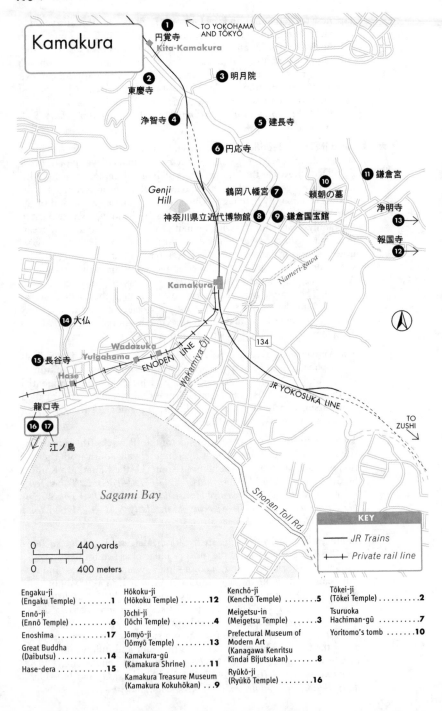

Kamakura

TO YOKOHAMA AND TŌKYŌ

1 円覚寺
Kita-Kamakura

3 明月院

2 東慶寺

浄智寺 **4**

5 建長寺

6 円応寺

11 鎌倉宮

10 頼朝の墓

Genji Hill

鶴岡八幡宮 **7**

浄明寺 **13** →

神奈川県立近代博物館 **8** **9** 鎌倉国宝館

報国寺 **12** →

Nameri-gawa

Kamakura

14 大仏

Wadazuka
Yuigahama
ENODEN LINE

Wakamiya Ōji

134

15 長谷寺

Hase

JR YOKOSUKA LINE

龍口寺

16 **17**

↙ 江ノ島

TO ZUSHI →

Sagami Bay

Shonan Toll Rd.

| 0 | 440 yards |
| 0 | 400 meters |

KEY
— JR Trains
+++ Private rail line

Engaku-ji (Engaku Temple) 1

Ennō-ji (Ennō Temple) 6

Enoshima 17

Great Buddha (Daibutsu) 14

Hase-dera 15

Hōkoku-ji (Hōkoku Temple) 12

Jōchi-ji (Jōchi Temple) 4

Jōmyō-ji (Jōmyō Temple) 13

Kamakura-gū (Kamakura Shrine) ...11

Kamakura Treasure Museum (Kamakura Kokuhōkan) ..9

Kenchō-ji (Kenchō Temple) 5

Meigetsu-in (Meigetsu Temple) 3

Prefectural Museum of Modern Art (Kanagawa Kenritsu Kindai Bijutsukan) 8

Ryūkō-ji (Ryūkō Temple) 16

Tōkei-ji (Tōkei Temple) 2

Tsuruoka Hachiman-gū 7

Yoritomo's tomb 10

4 In the Five Mountains hierarchy established by the Kamakura Shogunate for Zen Buddhist monasteries, **Jōchi-ji** (Jōchi Temple, 浄智寺) was ranked fourth. The buildings now in the temple complex are reconstructions; the Great Kantō Earthquake of 1923 destroyed the originals. The garden here is especially fine. Jōchi Temple is on the south side of the railway tracks, a few minutes' walk farther southwest of Tōkei Temple in the direction of Kamakura. Turn right off the main road (Route 21) and cross over a small bridge; a flight of moss-covered steps leads up to the temple. ✉ *1402 Yama-no-uchi* ☎ *0467/22–3943* 💴 *¥150* 🕐 *Daily 9–4:30.*

★ **5** Founded in 1250, **Kenchō-ji** (Kenchō Temple, 建長寺) was the foremost of Kamakura's five great Zen temples—and lays claim to being the oldest Zen temple in all of Japan. It was modeled on one of the great Chinese monasteries of the time and built for a distinguished Zen master who had just arrived in Japan from China. Over the centuries, fires and other disasters have taken their toll on Kencho Temple, and although many buildings have been authentically reconstructed, the temple complex today is half its original size. Near the Main Gate (San-mon) is a **bronze bell** cast in 1255; it's the temple's most important treasure. The Main Gate and the Lecture Hall (Hattō) are the only two structures to have survived the devastating Great Kantō Earthquake of 1923. Like Engaku Temple, Kencho Temple is a functioning temple of the Rinzai sect, where novices train and lay people can come to take part in Zen meditation. The entrance to Kencho Temple is about halfway along the main road from Kita-Kamakura Station to Tsuru-ga-oka Hachiman-gū, on the left. ✉ *8 Yama-no-uchi* ☎ *0467/22–0981* 💴 *¥300* 🕐 *Daily 8:30–4:30.*

★ **6** In the feudal period Japan acquired from China a belief in Enma, the lord of hell, who, with his court attendants, judges the souls of the departed and determines their destination in the afterlife. Kamakura's otherwise-undistinguished **Ennō-ji** (Ennō Temple, 円応寺) houses some remarkable statues of these judges—as grim and merciless a court as you're ever likely to confront. To see them is enough to put you on your best behavior, at least for the rest of your excursion. Ennō Temple is a minute's walk or so from Kencho Temple, on the opposite (south) side of the main road to Kamakura. A few minutes' walk along the main road to the south will bring you to Tsuru-ga-oka Hachiman-gū in downtown Kamakura. ✉ *1543 Yama-no-uchi* ☎ *0467/25–1095* 💴 *¥200* 🕐 *Mar.–Nov., daily 9–4; Dec.–Feb., daily 9–3:30.*

Kamakura 鎌倉

When the first Kamakura shōgun, Minamoto no Yoritomo, learned he was about to have an heir, he had the tutelary shrine of his family moved to Kamakura from nearby Yui-ga-hama and ordered a stately avenue to be built through the center of his capital from the shrine to the sea. Along this avenue would travel the procession that brought his son—if there were a son—to be presented to the gods. Yoritomo's consort did indeed bear him a son, Yoriie (yo-*ree*-ee-eh), in 1182; Yoriie was brought in great pomp to the shrine and then consecrated to his place in the shogunal succession. Alas, the blessing of the gods did

Yoriie little good. He was barely 18 when Yoritomo died, and the regency established by his mother's family, the Hōjō, kept him virtually powerless until 1203, when he was banished and eventually assassinated. The Minamoto were never to hold power again, but Yoriie's memory lives on in the street that his father built for him: Wakamiya Oji, "the Avenue of the Young Prince."

A bus from Kamakura Station (Sign 5) travels to the sights listed below, with stops at most access roads to the temples and shrines. However, you may want to walk out as far as Hōkoku-ji and take the bus back; it's easier to recognize the end of the line than any of the stops in between. You can also go by taxi to Hōkoku-ji—any cab driver knows the way—and walk the last leg in reverse. In any event, downtown Kamakura is a good place to stop for lunch and shop. Restaurants and shops selling local crafts objects, especially the carved and lacquered woodwork called Kamakura-*bori,* abound on Wakamiya Oji and the street parallel to it, Komachi-dōri.

★ **❼** The Minamoto shrine, **Tsuru-ga-oka Hachiman-gū** (鶴岡八幡宮), is dedicated to the legendary emperor Ōjin, his wife, and his mother, from whom Minamoto no Yoritomo claimed descent. At the entrance, the small, steeply arched, vermilion **Drum Bridge** (Taiko-bashi) crosses a stream between two lotus ponds. The ponds were made to Yoritomo's specifications. His wife, Masako, suggested placing islands in each. In the larger **Genji Pond,** to the right, filled with white lotus flowers, she placed three islands. Genji was another name for the Minamoto clan, and three is an auspicious number. In the smaller **Heike Pond,** to the left, she put four islands. Heike (*heh*-ee-keh) was another name for the rival Taira clan, which the Minamoto had destroyed, and four—homophonous in Japanese with the word for "death"—is very unlucky indeed.

On the far side of the Drum Bridge is the **Mai-den.** This hall is the setting for a story of the Minamoto celebrated in Nō and Kabuki theater. Beyond the Mai-den, a flight of steps leads to the shrine's Main Hall (Hon-dō). To the left of these steps is a ginkgo tree that—according to legend—was witness to a murder that ended the Minamoto line in 1219. From behind this tree, a priest named Kugyō leapt out and beheaded his uncle, the 26-year-old Sanetomo, Yoritomo's second son and the last Minamoto shōgun. The priest was quickly apprehended, but Sanetomo's head was never found. Like all other Shintō shrines, the Main Hall is unadorned; the building itself, an 1828 reconstruction, is not particularly noteworthy.

To reach Tsuru-ga-oka Hachiman-gū from the east side of Kamakura Station, cross the plaza, turn left, and walk north along Wakamiya Oji. Straight ahead is the first of three arches leading to the shrine, and the shrine itself is at the far end of the street. ✉ *2–1–31 Yuki-no-shita* ☎ *0467/22–0315* ✉ *Free* ☉ *Daily 9–4.*

❽ The **Prefectural Museum of Modern Art** (Kanagawa Kenritsu Kindai Bijutsukan, 神奈川県立近代博物館), on the north side of the Heike Pond at Tsuru-ga-oka Hachiman-gū, houses a collection of Japanese oil paintings and watercolors, wood-block prints, and sculpture. ✉ *2–1–53*

THE DOWNFALL OF YOSHITSUNE

ONCE A YEAR, *during the Spring Festival (early or mid-April, when the cherry trees are in bloom), the Mai-den hall at Tsuru-ga-oka Hachiman-gū is used to stage a heartrending drama about Minamoto no Yoritomo's brother. Although Yoritomo was the tactical genius behind the downfall of the Taira clan and the establishment of the Kamakura Shogunate in the late 12th century, it was his dashing half-brother, Yoshitsune, who actually defeated the Taira in battle. In so doing, Yoshitsune won the admiration of many, and Yoritomo came to believe that his sibling had ambitions of his own. Despite Yoshitsune's declaration of allegiance, Yoritomo had him exiled and sent assassins to have him killed. Yoshitsune spent his life fleeing from one place to another until, at the age of 30, he was betrayed in his last refuge and took his own life.*

Earlier in his exile, Yoshitsune's lover, the dancer Shizuka Gozen, had been captured and brought to Kamakura. Yoritomo and his wife, Masako, commanded Shizuka to dance at the family shrine as a kind of penance. Instead, she danced to the joy of her love for Yoshitsune and her concern for his fate. Yoritomo was furious, and only Masako's influence kept him from ordering her death. When he discovered, however, that Shizuka was carrying Yoshitsune's child, he ordered that if the child were a boy, he was to be killed. A boy was born. Some versions of the legend have it that the child was slain; others say he was placed in a cradle, like Moses, and cast adrift in the reeds.

Yuki-no-shita ☎ 0467/22–5000 🎟 ¥800–¥1,200, *depending on exhibition* ⊘ *Tues.–Sun. 9:30–4:30.*

⑨ The **Kamakura Treasure Museum** (Kamakura Kokuhōkan, 鎌倉国宝館) was built in 1928 as a repository for many of the most important objects belonging to the shrines and temples in the area. Many of these are designated Important Cultural Properties. The museum, located along the east side of the Tsuru-ga-oka Hachiman-gū shrine precincts, has an especially fine collection of devotional and portrait sculpture in wood from the Kamakura and Muromachi periods; the portrait pieces may be among the most expressive and interesting in all of classical Japanese art. ✉ 2–1–1 *Yuki-no-shita* ☎ 0467/22–0753 🎟 ¥300 ⊘ *Tues.–Sun. 9–4.*

The man who put Kamakura on the map, so to speak, chose not to leave it when he died: it's only a short walk from Tsuru-ga-oka Hachiman-gū to the tomb of the man responsible for its construction, Minamoto no Yoritomo. If you've already been to Nikkō and have seen how a later dynasty of shōguns sought to glorify its own memories, you may be surprised at the simplicity of **Yoritomo's tomb** (頼朝の墓). To get here, cross the Drum Bridge at Tsuru-ga-oka Hachiman-gū and turn left. Leave the grounds of the shrine and walk east along the main street (Route 204) that forms the T-intersection at the end of Wakamiya Oji. A 10-minute walk will bring you to a narrow street on the left—there's a bakery called Bergfeld on the corner—that leads to the tomb, about 100 yards off the street to the north and up a flight of stone steps. ⊠ *Free* ☉ *Daily 9–4.*

⑪ **Kamakura-gū** (Kamakura Shrine, 鎌倉宮) is a Shintō shrine built after the Meiji Restoration of 1868 and dedicated to Prince Morinaga (1308–36), the first son of Emperor Go-Daigo. When Go-Daigo overthrew the Kamakura Shogunate and restored Japan to direct imperial rule, Morinaga—who had been in the priesthood—was appointed supreme commander of his father's forces. The prince lived in turbulent times and died young: when the Ashikaga clan in turn overthrew Go-Daigo's government, Morinaga was taken into exile, held prisoner in a cave behind the present site of Kamakura Shrine, and eventually beheaded. The **Treasure House** (Hōmotsu-den), on the northwest corner of the grounds, next to the shrine's administrative office, is of interest mainly for its collection of paintings depicting the life of Prince Morinaga. To reach Kamakura Shrine, walk from Yoritomo's tomb to Route 204, and turn left; at the next traffic light, a narrow street on the left leads off at an angle to the shrine, about five minutes' walk west. ⊠ *154 Nikaidō* ☎ *0467/22–0318* ⊠ *Kamakura Shrine free, Treasure House ¥300* ☉ *Daily 9–4.*

⑫ Visitors to Kamakura tend to overlook **Hōkoku-ji** (Hōkoku Temple, 報国寺), a lovely little Zen temple of the Rinzai sect that was built in 1334. Over the years it had fallen into disrepair and neglect, until an enterprising priest took over, cleaned up the gardens, and began promoting the temple for meditation sessions, calligraphy exhibitions, and tea ceremony. Behind the main hall are a thick grove of bamboo and a small tea pavilion—a restful oasis and a fine place to go for *matcha* (tea-ceremony green tea). The temple is about 2 km (1 mi) east on Route 204 from the main entrance to Tsuru-ga-oka Hachiman-gū; turn right at the traffic light by the Hōkoku Temple Iriguchi bus stop and walk about three minutes south to the gate. ⊠ *2–7–4 Jōmyō-ji* ☎ *0467/ 22–0762* ⊠ *Hōkoku Temple free, bamboo grove ¥200, tea ceremony ¥500* ☉ *Daily 9–4.*

⑬ **Jōmyō-ji** (Jōmyo Temple, 浄明寺), founded in 1188, is the only one of the Five Mountains Zen monasteries in the eastern part of Kamakura. It lacks the grandeur and scale of the Engaku and Kenchō temples—naturally enough, as it was ranked behind them, in fifth place—but it still merits the status of an Important Cultural Property. To reach it from Hōkoku-ji, cross the main street (Route 204) that brought you the mile or so from Tsuru-ga-oka Hachiman-gū, and take the first narrow street north. The monastery is about 100 yards from the corner. ⊠ *3–8–31 Jōmyō-ji* ☎ *0467/22–2818* ⊠ *Jōmyō Temple ¥100, tea ceremony ¥500* ☉ *Daily 9–4:30.*

Hase   長谷

The single biggest attraction in Hase ("*ha*-seh") is the temple Kōtoku-in's **Great Buddha** (Daibutsu, 大仏)—sharing the honors with Mt. Fuji,

FodorsChoice
★

perhaps, as the quintessential picture-postcard image of Japan. The statue of the compassionate Amida Buddha sits cross-legged in the temple courtyard, the drapery of his robes flowing in lines reminiscent of ancient Greece, his expression profoundly serene. The 37-foot bronze figure was cast in 1292, three centuries before Europeans reached Japan; the concept of the classical Greek lines in the Buddha's robe must have come over the Silk Route through China during the time of Alexander the Great. The casting was probably first conceived in 1180, by Minamoto no Yoritomo, who wanted a statue to rival the enormous Daibutsu in Nara. Until 1495 the Amida Buddha was housed in a wooden temple, which washed away in a great tidal wave. Since then the loving Buddha has stood exposed, facing the cold winters and hot summers for more than five centuries.

It may seem sacrilegious to walk inside the Great Buddha, but for ¥20 you can enter the figure from a doorway in the right side and explore (until 4:15 PM) his stomach. To reach Kōtoku-in and the Great Buddha, take the Enoden Line from the west side of JR Kamakura Station three stops to Hase. From the east exit, turn right and walk north about 10 minutes on the main street (Route 32). ✉ *4–2–28 Hase* ☎ *0467/ 22–0703* 💲 *¥200* 🕙 *Apr.–Sept., daily 7–6; Oct.–Mar., daily 7–4:30.*

⓯ The only Kamakura temple facing the sea, **Hase-dera** (長谷寺) is one of the most beautiful, and saddest, places of pilgrimage in the city. On a landing partway up the stone steps that lead to the temple grounds are hundreds of small stone images of Jizō, one of the bodhisattvas in the Buddhist pantheon who have deferred their own ascendance into Buddhahood to guide the souls of others to salvation. Jizō is the savior of children, particularly the souls of the stillborn, aborted, and miscarried; the mothers of these children dress the statues of Jizō in bright red bibs and leave them small offerings of food, heartbreakingly touching acts of prayer.

FodorśChoice
★

The **Kannon Hall** (Kannon-do) at Hase-dera enshrines the largest carved-wood statue in Japan: the votive figure of Jūichimen Kannon, the 11-headed goddess of mercy. Standing 30 feet tall, the goddess bears a crown of 10 smaller heads, symbolizing her ability to search out in all directions for those in need of her compassion. No one knows for certain when the figure was carved. According to the temple records, a monk named Tokudo Shōnin carved two images of the Jūichimen Kannon from a huge laurel tree in 721. One was consecrated to the Hase-dera in present-day Nara Prefecture; the other was thrown into the sea in order to go wherever the sea decided that there were souls in need, and that image washed up on shore near Kamakura. Much later, in 1342, Ashikaga Takauji—the first of the 15 Ashikaga shōguns who followed the Kamakura era—had the statue covered with gold leaf.

The **Amida Hall** of Hase-dera enshrines the image of a seated Amida Buddha, who presides over the Western Paradise of the Pure Land. Minamoto no Yoritomo ordered the creation of this statue when he reached the age of 42; popular Japanese belief, adopted from China, holds that your 42nd year is particularly unlucky. Yoritomo's act of piety earned him another 11 years—he was 53 when he was thrown by a horse and died of his injuries. The Buddha is popularly known as the *yakuyoke* (good-luck) Amida, and many visitors—especially students facing entrance exams—make a point of coming here to pray. To the left of the main halls is a small restaurant where you can buy good-luck candy and admire the view of Kamakura Beach and Sagami Bay. To reach Hase-dera from Hase Station, walk north about five minutes on the main street (Route 32) towards Kōtoku-in and the Great Buddha, and look for a signpost to the temple on a side street to the left. ☒ *3–11–2 Hase* ☎ *0467/22–6300* ☺ *¥300* ⊗ *Mar.–Sept., daily 8–6; Oct.–Feb., daily 8–5:30.*

Ryūkō-ji & Enoshima 龍口寺・江ノ島

16 The Kamakura story would not be complete without the tale of Nichiren (1222–82), the monk who founded the only native Japanese sect of Buddhism and who is honored at **Ryūkō-ji** (Ryūkō Temple, 龍口寺). Nichiren's rejection of both Zen and Jōdo (Pure Land) teachings brought him into conflict with the Kamakura Shogunate, and the Hōjō regents sent him into exile on the Izu Peninsula in 1261. Later allowed to return, he continued to preach his own interpretation of the Lotus Sutra—and to assert the "blasphemy" of other Buddhist sects, a stance that finally persuaded the Hōjō regency, in 1271, to condemn him to death. Execution was to take place on a hill to the south of Hase. As the executioner swung his sword, legend has it a lightning bolt struck the blade and snapped it in two. Taken aback, the executioner sat down to collect his wits, and a messenger was sent back to Kamakura to report the event. On his way he met another messenger, who was carrying a writ from the Hōjō regents commuting Nichiren's sentence to exile on the island of Sado-ga-shima.

Followers of Nichiren built Ryūkō Temple in 1337, on the hill where he was to be executed, marking his miraculous deliverance from the headsman. There are other Nichiren temples closer to Kamakura—Myōhon-ji and Ankokuron-ji, for example—but Ryūkō not only has the typical Nichiren-style main hall with gold tassels hanging from its roof but also a beautiful pagoda, built in 1904. To reach it, take the Enoden Line west from Hase to Enoshima—a short, scenic ride that cuts through the hills surrounding Kamakura to the shore. From Enoshima Station walk about 100 yards east, keeping the train tracks on your right, and you'll come to the temple. ☒ *3–13–37 Katase, Fujisawa* ☎ *0466/25–7357* ☺ *Free* ⊗ *Daily 6–4.*

The Sagami Bay shore in this area has some of the closest beaches to Tōkyō, and in the hot, humid summer months it seems as though all of the city's teeming millions pour onto these beaches in search of a vacant patch of rather dirty gray sand. Pass up this mob scene and press **17** on instead to **Enoshima** (江ノ島). The island is only 4 km (2½ mi) around, with a hill in the middle. Partway up the hill is a shrine where the local fisherfolk used to pray for a bountiful catch—before it became a tourist attraction. Once upon a time it was quite a hike up to the shrine; now there's a series of escalators, flanked by the inevitable stalls selling souvenirs and snacks. The island has several cafés and restaurants, and on clear days some of them have spectacular views of Mt. Fuji and the Izu Peninsula. To reach the causeway from Enoshima Station to the island, walk south from the station for about 3 km (2 mi), keeping the Katase-gawa (Katase River) on your right.

To return to Tōkyō from Enoshima, take a train to Shinjuku on the Odakyū Line. From the island walk back across the causeway and take the second bridge over the Katase-gawa. Within five minutes you'll come to Katase-Enoshima Station. Or you can retrace your steps to Kamakura and take the JR Yokosuka Line to Tōkyō Station.

Where to Eat

Kita-Kamakura

★ $$$-$$$$ ✕ **Hachinoki Kita-Kamakura-ten** (鉢の木北鎌倉店). Traditional *shōjin ryōri* (the vegetarian cuisine of Zen monasteries) is served in this old Japanese house on the Kamakura Kaidō (Route 21) near the entrance to Jōchi Temple. There's some table service, but most seating is in tatami rooms, with beautiful antique wood furnishings. Allow plenty of time; this is not a meal to be hurried through. Meals, which are prix fixe only, are served Tuesday–Friday 11–2:30, weekends 11–3:30. ⊠ 7 *Yama-no-uchi, Kamakura* ☎ *0467/22–8719* ▤ *DC, V* ⊗ *Closed Mon. No dinner.*

$$-$$$ ✕ **Kyoraian** (去来庵). A traditional structure houses this restaurant known for its excellent Western-style beef stew. Half the seats are on tatami mats and half are at tables, but all look out on a peaceful patch of greenery. Kyoraian is on the main road from Kita-Kamakura to Kamakura on the left side; it's about halfway between Meigetsu Temple and Kenchō Temple, up a winding flight of stone steps. Meals are served 11–7:30. ⊠ *157 Yamanouchi, Kita-Kamakura* ☎ *0467/22–9835* ▤ *No credit cards* ⊗ *Closed Fri.*

Kamakura

$$-$$$$ ✕ **Tori-ichi** (鳥一). This elegant restaurant serves traditional Japanese kaiseki. In an old country-style building, waitresses in kimonos bring out sumptuous multicourse meals, including one or more subtle-tasting soups, sushi, tempura, grilled fish, and other delicacies. Meals are served Monday and Wednesday–Saturday noon–2 and 5–8, and Sunday 11:30–9. ⊠ *7–13 Onari-machi, Kamakura* ☎ *0467/22–1818* ▤ *No credit cards* ⊗ *Closed Tues.*

$-$$$ ✕ **T-Side.** Authentic, inexpensive Indian fare and a second-floor location looking down on Kamakura's main shopping street make this restaurant a popular choice for lunch and dinner. Curries are well-done, the various *thali* (sets) are a good value, and the kitchen also serves some Nepalese dishes. T-Side is at the very top of Komachi-dōri, on the left as you enter from Kamakura Station. ⊠ *1–6–2 Komachi, Kamakura* ☎ *0467/24–9572* ▤ *MC, V.*

¢ ✕ **Kaisen Misaki-ko** (海鮮三崎港). This *kaiten-zushi* (sushi served on a conveyor belt that lets you pick the dishes you want) restaurant on Komachi-dōri, Kamakura's main shopping street, serves eye-poppingly large fish portions that hang over the edge of their plates. All the standard sushi creations, from tuna to shrimp to egg, are prepared here for ¥170–¥500. The restaurant is on the right side of the road just as you enter Komachi-dōri from the east exit of Kamakura Station. ⊠ *1–7–1 Komachi, Kamakura* ☎ *0467/22–6228* ▤ *No credit cards.*

Hase

$$$–$$$$ ✕ **Kaseiro** (華正樓). This establishment, in an old Japanese house on the main street from Hase Station to the Great Buddha at Kōtoku-in, serves the best Chinese food in the city. The dining-room windows look out on a small, restful garden. Meals are served 11–7:30. ✉ *3–1–14 Hase, Kamakura* ☎ *0467/22–0280* 🖃 *AE, DC, MC, V.*

Kamakura A to Z

To research prices, get advice from other travelers, and book travel arrangements, visit www.fodors.com.

BUS TRAVEL

A bus from Kamakura Station (Sign 5) travels to most of the temples and shrines in the downtown Kamakura area.

TOURS

No bus company in Kamakura conducts guided tours in English. You can, however, take one of the Japanese tours, which depart from Kamakura Station eight times daily, starting at 9 AM; the last tour leaves at 1 PM. Purchase tickets at the bus office to the right of the station. There are two itineraries, each lasting a little less than three hours; tickets, depending on what the tour covers, are ¥2,250 and ¥3,390. These tours are best if you have limited time and would like to hit the major attractions but don't want to linger anywhere or do a lot of walking. Take John Carroll's book *Trails of Two Cities: A Walker's Guide to Yokohama, Kamakura and Vicinity* (Kodansha International, 1994) with you, and you'll have more information at your fingertips than any of your fellow passengers.

On the weekend the Kanagawa Student Guide Federation has a free guide service. Students show you the city in exchange for the chance to practice their English. Arrangements must be made in advance through the Japan National Tourist Organization in Tōkyō. You'll need to be at Kamakura Station between 10 AM and noon.

Sunrise Tours runs daily trips from Tōkyō to Kamakura; these tours are often combined with trips to Hakone. You can book through, and arrange to be picked up at, any of the major hotels. Before you do, however, be certain that the tour covers everything in Kamakura that you want to see, as many include little more than a passing view of the Great Buddha in Hase. Given how easy it is to get around—most sights are within walking distance of each other, and others are short bus or train rides apart—you're better off seeing Kamakura on your own.

🎫 **Tour Contacts Japan National Tourist Organization** ✉ Tōkyō Kōtsū Kaikan, 10F, 2-10-1 Yūraku-chō, Chiyoda-ku, Tōkyō ☎ 03/3201-3331 ⊕ www.jnto.go.jp Ⓜ JR Yamanote Line [Higashi-guchi/East Exit] and Yūraku-chō subway line [Exit A-8], Yūraku-chō Station. **Kanagawa Student Guide Federation** ☎03/3201-3331. **Sunrise Tours** ☎03/5796-5454 🖷 03/5495-0680 ⊕ www.jtb.co.jp/sunrisetour.

TRAIN TRAVEL

Traveling by train is by far the best way to get to Kamakura. Trains run from Tōkyō Station (and Shimbashi Station) every 10–15 minutes during the day. The trip takes 56 minutes to Kita-Kamakura and one hour to Kamakura. Take the JR Yokosuka Line from Track 1 downstairs in Tōkyō Station (Track 1 upstairs is on a different line and does not go to Kamakura). The cost is ¥780 to Kita-Kamakura, ¥890 to Kamakura (or use your JR [Japan Railways] Pass).

Local train service connects Kita-Kamakura, Kamakura, Hase, and Enoshima.

To return to Tōkyō from Enoshima, take a train to Shinjuku on the Odakyū Line. There are 11 express trains daily from here on weekdays, between 8:38 AM and 8:45 PM; 9 trains daily on weekends and national holidays, between 8:39 AM and 8:46 PM; and even more in summer. The express takes about 70 minutes and costs ¥1,220. Or you can retrace your steps to Kamakura and take the JR Yokosuka Line to Tōkyō Station.

🚃 **Japan Railways** ☎ 03/3423-0111 ⊕ www.japanrail.com.

VISITOR INFORMATION

Both Kamakura and Enoshima have their own tourist associations, although it can be problematic getting help in English over the phone. Your best bet is the Kamakura Station Tourist Information Center, which has a useful collection of brochures and maps. And since Kamakura is in Kanagawa Prefecture, visitors heading here from Yokohama can pre-plan their excursion at the Kanagawa Prefectural Tourist Association office in the Silk Center, on the Yamashita Park promenade.

🚃 **Tourist Information Enoshima Tourist Association** ✉ 4-3-17 Kugenuma Kaigan, Fujisawa-shi ☎ 0466/37-4141. **Kamakura Station Tourist Information Center** ✉ 1-1-1 Komachi, Kamakura-shi ☎ 0467/22-3350. **Kamakura Tourist Association** ✉ 1-12 Onari-machi, Kamakura-shi ☎ 0467/23-3050. **Kanagawa Prefectural Tourist Association** ✉ Silk Center 1F, 1 Yamashita-chō, Naka-ku, Yokohama-shi ☎ 045/681-0007 ⊕ www.kanagawa-kankou.or.jp.

YOKOHAMA 横浜

In 1639 the Tokugawa Shogunate adopted a policy of national seclusion that closed Japan to virtually all contact with the outside world. Japan adhered to this policy for more than 200 years, until 1853, when a fleet of four American warships under Commodore Matthew Perry sailed into the bay of Tōkyō (then Edo) and presented the reluctant Japanese with the demands of the U.S. government for the opening of diplomatic and commercial relations. The following year Perry returned and first set foot on Japanese soil at Yokohama—then a small fishing village on the mud-flats of the bay, some 20 km (12½ mi) southwest of Tōkyō.

Two years later New York businessman Townsend Harris became America's first diplomatic representative to Japan. In 1858 he was finally able to negotiate a commercial treaty between the two countries; part of the deal designated four locations—one of them Yokohama—as treaty ports. With the agreement signed, Harris lost no time in setting up his residence in Hangaku-ji, in nearby Kanagawa, another of the designated ports. Kanagawa, however, was also one of the 53 relay stations on the Tōkaidō, the highway from Edo to the imperial court in Kyōto, and the presence of foreigners—perceived as unclean barbarians—offended the

Japanese elite. Die-hard elements of the warrior class, moreover, wanted Japan to remain in isolation and were willing to give their lives to rid the country of intruders. Unable to protect foreigners in Kanagawa, in 1859 the shogunate created a special settlement in Yokohama for the growing community of merchants, traders, missionaries, and other assorted adventurers drawn to this exotic new land of opportunity.

The foreigners (predominantly Chinese and British, plus a few French, Americans, and Dutch) were confined here to a guarded compound about 5 square km (2 square mi)—placed, in effect, in isolation—but not for long. Within a few short years the shogunal government collapsed, and Japan began to modernize. Western ideas were welcomed, as were Western goods, and the little treaty port became Japan's principal gateway to the outside world. In 1872 Japan's first railway was built, linking Yokohama and Tōkyō. In 1889 Yokohama became a city; by then the population had grown to some 120,000. As the city prospered, so did the international community.

The English enjoyed a special cachet in the new Japan. Was not Britain, too, a small island nation? And did it not do great things in the wide world? These were people from whom they could learn and with whom they could trade, and the Japanese welcomed them in considerable numbers. (You can still watch the occasional game of cricket at the Yokohama Country and Athletic Club—once the exclusive bastion of British trading companies like Jardine Matheson.) The British, in turn, helped Japan recover its sovereignty over the original treaty ports, and by the early 1900s Yokohama was the busiest and most modern center of international trade in all of east Asia.

Then Yokohama came tumbling down. On September 1, 1923, the Great Kantō Earthquake devastated the city. The ensuing fires destroyed some 60,000 homes and took more than 40,000 lives. During the six years it took to rebuild the city, many foreign businesses took up quarters elsewhere, primarily in Kōbe and Ōsaka, and did not return.

Over the next 20 years Yokohama continued to grow as an industrial center—until May 29, 1945, when in a span of four hours, some 500 American B-29 bombers leveled nearly half the city and left more than half a million people homeless. When the war ended, what remained became—in effect—the center of the Allied occupation. General Douglas MacArthur set up headquarters here, briefly, before moving to Tōkyō; the entire port facility and about a quarter of the city remained in the hands of the U.S. military throughout the 1950s.

By the 1970s Yokohama was once more rising from the debris; in 1978 it surpassed Ōsaka as the nation's second-largest city, and the population is now inching up to the 3.5 million mark. Boosted by Japan's postwar economic miracle, Yokohama has extended its urban sprawl north to Tōkyō and south to Kamakura—in the process creating a whole new subcenter around the Shinkansen station at Shin-Yokohama.

The development of air travel and the competition from other ports have changed the city's role in Japan's economy. The great liners that once docked at Yokohama's piers are now but a memory, kept alive by a museum ship and the occasional visit of a luxury vessel on a Pacific cruise. Modern Yokohama thrives instead in its industrial, commercial, and service sectors—and a large percentage of its people commute to work in Tōkyō. Is Yokohama worth a visit? Not, one could argue, at the expense of Nikkō or Kamakura, and not if you are looking for history in the physical fabric of the city: most of Yokohama's late-19th- and early- 20th-century buildings are long gone. In some odd, undefinable way, however, Yokohama is a more *cosmopolitan* city than Tōkyō. The waterfront is fun, and city planners have made an exceptional success of their port redevelopment project. The museums are excellent. And if you spend time enough here, Yokohama can still invoke for you the days when, for intrepid Western travelers, Japan was a new frontier.

Exploring Yokohama

Large as Yokohama is, the central area is very negotiable. As with any other port city, much of what it has to offer centers on the waterfront—in this case, the Bund, on the west side of Tōkyō Bay. The downtown area is called Kannai (literally, "within the checkpoint"); this is where the international community was originally confined by the shogunate. Though the center of interest has expanded to include the waterfront and Ishikawa-chō, to the south, Kannai remains the heart of town.

Think of that heart as two adjacent areas. One is the old district of Kannai, bounded by Basha-michi on the northwest and Nippon-ōdori on the southeast, the Keihin Tōhoku Line tracks on the southwest, and the waterfront on the northeast. This area contains the business offices of modern Yokohama. The other area extends southeast from Nippon-ōdori to the Moto-machi shopping street and the International Cemetery, bordered by Yamashita Kōen and the waterfront to the northeast; in the center is Chinatown, with Ishikawa-chō Station to the southwest. This is the most interesting part of town for tourists.

Numbers in the text correspond to numbers in the margin and on the Yokohama map.

Central Yokohama 横浜市街

Whether you are coming from Tōkyō, Nagoya, or Kamakura, make Ishikawa-chō Station your starting point. Take the south exit from the station and head in the direction of the waterfront. Within a block of

❶ Ishikawa-chō Station is the beginning of **Moto-machi** (元町), the street that follows the course of the Nakamura-gawa (Nakamura River) to the harbor. This is where the Japanese set up shop 100 years ago to serve the foreigners living in Kannai. The street is now lined with smart boutiques and jewelry stores that cater to fashionable young Japanese consumers. ✉ *Naka-ku.*

❷ The **International Cemetery** (Gaijin Bochi, 外人墓地) is a Yokohama landmark and a reminder of the port city's heritage. It was established in 1854 with a grant of land from the shogunate; the first foreigners to be buried here were Russian sailors assassinated by xenophobes in the early days of the settlement. Most of the 4,500 graves on this hillside are English

Yokohama

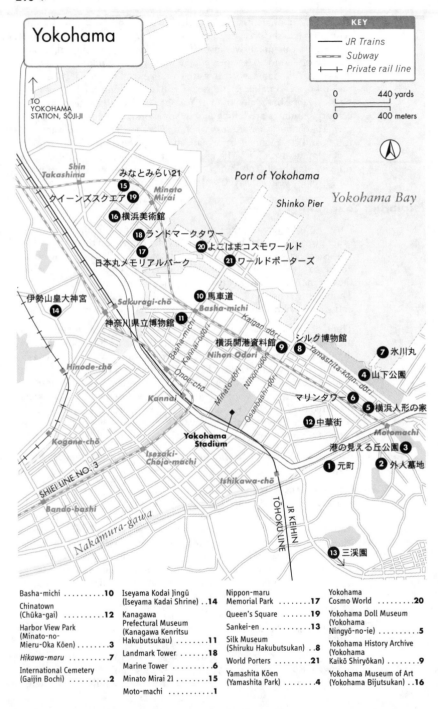

TO YOKOHAMA STATION, SŌJI-JI

Shin Takashima

みなとみらい21

Port of Yokohama

Shinko Pier

Yokohama Bay

⑮ ⑲ クイーンズスクエア

Minato Mirai

⑯ 横浜美術館

⑱ ランドマークタワー

⑰

日本丸メモリアルパーク

⑳ よこはまコスモワールド

㉑ ワールドポーターズ

伊勢山皇大神宮

⑭

Sakuragi-chō

⑩ 馬車道
Basha-michi

神奈川県立博物館 ⑪

Basha-michi

Kannai-ōdōri

Hinode-chō

横浜開港資料館 ⑨

Nihon Odori

Minato-ōdōri

Nihon-ōdōri

Onoe-chō

Kaigan-dōri

⑧ シルク博物館

Yamashita-kōen-dōri

⑦ 氷川丸

④ 山下公園

Kannai

Osanbashi-dōri

マリンタワー ⑥

⑤ 横浜人形の家

⑫ 中華街

Motomachi

Kogane-chō

Yokohama Stadium

Isezaki-Chōja-machi

港の見える丘公園 ③

① 元町

② 外人墓地

SHIEI LINE NO. 3

Ishikawa-chō

Bando-bashi

Nakamura-gawa

JR KEIHIN TŌHOKU LINE

⑬ 三渓園

Basha-michi 10

Chinatown
(Chūka-gai) 12

Harbor View Park
(Minato-no-
Mieru-Oka Kōen) 3

Hikawa-maru 7

International Cemetery
(Gaijin Bochi) 2

Iseyama Kodai Jingū
(Iseyama Kadai Shrine) . .14

Kanagawa
Prefectural Museum
(Kanagawa Kenritsu
Hakubutsukau) 11

Landmark Tower 18

Marine Tower 6

Minato Mirai 21 15

Moto-machi 1

Nippon-maru
Memorial Park 17

Queen's Square 19

Sankei-en 13

Silk Museum
(Shiruku Hakubutsukan) . .8

World Porters 21

Yamashita Kōen
(Yamashita Park) 4

Yokohama
Cosmo World 20

Yokohama Doll Museum
(Yokohama
Ningyō-no-ie) 5

Yokohama History Archive
(Yokohama
Kaikō Shiryōkan) 9

Yokohama Museum of Art
(Yokohama Bijutsukan) . .16

and American, and about 120 are of the Japanese wives of foreigners; the inscriptions on the crosses and headstones attest to some 40 different nationalities who lived and died in Yokohama. From Moto-machi Plaza, it's a short walk to the north end of the cemetery. ⊠ *Naka-ku.*

❸ Harbor View Park (Minato-no-Mieru-Oka Kōen, 港の見える丘公園), once the barracks of the British forces in Yokohama, affords a spectacular nighttime view of the waterfront, the floodlit gardens of Yamashita Park, and the Bay Bridge. The park is the major landmark in this part of the city, known, appropriately enough, as the Bluff (*yamate*). Foreigners were first allowed to build here in 1867, and it has been prime real estate ever since—an enclave of consulates, churches, international schools, private clubs, and palatial Western-style homes. ⊠ *Naka-ku.*

❹ Yamashita Kōen (Yamashita Park, 山下公園) is perhaps the only positive legacy of the Great Kantō Earthquake of 1923. The debris of the warehouses and other buildings that once stood here was swept away, and the area was made into a 17-acre oasis of green along the waterfront. The fountain, representing the Guardian of the Water, was presented to Yokohama by San Diego, California, one of its sister cities. To get here from Harbor View Park, walk northwest through neighboring French Hill Park and cross the walkway over Moto-machi. Turn right on the other side and walk one block down toward the bay to Yamashita-Kōen-dōri, the promenade along the park. ⊠ *Naka-ku.*

👋 **❺** The **Yokohama Doll Museum** (Yokohama Ningyō-no-ie, 横浜人形の家) houses a collection of some 4,000 dolls from all over the world. In Japanese tradition, dolls are less to play with than to display—either in religious folk customs or as the embodiment of some spiritual quality. Japanese visitors to this museum never seem to outgrow their affection for the Western dolls on display here, to which they tend to assign the role of timeless "ambassadors of good will" from other cultures. The museum is worth a quick visit, with or without a child in tow. It's just across from the southeast end of Yamashita Park, on the left side of the promenade. ⊠ *18 Yamashita-chō, Naka-ku* ☎ *045/671–9361* 💴 *¥300; multiple-entry ticket to museum, Marine Tower, and Hikawa-maru, ¥1,550* ⊙ *Daily 10–6; closed 3rd Mon. of month.*

For an older generation of Yokohama residents, the 348-foot-high **❻** decagonal **Marine Tower** (マリンタワー), which opened in 1961, was the city's landmark structure; civic pride prevented them from admitting that it falls lamentably short of an architectural masterpiece. The tower has a navigational beacon at the 338-foot level and purports to be the tallest lighthouse in the world. At the 328-foot level, an observation gallery provides 360-degree views of the harbor and the city, and on clear days in autumn or winter, you can often see Mt. Fuji in the distance. Marine Tower is in the middle of the second block northwest from the end of Yamashita Park, on the left side of the promenade. ⊠ *15 Yamashita-chō, Naka-ku* ☎ *045/641–7838* 💴 *¥700; multiple-entry ticket to Marine Tower and Hikawa-maru ¥1,300; multiple-entry ticket to Marine Tower, Hikawa-maru, and Yokohama Doll Museum ¥1,550* ⊙ *Jan. and Feb., daily 9–7; Mar.–May and Nov. and Dec., daily 9:30–9; June and July and Sept. and Oct., daily 9:30–9:30; Aug., daily 9:30–10.*

7 Moored on the waterfront, more or less in the middle of Yamashita Park, is the *Hikawa-maru* (氷川丸), which for 30 years shuttled passengers between Yokohama and Seattle, Washington, making a total of 238 trips. A tour of the ship evokes the time when Yokohama was a great port of call for the transpacific liners. The *Hikawa-maru* has a French restaurant, and in summer there's a beer garden on the upper deck. ⊠ *Naka-ku* ☎ *045/641–4361* ☞ *¥800; multiple-entry ticket to Hikawa-maru and Marine Tower ¥1,300; multiple-entry ticket to Hikawa-maru, Marine Tower, and Yokohama Doll Museum ¥1,550* ⊙ *Apr.–June, daily 9:30–7; July and Aug., daily 9:30–7:30; Sept. and Oct., daily 9:30–7; Nov.–Mar., daily 9:30–6:30.*

8 The **Silk Museum** (Shiruku Hakubutsukan, シルク博物館) pays tribute to the period at the turn of the 20th century when Japan's exports of silk were all shipped out of Yokohama. The museum houses an extensive collection of silk fabrics and an informative exhibit on the silk-making process. People on staff are very happy to answer questions. In the same building, on the first floor, are the main offices of the Yokohama International Tourist Association and the Kanagawa Prefectural Tourist Association. The museum is at the northwestern end of the Yamashita Park promenade, on the second floor of the Silk Center Building. ⊠ *1 Yamashita-chō, Naka-ku* ☎ *045/641–0841* ☞ *¥300* ⊙ *Tues.–Sun. 9–4.*

9 Within the **Yokohama History Archives** (Yokohama Kaikō Shiryōkan, 横浜開港資料館), housed in what was once the British Consulate, are some 140,000 items recording the history of Yokohama since the opening of the port to international trade in the mid-19th century. Across the street is a monument to the U.S.–Japanese Friendship Treaty. To get here from the Silk Center Building, at the end of the Yamashita Park promenade, walk west to the corner of Nihon-ōdori; the archives are on the left. ⊠ *3 Nihon-ōdori, Naka-ku* ☎ *045/201–2100* ☞ *¥200* ⊙ *Tues.–Sun. 9:30–4:30.*

10 Running southwest from Shinko Pier to Kannai is **Basha-michi** (馬車道), which literally translates into "Horse-Carriage Street." The street was so named in the 19th century, when it was widened to accommodate the horse-drawn carriages of the city's new European residents. This red-brick thoroughfare and the streets parallel to it have been restored to evoke that past, with faux-antique telephone booths and imitation gas lamps. Here you'll find some of the most elegant coffee shops, patisseries, and boutiques in town. On the block northeast of Kannai Station, as you walk toward the waterfront, is **Kannai Hall** (look for the red-orange abstract sculpture in front), a handsome venue for chamber music, Nō, classical recitals, and occasional performances by such groups as the Peking Opera. If you're planning to stay late in Yokohama, you might want to check out the listings. ⊠ *Naka-ku.*

11 One of the few buildings in Yokohama to have survived both the Great Kantō Earthquake of 1923 and World War II is the 1904 **Kanagawa Prefectural Museum** (Kanagawa Kenritsu Hakubutsukan, 神奈川県立博物館), a few blocks north of Kannai Station (use Exit 8) on Basha-michi. Most exhibits here have no explanations in English, but the galleries on the third floor showcase some remarkable medieval wooden sculptures (including one of the first Kamakura shōgun, Minamoto no Yoritomo), hanging scrolls, portraits, and armor. The exhibits of prehistory and of Yokohama in the early modern period are of much less interest. ✉ *5–60 Minami Naka-dōri, Naka-ku* ☎ *045/201–0926* 🎫 *¥300, special exhibits ¥800* ⊙ *Tues.–Sun. 9–4:30; closed last Tues. of month and the day after a national holiday.*

★ ⑫ Yokohama's **Chinatown** (Chūka-gai, 中華街) is the largest Chinese settlement in Japan—and easily the city's single most popular tourist attraction, drawing more than 18 million visitors a year. Its narrow streets and alleys are lined with some 350 shops selling foodstuffs, herbal medicines, cookware, toys and ornaments, and clothing and accessories. If China exports it, you'll find it here. Wonderful exotic aromas waft from the spice shops. Even better aromas drift from the quarter's 160-odd restaurants, which serve every major style of Chinese cuisine: this is the best place for lunch in Yokohama. Chinatown is a 10-minute walk southeast of Kannai Station. When you get to Yokohama Stadium, turn left and cut through the municipal park to the top of Nihon-ōdori. Then take a right, and you'll enter Chinatown through the Gembu-mon (North Gate), which leads to the dazzling red-and-gold, 50-foot-high Zenrin-mon (Good Neighbor Gate). ✉ *Naka-ku.*

Around Yokohama 横浜周辺

★ ⑬ Opened to the public in 1906, **Sankei-en** (三渓園) was once the estate and gardens of Hara Tomitarō, one of Yokohama's wealthiest men, who made his money as a silk merchant before becoming a patron of the arts. On the extensive grounds of the estate he created is a kind of open-air museum of traditional Japanese architecture, some of which was brought here from Kamakura and the western part of the country. Especially noteworthy is **Rinshun-kaku**, a villa built for the Tokugawa clan in 1649. There's also a tea pavilion, Chōshū-kaku, built by the third Tokugawa shōgun, Iemitsu. Other buildings include a small temple transported from Kyōto's famed Daitoku-ji and a farmhouse from the Gifu district in the Japan Alps (around Takayama).

Walking through Sankei-en is especially delightful in spring, when the flowering trees are at their best: plum blossoms in February and cherry blossoms in early April. In June come the irises, followed by the water lilies. In autumn the trees come back into their own with tinted golden leaves. To reach Sankei-en, take the JR Keihin Tōhoku Line to Negishi Station and a local bus from there for the 10-minute trip to the garden. ✉ *58–1 Honmoku San-no-tani, Naka-ku* ☎ *045/621–0635* 🎫 *Inner garden ¥300, outer garden ¥300, farmhouse ¥100* ⊙ *Inner garden daily 9–4, outer garden daily 9–4:30.*

⑭ **Iseyama Kodai Jingū** (Iseyama Kodai Shrine, 伊勢山皇大神宮), a branch of the nation's revered Grand Shrines of Ise, is the most important Shintō shrine in Yokohama—but probably worth a visit only if you have seen most of everything else in town. The shrine is a 10-minute walk west of Sakuragi-chō Station. ✉ *64 Miyazaki-chō, Nishi-ku* ☎ *045/241–1122* 🎫 *Free* ⊙ *Daily 9–7.*

⑮ If you want to see Yokohama urban development at its most self-assertive, **Minato Mirai 21** (みなとみらい21) is a must. The aim of this project, launched in the mid-1980s, was to turn some three-quarters of a square mile of waterfront property, lying east of the JR Negishi Line railroad tracks between the Yokohama and Sakuragi-chō stations, into a model "city of the future." As a hotel, business, international exhibition, and conference center, it's a smashing success. ⊠ *Nishi-ku.*

⑯ Minato Mirai 21 is the site of the **Yokohama Museum of Art** (Yokohama Bijutsukan, 横浜美術館), designed by Kenzō Tange. The 5,000 works in the permanent collection include paintings by both Western and Japanese artists, including Cézanne, Picasso, Braque, Klee, Kandinsky, Kishida Ryūsei, and Yokoyama Taikan. ⊠ *3–4–1 Minato Mirai, Nishi-ku* ☎ *045/221–0300* ⊠ *¥500* ⊙ *Mon.–Wed. and weekends 10–5:30, Fri. 10–7:30; closed day after a national holiday* Ⓜ *JR Line, Sakuragi-chō Station; Minato Mirai Line, Minato Mirai Station.*

⑰ On the east side of Minato Mirai 21, where the Ō-oka-gawa (Ō-oka River) flows into the bay, is **Nippon-maru Memorial Park** (日本丸メモリアルパーク). The centerpiece of the park is the *Nippon-maru,* a full-rigged three-masted ship popularly called the "Swan of the Pacific." Built in 1930 and now retired from service as a training vessel and an occasional participant in tall-ships festivals, it's open for guided tours. Adjacent to the ship is the **Yokohama Maritime Museum,** a two-story collection of ship models, displays, and archival materials that celebrate the achievements of the Port of Yokohama from its earliest days to the present. ⊠ *2–1–1 Minato Mirai, Nishi-ku* ☎ *045/221–0280* ⊠ *Ship and museum ¥600* ⊙ *Mar.–June and Sept. and Oct., daily 10–5; July and Aug., daily 10–6:30; Nov.–Feb., daily 10–4:30; closed day after a national holiday* Ⓜ *JR Line, Sakuragi-chō Station; Minato Mirai Line, Minato Mirai Station.*

⑱ The 70-story **Landmark Tower** (ランドマークタワー), in Yokohama's Minato Mirai, is Japan's tallest building. The observation deck on the 69th floor has a spectacular view of the city, especially at night; you reach it via a high-speed elevator that carries you up at an ear-popping 45 kph (28 mph). The Yokohama Royal Park Hotel occupies the top 20 stories of the building. On the first level of the Landmark Tower is the **Mitsubishi Minato Mirai Industrial Museum** (みなとみらい技術館), with rocket engines, power plants, a submarine, various gadgets, and displays that simulate piloting helicopters—great fun for kids.

The Landmark Tower complex's **Dockyard Garden,** built in 1896, is a restored dry dock with stepped sides of massive stone blocks. The long, narrow floor of the dock, with its water cascade at one end, makes a wonderful year-round venue for concerts and other events; in summer (July–mid-August), the beer garden installed here is a perfect refuge from the heat. ⊠ *3–3–1 Minato Mirai, Nishi-ku* ☎ *045/224–9031* ⊠ *Elevator to observation deck ¥1,000, museum ¥500* ⊙ *Museum Tues.–Sun. 10–5* Ⓜ *JR Line, Sakuragi-chō Station; Minato Mirai Line, Minato Mirai Station.*

⑲ The courtyard on the northeast side of the ⇨ **Landmark Tower** connects to **Queen's Square** (クイーンズスクエア), a huge atrium-style vertical mall with dozens of shops (mainly for clothing and accessories) and restaurants. The complex also houses the Pan Pacific Hotel Yokohama and Yokohama Minato Mirai Hall, the city's major venue for classical music. ✉ *Nishi-ku.*

🖑 ❷⓪ The **Yokohama Cosmo World** (よこはまコスモワールド) amusement park complex claims—among its 30 or so rides and attractions—the world's largest water-chute ride. It's west of Minato Mirai and Queen's Square, on both sides of the river. ✉ *11 Shin-minato-cho, Naka-ku* ☎ *045/641–6591* ▭ *Park free, rides ¥100–¥700 each* ⊙ *Mid-Mar.–Nov., weekdays 11–9, weekends 11–10; Dec.–mid-Mar., weekdays 11–8, weekends 11–9* Ⓜ *JR Line, Sakuragi-chō Station; Minato Mirai Line, Minato Mirai Station.*

❷① The **World Porters** (ワールドポーターズ) shopping center, on the opposite side of Yokohama Cosmo World, is notable chiefly for its restaurants that overlook the Minato Mirai area. Try arriving at sunset; the spectacular view of twinkling lights and the Landmark Tower, the Ferris wheel, and hotels will occasionally include Mt. Fuji in the background. Walking away from the waterfront area from World Porters will lead to **Aka Renga** (赤レンガ Redbrick Warehouses), two more shopping-and-entertainment facilities. ✉ *2–2–1 Shin-minato-cho, Naka-ku* ☎ *045/222–2000* ▭ *Free* ⊙ *Daily 10–9, restaurants until 11* Ⓜ *JR Line, Sakuragi-chō Station; Minato Mirai Line, Minato Mirai Station.*

off the beaten path

SŌJI-JI – One of the two major centers of the Sōtō sect of Zen Buddhism, Sōji-ji (総持寺), in Yokohama's Tsurumi ward, was founded in 1321. The center was moved here from Ishikawa, on the Noto Peninsula (on the Sea of Japan, north of Kanazawa), after a fire in the 19th century. There's also a Sōji-ji monastic complex at Eihei-ji in Fukui Prefecture. The Yokohama Sōji-ji is one of the largest and busiest Buddhist institutions in Japan, with more than 200 monks and novices in residence. The 14th-century patron of Sōji-ji was the emperor Go-Daigo, who overthrew the Kamakura Shogunate; the emperor is buried here, but his mausoleum is off-limits to visitors. However, you can see the **Buddha Hall,** the **Main Hall,** and the **Treasure House.** To get to Sōji-ji, take the JR Keihin Tōhoku Line two stops from Sakuragi-chō to Tsurumi. From the station walk five minutes south (back toward Yokohama), passing Tsurumi University on your right. You'll soon reach the stone lanterns that mark the entrance to the temple complex. ✉ *2–1–1 Tsurumi, Tsurumi-ku* ☎ *045/581–6021* ▭ *¥300* ⊙ *Daily dawn–dusk; Treasure House Tues.–Sun. 10–4.*

Where to Eat

$$$$ ✕ **Kaseiro** (華正樓). A smart Chinese restaurant with red carpets and gold-tone walls, Kaseiro serves Beijing cuisine—including, of course, Peking Duck and shark-fin soup—and is the best of its kind in the city. ✉ *164 Yamashita-chō, Chinatown, Naka-ku* ☎ *045/681–2918* ⋔ *Jacket and tie* ▭ *AE, DC, V.*

$$$$ ✕ **Scandia** (スカンディア). This Scandinavian restaurant near the Silk Center and the business district is known for its smorgasbord. It's popular for business lunches as well as for dinner. Scandia stays open until midnight, later than many other restaurants in the area. ⊠ *1–1 Kaigandōri, Naka-ku* ☎ *045/201–2262* ▭ *No credit cards* ☉ *No lunch Sun.*

$$$$ ✕ **Seryna** (瀬里奈). The hallmarks of this restaurant are *ishiyaki* steak, which is grilled on a hot stone, and shabu-shabu—thin slices of beef cooked in boiling water at your table and dipped in one of several sauces. "Shabu-shabu," by the way, is onomatapoeic for the sound the beef makes as you swish it through the water with your chopsticks. ⊠ *Shin-Kannai Bldg., B1, 4–45–1 Sumiyoshi-chō, Naka-ku* ☎ *045/681–2727* ▭ *AE, DC, MC, V.*

★ **$$$–$$$$** ✕ **Aichiya** (あいちや). One of the specialties at this seafood restaurant is fugu (blowfish)—a delicacy that must be treated with expert care, as chefs must remove organs that contain a deadly toxin before the fish can be consumed. Fugu is served only in winter. The crabs here are also a treat. Aichiya is open 3–10. ⊠ *7–156 Isezaki-chō, Naka-ku* ☎ *045/251–4163* 🏛 *Jacket and tie* ▭ *No credit cards* ☉ *Closed Mon.*

$$$–$$$$ ✕ **Rinka-en** (隣華苑). If you visit Sankei-en, you might want to have lunch at this traditional country restaurant, which serves kaiseki-style cuisine. The owner is the granddaughter of Hara Tomitaro, who donated the gardens of Sankei-en to the city. Rinka-en is open noon–5:30. ⊠ *Honmoku San-no-tani, Naka-ku* ☎ *045/621–0318* 🏛 *Jacket and tie* ▭ *No credit cards* ☉ *Closed Wed. and Aug. No dinner.*

$$–$$$$ ✕ **Rome Station** (ローマステーション). Rome Station, between Chinatown and Yamashita Park, is a popular venue for Italian food. The spaghetti *vongole* (with clam sauce) is particularly good. ⊠ *26 Yamashita-chō, Naka-ku* ☎ *045/681–1818* ▭ *No credit cards.*

★ **$$–$$$$** ✕ **Winds** (ウインズ). California-influenced cuisine, a spacious dining area, and windows that overlook the Minato Mirai waterfront make this one of Yokohama's finest restaurants. The seafood is particularly good; try the avocado-and-tuna entrée prepared with soy sauce and Japanese basil, or the linguine with sea crab. Winds has an extensive wine list of California labels. ⊠ *World Porters, 5F, 2–2–1 Shin-Minato-chō, Nishi-ku* ☎ *045/222–2570* ▭ *AE, MC, V.*

$$–$$$ ✕ **Saronikos** (サロニコス). The Akebono-chō district of Yokohama, west and south of Kannai Station, has long been home to a small cluster of Greek restaurants. Sailors off the Greek ships in port still drift over this way to bring gifts of feta cheese, spices, and *sirtaki* music tapes to friends and relatives of the owners. Saronikos is among the best of these restaurants, not the least because it invests more effort in the food than in tarted-up reproductions of the Parthenon and other pretensions to decor. Try the eggplant with garlic, the Greek salad, or the moussaka. Saronikos is open 6 PM–1 AM. ⊠ *3–30 Akebono-chō, Naka-ku* ☎ *045/251–8980* ▭ *No credit cards* ☉ *Closed 1st and 3rd Mon. of each month. No lunch.*

Yokohama A to Z

To research prices, get advice from other travelers, and book travel arrangements, visit www.fodors.com.

AIRPORTS & AIRPORT TRANSFERS
From Narita Airport, a direct limousine-bus service departs once or twice an hour between 6:45 AM and 10:20 PM for Yokohama City Air Ter-

minal (YCAT). The fare is ¥3,500. YCAT is a five-minute taxi ride from Yokohama Station. JR Narita Express trains going on from Tōkyō to Yokohama leave the airport every hour from 8:13 AM to 1:13 PM and 2:43 PM to 9:43 PM. The fare is ¥4,180 (¥6,730 for the first-class Green Car coaches). Or you can take the limousine-bus service from Narita to Tōkyō Station and continue on to Yokohama by train. Either way, the journey will take more than two hours—closer to three, if traffic is heavy.

The Airport Limousine Information Desk phone number provides information in English daily 9–6; you can also get timetables on its Web site. For information in English on Narita Express trains, call the JR Higashi-Nihon Info Line, available daily 10–6.

🈂 **Airport Limousine Information Desk** ☎ 03/3665-7220 ⊕ www.limousinebus.co.jp. **JR Higashi-Nihon Info Line** ☎ 03/3423-0111.

BUS TRAVEL

Most of the things you'll want to see in Yokohama are within easy walking distance of a JR or subway station, but this city is so much more negotiable than Tōkyō that exploring by bus is a viable alternative. Buses, in fact, are the best way to get to Sankei-en. The city map available in the visitor centers in Yokohama and Shin-Yokohama stations has most major bus routes marked on it, and the important stops on the tourist routes are announced in English. The fixed fare is ¥210. One-day passes are also available for ¥600 (contact the tourist office at Yokohama Station for more information).

EMERGENCIES

The Yokohama Police station has a Foreign Assistance Department.

🈂 **Ambulance or Fire** ☎ 119. **Police** ☎ 110. **Washinzaka Hospital** ✉ 169 Yamate-chō, Naka-ku ☎ 045/623-7688. **Yokohama Police station** ☎ 045/623-0110.

ENGLISH-LANGUAGE MEDIA

BOOKS Yūrindō has a good selection of popular paperbacks and books on Japan in English. The Minato-Mirai branch is open daily 11–8; the store on Isezaki-chō opens an hour earlier.

🈂 **Yūrindō** ✉ Landmark Plaza 5F, 3-3-1 Minato-Mirai, Nishi-ku ☎ 045/222-5500 ✉ 1-4-1 Isezaki-chō, Naka-ku ☎ 045/261-1231.

SUBWAY TRAVEL

One subway line connects Azamino, Shin-Yokohama, Yokohama, Totsuka, and Shōnandai. The basic fare is ¥200. One-day passes are also available for ¥740. The Minato Mirai Line, a spur of the Tōkyū Tōyoko Line, runs from Yokohama Station to all the major points of interest, including Minato Mirai, Chinatown, Yamashita Park, Moto-machi, and Basha-michi. The fare is ¥180–¥200, and one-day unlimited-ride passes are available for ¥450.

TAXIS

There are taxi stands at all the train stations, and you can always flag a cab on the street. Vacant taxis show a red light in the windshield. The basic fare is ¥660 for the first 2 km (1 mi), then ¥80 for every additional

350 meters (⅕ mi). Traffic is heavy in downtown Yokohama, however, and you will often find it faster to walk.

TOURS

Teiki Yuran Bus offers a full-day (9–3:45) sightseeing bus tour that covers the major sights and includes lunch at a Chinese restaurant in Chinatown. The tour is in Japanese only, but pamphlets written in English are available at most sightseeing stops. Buy tickets (¥6,360) at the bus offices at Yokohama Station (east side) and at Kannai Station; the tour departs daily at 9 AM from Bus Stop 14, on the east side of Yokohama Station. A half-day tour is also available, with lunch (9:30–1, ¥3,850) or without (2–5:30, ¥3,000).

The sightseeing boat *Marine Shuttle* makes 40-, 60-, and 90-minute tours of the harbor and bay for ¥900, ¥1,400, and ¥2,000, respectively. Boarding is at the pier at Yamashita Park. Boats depart roughly every hour between 10:20 AM and 6:30 PM. Another boat, the *Marine Rouge,* runs 90-minute tours departing from the pier at 11, 1:30, and 4, and a special two-hour evening tour at 7 (¥2,500).

🚩 Tour Contact *Marine Shuttle* ☎ 045/671-7719.

TRAIN TRAVEL

JR trains from Tōkyō Station leave approximately every 10 minutes, depending on the time of day. Take the Yokosuka, the Tōkaidō, or Keihin Tōhoku Line to Yokohama Station (the Yokosuka and Tōkaidō lines take 30 minutes; the Keihin Tōhoku Line takes 40 minutes). From there the Keihin Tōhoku Line (Platform 3) goes on to Kannai and Ishikawa-chō, Yokohama's business and downtown areas. If you're going directly to downtown Yokohama from Tōkyō, the blue commuter trains of the Keihin Tōhoku Line are best. The private Tōkyū Tōyoko Line, which runs from Shibuya Station in Tōkyō directly to Yokohama Station, is a good alternative if you leave from the western part of Tōkyō.

Yokohama Station is the hub that links all the train lines and connects them with the city's subway and bus services. Kannai and Ishikawa-chō are the two downtown stations, both on the Keihin Tōhoku Line; trains leave Yokohama Station every two to five minutes from Platform 3. From Sakuragi-chō, Kannai, or Ishikawa-chō, most of Yokohama's points of interest are within easy walking distance; the one notable exception is Sankei-en, which you reach via the JR Keihin Tōhoku Line to Negishi Station and then a local bus.

VISITOR INFORMATION

The Yokohama International Tourist Association arranges visits to the homes of English-speaking Japanese families. These usually last a few hours and are designed to give *gaijin* (foreigners) a glimpse into the Japanese way of life.

The Yokohama Tourist Office, in the central passageway of Yokohama Station, is open daily 9–7 (closed December 28–January 3). A similar office with the same closing times is in Shin-Yokohama Station. The head office of the Yokohama Convention & Visitors Bureau, open weekdays 9–5 (except national holidays and December 29–January 3), is in the Sangyō Bōeki Center Building, across from Yamashita Kōen. **🗷 Tourist Information** **Yokohama Convention & Visitors Bureau** ✉ 2 Yamashita-chō, Naka-ku ☎ 045/221-2111. **Yokohama International Tourist Association** ☎ 045/641-4759. **Yokohama Tourist Office** ✉ Yokohama Station, Nishi-ku ☎ 045/441-7300 ✉ Shin-Yokohama Station, Tsurumi-ku ☎ 045/473-2895.

FUJI-HAKONE-IZU
NATIONAL PARK 富士箱根伊豆国立公園

Fuji-Hakone-Izu National Park, southwest of Tōkyō between Suruga and Sagami bays, is one of Japan's most popular resort areas. The region's main attraction, of course, is Mt. Fuji, a dormant volcano—it last erupted in 1707—rising to a height of 12,388 feet. The mountain is truly beautiful, utterly captivating in the ways it can change in different light and from different perspectives. Its symmetry and majesty have been immortalized by poets and artists for centuries. Keep in mind that during spring and summer, Mt. Fuji often hides behind a blanket of clouds, to the disappointment of the crowds of tourists who travel to Hakone or the Fuji Five Lakes to see it.

Apart from Mt. Fuji itself, each of the three areas of the park—the Izu Peninsula, Hakone and environs, and the Five Lakes—has its own unique appeal. Izu is defined by its dramatic rugged coastline, beaches, and *onsen* (hot springs). Hakone has mountains, volcanic landscapes, and lake cruises, plus onsen of its own. The Five Lakes form a recreational area with some of the best views of Mt. Fuji. And in each of these areas there are monuments to Japan's past.

Although it's possible to make a grand tour of all three areas at one time, most people make each of them a separate excursion from Tōkyō. Because these are tourist attractions where people are accustomed to foreign visitors, there's always someone to help out in English if you want to explore off the beaten path.

Trains will serve you well in traveling to major points anywhere in the northern areas of the national-park region and down the eastern coast of the Izu Peninsula. For the west coast and central mountains of Izu, there are no train connections; unless you are intrepid enough to rent a car, the only way to get around is by bus.

Numbers in the text correspond to numbers in the margin and on the Fuji-Hakone-Izu National Park map.

Izu Peninsula 伊豆半島

Atami 熱海

❶ *48 min southwest of Tōkyō by Kodama Shinkansen.*

The gateway to the Izu Peninsula is Atami. Most Japanese travelers make it no farther into the peninsula than this town on Sagami Bay, so Atami itself has a fair number of hotels and traditional inns. When you arrive, collect a map from the **Atami Tourist Information Office**

(熱海市観光協会, ☎ 0557/85–2222) at the train station to guide you to the sights below.

★ The **MOA Museum of Art** (MOA Bijutsukan, MOA 美術館) houses the private collection of the messianic religious leader Okada Mokichi. Okada (1882–1955), who founded a movement called the Sekai Kyūsei Kyō (Religion for the Salvation of the World), also acquired more than 3,000 works of art, dating from the Asuka period (6th and 7th centuries) to the present day. Among these works are several particularly fine *ukiyo-e* (Edo-era wood-block prints) and ceramics. On a hill above the station and set in a garden full of old plum trees and azaleas, the museum also affords a sweeping view over Atami and the bay. ⊠ *26–2 Momoyama* ☎ *0557/84–2511* ✆ *¥1,600* ⊙ *Fri.–Wed. 9:30–5.*

Barely worth the 15-minute walk from Atami Station is the **Ōyu Geyser,** which used to gush on schedule once every 24 hours but stopped after the Great Kantō Earthquake of 1923. Not happy with this, the local chamber of commerce rigged a pump to raise the geyser for four out of every five minutes and gives it top billing in its tourist brochures.

The best time to visit the **Atami Plum Garden** (Atami Bai-en, 熱海梅園) is in late January or early February, when its 850 trees bloom. If you do visit, also stop by the small shrine in the shadow of an enormous old camphor tree: the tree has been designated a National Monument. Atami Bai-en is 15 minutes by bus from Atami or an eight-minute walk from Kinomiya Station, the next stop south of Atami served by local trains.

If you have the time and the inclination for a beach picnic, it's worth taking the 25-minute high-speed ferry (round-trip ¥2,340) from the pier over to **Hatsu-shima** (初島, ☎ 0557/81–0541 for ferry). There are nine departures daily between 7:30 and 5:20. You can easily walk around the island, which is only 4 km (2½ mi) in circumference, in less than two hours. Use of the **Picnic Garden** (open daily 10–3) is free.

WHERE TO STAY

★ **$$$$** ▦ **Taikansō** (熱海大観荘). The views of the sea must have been the inspiration for Yokoyama Taikan, the Japanese artist who once owned this villa that is now a traditional Japanese inn with exquisite furnishings and individualized service. The prices (¥31,000–¥47,000) are high, but bear in mind that they include a multicourse dinner of great artistry, served in your room, and breakfast the next morning. There are also indoor and outdoor hot-springs baths. The inn is a 10-minute walk from Atami Station. ⊠ *7–1 Hayashi-ga-oka-chō, Atami, Shizuoka-ken 413-0031* ☎ *0557/81–8137* ▤ *0557/83–5308* ⊕ *www.atami-taikanso.com* ⤴ *44 Japanese-style rooms with bath* ⚭ *Restaurant, pool, hot springs, sauna, meeting rooms* ▭ *AE, DC, MC, V* ❙◯❙ *MAP.*

$$–$$$$ ▦ **New Fujiya Hotel** (ニュー富士屋ホテル). Only the top rooms have a view of the sea at this modern, inland resort hotel, which makes a useful base for sightseeing. Service is impersonal but professional, and a foreign visitor is no cause for consternation. The hotel is a five-minute taxi ride from Atami Station. ⊠ *1–16 Ginza-chō, Atami, Shizuoka-ken 413-0013* ☎ *0557/81–0111* ⤴ *158 Western-style rooms with bath, 158 Japanese-style rooms with bath* ⚭ *3 restaurants, indoor pool, hot springs, bar* ▭ *AE, DC, MC, V.*

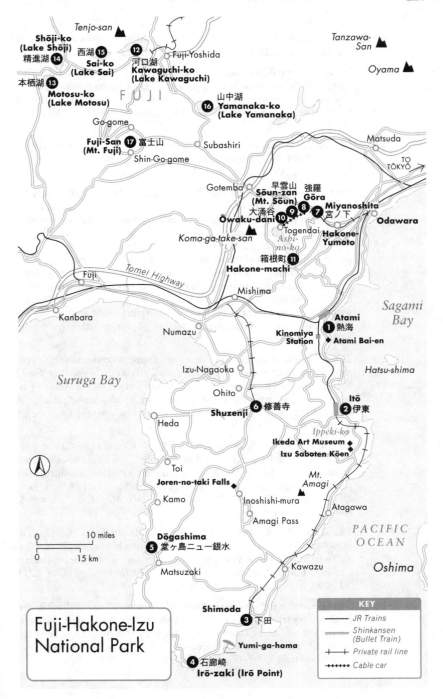

Tenjo-san

Shōji-ko (Lake Shōji) 精進湖 **⑭**

西湖 **⑮** **Sai-ko (Lake Sai)**

⑫ 河口湖 **Kawaguchi-ko (Lake Kawaguchi)**

Fuji-Yoshida

Tanzawa-San

Oyama

本栖湖 **⑬** **Motosu-ko (Lake Motosu)**

F U J I

山中湖 **⑯** **Yamanaka-ko (Lake Yamanaka)**

Matsuda

Go-gome

Fuji-San (Mt. Fuji) **⑰** 富士山

Subashiri

TO TŌKYŌ

Shin-Go-gome

Gotemba

早雲山 **Sōun-zan (Mt. Sōun)** 強羅 **Gōra**

⑧ **⑦** 宮ノ下 **Miyanoshita**

大涌谷 **Ōwaku-dani** **⑩** **⑨**

Hakone-Yumoto

Odawara

Koma-ga-take-san

Togendai

Ashi-no-ko

箱根町 **⑪** **Hakone-machi**

Sagami Bay

Tomei Highway

Fuji

Mishima

Kanbara

Atami **①** 熱海

Kinomiya Station

◆ **Atami Bai-en**

Numazu

Suruga Bay

Izu-Nagaoka

Hatsu-shima

Ohito

Shuzenji **⑥** 修善寺

Itō **②** 伊東

Heda

Ippeki-ko

Ikeda Art Museum ◆

Izu Saboten Kōen

Toi

Mt. Amagi

Joren-no-taki Falls ◆

Kamo

Inoshishi-mura

Amagi Pass

PACIFIC OCEAN

Atagawa

0 _____ 10 miles

0 _____ 15 km

Dōgashima **⑤** 堂ヶ島ニュー銀水

Kawazu

Oshima

Matsuzaki

Shimoda **③** 下田

Yumi-ga-hama

④ 石廊崎 **Irō-zaki (Irō Point)**

Fuji-Hakone-Izu National Park

KEY

—— JR Trains

══ Shinkansen (Bullet Train)

+-+-+ Private rail line

+++++ Cable car

Itō 伊東

② *25 min south of Atami by JR local; 1 hr, 40 min southwest of Tōkyō via Atami by Kodama Shinkansen, then JR local.*

There are some 800 thermal springs in the resort area surrounding Itō, 16 km (10 mi) south of Atami. These springs—and the beautiful, rocky, indented coastline nearby—remain the resort's major attractions, although there are plenty of interesting sights here. Some 150 hotels and inns serve the area.

Itō traces its history of associations with the West to 1604, when William Adams (1564–1620), the Englishman whose adventures served as the basis for James Clavell's novel *Shōgun*, came ashore.

Four years earlier Adams had beached his disabled Dutch vessel, *De Liefde,* on the shores of Kyūshū and became the first Englishman to set foot on Japan. The authorities, believing that he and his men were Portuguese pirates, put Adams in prison, but he was eventually befriended by the shōgun Ieyasu Tokugawa, who brought him to Edo (present-day Tōkyō) and granted him an estate. Ieyasu appointed Adams his adviser on foreign affairs. The English castaway taught mathematics, geography, gunnery, and navigation to shogunal officials and in 1604 was ordered to build an 80-ton Western-style ship. Pleased with this venture, Ieyasu ordered the construction of a larger ocean-going vessel. These two ships were built at Itō, where Adams lived from 1605 to 1610.

This history was largely forgotten until British Commonwealth occupation forces began coming to Itō for rest and recuperation after World War II. Adams's memory was revived, and since then the Anjin Festival (the Japanese gave Adams the name *anjin,* which means "pilot") has been held in his honor every August. A monument to the Englishman stands at the mouth of the river.

Izu Cactus Park (Izu Saboten Kōen, 伊豆サボテン公園) consists of a series of pyramidal greenhouses that contain 5,000 kinds of cacti from around the world. At the base of Komuro-san (Mt. Komuro), the park is 20 minutes south of Itō Station by bus. ⊠ *1317-13 Futo* ☎ *0557/51–5553* ⊠ *¥1,800, ¥800 after 5* ☉ *Mar.–Oct., daily 9–5; Nov.–Feb., daily 9–4.*

The **Ikeda 20th-Century Art Museum** (Ikeda 20-Seiki Bijutsukan, 池田20世紀美術館), at Lake Ippeki, houses works by Picasso, Dalí, Chagall, and Matisse, plus a number of wood-block prints. The museum is a 15-minute walk from Izu Cactus Park. ⊠ *614 Totari* ☎ *0557/45–2211* ⊠ *¥900* ☉ *Thurs.–Tues. 10–4:30.*

On the east side of **Komuro-san Kōen** (Mt. Komuro Park, 小室山公園) are 3,000 cherry trees of 35 varieties that bloom at various times throughout the year. A cable car takes you to the top of the mountain. The park is about 20 minutes south of Itō Station by bus. ⊠ *Free; round-trip cable car to mountain top ¥400* ☉ *Daily 9–4.*

ONSEN

JAPAN'S BIGGEST NATURAL HEADACHE—
the slip and slide of vast tectonic plates
deep below the archipelago that spawn
volcanoes and make earthquakes an
everyday fact of life—provides one of
Japan's greatest delights as well: thermal
baths. Wherever there are volcanic
mountains—and Japan is mostly volcanic
mountains—you can usually count on
drilling or tapping into springs of hot
water, rich in all sorts of restorative
minerals. Any place where this happens is
called, generically, an onsen; any place
where lots of spas have tapped these
sources, to cash in on the Japanese
passion for total immersion, is an onsen
chiiki (hot-springs resort area). The Izu
Peninsula is particularly rich in onsen. It
has, in fact, one-fifth of the 2,300-odd
officially recognized hot springs in Japan.

The spas in famous areas like Shuzenji take
many forms. The ne plus ultra is that small
secluded Japanese inn up in the mountains,
where you sleep on futons, in a setting of
almost poetic traditional furnishings and
design. Such an inn will have for the
exclusive use of its guests a rotemburo, an
open-air mineral-spring pool, usually in a
screened-off nook with a panoramic view.
For a room in one of these inns on a
weekend or in high season, you often have
to book months in advance. (High season is
late December to early January, late April to
early May, the second and third weeks of
August, and the second and third weeks of
October.) More typical is the large resort
hotel, geared mainly to groups, with one or
more large indoor mineral baths of its own.
Where whole towns and villages have
developed to exploit a local supply of hot
water, there will be several of these large
hotels, an assortment of smaller inns, and
probably a few modest public bathhouses,
with no accommodations, where you just
pay an entrance fee for a soak of whatever
length you wish.

The first challenge in bathing is
acknowledging that your Japanese bath
mates will stare at your body. Take solace,
however, in the fact that their apparent
voyeurism most likely stems from curiosity.
The second challenge is figuring out what
is required of you before you enter the hot
pool. Japanese custom dictates that your
body must be completely clean before
entering a communal pool. So help
yourself to the towels, soap, and shampoo
set out for this purpose, and grab a bucket
and a stool. At one of the shower stations
around the edge of the room, crouch on
your bucket (or stand if you prefer) and
use the handheld showers to wash yourself
thoroughly. A head-to-toe twice-over will
impress onlookers. Rinse off, and then you
may enter the public bath. All you need to
do then is lean back, relax, and
experience the pleasures of Shintō-style
purification—cleanse your body and
enlighten your spirit.

en route South of Itō the coastal scenery is lovely—each sweep around a headland reveals another picturesque sight of a rocky, indented shoreline. There are several spa towns en route to Shimoda. Higashi-Izu (East Izu) has numerous hot-springs resorts, of which **Atagawa** is the most fashionable. South of Atagawa is **Kawazu,** a place of relative quiet and solitude, with pools in the forested mountainside and waterfalls plunging through lush greenery.

Shimoda 下田
❸ *1 hr south of Itō by Izu Railways.*

Of all the resort towns south of Itō along Izu's eastern coast, none can match the distinction of Shimoda. Shimoda's encounter with the West began when Commodore Matthew Perry, bearing a commission from the U.S. government to open—by force, if necessary—diplomatic relations with Japan, anchored his fleet of black ships off the coast here in 1853. To commemorate the event, the three-day Black Ship Festival (Kurofune Matsuri) is held here every year in mid-May. Shimoda was also the site, in 1856, of the first American consulate.

The **Shimoda tourist office** (下田市観光協会, ☎ 0558/22–1531), in front of the station, has the easiest of the local English itineraries to follow. The 2½-km (1½-mi) tour covers most major sights. On request, the tourist office will also help you find local accommodations.

The first American consul to Japan was New York businessman Townsend Harris. Soon after his arrival in Shimoda, Harris asked the Japanese authorities to provide him with a female servant; they sent him a young girl named Saitō Okichi. The arrangement brought her only a new name—Tōjin (the Foreigner's) Okichi—and a tragic end. Harris soon sent her away, compounding poor Okichi's shame and ridicule. She tried and failed to rejoin a former lover, moved to Yokohama, and later returned to Shimoda in an unsuccessful attempt to run a restaurant. Okichi took to drink and drowned herself in 1890. Her tale is recounted in Rei Kimura's biographical novel *Butterfly in the Wind.* **Hōfuku-ji** (宝福寺) was Okichi's family temple. The museum annex displays a life-size image of her, and just behind the temple is her grave—where incense is still kept burning in her memory. The grave of her lover, Tsurumatsu, is at Tōden-ji, a temple about midway between Hōfuku-ji and Shimoda Station. ⊠ *18–26 1-chōme* ☎ *0558/22–0960* 🔁 *¥300* ☉ *Daily 8–5.*

Ryosen-ji (了仙寺) is the temple in which the negotiations took place that led to the United States–Japan Treaty of Amity and Commerce of 1858. The **Treasure Hall** (Hōmotsu-den) contains some personal articles that belonged to Tōjin Okichi. ⊠ *3–12–12 Shimoda* ☎ *0558/22–2805* 🔁 *Treasure Hall ¥500* ☉ *Daily 8:30–5.*

WHERE TO STAY
$$-$$$$ 🏨 **Shimoda Prince Hotel** (下田プリンスホテル). This modern V-shape resort hotel faces the Pacific, steps away from a white-sand beach. The decor is more functional than aesthetic, but the panoramic view of the ocean from the picture windows in the dining room makes this one of the best hotels in town. The Prince is just outside Shimoda, 10 minutes by taxi

from the station. ⊠ *1547–1 Shira-hama, Shimoda, Shizuoka-ken 415-8525* ☎ *0558/22–2111* 🖷 *0558/22–7584* ⊕ *www.princehotels.co.jp* 🛏 *70 Western-style rooms with bath, 6 Japanese-style rooms with bath* 🍴 *2 restaurants, 3 tennis courts, pool, hot springs, sauna, bar, nightclub, shops* ⊟ *AE, DC, MC, V.*

\$\$–\$\$\$\$ 🏨 **Shimoda Tokyū Hotel** (下田東急ホテル). Perched just above the bay, the Shimoda Tokyū has impressive views of the Pacific from one side (where rooms cost about 10% more) and mountains from the other. Unlike at most Japanese resort hotels, the lobby here is full of character and warmth, with an airy layout and floor-to-ceiling windows overlooking the bay. Prices are significantly higher in midsummer. ⊠ *5–12–1 Shimoda, Shimoda, Shizuoka-ken 415-8510* ☎ *0558/22–2411* ⊕ *www.tokyuhotels.co.jp* 🛏 *107 Western-style rooms with bath, 8 Japanese-style rooms with bath* 🍴 *3 restaurants, café, pool, hot springs, bar, shops* ⊟ *AE, DC, MC, V.*

¢ 🏨 **Pension Sakuraya** (ペンション桜家). There are a few Western-style bedrooms at this family-run inn just a few minutes' walk from Shimoda's main beach, but the best lodgings are the Japanese-style corner rooms, which have nice views of the hills surrounding Shimoda. The pleasant Japanese couple who run the pension speak English, and cheap meals are available in the dining room. Sakuraya has a wireless LAN network for PC users. ⊠ *2584–20 Shira-hama, Shimoda, Shizuoka-ken 415-0012* ☎ *0558/23–4470* 🖷 *0558/27–2130* 🛏 *4 Western-style rooms with bath, 5 Japanese-style rooms without bath* ⊕ *http://izu-sakuraya.jp/english* 🍴 *Dining room, Japanese baths, laundry facilities, Internet* ⊟ *AE, DC, MC, V.*

> **en route** The bus from Shimoda Station stops at **Yumi-ga-hama** (弓ヶ浜), one of the prettiest sandy beaches on the whole Izu Peninsula, before continuing to Irō-zaki, the last stop on the route.

Irō-zaki (Irō Point) 石廊崎
❹ *40 min by bus or boat from Shimoda.*

If you visit Irō-zaki, the southernmost part of the Izu Peninsula, in January, you're in for a special treat: a blanket of daffodils covers the cape. From the bus stop at the end of the line from Shimoda Station, it's a short walk to the **Irō-zaki Jungle Park** (石廊崎ジャングルパーク), with its 3,000 varieties of colorful tropical plants. Beyond the park you can walk to a lighthouse at the edge of the cliff. ⊠ *546–1 Irō-zaki, Minami-Izu* ☎ *0558/65–0050* 🎟 *¥900* ⊙ *Daily 8–5.*

Dōgashima 堂ヶ島
❺ *1 hr northwest of Shimoda by bus.*

The sea has eroded the coastal rock formations into fantastic shapes near the little port town of Dōgashima. A **Dōgashima Marine** (堂ヶ島マリン, ☎ *0558/52–0013*) sightseeing boat from Dōgashima Pier makes 20-minute runs to see the rocks (¥920). In an excess of kindness, a recorded loudspeaker—which you can safely ignore—recites the name of every rock you pass on the trip. The **Nishi-Izu Tourist Office** (西伊豆町観光協会, ☎ *0558/52–1268*) is near the pier, in the small building behind the bus station.

WHERE TO STAY

$$$$

🏠 **Dōgashima New Ginsui** (堂ヶ島ニュー銀水). Every guest room overlooks the sea at the New Ginsui, which sits atop cliffs above the water. This is the smartest luxury resort on Izu's west coast. Service is first class, despite its popularity with tour groups. The room rate includes a seafood kaiseki dinner served in your room and a buffet breakfast. ✉ *2977–1 Nishina, Nishi-Izu-chō, Dōgashima, Shizuoka-ken 410-3514* ☎ *0558/ 52–2211* 📠 *0558/52–1210* 🛏 *90 Japanese-style rooms with bath* ⚫ *Restaurant, 2 pools, hot springs, spa, nightclub, shops, laundry services, concierge, meeting rooms* ▭ *AE, DC, MC, V* 🍴 *MAP.*

Shuzenji 修善寺

6 *2 hrs north of Shimoda by bus, 32 min south of Mishima by Izu-Hakone Railway.*

Shuzenji—a hot-springs resort in the center of the peninsula, along the valley of the Katsura-gawa (Katsura River)—enjoys a certain historical notoriety as the place where the second Kamakura shōgun, Minamoto no Yoriie, was assassinated early in the 13th century. Don't judge the town by the area around the station; most of the hotels and hot springs are 2 km (1 mi) to the west.

If you've planned a longer visit to Izu, consider spending a night at **Inoshishi-mura** (いのしし村), en route by bus between Shimoda and Shuzenji. The scenery in this part of the peninsula is dramatic, and the specialty of the house at the local inns is roast mountain boar. In the morning, a pleasant 15-minute walk from Inoshishi-mura brings you to **Joren Falls** (Joren-no-taki).

WHERE TO STAY

★ $$$$

🏠 **Ryokan Sanyōsō** (旅館三養荘). The former villa of the Iwasaki family, founders of the Mitsubishi conglomerate, is as luxurious and beautiful a place to stay as you'll find on the Izu Peninsula. Museum-quality antiques furnish the rooms, the best of which have traditional baths made of fragrant cypress wood and overlooking exquisite little private gardens (note that these high-end rooms cost as much as ¥70,000). Breakfast and dinner, served in your room, are included in the rate. The Sanyōsō is a five-minute taxi ride from Izu-Nagaoka Station. ✉ *270 Mama-no-ue, Izu-Nagaoka-chō, Shizuoka-ken 410-2204* ☎ *0559/ 47–1111* 📠 *0559/47–0610* 🛏 *21 Western and Japanese-style rooms with bath* ⚫ *Restaurant, Japanese baths, bar, shops, laundry service, meeting rooms* ▭ *AE, DC, MC, V.*

$$ 🏠 **Kyorai-An Matsushiro-kan** (去来庵 松城館). Although this small family-owned inn five minutes by bus or taxi from Izu-Nagaoka Station is nothing fancy, the owners make you feel like a guest in their home. They also speak some English. Japanese meals are served in a common dining room. Room-only reservations (without meals) are accepted only on weekdays. ✉ *55 Kona, Izu-Nagaoka, Shizuoka-ken 410-2201* ☎ *0559/48–0072* 📠 *0559/48–4030* 🛏 *16 Japanese-style rooms with bath* ⚫ *Dining room* ▭ *AE, DC, MC, V* 🍴 *MAP.*

¢ 🏠 **Goyōkan** (五葉館). This family-run ryokan on Shuzenji's main street has rooms that look out on the Katsura-gawa, plus gorgeous stone-lined (for men) and wood-lined (for women) indoor hot springs. The staff speaks English and can make sightseeing arrangements for you. ✉ *765–2*

RYOKAN ETIQUETTE

UPON ENTERING, *take off your shoes, as you would do in a Japanese household, and put on the slippers that are provided in the entryway. A maid, after bowing to welcome you, will escort you to your room, which will have tatami (straw mats) on the floor and will probably be partitioned off with shōji (sliding paper-paneled walls). Remove your slippers before entering your room; you should not step on the tatami with either shoes or slippers. The room will have little furniture or decoration—perhaps one small low table and cushions on the tatami, with a long, simple scroll on the wall. Often the rooms overlook a garden.*

Plan to arrive in the late afternoon, as is the custom. After relaxing with a cup of green tea, have a long, hot bath. In ryokan with thermal pools, you can take to the waters anytime, although the doors to the pool are usually locked from 11 PM to 6 AM. In ryokan without thermal baths or private baths in guest rooms, guests must stagger visits to the one or two public baths. Typically the maid will ask what time you would like your bath and fit you into a schedule. In Japanese baths, washing and soaking are separate functions: wash and rinse off entirely, and then get in the tub. Be sure to keep all soap out of the tub. Because other guests will be using the same bathwater after you, it is important to observe this custom. After your bath, change into a yukata, a simple cotton kimono, provided in your room. Don't worry about walking around in what is essentially a robe—all other guests will be doing the same.

Dinner, included in the price, is served in your room at smaller and more personal ryokan; at larger ryokan, especially the newer ones, meals will be in the dining room. After you are finished, a maid will discreetly come in, clear away the dishes, and lay out your futon. In Japan futon means bedding, and this consists of a thin cotton mattress and a heavy, thick comforter. In summer the comforter is replaced with a thinner quilt. The small, hard pillow is filled with grain. The less expensive ryokan (under ¥7,000 for one) have become slightly lackadaisical in changing the sheet cover over the quilt with each new guest; feel free to complain (in as inoffensive a way as possible, of course, so as not to shame the proprietor). In the morning a maid will gently wake you, clear away the futon, and bring in your Japanese-style breakfast. If you are not fond of Japanese breakfasts, which often consist of fish, pickled vegetables, and rice, the staff will usually be able to rustle up some coffee and toast.

Because most ryokan staffs are small and dedicated, it is important to be considerate and understanding of their somewhat rigid schedules. Guests are expected to arrive in the late afternoon and eat around 6. Usually the doors to the inn are locked at 10, so plan for early evenings. Breakfast is served around 8, and checkout is at 10.

Bear in mind that not all inns are willing to accept foreign guests because of language and cultural barriers. This makes calling ahead for a room important so you can be sure to get one. Also, top-level ryokan expect even new Japanese guests to have introductions and references from a respected client of the inn, which means that you, too, might need an introduction from a Japanese for very top-level ryokan. On the other side of this issue, inns that do accept foreigners without introduction sometimes treat them as cash cows, which means giving you cursory service and a lesser room. When you reserve a room, try to have a Japanese make the call for you, or you can do it yourself if you know Japanese; this will convey the idea that you understand the customs of staying in a traditional inn.

Shuzenji-chō, Tagata-gun, Shizuoka-ken 410-24 ☎ 0558/72–2066
⊕ *www.goyokan.co.jp/english* ⌇ *11 Japanese-style rooms without*
bath ⌂ Refrigerators, hot springs, sauna ▤ AE, DC, MC, V.

Hakone 箱根

The national park and resort area of Hakone is a popular day trip from
Tōkyō and a good place for a close-up view of Mt. Fuji (assuming the
mountain is not swathed in clouds, as often happens in summer). Note
that on summer weekends it often seems as though all of Tōkyō has come
out to Hakone with you. Expect long lines at cable cars and traffic jams
everywhere.

You can cover the best of Hakone in a one-day trip out of Tōkyō, but
if you want to try the curative powers of the thermal waters or do some
hiking, then stay overnight. Two of the best areas are around the old
hot-springs resort of Miyanoshita and the western side of Koma-ga-take-
san (Mt. Koma-ga-take).

The typical Hakone route, outlined here, may sound complex, but this
is in fact one excursion from Tōkyō so well defined that you really can't
get lost—no more so, at least, than any of the thousands of Japanese
tourists ahead of and behind you. The first leg of the journey is from
Odawara or Hakone-Yumoto by train and cable car through the mountains to Tōgendai, on the north shore of Ashi-no-ko (Lake Ashi). The
scenery en route is spectacular, but if you have problems with vertigo
you might be better off on the bus. The long way around, from Odawara
to Tōgendai by bus, takes about an hour—in heavy traffic, an hour and
a half. The trip over the mountains, on the other hand, will take about
two hours. Credit the difference to the Hakone Tozan Tetsudō Line—
possibly the slowest train you'll ever ride. Using three switchbacks to
inch its way up the side of the mountain, the train takes 54 minutes to
travel the 16 km (10 mi) from Odawara to Gōra (38 minutes from
Hakone-Yumoto). The steeper it gets, the grander the view.

Trains do not stop at any station en route for any length of time, but
they do run frequently enough to allow you to disembark, visit a sight,
❼ and catch another train. **Miyanoshita** (宮ノ下), the first stop on the train
route from Hakone-Yumoto, is a small but very pleasant and popular
resort. Especially charming is the 19th-century Western-style **Fujiya
Hotel** here. Even if you're not staying at the hotel, drop in for a morning coffee on the first floor overlooking the garden. Before you leave
the hotel, take a peek at the vintage collection of old books and magazines in the library.

★ The **Hakone Open-Air Museum** (Hakone Chōkoku-no-mori Bijutsukan,
箱根彫刻の森美術館) houses an astonishing collection of 19th- and 20th-cen-
tury Western and Japanese sculpture, most of it on display in a spacious,
handsome garden. There are works here by Rodin, Moore, Arp, Calder,
Giacometti, Takeshi Shimizu, and Kōtarō Takamura. One section of the
garden is devoted to Emilio Greco. Inside are works by Picasso, Léger,
and Manzo, among others. The museum is within a minute's walk of
Miyanoshita Station; directions are posted in English. ✉ *1121 Mi-no-*

taira ☎0460/2–1161 ⊕*www.hakone-oam.or.jp* ✉¥1,600 ⊙*Mar.–Nov., daily 9–5; Dec.–Feb., daily 9–4.*

❽ **Gōra** (強羅), a small town at the end of the train line from Odawara and the lower end of the Sōun-zan cable car, is a good jumping-off point for hiking and exploring. Ignore the little restaurants and souvenir stands here: get off the train as quickly as you can and make a dash for the cable car at the other end of the station. If you let the rest of the passengers get there before you, and perhaps a tour bus or two, you may stand 45 minutes in line.

❾ The cable car from Gōra up to **Sōun-zan** (Mt. Sōun, 早雲山) departs every 20 minutes and takes 10 minutes (¥410; free with the Hakone Free Pass) to the top. There are four stops en route, and you can get off and reboard the cable car at any one of them if you've paid the full fare. At Kōen-kami, the second stop on the cable car from Gōra, is the **Hakone Museum of Art** (Hakone Bijutsukan), sister institution to the MOA Museum of Art in Atami. The museum, which consists of two buildings set in a garden, houses a modest collection of porcelain and ceramics from China, Korea, and Japan. ⊠ *1300 Gōra* ☎ *0460/2–2623* ✉ *¥900* ⊙ *Apr.–Nov., Fri.–Wed. 9:30–4:30; Dec.–Mar., Fri.–Wed. 9:30–4.*

★ ❿ At the cable-car terminus of Sōun-zan a gondola swings up over a ridge and crosses the valley called **Ōwaku-dani** (大涌谷) on its way to Tōgendai. The landscape here is blasted and desolate, with sulfurous billows of steam escaping through holes from some inferno deep in the earth—yet another reminder that Japan is a chain of volcanic islands. At the top of the ridge is one of the two stations where you can leave the gondola. From the station a ¾-km (½-mi) walking course wanders among the sulfur pits in the valley. Local entrepreneurs make a passable living boiling eggs in these holes and selling them to tourists at exorbitant prices. Just below the station is a restaurant; the food here is truly terrible, but on a clear day the view of Mt. Fuji is perfect. Next to the gondola station is the **Ōwaku-dani Natural History Museum** (Ōwaku-dani Shizen Kagakukan), an uninspired collection of exhibits on the ecosystems and volcanic history of the area, none of which have explanations in English. The museum is open daily 9–4:30; admission is ¥400. Remember that if you get off the gondola here, you—and others in the same situation—will have to wait for someone to make space on a later gondola before you can continue down to Tōgendai and Ashi-no-ko (but again, the gondolas come by every minute). ⊠ *Gondola in same bldg. as cable car terminus at Sōun-zan* ✉ *¥1,330, free with Hakone Free Pass* ⊙ *Gondolas depart every minute.*

From Ōwaku-dani the descent by gondola to Tōgendai on the shore of **Ashi-no-ko** (Lake Ashi, 芦ノ湖) takes 25 minutes. There's no reason to linger at Tōgendai; it's only a terminus for buses to Hakone-Yumoto and Odawara and to the resort villages in the northern part of Hakone. Head straight for the pier, a few minutes' walk down the hill, where boats set out on the lake for Hakone-machi. The ride is free with your Hakone Free Pass; otherwise, buy a ticket (¥970) at the office in the terminal. A few ships of conventional design ply the lake; the rest are astonishingly corny Disney knockoffs. One, for example, is rigged like a 17th-century warship. There are departures every 30 minutes, and the cruise to Hakone-machi takes about 30 minutes. With still water and good weather, you'll get a breathtaking reflection of the mountains in the waters of the lake as you go.

⓫ The main attraction in **Hakone-machi** (箱根町) is the **Hakone Barrier** (Hakone Sekisho). In days gone by, the town of Hakone was on the Tōkaidō, the main highway between the imperial court in Kyōto and the shogunate in Edo (present-day Tōkyō). The road was the only feasible passage through this mountainous country. Travelers could scarcely avoid passing through Hakone, which made it an ideal place for a checkpoint to control traffic. The Tokugawa Shogunate built the barrier here in 1618; its most important function was to monitor the *daimyō* (feudal lords) passing through—to keep track, above all, of weapons coming into Edo, and womenfolk coming out.

When Ieyasu Tokugawa came to power, Japan had been through nearly 100 years of bloody struggle among rival coalitions of daimyō. Ieyasu emerged supreme from all this, mainly because some of his opponents had switched sides at the last minute, in the Battle of Sekigahara in 1600. The shōgun was justifiably paranoid about his "loyal" barons—especially those in the outlying domains—so he required the daimyō to live in Edo for periods of time every two years. It was an inspired policy. The rotation system turned the daimyō into absentee landlords, which undercut their bases of power. They had to travel both ways in processions of great pomp and ceremony and maintain homes in the capital befitting their rank—expenses that kept them perennially strapped for cash. When they did return to their own lands, they had to leave their wives behind in Edo, hostages to their good behavior. A noble lady coming through the Hakone Sekisho without an official pass, in short, was a prima facie case of treason.

The checkpoint served the Tokugawa dynasty well for 250 years. It was demolished only when the shogunate fell, in the Meiji Restoration of 1868. An exact replica, with an exhibition hall of period costumes and weapons, was built as a tourist attraction in 1965. The restored barrier is a few minutes' walk from the pier, along the lakeshore in the direction of Moto-Hakone. ⊠ *Ichiban-chō, Hakone-machi* ☎ *0460/3–6635* 🎫 *¥300* ⊙ *Mar.–Nov., daily 9–4:30; Dec.–Feb., daily 9–4.*

Where to Stay

LAKE ASHI
★ $$–$$$$

🏨 **Hakone Prince Hotel** (箱根プリンスホテル). The location of this resort complex is perfect, with the lake in front and the mountains of Koma-ga-take in back. The Hakone Prince draws both tour groups and individual travelers, and it's also a popular venue for business conferences. The main building has both twin rooms and triples; the Japanese-style Ryū-gū-den annex, which overlooks the lake and has its own thermal bath, is superb. The rustic-style cottages in the complex sleep three to four guests; these are only open mid-April–November. ⊠ *144 Moto-Hakone, Hakone-machi, Ashigarashimo-gun, Kanagawa-ken 250-0522* ☎ *0460/3–1111* 🖷 *0460/3–7616* ⊕ *www.princehotels.co.jp* 🛏 *142 Western-style* *rooms with bath, 116 Western-style cottages with bath* ⚲ *2 restaurants, coffee shop, dining room, room service, 7 tennis courts, 2 pools, Japanese baths, bar, lounge, shops* ≡ *AE, DC, MC, V* 🍴 *CP.*

MIYANOSHITA
★ **$$–$$$$**

🏨 **Fujiya Hotel** (富士屋ホテル). Built in 1878, this Western-style hotel with modern additions is showing signs of age, but that somehow adds to its charm. The Fujiya combines the best of traditional Western decor with the exceptional service and hospitality of a fine Japanese inn. There are both Western and Japanese restaurants, and in the gardens behind the hotel is an old imperial villa that serves as a dining room. With its stacks of old books, the library would make a character out of Dickens feel positively at home. Hot-spring water is pumped right into the guest rooms. ✉ *359 Miyanoshita, Hakone-machi, Kanagawa-ken 250-0522* 📞 *0460/ 2–2211* 📠 *0460/2–2210* ⊕ *www.fujiyahotel.co.jp* 🛏 *149 Western-style rooms with bath* ⚲ *3 restaurants, room service, 18-hole golf course, 2 pools, hot springs, bar, convention center, meeting rooms, no-smoking rooms* ≡ *AE, DC, MC, V.*

SENGOKU
¢

🏨 **Fuji-Hakone Guest House** (富士箱根ゲストハウス). A small, family-run Japanese inn, this guesthouse has simple tatami rooms with the bare essentials. The owners, Mr. and Mrs. Takahashi, speak English and are a great help in planning trips off the beaten path. The inn is between Odawara Station and Tōgendai; take a bus from the station (Lane 4) and get off at the Senkyōro-mae stop. The family also operates the nearby Moto-Hakone Guest House (元箱根ゲストハウス), which has five Japanese-style rooms that share a typical Japanese-style bath. ✉ *912 Sengoku-hara, Hakone, Kanagawa-ken 250-0631, 103 Moto-Hakone for Moto-Hakone Guest House* 📞 *0460/4–6577 for Fuji-Hakone, 0460/3–7880 for Moto-Hakone* 🛏 *12 Japanese-style rooms with bath in Fuji-Hakone, 5 Japanese-style rooms without bath in Moto-Hakone* ⚲ *Hot springs, Japanese baths* ≡ *AE, MC, V.*

Fuji Go-ko (Fuji Five Lakes, 富士五湖)

To the north of Mt. Fuji, the Fuji Go-ko area affords an unbeatable view of the mountain on clear days and makes the best base for a climb to the summit. With its various outdoor activities, from skating and fishing in winter to boating and hiking in summer, this is a popular resort area for families and business conferences.

The five lakes are, from the east, Yamanaka-ko, Kawaguchi-ko, Sai-ko, Shōji-ko, and Motosu-ko. Yamanaka and Kawaguchi are the largest and most developed as resort areas, with Kawaguchi more or less the centerpiece of the group. You can visit this area on a day trip from Tōkyō, but unless you want to spend most of it on buses and trains, plan on staying overnight.

⑫ **Kawaguchi-ko** (Lake Kawaguchi, 河口湖), a 5- to 10-minute walk from Kawaguchi-ko Station, is the most developed of the five lakes, ringed with weekend retreats and vacation lodges—many of them maintained by companies and universities for their employees. Excursion boats depart from a pier here on 30-minute tours of the lake. The promise, not always fulfilled, is to have two views of Mt. Fuji: one of the thing itself and the other inverted in its reflection on the water. A gondola along the shore of Lake Kawaguchi (near the pier) quickly brings you to the top of the 3,622-foot-tall **Tenjō-san** (Mt. Tenjō, 天上山). From the observatory here the whole of Lake Kawaguchi lies before you, and beyond the lake is a classic view of Mt. Fuji.

One of the little oddities at Lake Kawaguchi is the **Fuji Museum** (Fuji Hakubutsukan, 富士博物館). The first floor holds conventional exhibits of local geology and history, but upstairs is an astonishing collection of—for want of a euphemism—phalluses (you must be 18 or older to view the exhibit). Mainly made from wood and stone and carved in every shape and size, these figures played a role in certain local fertility festivals. The museum is on the north shore of the lake, next to the Fuji Lake Hotel. ✉ *3964 Funatsu, Mizuminako, Kawaguchi-ko-machi* ☎ *0555/ 73–2266* 🎫 *1st fl. ¥200, 1st and 2nd fl. ¥500* ☉ *Mar.–Oct., daily 9–4; Nov.–Feb., Sat.–Thurs. 9–4; closed 3rd Tues. of month.*

Ⓒ The largest of the recreational facilities at Lake Kawaguchi is the **Fuji-kyū Highland** (富士急ハイランド). It has an impressive assortment of rides, roller coasters, and other amusements, but it's probably not worth a visit unless you have children in tow. In winter there's superb skating here, with Mt. Fuji for a backdrop. Fuji-kyū Highland is about 15 minutes' walk east from Kawaguchi-ko Station. ✉ *5–6–1 Shin Nishi Hara, Fujiyoshida-shi* ☎ *0555/23–2111* 🎫 *Full-day pass ¥4,300* ☉ *Weekdays 9–5, weekends 9–8.*

Buses from Kawaguchi-ko Station go to all the other lakes. The farthest
⑬ west is **Motosu-ko** (Lake Motosu, 本栖湖), the deepest and clearest of the Fuji Go-ko, which takes about 50 minutes.

⑭ Many people consider **Shōji-ko** (Lake Shōji, 精進湖), the smallest of the lakes, to be the prettiest—not least because it still has relatively little vacation-house development. The **Shōji Trail** (精進（湖畔）トレイル) leads from Lake Shōji to Mt. Fuji through Aoki-ga-hara (Sea of Trees), a forest with an underlying magnetic lava field that makes compasses go haywire. Any number of people go into Aoki-ga-hara every year and never come out, some of them on purpose—the forest seems to hold a morbid fascination for the Japanese as a place to commit suicide and disappear. If you're planning to climb Mt. Fuji from this trail, go with a guide.

⑮ **Sai-ko** (Lake Sai, 西湖), between Lakes Shōji and Kawaguchi, is the third-largest lake of the Fuji Go-ko, with only moderate development. From the western shore there is an especially good view of Mt. Fuji. Near Sai-ko there are two natural caves, an ice cave and a wind cave. You can either take a bus or walk to them.

⑯ The largest of the Fuji Go-ko is **Yamanaka-ko** (Lake Yamanaka, 山中湖), 35 minutes by bus to the southeast of Kawaguchi. Lake Yamanaka is the closest lake to the popular trail up Mt. Fuji that starts at Go-gōme, and many climbers use this resort area as a base.

Where to Stay

KAWAGUCHI-KO
$$$–$$$$

Fuji View Hotel (富士ビューホテル). This hotel on Lake Kawaguchi is a little threadbare but comfortable. The terrace lounge affords fine views of the lake and of Mt. Fuji beyond. The staff speaks English and is helpful in planning excursions. Many of the guests are on group excursions and take two meals—dinner and breakfast—in the hotel, but it's possible to opt for the room rate alone. Rates are significantly higher on weekends and in August. ⊠ *511 Katsuyama-mura, Fuji-Kawaguchiko-machi, Yamanashi-ken 401-0310* ☎ *0555/83–2211* ⊟ *0555/83–2128* ⊕ *www.fujiyahotel.co.jp* ↝ *40 Western-style rooms with bath, 30 Japanese-style rooms with bath* ♨ *2 restaurants, 9-hole golf course, 3 tennis courts, hot spring, boating* ⊟ *AE, DC, MC, V* ▯◯▯ *MAP.*

YAMANAKA-KO
$$

Hotel Mount Fuji (富士山ホテル). The best resort hotel on Lake Yamanaka, the Mount Fuji has all the facilities for a recreational holiday, and its guest rooms are larger than those at the other hotels on the lake. The lounges are spacious, and they have fine views of the lake and mountain. Rates are about 20% higher on weekends. ⊠ *1360-83 Yamanaka, Yamanaka-ko-mura, Yamanashi-ken 403-0017* ☎ *0555/62–2111* ↝ *153 Western-style rooms with bath, 4 Japanese-style rooms with bath* ♨ *3 restaurants, 2 tennis courts, pool, hot springs, ice-skating* ⊟ *AE, DC, MC, V.*

¢

Inn Fujitomita (旅館ふじとみた). One of the closest lodging options to the Mt. Fuji hiking trails, this inexpensive inn is a launching point for treks around the Fuji Go-ko area. Inn Fujitomita also has a swimming pool and tennis courts. The inn might not be much to look at from the outside, but the interior is spacious and homey. The staff speaks English and can help you plan an itinerary for visiting the area sights. Meals, including vegetarian options, are available at a very low price. Shuttle service is provided from Fuji Yoshida Station and the Lake Yamanaka bus stop. ⊠ *13235 Shibokusa, Oshinomura, Minami-Tsuru-gun, Yamanashi-ken 401-105* ☎ *0555/84–3359* ⊕ *www.tim.hi-ho.ne.jp/innfuji/* ↝ *10 Japanese-style rooms, 3 with bath* ♨ *Dining room, 3 tennis courts, pool, hot springs, fishing, laundry facilities; no TV in some rooms* ⊟ *AE, DC, MC, V.*

Fuji-san (Mt. Fuji) 富士山

⑰
Fodor's Choice
★

There are six routes to the summit of the 12,388-foot-high **Fuji-san** (Mt. Fuji, 富士山), but only two, both accessible by bus, are recommended: from Go-gōme (Fifth Station), on the north side, and from Shin-Go-gōme (New Fifth Station), on the south. The climb to the summit from Go-gōme takes five hours and is the shortest way up; the descent takes three hours. From Shin-Go-gōme the ascent is slightly longer and stonier, but the way down, via the *sunabashiri*, a volcanic sand slide, is faster. The quickest route is to ascend from Go-gōme and descend to Shin-Go-gōme via the sunabashiri.

The Climb

The ultimate experience of climbing Mt. Fuji is to reach the summit just before dawn and to greet the extraordinary sunrise. *Go-raikō* (The Honorable Coming of the Light [here *go* means "honorable"]), as the sunrise is called, has a mystical quality because the reflection shimmers across the sky just before the sun itself appears over the horizon. Mind you, there is no guarantee of seeing it: Mt. Fuji is often cloudy, even in the early morning.

The climb is taxing but not as hard as you might think scaling Japan's highest mountain would be. That said, the air *is* thin, and it *is* humiliating to struggle for the oxygen to take another step while some 83-year-old Japanese grandmother blithely leaves you in her dust (it happens: Japanese grannies are made of sterner stuff than most). Have no fear of losing the trail on either of the two main routes. Just follow the crowd—some 196,000 people make the climb during the official season, July 1–August 26 (outside of this season the weather is highly unpredictable and potentially dangerous, and climbing is strongly discouraged). In all, there are 10 stations to the top; you start at the fifth. There are stalls selling food and drinks along the way, but at exorbitant prices, so bring your own.

Also along the route are dormitory-style huts (about ¥7,000 with two meals, ¥5,000 without meals) where you can catch some sleep. A popular one is at the Hachi-gōme (Eighth Station), from which it's about a 90-minute climb to the top. However, these huts, which are open only in July and August, should be avoided at all costs. The food is vile, there's no fresh water, and the bedding is used by so many people and so seldom properly aired, you'd feel better sleeping on fish skins. Sensible folk leave the Go-gōme at midnight with good flashlights, climb through the night, and get to the summit just before dawn. Camping on the mountain is prohibited.

Be prepared for fickle weather around and atop the mountain. Summer days can be unbearably hot and muggy, and the nights can be a shocking contrast of freezing cold (bring numerous warm layers and be prepared to put them all on). Wear strong hiking shoes. The sun really burns at high altitudes, so wear protective clothing and a hat; gloves are a good idea, too. Use a backpack, as it keeps your hands free and serves a useful function on the way down: instead of returning to Go-gōme, descend to Shin-Go-gōme on the volcanic sand slide called the **sunabashiri** (砂走り)—sit down on your pack, push off, and away you go.

Fuji-Hakone-Izu National Park A to Z

To research prices, get advice from other travelers, and book travel arrangements, visit www.fodors.com.

BUS TRAVEL

Buses connect Tōkyō with the major gateway towns of this region, but except for the trip to Lake Kawaguchi or Mt. Fuji, the price advantage doesn't really offset the comfort and convenience of the trains. If you're interested only in climbing Mt. Fuji, take one of the daily buses directly to Go-gōme from Tōkyō; they run July through August and leave Shinjuku Station at 7:45, 8:45, 10:55, 4:50, 5:50, and 7:30. The last bus allows sufficient time for the tireless to make it to the summit before sunrise. The journey takes about 2 hours and 40 minutes from Shinjuku and costs

¥2,600. Reservations are required; book seats through the Fuji Kyūkō Highway Bus Reservation Center, the Keiō Highway Bus Reservation Center, the Japan Travel Bureau (which should have English-speaking staff), or any major travel agency.

To return from Mt. Fuji to Tōkyō, take an hour-long bus ride from Shin-Go-gōme to Gotemba (¥1,500). From Gotemba take the JR Tōkaidō and Gotemba lines to Tōkyō Station (¥1,890), or take the JR Line from Gotemba to Matsuda (¥480) and change to the private Odakyū Line from Shin-Matsuda to Shinjuku (¥750).

Direct bus service runs daily from Shinjuku Station in Tōkyō to Lake Kawaguchi every hour between 7:10 AM and 8:10 PM (¥1,700). Buses go from Kawaguchi-ko Station to Go-gōme (the fifth station on the climb up Mt. Fuji) in about an hour; there are eight departures a day (9:35, 10:10, 11:10, 12:10, 1:10, 2:10, 3:20, and 5:20) until the climbing season (July and August) starts, when there are 15 departures or more, depending on demand. The cost is ¥1,700.

From Lake Kawaguchi, you can also take a bus to Gotemba, then change to another bus for Sengoku; from Sengoku there are frequent buses to Hakone-Yumoto, Tōgendai, and elsewhere in the Hakone region. On the return trip, three or four buses a day make the two-hour journey from Lake Kawaguchi to Mishima (¥2,130), skirting the western lakes and circling Mt. Fuji; at Mishima you can transfer to the JR Shinkansen Line for Tōkyō or Kyōto. A shorter bus ride (70 minutes, ¥1,470) goes from Lake Kawaguchi to Gotemba with a transfer to the JR local line.

From Lake Kawaguchi, you can also connect to the Izu Peninsula. Take the bus to Mishima and from there go by train either to Shuzenji or Atami. From Shimoda, the end of the line on the private Izukyū Railway down the east coast of the Izu Peninsula, you must travel by bus around the southern cape to Dōgashima (¥1,360). From there, another bus takes you up the west coast as far as Heda and then turns inland to Shuzenji. From Shimoda, you can also take a bus directly north to Shuzenji through the Amagi Mountains (one departure daily at 10:45 AM, ¥2,180). The Tōkai Bus Company covers the west coast and central mountains of the Izu area well with local service; buses are not especially frequent, but they do provide the useful option of just hopping off and exploring if you happen to see something interesting from the window. Whatever your destination, always check the time of the last departure to make sure that you are not left stranded.

Within the Hakone area, buses run every 15–30 minutes from Hakone-machi buses to Hakone-Yumoto Station on the private Odakyū Line (40 minutes, ¥930), and Odawara Station (one hour, ¥1,150), where you can take either the Odakyū Romance Car back to Shinjuku Station or a JR Shinkansen to Tōkyō Station. The buses are covered by the Hakone Free Pass.

🚌 Bus Information **Fuji Kyūkō Highway Bus Reservation Center** ☎ 03/5376-2222. **Keiō Highway Bus Reservation Center** ☎ 03/5376-2222. Japan Travel Bureau ☎ 03/

3284-7605 ⊕ www.jtb.co.jp/eng. **Tōkai Bus Company** ☎ 0557/36-1112 for main office, 0557/22-2511 Shimoda Information Center.

CAR TRAVEL

Having your own car makes sense only for touring the Izu Peninsula, and only then if you're prepared to cope with less-than-ideal road conditions, lots of traffic (especially on holiday weekends), and the paucity of road markers in English. It takes some effort—but exploring the peninsula *is* a lot easier by car than by public transportation. From Tōkyō take the Tōmei Expressway as far as Ōi-matsuda (about 84 km [52 mi]); then pick up Routes 255 and 135 to Atami (approximately 28 km [17 mi]). From Atami drive another 55 km (34 mi) or so down the east coast of the Izu Peninsula to Shimoda.

One way to save yourself some trouble is to book a car through the Nippon or Toyota rental agency in Tōkyō and arrange to pick it up at the Shimoda branch. You can then simply take a train to Shimoda and use it as a base. From Shimoda you can drive back up the coast to Kawazu (35 minutes) and then to Shuzenji (30 minutes).

🚗 **Nippon Interrent** ☎ 03/3469-0919. **Toyota Rent-a-Car** ☎ 0070/800-0100 toll-free, 03/5954-8008 8 AM–8 PM.

DISCOUNTS & DEALS

For the Hakone area, the best way to get around is with a Hakone Free Pass, issued by the privately owned Odakyū Railways and valid for three days. This coupon ticket (¥5,500 from Shinjuku Station in Tōkyō) covers the train fare to Hakone and allows you to use any mode of transportation in the Hakone area, including the Hakone Tozan Railway, the Hakone Tozan bus, the Hakone Ropeway, the Hakone Cruise Boat, and the Sōun-zan cable car.

If you have a JR Pass, it's cheaper to take a Kodama Shinkansen from Tōkyō Station to Odawara and buy the Hakone Free Pass there (¥4,130) for travel within the Hakone region only.

TOURS

Once you are on the Izu Peninsula itself, sightseeing excursions by boat are available from several picturesque small ports. From Dōgashima, you can take the Dōgashima Marine short (20 minutes, ¥920) or long (45 minutes, ¥1,240) tours of Izu's rugged west coast. The Fujikyū Kōgyō company operates a daily ferry to Hatsu-shima from Atami (25 minutes, ¥2,340 round-trip) and another to the island from Itō (23 minutes, ¥1,150). Izukyū Marine offers a 40-minute tour (¥1,530) by boat from Shimoda to the coastal rock formations at Irō-zaki.

Sunrise Tours operates a tour to Hakone, including a cruise across Lake Ashi and a trip on the gondola over Ōwaku-dani (¥15,000 includes lunch and return to Tōkyō by Shinkansen; ¥12,000 includes lunch and return to Tōkyō by bus). Sunrise tours depart daily from Tōkyō's Hamamatsu-chō Bus Terminal and some major hotels.

🚢 **Dōgashima Marine** ☎ 0558/52-0013. **Fujikyū Kōgyō** ☎ 0557/81-0541. **Izukyū Marine** ☎ 0558/22-1151. **Sunrise Tours** ☎ 03/5796-5454 🖷 03/5495-0680 ⊕ www.jtb.co.jp/sunrisetour.

TRAIN TRAVEL

Trains are by far the easiest and fastest ways to get to the Fuji-Hakone-Izu National Park area. The gateway stations of Atami, Odawara, and Kawaguchi-ko are well served by comfortable express trains from Tōkyō, on both JR and private railway lines. These in turn connect to local trains and buses that can get you anywhere in the region you want to go. Call the JR Higashi-Nihon Info Line (10–6 daily, except December 31–January 3) for assistance in English.

The *Kodama* Shinkansen from Tōkyō to Atami costs ¥3,880 and takes 51 minutes; JR Passes are valid. The JR local from Atami to Itō takes 25 minutes and costs ¥320. Itō and Atami are also served by the JR Odoriko Super Express (not a Shinkansen train). The Tōkyō–Itō run takes 1¾ hours and costs ¥4,190; you can also use a JR Pass. The privately owned Izukyū Railways, on which JR Passes are not valid, makes the Itō–Shimoda run in one hour for ¥1,570.

The Izu–Hakone Railway Line runs from Tōkyō to Mishima (1 hour, 36 minutes; ¥4,090), with a change at Mishima for Shuzenji (31 minutes, ¥500); this is the cheapest option if you don't have a JR Pass. With a JR Pass, a Shinkansen–Izu Line combination will save about 35 minutes and will be the cheapest option. The Tōkyō–Mishima Shinkansen leg (62 minutes) costs ¥4,400; the Mishima–Shuzenji Izu Line leg (31 minutes) costs ¥500.

Trains depart every 12 minutes from Tōkyō's Shinjuku Station for Odawara in the Hakone area. The ¥5,500 Hakone Free Pass, which you can buy at the station, covers the train fare. Reservations are required for the upscale Romance Car, with comfortable seats and big observation windows, to Hakone (an extra ¥870 with Hakone Free Pass). The Romance Car goes one stop beyond Odawara to Hakone-Yumoto; buy tickets at any Odakyū Odakyū Travel Service counter or major travel agency, or call the Odakyū Reservation Center. Note that beyond Hakone-Yumoto, you must use the privately owned Hakone Tozan Tetsudō Line or buses.

The transportation hub, as well as one of the major resort areas in the Fuji Five Lakes area, is Kawaguchi-ko. Getting there from Tōkyō requires a change of trains at Ōtsuki. The JR Chūō Line Kaiji and Azusa express trains leave Shinjuku Station for Ōtsuki on the half hour from 7 AM to 8 PM (more frequently in the morning) and take approximately one hour. At Ōtsuki, change to the private Fuji-Kyūkō Line for Kawaguchi-ko, which takes another 50 minutes. The total traveling time is about two hours, and you can use your JR Pass as far as Ōtsuki; otherwise, the fare is ¥1,280. The Ōtsuki–Kawaguchi-ko leg costs ¥1,110. Also available are two direct service rapid trains for Kawaguchi-ko that leave Tōkyō in the morning at 6:08 and 7:10 on weekdays, 6:09 and 7:12 on weekends and national holidays.

The Holiday Kaisoku Picnic-gō, available on weekends and national holidays, offers direct express service from Shinjuku, leaving at 8:10 and arriving at Kawaguchi-ko Station at 10:37. From March through August, JR puts on additional weekend express trains for Kawaguchi-ko, but be aware that on some of them only the first three cars go all the way to the lake. Coming back, you have a choice of late-afternoon departures from Kawaguchi-ko that arrive at Shinjuku in the early evening. Check the express timetables before you go; you can also call either the JR Higashi-Nihon Info Line or Fuji-kyūukō Kawaguchi-ko Station for train information.

🚆 Train Information **Fuji-kyūukō Kawaguchi-ko Station** ☎ 0555/72-0017. **Hakone Tozan Railway** ☎ 0465/24-2115. **Izu-Hakone Railway** ☎ 0465/77-1200. **Izukyū Corporation** ☎ 0557/53-1111 for main office, 0558/22-3202 Izukyū Shimoda Station. **JR Higashi-Nihon Info Line** ☎ 03/3423-0111. **Odakyū Reservation Center** ☎ 03/3481-0130.

VISITOR INFORMATION

Especially in summer and fall, the Fuji-Hakone-Izu National Park area is one of the most popular vacation destinations in the country, so most towns and resorts have local visitor information centers. Few of them have staff members who speak fluent English, but you can still pick up local maps and pamphlets, as well as information on low-cost inns, pensions, and guesthouses.

🚩 Tourist Information **Atami Tourist Association** ✉ 12-1 Ginza-chō, Atami-shi ☎ 0557/85-2222. **Fuji-Kawaguchiko Tourist Association** ✉ 890 Funatsu, Kawakuchiko-machi, Minami-Tsurugun ☎ 0555/72-2460. **Hakone-machi Tourist Association** ✉ 698 Yūmoto, Hakone-machi ☎ 0460/5-8911. **Nishi-Izu Tourist Office** ✉ Dogashima, Nishi-Izu-chō, Kamo-gu ☎ 0558/52-1268. **Shimoda Tourist Association** ✉ 1-1 Soto-ga-oka, Shimoda-shi ☎ 0558/22-1531.

THE DISCREET CHARM OF JAPANESE CUISINE

THE ESSENTIALS OF A JAPANESE MEAL

CULTURE: THE MAIN COURSE

KAISEKI RYŌRI: JAPANESE HAUTE CUISINE

SHŌJIN RYŌRI: ZEN-STYLE VEGETARIAN CUISINE

SUSHI, SUKIYAKI, TEMPURA & NABEMONO:
A COMFORTABLE MIDDLE GROUND

BENTŌ, SOBA, UDON & ROBATAYAKI:
FEASTING ON A BUDGET

REGIONAL DIFFERENCES

THE BOTTOM LINE

EAVE BEHIND THE HUMIDITY OF JAPAN IN SUMMER and part the crisp linen curtain of the neighborhood sushi-ya some hot night in mid-July. Enter a world of white cypress and chilled sea urchin, where a welcome oshibori (hot towel for cleaning your hands) awaits and a master chef stands at your beck and call. A cup of tea to begin, a tiny mound of ginger to freshen the palate, and you're ready to choose from the colorful array of fresh seafood on ice inside a glass case before you. Bite-size morsels arrive in friendly pairs, along with a glass of ice-cold beer. The young apprentice runs up and down, making sure everyone has tea—and anything else that might be needed. The chef has trained for years in his art, and he's proud, in his stoic way, to demonstrate it. The o-tsukuri (a kind of sashimi) you've ordered arrives; today the thinly sliced raw tuna comes in the shape of a rose. The fourth round you order brings with it an unexpected ribbon of cucumber, sliced with a razor-sharp sushi knife into sections that expand like an accordion. The chef's made your day . . .

Red-paper lanterns dangling in the dark above 1,000 tiny food stalls on the backstreets of Tōkyō . . . To the weary Japanese salaryman on his way home from the office, these akachōchin (red) lanterns are a prescription for the best kind of therapy known for the "Subterranean Homesick Blues," Japanese style: one last belly-warming bottle of sake, a nerve-soothing platter of grilled chicken wings, and perhaps a few words of wisdom for the road. Without these nocturnal way stations, many a fuzzy-eyed urban refugee would never survive that rumbling, fluorescent nightmare known as the last train home.

And where would half of Japan's night-owl college students be if not for the local shokudō, as the neighborhood not-so-greasy spoon is known? Separated at last from mother's protective guidance (and therefore without a clue as to how to boil an egg or heat a bowl of soup), the male contingent of young lodging-house boarders put their lives in the hands of the old couple who run the neighborhood café. Bent furtively over a platter of kare-raisu (curry and rice) or tonkatsu teishoku (pork cutlet set meal), these ravenous young men thumb through their baseball comics each night, still on the road to recovery from a childhood spent memorizing mathematical formulas and English phrases they hope they'll never have to use.

Down a dimly lit backstreet not two blocks away, a geisha in all her elaborate finery walks her last silk-suited customer out to his chauffeur-driven limousine. He has spent the evening being pampered, feasted, and fan-danced in the rarefied air of one of Tōkyō's finest ryōtei. (You must be invited to these exclusive eateries—or be a regular patron, introduced by another regular patron who vouched for your reputation with his own.) There have been the most restrained of traditional dances, some shamisen playing—an oh-so-tastefully suggestive tête-à-tête. The customer has been drinking the very finest sake, accompanied by a succession of exquisitely presented hors d'oeuvres—what amounts to a seven-course meal in the end is the formal Japanese haute cuisine known as kaiseki. If it were not for his company's expense account, by now he would have spent the average man's monthly salary. Luckily for him, he's not the average man.

On a stool now, under the flimsy awning of a street stall, shielded from the wind and rain by flapping tarps, heated only by a portable kerosene stove and the steam from a vat of boiling noodles, you'll find neither tourist nor ptomaine. Here sits the everyday workingman, glass of shōchū (a strong liquor made from sweet potatoes) in sun-baked hand, arguing over the Tigers' chances of winning the Japan Series as he zealously slurps down a bowl of hot noodle soup sprinkled with red-pepper sauce—more atmosphere and livelier company than you're likely to find anywhere else in Japan. The yatai-san, as these inimitable street vendors are known, are an amiable, if disappearing, breed.

Somewhere between the street stalls and the exclusive ryōtei, a vast culinary world exists in Japan. Tiny, over-the-counter restaurants, each with its own specialty—from familiar favorites, such as tempura, sukiyaki, or sushi to exotic delicacies, like *unagi* (eel) or *fugu* (blowfish)—inhabit every city side street. Comfortable, country-style restaurants abound, serving a variety of different *nabemono,* the one-pot stew dishes cooked right at your table. There are also lively neighborhood *robatayaki* grills, where cooks in *happi* coats wield skewered bits of meat, seafood, and vegetables over a hot charcoal grill as you watch.

A dozen years ago, sukiyaki and tempura were exotic enough for most Western travelers. Those were the days when raw fish was still something a traveler needed fortitude to try. But with *soba* (buckwheat noodle) shops and sushi bars popping up everywhere from Los Angeles to Paris, it seems that—at long last—the joy of Japanese cooking has found its way westward.

There *is* something special, however, about visiting the tiger in his lair—something no tame circus cat could ever match. Although tours to famous temples and scenic places can provide important historical and cultural background material, there's nothing like a meal in a local restaurant— be it under the tarps of the liveliest street stall or within the quiet recesses of an elegant Japanese inn—for a taste of the real Japan. Approaching a platter of fresh sashimi in Tōkyō is like devouring a hot dog smothered in mustard and onions in Yankee Stadium. There's nothing like it in the world.

The Essentials of a Japanese Meal

The basic formula for a traditional Japanese meal is deceptively simple. It starts with soup, followed by raw fish, then the entrée (grilled, steamed, simmered, or fried

fish, chicken, or vegetables), and ends with rice and pickles, with perhaps some fresh fruit for dessert, and a cup of green tea. It's as simple as that—almost.

An exploration of any cuisine should begin at the beginning, with a basic knowledge of what it is you're eating: rice, of course— the traditional staple; and seafood—grilled, steamed, fried, stewed, or raw; chicken, pork, or beef, at times—in that order of frequency; a wide variety of vegetables (wild and cultivated), steamed, sautéed, blanched, or pickled, perhaps—but never overcooked; soybeans in every form imaginable, from tofu to soy sauce; and seaweed, in and around lots of things.

The basics are just that. But there are, admittedly, a few twists to the story. Beyond the raw fish, it's the incredible variety of vegetation used in Japanese cooking that still surprises the Western palate: *take-no-ko* (bamboo shoots), *renkon* (lotus root), and the treasured *matsutake* mushrooms (which grow wild in jealously guarded forest hideaways and sometimes sell for more than $60 apiece), to name a few.

Tangy garnishes, both wild and domestic, such as *kinome* (leaves of the Japanese prickly ash pepper tree), *mitsuba* (trefoil, of the parsley family), and *shiso* (a member of the mint family), are used as a foil for oily foods. The more familiar-sounding ingredients, such as sesame and ginger, appear in abundance, as do the less familiar—*wasabi* (Japanese horseradish), *yuri-ne* (lily bulbs), *ginnan* (gingko nuts), and *daikon* (gigantic white radishes). Exotic? Perhaps, but delicious, and nothing here bites back. Simple? Yes, if you understand a few of the ground rules.

Absolute freshness is first. According to world-renowned Japanese chef Shizuo Tsuji, soup and raw fish are the two test pieces of Japanese cuisine. Freshness is the criterion for both: "I can tell at a glance by the texture of their skins—like the bloom of youth on a young girl—whether the fish is really fresh," Tsuji says in *The Art of Japanese Cooking.* A comparison as startling, perhaps, as it is revealing. To a Japanese chef, freshness is an unparalleled virtue, and much of a chef's reputation relies on the ability to obtain the finest ingredients at the peak of season: fish brought in from the sea this morning (not yesterday) and vegetables from the earth (not the hothouse), if at all possible.

Simplicity is next. Rather than embellishing foods with heavy spices and rich sauces, the Japanese chef prefers flavors au naturel. Flavors are enhanced, not elaborated, accented rather than concealed. Without a heavy dill sauce, fish is permitted a degree of natural fishiness—a garnish of fresh red ginger will be provided to offset the flavor rather than to disguise it.

The third prerequisite is beauty. Simple, natural foods must appeal to the eye as well as to the palate. Green peppers on a vermilion dish, perhaps, or an egg custard in a blue bowl. Rectangular dishes for a round eggplant. So important is the seasonal element in Japanese cooking that maple leaves and pine needles will be used to accent an autumn dish. Or two small summer delicacies, a pair of freshwater *ayu* fish, will be grilled with a purposeful twist to their tails to make them "swim" across a crystal platter and thereby suggest the coolness of a mountain stream on a hot August night.

Mood can make or break the entire meal, and the Japanese connoisseur will go to great lengths to find the perfect yakitori stand—a smoky, lively place—an environment appropriate to the occasion, offering a night of grilled chicken, cold beer, and camaraderie.

Atmosphere depends as much on the company as it does on the lighting or the color of the drapes. In Japan this seems to hold particularly true. The popularity of a particular *nomiya,* or bar, depends entirely on the affability of the *mama-san,* that long-suffering lady who's been listening to your troubles for years. In fancier places, mood becomes a fancier problem, to the point of quibbling over the proper amount of "water music" trickling in the basin outside your private room.

Culture: The Main Course

Sipping coffee at a sidewalk café on the Left Bank, you begin to feel what it means to be a Parisian. Slurping noodles on tatami in a neighborhood soba shop overlooking a tiny interior garden, you start to understand what it's like to live in Japan. Food, no matter which country you're in, has much to say about the culture as a whole.

Beyond the natural dictates of climate and geography, Japanese food has its roots in the centuries-old cuisine of the imperial court, which was imported from China— a religiously formal style of meal called *yūsoku ryōri.* It was prepared only by specially appointed chefs, who had the status of priests in the service of the emperor, in a culinary ritual that is now nearly a lost art. Although it was never popularly served in centuries past (a modified version can still be found in Kyōto), much of the ceremony and careful attention to detail of yūsoku ryōri are reflected today in the formal kaiseki meal.

Kaiseki Ryōri: Japanese Haute Cuisine

Kaiseki refers to the most elegant of all styles of Japanese food available today, and *ryōri* means cuisine. Rooted in the banquet feasts of the aristocracy, by the late 16th century it had developed into a meal to accompany ceremonial tea. The word *kaiseki* refers to a heated stone (*seki*) that Buddhist monks placed inside the folds (*kai*) of their kimonos to keep off the biting cold in the unheated temple halls where they slept and meditated.

Cha-kaiseki, as the formal meal served with tea (*cha*) is called, is intended to take the edge off your hunger at the beginning of a formal tea ceremony and to counterbalance the astringent character of the thick green tea. In the tea ceremony balance—and the sense of calmness and well-being it inspires—is the keynote.

The formula for the basic Japanese meal derived originally from the rules governing formal kaiseki—not too large a portion, just enough; not too spicy, but perhaps with a savory sprig of trefoil to offset the bland tofu. A grilled dish is served before a steamed one, a steamed dish before a simmered one; a square plate is used for a round food; a bright green maple leaf is placed to one side to herald the arrival of spring.

Kaiseki ryōri appeals to all the senses at once. An atmosphere is created in which the meal is to be experienced. The poem in calligraphy on a hanging scroll and the flowers in the alcove set the seasonal theme, a motif picked up in the pattern of the dishware chosen for the evening. The colors and shapes of the vessels complement the foods served on them. The visual harmony presented is as vital as the balance and variety of flavors of the foods themselves, for which the ultimate criterion is freshness. The finest ryōtei will never serve a fish or vegetable out of its proper season—no matter how marvelous a winter melon today's modern greenhouses can guarantee. Melons are for rejoicing in the summer's bounty . . . period.

Kaiseki ryōri found its way out of the formal tearooms and into a much earthier realm of the senses when it became the fashionable snack with sake in the teahouses of the geisha quarters during the 17th and 18th centuries. Not only the atmosphere but the Chinese characters used to write the word *kaiseki* are different in this context; they refer to aristocratic "banquet seats." And banquets they are. To partake in the most exclusive of these evenings in a teahouse in Kyōto still requires a personal introduction and a great deal of money, though these days many traditional restaurants serve elegant kaiseki meals (without the geisha) at much more reasonable prices.

One excellent way to experience this incomparable cuisine on a budget is to visit a kaiseki restaurant at lunchtime. Many of them offer *kaiseki bentō* lunches at a fraction of the dinner price, exquisitely presented in lacquered boxes, as a sampler of their full-course evening meal.

Shōjin Ryōri: Zen-Style Vegetarian Cuisine

Shōjin ryōri is the Zen-style vegetarian cuisine. Traditional Japanese cuisine emphasizes the natural flavor of the freshest ingredients in season, without the embellishment of heavy spices and rich sauces. This probably developed out of the Zen belief in the importance of simplicity and austerity as paths to enlightenment. Protein is provided by an almost limitless number of dishes made from soybeans—such as *yu-dōfu,* or boiled bean curd, and *yuba,* sheets of pure protein skimmed from vats of steaming soy milk. The variety and visual beauty of a full-course shōjin ryōri meal offer new dimensions in dining to the vegetarian gourmet. *Goma-dōfu,* or sesame-flavored bean curd, for example, is a delicious taste treat, as is *nasu-dengaku,* grilled eggplant covered with a sweet *miso* sauce.

There are many fine restaurants—particularly in the Kyōto area—that specialize in shōjin ryōri, but it's best to seek out one of the many temples throughout Japan that open their doors to visitors; here you can try these special meals within the actual temple halls, which often overlook a traditional garden.

Sushi, Sukiyaki, Tempura & Nabemono: A Comfortable Middle Ground

Leaving the rarefied atmosphere of teahouses and temples behind, an entire realm of more down-to-earth gastronomic pleasures waits to be explored. Sushi, sukiyaki, and tempura are probably the three most commonly known Japanese dishes in the Western world. Restaurants serving these dishes are to be found in abundance in every major hotel in Japan. It is best, however, to try each of these in a place that specializes in just one.

An old Japanese proverb says "*Mochi wa mochi-ya e*"—if you want rice cakes, go to a rice-cake shop. The same goes for sushi. Sushi chefs undergo a lengthy apprenticeship, and the trade is considered an art form. Possessing the discipline of a judo player, the *itamae-san* (or, "man before . . . or behind . . . the counter," depending on your point of view) at a sushi-ya is a real master. Every neighborhood has its own sushi shop, and everyone you meet has his or her own secret little place to go for sushi.

The Central Wholesale Market district in Tōkyō is so popular for its sushi shops that you usually have to wait in line for a seat at the counter. Some are quite expensive, while others are relatively cheap. "Know before you go" is the best policy; "Ask before you eat" is next. Among the dozens types of sushi available, some of the most popular are *maguro* (tuna), *ebi* (shrimp), *hamachi* (yellowtail), *uni* (sea urchin), *anago* (conger eel), *tako* (octopus), *awabi* (abalone), and *akagai* (red shellfish). The day's selection is usually displayed in a glass case at the counter, which enables you to point at whatever catches your eye.

Tempura, the battered and deep-fried fish and vegetable dish, is almost certain to taste better at a small shop that serves nothing else. The difficulties of preparing this seemingly simple dish lie in achieving the proper consistency of the batter and the right temperature and freshness of the oil in which it is fried.

Sukiyaki is the popular beef dish that is sautéed with vegetables in an iron skillet at the table. The tenderness of the beef is the determining factor here, and many of the best sukiyaki houses also run their own butcher shops so that they can control the quality of the beef they serve. Although beef did not become a part of the Japanese diet until the turn of the 20th century, the Japanese are justifiably proud of

their notorious beer-fed and hand-massaged beef (e.g., the famous Matsuzaka beef from Kōbe and the equally delicious Ōmi beef from Shiga Prefecture).

Shabu-shabu is another possibility, though this dish has become more popular with tourists than with the Japanese. It's similar to sukiyaki in that it is prepared at the table with a combination of vegetables, but it differs in that shabu-shabu is swished briefly in boiling water, while sukiyaki is sautéed in oil and, usually, a slightly sweetened soy sauce. The word *shabu-shabu* actually refers to this swishing sound.

Nabemono, or one-pot dishes, are not as familiar to Westerners as the three mentioned above, but the possibilities are endless, and nothing tastes better on a cold winter's night. Simmered in a light, fish-based broth, these stews can be made of almost anything: chicken (*tori-nabe*), oysters (*kaki-nabe*), or the sumō wrestler's favorite, the hearty *chanko-nabe* . . .with something in it for everyone. Nabemono is a popular family or party dish. The restaurants specializing in nabemono often have a casual, country atmosphere.

Bentō, Soba, Udon & Robatayaki: Feasting on a Budget

Tales of unsuspecting tourists swallowed up by money-gobbling monsters disguised as quaint little restaurants on the backstreets of Japan's major cities abound. There are, however, many wonderful little places that provide excellent meals and thoughtful service—and have no intention of straining anyone's budget. To find them, you must not be afraid to venture outside your hotel lobby or worry that the dining spot has no menu in English. Many restaurants have menus posted out front that clearly state the full price you can expect to pay (some do add a 10% tax, and possibly a service charge, so ask in advance).

Here are a few suggestions for Japanese meals that do not cost a fortune and are usually a lot more fun than relying on the familiar but unexciting international fast-food chains for quick meals on a budget: *bentō* (box) lunches, *soba* or *udon* (noodle) dishes, and the faithful neighborhood *robatayaki* (grills), ad infinitum.

The Bentō. This is the traditional Japanese box lunch, available for takeout everywhere and usually comparatively inexpensive. It can be purchased in the morning to be taken along and eaten later, either outdoors or on the train as you travel between cities. The bentō consists of rice, pickles, grilled fish or meat, and vegetables, in an almost limitless variety of combinations to suit the season. The basement levels of most major department stores sell beautifully prepared bentō to go. In fact, a department-store basement is a great place to sample and purchase the whole range of foods offered in Japan: among the things available are French bread, imported cheeses, traditional bean cakes, chocolate bonbons, barbecued chicken, grilled eel, roasted peanuts, fresh vegetables, potato salads, pickled bamboo shoots, and smoked salmon.

The *o-bentō* (the *o* is honorific) in its most elaborate incarnation is served in gorgeous, multilayer lacquered boxes as an accompaniment to outdoor tea ceremonies or for flower-viewing parties held in spring. Exquisite *bentō-bako* (lunch boxes) made in the Edo period (1603–1868) can be found in museums and antiques shops. They are inlaid with mother-of-pearl and delicately hand-painted in gold. A wide variety of sizes and shapes of bentō boxes are still handmade in major cities and small villages throughout Japan in both formal and informal styles. They make excellent souvenirs.

A major benefit to the bentō is its portability. Sightseeing can take you down many an unexpected path, and if you bring your own bentō you won't need to worry about finding an appropriate place to stop for a bite to eat. No vacationing Japanese family would ever be without one tucked carefully inside their rucksacks right beside the thermos bottle of tea. If they do somehow run out of time to prepare one in advance—no problem—there are hundreds of wonderful options in the form of the beloved *eki-ben* (train-station box lunch).

Each whistle-stop in Japan takes great pride in the uniqueness and flavor of the special box lunches, featuring the local delicacy, sold right at the station or from vendors inside the trains. The pursuit of the eki-ben has become a national pastime in this nation in love with its trains. Entire books have been written in Japanese explaining the features of every different eki-ben available along the 26,000 km (16,120 mi) of railways in the country. This is one of the best ways to sample the different styles of regional cooking in Japan and is highly recommended to any traveler who plans to spend time on the Japan Railway trains.

Soba and Udon. Soba and udon (noodle) dishes are another lifesaving treat for stomachs (and wallets) unaccustomed to exotic flavors (and prices). Small shops serving soba (thin, brown buckwheat noodle) and udon (thick, white-wheat noodle) dishes in a variety of combinations can be found in every neighborhood in the country. Both can be ordered plain (ask for *o-soba* or *o-udon*), in a lightly seasoned broth flavored with bonito and soy sauce, or in combination with things like tempura shrimp (*tempura soba* or *udon*) or chicken (*tori-namban soba* or *udon*). For a refreshing change in summer, try *zaru soba,* cold noodles to be dipped in a tangy soy sauce. *Nabeyaki-udon* is a hearty winter dish of udon noodles, assorted vegetables, and egg served in the pot in which it was cooked.

Robatayaki. Perhaps the most exuberant of inexpensive options is the robatayaki (grill). Beer mug in hand, elbow to elbow at the counter of one of these popular neighborhood grills—that is the best way to relax and join in with the local fun. You'll find no pretenses here—just a wide variety of plain, good food (as much or as little as you want) with the proper amount of alcohol to get things rolling.

Robata means fireside, and the style of cooking is reminiscent of old-fashioned Japanese farmhouse meals cooked over a charcoal fire in an open hearth. It's easy to order at a robatayaki shop because the selection of food to be grilled is lined up behind glass at the counter. Fish, meat, vegetables, tofu—take your pick. Some popular choices are *yaki-zakana* (grilled fish), particularly *karei-shio-yaki* (salted and grilled flounder) and *asari saka-mushi* (clams simmered in sake). Try the grilled Japanese shiitake mushrooms, *ao-tō* (green peppers), and the *hiyayakko* (chilled tofu sprinkled with bonito flakes, diced green onions, and soy sauce). Yak-itori can be ordered in most robatayaki shops, though many inexpensive drinking places specialize in this popular bar-becued chicken dish.

The budget dining possibilities in Japan don't stop there. **Okonomiyaki** is another choice. Somewhat misleadingly called the Japanese pancake, it is actually a mixture of vegetables, meat, and seafood in an egg-and-flour batter grilled at your table, much better with beer than with butter. It's most popular for lunch or as an after-movie snack.

Another is **kushi-age**, skewered bits of meat, seafood, and vegetables battered, dipped in bread crumbs, and deep-fried. There are many small restaurants serving only kushi-age at a counter, and many of the robatayaki serve it as a side dish. It's also a popular drinking snack.

Oden, a winter favorite, is another inex-pensive meal. A variety of meats and veg-etables slowly simmered in vats, it goes well with beer or sake. This, too, may be or-dered piece by piece (*ippin*) from the as-sortment you see steaming away behind the counter or *moriawase*, in which case the cook will serve you up an assortment.

Regional Differences

Tōkyō people are known for their candor and vigor, as compared with the refined re-straint of people in the older, more provin-cial Kyōto. This applies as much to food as it does to language, art, and fashion. Foods in the Kansai district (including Kyōto, Nara, Ōsaka, and Kōbe) tend to be lighter, the sauces less spicy, the soups not as hardy as those of the Kantō district, of which Tōkyō is the center. How many Tōkyōites have been heard to grumble about the "weak" soba broth on their vis-its to Kyōto? You go to Kyōto for the del-icate and formal kaiseki, to Tōkyō for sushi.

Nigiri zushi (note that the pronunciation of "sushi" changes to "zushi" when com-bined with certain words), with pieces of raw fish on bite-size balls of rice (the form with which most Westerners are famil-iar), originated in the Kantō district, where there is a bounty of fresh fish. *Saba zushi* is the specialty of landlocked Kyōto. Ac-tually the forerunner of nigiri zushi, it is made by pressing salt-preserved mackerel onto a bed of rice in a mold.

Every island in the Japanese archipelago has its specialty, and within each island every province has its own *meibutsu ryōri*, or specialty dish. In Kyūshū try *shippoku-ryōri*, a banquet-style feast of different dishes in which you eat your way up to a large fish mousse topped with shrimp. This dish is the local specialty in Nagasaki, for centuries the only port through which Japan had contact with the West.

On the island of Shikoku, try *sawachi-ryōri*, an extravaganza of elaborately pre-pared platters of fresh fish dishes, which is the specialty of Kōchi, the main city on the Pacific Ocean side of the island. In Hokkaidō, where salmon dishes are the local specialty, try *ishikari-nabe*, a hearty salmon-and-vegetable stew.

The Bottom Line

A couple of things take some getting used to. Things will be easier for you in Japan if you've had some experience with chop-sticks. Some of the tourist-oriented restau-rants (and, of course, all those serving Western food) provide silverware, but most traditional restaurants in Japan offer only chopsticks. It's a good idea to practice. The secret is to learn to move only the chopstick on top rather than trying to move both at once.

Sitting on the floor is another obstacle for many, including the younger generation of Japanese, to whom the prospect of sitting on a cushion on tatami mats for an hour or so means nothing but stiff knees and numb feet. Because of this, many restaurants now have rooms with tables and chairs. The most traditional restaurants, however, have kept to the customary style of dining in tatami rooms. Give it a try. Nothing can compare with a full-course kaiseki meal brought to your room at a traditional inn. Fresh from the bath, robed in a cotton kimono, you are free to relax and enjoy it all, including the view. After all, the carefully landscaped garden outside your door was designed specifically to be seen from this position.

The service in Japan is usually superb, particularly at a *ryōri-ryokan,* as restaurant-inns are called. A maid is assigned to anticipate your every need (even a few you didn't know you had). "*O-kyakusan wa kamisama desu*" (the customer is god), as the old Japanese proverb goes. People who prefer to dine in privacy have been known to say the service is too much.

Other problems? "The portions are too small" is a common complaint. The solution is an adjustment in perspective. In the world of Japanese cuisine, there are colors to delight in, and shapes, textures, and flavors are balanced for your pleasure. Naturally, the aroma, flavor, and freshness of the foods have importance, but so do the dishware, the design of the room, the sound of water in a stone basin outside. You are meant to leave the table delighted—not stuffed. An appeal is made to all the senses through the food itself, the atmosphere, and appreciation for a carefully orchestrated feast in every sense of the word—these, and the luxury of time spent in the company of friends.

This is not to say that every Japanese restaurant offers aesthetic perfection. Your basic train-platform, stand-up, gulp-it-down noodle stall ("eat-and-out" in under six minutes) should leave no doubts as to the truth of the old saying that "all feet tread not in one shoe."

In the end you'll discover that the joy of eating in Japan lies in the adventure of exploring the possibilities. Along every city street you'll find countless little eateries specializing in anything you can name—and some you can't. In the major cities, you'll find French restaurants, British pubs, and little places serving Italian, Chinese, Indian, and American food. In country towns you can explore a world of regional delicacies found nowhere else. Each meal can be paired with a suitable drink, too, usually sake or beer. (For more on what to drink in Japan drinks, see the box "Japanese Beer, Wine, Spirits & Sake" in Chapter 2.)

There's something for everyone and every budget—from the most exquisitely prepared and presented formal kaiseki meal to a delicately sculpted salmon mousse à la nouvelle cuisine, from skewers of grilled chicken in barbecue sauce to a steaming bowl of noodle soup at an outdoor stall. And much to the chagrin of culinary purists, Japan has no dearth of international fast-food chains—from burgers to spareribs to fried chicken to doughnuts to 31 flavors of American ice cream.

Sometimes the contradictions of this intriguing culture—as seen in the startling contrast between ancient traditions and modern industrial life—seem almost overwhelming. Who would ever have thought you could face eating a salad that included seaweed along with lettuce and tomatoes, or that you could happily dig into green-tea ice cream? As the famous potter Kawai Kanjiro once said, "Sometimes it's better if you don't understand everything . . . It makes life so much more exciting."

— *Diane Durston*

ARTS & CULTURE

PAPERMAKING & CALLIGRAPHY

CERAMICS & LACQUERWARE

JAPANESE GARDENS

JAPANESE TEXTILES

BATHING: AN IMMERSION COURSE

RITUAL & RELIGION

THE TEA CEREMONY

GEISHA

JAPANESE SOCIETY: A FACTORY OF FADS

BOOKS & MOVIES

PAPERMAKING & CALLIGRAPHY

Papermaking

Handmade paper and shōji (paper screens) are unique and beautiful Japanese creations that are surprisingly affordable, unlike other traditional crafts. *Washi*, Japanese paper, can have a translucent quality that seems to argue against its amazing durability.

The use of paper as a decorative symbol in Shintō shrines—probably due to its purity when new—gives an added importance to the already high esteem the Japanese hold for paper and the written word. Paper is a symbol of *kami* (god), and the process to make it is almost ritualistic. Usually, the inner bark of the paper mulberry is used, but leaves, ropelike fibers, even gold flake can be added in the later steps of the process for a dramatic effect. The raw branches are steamed and bleached by exposure to cold or snow. The fibers are boiled with ash lye and subsequently rinsed. After chopping and beating the pulp, it's soaked in a starchy taro solution, and the textures or leaves are added for decoration. A screen is dipped in the floating fibers, and when the screen is pulled up evenly, a sheet of paper is formed. Amazingly, wet sheets when stacked do not stick together.

The best places to view the papermaking process are Kurodani, near Kyōto; Mino, in central Japan; and Yame, near Kurume. Different parts of Japan specialize in different products. Gifu is known for its umbrellas and lanterns, Nagasaki for its distinctive kites, and Nara for its calligraphy paper and utensils. A light, inexpensive, and excellent gift, Japanese paper is a handicraft you can easily carry home as a souvenir.

Calligraphy

Calligraphy in Japan arrived around AD 500 with Chinese characters. By 800 the *kana* of Japanese language—the two alphabets—began to be artistically written as well. The art of calligraphy lies not only in the creative execution of the characters, as in Western calligraphy, but also in the direct expression of the artist's personality and message. Thick, heavy splotches or delicate, watery lines should be viewed first without respect to their meaning, as creative forms displaying emotion. Then the meaning can come to the fore, adding substance to the art.

As with all traditional arts in Japan, there are various schools and styles of calligraphy—five in this case—each with more or less emphasis on structure and expression. The Chinese exported the *tenshō* (a primitive style called "seal") and *reishō* (scribe's style, an advanced primitive form) to Japan with written Buddhist scripture. The Japanese developed three other styles: *sōshō* (cursive writing), the looser *gyōshō* (semicursive, or "running" style), and *kaishō* (block, or standard style). The first two demonstrate the Japanese emphasis on expression to convey an impromptu, flowing image unique to the moment—retouching and erasing is impossible. Kaishō has since developed into carved calligraphy on wood—either engraved or in relief—and the traditional stamp art seen at temples and in print. Avant-garde styles now popular, which are difficult even for Japanese to read, can seem the most interesting to foreigners as an art form. You'll see this style in many traditional restaurants.

Go to visitor centers if you would like to try out a brush. Reading: *The Art of Japanese Calligraphy,* by Yujiro Nakata.

— David Miles & Barbara Blechman

CERAMICS & LACQUERWARE

Ceramics

With wares that range from clean, flawlessly decorated porcelain to rustic pieces so spirited that they almost breathe, Japanese pottery attracts its share of enthusiasts and ardent collectors for good reason. During the past several decades, it has significantly influenced North American ceramic artists. The popularity of Raku firing techniques, adapted from those of the famous Japanese pottery clan of the same name, is one example.

Japanese ceramic styles are defined regionally. Arita *yaki* (ceramic ware from Arita on Kyūshū), Tobe yaki, Kutani yaki, and Kyōto's Kyō yaki and Kiyomizu yaki are all porcelain ware. True to the nature of porcelain—a delicate fine-particled clay body—these styles are either elaborately decorated or covered with images. Stoneware decoration tends to have an earthier but no less refined appeal, befitting the rougher texture of the clay body. Mashiko yaki's brown, black, and white glazes are often applied in splatters. Celebrated potter Shōji Hamada (1894–1978) worked in Mashiko.

Other regional potters use glazes on stoneware for texture and coloristic effects—mottled, crusty Tokoname yaki; speckled, earth-tone Shigaraki yaki made near Kyōto; and the pasty white or blue-white Hagi yaki come to life with the surface and depth of their rustic glazes. Bizen yaki, another stoneware, has no liquid glaze applied to its surfaces. Pots are buried in ash, wrapped in straw, or colored in the firing process by the potters' manipulations of kiln conditions.

Unless your mind is set on the idea of kiln hopping in pottery towns like Hagi, Bizen, and Arita, you can find these wares in department stores. If you do go on a pilgrimage, call local kilns and tourist organizations to verify that what you want to see will be open and to ask about yearly pottery sales, during which local wares are discounted. Reading: *Inside Japanese Ceramics* (Weatherhill, 1999) by Richard L. Wilson.

Lacquerware

Japanese lacquerware has its origins in the Jōmon period (8,000–300 BC), when basic utensils were coated with lacquer resin made from tree sap. By the Nara period (AD 710–AD 784) most of the techniques we recognize today were being used. For example, *maki-e* (literally, "sprinkled picture") refers to several different techniques that use gold or silver powder in areas coated with liquid lacquer. In the Azuchi-Momoyama period (1568–1600), lacquerware exports made their way to Europe. The following period, the Edo (1603–1868), saw the broadening of the uses of lacquer for the newly prosperous merchant class.

The production of lacquerware starts with the draining, evaporation, and filtration of sap from lacquer trees. Successive layers of lacquer are carefully painted on basketry, wood, bamboo, woven textiles, metal, and even paper. The lacquer strengthens the object, making it durable for eating, carrying, or protecting fragile objects, such as fans. Lacquerware can be mirrorlike if polished; often the many layers contain inlays of mother-of-pearl or precious metals inserted between coats, creating a complicated design of exquisite beauty and delicacy. The best places to see lacquerware are Hōryū-ji in Nara—the temple has a beautiful display—and Wajima in Ishikawa. Expensive yet precious lacquerware remains one of the most distinctive and highest-quality crafts of Japan.

— David Miles & Barbara Blechman

JAPANESE GARDENS

WHAT MIGHT STRIKE US only second to the sense of beauty and calm that pervades Japanese gardens is how different they are from our own Western gardens. One key to understanding—and more fully enjoying—them is knowing that garden design, like all traditional Japanese arts, emerged out of the country's unique mixture of religious, philosophical, and artistic ideas.

Shintoism, Taoism, and Buddhism all stress the contemplation and re-creation of nature as part of the process of achieving understanding and enlightenment, and from these come many of the principles that most influence Japanese garden design.

From Shintoism, Japan's ancient religion, comes *genus loci* (the spirit of place) and the search for the divine presence in remarkable natural features: special mountains, trees, rocks, and so forth. Prevalent features of Tao influence are islands that act as a symbolic heaven for souls who achieve perfect harmony. Here sea turtles and cranes—creatures commonly represented in gardens—serve these enlightened souls.

Buddhist gardens function as settings for meditation, the goal of which is enlightenment. Shōgun and samurai were strongly drawn to Zen Buddhism and the achievement of enlightenment, and Zen gardens evolved as spaces for individuals to use almost exclusively for meditation and growth. The classic example from this time is the *karesansui*—dry landscape—consisting of meticulously placed rocks and raked gravel. It's a highly challenging style that reflects the skill of the designer.

Historically, the first garden designers in Japan were temple priests. Later, tea masters created gardens in order to refine the tea ceremony experience. A major contribution of the tea masters was the *roji*, the path or dewy ground that emotionally and mentally prepares participants for the ceremony as it leads them through the garden to the teahouse.

Gradually gardens moved out of the exclusive realm to which only nobles, *daimyō*, (feudal lords) wealthy merchants, and poets had access, and the increasingly affluent middle class began to demand professional designers. In the process, aesthetic concerns came to override those of religion.

In addition to genus loci, karesansui style, and the roji mentioned above, here are a few terms that will help you more fully experience Japanese gardens.

Change and movement. Change is highlighted in Japanese gardens with careful attention to the seasonal variations that plants undergo: from cherry blossoms in spring to summer greenery to autumn leaf coloring to winter snow clinging to the garden's bare bones. A water element, either real or abstract, often represents movement, as with the use of raked gravel or a stone "stream."

Mie gakure. The "reveal-and-hide" principle dictates that from no point should all of a garden be visible, that there is always mystery and incompleteness, and that viewers move through a garden to contemplate its changing perspectives.

Miniaturized landscapes. Depicting celebrated natural and literary sites, these references have been one of the most frequently utilized design techniques in Japanese gardens. They hark back to their original inspiration—Fuji-san represented by a truncated cone of stones; Ama-no-Hashidate, the famous spit of land, by a stone bridge; or a mighty forest by a lone tree.

Shakkei. "Borrowed landscape" extends the boundaries of a garden by integrating a nearby attractive mountain, grove of trees, or a sweeping temple roofline, for example, and framing and capturing the view by echoing it with elements of similar shape or color inside the garden itself.

Symbolism. Abstract concepts and mythological legends, readily understood by Japan's homogeneous population, are part of the garden vocabulary. The use of boulders in a streambed can represent life's surmountable difficulties, a pine tree can stand for stability, or islands in a pond for a faraway paradise.

— David Miles & Barbara Blechman

JAPANESE TEXTILES

THE TOPIC OF TEXTILES is invariably linked to the history and nature of kimonos and costumes, which offered the best opportunity for weavers, dyers, and designers to exhibit their skills. Both Buddhism and Confucianism helped to create the four castes in Japan: samurai, Buddhist clerics, farmers, and townspeople (merchants and artisans) in descending order of importance. Courtesans and actors often slipped through the cracks and thus were exempt from the targets of the laws that reinforced these strata by making certain types of dress illegal for lower castes. Outer appearance helped to identify social rank and maintained order. Styles of embroidery and decoration and sumptuous clothing changed legal status in reaction to social upheavals and the eventual rise of the merchant class.

The types of the kimono—Japanese traditional dress attire is unisex in cut—are made from flat woven panels that provide the most surface for decoration. Although Western clothing follows the body line in a sculptural way, the Japanese use of fabric is more painterly and has little concern for body size and shape. No matter the wearer's height or weight, a kimono is made from one bolt of cloth cut and stitched into four panels and fitted with a collar. When creating a kimono, or the Buddhist clerics' *kesa* (a body wrap), no fabric is wasted. Shintō's emphasis is evident in the importance of natural fabrics, as the way of the gods was always concerned with purity and defilement.

Regional designs are the rule in textiles. Kyōto's heavily decorated Nishijin Ori is as sumptuous as Japanese fabric comes. Okinawa produces a variety of stunning fabrics, and both Kyōto's and Tōkyō's stencil dyeing techniques yield intricate, elegant patterns. The most affordable kimonos are used kimonos—which can be nearly flawless or in need of minor stitching. Kyōto's flea markets are a good venue for this. Also look for lighter weight *yukata* (robes), *obi* (sashes), or handkerchiefs from Arimatsu, near Nagoya, for example. Good places to see fabrics are Kyōto's Fūzoku Hakubutsukan (Costume Museum), Nishijin Orimono (Textile Center), and the Tōkyō National Museum, which displays garments of the Edo period.

BATHING:
AN IMMERSION COURSE

MANY JAPANESE CULTURAL PHE-
NOMENA confound first-time
visitors to the country, but few
rituals are as opaque to foreigners as those surrounding bathing.
Partly because of the importance of purification rites in Shintō, Japan's ancient
indigenous religion, the art of bathing has
been a crucial element of Japanese culture
for centuries. Baths in Japan are as much
about pleasure and relaxation as they are
about washing and cleansing. Traditionally, communal bathhouses served as centers for social gatherings, and even though
most modern houses and apartments have
bathtubs, many Japanese still prefer the
pleasures of communal bathing—either
at *onsen* (hot springs) while on vacation
or in public bathhouses closer to home.

Japanese bathtubs themselves are different from those in the West—they're deep
enough to sit in upright with (very hot)
water up to the neck—and the procedures
for using them are quite different as well.
You wash yourself in a special area outside the tub first. The tubs are for soaking, not washing; soap must not get into
the bathwater.

Many hotels in major cities offer only
Western-style reclining bathtubs, so to in-
dulge in the pleasure of a Japanese bath
you'll need to stay in a Japanese-style inn
or find an *o-furo-ya* (public bathhouse).
The latter are clean, hygienic, and easy to
find. Japanese bath towels, which are typically called (*ta*-o-ru), are available for a
fee at onsen and bathhouses. They are no
larger than a hand towel, and they have
three functions: covering your privates
(and breasts in mixed bathing), washing before you bathe and scrubbing while you
bathe (if desired), and drying off (wring
them out hard and they will dry you quite
well). If you want a larger towel to dry
yourself off, you will have to bring one
along.

You may at first feel justifiably appre-
hensive about bathing (and bathing *properly*) in an o-furo, but if you're well versed
in bathing etiquette, you should soon feel
at ease. And once you've experienced a variety of public baths—from the standard
bathhouses found in every neighborhood
to idyllic outdoor hot springs—you may
find yourself an unlikely advocate of this
ancient custom.

The first challenge in bathing is acknowledging that your Japanese bath mates will
stare at your body. Take solace, however,
in the fact that their apparent voyeurism
most likely stems from curiosity.

When you enter the bathing room, help
yourself to two towels, soap, and shampoo (often included in the entry fee), and
grab a bucket and a stool. At one of the
shower stations around the edge of the
room, crouch on your bucket (or stand if
you prefer) and use the handheld showers, your soap, and one of your towels to
wash yourself thoroughly. A head-to-toe
twice-over will impress onlookers. Rinse
off, and then you may enter the public
bath. When you do, you'll still have one
dry towel. You can use it to cover yourself, or you can place it on your head (as
you'll see many of your bath mates doing)
while soaking. The water in the bath is as
hot as the body can endure, and the reward
for making it past the initial shock of the
heat is the pleasure of a lengthy soak in
water that does not become tepid. All you
need to do then is lean back, relax, and
experience the pleasures of Shintō-style
purification—cleanse your body and enlighten your spirit. It seems, in Japan,
cleanliness is next to godliness.

— David Miles

Buddhism

Buddhism in Japan grew out of a Korean king's symbolic gift of a statue of Shaka—the first Buddha, Prince Gautama—to the Yamato court in AD 538. The Soga clan adopted the foreign faith and used it as a vehicle for changing the political order of the day. After battling for control of the country, the Soga clan established itself as political rulers, and Buddhism took permanent hold of Japan. Shōtoku Taishi, the crown prince and regent during this period, sent the first Japanese ambassadors to China, which inaugurated the importation of Chinese culture, writing, and religion in Japan. Since that time several eras in Japanese history have seen the equation of consolidating state power with promulgating Buddhist influence and building temples. By the 8th century AD Japanese Buddhism's six schools of thought were well established, and priests from India and Persia came for the ceremonial opening of Tōdai-ji in Nara. Scholars argue that the importation of architectural styles and things Buddhist in this period may have had more to do with the political rather than religious needs of Japanese society. Likewise, the intertwining of religion and state and the importation of foreign ideas had undeniably political motivations during the Meiji Restoration and Japanese colonial expansion early in the 20th century. And the use of foreign ideas continues to be an essential component of understanding the social climate in Japan today.

Three waves in the development of Japanese Buddhism followed the religion's Nara-period (710–84) florescence. In the Heian period (794–894), two priests who studied in China—Saichō and Kūkai—introduced esoteric Buddhism. Near Kyōto, Saichō established a temple on Mt. Hiei—making it the most revered mountain in Japan after Mt. Fuji. Kūkai

established the Shingon sect of Esoteric Buddhism on Mt. Kōya, south of Nara. It's said he is still in a state of meditation and will remain so until the arrival of the last bodhisattva (Buddhist messianic saint, *bosatsu* in Japanese). In Japanese temple architecture, Esoteric Buddhism introduced the separation of the temple into an interior for the initiated and an outer laypersons' area. This springs from Esoteric Buddhism's emphasis on *mikkyō* (secret rites) for the initiated.

Amidism was the second wave, and it flourished until the introduction of Zen in 1185. Its adherents saw the world emerging from a period of darkness, during which Buddhism had been in decline, and asserted that salvation was offered only to the believers in Amida, a Nyorai (Buddha), an enlightened being. Amidism's promise of salvation and its subsequent versions of heaven and hell earned it the appellation "Devil's Christianity" from visiting Christian missionaries in the 16th century.

The influences of Nichiren and Zen Buddhist philosophies pushed Japanese Buddhism in the unique direction it heads today. Nichiren (1222–82) was a monk who insisted that repetition of the phrase "Hail the miraculous law of the Lotus Sutra" would bring salvation, the Lotus Sutra being the supposed last and greatest sutra of Shaka. Zen Buddhism was attractive to the samurai class's ideals of discipline and worldly detachment and thus spread throughout Japan in the 12th century.

Japanese Buddhism today, like most religions in Japan, plays a minimal role in the daily life of the average Japanese. Important milestones in life provide the primary occasions for religious observance. Most Japanese have Buddhist burials. Weddings are usually in the Shintō style; recently, ceremonial references to Christian weddings have crept in, added mainly for romantic effect. (This mixing of religions may seem strange in the West, but it is wholly acceptable in Japan.) Outsiders have criticized the Japanese for lacking spirituality, and it is true that many Japanese don't make some kind of religious observance part of their daily or weekly lives. That said, there is a spiritual element in the people's unflinching belief in the group, and Japanese circles around very spiritual issues.

For more information on religious and political history, statuary manifestations of bosatsu and the Buddha, and architectural styles, consult *Buddhism, A History,* by Noble Ross Reat, and *Sources of Japanese Tradition,* by Tsunoda, De Bary, and Keene.

Shintō

Shintō—literally, "the way of the *kami* (god)"—does not preach a moral doctrine or code of ethics to follow. It's a form of animism, nature worship, based on myth and rooted to the geography and holy places of the land. Fog-enshrouded mountains, pairs of rocks, primeval forests, and geothermal activity are all manifestations of the *kami-sama* (honorable gods). For many Japanese the Shintō aspect of their lives is simply the realm of the kami-sama, not attached to a religious framework as it would be in the West. In that sense, the name describes more a philosophy than a religion.

Shintō rites that affect the daily lives of Japanese today are the wedding ceremony, the *matsuri* (festivals), and New Year's Day. The wedding ceremony uses an elaborate, colorful kimono for the bride and a simple, masculine *montsuki* (crested) kimono and *haori* overcoat with *hakama* pants for the groom. The number three is significant, and sake, of the fruits of the earth from the gods, is the ritual libation.

The neighborhood shrine's annual matsuri is a time of giving thanks for prosperity and of the blessing of homes and local businesses. *O-mikoshi,* portable shrines for the gods, are enthusiastically carried around the district by young local men. Shouting and much sake drinking are part of the celebration.

New Year's Day entails visiting an important local shrine and praying for health, happiness, success in school or business, or the safe birth of a child in the coming year. A traditional meal of rice cakes and sweet beans is served in stacked boxes at home, as part of a family time not unlike those of traditional Western winter holidays.

Like Buddhism, Shintō was used throughout Japanese history as a tool for affirming the might of a given ruling power. The Meiji Restoration in 1868 used Shintoism to reclaim the emperor's sacred right to rule and to wrest control from the last Tokugawa shōgun. Today shrines are more often visited for their beauty than for their spiritual importance, though there is no denying the ancient spiritual pull of shrines like the Ise Jingū, south of Nagoya.

— David Miles

THE TEA CEREMONY

THE TEA CEREMONY was formalized by the 16th century under the patronage of the Ashikaga shōguns, but it was the Zen monks of the 12th century who started the practice of drinking tea for a refresher between meditation sessions. The samurai and tea master Sen-no-Rikyū elucidated "the Way," the meditative and spiritual aspect of the ceremony, and is the most revered figure in the history of tea. For samurai, the ceremony appealed to their ideals and their sense of discipline, and diversions in time of peace were necessary. In essence, tea ceremony is a spiritual and philosophical ritual whose prescribed steps and movements serve as an aid in sharpening the aesthetic sense.

Tea ceremony has a precisely choreographed program. Participants enter the teahouse or room and comment on the specially chosen art in the entryway. The ritual begins as the server prepares a cup of tea for the first patron. This process involves a strictly determined series of movements and actions, common to every ceremony, which include cleansing each of the utensils to be used. One by one the participants slurp up their bowl of tea, then eat the sweet cracker served with it. Finally, comments about the beauty of the bowls used are exchanged. The entire ritual involves contemplating the beauty in the smallest actions, focusing their meaning in the midst of the impermanence of life.

The architecture of a traditional teahouse is also consistent. There are two entrances: a service entrance for the host and server and a low door that requires that guests enter on their knees, in order to be humbled. Tearooms often have a flower arrangement or piece of artwork in the alcove, for contemplation and comment, and tatami (grass mat) flooring. Though much of the process may seem the same wherever you experience the ceremony, there are different schools of thought on the subject. The three best-known schools of tea are the Ura Senke, the Omote Senke, and the Musha Kōji, each with its own styles, emphases, and masters.

Most of your tea experiences will be geared toward the uninitiated: the tea ceremony is a rite that requires methodical initiation by education. If you don't go for instruction before your trip, keep two things in mind if you attend or are invited to a tea ceremony: first, be in the right frame of mind when you enter the room. Though the tea ceremony is a pleasant event, some people take it quite seriously, and boisterous behavior beforehand is frowned upon. Instead, make conversation that enhances a mood of serenity and invites a feeling of meditative quietude. Second, be sure to sit quietly through the serving and drinking—controlled slurping is expected—and openly appreciate the tools and cups afterward, commenting on their elegance and simplicity. This appreciation is an important final step of the ritual. Above all, pay close attention to the practiced movements of the ceremony, from the art at the entryway and the kimono of the server to the quality of the utensils. Reading: *The Book of Tea,* by Kakuzo Okakura; *Cha-no-Yu: The Japanese Tea Ceremony,* by A. L. Sadler.

— David Miles

GEISHA

ECAUSE THE CHARACTER FOR the *gei* in *geisha* stands for arts and accomplishments (*sha* in this case means person), the public image of geisha in Japan is one of high status. Although it's a common misconception in the West, geisha are not prostitutes. To become a geisha, a woman must perfect many talents. She must have grace and a thorough mastery of etiquette. She should have an accomplished singing voice and dance beautifully. She needs to have a finely tuned aesthetic sense—with flower arranging and tea ceremony—and should excel at the art of conversation. In short, she should be the ultimate companion.

These days geisha are a rare breed. They numbered a mere 10,000 in the late 1980s, as opposed to 80,000 in the 1920s. This is partly due to the increase of bar hostesses—who perform a similar function in nightclubs with virtually none of a geisha's training—not to mention the refinement and expense it takes to hire a geisha. Because she is essentially the most personal form of entertainer, the emphasis is on artistic and conversational skills, not solely on youth or beauty. Thus the typical geisha can work to an advanced age.

Geisha will establish a variety of relations with men. Besides maintaining a dependable amount of favorite customers, one might choose a *danna*, one man for emotional, sexual, and financial gratification. The geisha's exercise of choice in this matter is due partly to the fact that wages and tips alone must provide enough for her to survive. Some geisha marry, most often to an intimate client. When they do, they leave the profession.

A geisha typically starts her career as a servant at a house until 13. She continues as a *maiko* (dancing child) until she masters the requisite accomplishments at about 18. Before World War II full geisha status was achieved after a geisha experienced a *mizuage* (deflowering), with an important client of the house. Maiko must master the shamisen and learn the proper hairstyles and kimono fittings. They are a sight to see on the banks of the Kamogawa in the Gion district of Kyōto, or in Shimbashi, Akasaka, and Ginza in Tōkyō. Today geisha unions, restaurant unions, and registry offices regulate the times and fees of geisha. Fees are measured in "sticks"—generally, one hour—which is the time it would take a stick of *senkō* (incense) to burn.

Arthur Golden's minutely researched novel, *Memoirs of a Geisha,* offers a balanced and intelligent view of this society seldom to be found in English-language books.

— David Miles

JAPANESE SOCIETY:
A FACTORY OF FADS

T IS IMPOSSIBLE TO SUMMARIZE the life of a people in brief. Still, there are a few fascinating points about the Japanese that are nonetheless important to mention, even if only in passing.

The Japanese communicate among themselves in what Dr. Chie Nakane, in her *Japanese Society* (1972), calls a "vertical society." In other words, the Japanese constantly vary the way they speak with each other according to the gender, family and educational background, occupation and position, and age of the speakers. Japanese grammar reflects this by requiring different verbs for different levels of interaction. Since it is necessary for individuals to vary the way they speak according to the person, they are always considering the levels of the people around them. In a crowded country, this means the Japanese are often wondering what other people are thinking—often in an effort to gauge where they belong themselves. This constant consideration toward other members of their group makes the Japanese keen readers of other people's emotions and reactions.

Where much of the West—the United States in particular—has shed nearly everything but wealth as an indicator of position in society, the Japanese maintain concepts of social order that have feudal echoes, as in the ideas of *uchi* and *soto*. Uchi refers to the home, the inside group, and, ultimately, Japan and Japaneseness. Soto is everything outside. Imagine uchi being a set of concentric rings, where the most central group is the family; the next is the neighborhood or extended family; then the school, company, or association; then the prefecture, the family of companies, or the region in which they live; and, finally, Japan itself. Japanese verb forms are more casual within the various uchi, as opposed to the more polite forms for

those "outside." Interestingly enough, the *gai* in the Japanese word for foreigner, *gaijin*, is the same character as *soto*. Soto—not belonging—is an undeniable barrier for non-Japanese. Translated into feelings, being the "other" can be frustrating and alienating. At the same time, it makes instances of crossing the boundary into some level of uchi that much more precious.

Despite the belief that the American presence after World War II was what built Japan, it is more correctly the sense of tribe or group the Japanese have utilized to their advantage since the Meiji Restoration that really created modern Japan. In the West we might have trouble understanding what we perceive as a lack of individuality in Japanese society, but we tend to ignore the sense of togetherness and joy that comes from a feeling of homogeneity. We might also miss any number of subtleties in interpersonal communication because we are wholly unaccustomed to them. It can take a lifetime to master the finer points of Japanese ambiguities, but even a basic appreciation of shades of meaning and the Japanese vigilance in maintaining the tightness of the group helps to see the beauty of this different way of life.

This beauty might be that much more precious in the face of change. With more of the younger generation traveling and living abroad, women especially, the group mentality and its role in supporting the Japanese socioeconomic structure are eroding rapidly.

You're bound to notice that the Japanese are extremely fond of animation, and they use it in communicating ideas and in advertising far more than we do in the West. So you'll see the anthropomorphizing of garbage cans, signage, and even huge, cute-squid telephone booths. The Japanese also seem to lead the world in the production of purposeless gadgets that astound and delight, if only for a minute or two. If this is your thing, don't miss the shops in downtown Ōsaka, or Harajuku and Shibuya in Tōkyō, because you'll never find these items anywhere else. Some of them are expensive—the mooing cow clock that wakes you up with "Don't-o suleepu yo-ah liefoo eh-way" looks hardly worth more than $10 but is nearly four times that, if you can even find one available; and the "waterfall sounds" player for shy women using the toilet can run up to $300.

There are reams of books and articles on Japanese English—and how they use and abuse it—but the topic might not come to mind until you set foot in Japan. Throughout the country, on billboards and in stores, on clothes, bags, hats, and even on cars, baffling, cryptic, often side-splitting English phrases leap out at you in the midst of your deepest cultural encounters. For example: "Woody goods: We have a woody heart, now listen to my story." What could this possibly mean? Did it make sense in the original Japanese?

Alas, friends and family might not understand why you find funny English so hilarious, without a firsthand encounter with something like CREAM SODA earnestly printed on a bodybuilder's T-shirt—or a fashion catalog that cryptically asserts "optimistic sunbeam shines beautifully for you." These tortured meanings are no doubt a compliment to the ascendancy of the English language, which on the world popular-culture stage is, in whatever form, chic and cool. You might find that on a heavy day of temple viewing, funny English might be the straightest path toward *satori* (enlightenment).

The latest obsessions in Japan can take a long time to get rolling, but when they do, they can take over the country. And Japanese homogeneity makes for a certain lemming quality that is utterly intriguing when it comes to observing fads. Take the wild popularity of Tamagotchi and Pokèmon. The international success of these techno-obsessions just goes to show how adept the Japanese are at catering to the world's unrecognized needs.

Whatever the fad is, when you're in Japan, make a note of it and try to remember the Japanese name or words associated with it. When you try to pronounce them, Japanese friends and colleagues will be immensely humored and impressed. Such is the intensity of fads that they act as barometers of the atmosphere of Japan at any given time.

— David Miles

Books

The incredible refinement of Japanese culture has produced a wealth of literature. Yet in the face of thousands of such books, where should you begin? If you are a newcomer to the subject of Japan, start with Pico Iyer's *The Lady and the Monk*, which will charm you through the first five phases of stereotypical infatuation with Japan and leave you with five times as many insights. Then read Seichō Matsumoto's *Inspector Imanishi Investigates*, a superb detective novel that says volumes about Japanese life (make a list of characters' names as you read to keep them straight). For those wanting to know more about the atomic bombing, John Hersey's *Hiroshima*, in which he records the stories of survivors, is essential reading. For a fictional retelling of this terrible period in Japan's history read Ibuse Masuji's classic novel *Black Rain*.

Art & Architecture. A wealth of literature exists on Japanese art. Much of the early writing has not withstood the test of time, but R. Paine and Alexander Soper's *Art and Architecture of Japan* remains a good place to start. A more recent survey, though narrower in scope, is Joan Stanley-Smith's *Japanese Art*.

The multivolume *Japan Arts Library* covers most of the styles and personalities of the Japanese arts. The series has volumes on castles, teahouses, screen painting, and wood-block prints. A more detailed look at the architecture of Tōkyō is Edward Seidensticker's *Low City, High City*. Kazuo Nishi and Kazuo Hozumi's *What Is Japanese Architecture?* treats the history of Japanese architecture and uses examples of buildings you will actually see on your travels.

Fiction & Poetry. The great classic of Japanese fiction is the *Tale of Genji*, written by Murasaki Shikibu, a woman of the imperial court around 1000 AD. Genji, or the Shining Prince, has long been taken as the archetype of ideal male behavior. From the same period, Japanese literature's golden age, *The Pillow Book of Sei Shōnagon* is the stylish and stylized diary of a woman's courtly life. *The Tale of Heike* is the poetic and highly moving story of the battles and eventual defeat of the ancient Taira clan by the Minamotos.

The Edo period is well covered by literary translations. Howard Hibbett's *Floating World in Japanese Fiction* gives an excellent selection with commentaries. For a selection of Edo ghost stories try Akinari Ueda's *Ugetsu Monogatari: Tales of Moonlight and Rain*, translated by Leon Zolbrod. The racy prose of late-17th-century Saikaku Ihara is translated in various books, including *Some Final Words of Advice* and *Five Women Who Loved Love*.

Modern Japanese fiction is more widely available in translation. One of the best-known writers among Westerners is Yukio Mishima, author of *The Sea of Fertility* trilogy and *The Temple of The Golden Pavilion*, among many other works. His books often deal with the effects of postwar Westernization on Japanese culture. Two superb prose stylists are Junichirō Tanizaki, author of *The Makioka Sisters, Some Prefer Nettles,* and the racy 1920s *Quicksand*; and Nobel Prize winner Yasunari Kawabata, whose superbly written novels include *Snow Country* and *The Sound of the Mountain*. Kawabata's *Thousand Cranes,* which uses the tea ceremony as a vehicle, is an elegant page-turner. Jirō Osaragi's *The Journey* is a lucid, entertaining rendering of the clash of tradition and modernity in postwar Japan. Also look for Natsume Sōseki's charming *Botchan* and delightful *I Am a Cat*.

Other novelists and works of note are Kōbō Abe, whose *Woman in the Dunes* is a 1960s landmark, and Shūsaku Endō, who brutally and breathlessly treated the early clash of Japan with Christianity in *The Samurai.*

Novelists at work in Japan today are no less interesting. Fumiko Enchi's *Masks* poignantly explores the fascinating public-private dichotomy. Haruki Murakami's *Wild Sheep Chase* is a wild ride indeed; his short stories are often bizarre and humorous, with a touch of the science fiction thrown in for good measure. Murakami's more recent *The Wind-up Bird Chronicle,* a dense and daring novel, fantastically juxtaposes the banality of modern Japanese suburbia with the harsh realities of 20th-century Japanese history. Along with Murakami's books, Banana Yoshimoto's *Kitchen* and other novels are probably the most fun you'll have with any Japanese fiction. Kōno Taeko's *Toddler-Hunting* and Yūko Tsushima's *The Shooting Gallery* are as engrossing and well crafted as they are frank about the burdens of tradition on Japanese women today. Nobel Prize winner Kenzaburō Ōe's writing similarly explores deeply personal issues, among them his compelling relationship with his disabled son. His two most important works are *A Personal Matter* and *Silent Scream.*

Haiku, the 5-7-5 syllable form that the monk Matsuo Bashō honed in the 17th century, is the flagship of Japanese poetry. His *Narrow Road to the Deep North* is a wistful prose-and-poem travelogue that is available in a few translations. But there are many more forms and authors worth exploring. Three volumes of translations by Kenneth Rexroth include numerous authors' work from the last 1,000 years: *One Hundred Poems from the Japanese, 100 More Poems from the Japanese,* and *Women Poets of Japan* (translated with Akiko Atsumi). Each has notes and brief author biographies. *Ink Dark Moon,* translated by Jane Hirshfield with Mariko Aratani, presents the remarkable poems of Ono no Komachi and Izumi Shikibu, two

of Japan's earliest women poets. The Zen poems of Ryōkan represent the sacred current in Japanese poetry; look for *Dew Drops on a Lotus Leaf.* Other poets to look for are Issa, Buson, and Bonchō. Two fine small volumes that link their haiku with those of other poets, including Bashō, are *The Monkey's Raincoat* and the beautifully illustrated *A Net of Fireflies.*

Another way into Japanese culture is riding on the heels of Westerners who live or have lived in Japan. The emotional realities of such experience are engagingly rendered in *The Broken Bridge: Fiction from Expatriates in Literary Japan,* edited by Suzanne Kamata. The enormously popular tale *Memoirs of a Geisha,* by Arthur Golden, recounts the dramatic life of a geisha in the decades surrounding World War II.

History & Society. Fourteen hundred years of history are rather a lot to take in when going on a vacation, but two good surveys make the task much easier: Richard Storry's *A History of Modern Japan* (by modern, he means everything post-pre-historic) and George Sansom's *Japan: A Short Cultural History.* Sansom's three-volume *History of Japan* is a more exhaustive treatment.

If you're interested in earlier times, Yamamoto Tsunetomo's *Hagakure (The Book of the Samurai)* is an 18th-century guide of sorts to the principles and ethics of the "Way of the Samurai," written by a Kyūshū samurai. Dr. Junichi Saga's *Memories of Silk and Straw: A Self-Portrait of Small-Town Japan* is his 1970s collection of interviews with local old-timers in his hometown outside Tōkyō. Saga's father illustrated the accounts. Few books get so close to the realities of everyday life in early modern rural Japan. Elizabeth Bumiller's 1995 *The Secrets of Mariko* intimately recounts a very poignant year in the life of a Japanese woman and her family.

The Japanese have a genre they refer to as *nihon-jin-ron,* or studies of Japaneseness. A fine study of the Japanese mind is found in Takeo Doi's *The Anatomy of Dependence* and Chie Nakane's *Japanese Society.*

Karel van Wolferen's *The Enigma of Japanese Power* is an enlightening book on the Japanese sociopolitical system, especially for diplomats and businesspeople intending to work with the Japanese. And as a sounding of the experience of his years in the country, Alex Kerr's *Lost Japan* examines the directions of Japanese society past and present. This book was the first by a foreigner ever to win Japan's Shinchō Gakugei literature prize.

Language. There's an overwhelming number of books and courses available for studying Japanese. *Japanese for Busy People* uses conversational situations (rather than grammatical principles) as a means of introducing the Japanese language. With it you will also learn the two syllabaries, *hiragana* and *katakana,* and rudimentary *kanji* characters.

Religion. Anyone wanting to read a Zen Buddhist text should try *The Platform Sutra of the Sixth Patriarch,* one of the Zen classics, written by an ancient Chinese head of the sect and translated by Philip B. Yampolsky. Another Buddhist text of high importance is the *Lotus Sutra*; it has been translated by Leon Hurvitz as *The Scripture of the Lotus Blossom of the Fine Dharma: The Lotus Sutra.* Stuart D. Picken has written books on both major Japanese religions: *Shintō: Japan's Spiritual Roots* and *Buddhism: Japan's Cultural Identity.* William R. LaFleur's *Karma of Words: Buddhism and the Literary Arts in Medieval Japan* traces how Buddhism affected medieval Japanese mentality and behavior.

Travel Narratives. Two travel narratives stand out as superb introductions to Japanese history, culture, and people. Donald Richie's classic *The Inland Sea* recalls his journey and encounters on the fabled Seto Nai-kai. Leila Philip's year working in a Kyūshū pottery village became the eloquent *Road Through Miyama.*

Movies

The Japanese film industry has been active since the early days of the medium's invention. A limited number of Japanese films, however, have been transferred to video for Western audiences, and even these may be hard to locate at your local video store. Many Japanese movies fall into two genres: the *jidai-geki* period-costume films and the *gendai-geki* films about contemporary life. Period films often deal with romantic entanglements, ghosts, and samurai warriors, as in *chambara* (sword-fight) films. Movies set in more recent times often focus on lower- or middle-class family life and the world of gangsters.

Western viewers have typically encountered Japanese cinema in the works of Japan's most prolific movie directors, Kenji Mizoguchi, Yasujirō Ozu, and Akira Kurosawa. Mizoguchi's career spanned a 34-year period beginning in 1922, and three of his finest films investigate the social role of a female protagonist in feudal Japan: *The Life of Oharu* (1952), *Ugetsu* (1953), and *Sanchō the Bailiff* (1954). Ozu directed 54 films from 1927 to 1962; most of his movies explore traditional Japanese values and concentrate on the everyday life and relationships of middle-class families. Among his best works are *Late Spring* (1949), *Early Summer* (1951), *Tōkyō Story* (1953), and *An Autumn Afternoon* (1962).

Kurosawa, who began directing movies in 1943, is the best-known Japanese filmmaker among Western audiences. His film *Rashōmon* (1950), a 12th-century murder story told by four different narrators, brought him international acclaim and sparked world interest in Japanese cinema. Among his other classic period films are *Seven Samurai* (1954), *The Hidden Fortress* (1958), *Yōjimbō* (1961), *Red Beard* (1965), *Dersu Uzala* (1975), and *Kagemusha* (1980). The life-affirming

Ikiru (1952) deals with an office worker dying of cancer. *High and Low* (1963), about a kidnapping, was based on a detective novel by Ed McBain. Two of Kurosawa's most honored films were adapted from Shakespeare plays: *Throne of Blood* (1957), based on *Macbeth,* and *Ran* (1985), based on *King Lear.*

Another director in the same generation as Mizoguchi and Ozu was Teinosuke Kinugasa, whose *Gate of Hell* (1953) vividly re-creates medieval Japan. *The Samurai Trilogy* (1954), directed by Hiroshi Inagaki, follows the adventures of a legendary 16th-century samurai hero, Musashi Miyamoto. A whole new group of filmmakers came to the forefront in postwar Japan, including Kon Ichikawa, who directed two powerful antiwar movies, *The Burmese Harp* (1956) and *Fires on the Plain* (1959); and Masaki Kobayashi, whose samurai period film *Harakiri* (1962) is considered his best work. In the late '60s and '70s several new directors gained prominence, including Hiroshi Teshigahara, Shōhei Imamura, and Nagisa Ōshima. Teshigahara is renowned for the allegorical *Woman in the Dunes* (1964), based on a novel by Kōbō Abe. Among Imamura's honored works are *The Ballad of Narayama* (1983), about the death of the elderly, and *Black Rain* (1989), which deals with the atomic bombing of Hiroshima. Ōshima directed *Merry*

Christmas, Mr. Lawrence (1983), about a British officer in a Japanese prisoner-of-war camp in Java during World War II.

Other Japanese filmmakers worth checking out are Yoshimitsu Morita, Jūzō Itami, Masayuki Suo, Kitano Takeshi and Iwai Shunji. Morita's *The Family Game* (1983) satirizes Japanese domestic life and the educational system. Itami won international recognition for *Tampopo* (1986), a highly original comedy about food. His other films include *A Taxing Woman* (1987), which pokes fun at the Japanese tax system, and *Mimbō* (1992), which dissects the world of Japanese gangsters. Suo's *Shall We Dance?* (1997) is a bittersweet comedy about a married businessman who escapes his daily routine by taking ballroom dance lessons. *Fireworks* (1997), by Kitano Takeshi, depicts a cop's struggle with loss in modern, frenetic Japan. Iwai Shunji's *Love Letter* (1995) is a touching story about a girl who receives a lost letter from her boyfriend after he has died.

The Japanese film industry also produces some of the best animated or anime movies in the world. The Academy Award-winning picture, *Spirited Away* (2002), available in English, is a good place to start for those interested in these kind of movies. *Kiki's Delivery Service* (1989), starring Kirsten Dunst as the voice of Kiki, is another very good choice.

FACTS & FIGURES

JAPAN AT A GLANCE

TŌKYŌ AT A GLANCE

CHRONOLOGY

JAPAN AT A GLANCE

Fast Facts

Capital: Tōkyō
National anthem: *Kimigayo (The Emperor's Reign)*
Type of government: Constitutional monarchy with a parliamentary government
Administrative divisions: 47 prefectures
Independence: 660 BC (traditional founding)
Constitution: May 3, 1947
Legal system: Modeled after European civil law system with English-American influence; judicial review of legislative acts in the Supreme Court
Suffrage: 20 years of age; universal
Legislature: Bicameral Diet or Kokkai with House of Councillors (247 seats, members elected for six-year terms, half reelected every three years, 149 members in multiseat constituencies and 98 by proportional representation); House of Representatives (480 seats, members elected for four-year terms, 300 in single-seat constituencies, 180 members by proportional representation in 11 regional blocs)
Population: 127.3 million
Population density: 340 people per square km (880 people per square mi)
Median age: Female: 44.1, male: 40.5
Life expectancy: Female: 84.5; male: 77.7
Infant mortality rate: 3.3 deaths per 1,000 live births
Literacy: 99%
Language: Japanese
Ethnic groups: Japanese 99%; other (Korean, Chinese, Brazilian, Filipino) 1%
Religion: Shintō and Buddhist 84%; other 16%

In fact, the whole of Japan is a pure invention. There is no such country, there are no such people . . . The Japanese people are . . . simply a mode of style, an exquisite fancy of art.

–Oscar Wilde

Geography & Environment

Land area: 374,744 square km (144,689 square mi), slightly smaller than California
Coastline: 29,751 km (11,487 mi)
Terrain: Mostly rugged and mountainous
Islands: Bonin Islands (Ogasawara-guntō), Daito-shotō, Minami-jima, Okino-tori-shima, Ryukyu Islands (Nansei-shotō), and Volcano Islands (Kazan-rettō)
Natural resources: Fish, mineral resources
Natural hazards: Japan has about 1,500 seismic occurrences (mostly tremors) every year; tsunamis; typhoons, volcanoes
Environmental issues: Air pollution from power plant emissions results in acid rain; acidification of lakes and reservoirs degrading water quality and threatening aquatic life; Japan is one of the largest consumers of fish and tropical timber, contributing to the depletion of these resources in Asia and elsewhere

Economy

Currency: Yen
Exchange rate: 110 yen
GDP: $3.6 trillion
Per capita income: 4 million yen ($35,610)
Inflation: -0.4%

Unemployment: 5.3%
Work force: 66.7 million; services 70%; industry 25%; agriculture 5%
Major industries: Chemicals, electronic equipment, machine tools, motor vehicles, processed foods, ships, steel and nonferrous metals, textiles
Agricultural products: Dairy products, eggs, fish, fruit, pork, poultry, rice, sugar beets, vegetables
Exports: $447.1 billion
Major export products: Chemicals, motor vehicles, office machinery, semiconductors
Export partners: U.S. 28.8%; China 9.6%; South Korea 6.9%; Taiwan 6.3%; Hong Kong 6.1%

Imports: $346.6 billion
Major import products: Chemicals, foodstuffs, fuels, machinery and equipment, raw materials, textiles
Import partners: China 18.3%; U.S. 17.4%; South Korea 4.6%; Indonesia 4.2%; Australia 4.1%

Japan has distorted its economy and depressed its living standard in order to keep its job structure and social values as steady as possible. At the governmentís direction, the entire economy has tried to flex almost as one, in response to the ever-changing world.

—James Fallows

Political Climate

Japan has more than 10,000 political parties and most are small, regional bodies without mass appeal. The Liberal Democratic party (LDP) held the majority of seats in the legislature since 1955, when the party was formed, with a brief ouster in the 1990s. The LDP is considered a conservative party and has supported close ties with the U.S., especially concerning security. The Democratic Party of Japan and New Kōmeitō form the largest opposition groups. Economically, deregulation and growth in the free market are important policy issues. Japan's aging population is also becoming a crucible for politicians, as the balance between the structure of the labor force and pensions and benefits for the elderly makes the governmentís budget a tough one to balance.

Did You Know?

• Japanese engineers have built a car that can go 11,193 miles on one gallon of fuel, a world record. The car performs best at 15 mi per hour and engineers are adapting the technology for commercial production. Japan is also home to the world's first environmentally friendly rental car company. Kōbe-Eco-Car in Kōbe has rented electric vehicles, compressed natural gas vehicles, and hybrid cars since it was founded in 1998.

• With an average life expectancy of 77.7 years for men and 84.5 years for women, the Japanese live longer than anyone else on the planet.

• To take any of the 2,200 daily trips on the East Japan Railway is to ride the world's busiest train system. It carries 16 million passengers over 4,684 mi of track, stopping at a dizzying 1,707 stations.

• The world's worst single-aircraft accident occurred in 1985 over Japan when a JAL Boeing 747 lost control over the rear of the aircraft. Fifteen crew members and 520 passengers were killed.

• The largest sumō wrestling champion in the history of the sport isn't Japanese, but American. Chad Rowan, whose sumō name is Akebono, was born in Hawaii, and reached the top ranking of *yokozuna* in 1983. He was 6 feet 8 inches and 501 pounds.

• The Japanese prime minister earns an annual salary of 69.3 million yen ($676,000), the highest of any prime minister in the world.

• Japan's Yomiuri Shimbun has more readers than any other newspaper on earth. Its combined morning and evening circulation is 14.3 million, more than 10 times larger than the New York Times.

• Japan is the third-largest consumer of cigarettes. The Japanese smoke about 325 billion cigarettes each year, about 100 billion less than Americans and more than a trillion less than the Chinese.

TŌKYŌ AT A GLANCE

Fast Facts

Type of government: Metropolitan prefecture with democratically elected governor and assembly. Wards and other subsidiary units have local assemblies.
Population: 12.4 million (city), 28 million (metro)
Population density: 5,656 people per square km (14,655 people per square mi)
Crime rate: Roughly 225 criminal cases per 10,000 residents per year

Median age: Female 41.2, male 38.2
Language: Japanese (official)
Ethnic groups: Japanese: 99.4%; other 0.6%

The Metropolis should have been aborted long before it became New York, London or Tōkyō.
— John Kenneth Galbraith

Geography & Environment

Latitude: 35°N (same as Albuquerque, New Mexico; Kabul, Afghanistan; Memphis, Tennessee)
Longitude: 139° E (same as Adelaide, Australia)
Elevation: 17 meters (59 feet)
Land area: 2,187 square km (844 square mi)
Terrain: Tōkyō sits on the Kantō plain, at the head of Tōkyō Bay, near the center of the Japanese archipelago. Edogawa River is to the east, mountains are to the west, and Tamagawa River is to the south. Mount Fuji, Japan's highest mountain, rises up 12,388 feet about 60 mi (100 km) west of Tōkyō.
Natural hazards: Earthquakes, typhoons
Environmental issues: Tōkyō has banned trucks that don't meet strict emissions standards and ordered filters placed on many other diesel vehicles. As a result, the air quality has improved. Studies are being conducted on the so-called heat island effect, which is the raising of temperatures by air-conditioners and other exhausts emitted by buildings in the dense downtown area. Also, finding landfills for the city's garbage is a growing problem.

Economy

Per capita income: ¥4.1 million ($37,661)
Unemployment: 4.6%
Work force: 6.5 million; clerical, technical and management 46.3%; sales and services 29.2%; manufacturing and transportation 24%; agriculture, forestry and fisheries 0.5%
Major industries: Automobiles, banking, cameras and optical goods, consumer items, electronic apparatus, equipment, financial services, furniture, publishing and printing, textiles, transport

Did You Know?

• The average Tōkyō residence is only slightly larger than a two-car garage in the U.S.

• Tōkyō has the lowest population of children aged 0 to 14 of any area of Japan.

• Japanese inventors have created a material that absorbs nitrogen and sulphur oxide gases, reducing smog. The product is now in use on bridges, buildings, and highways across Tōkyō.

• Tōkyō has the second largest homeless population in Japan. In 2003, the city counted 5,927 people. About half are estimated to be sleeping in parks and on the streets, the rest are in government shelters.

• There are eight U.S. military bases within Tōkyō, covering more than 6 square mi.

• Tōkyō's daytime population is 2.7 million people higher than its nighttime population. The change is most dramatic in the city's downtown wards—Chiyoda, Chuo, and Minato—which have only 268,000 persons by night and 2.3 million by day.

• The ginkgo biloba is the most common tree in Tōkyō and has even been adopted as the city's symbol. It's fan-shaped green leaves turn yellow every fall.

CHRONOLOGY

10,000 BC– AD 300	Neolithic Jōmon hunting and fishing culture leaves richly decorated pottery.
AD 300	Yayoi culture displays knowledge of farming and metallurgy imported from Korea.
after 300	The Yamato tribe consolidates power in the rich Kansai plain and expands westward, forming the kind of military aristocratic society that will dominate Japan's history.
ca. 500	Yamato leaders, claiming to be descended from the sun goddess, Amaterasu, take the title of emperor.
538–552	Buddhism, introduced to the Yamato court from China by way of Korea, complements rather than replaces the indigenous Shintō religion.
593–622	Prince Shōtoku encourages the Japanese to embrace Chinese culture and has Buddhist temple Hōryū-ji built at Nara in 607 (its existing buildings are among the oldest surviving wooden structures in the world).

Nara Period

710–784	Japan has first permanent capital at Nara; great age of Buddhist sculpture, piety, and poetry.

Fujiwara or Heian (Peace) Period

794–1160	The capital is moved from Nara to Heian-kyō (now Kyōto), where the Fujiwara family dominates the imperial court. Lady Murasaki's novel *The Tale of Genji*, written circa 1020, describes the elegance and political maneuvering of court life.

Kamakura Period

1185–1335	Feudalism enters, with military and economic power in the provinces and the emperor a powerless, ceremonial figurehead in Kyōto. Samurai warriors welcome Zen, a new sect of Buddhism from China.
1192	After a war with the Taira family, Yoritomo of the Minamoto family becomes the first shōgun; he places his capital in Kamakura.
1274 and 1281	The fleets sent by Chinese emperor Kublai Khan to invade Japan are destroyed by typhoons, praised in Japanese history as kamikaze, or divine wind.

Ashikaga Period

1336–1568	The Ashikaga family assumes the title of shōgun and settles in Kyōto. The Zen aesthetic flourishes in painting, landscape gardening, and tea ceremony. Nō theater emerges. The Silver Pavilion, or Ginkaku-ji, in Kyōto, built in 1483, is the quintessential example of Zen-inspired architecture. The period is marked by constant warfare but also by

increased trade with the mainland. Ōsaka develops into an important commercial city, and trade guilds appear.

1467–77   The Ōnin Wars that wrack Kyōto initiate a 100-year period of civil war.

1543   Portuguese sailors, the first Europeans to reach Japan, initiate trade relations with the lords of western Japan and introduce the musket, which changes Japanese warfare.

1549–51   St. Francis Xavier, the first Jesuit missionary, introduces Christianity.

Momoyama Period of National Unification

1568–1600   Two generals, Nobunaga Oda and Hideyoshi Toyotomi, are the central figures of this period. Nobunaga builds a military base from which Hideyoshi unifies Japan.

1592, 1597   Hideyoshi invades Korea. He brings back Korean potters, who rapidly develop a Japanese ceramics industry.

Tokugawa Period

1600–1868   Ieyasu Tokugawa becomes shōgun after the battle of Sekigahara. The military capital is established at Edo (now Tōkyō), which shows phenomenal economic and cultural growth. A hierarchical order of four social classes—warriors, farmers, artisans, then merchants—is rigorously enforced. The merchant class, however, is increasingly prosperous and effects a transition from a rice to a money economy. Merchants patronize new, popular forms of art: Kabuki, haiku, and the ukiyo-e school of painting. The life of the latter part of this era is beautifully illustrated in the wood-block prints of the artist Hokusai (1760–1849).

1618   Japanese Christians who refuse to renounce their foreign religion are persecuted.

1637–38   Japanese Christians are massacred in the Shimabara uprising. Japan is closed to the outside world except for a Dutch trading post in Nagasaki harbor.

1853   U.S. commodore Matthew Perry reopens Japan to foreign trade.

Meiji Restoration

1868–1912   Opponents of the weakened Tokugawa Shogunate support Emperor Meiji and overthrow the last shōgun. The emperor is restored (with little actual power), and the imperial capital is moved to Edo, which is renamed Tōkyō (Eastern Capital). Japan is modernized along Western lines, with a constitution proclaimed in 1889; a system of compulsory education and a surge of industrialization follow.

1902–05   Japan defeats Russia in the Russo-Japanese War and achieves world-power status.

1910   Japan annexes Korea.

1914–18 Japan joins the Allies in World War I.

1923 The Great Kantō Earthquake devastates much of Tōkyō and Yokohama.

1931 As a sign of growing militarism in the country, Japan seizes the Chinese province of Manchuria.

1937 Following years of increasing military and diplomatic activity in northern China, open warfare breaks out (and lasts until 1945); Chinese Nationalists and Communists both fight Japan.

1939–45 Japan, having signed anti-Communist treaties with Nazi Germany and Italy (1936 and 1937), invades and occupies French Indochina.

1941 The Japanese attack on Pearl Harbor on December 7 brings the United States into war against Japan in the Pacific.

1942 Japan's empire extends to Indochina, Burma, Malaya, the Philippines, and Indonesia. Japan bombs Darwin, Australia. U.S. defeat of Japanese forces at Midway turns the tide of the Pacific war.

1945 Tōkyō and 50 other Japanese cities are devastated by U.S. bombing raids. The United States drops atomic bombs on Hiroshima and Nagasaki in August, precipitating Japanese surrender.

1945–52 The American occupation under General Douglas MacArthur disarms Japan and encourages the establishment of a democratic government. Emperor Hirohito retains his position.

1953 After the Korean War, Japan begins a period of great economic growth.

1964 Tōkyō hosts the Summer Olympic games.

late 1960s Japan develops into one of the major industrial nations in the world.

mid-1970s Production of electronics, cars, cameras, and computers places Japan at the heart of the emerging Pacific Rim economic sphere and threatens to spark a trade war with the industrial nations of Europe and the United States.

1989 Emperor Hirohito dies.

1990 Coronation of Emperor Akihito. Prince Fumihito marries Kiko Kawashima.

1992 The Diet approves use of Japanese military forces under United Nations auspices.

1993 Crown Prince Naruhito marries Masako Owada.

1995 A massive earthquake strikes Kōbe and environs. Approximately 5,500 people are killed and 35,000 injured; more than 100,000 buildings are destroyed.

Members of a fringe religious organization, the Aum Shinri Kyō, carry out a series of poison-gas attacks on the transportation networks of Tōkyō and Yokohama, undermining, in a society that is a model of decorum and mutual respect, confidence in personal safety.

1997   The deregulation of rice prices and the appearance of discount gasoline stations mark a turn in the Japanese economy toward genuine privatization. These small indications constitute a break from traditional price control policies that support small merchants and producers.

1998   The Japanese economy is crippled from slumps throughout Asia. Banks merge or go bankrupt, and Japanese consumers spend less and less.

1999   In the international arena Japanese toys, films, and other accoutrements of pop culture find themselves in the spotlight like never before. The economy, however, continues to suffer as politicians debate economic measures that foreign economists have been recommending for years. Small businesses are most affected, and the attitude of the average Japanese is grim.

    A nuclear accident 112 km (70 mi) northeast of Tōkyō injures few but raises many questions about Japan's vast nuclear-power industry.

2001   In support of the U.S. war against terrorism in Afghanistan, the Japanese government extends noncombat military activities abroad for the first time since World War II by sending support ships to the Indian Ocean under a reinterpretation of the existing post-1945, pacifist constitution. Asian leaders express some concern for a first step for Japanese military presence abroad since 1945.

2002   North Korea admits to the kidnapping of 11 Japanese civilians in the 1970s and '80s for use as language teachers. Japan negotiates the return of several of its citizens.

2003   Prime Minister Koizumi sends Japanese combat troops to Iraq in the first deployment of Japanese troops since WWII.

VOCABULARY &
MENU GUIDE

ABOUT JAPANESE

ESSENTIAL PHRASES

MENU GUIDE

ABOUT JAPANESE

Japanese sounds and spellings differ in principle from those of the West. We build words letter by letter, and one letter can sound different depending where it appears in a word. For example, we see *ta* as two letters, and *ta* could be pronounced three ways, as in *tat, tall,* and *tale.* For the Japanese, *ta* is one character, and it is pronounced one way: *tah.*

The *hiragana* and *katakana* (tables of sounds) are the rough equivalents of our alphabet. There are four types of syllables within these tables: the single vowels *a, i, u, e,* and *o,* in that order; vowel-consonant pairs like *ka, ni, hu,* or *ro;* the single consonant *n,* which punctuates the upbeats of the word for bullet train, *Shinkansen* (shee-n-ka-n-se-n); and compounds like *kya, chu,* and *ryo.* Remember that these compounds are one syllable. Thus Tōkyō, the capital city, has only two syllables—*tō* and *kyō*—not three. Likewise pronounce Kyōtō *kyō-tō,* not *kee-oh-to.*

Japanese vowels are pronounced as follows: *a*–ah, *i*–ee, *u*–oo, *e*–eh, *o*–oh. The Japanese *r* is rolled so that it sounds like a bounced *d.*

No diphthongs. Paired vowels in Japanese words are not slurred together, as in our words *coin, brain,* or *stein.* The Japanese separate them, as in *mae* (*ma*-eh), whch means in front of; *kōen* (*ko*-en), which means park; *byōin* (*byo*-een), which means hospital; and *tokei* (to-*keh*-ee), which means clock or watch.

Macrons. Many Japanese words, when rendered in *romaji* (roman letters), require macrons over vowels to indicate correct pronunciation, as in Tōkyō. When you see these macrons, double the length of the vowel, as if you're saying it twice: to-o-kyo-o. Likewise, when you see double consonants, as in the city name Nikkō, linger on the Ks—as in "bookkeeper"—and on the O.

Emphasis. Some books state that the Japanese emphasize all syllables in their words equally. This is not true. Take the words *sayōnara* and *Hiroshima.* Americans are likely to stress the downbeats: sa-yo-*na*-ra and hi-ro-*shi*-ma. The Japanese actually emphasize the second beat in each case: sa-*yō*-na-ra (note the macron) and hi-*ro*-shi-ma. Metaphorically speaking, the Japanese don't so much stress syllables as pause over them or race past them: Emphasis is more a question of speed than weight. In the vocabulary below, we indicate emphasis by italicizing the syllable that you should stress.

Three interesting pronunciations are in the vocabulary below. The word *desu* roughly means "is." It looks like it has two syllables, but the Japanese race past the final *u* and just say "dess." Likewise, some verbs end in *-masu,* which is pronounced "mahss." Similarly, the character *shi* is often quickly pronounced "sh," as in the phrase meaning "pleased to meet you:" ha-ji-me-*mash(i)*-te. Just like *desu* and *-masu,* what look like two syllables, in this case *ma* and *shi,* are pronounced *mahsh.*

Hyphens. Throughout *Fodor's Tokyo*, we have hyphenated certain words to help you recognize meaningful patterns. This isn't conventional; it is practical. For example, *Eki-mae-dori*, which literally means "Station Front Avenue," turns into a blur when rendered Ekimaedori. And you'll run across a number of sight names that end in *-jingu* or *-jinja* or *-taisha*. You'll soon catch on to their meaning: Shinto shrine.

ESSENTIAL PHRASES

Basics

Yes/No	*ha*-i/*ii*-e	はい／いいえ
Please	o-ne-*gai* shi-masu	お願いします
Thank you (very much)	(*dō*-mo) a-*ri*-ga-to go-*zai*-ma su	（どうも）ありがとう ございます
You're welcome	*dō* i-ta-shi-ma-shi-te	どういたしまして
Excuse me	su-mi-ma-*sen*	すみません
Sorry	*go*-men na-*sai*	ごめんなさい
Good morning	o-*ha*-yō *go*-zai-ma-su	お早うございます
Good day/afternoon	kon-*ni*-chi-wa	こんにちは
Good evening	kom-*ban*-wa	こんばんは
Good night	o-*ya*-su-mi na-*sai*	おやすみなさい
Goodbye	sa-*yō*-na-ra	さようなら
Mr./Mrs./Miss	-san	一さん
Pleased to meet you	*ha*-ji-me-*mashi*-te	はじめまして
How do you do?	*dō*-zo yo-*ro*-shi-ku	どうぞよろしく

Numbers

The first reading is used for reading numbers, as in telephone numbers, and the second is often used for counting things.

1	*i*-chi / hi-*to*-tsu	一／一つ	17	*jū*-shi-chi	十七
2	ni / fu-*ta*-tsu	二／二つ	18	*jū*-ha-chi	十八
3	san / *mit*-tsu	三／三つ	19	*jū*-kyū	十九
4	shi / *yot*-tsu	四／四つ	20	*ni*-jū	二十
5	go / i-*tsu*-tsu	五／五つ	21	*ni*-jū-i-chi	二十一
6	*ro*-ku / *mut*-tsu	六／六つ	30	*san*-jū	三十
7	*na*-na / *na*-na-tsu	七／七つ	40	*yon*-jū	四十
8	*ha*-chi / *yat*-tsu	八／八つ	50	*go*-jū	五十
9	kyū / *ko*-ko-no-*tsu*	九／九つ	60	*ro*-ku-jū	六十
10	jū / tō	十／十	70	na-na-jū	七十
11	*jū*-i-chi	十一	80	*ha*-chi-jū	八十
12	*jū*-ni	十二	90	kyū-jū	九十
13	*jū*-san	十三	100	*hya*-ku	百
14	*jū*-yon	十四	1000	sen	千
15	*jū*-go	十五	10,000	*i*-chi-man	一万
16	*jū*-ro-ku	十六	100,000	*jū*-man	十万

Days of the Week

Sunday	*ni*-chı yō-bı	日曜日
Monday	*ge*-tsu yō-bi	月曜日
Tuesday	*ka* yō-bi	火曜日
Wednesday	*su*-i yō-bi	水曜日
Thursday	*mo*-ku yō-bi	木曜日
Friday	*kin* yō-bi	金曜日
Saturday	*dō* yō-bi	土曜日
Weekday	hei-ji-tsu	平日
Weekend	shū-ma-tsu	週末

Months

January	*i*-chi *ga*-tsu	一月
February	*ni* ga-tsu	二月
March	*san* ga-tsu	三月
April	*shi* ga-tsu	四月
May	*go* ga-tsu	五月
June	*ro*-ku *ga*-tsu	六月
July	*shi*-chi *ga*-tsu	七月
August	*ha*-chi *ga*-tsu	八月
September	*ku* ga-tsu	九月
October	*jū* ga-tsu	十月
November	*jū*-i-chi *ga*-tsu	十一月
December	*jū*-ni *ga*-tsu	十二月

Useful Expressions, Questions, and Answers

Do you speak English?	*ei*-go ga wa-*ka*-ri-ma-su *ka*	英語が わかりますか。
I don't speak Japanese.	*ni*-hon-go ga wa-*ka*-ri-ma-*sen*	日本語が わかりません。
I don't understand.	wa-*ka*-ri-ma-*sen*	わかりません。
I understand.	wa-*ka*-ri-ma-shi-*ta*	わかりました。
I don't know.	*shi*-ri-ma-*sen*	知りません。
I'm American (British).	wa-*ta*-shi wa a-*me*-ri-ka (i-*gi*-ri-su) jin *desu*	私はアメリカ (イギリス) 人 です。
What's your name?	o-*na*-ma-e wa *nan* desu *ka*	お名前は何ですか。
My name is . . .	. . . to *mo*-shi-*ma*-su	.....と申します。
What time is it?	*i*-ma *nan*-ji desu *ka*	今何時ですか。

How?	*dō* yat-te	どうやって。
When?	*i*-tsu	いつ。
Yesterday/today/tomorrow	ki-*nō*/kyō/*ashi*-ta	きのう／きょう／あした
This morning	*ke*-sa	けさ
This afternoon	*kyō* no *go*-go	きょうの午後
Tonight	*kom*-ban	こんばん
Excuse me, what?	su-*mi*-ma-*sen, nan* desu *ka*	すみません、何ですか。
What is this/that?	*ko*-re/*so*-re wa *nan* desu *ka*	これ／それは何ですか。
Why?	*na*-ze desu *ka*	なぜですか。
Who?	*da*-re desu *ka*	だれですか。
I am lost.	*mi*-chi ni ma-yo-i-*mash*-ta	道に迷いました。
Where is [place]	[place] wa *do*-ko desu *ka*	.....はどこですか。
Train station?	e-ki	駅
Subway station?	chi-*ka*-te-tsu-no eki	地下鉄の駅
Bus stop?	*ba*-su *no*-ri-*ba*	バス乗り場
Taxi stand?	*ta*-ku-shi-i *no*-ri-*ba*	タクシー乗り場
Airport?	kū-kō	空港
Post office?	*yū*-bin-*kyo*-ku	郵便局
Bank?	*gin*-kō	銀行
the [name] hotel?	[name] ho-*te*-ru	ホテル
Elevator?	e-re-bē-tā	エレベーター
Where are the restrooms?	*to*-i-re wa *do*-ko desu *ka*	トイレはどこですか。
Here/there/over there	*ko*-ko/*so*-ko/*a*-so-ko	ここ／そこ／あそこ
Left/right	hi-*da*-ri/*mi*-gi	左／右
Straight ahead	mas-*su*-gu	まっすぐ
Is it near (far)?	chi-*ka*-i (*to*-i) desu *ka*	近い (遠い) ですか。
Are there any rooms?	*he*-ya *ga* a-ri-masu *ka*	部屋がありますか。
I'd like [item]	[item] ga ho-*shi*-i no desu ga	.....がほしいのですが。
Newspaper	*shim*-bun	新聞
Stamp	*kit*-te	切手
Key	*ka*-gi	鍵
I'd like to buy [item]	[item] o kai-*ta*-i no desu ke do	.....を買いたいのですけど。

a ticket to [event]	[event] *ma*-de no *kip*-pu	…..までの切符
Map	*chi*-zu	地図
How much is it?	i-*ku*-ra desu *ka*	いくらですか。
It's expensive (cheap).	ta-*ka*-i (ya-*su*-i) de su *ne*	高い (安い) ですね。
A little (a lot)	su-*ko*-shi (*ta*-ku-san)	少し (たくさん)
More/less	*mot*-to o-ku/ *su*-ku-*na*-ku	もっと多く／少なく
Enough/too much	*jū*-bun/o-su-*gi*-ru	十分／多すぎる
I'd like to exchange . . .	. . . *ryō*-ga e shi-*te* i-*ta*-da-ke-masu *ka*	…..両替して 頂けますか。
dollars to yen	*do*-ru o *en* ni	ドルを円に
pounds to yen	*pon*-do o *en* ni	ポンドを円に
How do you say . . . in Japanese?	ni-*hon*-go de . . . wa *dō* i-i-masu *ka*	日本語で…..は どう言いますか。
I am ill/sick.	wa-*ta*-shi wa *byō*-ki desu	私は病気です。
Please call a doctor.	*i*-sha o *yon*-de ku-da-*sa*-i	医者を呼んで 下さい。
Please call the police.	*ke*-i-sa-tsu o *yon*-de ku-da-*sa*-i	警察を 呼んで下さい。
Help!	*ta*-su-*ke*-te	助けて！

More Useful Phrases

Temple	otera/-dera/-ji/-in/-dō	堂／寺
Shrine	jinja/jingū/-gū/-dō/taisha	神社／神宮／大社
Castle	-jō	城
Park	kōen	公園
River	-kawa/-gawa	川
Bridge	hashi/bashi	橋
Museum	hakubutsukan	博物館
Zoo	dōbutsu-en	動物園
Botanical gardens	shokubutsu-en	植物園
Island	shima/jima/tō	島
Slope	saka/zaka	坂
Hill	oka	丘
Lake	-ko	湖
Marsh	shitsugen	湿原
Pond	-ike	池
Bay	-wan	湾

Plain	hara/bara/taira/daira	平
Peninsula	hantō	半島
Mountain	yama/-san/-take	山
Cape	misaki/saki	岬
Sea	-kai/-nada	海
Gorge	kyōkoku	峡谷
Plateau	kōgen	高原
Train line	sen	線
Prefecture	-ken/-fu	県／府
Ward	-ku	区
Exit	deguchi/-guchi	出口
Street, avenue	dōri/-dō/michi	道
main road	kaidō/kōdō	街道／公道
In front of	mae	前
North	kita	北
South	minami	南
East	higashi	東
West	nishi	西
Shop, store	mise/-ya	店
Hot-spring spa	onsen	温泉

MENU GUIDE

Restaurants

Basics and Useful Expressions

A bottle of . . .	. . . *ip*-pon	.....一本
A glass/cup of . . .	. . . *ip*-pai	.....一杯
Ashtray	*ha*-i-*za*-ra	灰皿
Plate	*sa*-ra	皿
Bill/check	kan-*jō*	かんじょう
Bread	pan	パン
Breakfast	*chō*-sho-ku	朝食
Butter	ba-*tā*	バター
Cheers!	kam-*pai*	乾杯！
Chopsticks	*ha*-shi	箸
Cocktail	*ka*-ku-*te*-ru	カクテル
Does that include dinner?...	*yū*-sho-ku *ga* tsu-ki-ma-*su*-ka	夕食が付きますか。
Excuse me!	su-mi-ma-*sen*	すみません。
Fork	*fō*-ku	フォーク
I am diabetic.	wa-*ta*-shi wa tō-*nyō*-byō de su	私は糖尿病です。
I am dieting.	*da*-i-et-to *chū* desu	ダイエット中です。
I am a vegetarian.	sa-i-*sho*-ku *shū*-gi-sha de-su	菜食主義者です。
I cannot eat [item]	[item] wa *ta*-be-ra-re-ma-*sen*	.....は食べられません。
I'd like to order.	*chū*-mon o shi-*tai* desu	注文をしたいです。
I'd like [item]	[item] o o-ne-*gai*-shi-ma su	.....をお願いします。
I'm hungry.	o-na-ka ga *su*-i-te i-*ma* su	お腹が空いています。
I'm thirsty.	*no*-do ga ka-*wa*-i-te i-*ma* su	喉が渇いています。
It's tasty (not good)	*o*-i-shi-i (ma-*zu*-i) desu	おいしい (まずい) です。
Knife	*na*-i-fu	ナイフ
Lunch	*chū*-sho-ku	昼食
Menu	me-nyū	メニュー
Napkin	*na*-pu-*kin*	ナプキン
Pepper	ko-*shō*	こしょう
Please give me [item]	[item] o ku-da-*sa*-i	.....を下さい。

Salt	*shi*-o	塩
Set menu	*te*-i-sho-ku	定食
Spoon	su-*pūn*	スプーン
Sugar	sa-to	砂糖
Wine list	*wa*-i-n *ri*-su-*to*	ワインリスト
What do you recommend?	*o*-su-su-me *ryō*-ri wa *nan* desu *ka*	お勧め料理は何ですか。

Meat Dishes

焼き肉	yaki-niku	Thinly sliced meat is marinated then barbecued over an open fire at the table.
すき焼き	sukiyaki	Thinly sliced beef, green onions, mushrooms, thin noodles, and cubes of tōfu are simmered in a large iron pan in front of you. These ingredients are cooked in a mixture of soy sauce, mirin (cooking wine), and a little sugar. You are given a saucer of raw egg to cool the sukī-yakī morsels before eating. Using chopsticks, you help yourself to anything on your side of the pan and dip it into the egg and then eat. Best enjoyed in a group.
しゃぶしゃぶ	shabu-shabu	Extremely thin slices of beef are plunged for an instant into boiling water flavored with soup stock and then dipped into a thin sauce and eaten.
肉じゃが	niku-jaga	Beef and potatoes stewed together with soy sauce.
ステーキ	sutēki	steak
ハンバーグ	hambāgu	Hamburger pattie served with sauce.
トンカツ	tonkatsu	Breaded deep-fried pork cutlets.
しょうが焼	shōga-yaki	Pork cooked with ginger.
酢豚	subuta	Sweet and sour pork, originally a Chinese dish.
からあげ	kara-age	deep-fried without batter
焼き鳥	yaki-tori	Pieces of chicken, white meat, liver, skin, etc., threaded on skewers with green onions and marinated in sweet soy sauce and grilled.
親子どんぶり	oyako-domburi	Literally, "mother and child bowl"—chicken and egg in broth over rice.

他人どんぶり	tanin-domburi	Literally, "strangers in a bowl"— similar to oyako domburi, but with beef instead of chicken.
ロール・キャベツ	rōru kyabetsu	Rolled cabbage; beef or pork rolled in cabbage and cooked.
はやしライス	hayashi raisu	Beef flavored with tomato and soy sauce with onions and peas over rice.
カレーライス	karē-raisu	Curried rice. A thick curry gravy typically containing beef is poured over white rice.
カツカレー	katsu-karē	Curried rice with tonkatsu.
お好み焼き	okonomi-yaki	Sometimes called a Japanese pancake, this is made from a batter of flour, egg, cabbage, and meat or seafood, griddle-cooked then covered with green onions and a special sauce.
シュウマイ	shūmai	Shrimp or pork wrapped in a light dough and steamed.
ギョウザ	gyōza	Pork spiced with ginger and garlic in a Chinese wrapper and fried or steamed.

Seafood Dishes

焼き魚	yaki-zakana	broiled fish
塩焼	shio-yaki	Fish sprinkled with salt and broiled until crisp.
さんま	samma	saury pike
いわし	iwashi	sardines
しゃけ	shake	salmon
照り焼き	teri-yaki	Fish basted in soy sauce and broiled.
ぶり	buri	yellowtail
煮魚	nizakana	soy-simmered fish
さばのみそ煮	saba no miso ni	Mackerel stewed with soy-bean paste.
揚げ魚	age-zakana	deep-fried fish
かれいフライ	karei furai	deep-fried breaded flounder
刺身	sashimi	Very fresh raw fish. Served sliced thin on a bed of white radish with a saucer of soy sauce and horseradish. Eaten by dipping fish into soy sauce mixed with horseradish.
まぐろ	maguro	tuna

あまえび	ama-ebi	sweet shrimp
いか	ika	squid
たこ	tako	octopus
あじ	aji	horse mackerel
さわら	sawara	Spanish mackerel
しめさば	shimesaba	Mackerel marinated in vinegar.
かつおのたたき	katsuo no tataki	Bonito cooked just slightly on the surface. Eaten with cut green onions and thin soy sauce.
どじょうの 柳川なべ	dojo no yanagawa nabe	Loach cooked with burdock root and egg in an earthen dish. Considered a delicacy.
うな重	una-jū	Eel marinated in a slightly sweet soy sauce is charcoal-broiled and served over rice. Considered a delicacy.
天重	ten-jū	Deep-fried prawns served over rice with sauce.
海老フライ	ebi furai	Deep-fried breaded prawns.
あさりの酒蒸し	asari no sakamushi	Clams steamed with rice wine.

Sushi

寿司	sushi	Basically, sushi is rice, fish, and vegetables. The rice is delicately seasoned with vinegar, salt, and sugar. There are basically three types of sushi: nigiri, chirashi, and maki.
にぎり寿司	nigiri zushi	The rice is formed into a bite-sized cake and topped with various raw or cooked fish. The various types are usually named after the fish, but not all are fish. Nigiri zushi is eaten by picking up the cakes with chopsticks or the fingers, dipping the fish side in soy sauce, and eating.
ちらし寿司	chirashi zushi	In chirashi zushi, a variety of seafood is arranged on the top of the rice and served in a bowl.
巻き寿司	maki zushi	Raw fish and vegetables or other morsels are rolled in sushi rice and wrapped in dried seaweed. Some popular varieties are listed here.
まぐろ	maguro	tuna
とろ	toro	fatty tuna

たい	tai	red snapper
さば	saba	mackerel
こはだ	kohada	gizzard shad
しゃけ	shake	salmon
はまち	hamachi	yellowtail
ひらめ	hirame	flounder
あじ	aji	horse mackerel
たこ	tako	octopus
あなご	anago	conger eel
えび	ebi	shrimp
甘えび	ama-ebi	sweet shrimp
いか	ika	squid
みる貝	miru-gai	giant clam
あおやぎ	aoyagi	round clam
卵	tamago	egg
かずのこ	kazunoko	herring roe
かに	kani	crab
ほたて貝	hotate-gai	scallop
うに	uni	sea urchin
いくら	ikura	salmon roe
鉄火巻	tekka-maki	tuna roll
かっぱ巻	kappa-maki	cucumber roll
新香巻	shinko-maki	shinko roll (shinko is a type of pickle)
カリフォルニア巻	kariforunia-maki	California roll, containing crab-meat and avocado. This was invented in the U.S. but was re-exported to Japan and is gaining popularity there.
うに	uni	Sea urchin on rice wrapped with seaweed.
いくら	ikura	Salmon roe on rice wrapped with seaweed.
太巻	futo-maki	Big roll with egg and pickled vegetables.

Vegetable Dishes

おでん	oden	Often sold by street vendors at festivals and in parks, etc., this is vegetables, octopus, or egg simmered in a soy fish stock.

天ぷら	tempura	Vegetables, shrimp, or fish deep-fried in a light batter. Eaten by dipping into a thin sauce containing grated white radish.
野菜サラダ	yasai sarada	vegetable salad
大学いも	daigaku imo	fried yams in a sweet syrup
野菜いため	yasai itame	stir-fried vegetables
きんぴらごぼう	kimpira gobō	Carrots and burdock root, fried with soy sauce.
煮もの	nimono	vegetables simmered in a soy- and sake-based sauce
かぼちゃ	kabocha	pumpkin
さといも	satoimo	taro root
たけのこ	takenoko	bamboo shoots
ごぼう	gobō	burdock root
れんこん	renkon	lotus root
酢のもの	sumono	Vegetables seasoned with ginger.
きゅうり	kyūri	cucumber
和えもの	aemono	Vegetables dressed with sauces.
ねぎ	tamanegi	onions
おひたし	o-hitashi	Boiled vegetables with soy sauce and dried shaved bonito or sesame seeds.
ほうれん草	hōrenso	spinach
漬物	tsukemono	Japanese pickles. Made from white radish, eggplant or other vegetables. Considered essential to the Japanese meal.

Egg Dishes

ベーコン・エッグ	bēkon-eggu	bacon and eggs
ハム・エッグ	hamu-eggu	ham and eggs
スクランブル・エッグ	sukuramburu eggu	scrambled eggs
ゆで卵	yude tamago	boiled eggs
目玉焼	medama-yaki	fried eggs, sunny-side up
オムレツ	omuretsu	omelet
オムライス	omuraisu	Omelet with rice inside, often eaten with ketchup.
茶わんむし	chawan mushi	Vegetables, shrimp, etc., steamed in egg custard.

Tōfu Dishes

Tōfu, also called bean curd, is a white, high-protein food with the consistency of soft gelatin.

冷やっこ	hiya-yakko	Cold tōfu with soy sauce and grated ginger.
湯どうふ	yu-dōfu	boiled tōfu
あげだしどうふ	agedashi dōfu	Lightly fried plain tōfu dipped in soy sauce and grated ginger.
マーボーどうふ	mābō dōfu	Tōfu and ground pork in a spicy red sauce. Originally a Chinese dish.
とうふの田楽	tōfu no dengaku	Tōfu broiled on skewers and flavored with miso.

Rice Dishes

ごはん	gohan	steamed white rice
おにぎり	onigiri	Triangular balls of rice with fish or vegetables inside and wrapped in a type of seaweed.
おかゆ	okayu	rice porridge
チャーハン	chāhan	Fried rice; includes vegetables and pork.
ちまき	chimaki	A type of onigiri made with sticky rice.
パン	pan	Bread, but usually rolls with a meal.

Soups

みそ汁	miso shiru	Miso soup. A thin broth containing tōfu, mushrooms, or other morsels in a soup flavored with miso or soy-bean paste. The morsels are taken out of the bowl and the soup is drunk straight from the bowl without a spoon.
すいもの	suimono	Soy sauce flavored soup, often including fish and tofu.
とん汁	tonjiru	Pork soup with vegetables.

Noodles

うどん	udon	Wide flour noodles in broth. Can be lunch in a light broth or a full dinner called *nabe-yaki udon* when meat, chicken, egg, and vegetables are added.

そば	soba	Buckwheat noodles. Served in a broth like udon or, during the summer, cold on a bamboo mesh and called *zaru soba*.
ラーメン	rāmen	Chinese noodles in broth, often with *chashu* or roast pork. Broth is soy sauce, miso or salt flavored.
そう麺	sōmen	Very thin wheat noodles, usually served cold with a tsuyu or thin sauce. Eaten in summer.
ひやむぎ	hiyamugi	Similar to somen, but thicker.
やきそば	yaki-soba	Noodles fried with beef and cabbage, garnished with pickled ginger and vegetables.
スパゲッティ	supagetti	Spaghetti. There are many interesting variations on this dish, notably spaghetti in soup, often with seafood.

Fruit

アーモンド	āmondo	almonds
あんず	anzu	apricot
バナナ	banana	banana
ぶどう	budō	grapes
グレープフルーツ	gurēpufurūtsu	grapefruit
干しぶどう	hoshi-budō	raisins
いちご	ichigo	strawberries
いちじく	ichijiku	figs
かき	kaki	persimmons
キーウィ	kiiui	kiwi
ココナッツ	kokonattsu	coconut
くり	kuri	chestnuts
くるみ	kurumi	walnuts
マンゴ	mango	mango
メロン	meron	melon
みかん	mikan	tangerine (mandarin orange)
桃	momo	peach
梨	nashi	pear
オレンジ	orenji	orange
パイナップル	painappuru	pineapple
パパイヤ	papaiya	papaya

ピーナッツ	piinattsu	peanuts
プルーン	purūn	prunes
レモン	remon	lemon
りんご	ringo	apple
さくらんぼ	sakurambo	cherry
西瓜	suika	watermelon

Dessert

アイスクリーム	aisukuriimu	ice cream
プリン	purin	caramel pudding
グレープ	kurēpu	crepes
ケーキ	kēki	cake
シャーベット	shābetto	sherbet
アップルパイ	appuru pai	apple pie
ようかん	yōkan	sweet bean paste jelly
コーヒーゼリー	kōhii zeri	coffee-flavored gelatin
和菓子	wagashi	Japanese sweets

Drinks

Alcoholic

ビール	biiru	beer
生ビール	nama biiru	draft beer
カクテル	kakuteru	cocktail
ウィスキー	uisukii	whisky
スコッチ	sukocchi	scotch
バーボン	bābon	bourbon
日本酒 （酒）	nihonshu (sake)	Sake, a wine brewed from rice.
あつかん	atsukan	warmed sake
ひや	hiya	cold sake
焼酎	shōchū	Spirit distilled from potatoes.
チューハイ	chūhai	Shōchū mixed with soda water and flavored with lemon juice or other flavors.
ワイン	wain	wine
赤	aka	red
白	shiro	white
ロゼ	roze	rose
シャンペン	shampen	champagne
ブランデー	burandē	brandy

Non-alcoholic

コーヒー	kōhii	coffee
アイスコーヒー	aisu kōhii	iced coffee
日本茶	nihon cha	Japanese green tea
紅茶	kō-cha	black tea
レモンティー	remon tii	tea with lemon
ミルクティー	miruku tii	tea with milk
アイスティー	aisu tii	iced tea
ウーロン茶	ūron cha	oolong tea
ジャスミン茶	jasumin cha	jasmine tea
牛乳／ミルク	gyū-nyū/miruku	milk
ココア	kokoa	hot chocolate
レモンスカッシュ	remon sukasshu	carbonated lemon soft drink
ミルクセーキ	miruku sēki	milk shake
ジュース	jūsu	juice, but can also mean any soft drink
レモネード	remonēdo	lemonade

INDEX

A

Addresses, F25
Adjanta ✕, 98
Advertising Museum Tōkyō, 47
Aichiya ✕, 216
Airports and transfers, F28–F29
Yokohama, 216–217
Air travel, F25–F28
booking your flight, F26
carriers, F26
check-in and boarding, F26
with children, F33
complaints, F28
cutting costs, F26–F27
discount reservations, F37
enjoying the flight, F27–F28
flying times, F28
luggage concerns, F45
reconfirming, F28
Akasaka
dining, 86, 88
nightlife, 140
Akasaka-mitsuke
dining, 89
lodging, 108
Akasaka Prince Hotel 🖭, 108
Akechi-daira, 189
Akihabara, F14
exploring, 18–23
shopping, 155–156
Ame-ya Yoko-chō Market, 27
Amida Hall, 203–204
Amusement centers
Fuji-Hakone-Izu National Park, 232
Tōkyō, 75–77
Yokohama, 215
ANA Hotel Narita 🖭, 126–127
ANA Hotel Tōkyō 🖭, 124
Antiques shops, 164–165
Aoi-Marushin ✕, F22, 92
Aoyama, F15
dining, 89, 92
exploring, 59–68
shopping, 156
Apartment rentals, 122
Aquariums, 77–78
Art galleries and museums
Aoyama, Harajuku and Shibuya, 64–65, 66, 67
Fuji-Hakone-Izu National Park, 220, 222, 228–229
Imperial Palace District, 12–13, 16

Kamakura, 200–201
Nihombashi, Ginza and Yūraku-chō, 56, 57, 58
Shinjuku, 73–74
Shitamachi, 78
Ueno, 28, 31–32, 33
Yokohama, 214
Asakura Sculpture Gallery, 78
Asakusa, F14
dining, 92
exploring, 33, 36–43
lodging, 108, 110–111
shopping, 156
Asakusa Jinja, 40
Asakusa View Hotel 🖭, 108, 110
Ashi-no-ko, 229–230
Ashoka ✕, 94
Asia Center of Japan 🖭, 121, 123
Asuka-yama Ōji Paper Museum, 83
Atagawa, 224
Atami, 219–220
Atami Plum Garden, 220
ATMs, F43
Attore ✕, 97
Auto clubs, F32
Azabu-jūban
dining, 92–93

B

Babysitting services, F33
Backstreet shops of Tsukiji, F24, 47–48
Bank hours, F30
Bank of Japan, 55–56
Barbacoa Grill ✕, 98–99
Bars, 141–142, 147
Baseball, 149–150
Bathing, art of, 254
Beer, 96
Beer halls, 142–143
Belfry, 40–41
Benzaiten, 27, 29
Boat and ferry travel, F29–F30
Books on Japan, 261–263
Bookstores, F39, 165–166
Jimbō-chō, 20–21
Bridges
Imperial Palace District, 16
Nihombashi, Ginza and Yūraku-chō, 58
Nikkō, 182–183
Bridgestone Museum of Art, 56

Buddhism, 255–256
Bunka-mura, 64–65
Bunraku puppet theater, 136, 139
Business etiquette, 14–15
Business hotels, 114
Business hours, F30
Bus travel, F30
Fuji-Hakone-Izu National Park, 234–236
Kamakura, 206
Nikkō, 193
Yokohama, 217
Butō dance, 132
Butsunichi-an, 196–197

C

Cactus Park, 222
Calligraphy, 249
Cameras, F30–F31
Capitol Tōkyū Hotel 🖭, 119
Capsule hotels, 115
Car rentals, F31–F32
discount reservations, F37
Car travel, F32–F33
emergency road service, F32
Fuji-Hakone-Izu National Park, 236
Nikkō, 193
Cemeteries, 209, 211
Century Hyatt Hotel 🖭, 120
Ceramics, 250
Ceramics shops, 166
Cherry trees, 222
Chez Inno ✕, 97
Chez Matsuo ✕, 103
Chidori-ga-fuchi Boathouse, 10
Chidori-ga-fuchi National Memorial Garden, 10
Children and travel, F33–F34
Children's attractions, F34
Akihabara and Jimbō-chō, 22
Fuji-Hakone-Izu National Park, 232
Nihombashi, Ginza and Yūraku-chō, 57
Nikkō, 188–189
shops, 168, 170, 171, 175
Tōkyō amusement centers, 75–77
Ueno, 29, 33
Yokohama, 211, 214, 215
zoos and aquariums, 33, 77–78
Chūgū-shi, 190
Churches, 22

Chūzenji, *190*
Chūzenji Kanaya , *192*
Chūzenji-ko, *189–190, 192*
Climate, *F18*
Clothing boutiques, *166–167*
Computers, *F34*
Consumer protection, *F34*
Credit cards, *F43*
Currency, *F43–F44*
Currency Museum, *56*
Customs, *F34–F36*

D

Dai-ichi Mutual Life Insurance
 Company Building, *56*
Daikanyama
 dining, 94
Dance, *131–132*
Dance clubs, *143–144*
Dembō-in, *41*
Den-En Kyo ✕, *102*
Dentists, *F38*
Department stores, *160–164*
Dining, *F21, 85–86. ⇨ Also
 specific Tōkyō
 neighborhoods; specific
 cities and towns*
*beer, wine, sake and spirits,
 96*
with children, F33
dress, 87
*essentials of a Japanese meal,
 240–247*
fast food, 100
Fodor's Choice, F22
price categories, 87, 181
reservations, 87
*side trips from Tōkyō, 177,
 180, 181*
sushi, 88
symbols related to, F9
tempura, 88
tips on dining in Japan, 93
vocabulary for, 283–292
water and restrooms, 87
Directory and operator
 assistance, *F50*
Disabilities and accessibility,
 F36–F37
Discounts and deals, *F37*
*Fuji-Hakone-Izu National Park,
 236*
Disneyland of Tōkyō, *76*
Dockyard Garden, *214*
Doctors, *F38*
Dōgashima, *225–226*
Dōgashima New Ginsui ,
 226
Doll shops, *167–168*

Dragon's Head Falls, *190*
Drum Bridge, *200*
Duties, *F34–F36*

E

Ebisu
 lodging, 111
Ecotourism, *F37*
Edo-Gin ✕, *103–104*
Edo-Tōkyō Museum, *81*
Electricity, *F37*
Electronics shops, *168*
Embassies and consulates,
 F37–F38
Emergencies
 lost and found, F38–F39
 medical services, F38
 road service, F32
 Yokohama, 217
Engaku-ji, *196–197*
English-language media, *F39*
 Yokohama, 217
Ennō-ji, *199*
Enoshima, *204–205*
Erawan ✕, *101*
Etiquette and behavior,
 14–15
Exchanging money,
 F43–F44
Excursions, *F47*

F

Fads, *259–260*
Festivals and seasonal events,
 F19–F20
Film, *132–133*
Films about Japan, *263–264*
Fitness centers, *151–152*
Five-Story Pagoda, *185*
Fodor's Choice, *F22–F24*
Folk crafts shops, *168–169*
Foodstuffs and wares shops,
 169–170
Four Seasons Hotel Chinzan-sō
  , *F22, 123*
Four Seasons Hotel Tōkyō at
 Marunouchi , *118*
Fuji Go-ko, *231–233*
Fuji-Hakone Guest House ,
 231
Fuji-Hakone-Izu National Park,
 219–238
 Fuji Go-ko, 231–233
 Fuji-san, F23, 233–234
 Hakone, 228–231
 *Izu Peninsula, 219–220, 222,
  224–226, 228*
 *lodging, 220, 224–225, 226,
  228, 230–231, 233*

 *transportation and services,
  234–238*
 visitor information, 238
Fuji-kyū Highland, *232*
Fujimi Tamon, *11*
Fujimoto ✕, *191*
Fuji Museum, *232*
Fuji-san, *F23, 233–234*
Fuji Television Nippon
 Broadcasting Building, *79*
Fuji View Hotel , *233*
Fujiya Hotel , *228, 231*
Futara-san Jinja, *187*

G

Ganchan ✕, *F22, 101*
Gardens, *251–252*
 *Aoyama, Harajuku and
  Shibuya, 66*
 *Fuji-Hakone-Izu National Park,
  220*
 Imperial Palace District, 10–12
 Shinjuku, 74
 Tsukiji and Shiodome, 48
 Yokohama, 213, 214
Gasoline, *F32*
Gate at the Foot of the Hill,
 187
Gate of Sunlight, *186*
Gates
 Asakusa, 41–43
 Imperial Palace District, 10, 13
 Nikkō, 186, 187, 188
Gay and lesbian travel,
 F39–F40
Geisha, *258*
Genji Pond, *200*
Ginza, *F14*
 dining, 94–95
 exploring, 50–59
 lodging, 111, 116
 nightlife, 140
 shopping, 156, 162–163
Gohōten-dō, *183, 185*
Golf, *150*
Gōra, *229*
Government buildings
 Imperial Palace District, 12, 13
 Shinjuku, 74–75
Goyokan , *226, 228*
Grand Hyatt Tōkyō at
 Roppongi Hills , *F22,
 121*
Great Bell, *196*
Great Buddha, *F24, 202–203*
Great Ferris Wheel of
 Diamonds and Flowers, *75*
Green Plaza Shinjuku , *117*
Gyōshintei ✕, *190–191*

H

Hachinoki Kita-Kamakura-ten
✕, 205
Hai-den, 188
Hakone, 228–231
Hakone-machi, 230
Hakone Museum of Art, 229
Hakone Open-Air Museum,
228–229
Hakone Prince Hotel 🏨,
230–231
Hakozaki
lodging, 116
Hall of the Holy Relic of
Buddha, 196
Hama Rikyū Tei-en, 48
Hanazono Jinja, 72–73
Haneda Airport, F28, F29
Hanzō-mon, 10
Harajuku, F15
exploring, 59–68
shopping, 156, 158
Harbor View Park, 211
Hase, 202–204, 206
Hase-dera, F24, 203–204
Hatsu-shima, 220
Health concerns, F40
Heichinrou ✕, 104
Heike Pond, 200
Heiroku-zushi ✕, 99
Hibiya
lodging, 116–117
Higashi-Gotanda
lodging, 117
Higashi-Shinjuku
lodging, 117
Higo-no-ya ✕, 89
Hikawa-maru, 212
Hilton Tōkyō 🏨, 119–120
Hirakawa-mon, 10
Hōfuku-ji, 224
Hōkoku-ji, 202
Holiday Inn Tōbu Narita 🏨,
127
Holidays, F40
Home exchanges, 122
Home visits, 122
Homeworks ✕, 92–93
Hospitals, F38
Hostels, 115, 126
Hotel Arca Torre 🏨, 121
Hotel Mount Fuji 🏨, 233
Hotel New Otani Tōkyō and
Towers 🏨, 108
Hotel Nikkō Winds Narita 🏨,
127
Hotel Okura 🏨, F22, 125
Hotels. ⇨ See Lodging

Hotel Seiyō Ginza 🏨,
117–118
Hotel Yaesu Ryūmeikan 🏨,
125–126
Hot springs, F21, 223
Fuji-Hakone-Izu National Park,
222, 224
Odaiba, 79–80
Hot Spring Theme Park, 79–80
House rentals, 122
Housewares shops, 170–171
Hōzō-mon, 42–43
Hundred-Man Guardhouse, 11

I

Ichiyaga
dining, 95
Idemitsu Museum of Art, 57
Ikebukuro
dining, 95, 97
shopping, 163
Ikeda 20th-Century Art
Museum, 222
Imperial Hotel 🏨, 116–117
Imperial Palace District, F14
exploring, 4–13, 16–17
Imperial Palace East Garden,
F23, 10–12
Imperial Palace Outer Garden,
12
Inakaya ✕, F22, 100–101
Inner Garden, 66
Inn Fujitomita 🏨, 233
Inoshishi-mura, 226
Insurance
for car rentals, F31
travel insurance, F40–F41
International Cemetery, 209,
211
Irō-zaki, 225
Iseyama Kodai Jingū, 213
Itineraries, F16–F17
Itō, 222
Izakaya, 144–145
Izu Peninsula, 219–220, 222,
224–226, 228

J

Jakko Falls, 189
Japan
books and films about,
261–264
facts about, 266–268
history of, 271–274
Japanese Sword Museum, 65
Japan Martial Arts Hall, 12
Jazz clubs, 145
Jidaiya restaurants ✕, 88,
101

Jigen-dō, 188
Jimbō-chō, F14
exploring, 18–23
shopping, 155–156
Jōchi-ji, 199
Jōmyō-ji, 202
Joren Falls, 226

K

Kabuki-chō, 73
Kabuki theater, 136–137, 138
Kabuki-za, F23, 48, 136
Kabuto Jinja, 57
Kagura-den, 187
Kaisen Misaki-kō ✕, 205
Kamakura, 194–207
dining, 205–206
exploring, 195–205
transportation and services,
206–207
visitor information, 207
Kamakura-gū, 202
Kamakura Treasure Museum,
201
Kaminari-mon, 41–42
Kanagawa Prefectural
Museum, 212–213
Kanda Myōjin, 21–22
Kanei-ji, 27–28
Kannai Hall, 212
Kappa-bashi, 43
Karaoke, 146
Kasai Seaside Park, 75–76
Kaseiro restaurants ✕, 206,
215
Kawaguchi-ko, 231–232, 233
Kawazu, 224
Kayaba-chō Pearl Hotel 🏨,
116
Keawjai ✕, 98
Kegon Falls, F23, 190
Kenchō-ji, 199
Kimono shops, 171–172
Kisoji ✕, 88
Kite Museum, 57
Knife shops, 174–175
Kōgeikan, 12
Koka-mon, 188
Koma Gekijō, 73
Komuro-san Kōen, 222
Kōrakuen, 76
Kyō-bashi
dining, 97
lodging, 117–118
Kyōgen theater, 139
Kyoraian ✕, 205
Kyorai-An Matsushiro-kan 🏨,
226
Kyūkyodō, 57

L

Lacquerware, *250*
Lacquerware shops, *172*
La Granata ✕, *86*
Landmark Tower, *214*
Language, *F21, F41–F42*
basics of Japanese, *276–277*
essential phrases, *278–282*
menu guide, *283–292*
sightseeing glossaries, *3,
178–179*
LAOX, *22*
LaQua, *76*
Le Meridien Pacific Tōkyō ⌂,
123–124
Le Papillon de Paris ✕, *99*
Libraries
Nikkō, *185*
Yokohama, *212*
Live houses, *146–147*
Living-history theme parks,
188–189
Lodging, *F42, 107.* ▷ *Also
specific Tōkyō
neighborhoods; specific
cities and towns*
alternatives to hotels, *122*
with children, *F34*
for disabled travelers, *F36*
discount reservations, *F37*
facilities, *109*
Fodor's Choice, *F22*
hotel types, *114–115*
meal plans, *109*
price categories, *110, 181*
reservations, *109–110*
side trips from Tōkyō, *180–181*
symbols related to, *F9*
taxes on hotel bills, *F49*
tipping, *F51*
Long-distance services, *F50*
Lost and found, *F38–F39*

M

MacArthur, Gen. Douglas, *56*
Magazines, *F39*
Mai-den, *200*
Mail and shipping, *F42–F43*
Maisen ✕, *89*
Malls and shopping centers,
160
Manhattan Grill ✕, *102*
Maps for driving, *F32–F33*
Marine Tower, *211*
Martial arts, *12*
Marunouchi
lodging, *118*
Masudaya ✕, *191*

Matsugaoka Treasure House,
197
Matsuzakaya, *57*
Medical services, *F38*
Meguro
dining, *97–98*
Meigetsu-in, *197*
Meiji Memorial Picture
Gallery, *66*
Meiji-no-Yakata ✕, *191*
Meiji Shrine, *65–66*
Meiji Shrine Outer Garden, *66*
Mikimoto, *56–57*
Minato Mirai 21, *214*
Minshuku, *114–115*
Mitsubishi Minato Mirai
Industrial Museum, *214*
Mitsukoshi, *57–58*
Miyanoshita, *228, 231*
MOA Museum of Art, *220*
Mobile phones, *F50–F51*
Money matters, *F43–F44*
Monsoon Cafe ✕, *94*
Montoak, *F23, 141–142*
Monument to Masatuna
Matsudaira, *183*
Mosquitoes, *F40*
Moti restaurants ✕, *86, 89,
100*
Motosu-ko, *232*
Mt. Fuji, *F23, 233–234*
Museum of Maritime Science,
79
Museums. ▷ *Also Art
galleries and museums*
advertising, *47*
in Akihabara and Jimbō-chō,
22
in Aoyama, Harajuku and
Shibuya, *65, 68*
business hours of, *F30*
currency, *56*
dolls, *211*
Edo period, *81*
Fodor's Choice, *F23*
in Fuji-Hakone-Izu National
Park, *224, 229, 232*
history, *212–213*
industry, *214*
kites, *57*
maritime history, *79, 214*
natural history, *229*
in Nihombashi, Ginza and
Yūraku-chō, *56, 57*
in Odaiba, *79*
in Ōji, *83*
Okichi tragedy, *224*
paper, *83*
phalluses, *232*

in Ryōgoku, *81–82*
science, *29, 79*
silk, *212*
sumō wrestling, *81–82*
swords, *65*
tobacco and salt, *68*
transportation, *22*
in Tsukiji and Shiodome, *47*
in Ueno, *29–30*
urban life, *29–30*
in Yokohama, *211, 212–213,
214*
Music, *134–136*

N

Nagata-chō
lodging, *119*
Nantai-san, *189*
Naokyu ✕, *95*
Narita Airport, *F28–F29*
nearby hotels, *126–128*
Narita Airport Rest House ⌂,
128
Narita View Hotel ⌂, *127*
National Diet Building, *12*
National Museum of Emerging
Science and Innovation, *79*
National Museum of Modern
Art, Tōkyō, *12–13*
National Museum of Western
Art, *28*
National Science Museum, *29*
National Stadium, *66*
National Theater, *13*
National Yoyogi Sports Center,
66
New Fujiya Hotel ⌂, *220*
Newspapers, *F39*
Nezu Institute of Fine Arts,
F23, 67
NHK Broadcasting Center, *67*
Niban-chō
dining, *98*
Nightlife, *137, 140–147*
Fodor's Choice, *F23*
Nihombashi, *F14*
dining, *98*
exploring, *50–59*
shopping, *162–163*
Nihombashi (bridge), *58*
Nikkō, *181–194*
dining, *190–191*
exploring, *182–190*
lodging, *191–192*
transportation and services,
193–194
visitor information, *194*
Nikkō Edo Village, *188–189*

Nikkō Kanaya Hotel ⌧ , *183, 191–192*
Nikkō Lakeside Hotel ⌧ , *192*
Nikkō Prince Hotel ⌧ , *192*
Nikolai Cathedral, *22*
Ningyō-chō
lodging, 119
Nippon-maru Memorial Park, *214*
Nippon Token, *F23, 175*
Nishi-Shinjuku
lodging, 119–121
Nō theater, *137, 138–139*

O

Obai-in, *197*
Odaiba, *78–80*
Odaiba Kaihin Kōen, *79*
Office hours, *F30*
Ōji, *83*
Omotesandō
dining, 98–99
shopping, 158
Onsen, *F21, 223*
Orientation tours, *F47–F48*
Ōshima ✕ , *94–95*
Ōta Memorial Museum of Art, *67*
Ōte-mon, *13*
Ōwaku-dani, *229*
Ōwaku-dani Natural History Museum, *229*
Oya Geyser, *220*

P

Package deals, *F37, F51–F52*
Packing, *F44–F45*
Palace Hotel ⌧ , *118*
Palette Town, *80*
Papermaking, *249*
Paper shops, *173–174*
Park Hyatt Tōkyō ⌧ , *120*
Parks. ⇨ *Also* Fuji-Hakone-Izu National Park
Aoyama, Harajuku and Shibuya, 68
Yokohama, 211, 214
Passports, *F45–F46*
Pearl shops, *174*
Pension Sakuraya ⌧ , *225*
Performing arts, *F21, 130–137*
Personal guides, *F48*
Pharmacies, *F38, F40*
Phone cards, *F51*
Photography, *F30–F31*
Prefectural Museum of Modern Art, *200–201*

Price categories
side trips from Tōkyō, 181
Tōkyō dining, 87
Tōkyō lodging, 110
Public phones, *F51*
Pubs, *142–143*
Puppet theater, *136, 139*

Q

Queen's Square, *214–215*

R

Radio, *F39*
Radisson Hotel Narita Airport ⌧ , *127*
Rakugo theater, *137*
Rangetsu ✕ , *95*
Religion, *255–256*
Renaissance Tōkyō Hotel Ginza Tōbu ⌧ , *111*
Restaurants. ⇨ *See* Dining
Restorante Carmine ✕ , *95*
Restrooms, *F46, 87*
Rinka-en ✕ , *216*
Rinnō-ji, *183, 185*
Rinshun-kaku, *213*
Robata ✕ , *F22, 104–105*
Rome Station ✕ , *216*
Rooftop bars, *147*
Roppongi
dining, 99–101
exploring, 80–81
lodging, 121, 123
nightlife, 140
Roti ✕ , *100*
Royal Park Hotel ⌧ , *116*
Running, *150*
Ryōgoku, *F24, 81–82*
Ryokan, *114*
etiquette for, 227
Ryokan Katsutarō ⌧ , *125*
Ryokan Sansuisō ⌧ , *117*
Ryokan Sanyōsō ⌧ , *226*
Ryokan Shigetsu ⌧ , *110–111*
Ryosen-ji, *224*
Ryūkō-ji, *204*

S

Sabado Sabadete ✕ , *102–103*
Sacred Bridge, *182–183*
Sacred Stable, *185*
Safety, *F46*
Sai-ko, *232*
Sake and spirits, *96*
Sakurada-mon, *13*
Sankei-en, *213*

Sankō-en ✕ , *93*
Saronikos ✕ , *216*
Sasa-no-yuki ✕ , *104*
Sasashin ✕ , *98*
Sasashū ✕ , *F22, 95, 97*
Sawamoto ✕ , *191*
Sawanoi ✕ , *89*
Sawanoya Ryokan ⌧ , *F22, 126*
Scandia ✕ , *215–216*
Seiji Tōgō Memorial Sompo Japan Museum of Art, *73–74*
Sekiguchi
lodging, 123
Sekirei, *F23, 142*
Sengaku-ji, *82–83*
Sengoku, *231*
Senior-citizen travel, *F46–F47*
Sensō-ji Complex, *F24, 40–43*
Sensō-ji Main Hall, *42*
Seryna ✕ , *216*
Shiba Daimon Hotel ⌧ , *123*
Shiba Kōen
lodging, 123
Shibuya, *F15*
dining, 101–102
exploring, 59–68
nightlife, 141
shopping, 158, 163
Shimoda, *224–225*
Shimoda Prince Hotel ⌧ , *224–225*
Shimoda Tokyū Hotel ⌧ , *225*
Shinagawa
dining, 102
lodging, 123–124
Shinagawa Aquarium, *77*
Shinjuku, *F15*
exploring, 69–75
nightlife, 141
shopping, 159, 163–164
Shinjuku Gyo-en National Garden, *74*
Shinjuku Park Tower Building, *74*
Shinjuku Washington Hotel ⌧ , *120–121*
Shinobazu Pond, *29*
Shintō, *256*
Shinyosha, *186*
Shiodome, *F14*
exploring, 43–50
Shirokanedai
dining, 102–103
Shitamachi, *78*
Shitamachi Museum, *29–30*
Shobu-ga-hama, *192*
Shōgitai Memorial, *30*

Shōji-ko, 232
Shopping, F21, F47,
155–175
blitz tour, 157
business hours, F30
Fodor's Choice, F23
souvenirs, 161
Shōtō
dining, 103
Shrines. ➪ See Temples and
shrines
Shuzenji, 226, 228
Sightseeing guides, F47–F48
Silk Museum, 212
Soccer, 150–151
Sōgetsu School, 83
Sōji-ji, 215
Sōun-zan, 229
Souvenirs, 161
Spago ✕, 99
Special-interest tours, F48
Sports and the outdoors,
149–153
Stadiums, 66
Statue of Hachiko, 68
Statue of Takamori Saigō, 30
Student travel, F48
Subway travel, F48–F49
Yokohama, 217
Sukiya-bashi, 58
Sumishō Hotel 🏨, 119
Sumō Museum, 81–82
Sumō wrestling, 151, 152
Sunshine International
Aquarium, 77
Supreme Court, 13
Sutra Library, 185
Suwa Tea Pavilion, 11
Suzumoto, 30
Sweet Basil 139, F23, 145
Swimming, 151–152
Sword shops, 174–175
Symbols, F9

T

Tableaux ✕, F22, 94
Tachi-ki Kannon, 190
Taikansō 🏨, 220
Taiyū-in Mausoleum, 188
Takanawa Tōbu Hotel 🏨, 124
Takashimaya, F23, 162–163
Takeno ✕, 104
Tama Zoo, 77
Tatsumiya ✕, 92
Taxes, F49
Taxis, F49–F50
Nikkō, 193
Yokohama, 217–218
Tea ceremony, 257

Telephones, F50–F51
Television, F39
Television facilities, 67, 79
Temples and shrines
accommodations in Buddhist
temples, 122
Akihabara and Jimbō-chō,
21–23
Aoyama, Harajuku and
Shibuya, 65–66
Asakusa, 40–43
Fodor's Choice, F24
Fuji-Hakone-Izu National Park,
224
Imperial Palace District, 16–17
Kamakura, 196–197, 199, 200,
202–204
Nihombashi, Ginza and
Yūraku-chō, 57
Nikkō, 183, 185–188, 190
Sengaku-ji, 82–83
Shinjuku, 72–73
Tsukiji and Shiodome, 49–50
Ueno, 27–28, 30–31, 32
Yokohama, 213, 215
Tenjo-san, 232
Tenmatsu ✕, 101–102
Tennis, 152–153
Textiles, 253
Theater
modern, 133–134
traditional, 136–137, 138–139
Theater buildings
Imperial Palace District, 13
Shinjuku, 73, 75
Tsukiji and Shiodome, 48
Ueno, 30
Ticket outlets, 131
Time, F51
Tipping, F51
Tobacco and Salt Museum, 68
Toden Arakawa Line, 83
Toh-Ka-Lin ✕, 103
Toka Music Hall, 11
Tōkei-ji, 197
Tokudai-ji, 30–31
Tōkyō. ➪ Also specific
neighborhoods
facts about, 269–270
history of, 34–35
nightlife, 137, 140–147
performing arts, 130–137
sports and the outdoors,
149–153
Tōkyō Central Wholesale
Market, 48–49
Tōkyō Disneyland, 76
Tōkyō International Forum,
58–59

Tōkyō International Youth
Hostel 🏨, 126
Tōkyō Metropolitan Art
Museum, 31
Tōkyō Metropolitan
Government Office, 74–75
Tōkyō National Museum, F23,
31–32
Tōkyō Opera City, 75
Tōkyō Sea Life Park, 75, 78
Tōkyō Station, 16
Tōkyō Tower, 76–77
Tonki ✕, 97
Tora-no-mon
dining, 103
lodging, 124–125
Tori-ichi ✕, 205
Toshima-en, 77
Tōshō-gū (Nikkō), F24,
185–187
Tōshō-gū (Tōkyō), 32
Tour operators, F51–F52
Fuji-Hakone-Izu National Park,
236
Kamakura, 206
Nikkō, 193
Yokohama, 218
Towers
Shinjuku, 74
Tōkyō Tower, 76–77
Yokohama, 211, 214
Toy shops, 175
Train travel
cutting costs, F52–F53
for disabled travelers, F36–F37
fares and schedules, F53
Fuji-Hakone-Izu National Park,
237–238
Kamakura, 206–207
Nikkō, 193–194
reservations, F53
Tōkyō (to and from), F52–F53
Tōkyō (within), F53–F54
Yokohama, 218
Transportation around Tōkyō,
F54
Transportation Museum, 22
Travel agencies
for disabled travelers, F37
selecting an agent, F54–F55
for tour bookings, F51
Traveler's checks, F44
Travel insurance, F40–F41
T-Side ✕, 205
Tsukiji, F14
dining, 103–104
exploring, 43–50
shopping, 159
Tsukiji Hongan-ji, 49–50

Tsuru-ga-oka Hachiman-gū,
   200
Turtle Inn Nikkō 🏨 , 192
Two-Tiered Bridge, 16
T. Y. Harbor Brewery ✕ , 102

U

Uchisaiwai-chō
dining, 104
Ueno, *F14*
dining, 104
exploring, 23–33
lodging, 125
Ueno Royal Museum, 33
Ueno Zoo, 33
Umagaeshi, 189
Ume no Hana ✕ , *F22*, 92
Urami Falls, 189

V

Value-added tax (V.A.T.),
   F49
Venus Fort, 80
Visas, *F45–F46*
Visitor information, *F55–F56*
Fuji-Hakone-Izu National Park,
   238
Kamakura, 207
Nikkō, 194
Yokohama, 218–219

W

Wako, 56
Waterfalls
Fuji-Hakone-Izu National Park,
   226
Nikkō, 189, 190
Weather information, *F18*
Web sites, *F56*
Westin Tōkyō 🏨 , 111
When to go, *F18*
Winds ✕ , 216
Wine, 96
World Porters, 215

Y

Yaesu
lodging, 125–126
Yakushi-dō, 185–186
Yamada Heiando, *F23*, 172
Yamagiwa, 22
Yamanaka-ko, 232, 233
Yamashita Kōen, 211
Yamatane Museum of Art, 16
Yanaka
lodging, 126
Yasha-mon, 188
Yasukuni Jinja, 16–17
YMCA Asia Youth Center 🏨 ,
   126

Yokohama, 207–219
Chinatown, 213
dining, 215–216
emergencies, 217
exploring, 209–215
transportation and services,
   216–219
visitor information, 218–219
Yokohama Cosmo World, 215
Yokohama Doll Museum, 211
Yokohama History Archives,
   212
Yokohama Maritime Museum,
   214
Yokohama Museum of Art,
   214
Yoritomo's tomb, 201–202
Yoshimizu Ginza 🏨 , *F22*,
   111, 116
Yoyogi Kōen, 68
Yumi-ga-hama, 225
Yūraku-chō, *F14*
dining, 104–105
exploring, 50–59
Yūshima Seidō, 22–23

Z

Zoos, 33, 77

NOTES

NOTES

NOTES

NOTES

NOTES

NOTES

NOTES

NOTES

NOTES

NOTES

NOTES

NOTES

NOTES